Fundamentals of Human Communication

Social Science in Everyday Life

Fourth edition

Margaret H. DeFleur

Louisiana State University

Patricia Kearney

California State University, Long Beach

Timothy G. Plax

California State University, Long Beach

Melvin L. DeFleur

Louisiana State University

Mc Graw Hill

Connect
Learn
Succeed™

FUNDAMENTALS OF HUMAN COMMUNICATION: SOCIAL SCIENCE IN EVERYDAY LIFE, FOURTH EDITION

1 2 3 4 5 6 7 8 9 0 QFR/QFR 1 0 9 8 7 6 5 4 3

ISBN 978-0-07-803689-7
MHID 0-07-803689-5

Vice President & Editor-in-Chief: *Michael Ryan*
Executive Director of Development: *Lisa Pinto*
Managing Director: *Gina Boedeker*
Marketing Specialist: *Alexandra Schultz*
Managing Development Editor: *Penina Braffman*
Editorial Coordinator: *Adina Lonn*
Senior Project Manager: *Joyce Watters*
Buyer: *Nichole Birkenholz*
Media Project Manager: *Sridevi Palani*
Cover Designer: *Studio Montage, St. Louis, MO*
Typeface: *10/12 Sabon*
Compositor: *Cenveo® Publisher Services*
Printer: *Quad/Graphics*

Library of Congress Cataloging-in-Publication Data

Fundamentals of human communication: social science in everyday life / Margaret H. DeFleur, Louisiana State University, Patricia Kearney, California State University, Long Beach, Timothy G. Plax, California State University, Long Beach, Melvin L. DeFleur, Louisiana State University.—Fourth edition.
        pages cm.
    ISBN 978-0-07-803689-7 — ISBN 0-07-803689-5
    1. Communication. I. DeFleur, Margaret H.   II. Kearney, Patricia, 1949-   III. Plax, Timothy G.
IV. DeFleur, Melvin L. (Melvin Lawrence), 1923-
P90.D4415   2013
302.2—dc23   2012044651

Contents in Brief

P
90
.D4415
2014

Contents

part one   Basics of Communication

part three   Managing Personal Communication Processes

chapter 11   Influencing Others   293

chapter 12   Coping with Conflict   321

Preface

The authors wish to thank the many instructors and students who have sent us invaluable comments and advice as to how to craft this fourth edition. We hope it will continue to meet the needs of those who adopt it for their courses. We also hope that it will prove useful to the students who use it.

Our Goals

One of the goals of this textbook was to recognize the contribution of the discipline of communication to the social sciences. Communication is the basis of both social life and of personal cognitive functioning. As such it is perhaps the single most important form of human behavior. We all communicate, all day, every day, in an enormous variety of contexts, to many kinds of people and for an enormous variety of purposes. It follows that the better we understand that process the more effective we will be in relating to other human beings.

For that reason an effort was made to incorporate relevant theories and findings from all of the social science disciplines into the study of human communication. Contributions from those fields provide significant insights into the ways people communicate and the influence that communication has on their lives. By pursuing this objective we hope to bring social science into the everyday lives of our readers so

that they may develop a better understanding of the processes, problems, and consequences of human communication.

Within that framework, this book presents a number of innovative theories and perspectives as well as the more traditional introductory material in order to help students develop strategies for thinking about and engaging in communication. We do not want students to leave the course with only a list of memorized concepts and definitions. We want them to cultivate a working command of the tools of effective communication so that they can competently manage everyday situations long after they have completed the course. We have drawn from a growing body of classical and contemporary theory and research and have brought together ideas and findings from several disciplines—communication, psychology, sociology, biology, anthropology, and education—that provide a rich variety of insight into the communication process.

Another major goal is to discuss communication in ways that are sensitive to the needs and interests of diverse categories of students. Although most fundamental communication theory and its applications are not unique to either gender or to any particular racial, ethnic, or cultural category, we have tried to provide material that acknowledges the variety of communication styles and customs that exist in the American society. Related to this, we use many examples, concepts, and explanations that are relevant to the workplace so that the content will be of value to students when they enter the labor force. Of course, many students are already in the labor force.

In short, the purpose of this book is to present basic theoretical and practical analyses of the human communication process. To do that, the book makes extensive use of examples, concepts, theories, and research from many sources that help clarify fundamental issues that are an important part of that process.

Organization

After an overview of the communication process, the book moves from the discussion of simple messages between two people to more complex communication contexts, such as intercultural, organizational, and mass communication. Part One presents the basics of verbal and nonverbal interaction, their personal and social implications (Chapters 1–4). Part Two explains how communication takes place in distinct contexts (Chapters 5–8). These beginning chapters provide the student with a strong foundation of concepts, principles, and research-supported theories that explain the nature and consequences of human communication.

The third part of the book (Chapters 9–12) focuses on practical applications and is intended to improve the student's ability to communicate effectively in a variety of situations and settings. The final part of the book looks at three major topics. These are effective communication with new media technologies (Chapter 13), the process and effects of mass communication (Chapter 14), and, finally, the design and conduct of research on the communication process (Chapter 15).

The fourth edition, therefore, consists of 15 chapters, one less than the previous edition of this text. At the suggestion of our reviewers, we removed a chapter on professional communication, which acquainted students with the fields of public relations and advertising. This was done in order to allow the number of chapters to be a better fit for the number of weeks of instruction time in a semester.

Features

A number of innovative approaches make this book unique. For example, starting with the first chapter, both linear and transactional approaches are used to analyze the basics of the communication process. A second example is the developmental format used to discuss interpersonal communication (Chapter 5). That format discusses how people use particular forms of messages to initiate interpersonal relationships, to maintain them, and (possibly) to disengage from each other if things do not work out.

Another innovative theoretical perspective is used in the discussion of small groups (Chapter 6). This expands on traditional approaches by showing the influence of patterns of behavior based on norms, roles, ranks, and controls that indicate who can talk to whom, in what way for what purpose. Still another innovation is the development in Chapter 7 of a theory of group cohesion based on such factors as sentiment, personal reward considerations, interlocking work assignments, or mutual role dependency.

A feature that has been retained and updated from previous editions is *A Closer Look*, boxes which provide skills-based tips, bulleted summaries, narrative examples, or relevant theories in each chapter. In addition, several chapters feature *Ethical Concerns* boxes which underscore ever-important questions and issues of ethics within the discipline of communication.

A feature from an earlier edition that we are bringing back is the inclusion of self-assessment scales for students to evaluate their communication competence, listening skills, nonverbal immediacy, comfort with technology, and other issues. Our reviewers suggested this as another way to engage our students, and we agree.

Changes in the Fourth Edition

Overall, the fourth edition has been streamlined considerably, removing information that our reviewers have indicated is redundant or unnecessary. Thus, we believe the reading experience for students will be improved. In addition, there are many new chapter openings that highlight important issues covered in the chapters, and updated references to the use of new technology throughout the book.

In every chapter an effort has been made to incorporate recent research developments and to cite noteworthy contributions of communication scholars. Additional theoretical perspectives have been added, such as social information processing theory (SIP), which is helpful for understanding how relationships are formed online. Many new examples have been added. Definitions of key terms have been simplified. Selected chapters contain new *Workplace Perspective* boxes, which highlight important communication issues in career settings, including such topics as social networking etiquette and how to communicate effectively with your manager. And, as already mentioned, most chapters include an interactive self-assessment feature to help students evaluate their communication skills.

Of particular note in the fourth edition is the inclusion of discussions about social media and new media technologies throughout the book, and especially in Chapter 13 (Using Media to Communicate Interpersonally) and Chapter 14 (Understanding Mass Communication). Clearly, communication technologies have changed considerably since the third edition was published, and we have incorporated those changes throughout. As a result, we hope the fourth edition will continue to be instructive, useful and relevant for all of our students.

Acknowledgments

We are indebted to the following people who made important contributions to this book, including the reviewers who provided many insightful comments for the previous editions as well as in revising this book for the fourth edition: Terre and Scott Allen, California State University, Long Beach; Jack M. Bain, Michigan State University; Michael J. Beatty, Cleveland State University; Julie A. Burke, Bowling Green State University; Karen Buzzard, Southwest Missouri State University; Lynn Cockett, Juniata College; Karen Cristiano, Drexel University; Ann L. Darling, University of Utah; Sharon Downey, California State University, Long Beach; Lawrence W. Hugenberg, Youngstown State University; Karen Isaacs, University of New Haven; Robert Kastenbaum, Arizona State University; Richard A. Katula, Northeastern University; Joann Keyton, University of Kansas; Jay Libby, University of New Haven; Anne F. Mattina, Northeastern University; Matt McAllister, Virginia Tech; Raymie E. McKerrow, Ohio University; Joquina Reed, Texas A&M University; Heidi M. Rose, Villanova University; Carolyn Shepard, University of California at Santa Barbara; Jennifer Thackaberry, University of Colorado; Bryan C. Taylor, University of Colorado; Lisa Waite, Kent State University; Jennifer Waldeck, University of California at Santa Barbara; Larry J. Whatule, University of Pittsburgh at Greensburg; John L. Williams, California State University, Sacramento; and Donald D. Yoder, University of Dayton.

The authors would like to offer a special thanks to the following from McGraw-Hill for their important contributions to this book: Craig Leonard, development editor; Deb Hash, sponsoring editor; Penina Braffman, managing development editor; and Joyce Watters, project manager.

The Communication Process: An Overview

W ell son," Mr. Andrews said. "It's really nice to have you home, even if it's only for the few days of the Thanksgiving holiday. Your mom and I are so proud of you."

Tom chuckled, saying, "Well, Dad, it's sure nice to be here. The dorms are really OK, and I like the friends I've made. College is cool, but it's nice to get away, and I'm really looking forward to mom's Thanksgiving dinner."

"Tell me how things are going," Mr. Andrews said. "How are the grades shaping up?" Recognizing the note of parental concern in his Dad's voice, Tom explained that he had a solid grade point average, and that with some hard work he might be able to raise it even higher.

"Well that's just fine, Tom," Mr. Andrews replied with a smile. "Maybe next year you will be able to qualify for a scholarship. With both you and your sister in college, those tuition bills are really starting to add up. Mom and I are glad to do it though, we want both of you to have the best possible chances to get really good jobs when you finish."

"I really appreciate that Dad. I know that it has been a financial sacrifice. But I think it will be worth it once I finish my degree and start working."

"Have you given any more thought to what you will major in?" Mr. Andrews asked.

"Yes I have. I have to finish my required courses in sciences and humanities first, of course, but I've thought about it a lot, and I have looked into what kind of work I might really want to do after I graduate. Dad, I have decided to major in communication, and I have already taken an introductory course in that program. It's really interesting."

Tom saw his father's eyes widen and a disbelieving look on his face. Tom sensed immediately that he had a problem.

"You're going to major in *what*? Did I hear you say you're going to major in 'communication'?"

"Yes, Dad, communication!"

"Tom, I'm concerned. Mom and I want you to be able to get a job and earn some money after you graduate. We have been hoping that you would select something practical like accounting or computer science. Those people get real jobs."

"But it is really an interesting major, Dad. I don't want to just juggle some company's profit and loss statement, or sit in a cubicle staring into a computer all day—unable to have an intelligent conversation with another human being. People spend immense amounts of time every day communicating. They talk, listen, read, write, use media, and spend more time communicating than any other activity. It is one of the most important aspects of human life."

"Well I'll tell you what kind of 'intelligent conversation' you will probably have if you major in communication."

(Tom detected the obviously negative tone that his Dad used with the word "communication.")

"You'll be able to have great discussions with people that you drive around in your taxicab.

You might as well have selected Medieval studies, Latin, or Icelandic literature. In fact, people who pick those majors may actually have a better chance."

"I don't think that you understand the situation very well, Dad. I have looked into the employment picture pretty thoroughly. People who have a solid command of communication skills have excellent chances in the labor force. The study of communication is a social science—one devoted to understanding how we communicate and how we can do it well. It really does help people who want to excel in their jobs."

In spite of his parents' views, Tom became even more firmly committed to his major during his sophomore year, and he went on to establish an outstanding record in the communication courses he took. Although his father was worried that he and his wife would never get "a decent return on their investment" in Tom's tuition, they learned over time that communication was indeed a practical skill after all. They discovered how much employers valued communication skills in virtually every job in the workplace. Employees who can communicate complex information effectively have an edge over those who cannot.

While Tom had decided to study communication, it is clear that his father had serious reservations. So, an appropriate way to begin the first chapter is to ask, what is the discipline of communication anyway? Where did it come from? What do people in the discipline study? A second important question is to ask what value does the knowledge it develops have someone like Tom who decides to major in

Answers to the first question can be both simple and complex. The simple version is that the central focus of the discipline is **human communication** *in all its aspects*. Stated briefly, communication is the study of the many ways that human beings relate to each other by exchanging messages, using a number of different processes of communication in a variety of settings and **contexts,** and the consequences of those exchanges.

A more complex answer to the first question above is that communication is an academic discipline that makes use of the strategies and perspectives of social science to discover and teach others about the processes and consequences of human communication. Actually, the discipline had its origins centuries before any kind of social scientific strategies for study were available. Its prescientific roots extend back to ancient Greece, and the writings of philosophers such as Aristotle and Quintillian. In the fourth century B.C. they recognized the importance of communication in human affairs and they systematically studied the use of *rhetoric*. The term refers to the art of expressive discourse, including the rules of message composition used in speaking (and writing) to achieve specific kinds of results and influences on audiences. Indeed, public speaking remains one of the discipline's central concerns today. In addition, contemporary communication scholars conduct research, using the intellectual tools of science. They seek to push forward the cutting edge of knowledge about how human beings communicate, either orally or with media, and what consequences results from such exchanges. To do this they not only conduct their own research projects but they also incorporate knowledge about human communication that has been discovered by several related social sciences—anthropology, linguistics, social psychology, psychology, and sociology. Thus, this complex discipline is *interdisciplinary,* focusing on human communication in all its many aspects. It includes how communication takes place between individuals, in various kinds of group settings, through the use of many kinds of media.

Using this broad explanation of communication as a guide, the purpose of the present chapter is to explain in considerable detail how human beings communicate at an interpersonal level, and the consequences of doing it well. That explanation will be based on an examination of two so-called "models" of the process. These are detailed discussions and portrayals of the exact stages and steps that take place when *one person communicates with another in a face-to-face setting*. First, however, why is the study of communication so important?

The Significance of Communication in Human Life

An old joke, familiar to any sixth grader, begins with the question, "Where in the jungle does the 800-pound gorilla sleep?" The answer, of course, is "Anywhere he wants!" Perhaps a more relevant version of that question is this: "Where does a person with a degree in communication work?" Perhaps, surprisingly, the answer is much the same: "Anywhere he or she wants!" Of course that is an overstatement, because there are many occupations that require very specific technical training. Nevertheless, in contemporary society there is one kind of skill that stands out sharply as more critical to success in the workplace than any other. That skill is the *ability to communicate effectively*—that is, to communicate clearly and accurately in such a way that others have no difficulty in understanding what you are saying or writing.

In virtually any survey, or other research study, of what employers say they want when they hire new people, they say "the ability to communicate effectively."[1] For example, in a recent survey of employers conducted on behalf of the Association of American Colleges and Universities, 89% of employers ranked the ability to communicate effectively, orally and in writing, as one of the most important skills on which more emphasis should be placed. The employers also insist that new employees have a broader set of skills and higher levels of

What can you do with a degree in Communication? Communication skills are highly valued in the workplace, with applications in almost all business and professional settings.

learning and knowledge than in the past in order to meet the increasingly complex demands necessary for today's workplace (See Table 1.1).[2] There is no question that other skills are also important in the workplace. Employers want people who can expertly perform the duties of accountants, investment managers, nurses, or other specialized roles. However, all use communication skills to relate to customers, colleagues, and clients in ways that bring them to buy, invest, perform, donate, cooperate, join, be satisfied, vote, approve, or engage in some other form of action that their employers value. Becoming an expert **communicator,** therefore, *lays the foundation for success* in the contemporary labor force.

Jobs are not the only setting in which communication can be critical. There are compelling reasons beyond the world of work for developing refined skills as a **communicator.** We must all relate effectively to those whom we like, love, honor, admire, or otherwise value. People who are unable to do this often experience problems. If they fail to interact comfortably with their families, friends, lovers, neighbors, and others with whom they are in frequent contact, they may remain "outsiders" who live less rewarding lives. The divorce court constantly process people who were unable communicate effectively with their spous Children in homes where effective commun tion with parents is not possible are at r

TABLE 1.1 Proportion of Employers Who Want Colleges to Place *More* Emphasis on Selected Skills and Knowledge

	%
The ability to communicate effectively orally and in writing	89
Critical thinking and analytical reasoning skills	81
The ability to apply knowledge and skills to real-world settings through internships or other hands-on experiences	79
The ability to analyze and solve complex problems	75
The ability to connect choices and actions to ethical decisions	75
Teamwork skills and the ability to collaborate with others in diverse group settings	71
The ability to innovate and be creative	70
Concepts and new developments in science and technology	70
The ability to locate, organize, and evaluate information from multiple sources	68
The ability to understand the global context of situations and decisions	67
Global issues and developments and their implications for the future	65
The ability to work with numbers and understand statistics	63
The role of the United States in the world	57
Cultural diversity in America and other countries	57
Civic knowledge, civic participation, and community engagement	52
Proficiency in a foreign language	45
Democratic institutions and values	40

Source: "Raising the Bar: Employers' Views on College Learning in the Wake of the Economic Downturn." Survey of Employers conducted on behalf of The Association of American Colleges and Universities by Hart Research Associates.

Effective communication is crucial in the relationship between physicians and their patients, and for designing campaigns to persuade individuals to adopt behaviors that promote good health.[3] Men or women who cannot communicate in acceptable ways with persons of the opposite gender don't get a second date—and maybe not even a first one! And so it goes. The bottom line is that ability to communicate effectively at both a *personal* level and in the *workplace* is one of the most important skills characterizing modern life.

Human communication is a truly remarkable process. Think about it! It is our most complicated form of behavior. Because it is so complicated, it sharply separates us from other members of the animal kingdom. Through the use of words, along with other signs and **symbols** for which we share meanings, we perceive, evaluate, and respond to the physical and social world around us as only human beings can.

Communication can be looked at from both an individual and a social or collective viewpoint. For example, it is not only the means by which we are able to engage in human *thought* (an individual activity), but also it provides us with the ability to develop and maintain a *society* (clearly a social activity). At a personal level communication enables each of us to acquire a *personality*. We each become a separate and unique individual—with our own special patterns of beliefs, attitudes, and habits of behavior that are not identical to those of anyone else in the world. Not only that, but because we engage in extensive communication with other people we develop shared understandings about what is expected and acceptable in social relationships—a host of *shared guides for behavior* (informal norms, laws, etc.). In an overall sense, then, communication is critical to everything that we are. It is the foundation of virtually everything that is human and that we do not share with other biological organisms.[4]

But how important is the ability to communicate *effectively* to each of us personally? As we noted, communicating well or poorly can spell the difference between success and failure in almost every kind of human relationship. The American society today is no longer one in which those who work in factories are likely to achieve significant economic success—as was the case only a few decades ago. For most of the 1900s, blue-collar workers producing "things" of many kinds could earn relatively high incomes. Those days have all but come to a close. By the mid-20th century, the United States was already becoming an "information society" in which more people were working with symbols—words and numbers—than were producing things with their hands.[5] Today, educated workers who are skilled communicators command the highest salaries. Those who lack the ability to communicate ideas persuasively and accurately are at a distinct economic disadvantage.

Improving your ability to communicate is precisely what this book is about. It examines the fundamental nature of human communication and discusses how this process is influenced in a variety of settings. No one will claim that this is easy. You will have to work hard to achieve this goal, but it will be worth it. In other words, this text is not just a "how-to" manual like the ones people get with a new software program. Acquiring effective communication skills requires *detailed analysis of every feature of the process*. Becoming a truly competent communicator rests upon a full understanding of the nature of speech and language as used in both verbal and nonverbal communication, as well as how different situations influence the communication process, and of how to listen effectively. Furthermore, communicating with media, including social media, is another important feature. In other words,

practical skills are built on an understanding of concepts, principles, and theories that explain the human communication process as it takes place in a variety of contexts for many purposes. That knowledge has emerged from decades of systematic study and research on how communication takes place, how it can go wrong, and what the consequences are likely to be. This text will help in understanding these issues. It brings together the main ideas from these analyses and shows how they can be usefully applied.

Why is human communication complex? For many reasons. For example, the number of *settings* or *contexts* in which people communicate is almost unlimited. Think about it. The range includes such settings as intimate conversations between lovers, discussions in small groups such as families and friends, sending or receiving messages that move through large organizations, and making public speeches with one person talking to a large audience—to name only a few. People also communicate using various *media* such as a cell phone or "smart" phone, social media such as Facebook or Twitter, the Internet, and various computer systems for sending and receiving e-mail—as well as by using traditional mass media such as newspapers, magazines, the movies, and television, whereby messages may go out to millions of people. Unique factors characterize communication in each such context, with each medium posing its own problems. OK, so communication can be complex, but how it works in various settings and what difference it makes will be addressed in chapters that follow.

Defining Communication

But wait a minute! What exactly is communication? That may sound like an obvious question because you do it all the time and you m: think you do it very well. However, the ex: nature of the process has fascinated human ings and has been debated throughout histo

From ancient times to the present, philosophers, scholars, and teachers have examined how people are influenced, both in personal terms by thinking and knowing the world around them, and in terms of rational discourse and public speaking as forms of human communication.[7] They have left a legacy of important treatises on many topics, such as oratory, rhetoric, dialogue, persuasion, elocution, syntax, and grammar, that deepen our contemporary understanding of human communication.[8] A brief look at what a few of them have said can be helpful.

By the beginning of the 1900s, social scientists had put together comprehensive definitions of human communication that more or less included all its basic features. For example, pioneer student of communication Charles Horton Cooley, writing in 1909, developed the early foundations of a broad *paradigm*—that is, a general and comprehensive theory—explaining that the origins and nature of the human mind as well as society itself was in the use of language. That paradigm came to be called "symbolic interactionism," and it remains an important way today to look at individual human personality and the social order. This view stresses the idea that *human nature* (what makes us different from animals) is developed in a process of communication using language symbols (mainly words) that are passed on as part of culture through generations. His definition was an interesting one:

> By Communication is here meant the mechanism through which human relations exist and develop—all the symbols of the mind, together with the means of conveying them through space and preserving them in time. It includes the expression of the face, attitude and gesture, the tones of the voice, words, writing, printing, railways, telegraphs, telephones, and whatever else may be the latest achievements in the conquest of time and space.[9]

If you look closely at Cooley's definition you can see that it recognizes that communication can take place not only by *verbal* means but also by *nonverbal* means as well. He also noted that communicating via *media* that surmount space and time can be part of what he called the "mechanism" (by which people relate to each other). Although he had no knowledge of media to come—such as radio, television, movies, and the Internet—his definition is as modern as the latest technological triumphs of digital television, wireless cellular phones, and the Internet. However, note also that his definition says nothing about exactly how the "mechanism" works. That is, it really does not explain *how* communication actually takes place, either between individuals or via media. A necessary feature of an acceptable definition today is that it must set forth the nature of the *process* by which the intended meanings of a person sending a message are reconstructed by a **receiver** in such a way that both of their meanings are reasonably similar. Nevertheless, Cooley's definition did set forth the important ideas of *verbal, nonverbal,* and *mediated* communication.

We noted earlier that communication scholars make use of perspectives and findings from all of the social sciences that are concerned with communication. In that spirit, let's look at what psychologists have to say about the process. First, however, we need to understand that their discipline is a very general one, which tries to find ways in which all living organisms share patterns of behavior. Thus, in recent times, psychologists have taken an interesting approach to try to identify the nature of communication *as it occurs across species.* In other words, they have done so by studying communication among both animals and human beings to see what they have in common.

The classic strategy of psychology is to develop a *comparative perspective*—comparing the ways in which communication occurs among all animal forms, from simple to complex, and then sorting out what is common to all, or different among them. This strategy can be a very useful one and it has led to a very general definition of communication that actually can be applied to all living forms. Perhaps there are some important clues here that will help us to develop a really useful definition of human communication:

> Communication occurs when one organism (the source) encodes **information** into a signal that passes to another organism (the receiver), who decodes the signal and is capable of responding appropriately.[10]

This very broad definition from comparative psychology is one into which both human and animal communication can fit. However, that may be of only limited help in understanding what is actually unique about human communication. That is, what is there about human communication that very clearly *sets it apart* from that of animals? Or, is there actually little or nothing that makes the human communication process unique and distinct?

In spite of its limitations, this very general definition from psychology does add to the factors that were included in Cooley's definition in that it provides an elementary view of his "mechanism." For example, it shows that when an act of communication takes place, one "organism" initiates the process by serving as a **source or sender.** Then, some sort of **encoding** occurs. Following that, "information" *moves across space.* Following that, **decoding** is accomplished by a *receiver.* Finally, a *response* is made.

These ideas are important because they are indeed essential features of any act of communication—whether among animals or human beings. However, more is needed for understanding this form of behavior among human beings because people communicate in very complex ways that never occur among animals. For example, while animals clearly do signal each other about food, mating, and danger, they do not chat with friends, give speeches, write letters, or read the newspaper, making use of verbal and nonverbal communication in both oral and written form. So, human communication *is really not just like that of animals,* and much more has to be added to describe the process more realistically. So, bringing together both Cooley's sociological concepts and those from comparative psychology, we can (finally) formulate a foundation definition for discussing how two human beings in face-to-face settings communicate with each other:

> Human communication is a *process* during which a *source* (individual) initiates a *message* using *verbal and nonverbal symbols* and *contextual cues* to express *meaning* by transmitting *information* in such a way that similar or parallel *understandings* are constructed by the intended *receiver(s).*

At first glance, this definition looks complicated. Yet, if you look more closely, it is essentially a sort of list of the important factors that are involved when two people communicate with one another.

Let's look carefully at each of the factors that is included in this definition. For example, note that the definition begins by stating that communication is a *process.* That is really an important idea—and it is not very difficult to understand. To explain, any "process" is a series of *stages* in which something undergoes *transformation* at each step. Lots of things that you already know about take place as "processes." An example would be transforming food that you chew, eat, and digest (in a series of stages) into energy for your body plus waste.

In the communication process human beings serve as *sources* and begin by selecting meanings that will make up their messages. It is these meanings that are transformed during the process. In the first stage, the source's thoughts and ideas—his or her meanings—are transformed into messages by selecting appropriate symbols. This is the stage that is referred to as *encoding.* Then, these messages are transformed once again, this time into *information*—that is, physical events, like verbal sounds, visible nonverbal signals (like printed letters), or both, that can move across space. In the next stage, receiving individuals then see or hear the messages and transform them back to the person's own symbolic understandings of thoughts and ideas—meanings—aroused by the message.

For communication to be accurate, of course, the meanings constructed by both sender and receiver must be similar. So, communication can be thought of as a series of stages—that is, a process.

A critical idea included in the definition is the idea that a message typically consists of a set of words with agreed-upon meanings, plus arrangements of grammar and syntax that are part of language. It may also include standardized nonverbal cues and contextual factors that imply meanings. Thus, a source normally expresses intended meanings with words, gestures, and actions. However, features from the social and physical settings within which the communication takes place can *add additional meanings.*

Note also that the definition highlights the idea of *parallel meanings* in each of the communicators. As we will see, *meaning* is a form of internal or subjective behavior that occurs as responses *within a person* to words or other standardized signs and signals. To the degree that the subjective meanings aroused in each person are *similar,* they can be said to be "parallel." If that is the case, the communication between the individuals is reasonably complete or accurate. If the meanings are *different,* the communication process has suffered some kind of **distortion,** and the result is limited **accuracy.**

Although the word *communicator* in everyday language commonly designates the person who initiates a message, in the present analysis both the source and the receiver are "communicators." Therefore, the term *source,* or *sender,* will be used to identify a person who formulates and transmits a message. The term *receiver* will identify the communicator to whom that message is directed and who constructs his or her version of what it means.

Now here is an unusual notion: The foundation definition stated above conceptualizes communication somewhat artificially as a **linear** process—one that starts, goes through stages, one after the other like a straight line, and then stops. Is this realistic? Is it a truly adequate way to describe the complex process of

human communication? The answer is definitely "No!" In many ways this linear description of the process is *unrealistic.* This view implies that communication occurs when one person begins the action and another, who waits for the message to arrive, completes it. In reality, ongoing communication between two interacting parties is *far more complex* than this linear view implies. However, even though this is not the final way that we will define and discuss human communication, it does provide a good point of departure.

An important advantage of looking first at communication as a linear process is that it provides a foundation for understanding in detail what two human beings do when they communicate. In reality, human communicators engage in a complex and ongoing *exchange.* They repeatedly go through linear stages as they communicate back and forth. Thus, when one person is acting as a sender, she or he can also be acting as a receiver while formulating an outgoing message to be transmitted to the other. Similarly, the receiver can be serving as a source, both listening and sending back a response.

Usually, people quickly take turns in such interactions. In fact, they may perform them *simultaneously,* providing subtle messages to each other before, during, and after their turns. However, even subtle messages must be formulated, transmitted, and received. Thus, ongoing stages of message transmission and reception, as in a conversation, are made up of patterns of linear exchanges that are embedded in a complex process of simultaneous interactions. That sounds complicated, and in many ways it is. We will discuss it after beginning with the linear view.

Communication as Linear Process: An Analytic Model

The stages or steps involved in the person-to-person human communication process can be illustrated by considering an elementary communicative act involving only two people. The source will initiate the exchange with a sentence consisting of three words, and the receiver will respond with a single nonverbal gesture. Using that example, we can examine a very basic linear model of the communication process.

A *model* in science is a "representation"—a careful and concise *description* that summarizes and illustrates what takes place in some situation or process. Some models are verbal—set forth in ordinary words and descriptive sentences. These are probably the easiest to understand. Others use graphics, abstract symbols, or even mathematical equations to portray what they represent. The model of communication presented in Figure 1.1 is both verbal and graphic.

What about a "linear" model? This is really a simple idea. As noted earlier, the term *linear* indicates that the process being depicted moves rather like a straight line, from a beginning point to an end point through specific stages—one after the other. Our basic strategy of analysis using the linear model will be to start a conversation between two people at a point when one person decides to transmit a message to another. We will then enter the process and artificially slow it down to look at what happens stage by stage—like looking at a film projected slowly, one frame at a time. We will examine every stage of the communicative act in detail. We will start from the point at which one human being constructs a meaningful message, transmits it to another, who attends to it

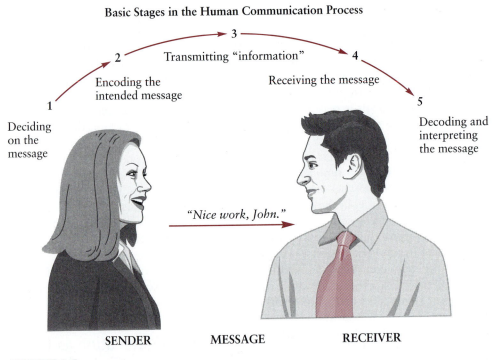

Basic Stages in the Human Communication Process

3

2   Transmitting "information"   4

Encoding the   Receiving the message
intended message

1   5

Deciding   Decoding and
on the   interpreting
message   the message

"Nice work, John."

SENDER   **MESSAGE**   **RECEIVER**

FIGURE 1.1

A Linear Model
With the basic linear perspective, we can understand what is happening at each stage in the communication process: A message is decided on and formulated by the sender; the message is encoded and transmitted; it is decoded and interpreted by the receiver, who applies meanings stored in memory.

and then reconstructs the meaning and ultimately understands the message. We will also indicate that the receiver then transmits an acknowledgment back to the initiator.

We can start with the example shown in Figure 1.1, our linear model. The sender says to the receiver, "Nice work, John," and the receiver smiles in return. Despite its simplicity, this exchange, using only three words (and a nonverbal gesture) provides a basis for understanding each of the steps or stages involved in human communication. Essentially, the process involves *five distinct stages,* summarized as follows:

Stage 1: *Deciding on the message.* A person serving as a source decides on a message to be sent to a receiver (or receivers) to achieve a desired *goal.*

Stage 2: *Encoding the intended meanings.* The source searches his or her *memory* for specific *symbols,* such as words and gestures, and their associated *meanings* that can be put together into a *pattern* that will describe the desired facts, ideas and images.

Stage 3: *Transmitting the message as information.* The message is transformed by voice or other means into physical *information* (like sound waves) so that it can overcome distance, and the message moves in this form from sender to receiver.

Stage 4. *Perceiving the information as a message.* The receiver attends to the physical information as it arrives and *perceives,* that is, identifies, the symbols into which it has been coded.

Stage 5: *Decoding and interpreting the message.* The receiver searches and compares the incoming symbols with meanings stored in her or his memory and selects those that seem best for *interpreting* the message.

Look at those steps again. There are a lot of concepts in them that need to be discussed.

These include *encoding, decoding, symbols, goal, memory, meaning, pattern, information, perceiving,* and *interpreting.* This is quite a list. However, to understand human communication fully, each step has to be explained because these steps are the human activities that make the process possible. Therefore, let's take a closer look at each of the five stages, and see how these concepts are involved:

Stage One: Deciding on the Message

Any person initiating an act of communication has some *intention* in mind—that is, a *goal.* The goal may be to sell something, improve a relationship, or teach something to another person. Of the many goals that people attempt to achieve through communication, most are simple and obvious, but others can be complex, and vague, and are often difficult to ascertain. Indeed, on many occasions, the person initiating a message may not have consciously thought much about achieving some sort of "goal." For example, when you see your friend walking toward you in the morning, and you say, "Hi, how are you?" you do not consciously think, *Hmmm, I have a goal of sending a nice greeting to this person who is my friend because that will help maintain that relationship, which I value.* Nevertheless, on close analysis, that is what such a communication is all about. You plan and execute it so fast that you are not even aware of having a goal in mind.

Even though such planning and stating such a greeting takes place swiftly, it is a deliberate act. We formulate messages so that they fit with what we are involved in and intending at the moment. For example, in Figure 1.1, where the three-word message is, "Nice work, John," the source's purpose is simple: *to express a sentiment that will reinforce a meaningful relationship.* Whatever the intention, a key principle here is that communication begins when the sender mentally constructs a message that she or he feels the receiver can interpret with reasonable accuracy so as to accomplish whatever goal or purposes the person seeks.

Stage Two: Encoding the Intended Meanings

After the goal or goals have been set, whether vaguely or clearly, the source must construct (mentally) a message consistent with his or her purpose. This is done by selecting from *memory* whatever *signs and symbols*—usually words and maybe gestures—are needed to represent the *intended meanings*. This is what takes place in the encoding stage and it can be complex because it involves more than merely selecting particular words. Often, our messages include gestures, postures, or even objects and other nonverbal symbols associated with particular meanings.

The term *symbol,* as used here, is any word, number, gesture, object, or other cue (verbal or nonverbal) that has associated with it in our "language community" a *conventional* meaning. The term **convention** implies that people share a rule as to how they are expected to understand it. In other words, the symbol arouses in our minds an interpretation that is very similar to the interpretations that others are likely to experience when they use, see, read or hear the same one. Even a bodily posture can serve as a symbol. Imagine a person who is upset, has folded arms, is glaring at you with a frown, and is tapping his or her foot. Few of us would assume that such a person is happy. Physical objects can serve as symbols. Examples are a police badge, a flag, a cross, and even a limousine. Clothing is often used to send messages (as when we wear a military uniform, a tuxedo, or a long evening gown, versus when we are in shorts and sandals).

While actions and objects can be important, our principle "mechanism" (as Cooley stated it) for communicating with other people is the use of *words* as standardized symbols. That is, in verbal communication words are most often the tools that permit meanings to be encoded. Moreover, words are the most deeply established of all signs and signals in our language culture. Words are truly a remarkable invention. Because words have such well-standardized meanings in our language community, and can be translated with reasonable accuracy from one to another, we can interpret the thoughts and ideas of writers who have been dead for thousands of years. Cooley explained the idea in a colorful way:

> A word is a vehicle, a boat floating down from the past with the thought of men we never saw; and in coming to understand it we enter not only into the minds of our contemporaries, but into the general mind of humanity continuous through time.[11]

The term *sign* refers to much the same idea, but it is even broader. Words are one form of signs, but even events can serve as signs. For example, a lightning stroke can be a "sign" that a peal of thunder will follow, or a snarling dog may be a "sign" for an intruder that an attack is likely. Animals use signs to adjust to their world, as when a dog whines at the door to be let out. Symbols, on the other hand, are a form of signs that are used *exclusively by human beings* who share their links to meanings in a specific language community. For example, two persons who live together quickly learn to read signs in the behavior of one another that tell them what mood the other person is in, or what has pleased or angered them. They don't need verbal messages to understand such meanings. So, signs in this sense are part of the human communication experience as well—although they may be used at a less conscious level than when we use words.

Although the example shown in Figure 1.1 is elementary, involving only the symbols "nice," "work," and "John," plus a slight smile, most people in the English-speaking language community will have conventional (standardized) meanings for each of these words. Even so, selecting just the right symbols is not all the sender must consider. Not only must each of the symbols selected be *linked in our language community with our desired meanings,* but also we must believe that they will be *understood in the same way by both sender and receiver.*

In addition, there is the problem of the *sequence* or pattern of these signs and symbols.

This is called *syntax*. For example, suppose we rearranged the order of the three words of the message in Figure 1.1 into another pattern, such as "Work nice John." That expresses a very different overall meaning—even though it contains exactly the same three words! Or consider this case: "The bear ate the man." That's clear enough. But what about "The man ate the bear?" Obviously, in each case, these are very different overall meanings that are introduced by the distinct patterns. So, meaning is associated not only with specific symbols, but the *order* in which they are presented. In other words, syntax matters, and it matters a lot! The lesson here is that our language community sets rules, not only about the meanings aroused in our heads for specific symbols (words, numbers, gestures, objects, and so on), but also for the sequences or patterns in which they are used.

The next step in gaining a perspective on the human communication process is to examine the *nature of meaning* itself and the relationship it implies between symbols, patterns, and memory. Then we can look at ways in which senders try to anticipate whether the receiver actually will understand their encoded message.

The meaning of meaning. Quite obviously, understanding the concept of meaning is essential to a full understanding of the encoding process. Meaning can be difficult to define, study, and analyze. Nevertheless, we need to do it because it is at the very heart of the human communication process. We can start by noting that meanings are *subjective*. What that means is that they are experiences that occur "in our heads," where only we—and no one else—can experience them. For that reason, we have no way of directly observing another person's meanings. Nevertheless, we can make some *assumptions* about meaning that will make it less mysterious and easier to define.

First, meanings are not ethereal, spiritual, or in any other way unnatural. They are a form of internal, that is, "mental" *behavior*. In short, meaning consists of *responses* we make (within

ourselves) to objects, events, and situations we encounter in the world around us. Those subjective responses are the different kinds of images, feelings, and beliefs that are aroused within us when we encounter some part of reality—a dog, a house, mom, a football game, and so on. Thus, meanings are *learned* internal behaviors. We encounter such realities (dog, mom, house, etc.) through our senses—by seeing, feeling, hearing, smelling, or even tasting. After many such encounters, we learn to make a specific pattern of internal subjective responses (a set of meanings) that we and our fellow members of our language community assign to each kind of object, event, and situation.

What about meanings for words, as opposed to objects and events? We learn to make responses to words or other symbols *in the same way we experience meaning for things that exist in reality*. In other words, the term *meaning* has a double implication: Not only does it imply subjective responses to aspects of reality—when we actually see, hear, or feel something that exists—but it also implies the same kinds of responses *to the words that we use to label that reality*. To illustrate this point, consider this: We will have an internal meaning experience when we see a small animal, such as a squirrel. At the same time, we have a very similar internal experience when we hear or read the *word* "squirrel." If we were talking and I mentioned that I saw a squirrel, you would have a kind of internal image (a meaning) of that little animal associated with that word. Thus, both the reality and the symbol we use as its label arouse much the same inner meaning. Recognizing this double implication of *meaning* (as a response both to reality and to labels for that reality), we can set forth a rather simple definition. *Meaning* can be defined as:

> Subjective responses that individuals in a given language community learn to make, either to things they directly experience in reality or to particular symbols they use to label that reality.

We learn such links between reality, symbols, and meaning because we live among other people, all of whom have been taught the rules to use to associate specific patterns of inner experiences with particular words we share with them. It is this remarkable "language community" feature of human social life that permits human beings to communicate *with each other* as they do. In addition, this ability also makes it possible to communicate *with ourselves* (to think) by using language to arouse internal meanings. Meaning, then, is the key to understanding human beings as both thinking and communicating creatures.

But are we sure that others in our language community understand reality as we do? Interesting question, and one that has been debated for centuries. The answer is that we can't be certain, but we normally assume that the meanings one person experiences for a particular aspect of reality or a word used to label it are basically the same as another's. For example, we assume that a banana looks the same to everyone and has the same smell, feel, and taste. The symbol we use to label that reality, "banana," is also supposed to arouse pretty much the same experiences in everyone. Unfortunately, a sender's subjective meanings may not always be precisely and exactly the same as the receiver's, which can result in distortion and misinterpretation of the message.

Types of meanings: Denotations versus connotations. One potential source of confusion in communication is the problem of *unique personal meanings* versus shared or *standardized meanings*. This can be a significant source of inaccuracy in communications. For the most part,

How do you interpret what is going on in this photo? What meanings do you ascribe? Is she sharing her fries or is he pilfering them?

a symbol in a message transmitted to a receiver will evoke only its *denotative* or standardized meaning within the relevant culture. If that is the case, accuracy will be high. The meanings aroused in each will be restricted to those in dictionaries. However, there is always the problem of *connotative meanings*. These may be part of the personal meanings that an individual uniquely associates with a word because of past experience, or as a result of membership in a specific culture. If that is the case, use of the symbol in a message will arouse those private and unshared meanings and reduce the accuracy of the communication.

Connotative meanings can be illustrated easily. For example, in 2001, President George W. Bush initially described to the public the struggle against terrorism that he was designing as a "crusade." What he meant, of course, was a spirited and determined effort to apprehend and bring to justice those who commit attacks against civilians—such as the assault by airliner on the World Trade Center that occurred on Tuesday, September 11, 2001.[12]

In contemporary English, a "crusade" can be conducted against anything that needs to be strongly opposed—disease, poverty, crime, ignorance, or whatever. The meaning of *crusade* in that context was clear to most Americans who heard the president's speech. However, that term has additional and much more emotional meanings for those of the Muslim faith. They remain deeply aware of the great armed expeditions initiated by Pope Urban II, beginning in the 1100s to force the Muslims out of Jerusalem. Over two centuries there were a number of bitterly fought crusades, led by knights and their followers, who were intent on ejecting Muslims from the Holy Land, and indeed the complete destruction of Islam. To many in the Arabic world, then, the president's use of the word *crusade* had ominous connotative meanings indeed.

In less global terms, suppose that you ask me if I have a pet and I say, "Yes, I have a dog." It may appear that communication has been complete and accurate. After all, the word *dog* has

a specific denotative meaning set forth in English language dictionaries. However, I may have private (connotative) meanings for the word that bring to mind the attributes of my large, brown, friendly, and gentle dog that wags its tail when petted. Your dog, however, is different. It is a little, white mutt that barks constantly and nips at the heels of strangers. Our mutual connotative meanings have limited the degree to which our communication can be accurate.

Although connotations often bring about inaccuracy, they are not always undesirable. They can be a source of delight in certain kinds of messages. Poets, novelists, and even spellbinding orators often try to arouse a flow of colorful subjective meanings within their audiences by a rich attachment of connotative meanings to the symbols they select.

While the use of connotative meanings may be accepted for some purposes, accurate communication normally requires denotative meanings. To do otherwise, and let people use whatever meanings they wished for a particular word or nonverbal symbol, would result in an *Alice in Wonderland* world of chaos and would make communication impossible. It is for this reason that dictionaries provide relatively fixed meanings—at least for verbal symbols.

Storing symbols and meanings in memory. The way symbols and meanings are stored in memory is also an important consideration for understanding the encoding stage. But how does this work? No one is completely certain, but scientists in recent years have developed a couple of theories to explain how our memories work.[13] One way of explaining the process (by analogy) is to think of our memory structure as like that of a computer that records information on a magnetic disk, but infinitely more intricate. The key concepts that scientists have identified are *traces* and *schemas*.

Traces are imprinted records of experience registered in the brain's nerve cells. The computer analogy would be the magnetic areas on a disc that record the digital patterns for letters and numbers. But a word of caution: It may not be helpful to carry the computer analogy too far. We are talking about a biological rather than a mechanical process. In any case, traces can be thought of as neural "imprints" of the images, recollections, and other elements of experience that we associate with every word or symbol we know. This gets a bit murky because neurologists differ in their explanations of exactly how traces are imprinted. It may be a biochemical process, the result of tiny electrical currents, or alterations of nerve-cell structure. But one thing seems clear: A large body of research indicates that everything we experience, either in waking life or in our dreams, *leaves memory traces in our brain cells.* Even though we may not be able to recover those traces into consciousness at will, they appear to be there. One model, the selective activation, reconstruction and anchoring (SARA) model, suggests that memories are associated with each other with links of varying strength that indicate the probability of retrieval. The closer certain memories are related, the greater the strength of their association and the higher the probability that activation of one will lead to the activation of the other.[14] We do know that many memories can be recovered through hypnosis, drugs, or psychotherapy.

Looking at memory *psychologically* (rather than physiologically), how do we recover into consciousness memories of our experience from these traces? That is, how do we *organize our memories* so that we can recall past episodes in our life, meanings for words, and so forth? Psychologists who study memory conclude that as we send our experiences to our memory system, our brain organizes them into *schemas.* A **schema** *is a pattern or configuration of traces of symbols, images, experiences and their meanings that have been organized and recorded in a person's memory.*[15] What this implies is that our memory is not just a random jumble of imprinted traces. We store and recall organized schemas made up of all the memory traces of understanding, feeling, imagery, or other interpretations that we associate with

experiences that we have, or even with the word labeling that aspect of reality.

To illustrate, some schemas are simple, like the organization of the recall we experience for such words as *chair, fork,* or *shoe.* Others are more elaborate, like *circus.* Here we have a number of ideas in a kind of hierarchy, with big tents, animals, people, acts, and so on. The ideas included get more and more specific as one goes down the levels, with the most general and inclusive at the top and the most detailed at the bottom. (See Figure 1.2.)

You have used schemas many times—indeed every day. For example, when your friend says the phrase "Fourth of July," what organized meanings will you both recall? Probably you will experience a pattern of meanings that includes fireworks, flags, parades, and perhaps picnics or barbecues. But shame on you! You forgot the Declaration of Independence, which was announced on that date, and all the other patriotic reasons we celebrate that date. In any case, the Fourth of July schema brings together a number of meanings into an organized configuration.

Some schemas are related to more abstract terms, like "democracy" or "freedom." But even though these terms are abstractions, we do have some experiences that "come to mind" when we hear or read them. We also have schemas for particular episodes in our life, such as our high school graduation ceremony or the wedding of a good friend. Thus, we organize our meanings psychologically into schematic patterns of varying complexity that help in the recall of "clusters" of related traces.

What do all these ideas and concepts—memory traces and schemas—have to do with encoding intended meanings in a message? The schema idea is essential in describing the structure of a particular message that is selected and encoded for transmission to others. We can think of any message we formulate as *a number of organized schemas,* one associated with each word we select. Referring again to the example in Figure 1.1, the sender constructs an organized message from the separate schemas for

FIGURE 1.2

A Schema for "Circus"

The schema for "circus" includes meaningful categories of experience, such as animals, people, and things. Each person's schema for "circus" will vary according to the person's subjective experiences and memories.

"nice," "work," and "John." The sender then organizes these individual schemas into a sequence that meets the requirements of syntax (and of course grammar) in our language community. We noted earlier that these rules are also recorded as traces that can be recalled as organized schemas. For example, the sender in this case uses the recalled schemas of meanings for each word and rules of syntax to bring together the message of "Nice work, John" into one overall configuration of meaning. The sender fully believes that the message represents her intended meanings and that John will be able to interpret it in his own head by experiencing parallel meanings.

In summary, at the encoding stage the sender has to sort among his or her traces and organized schemas and decide which symbols match the meanings he or she intends. The individual then selects those symbols, plus the appropriate rules for their combination, in order to form a message that is both appropriate to the occasion and consistent with the goal. Then, as the encoding stage of the process proceeds, he or she tentatively constructs the message pattern to be used.

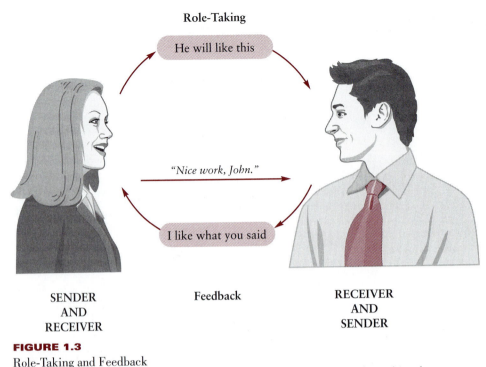

Role-Taking

He will like this

"Nice work, John."

I like what you said

SENDER
AND
RECEIVER

Feedback

RECEIVER
AND
SENDER

FIGURE 1.3

Role-Taking and Feedback
Adding feedback to the linear model modifies the communication process by making the receiver now a sender and the original sender now a receiver. Role-taking further modifies the model by making it more interactive.

Role-taking to assess probable receiver interpretations. Even when the message has been tentatively constructed, the encoding process is not complete. A remaining problem for the sender is to decide whether the receiver is likely to understand the message as formulated. The sender decides this by an activity called **role-taking**—which means "taking the role of the other."[16] Role-taking refers to an activity of the sender or source, who figuratively places herself or himself (psychologically) in the position of the receiver. The purpose of role-taking for the sender is to try to understand the best way to encode intended meanings so that the receiver will be able to interpret them as they were intended. This is not difficult if the sender knows the receiver well, but it can be a problem if the receiver is a stranger. If role-taking suggests the receiver is *not* likely to understand the message as formulated, the sender must quickly revise the message before transmission. (See Figure 1.3.)

We all engage in role-taking every time we communicate, and we do it in different ways, depending on the nature of the receiver. For example, we engage in role-taking when we communicate with a child—encoding the message in simple symbols associated with appropriate meanings the child is likely to understand. We also use role-taking every time we hope to convey a message that may not be easily understood or that could arouse unwanted feelings. The assessment of probable interpretations by role-taking, then, is a significant part of the message-encoding process.

An important, and more complex, role-taking activity is the construction of an *implicit personality*. That is, when we look at someone, especially for the first time, we observe what are called "salient characteristics." These are prominent, or at least readily noticeable, features of the person—a nice smile, bold jewelry, an attractive hair style, inappropriate clothing, or anything that stands out. We use these features to make assumptions about that person's character and probable behavior.

Encoding as automated behavior. By explaining the encoding process in such great detail, it may seem cumbersome and slow. That is incorrect. In fact, the encoding process is unbelievably fast—so fast that it rivals the speed of even the most sophisticated computer. In an instant we can formulate a message, engage in role-taking, and revise what we want to say if needed. We can achieve this speed because encoding behavior is *automated*. It takes place so fast and automatically that we are not usually aware of the steps we follow while doing it.[17]

Examples of automated behavior, other than what we do when communicating, include typing on a keyboard, playing a piano, and driving a car. When we do these things, we do not carefully plan, select, and then execute each finger or arm movement or other action with conscious awareness. In the communication process, encoding messages that incorporate the meanings we intend is done even faster.

Stage Three: Transmitting the Message as Information

The third stage in the linear model of the communication process requires that the message span the distance between the parties as *information*.[18] The term *information* refers to *patterned physical events*. For example, in the example in Figure 1.1 the message "Nice work, John" is transformed into agitations of air molecules that we know as sound. That transformation is accomplished by the parts of the body the sender uses to produce the sound waves relevant to the phrase "Nice work, John." In this form, the information moves across space in physical patterns representing words and related aspects of the message. This information serves as *stimuli* (a term from

psychology) that the receiver's sensory organs can detect.

If the message had been transmitted in written form, the information would conquer distance as visible patterned marks on paper. In a movie the information is patterns of light waves. Here, in both cases, the information stimuli are visual. If a medium such as a telephone, computer, or broadcasting had been involved, electronic impulses traveling along a wire or radiated electromagnetic waves would move the information from one communicator to another.

Stage Four: Perceiving the Information as a Message

In the fourth stage of our linear model, the person to whom the message is directed becomes the principal actor. Briefly stated, the receiver first *perceives* the incoming information stimuli and then assigns meanings to it so as to interpret it as a message. **Perception** is a rather complex psychological process. What happens is this: Patterns of information transmitted by the message source are picked up as stimuli by the receiver's sensory organs—usually eyes or ears. These are then identified as specific words, in a recognizable pattern, along with any nonverbal or other observable cues. Only then will the assignment of meanings (decoding) actually begin.

The term *perception* is a very important one in understanding human communication. It comes from psychology and has both common-use and technical meanings. Many people use the term loosely as a synonym for *belief* when they say something like, "It is my perception that our candidate will win the election." A more precise and technical meaning is used by psychologists and other social scientists. When they use the term *perception*, it means seeing, hearing, or feeling something (with the senses) and then *identifying* what it is, based on knowledge and prior experience that the person has obtained from his or her culture. To illustrate, when we see a person with a round semispherical shape of cloth on the end of a shaft held over the individual's head while it is raining (a stimulus) we have no trouble in identifying (perceiving) it as an "umbrella."

Thus, perceiving refers to identifying and classifying a stimulus apprehended by the senses. It could be a physical stimulus—like recognizing a small, red spherical object as an apple—or it could be identifying the pattern of sounds for the spoken word *apple* as a label for that fruit. Other stimuli may be identified as abstractions, such as "triangle," or as complex ideas, such as "justice." Perception is of critical importance in human communication because receivers have to identify the words that make up a message before they interpret it in full by arousing within themselves the appropriate meanings they have stored for those words.

Stage Five: Decoding and Interpreting the Message

After the words and other symbols of the message have been perceived and identified, the process of *decoding* can take place. This occurs at a very rapid rate (again, automated). One need not listen step by step to a message, then carefully decide what specific words have been used, then figure out each word's meaning, then decide what their overall pattern implies, and then interpret what has been said. That would take a while, to say the least. Thus, decoding, as well as encoding, is automated behavior that takes place almost instantaneously.

How can all of this take place so fast? The automated memory processes that enable the sender to sort and select appropriate symbols for the message are also used by the receiver to interpret the information. Stored in the receiver's memory are many thousands of schemas, organized structures of verbal and nonverbal symbols and grammatical patterns that have standardized and recognizable meanings that are *part of our shared language culture*. The incoming symbols are quickly distinguished from others similar to them and specifically identified. For each symbol, a quick search is made for possible interpretations. In the case of our simple three-word example (Figure 1.1), the receiver (John) almost instantly perceives the message as "Nice work, John"—and then instantly sorts out the associated meanings stored in his memory. When these are understood, the linear process is complete.

Note that even within this linear view of the communication process, it is the receiver who actively constructs meanings for the incoming information. In so doing, he or she draws on enormous personal resources of learned meaning responses, based on traces organized into schemas, plus habits, opinions, beliefs, attitudes, values, and factual information stored in memory. Clearly, the receiver's interpretations are certainly related to the sender's intended meanings, but they are not just passive duplications of the sender's meanings. They are *active reconstructions of meanings* derived from the receiver's own traces, schemas, and other experiences stored in memory. Because each participant constructs and interprets meanings separately, things can always go wrong!

Let's pause at this point and reconsider for a moment. As we have already indicated, face-to-face communication is seldom as simple (and never as slow!) as in this example. And, it is much more than the start-stop linear process that has been discussed up to this point. In reality, communication flows back and forth between people as they engage in ongoing conversations, and what they have said or done earlier shapes what they say next. It is for these reasons that we need to look at a more realistic *interactive model* of the process.

Interactive Communication: A Simultaneous Transactions Model

The basic linear model can be easily transformed into a much more realistic interactive representation of ongoing human communication by recognizing that both people in a conversation are communicators. They constantly respond to each other, simultaneously initiating messages and sending responses back and forth.

This calls attention to the importance of messages *sent back by the receiver to the source as responses.* For example, depicted in the linear model, after the source said, "Nice work, John," the receiver responded with a smile. In other words, John sent a message back! A smile under such circumstances is a nonverbal gesture used as *feedback.*[19] The term **feedback** indicates that some sort of message is returned to the sender as the message is being perceived and interpreted by the receiver. The smile is a good example of nonverbal communication—a conventionalized gesture that functions like a word because it has a standardized meaning in our society. We all understand that it implies a positive, rather than a negative, interpretation of meaning—something like "I like what you said."

Introducing feedback into the model makes the process *interactive.* That is, the communication process is no longer simply linear—a one-way series of stages from sender to receiver—but one in which both parties are *simultaneously* sending and receiving messages to and from one another at the same time. This simultaneous interaction feature of the process makes it necessary to develop a somewhat different model to portray human communication more realistically.

You will be relieved to know that to understand feedback, no new concepts or stages are required. A feedback message may be little more than a simple facial expression, like smiling or yawning, or the feedback may be a complex verbal statement or question, as in ordinary conversation. A feedback message, like any other, begins with a goal—to supply the sender with a return message. Words or gestures are selected to arouse an intended meaning. The message is transmitted (the smile in our example), and it is then perceived and decoded for interpretation by the source, *who is now a receiver.* Thus, feedback follows the step-by-step linear process between the two communicators that was discussed earlier.

However, we can now put together a more realistic model of human communication by incorporating both the role-taking and feedback activities of sender and receiver. This new version can be called a *simultaneous transactions model.* When used to describe the communication process, "simultaneous" implies that both communicators are undergoing the same kind of experience *at the same time.* That is not a complex idea. Equally simple is the term **transaction.** It refers to any kind of *exchange*—that is, an activity that occurs between, and mutually influences, all individuals acting with each other in some way. You have transactions every time you buy something, exchanging money for your purchase.

The simultaneous transactions model does not challenge the validity of the linear view of the communication process. On the contrary, it subsumes or *incorporates* it. To explain, the linear model helped us to *analyze* the act of communication, to break it down into its constituent parts and stages. Our task now is to take that linear process and *synthesize* (combine) it with other critical features of the process to provide a more realistic description of what happens when people communicate.

We can sum up the essential ideas of a simultaneous transactions model of the human communication process in six basic propositions. Communicators *simultaneously:*

1. *Encode and decode messages.* All individuals involved act as sources and receivers at the same time.

2. *Engage in role-taking and feedback.* These processes take place as each person decodes messages and encodes replies.

3. *Are influenced by their prior acts of communication.* What people say and the way they respond during a given transaction depend greatly on what has been said before.

4. *Are influenced by the physical surroundings within which their transaction takes place.* People communicate differently in different places.

5. *Are influenced by the sociocultural situation within which their communication takes*

place. What people say is almost always part of an ongoing social situation that has behavioral rules, such as a family dinner, a date, or workplace activity.

6. *Are influenced by the relationship that exists between them.* The type of social relationship between communicators (they may be strangers or intimates) significantly influences their transaction.

Taken together, these six propositions form a realistic description of the nature of face-to-face communications. They provide the basis for setting forth a model of how it occurs under a wide variety of circumstances, ranging from an intimate conversation between friends to a speech before a live audience of strangers.[20] Figure 1.4 illustrates this model. It is most applicable to face-to-face communication, and is less applicable to "mediated" communication, such as when communicators write letters, talk on the telephone, respond to a "tweet" or a text message, or use e-mail. It is clearly not relevant to communication with mass media,

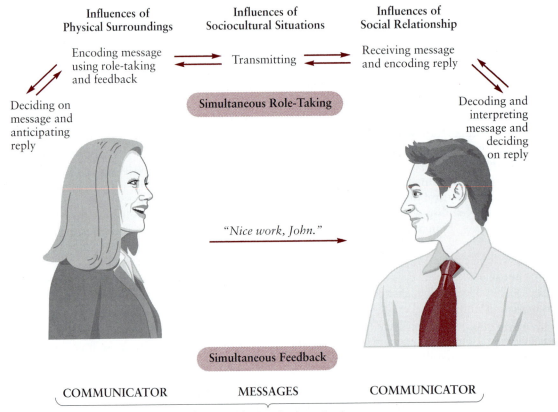

FIGURE 1.4

A Simultaneous Transactions Model
The simultaneous transactions model depicts the process of face-to-face communication as reciprocal activities that both parties engage in at the same time. While the messages are encoded and decoded, transmitted and received, role-taking and feedback are also applied. Moreover, significant influences on the process arise from what they have said before, the physical setting, the sociocultural nature of their activity, and the relationship between them.

where professional writers or broadcasters transmit messages to large audiences of individuals whom they do not know and never see.

Encoding and Decoding

The first proposition in the model indicates that while encoding messages, people also receive and decode incoming verbal or nonverbal messages from others. Thus, even as one person is speaking, the other may be encoding a reply. This is not inconsistent with the linear model described earlier. What this proposition implies is that those processes occur *simultaneously* as each party formulates and interprets messages continuously, speaking and responding, listening and replying.

Role-Taking and Feedback

The second proposition in the model is an extension of the first: The messages of each party, and the interpretations constructed by each, are simultaneously influenced by the role-taking assessments and the feedback they mutually provide. Thus, even as a person speaks, he or she is simultaneously assessing the listener's response on the basis of feedback and may be modifying parts of the message as that feedback is being transmitted.

Influences of Prior Communication

The third proposition in the model is obvious: What people have already said or heard determines what will follow. Thus, the encoding, decoding, and interpretation of messages usually builds on, or is an extension of, prior message content. Communicators simultaneously take this prior message content into account as the exchange continues.

Influences of Physical Surroundings

The influence of physical surroundings on communication is not always clear, but in many cases the setting in which it takes place has a strong influence on both what and how messages are exchanged. Consider how the physical context influences a discussion among close friends at a favorite restaurant, in the home of one's parents, at a funeral, or at a New Year's Eve party.

Influences of Sociocultural Situations

People do not usually get together in random groupings and begin communicating. Instead, communication is part of social situations that have meanings within their culture. These can be one-time get-togethers such as weddings, parties, or religious ceremonies, or ongoing situations such as at home, school, or work. What is said, to whom, and in what way is heavily influenced by the sociocultural situation. At a party where people have only recently met, for example, the conversation will likely focus on *small talk*, as people size up one another without revealing much about themselves. When it's a fishing vacation among close friends, however, conversation topics are quite different, and a great deal of self-disclosure takes place. Thus, the situation that brings people together is an important feature of a transactions model.

Influences of Social Relationships

Finally, the model's sixth proposition states that communicators are simultaneously influenced by any *social relationships* that already exist between them. Relationships such as those between spouses, friends, acquaintances, or supervisors and subordinates at work, can strongly influence both the content of messages and the way in which they are transmitted and received. Even if the communicators have never met before, the absence of a relationship heavily influences what they communicate to each other. Thus, the social expectations and rules of relationships shape many aspects of the exchange. These include the way messages are encoded or decoded, the effectiveness of role-taking assessments, the amount and kind of feedback, and even the amount of self-disclosure each party provides for the other.

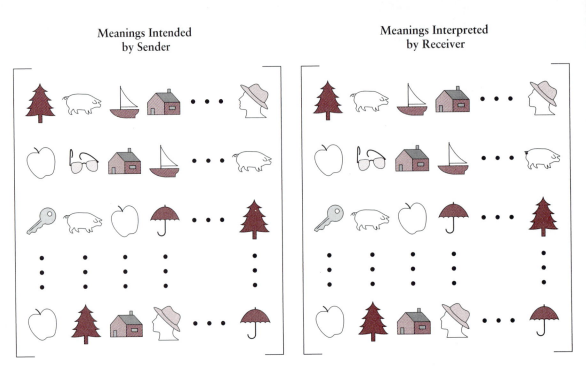

Meanings Intended by Sender

Meanings Interpreted by Receiver

FIGURE 1.5

Totally Accurate Communication
In totally accurate communication, every element and nuance of meaning in the message encoded by the sender would be decoded and interpreted by the receiver precisely as the sender intended. This accuracy is probably only possible for very trivial messages.

In summary, the simultaneous transactions model is a general view that applies to a broad spectrum of situations, relationships, and contexts within which people communicate. It brings together all the elements and stages discussed in the linear model and adds the influence of factors that affect the human communication process as it takes place in various settings for various purposes.

Accuracy in Communication

Totally accurate communication means that all the source's intended meanings, element by element, are reconstructed by the receiver so that they match each other perfectly and completely. (See Figure 1.5.) Unfortunately, communication between human beings is seldom if ever completely accurate in this sense. The meanings of the message as interpreted by the receiver almost always differ to some degree from those intended by the source. It was the realization of this fact during the 1940s that led two physical scientists to put together the very first linear model of the communication process on which our discussion is based. (See Figure 1.6.)

Claude Shannon and Warren Weaver, physicists working in Bell Telephone Laboratories, were considering the problems of distortion and inaccuracy that can take place in a mechanical communication medium—in this case the telephone. At first, they were not concerned with how the words or patterns of a message could become distorted by language problems or misunderstandings on the part of human communicators. They were trying to understand the *physical* problems that could introduce

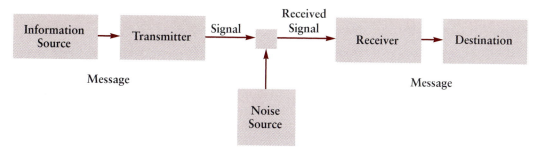

FIGURE 1.6
The Shannon and Weaver Conceptualization of the Communication Process.

what they called "noise" into the exchange.[21] To do this they set about to design a model of the mediated communication process.

What they came up with was a linear view of mediated communication that included a *source*, a *transmitter*, a *signal*, a *receiver*, and, finally, a *destination*. As is obvious, these terms look very much like those used in our linear model. The reason they seem similar is that the Shannon-Weaver model was adopted by communication scholars considering how people communicate interpersonally—with or without media. Thus, ideas from physical science provided a useful way of looking at interpersonal communication as we are discussing it.

The Shannon-Weaver view of the communication process (see Figure 1.6) was a mathematical one. It incorporated a number of ideas that did not become a part of the models later developed by communication scholars. However, one that was long regarded as useful was the term "noise." What that means is that various kinds of distortions that reduce accuracy can be introduced in the exchange between source and destination. Obviously, *physical* factors can reduce accuracy—such as trying to communicate with someone who is listening to music on an iPod. In interpersonal communication, many kinds of *psychological, social,* and *cultural* factors can reduce accuracy. These would include problems of perception, lack of familiarity with language, faulty memory, and perhaps animosities between the communicators. All of these can introduce "noise" (reduced accuracy) into an exchange.

In fact, there are an almost unlimited number of ways in which unintended meanings, constructed by a receiver, can displace or become compounded with those that the sender wanted to arouse. In large part, distortion arises because communication is much more than just using words and other symbols to express ideas.

Three broad categories of techniques are used, either deliberately or unwittingly, to arouse meanings in others. Each offers abundant opportunities for distortion. First, messages can be distorted *verbally,* through the spoken, written, or printed symbols and patterns (grammar and syntax) of language itself. Although words are deliberately selected, the sender may make poor choices that distort meaning for the receiver. For example, the use of the term *man* to refer to all human beings implies a lesser status for women. Although the sender may not intend this implication, poor word choice caused the distortion.

A second opportunity for distortion is provided by **nonverbal communication,** which can be very complex and confusing. For example, winking at a child while scolding her in front of others can be intended to negate the meanings included in the verbal scolding. However, the child may not understand. Whether nonverbal cues are used deliberately or unintentionally, they can cause others to construct distorted meanings. Third, distortion may arise from features of the setting or *context* within which the communication takes place. A message such as "I love you" said sincerely after a romantic candlelight dinner,

BOX 1.1   *A Closer Look*

Distortion in Communication

Although achieving complete and accurate communication is virtually impossible, examining those factors that interfere with our ability to get our intended meaning across to others will help us minimize distortion.

- *First, select your words carefully.* Even though you and your communication partner may both speak English, you probably do not share the exact same connotative meaning for any given word or phase. Verbal word choice becomes increasingly more important when you communicate with people whose experiences have been very different from yours. They may not understand what you mean or, worse, they may think you intend to hurt, demean, or exclude them by the words you use. For example, to refer to Asian-Americans as "Orientals" or adult women as "girls" can unintentionally distort what you mean to convey.
- *Second, give special attention to the nonverbal messages you send.* Nonverbal gestures,

hand movements, eye contact, smiling or frowning, and leaning body forward or backward all send a message—whether intended or not. Know that others will read those nonverbal signals even if you did not consciously send them. In fact, should you happen to send a nonverbal message that appears to contradict your words, you may confuse people.

- *Third, consider what you say always takes place within a certain context.* People often look to the context to help them understand the meanings of your message. A verbal message that may be appropriate and reinforced in one context might be totally distorted in another. For example, suppose you say "I do" when standing before a justice of the peace. Contrast the meaning of those same words when spoken as a trial witness in a county courtroom. Although both may connote a promise, what is being promised is altogether different.

---

may be interpreted differently from the same words uttered to someone met an hour earlier in a singles bar. Later chapters will discuss the influences of contexts at length. For now, note the sociocultural and physical settings within which communication takes place can introduce subtle or obvious cues into the process. These cues often influence the meanings intended by the source and those constructed by the receiver, resulting in distortion without awareness on the part of either. Shannon and Weaver would refer to such distortions as "noise." (See Box 1.1.)

Remember that receivers are always *active parties* in the communication process. They bring their own individual memories and meanings to the act of interpreting the message. The receiver's private and subjective meanings or connotations for words, things, actions, and settings may not be shared by the source.

Nevertheless, they may be used in the receiver's construction and interpretation of the source's message. It is little wonder, then, that human communication can often be a flawed process.

This discussion of incompleteness and distortion may make it seem that we can never communicate with other human beings at a level of accuracy needed to conduct our affairs. In reality, we seldom need to communicate perfectly. Other features of the human communication process permit people to get along pretty well *without* totally complete and perfectly accurate meaning constructions. To illustrate, let us assume that you're at work and your boss comes by one morning and says:

"I wonder if you would mind going down to the legal department and talk with Mr. Murakita. He has a mortgage contract that was signed a couple of

BOX 1.2   *Ethical Concerns*

DILEMMAS IN COMMUNICATION

Communication ethics develops guidelines to help us make good communication decisions. Consider the following ethical dilemmas. How would you answer each? What set of moral rules or principles do you rely on to help you respond to various communication situations? In other words, what are your personal ethics about communicating?

- Should I always tell the truth, even if the truth may hurt? Shouldn't some people be protected from the truth?
- Is there a difference between self*less* lies (Lying to protect someone else) and self*ish* lies (lying to protect myself)? Is one more acceptable than the other?
- Should others always be able to trust my word? Should I assume that I can trust someone else's word?

- Am I obligated to listen intently to my friend's concerns even when I think her problems are trivial?
- Should I attempt to persuade my partner to vote for the Democratic presidential nominee, or should I let him make up his own mind?
- If I am anxious to get off the phone and back to work, should I lie and say, "Someone's at the door. I have to go now"?
- When is it okay to reveal a confidence?
- When is it okay to interrupt someone else's talk? What if his or her topic is boring and I want to talk about something else?
- In an effort to avoid conflict, is it okay to be intentionally ambiguous or to simply refrain from stating my opinion?
- What responsibility do I have to keep the conversation going in social situations? Can't I just sit back and listen quietly if I want to?

days ago, and we may need it for the three o'clock meeting this afternoon. You might want to go over it with him so that you will understand the terms."

Suppose now that another person comes up a few moments later and asks, "Exactly what did the boss say?" Your response might be:

"Well, she told me to go see Mr. Murakita to get a contract that was just signed. Then she said she wanted me to read it in time for the meeting this afternoon."

Your version may sound pretty close, but looking at the two it is clear that it is different in a number of ways. In fact, if the two messages are directly compared, the accuracy level is rather low. For example, the boss asked you "if you would mind"—but you didn't say that. Furthermore, she did not specifically say that she wanted you to *read* the document; she merely implied that by saying that, "You might want to go over it."

Thus, the two messages above contain a number of differences between the version encoded and transmitted by the boss and that decoded and interpreted by you. At the same time, the basic elements of meaning *are close enough* so that you can do what the boss expects. The source's and receiver's combinations of meaning schemas contain enough similarity *for practical purposes*. That is: (1) You understand that there is a document, (2) you know that you are to get it, and (3) you realize that you are supposed to read it and be ready for the meeting. Those elements are all you really need to comply rather closely with the boss's wishes.

The point is that in any message there are two levels of meaning in most messages we initiate and transmit: The **surface meaning** refers to the whole range of intended elements we formulate into our message, exactly as we word it, but the **deep meaning** is the basic ideas that can be understood well enough for practical purposes. Despite this flexibility, even deep meanings

BOX 1.3 *Communication Competence Scale (CCS)*

Instructions

The following are statements about how people generally communicate with others. Answer each item as it relates to your *general* style of communicating in *most* social situations. Complete the questionnaire by indicating the extent to which you agree or disagree with each statement—by noting whether you:

5 = Strongly Agree
4 = Agree
3 = Neutral/Undecided
2 = Disagree
1 = Strongly Disagree

_____ 1. I find it easy to get along with others.
_____ 2. I adapt to changing situations.
_____ 3. I treat people as individuals.
_____ 4. I interrupt others too much.
_____ 5. Others find it "rewarding" to talk with me.
_____ 6. I deal with others effectively.
_____ 7. I am a good listener.
_____ 8. My personal relationships are cold and distant.
_____ 9. I am easy to talk to.
_____ 10. I won't argue with someone just to prove I am right.
_____ 11. My conversation behavior is not "smooth."
_____ 12. I ignore other people's feelings.
_____ 13. I generally know how others feel.
_____ 14. I let others know I understand what they mean.
_____ 15. I understand other people.
_____ 16. I am relaxed and comfortable when speaking.
_____ 17. I listen to what people say to me.
_____ 18. I like to be close and personal with people.
_____ 19. I generally know what type of behavior is appropriate in any given situation.
_____ 20. I usually do not make unusual demands on my friends.
_____ 21. I am an effective conversationalist.
_____ 22. I am supportive of others.
_____ 23. I do not mind meeting strangers.
_____ 24. I can easily put myself in another person's shoes.
_____ 25. I pay attention to the conversation.
_____ 26. I am generally relaxed when conversing with a new acquaintance.
_____ 27. I am interested in what others have to say.
_____ 28. I don't follow conversations very well.
_____ 29. I enjoy social gatherings where I meet new people.
_____ 30. I am a likeable person.
_____ 31. I am flexible.
_____ 32. I am not afraid to speak with people in authority.
_____ 33. People can come to me with their problems.
_____ 34. I generally say the right thing at the right time.
_____ 35. I like to use my voice and body expressively to communicate.
_____ 36. I am sensitive to others' needs of the moment.

Calculating Your Score:

1. Add together your responses to items 4, 8, 11, 12, and 28 = _____.
2. Add together your responses to all the other items.
3. Then, complete the following formula:
   CCS = 30 – Total from Step 1 = _____.
   Then, + Total from Step 2. YOUR TOTAL SCORE = _____.

Interpreting Your Score:

Possible range of scores: 36–180. (If your own final CCS score does not fall within that range, you made a computational error). The absolute mean = 108.

Individuals high in CCS (above 108) are generally more sensitive, flexible and assertive communicators than those lower in CCS. Of course, the higher your score, the more competent the communicator you perceive yourself to be. Importantly, this score only reflects how YOU perceive yourself as a communicator. You might want to let a partner, parent, brother/sister, or co-worker complete the scale on you as well. Then compare their total scored responses with your own!

Reference:

Wiemann, J. M. (1977). Explication and test of a model of communicative competence. *Human Communication Research, 3,* 195–213.

are often interpreted incorrectly. However, if a reasonable amount of accuracy can be attained at the deep meaning level, the transaction can usually serve well enough. Unfortunately, even modest levels of accuracy are not always easy to attain. (See Box 1.3.)

Communication that is complete and relatively free of distortion doesn't just "happen." The most important lesson that can be learned from all of these considerations is that the messages we put together for any purpose that is important to us must be *carefully managed at every stage.* That is true whether we are among family, friends, work associates or others with whom we need to have effective communication. The chapters that follow offer insights into the ways in which all of us, as either senders or receivers, can improve our ability to communicate.

Brief Chapter Review

- The central focus of the chapter is *human communication in all its aspects.* Stated briefly, communication is the study of the many ways that human beings relate to each other by exchanging messages, using a number of different processes of communication, and the consequences of those exchanges.

- In today's society, whether in the workplace, among friends, family, or in other kinds of settings, understanding the process of communication and acquiring effective communication skills is essential. Communication is defined as a process in which an individual initiates messages using verbal and nonverbal symbols to express meanings in such a way that similar or parallel understandings are aroused in all the communicators involved.

- The act of human communication can be visualized using a "linear model," which has been derived from an earlier version developed by Shannon and Weaver. The model is somewhat unrealistic in that it does not take into account the processes or role-taking or feedback, but it does break down the act of communication into a series of stages for purposes of detailed analysis.

- The linear model depicts communication as taking place when a person identifies a goal, constructs a message, and then transmits that message using various parts of the body and brain. With the use of the senses, a receiver then detects and identifies (perceives) the symbols, decodes the message, and interprets the meaning. Often, the receiver formulates a return message to provide feedback to the original source.

- Meaning is at the heart of communication. *Meaning* is the internal or subjective responses we make, either to aspects of the reality around us or to the labels we impose on that reality.

- A more accurate depiction of the human communication process is provided by the "simultaneous transactions model," which indicates that communicators simultaneously encode and decode messages and engage in role-taking and feedback. The model also indicates that communicators are influenced by their prior interactions, the physical setting, the social situation, and the nature of their relationship.

- Complete and totally accurate communication between communicators is unlikely because a variety of factors create distortion. However, total accuracy is not necessary in routine exchanges. Most message transactions arouse deep meanings that serve the practical needs of the communicators. Even so, it is likely that inaccuracies will occur in communication.

Key Terms

human communication
context
communicator
symbols
receiver
information
source or sender
encoding

decoding
distortion
accuracy (in communication)
linear
convention
trace
schema

role-taking
perception
feedback
transaction
nonverbal communication
meaning (surface)
meaning (deep)

Notes

1. See, for example: Gray, E., & Murray, N. (2011). A distinguishing factor: Oral communication skills in new accountancy graduates. *Accounting Education*, 20, 275-294; Stewart, J., & Knowles, V. (2000). Graduate recruitment and selection: Implications for HE, graduates and small business recruiters. *Career Development International*, 65–80; Ritter, M. A., Starbuck, R. R., & Hogg, R. V. (2001). Advice from prospective employers on training BS statisticians. *The American Statistician*, 14–18; Napoli, P. M., Taylor, M., & Powers, G. (1999). Writing activities of public relations practitioners: The relationship between experience and writing tasks. *Public Relations Review*, 25, 3, 369–380; Ugbah, S. D., & Majors, R. E. (1992). Influential communication factors in employment interviews. *The Journal of Business Communication*, 145.

2. Hart Research Associates (2010). *Raising the bar: Employers' views on college learning in the wake of the economic downturn*. Retrieved from http://www.aacu.org/leap/documents/2009EmployerSurvey.pdf

3. Levinson, W., Lesser, C. S., & Epstein, R. M. (2010). Developing physician communication skills for patient-centered care. *Health Affairs*, 29,1310-1317; Ratzan, S. C. (2011). Health communication: Beyond recognition to impact. *Journal of Health Communication*, 16, 109–111; Wakefield, M. A., Loken, B., & Hornik, R. C. (2010). Use of mass media campaigns to change health behavior. *The Lancet*, 376, 1261–1271.

4. The relationship between language, thought, and social life has been well established for many decades in such disciplines as anthropology, linguistics, philosophy, social psychology,

and sociology. See, for example: J. B. Carol, *Language, thought and reality*. Cambridge, MA: MIT Press; Mead, G. H. (1934). *Mind, self and society from the standpoint of a social behaviorist*. Chicago: University of Chicago Press; Bronowski, J. (1978). *The origins of knowledge and imagination*. New Haven, CT: Yale University Press, and Hymes, D. (1964) *Language in culture and society*. New York: Harper and Row, Publishers.

5. See: Bell, D. (1973). *The coming of post-industrial society: A venture in social forecasting*. New York: Basic Books.

6. Locke, J. (1975). In P. Nidich (Ed.), *An essay concerning human understanding* (p. 402). Oxford: Clarendon Press. (First published in 1690.)

7. Becker, H., & Barnes, H. E. (1961). *Social thought from lore to science* (3rd ed., pp. 3–131). New York: Dover Publications. Also: Cornford, F. M. (Trans.). (1941). *The Republic of Plato*. London: Oxford University Press. See especially Part III, Books XXIV–XXVIII, pp. 221–264.

8. See: Harper, N. (1979). *Communication theory: The history of a paradigm*. Rochelle Park, NJ: Hayden Book Company; Littlejohn, S. W., & Foss, K. A. (2011). *Theories of human communication* (10th ed.). Long Grove, IL: Waveland Press.

9. Cooley, C. H. (1909). *Social organization*. New York: Charles Scribner's Sons (p. 61).

10. Ellis, A., & Beattie, G. (1986). *The psychology of language and communication* (p. 19). New York: Guilford Press.

11. Cooley, *Social organization*, p. 69.

12. See: Kornblut, A. E., & Radin, C. (Sept. 18, 2001). Bush image of crusade upsets some potential allies. *The Boston Globe*, p. A22; Ford, P. (September 19, 2001). Europe cringes at Bush "crusade" against terrorists. *The Christian Science Monitor*, p. 12.

13. Detailed reviews of this developing field are found in the following sources: Nadel, L., & Hardt, O. (2011). Update on memory systems and processes. *Neuropsychopharmacology*, 36, 251-273; Frankland, P. W., & Bontempi, B. (2005). The organization of recent and remote memories. *National Review of Neuroscience*, 6, 119-130; Cermak, L. S., & Craik, F. I. M. (Eds.). (1979). *Levels of processing in human memory*. Hillsdale, NJ: Lawrence Erlbaum; and Bower, G. (Ed.). (1977). *Human memory: Basic processes*. New York: Academic Press; Green, J. (1984). A cognitive approach to human communication: An action assembly theory. *Communication Monographs*, 51, 289–306; Green, I. (1989). Action assembly theory: Metatheoretical commitments, theoretical propositions, and empirical allocations. In B. Dervin, L. Grossberg, B. J. O'Keefe, & E. Wartella (Eds.), *Rethinking communication* (Vol. 2, pp. 117–128). Newbury Park, CA: Sage.

14. Hardt, O., Einarsson, E., & Nader, K. (2010). A bridge over troubled water: Reconsolidation as a link between cognitive and neuroscientific memory research traditions. *Annual Review of Psychology*, 61, 141–167.

15. The schema concept was first used by Frederick C. Bartlett in his classic work *Remembering* (1932). London: Cambridge University Press. See also: Crocket, W. H. (1988). Schemas, affect and communication. In L. Donahue, H. E. Sypher, & E. T. Higgins (Eds.), *Communication, social cognition and affect* (pp. 32–51). Hillsdale, NJ: Lawrence Erlbaum;

16. The activity of role-taking, sometimes called "taking the role of the other," comes originally from the writings of George Herbert Mead, a philosopher and sociologist of the early 20th century. He developed a general theory called "symbolic interactionism," which maintains that human communication, using symbols with conventional rules of meaning, is the basis for the thinking abilities of human beings, and of the social rules that we share for behaving predictably in society. See: Mead, G. H. (1934). *Mind, self and society. From the standpoint of a social behaviorist*. Chicago: University of Chicago Press. For excellent discussions of role-taking and of symbolic interactionism more generally, see: Littlejohn, S. W., Symbolic interactionism as an approach to the study of human communication. *Quarterly Journal of Speech*, 63, 84–91; and Delia, J. G., & Grossberg, L. (1977). Interpretation and evidence. *Western Journal of Speech Communication*, 41, 32–42.

17. For a readable account of the implications of automaticity, see: Bargh, J. A. (1988). Automatic information processing: Implications for communication and affect. In L. Donahew, H. E. Sypher, & E. T. Higgins (Eds.), *Communication, social cognition and affect* (pp. 9–32). Hillsdale, NJ: Lawrence Erlbaum.

18. The term *information* as physical events that permit a message to conquer long or short distances, such as sound and light waves, electric pulses moving along a wire, or electromagnetic radiations that instantly transverse space, was developed in the work of Claude Shannon and Warren Weaver. See: Shannon, C., & Weaver, W. (1949). *The mathematical theory of communication.* Urbana: University of Illinois Press.

19. The term *feedback* comes from the field of cybernetics, which is the study of the automatic control systems formed by the nervous system and the brain that stabilize functions of the human body. It came into the study of communication through the work of Norbert Wiener (1954) in his seminal book, *The human use of human beings: Cybernetics and society.* Boston: Houghton Mifflin.

20. This view of human communication parallels in part what has been described as the "rules perspective." Communication scholars arguing this perspective indicate that people learn the rules for communication within differing situations and that the use of these rules is highly contextualized. For complete discussions of the rules perspective, see: Shimanoff, S. B. (1980). *Communication rules: Theory and research.* Beverly Hills, CA: Sage; and Sigman, S. J. (1980). On communication rules from a social perspective. *Human Communication Research, 7,* 31–51.

21. The term *noise* is often used to lump together and label various kinds of physical and other influences that reduce the accuracy of communication. It comes originally from the classic formulation of Shannon and Weaver's information theory (page 25). For elaborations of Shannon and Weaver's formulation, see: Broadhurst, A. R., & Darnell, D. K. (1965). An introduction to cybernetics and information theory. *Quarterly Journal of Speech, 51,* 442–435; Krippendorf, K. (1975). Information theory. In G. Hanneman & W. McEwen (Eds.). *Communication and behavior* (pp. 351–389). Reading, MA: Addison-Wesley; and Littlejohn, S. W. (2002). *Theories of human communication* (7th ed., pp. 43–56). Belmont, CA: Wadsworth.

Verbal Communication: Using Speech and Language

Look, Jennifer, I know I'm right," Gary said firmly. "My dog Sparky understands every word I say. He even talks back! When I get my car keys out and say 'Do you want to go for a ride?' he barks with enthusiasm. Or, when I scold him, he hangs his head and looks sorry. Don't tell me that animals can't use language. Sparky is a smart dog and, I say again, he understands every word I say. I have no doubt that he is engaging in verbal communication."

"But Gary," Jennifer replied, patiently. "What you are seeing is not really verbal communication. What is actually happening is that Sparky is an intelligent animal. He has lived with you long enough to pick up on your every action, your tone of voice and even all the distinctive patterns of sounds and signals that you use with him frequently—like letting him see the keys and asking him if he 'wants to go for a ride.' He does not remotely understand the words in the same way we do. He recognizes that particular pattern of signs and signals, and he has learned that a pleasant experience is likely to follow. It's no wonder that Sparky gets excited and barks.

"Psychologists say that animals learn to respond to natural signs that occur in their environment. You are Sparky's environment. All animals are capable of learning, and they catch on quickly about what will follow when they detect a particular stimulus. It's like pigeons who see someone eating from a sack of popcorn on a park bench.

They have learned that if they approach and strut around they are likely to get some. They don't have to understand language at all. Neither does Sparky. Let me say it again, and watch my lips. Animals just do not understand or use language."

"Oh yeah! What about whales? I read that they have their own language. Whales are highly intelligent and can make complex sounds that other whales can detect, even miles away. Their singing has even been recorded and set to music! I think dolphins also have their own language. I saw a thing on TV where dolphins followed the commands of a trainer who asked them to do all kinds of really complicated things."

"It is a wonderful idea, Gary. I personally would love to have a conversation with a whale or a dolphin but it just isn't going to happen. It is certainly true that they engage in complex signaling to each other, but all animals in the wild do that. Geese, deer, wolves, and even insects provide signals to indicate the presence of danger, their readiness to mate, or the availability of food. Some do it with sounds, others with body movements or even odors. But they are not having conversations about the weather or setting up meetings for later in the week. They are using inherited or learned systems of signals to communicate basic messages. So, I am saying that animals can certainly communicate. But they do not develop and share languages."

"Jennifer, you need to read up on the experiments psychologists have done in teaching chimpanzees and even a gorilla to use sign language. Some of those animals were able to learn more than a hundred different signs and use them to understand various messages that their trainers sent to them. Sure, they couldn't actually speak, as we do, but they were able to respond to signs. You have to agree that this clearly is verbal communication, even if it is not speaking like we are now."

"Gary, I'm not going to argue with you any more. Your head is filled with incorrect interpretations and false conclusions. I don't want to waste my time discussing this any more. You can just have a nice chat with your dog."

We can hope that Gary and Jennifer found some other topic to discuss. But who was right? Was Jennifer correct in her conviction that animals can communicate, but only by using a variety of nonverbal and nonlanguage behaviors? Or, is Gary right in concluding that his dog, Sparky, and indeed other kinds of animals, such as whales, dolphins, and chimpanzees, have been able to master forms of verbal communication and the use of a language of their own under the right circumstances?

First, why is this important? One answer is that the study of how animals communicate has been an important topic in the social sciences—particularly in psychology. Psychologists search for "universal laws of behavior"— conduct and actions that can be found among many kinds of species. The question is this: Do human beings communicate in ways that are *unique* to them, or are they just one more animal that communicates in basically the same way? We can find the answer to that question by a very brief look at the communication process in *comparative perspective*—which means comparing and contrasting the communication processes used by animals with that used among human beings. Are they essentially the same or starkly different?

It can be instructive to look very briefly at what takes place among animals as a starting point for gaining a better understanding of human verbal communication using speech and

Communication using language is unique to humans. Verbal communication is based on learning but also requires shared conventions of meaning among those who use a language.

language. As Jennifer pointed out, animals certainly are able to communicate with each other—using **natural signs**—sounds, movements, odors, and postures that they are capable of performing—often in remarkably complex ways. But is it the equivalent, as Gary claimed, to the use of language to communicate the way people do constantly? The value in sorting out this issue as a foundation for discussing verbal behavior among human beings is *not* to become an expert in the ways of animals. Its value lies in understanding more thoroughly the unique nature of words, their meanings within a language, and what human communication does for us as thinking, remembering human beings who know their environment, develop solutions to problems, and lead complex social lives.

The Animal Kingdom: Communicating without Language

The idea is an old one that animals can communicate as do human beings, and at least in some cases, understand **language** as fully as we do. The idea of talking animals can be found in legends and tales in almost every society throughout history. Talking animals were common in classic Greek fables (e.g, Aesop's tale of "The Fox and the Grapes") as well as in more modern literature (e.g., Lewis Carol's *Through the Looking Glass*) and on into today's funny papers. But there is one account that for our purposes truly stands out. Over a hundred years ago, a particular animal came to public attention that seemed to offer convincing proof that an animal could understand language in remarkably complex ways. The animal seemed to possess an extraordinary level of intelligence. It was startling because no one had ever before suspected such capacity among members of the animal kingdom. This is what happened:

The Case of Clever Hans

In 1900 a retiring Berlin schoolteacher of mathematics, Wilhelm von Osten, bought a horse. He called him Hans. The horse was an attractive animal who soon bonded with his master. As a hobby, Herr von Osten began to train Hans in a most unusual way. With the aid of a blackboard and other devices, he taught the horse to recognize numbers and count out their value by tapping his forefoot on a small wooden platform. At first, he had to assist Hans in learning the tapping routine, but the schoolteacher was very patient with his new pupil and aided him in getting it right. In the early lessons he had to take the horse's hoof in his hands and show him just how to tap, over and over, until Hans could do it by himself. He then taught him the right answers to some very basic problems. For example, when shown a number (such as 7 or 9) on a blackboard that Hans could see, and then when asked verbally what it was, Hans would obediently tap the correct number of times. Hans progressed rapidly and could soon do fairly large numbers, even those over one hundred.

The teacher was pleased and decided to go on to more advanced problems. To his delight, Hans caught on very quickly, and soon the horse could answer amazingly complex arithmetic questions put to him by his trainer. He seemed to be able to add and subtract, and even to multiply and divide, always signaling the correct answers to his trainer by taps of his hoof on the little platform. Herr von Osten was not a showman or a professional animal trainer, and he was as surprised as anyone at how clever Hans was.

As the neighbors saw what Hans could do, and stories began to appear in the press, the horse's reputation grew rapidly. Soon Hans was attracting nationwide, and later even worldwide, attention. The idea that an animal could communicate with human beings was very exciting. Furthermore, the level of intelligence required to perform the tasks accomplished by Hans was far beyond what anyone had attributed to a horse before. Finally, experts were coming from all over Europe, and even other parts of the world, to see *Kluge Hans* ("Clever Hans," as he became known).

Some were convinced that it was all a fake, and they tried to expose Herr von Osten as a fraud. But no one was able to detect any deception. As time went on, many came to believe that Clever Hans might provide the key to a whole new understanding of animals. Some authorities felt that the discovery of the horse's amazing capacity posed an important ethical breakthrough. It seemed clear that the animal—and perhaps all animals—had a level of intelligence very close to that of human beings. In particular, it appeared that Hans was *understanding and using language as effectively as a human being.* Although he lacked a voice, his hoof-tapping seemed like an acceptable alternative.

Then, in 1904, a German psychologist, Professor Oskar Pfungst, persuaded the owner to let him make a thorough study of the remarkable horse to determine once and for all whether the animal was actually able to understand and use human language.[1] With the owner's permission, the psychologist conducted all kinds of tests to determine the animal's true abilities.

What Professor Pfungst discovered was that Hans was a very clever horse indeed—but not in the way people thought. Actually, Hans was receiving unintentional "cues" from his owner that enabled him to start and stop tapping in exactly the right way! The bond between the animal and his owner was so strong that Hans could detect the *most subtle movements and facial expressions* of the schoolteacher when he was standing in front of Hans and waiting for him to tap out answers. What Herr von Osten was doing, without realizing it, was nodding his head in an almost undetectable manner as he silently counted to see whether Hans would reach the correct number of taps. Such unintended movements (some as small as a fraction of a millimeter) were cues to Hans to keep tapping. When the owner stopped moving his head, changed expression, moved back, or smiled as the correct number was reached, Hans simply stopped tapping.

What confused many observers was the fact that Hans was able to tap out the right number to answer problems posed by a stranger—even if his master was not present. That certainly ruled out deliberate deception with secret signals; but eventually, Professor Pfungst found out that Hans could not correctly solve a problem if the answer was not known to the questioner or if Hans could not see or hear the person standing in front of him.

The conclusion finally reached was that Clever Hans had no grasp of human language whatsoever. What he was doing was much simpler. The horse had learned to read a great variety of *subtle cues* as to when he should start and stop tapping. In fact, he learned to read amazingly subtle forms of behavior from strangers as well as his master. When other people came to watch Hans perform he was able to read their expressions of anticipation, encouragement, and satisfaction, just as well as those of his master. When such cues were absent, Hans was just another nice horse.

Communicating with Learned Signs

The story of Clever Hans helps us understand the nature of language by showing the sharp contrast between human and animal communication. It is very easy to be misled by clever animals that seem to understand language. What can be observed in their behavior is often called the **Clever Hans effect**—responses to subtle actions and cues provided unwittingly by owners or experimenters. Nevertheless, the question whether animals are capable of using language still remains an open one within the scientific community.

It is easy to assume mistakenly that a clever animal, like Hans, can learn to use language.

Anyone who has lived with a much-loved pet understands that communication between a human being and an animal can be both subtle and extensive. Like Hans, dogs, cats, and parrots are much more intelligent than most people realize. It doesn't take them long to figure out how to master their environment, whether it is a backyard or an urban apartment. They develop ways to let people know that they want to be fed, that they want out (or in), that strangers are present, and so forth. They have little trouble in initiating **signals** to beg for treats, to indicate that they want to go along in the car, or that they want to play. Like Clever Hans, pets quickly learn to pick up subtle cues related to human habits and family routines. Anyone who has seen pets suddenly make themselves scarce at bath time will realize the subtlety of the cues they can read. No wonder owners sometimes conclude that their pets really can understand human language.

Where are we in this debate now? At present, psychologists who compare animal and human behavior have concluded that animal communication is based on inherited biological abilities, that is, *instincts* (among simpler animals like insects) and on *learned* **signs** for those closer to human beings on the evolutionary scale. Human beings, in contrast not only learn various kinds of **symbols** but also learn to interpret them in ways that are parallel to their meanings to others in their **language community**. Animals do not do this. Individually, they can respond to signs, often in remarkable ways as was the case with Hans, but they have yet to develop a system of language in which meanings for signs are shared with others of their species in a language community. (See Figure 2.1.)

In spite of all these considerations, there is one important question that needs to be addressed: Isn't it possible that some intelligent animals would be capable of learning to use language *if human beings took the trouble to teach them?* This question has been vigorously studied in recent decades, and a considerable controversy has raged around the conclusions reached.

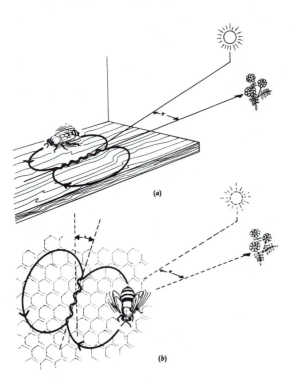

FIGURE 2.1

(a) The bee uses a dance to indicate to other bees the distance (*x*) to food source; (b) the bee circles in the hive to direct other bees to direction and distance to food.

Trying to Teach Apes to Talk

Are any animals at all capable of learning to speak and use language, even at a very elementary level? Can any creature *other* than a human being be taught to speak? This is a very interesting, even critical, question—and it has been systematically explored.

The capacity to learn is at a maximum among animals near the top of the **phylogenetic continuum** or scale (those nearest us in the evolutionary chain), such as chimpanzees, gorillas, and other large primates. Decades ago a number of systematic attempts were made by psychologists to teach chimpanzees to speak and also to instruct gorillas or other primates to use sign language, special symbols, and computers. In many ways, the results of these attempts are surprising. They also remain controversial.

In the first of a series of classic experiments, psychologists Winthrop and Louise Kellogg decided in 1931 to see whether a chimpanzee could learn to speak.[2] At the time, they did not understand the limitations of chimpanzee anatomy that would make this impossible (like the problem with early human beings). They believed that one reason apes did not do so was because they were not raised in a language environment. Human infants, on the other hand, are in constant contact with language-using adults who offer rewards and encouragement for attempts to learn to talk. Why not, then, raise a chimp in a completely human environment and teach the animal to speak as though it were a human child?

As it happened, the Kelloggs were expecting a baby. They decided to conduct an experiment by acquiring an infant chimpanzee to raise in an identical manner with their own child. As soon as their infant son, Donald, was born, they were able to get a baby chimp. Donald and the baby chimp, Gua, were bathed, fed, diapered, and treated affectionately in exactly the same manner. Both were equally encouraged to use words and were coached extensively.

It didn't work. The chimp and the baby got along very well, but at the end of three years, Donald was growing up to be a normal boy while Gua was developing into a normal chimp. Donald learned speech in the manner typical of his age, putting together words into simple sentences. Gua was never able to speak a word.

In 1947 a somewhat similar project was undertaken. There was no human baby present, but Keith and Catherine Hayes raised a chimp, Vicki, in their home.[3] They coached her constantly in the use of specific words, helping her to form sounds by manipulating her lips. After six years, however, the chimp had learned to vocalize only three crude approximations of English words—"mama," "papa," and "cup." She did so only on command in a hoarse whisper with great difficulty, and there was no firm indication that these "words" had the same meanings they have for people. Vicki's accomplishments were not much different from those of a dog that learns to "speak" at the owner's command.

The home-rearing experiments with Gua and Vicki were generally failures in terms of their original goals. Yet, in one way they were great successes. They forced a clear recognition that the animals had difficulty because their vocal physiology was not able to form speech sounds. We know now that the vocal tract, larynx, and other soft tissue structures that human beings use to generate and control complex sounds are quite different in other primates.

Even more significant, an elaborate brain is required for speech. The chimpanzee brain does not appear to have clear counterparts of the areas in the human brain that are essential to human speech (Broca's and Wernicke's areas).[4] What all of this means is that apes are not going to learn to talk, no matter how they are coached. Their bodies are not designed for it, and it would be rather pointless to make further attempts.

If apes can't speak, is there another way that they can communicate using language? As an alternative to speech, sign language has been the subject of several classic experiments. Young apes are far better at manual dexterity than are young human beings. They spontaneously make many expressive gestures and finger movements. This fact led comparative psychologists to conclude that they should try to take advantage of their manual dexterity, by using a means of communication not requiring the apes to speak. If this could be done, then perhaps apes could be taught to "talk" with human beings without the use of the voice.

Thinking along these lines, psychologists Beatrice and Allan Gardner decided to try to teach a chimp the finger positions, movements, and other language signs and symbols used by people who are deaf. In 1966 they acquired Washoe (whom they named after the Nevada county where they lived). They immediately began to teach her ASL—American Sign Language—which is used by the deaf community.[5] Here, no vocalization was involved, and the chimp could take advantage of her natural agility.

Teaching Washoe the signs wasn't easy. The chimp was housed in a special trailer surrounded by a big yard with a high fence—a rich environment somewhat like a human home. Both the Gardners and other teachers spent long periods with Washoe every day, conditioning her to make the right signs for various objects and actions. At the end of the four-year experiment, the researchers believed she was able to respond to some 160 signs.

What seemed even more exciting to them was that the chimp sometimes spontaneously put two, or even three, signs together. At least some of these combinations appeared to "make sense." The chimp produced such combinations as "gimme tickle," "go sweet" (which the experimenters interpreted as a request to be taken to raspberry bushes to eat fruit), and even "Roger Washoe tickle" (seen as a request to play with her trainer).

While the results seemed gratifying, there were serious limitations in what Washoe could do. On no occasion did she put together anything abstract, novel, or inventive, although she lived in an environment where there were numerous possibilities to make such combinations. Her signing behavior was restricted to the *here and now,* never referring to the past or future. Virtually all her spontaneous signing was related to food, treats, or other personal needs of the moment. Most important, there was no evidence that she developed an understanding of **syntax,** that is, rules for putting signs together in consistent patterns that themselves provide meaning. In short, the effort was inconclusive.

Perhaps the most dramatic of the sign language experiments was the effort by psychologist Francene Patterson to teach Koko, an African gorilla, to communicate with ASL. She acquired the animal as an infant and established it in special quarters. Working with several assistants, Patterson patiently taught the animal to make signs and associate them with specific meanings (such as "food," "drink," and "more"). Later, this was extended to include many more signs and their associated meanings.

The animal was able to make a great many signs which she produced in many sequences. Some of them seemed to Patterson to be appropriate to communicate simple requests and responses to queries from the trainers. Generally, Koko seemed to be the equal or even superior of Washoe in the use of signs.[6]

Many critical psychologists have rejected the conclusion that these animal experiments show any language usage or capacity at all. They base their rejection on two grounds. First, careful studies of films and videotapes taken to record the training of many of the chimps, and the gorilla Koko, seem to show the Clever Hans effect. That is, there was evidence that these intelligent animals could detect what their trainers wanted them to sign, and they obligingly complied to get approval or rewards. This interpretation has raised serious doubts about whether the animals involved had any real conceptual ability or had mastered even the crudest idea of syntax.

In more recent years, psychologists have tried to go beyond the close contact between trainer and chimp required by learning sign language. In various experiments chimps learned to use "artificial languages." For example, a chimp called Sarah was taught by David Premack to manipulate pieces of plastic of various colors and random shapes.[7] Through conditioning, the ape was taught to associate various objects and actions with these plastic "words." Then, to try to develop primitive rules of syntax, various combinations were given meanings. Sarah did learn to use sequences of her pieces of plastic. In fact, after extensive training it seemed to the experimenters that she had mastered simple abstractions and conceptual relationships, such as identifying things by color and indicating whether an object was "over," "under," or "beside" another.

Perhaps the most significant finding from the work with Sarah was that she could learn and use simple rules for associating meaning with combinations of her plastic pieces. On the other hand, she was limited by the characteristics of all apes: She had a very short memory span and

her use of the synthetic "language" was restricted completely to the here and now.

Even more recently, elaborate experiments have been tried in attempts to rule out the Clever Hans effect. Chimps have been placed in computer-controlled environments that did not require the presence of a human handler.[8] Typically, these are laboratory-like rooms that contain a kind of keyboard. Each key corresponded to a "word" in an artificial language called "Yerkish" (after Robert Yerkes, a famous comparative psychologist). Pressing the key, on which is displayed a special symbol, causes a visual display with the same symbol to light up. The chimp subject can press several keys and get a string of symbols lit up on the special display. Outside the room, the experimenter has a similar keyboard. Because it is also wired to the visual display, two-way signaling with the ape is possible. A computer interfaces the two devices and keeps track of the results. Overall, however, no startling findings have come forth.[9]

The most damaging criticism of the animal communication studies comes from statistical evidence. The number of times the animals used various signs and signals both singly and in various combinations has been carefully tallied in a number of these experiments. Out of the thousands of such usages, a certain number of combinations would be expected *if only chance were at work*. That is, even in the most random set of events, at least some combinations will be found that "look" meaningful. In fact, such analyses reveal that the combinations of sign usage occur almost exactly in proportion to what one would expect in distributions produced solely by chance. Thus, enthusiastic experimenters may have focused on those few random accidental occurrences and unrealistically concluded that they represent language usages, while ignoring the huge numbers of meaningless combinations far more typical of animal behavior.

At present, it seems that even the animals closest to human beings on the phylogenetic continuum will not be shown to be able either to speak or to use language in any realistic way as do human beings. Yet, studies of this issue should continue. Who knows? Perhaps a clever experimenter in the future will show us a way in which Gary can have that nice chat with his dog Sparky.

The Human Experience: The Development of Speech and Language

But have we always, since our very beginnings, been able to use speech and language? Or, were we like animals long ago, at some prehistoric point before we acquired those remarkable features of human life? Analysis of fossil remains indicate that the earliest hominids (human-like creatures) split off in the evolutionary tree of apelike animals about 8 million years ago.[10] Those prehistoric human ancestors (*homo australopithicus*) could use only signs and signals to communicate. That is, they could use their arms, hands, and various bodily actions to transmit simple commands or other signals to each other. It seems likely that they could supplement these signs and signals with sounds, but these appear to have been relatively uncontrolled vocal noises, rather like apes and monkeys make. They would not be able to speak as we do until their brains became much larger, their vocal chords moved to their present position (from a much lower area in the upper chest) and their lip and tongue structures became more refined to resemble those of contemporary human beings. All of that gradually took place over millions of years as *Homo sapiens, sapiens* (modern human beings) gradually evolved.

The Beginnings: Gaining the Ability to Talk

What all this means is that we began speaking and using language—that is engaging in verbal communication—only a relatively short time ago, considering the millions of years that human creatures have lived on this planet.[11] According to the best available evidence put together by paleoanthropologists who study ancient human beings, *speech*—the ability to pronounce words using vocal chords with refined movements of tongue, lips, and air passages—as we know it today did not come until the appearance of the *Cro-Magnon people*, our immediate human ancestors. The most important feature of the *Cro-Magnon* is that they appear to be the first in the chain of human evolution *who could make and control the sounds* that we use today when we talk.

Our best estimates place these changes back somewhere between 90,000 and 35,000 years ago. (No one really knows in any more precise way.) It seems very likely that by about 30,000 years ago, the ability to speak was well-developed and local groups in many parts of the world could talk with each other, tell stories, teach their young, and generally communicate with speech, much as we do now. To do so they had to use a *language*—that is, a standardized vocabulary, with agreed-upon rules of pronunciation, syntax, and grammar.

Expanding Verbal Communication: Conquering Time and Distance

Acquiring the ability to speak and use language brought remarkable benefits to human beings. For example, somewhere around 10,000 years back our ancestors began to invent *agriculture*—techniques for farming and the domestication of animals. This enabled them to make a transition from hunting and gathering as a means of subsistence to living in fixed locations—in villages where they could tend their crops and raise their animals. Agriculture along with techniques for preserving food made life far easier. It also meant great progress toward a more stable existence.

Being able to talk allowed each new generation to invent new ideas, procedures, and technologies for solving problems and pass them on orally. One consequence was a development of ever more efficient techniques of agriculture and food preservation. As a result, there was a steady and significant growth in the world's human population and a gradual increase in life expectancy (average age at death). Still, the ability to pass on knowledge was limited to the capacity of human memory, so even small advances took many generations. The expansion of human knowledge, then, was slow and limited in an era of purely oral communication. More rapid improvements in life would not come about until more recent times with the invention of writing. Improvements would accelerate greatly after the 15th century, with the invention and widespread use of printing. Finally, in very recent times, over the last two centuries, human communication would cease to be bound by time or distance with the invention and adoption of modern mass media.

Writing: Recording and recovering thoughts. Today, few of us truly understand that the development of writing was one of the most remarkable human accomplishments in verbal communication of all time. Some authorities link it to cave paintings, such as those found in southern France and in Spain. In some cases, these go back at least 15,000 years. Yet, their purpose remains unclear and no one really knows whether they were the first steps in developing writing.

Much clearer are techniques for using graphic pictures and abstract symbols for *recording ideas* that began between 5,000 and 6,000 thousand years ago. At first they were very simple, to be sure, but they were indeed systems for writing as we think of it today. People of the time (in various parts of the Mesopotamian area) began to carve or scratch simple pictures on flat stone slabs. They used lines to separate different parts of their messages into small squares (like is still done in the comic strips in the daily paper). Within such squares they carved representations of objects that had associated familiar meanings, such as animals, parts of the human body, or other features of their environment. For example, a simple

depiction of a foot represented a man walking. A simplified sun indicated one day, and a wavy line meant water, such as a lake. A person seeing these symbols and recovering their meaning would read them as: "A man walked for one day alongside a lake." It was a remarkable achievement. *It even permitted living people to communicate with the dead!* That hitherto impossible feat gave even early writing a special significance.

The key to understand such a written message using *pictographs* (simplified pictures representing ideas) was that agreements had to be in place (among both those who prepared them and those who tried to interpret them) that a particular little pictograph (e.g., a sun) was always supposed to arouse the standardized meaning of *one day*. With such agreements in place, such a system of writing really worked. Each symbol represented a particular word or idea and could indeed be prepared by, or later interpreted by, anyone who knew the rules. In fact, many of the writing systems used in the world today are still based on this process. Examples are Arabic, Chinese and Japanese—to mention only a few.

Eventually, some of the ancient people who inhabited regions around the Mediterranean began to improve their way of writing. One great improvement was that they began to have the graphic forms—the symbols—whether carved, painted with a brush, or written with a pen represent *sounds*, rather than words or whole ideas. This was a really important advance. To develop "sound" writing, a way had to be invented so that each of the different noises human beings can make with their voice boxes, lips, tongues and so on, has its own characteristic written mark. Over time a link was made between sounds and written symbols or *characters* to represent them.

Eventually, by around 900 B.C., the Greeks produced a remarkably different system based on *letters*, each of which represented its own sound. The letters could be placed into sequences to make the sound of an entire word. Eventually, they standardized these characters throughout their various regions. This made written communication based on the oral sounds of spoken language much simpler, easier to learn, and far easier to write. The Greeks used common names of things in their environment, such as *alef* (the bull), to label their letters. Thus the first letter was *alpha* from that source. Their second was *beta,* and from those two we get *alphabet.*

Using an alphabet to represent sounds greatly simplified learning both reading and writing. There are only a certain number of distinct sounds that a human being can make with his or her voice. Generally, we can make sounds that we know today as *vowels* (softer ooohs, aaahs, and eeehs). We can also make harsher sounds—consonants like the *t*, the *k, b,* and *d.* Although it took thousands of years to produce and standardize the way we do this today, using a set of letters for sounds did get conventionalized. The standardized Greek alphabet made it possible for Plato (428–348 B.C.) to write his *Republic,* and for his student Aristotle (384–322) to produce not only his great works *Ethics* and *Politics,* but also his system of Aristotelian logic, which became the established route to valid knowledge for religious scholars more than a thousand years afterward. Their ideas have remained a part of Western culture since that time. They also made it possible for many to learn to read.

Beginning in about the first century before Christ, the Romans developed a modified alphabet derived from the Etruscan and Greek versions. They also standardized the appearance of the letters. The Roman letters they developed are still widely used when we write in English as well as in many other languages. Today, we have only 26 letters, plus some punctuation characters, that represent in graphic form the phonograms we use in speech.

In overview, it took many centuries for human verbal communication to get here from there, but both human speech and the ability to record it as writing represent advances of staggering proportions. We often think today that inventions like the telephone, the automobile and the computer represent immense steps forward. And, of course they do. But they all pale in comparison with the development of speech and writing as modes of verbal communication which made possible the very foundations of human existence and civilization.

Printing: Expanding the dissemination of ideas. With speech and writing well developed, humankind still faced a significant problem. There was a serious need for extensive written documents that could preserve the growing bodies of knowledge that were being produced by the world's great religions, by early mathematicians and astronomers, by some of the founding fathers of science and other intellectuals. Books were badly needed to record that knowledge and to pass it on to others. The skill of writing books by hand did not provide well for that need. Books written by hand, that is, *manuscripti,* prepared letter by letter, word by word and sentence by sentence, were very difficult to produce and demand far outstripped supply.

During the 1200s, a new kind of more secular institution began to be established in major capitals of European countries. They were schools whose curricula focused on the "learned professions." These were the liberal arts, canon and civil law, medicine and theology. While they educated students who were mainly from the upper levels of society, their importance for the study of verbal communication is that *they required both libraries and textbooks.* But at the time, books for both uses were still dreadfully difficult to obtain. All were handwritten in (secular) *scriptoria* to be sold for very high prices, or were copied word for word from rented chapters by students themselves. A new technology for producing books was sorely needed. However, it was simply not available.

The person who developed the technology for printing was Johannes Gutenberg, the son of a goldsmith in Mainz (in what is now Germany). It was a remarkable new technology. He experimented for more than 20 years and finally developed a press (based on the principles of a wine press). He cast individual letters in metal, one letter at a time, and prepared a suitable printers' ink (made of lampblack and varnish). Finally he had all the procedures needed to produce a large number of identical pages free from the usual errors of the *manu-scriptus*. His first effort was an elegant Bible. However, he did not profit from his invention. He had to borrow money for supplies but was unable to repay the loan. The lender threw him out of his print shop, took over his press and the 200 copies of the Bible he had printed. He had the Bibles bound and sold them at a considerable profit. The penniless Gutenberg wandered around for a few years after that, living miserably on charity, went blind, and died in utter poverty. As you read these lines today, think of the remarkable contribution that he made to your personal education, and indeed human existence.

By the time that Columbus set out for the new world, there was a printing press in virtually every major city in Europe, from which it quickly spread to most other parts of the world. The use of print as a means of extending speech as a mode of verbal communication entered a new and truly important era. Now, books could be printed in large numbers of identical copies. With the alphabet as a basis for written language, and books available to read, the rate of literacy in populations rose sharply. The new books not only served the universities and churches well, but it expanded the ability of humankind to pass on culture to new generations. As science began, religion expanded and writers produced an increasing body of literature. Thus, verbal communication was serving human beings as never before. By the 1500s, a few primitive news sheets began to appear on the street of major cities. Limited though they were, they were the forerunners of the newspapers we know today. The era of mass media based on print as verbal communication was getting its earliest start.

Contemporary media: The proliferation of channels. The pace of development in conquering distance and time in verbal communication gradually accelerated in Western societies.

However, at the time the first settlers arrived in the new world (early in the 1600s), printing technology was virtually identical with that first used by Gutenberg. Books and other printed documents (e.g., simple newspapers) were produced with a hand-operated flatbed press, with letters individually cast in metal, and indeed with all the technology that had been used by Gutenberg to print the pages of his Bible. As newspapers gradually developed during the 1700s, they played an important part in defining the ideals underlying the American Revolution. They were not like those of today. Subscribing was very expensive and distribution beyond the city where they were published was very limited, but the newspapers were developing. The political information they contained was important in developing a new form of government in the colonies, but they were of interest primarily to the commercial elite who were well educated and affluent. Nevertheless, in the British Colonies in North America, literacy was slowly expanding, books were being printed, and even a few magazines began to appear.

The great breakthrough in extending human verbal communication beyond print and across the barriers of time and distance took place in the first half of the 1800s. Within a few decades after the 19th century began, the steam engine was rapidly replacing wind, water, and muscle as a source of power. The great Industrial Revolution had begun.

Within a remarkably short time, steam power was used for a long list of applications. Ships were built to be driven by steam. Carriages on rails moved goods and people far more swiftly than ever before. Above all, factories made use of steam to power their machines. Along with these, steam was applied to the printing press. When the publishers began to pay the costs of production by selling advertising, the modern mass newspaper was born (in New York in 1834). Newspapers were sold for only a penny, which made it possible for ordinary people to participate in a rapid and extended flow of information for the first time ever. Channels for verbal communication were expanding.[12]

A decade later, the telegraph was developed. The name itself indicates what it did (*tele*, the Greek word for "at a distance," plus *graphos*, "to write"). Samuel F. B. Morse sent his first message, "What hath God Wrought?" over 35 miles of wire (between Washington, D.C., and Baltimore, Maryland) at the speed of light (186,000 miles per second). At that point, verbal communication between human beings entered a totally new era. Device after device greatly expanded the channels available for verbal (and even visual) communications—the telephone at the end of the 1800s, the wireless telegraph (dot and dash radio) at the turn of the century, the radio-telephone in the first decade of the 1900s, the movies during the same period, regularly scheduled broadcasts to radio receivers in peoples' homes in the 1920s, television in homes by the late 1940s, the Internet and the World Wide Web by the end of the 1900s, and the advent of social media in the early years of the present century.

Where is all this development leading? No one can tell. People talk of a "global village," united by common interests and brought together by open channels of communication. Obviously, we are not there yet. Yet, as we continue to travel through the centuries ahead, perhaps that is not really such a far-fetched dream after all. Our ability to engage in human verbal communication, overcoming distance and time, to relate to each other in more harmonious ways may prove to be the most remarkable of all of the accomplishments of our species.

The Basic Nature of Language

Human beings use many different kinds of cues, signs, and labels to refer to the various types of organized and shared meanings we have discussed. We noted in Chapter 1 that one convenient way of referring to all of those many kinds is simply to call them "symbols." This term has come into wide use for that purpose.

Language Symbols and Their Referents

Human beings communicate with patterns of *symbols* whose meanings are understood by both the individual initiating a message and the person or persons who perceive, decode and construct its meanings. As explained in Chapter 1, this can be a complex process involving a number of stages. It can also include role-taking, feedback, and considerations of contexts. In interpersonal communication this complex process is best understood in terms of simultaneous transactions in which each of the communicating parties plays an active part.

Included in any spoken language are two basic categories of symbols—*verbal* and *nonverbal*—plus a number of patterns (i.e., grammatical structures, word order, or syntax) that serve the same functions as words (in that they too arouse meanings in people who are communicating). In each case, such symbols and patterns are used to encode and decode meanings. An important point here, one that aids in understanding the basic nature of language, is that there is a socially accepted and standardized *rule* or "convention" that defines the relationship between *every symbol in a language and its referent*. The term **referent** is used by language scholars to indicate whatever the symbol "refers to"—that is what it "labels," or "stands for." Each of these ideas requires clarification.

Most of the symbols we use in communication are ordinary words that are formally or "officially" defined in standard dictionaries in terms of their **denotative meanings**. The most significant point that can be made about this broad category of symbols is that each of them serves as a *label* in some way for some organized set or sets of meanings. That is, each provides an identifier, or a guide to how people are expected to respond to its sound or appearance in writing by experiencing internal images, feelings, and understandings. In terms of the explanations developed in previous sections, we can put all the ideas together in the following definition:

Symbols are socially agreed-upon labels that we use to identify and arouse conventionalized meanings stored in schemata within our memory system.

This formulation provides an extension of the definition of communication that we formulated in Chapter 1. It does so by specifying more precisely the nature of symbols—including nonverbal symbols and signs.

Nonverbal symbols: Communicating without words. Much of what human beings communicate takes place without words. Included in the messages we transmit to each other are actions, gestures, and tones of voice. These too have referents. That is, they arouse conventionalized meanings in ourselves and others in much the same way as words.[13] For example, a frown is an action that communicates an emotional state as its referent. In addition to such actions, many other symbols we use in communication are also not actually words but nonverbal cues, such as special clothing (e.g., a police officer's or nurse's uniform that implies a specific set of meanings). These are also used to identify and arouse within us particular **connotative** (that is subtle) meanings and interpretations. The list is long and can include military insignia, tattoos, and jewelry. In each case, however, the nonverbal symbol has an associated meaning that is more-or-less standardized.

Sources of symbols: The principle of arbitrary selection. Where do such verbal and nonverbal symbols come from? That is, how does a given language community originally select a particular word, a nonverbal gesture, an object, or another symbol for its members to use as a label for a given set of meanings? The fact is that there is no clear answer to that question. No clear rules precisely explain the origins of most of our words or other symbols. The most accurate statement we can make is that the selection process is **arbitrary.** This means that it is often rather random and sometimes even capricious.[14] For example, in English we say *horse*, in Spanish *caballo*, and in German *pferd*. These

The Principles of Symbols

Symbols are the labels we agree to use to arouse meanings that are associated with some reality we've experienced. Most of the symbols we use are words. But where do these symbols come from? And why do all of us, within the same language community, decide that we should use this word as a label, and not some other symbol? The following principles apply to symbols:

- *The principle of arbitrary selection.* The particular symbol or word we select is arbitrary. In other words, we could just as easily have chosen the symbol *chair* to refer to table or *dad* to refer to *mother.* Consider how this principle is applied by special groups, like teenagers: *Bad, tight,* and *phat* all refer to something that is good. What other labels have you or your friends arbitrarily chosen to refer to something else?
- *The principle of conventions.* Once a symbol has been arbitrarily assigned, the rules change. To use the symbol to communicate, we need to stabilize its use. That is, all individuals within a shared language community must now agree to use that particular symbol. This principle, then, asserts that once a symbol is assigned, we must always use that particular symbol, and no other, to refer to that particular thing. Without this principle, people would arbitrarily use any word at any time to refer to anything at all. Imagine how difficult it would be to communicate with others without this principle!

sounds and spellings have nothing in common. No one can say exactly how these very different labels came to be associated with that particular kind of animal. Someone in the history of the people speaking those languages decided that the word was an acceptable label for that aspect of reality. Most of our words are like that—their original selection was arbitrary.

For some words, clearly, we can uncover historical origins. Many contemporary words in English, which is a composite of a number of ancient and relatively modern languages, can be traced back to historic or even prehistoric sources. For example, the term *father* is an obvious derivation of the Latin and Greek *pater*. That, in turn, is almost identical to the earlier term *pitar* found in ancient Sanskrit. In fact, there are indications that it originated as part of the very earliest languages used by human beings.[15]

Aside from this heritage, the process of selecting words to signify and arouse particular meanings appears to be rather capricious. Whoever those ancient people were who began using *pitar* to signify male parenthood could just as easily have chosen something quite different. Thus, their choice was also arbitrary.

The same can be said about nonverbal symbols. Why does a middle finger, pointed upward, with the other fingers pointed down, have as its referent a rude meaning? Why does a thumb and finger held in a circle imply *"OK"* or general approval (at least for English speakers)? There probably are historical origins, but someone back then selected those gestures in an arbitrary manner.

The principle of arbitrary selection, then, indicates that when new sets of related meanings are formed, the process of labeling them does not follow some rigid or systematic rule. The reason a particular sound comes into use is seldom easy to explain. Someone proposes a label; it starts to be used, becomes more common; and when usage stabilizes it has become a part of the standard vocabulary within a language community. For that reason, Americans use "gasoline" in their cars, the British use "petrol," and people in Argentina use *nafta,* even though they are all chemically the same.

Language as Conventions

The term *convention* refers to a standard *rule* that has been accepted by a particular community or society to engage in some action in a particular way. For example, it is a convention among the military that enlisted personnel will always salute an officer who approaches them. There are many kinds of conventions, and those of concern here are the ones that link certain symbols and their standardized meanings.

While the original assignment of a symbol as a label for a common set of meanings can be arbitrary, once the assignment has been made the situation changes sharply. To be used as a tool for communication, the link between a symbol and its referent—the object, situation, or event to which it refers—has to be *predictable, stable, and relatively unchanging.* Otherwise, its use in communication would be impossible. No one could be sure of what meaning was implied. This stability is achieved by the use of the *principle of conventions* for defining and using symbols.

Convention has a broad meaning, implying any kind of rule that a given people agree to follow. In verbal (and nonverbal) communication, it refers to a rule that people within a given language community have devised and accepted. That rule links a particular meaning to a particular word (or nonverbal symbol). Such conventions state that whenever a person initiates a particular sound pattern or written mark (as in a given word) or a specific nonverbal symbol, the expected meaning experience is standardized.

We can now bring together the ideas and principles we have discussed concerning symbols, their referents (the objects or situations that are labeled), and their meanings to raise again the issue of how we know the world outside our heads. The relationships between all three can be represented by the simple diagram. This diagram is a version of one that was first proposed in 1946 by Ogden and Richards, who aptly called it the **meaning triangle.**[16] (See Figure 2.2.)

The diagram shows that meaning, the symbol, and referent constitute a kind of system. That is, within a specific language community, each pair of elements is linked by a convention. The referent is the object, situation, or thing (or even make-believe idea) to which we have assigned some meaning. The meaning, as was explained in detail earlier, is the internal psychological configuration or *schema* of memory traces subjectively aroused in us. That arousal takes place either by apprehending the referent itself with our senses or by receiving a communicated cue from another person. The symbol, of course, is the word, gesture, object, or behavior we use as a cue to arouse the meaning in another person (or even in ourselves).

The conventions, C1, C2, and C3 are the rules of our particular language community that stabilize the meaning triangle. The first, C1, links the *referent* and the *person's meaning*

with a rule that a specific pattern of internal experiences is the expected way of perceiving and understanding that aspect of reality. A second convention, C2, links the *symbol* and the *person's meaning* with an agreement that **perception** of the symbol will arouse the same meanings (in us or in another person) as does the referent itself—even though the latter may not actually be present. Still another convention, C3, completes the system with a shared agreement that the particular symbol *will stand for*, and *will be the socially accepted label of*, the referent. The arrows in the meaning triangle show these relationships.

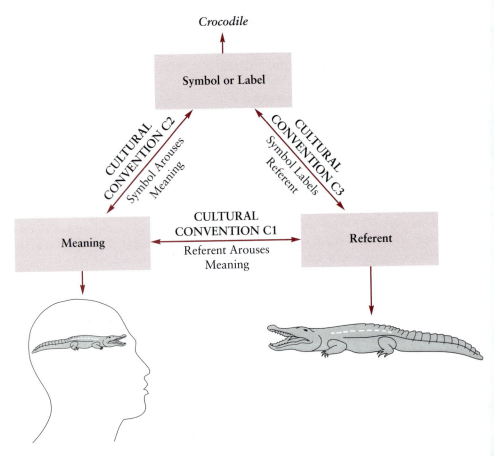

FIGURE 2.2

The Meaning Triangle

Every symbol in our vocabulary can be thought of as a *meaning triangle*, depicting the relationship between the symbol, what it labels in reality, and the meaning experience we have for both. Cultural conventions provide rules for linking the symbol, referent, and meaning.

Conceptualizing language symbols in terms of configurations of schemata and meaning triangles probably will not, just by themselves, be of immediate practical utility in communicating effectively with one's boss, roommate, or special friend. Nevertheless, such theoretical models do identify the nature and definitions of the most basic features of the communication process that may otherwise be difficult to understand—and they do so far better than vague descriptions. For that reason, models are an important part of the foundation on which effective communication skills are acquired.

Mastering a particular language requires a thorough familiarity with a host of different types of conventions. For example, every language has a large formal or official *vocabulary*, specific words with particular meanings that must be well understood, both to express meanings and to understand the meanings of others. These are the building blocks out of which messages are constructed. The authoritative *Oxford English Dictionary* lists about 500,000 words. To this could be added about another half-million terms used in specialized technical and scientific fields by English speakers.[17] In contrast, German has about 185,000 words, and Chinese has at most about 50,000 characters, each standing for a word. However, each of these languages provides for the same level of richness of expression as words can be combined to indicate virtually any intended meaning.

To represent the entire English vocabulary, including all technical words, in the form of meaning triangles we would need up to 1 million diagrams (there would have to be a separate diagram for every word). This is a staggering thought, to say the least. However, none of us carry around anything even close to a million meaning triangles in our head. In order to conduct our daily routine, most of us can get by nicely with about 5,000 words. On average, an educated person will have a vocabulary of about 15,000 words. Truly able communicators will have many more. For example, William Shakespeare, who had one of the largest vocabularies of any English writer, used an estimated 30,000 different words to write his plays and sonnets.[18] Included in the vocabulary of every language are numerous synonyms—words that actually are associated with very similar meanings.

Each language has conventions of *pronunciation*. Even minor errors in the way a word is pronounced can cause confusion. Significant regional accents can also muddy meanings for people not familiar with them. The rules of pronunciation are acquired in a language community, starting at a very early age.

If you've ever wondered how a word is pronounced, there is a handy web site that helps people learn pronunciations of words in 279 languages. If you ask for a word at Forvo.com, another user will pronounce it for you.

To the conventions of vocabulary and pronunciation we can add those of *grammar*—a critical aspect of any language. The important point is that grammatical structures themselves imply meanings. That is, different variants of symbols (tenses, verb forms, and so on) arranged into grammatically conventionalized sequences, indicate meanings that are not implied in the specific words in a message. The same words in different grammatical patterns form distinct messages.[19]

The grammatical conventions of some languages are far more complex than those of others, and many languages use forms that have no counterparts in English. For example, English speakers do not assign a masculine or feminine status to nouns, as some languages require. In Spanish, any house (*casa*) is feminine and takes an "a" ending, whereas any "building" (*edificio*) is masculine and takes an "o" ending. For every noun one must remember whether it is masculine or feminine and pronounce it accordingly. Native English speakers learning Spanish often find this difficult.

By comparison with those of some languages, English grammar is simple. We use nouns to indicate objects and verbs for action. Our system of nouns is neuter in terms of the masculine-feminine distinctions noted above. We do make an important distinction between actions that occurred in the past, those that are occurring in the present, and those that will occur in the future, and we conjugate our verbs differently in each of these tenses. Furthermore, we use separate sets of adjectives and adverbs to modify the meanings of nouns and verbs.

Some languages do all of this very differently. For example, the Navajo language uses only two major categories of verbs—neuter and active—for which English has no counterparts. However, in each category, the Navajo have from five to seven different ways of conjugating their verbs that imply important distinctions. In addition, the implications of nouns, verbs, adjectives, and adverbs can be compounded into a single term. In the Navajo language it is possible to indicate, with only one word, the meaning "the round solid object that was formerly in motion is now at rest."[20]

Finally, as we have noted and illustrated earlier, using the accepted rules for syntax is essential to avoid serious misinterpretations. Thus, the principle of conventions extends beyond linking words and nonverbal symbols to meanings. It is also the foundation for the use of pronunciation, grammar and syntax in verbal communication.

How Language Serves Us Today: Individually and Collectively

As has been suggested, human life changed greatly and continuously in that short period between the first development of language by

Have you ever wondered how a word is pronounced? FORVO is a website that helps people learn pronunciations of words in 279 languages. If you ask for a word at Forvo.com, another user will pronounce it for you.

WHAT SIGNIFICANCE SHOULD WE PUT ON GRAMMAR?

Not too long ago when my sister was visiting from out of state, I invited her to accompany me to a public speaking class that I was teaching. Together we listened to a young Latina student give a heartfelt presentation on the status of illegal immigrants trying to make a living in southern California.

After class, I turned to my sister and asked, "What did you think of Dolores's speech?" Dianne replied that she really enjoyed it and thought Dolores had made several good points.

But I persisted, "Yes, but what did you think of Dolores's presentation?" Again, Dianne discussed the relative merits of the student's arguments.

"Okay, but let me ask you this: What if your daughter spoke the way Dolores had? How would you have evaluated her presentation then?"

Dianne was quick to respond. "I would expect my daughter to talk with a better vocabulary and grammar than this student did. After all, Dolores mispronounced and misused a number of words and phrases in her presentation."

Do we, should we, hold others to the same high standards of grammar and vocabulary that we do ourselves? Do we, should we, lower our standards when the speaker represents a culture that is different from our own? Does incorrect grammar or word pronunciation interfere with our ability to understand a speaker? Does it influence our perceptions of a speaker's credibility? Does it make it more difficult to listen?

What happens when individuals do not follow the conventions for "good" grammar? What does "poor" grammar communicate about the individual, if anything? Should we expect everyone to share our grammatical conventions—even people for whom English is not their first language? Should we expect individuals who represent different ethnic groups to share U.S. standards for grammar? Why or why not?

This chapter discusses the importance of grammar and conventions: that is, different word arrangements, word pronunciations, and verb tenses all communicate particular meanings. The grammatical conventions or rules for English are very complex. Children are taught rules for English grammar even before they begin school, and that instruction continues through grade school, high school, and college. What ethical responsibility do we have to comply with the conventions of grammar that we are taught? What ethical responsibility do we have to overlook another's grammatical mistakes?

the *Cro-Magnon* and the present with our current world-wide use of instantaneous mass media. But how has the use of speech and language made a difference in our lives today? There are two important questions. First, how does language shape the way we function psychologically as individual human beings who continuously experience and respond to our environment? The answer is that it does so in very complex ways. Second, how has language enabled us to live together collectively and harmoniously in groups and societies with stable and predictable ways of life and with a continuous development of new solutions to problems of living? Again, the answer is in complex ways.

First, language made it possible for people to *know the world* through internal meanings. We are able to understand our physical environment through a process of **perception** that is dependent on the language community in which we exist. Second, language enabled human beings to *think analytically*—to solve problems by examining facts and premises, to reason from them to reach conclusions and decide on what actions to take or what interpretations should be reached. Third, language enabled human beings to *remember* the events of their daily experiences in an organized manner. Thus, our language provides each of us with the means to *accumulate knowledge,* records of experience, that can guide future decisions and actions. Those three great changes in psychological functioning are what psychologists currently call "cognitive processing."

Language also changed the way people *relate collectively* to their fellow human beings. After acquiring the ability to speak, our ancestors evolved from small hunting and gathering groups of related families to ever-larger populations living in fixed villages and practicing agriculture. Eventually, large societies developed, composed of many kinds of groups with complex relationships. To stabilize those relationships between people, shared rules for acceptable behavior were needed, so that individuals and families could lead well-regulated lives. Language made this possible. Putting it very simply, language permitted the development of a uniquely human existence that forever separated us from other species on our planet.

Language and the Social Construction of Reality

For more than 2,000 years, philosophers have pondered how it is that human beings can develop internal understandings that enable them to cope with the physical and social worlds that exist outside their heads. This seemingly arcane question was of great concern to ancient scholars who were first trying to understand human mental processes.

Social construction of reality: How do environmentalists influence our perceptions using language?

They posed the issue in terms of the question "How do we know reality?" Indeed, that question has continued to hold the attention of many kinds of scholars right up to the present day.[21]

The answer to this very basic question provides the key to understanding how human beings interpret their physical and social environment, think about the world around them, and communicate their thoughts to others and themselves. Thus, the issue of how we know reality must be resolved before insight can be gained into communication transactions as well as into such critical "mental" activities as perceiving, reasoning, and remembering. As we have noted, it is these activities that enable human beings to lead elaborate social lives and to develop and pass on complex cultures.[22]

Constructing reality by communicating. Almost 400 years before the birth of Christ, a remarkable man began to clarify the issue of how we know reality. Plato wrote in his *Republic* of an imaginary experiment that wonderfully illustrates the issue. In his "Allegory of the Cave," he set forth this passage:

> Imagine the condition of men living in a sort of cavernous chamber underground, with an entrance not open to the light and a long passage all down the cave. Here they have been from childhood, chained by the leg and also by the neck, so that they cannot move and see only what is in front of them, because the chains will not let them turn their heads.[23]

Obviously, such an experiment would not actually or ethically be possible, but suppose there were men in such a condition. Now we can add additional conditions that Plato described. Behind the men (who are presumably seated on a bench), he wrote, is a high wall. The men, facing outward, cannot see this, but on the back of the other side of the wall is a walkway, along which other men can move while holding up long sticks, each of which has a shape attached (like a silhouette figure of men or animals, or any kind of shape formed of wood or other material). Still farther back from the wall, and high up, is a brightly burning fire. The fire casts a bright light onto the wall of the cave that the chained men can see (Plato obviously did not have electricity for this purpose).

These arrangements result in the chained men seeing *shadows* on the cave wall in front of them—shadows with various silhouette shapes moving along (as the men behind the wall on the walkway march along holding up their sticks with the figures).

These shadows *are all the reality that the chained men ever see.* As they talk to each other, they discuss the shadows, give each different one a name, and try to see who among them can best forecast their sequences of appearances. Since the shadows are their only reality, they come to know them well indeed.

Now suppose that one of the men were unchained, released, shown the fire, the sticks, the walkway and the silhouette shapes that the other men used to produce the shadows. He would be told that the reality that he and his fellows had worked out with the shadows was only an illusion! Then, imagine further that he was taken out of the cave altogether, and shown the real world that existed out there—its stars, sun, moon, houses, roads, sheep, wagons, and all the other things that the Greeks of the time saw and used.

Finally, suppose that he were to be brought back into the cave and chained once again in his original position. Now he would have the task of explaining to his comrades where he had been and what he had learned. He would try to explain to them that what they regarded as reality was *only an illusion*, and that he had a true grasp of the real world. He would describe what he had seen and heard during his absence.

Would those still in the chains believe him? Plato said no. After all, they already knew the nature of reality. They had worked it out together, communicating again and again about the shadows and agreeing on the names and meaning of each. They would laugh at the man who had returned, and at his preposterous ideas. In fact, they would probably see him as a raving lunatic. Indeed, said Plato, the men who had remained in the cave might be inclined to kill him because he was a dangerous madman.

The lesson from Plato? *It is through an extended process of verbal and nonverbal communication within our language community that we come to know reality.* Plato had an incredible insight that is as true today as it was in his time. Today we can revise that principle by adding the influences of *mass-mediated visual communication*—and especially its *visual* forms (such as movies, television, and the Internet). To illustrate this revised principle and show its practical implications, a large-scale study of teenagers in 12 countries shows the influence of mass-communicated entertainment on teenagers who have little or no direct knowledge of Americans or their society. From their exposure to American popular culture they gain impressions of the reality of ordinary people and their ways of life in the United States. If they lack contact with Americans, the impressions, beliefs, and attitudes that they unwittingly form about Americans from media-delivered entertainment may be distorted. This comes about because many countries have no facilities for producing their own movies or TV programming. However, they do have cinemas for providing movies and cable or broadcast systems to deliver TV content to their populations. Satellite dishes are also common, from which they can receive programming from the United States (and other Western societies).

In this way, people in developing countries receive entertainment and news programs on their TV sets, and see films at their local cinemas. In all areas of the globe, then, people see *Oprah, Sex and the City, Jersey Shore,* crime dramas, and much the same programs depicting Americans that are seen by families in cities and towns in the United States. This popular content seems to them to depict life among ordinary people in the United States. It seems obvious to many such viewers (who have no other sources from which to gain knowledge) that Americans and life in the United States are characterized by crime, violence, open and nonmarital sexual liaisons, materialism, and little or no interest in religious or spiritual matters. American movies and TV entertainment are designed as *entertainment* and not as documentaries or educational materials, but it is from such popular mass communications that millions of people around the world build **social constructions of reality** concerning the nature of American people and their ways of life.

Needless to say, the consequent understandings and beliefs about Americans and lifestyles in the United States can be seriously flawed.[24] One need look no further than the tragic events of September 11, 2001, and other terrorist events, to understand that very real and dire consequences can result from such views.[25] At the same time, Americans often receive incorrect views of other nations and their people.

It would be incorrect, however, to assume that such misinterpretations may result only when those in other nations view media content portraying people in the United States, or when citizens of the United States view content about those living in other nations. Think about the ways in which people living in one region of the United States are sometimes portrayed to those who live elsewhere in the nation.

For example, the History Channel's reality television program, *Swamp People*, depicts Cajun alligator hunters in Louisiana fighting and harvesting as many alligators as possible during the season. The hunters speak with a thick Cajun accent, live in shacks, and argue with each other while shooting alligators in the head. So what can others learn about people who live in Louisiana? According to one newspaper columnist, the program can give the impression that people who live in Louisiana can barely speak English, live in shacks, are all missing teeth, wear shrimp boots, and spend their time "killin gators."[26]

What about the HBO comedy series *Big Love*, which tells about the trials and tribulations of a polygamist and his three wives in suburban America? Many criticize the program for dredging up old stereotypes about the Mormon religion, which banned polygamy more than 100 years ago. And what impressions of New Jersey may result after viewing episodes of the program *Jersey Shore?* [27]

Thus, modern mass communications have been added to what existed in Plato's time. The social construction of reality is a process of communication during which labels and definitions are provided for all the things that make up the physical and social worlds that we experience. This is a process that has been going on since language came into existence.

Linguistic relativity: Different cultures, different names, different realities. As the foregoing suggests, not all language communities construct the same interpretations of reality. Even without considering the influence of television, movies, and the Internet, the way a language is organized can bring people to define and experience reality in quite different ways.[28] This is a simple way of defining the principle of **linguistic relativity.** When populations began to grow (as agriculture produced more food) people began to live longer. Slowly, people began to drift away from where humankind originated. When this dispersion of populations to what is now Europe, Asia, and the Americas took place, new languages were developed and older ones were modified. Distinct cultures came to be developed as people adapted in different ways in different regions and continents. Some remained as hunting and gathering people (e.g., many Native American and Eskimo groups as well as others in Africa and Australia). Others improved their agriculture and built remarkable cities and monuments (e.g., the Aztecs and Maya in the Western Hemisphere). Still others industrialized to become modern societies.

One major result of all these changes was the development of thousands of local languages, each very different from all others. Different word categories developed with distinct meanings attached to each symbol. For example, among Native American language groups even the realities of colors are divided up differently from one group to the next. Some indigenous people lumped all the greens and blues together and gave them a single name,[29] and some had dozens of different names for what we currently refer to simply as "snow." For example, among the Greenland Eskimos there are many kinds of snow—some suitable for building igloos, others unsuitable. Still other named categories provide excellent surfaces for sleds; others make sled travel more difficult. Each type has a different name. Of course, the principle that different kinds of people divide up what they see around them and name them in special ways is not confined to people who live in remote places.

Thus, when people construct specific sets of labels and meanings through a process of communication, they interpret the physical and social world in distinct ways. Plato established the principle long ago and it is still relevant today. People watching a TV set and seeing the United States portrayed in programs produced to entertain, are likely to develop a set of terms to describe the characteristics of Americans that is different from the set of terms developed by suburbanites in the American Midwest who view the same content.

Human Cognitive Processing

The individual counterpart to the social construction of reality—which is a *collective process* that takes place between people—is what takes place *within each of us* as we personally experience the reality to which we must respond. This activity is profoundly influenced by our language. Today, more than 2,000 years after Plato, we understand that human beings continuously engage in complex internal or subjective processes as they sort out meanings for, and respond to, what they encounter in their environment. The phrase "cognitive processing" refers to such human activities as *perception, judgment* (that is, systematic reasoning or thinking), and *memory*. Cognitive functions are distinct from other internal human behaviors such as emotions, including fear, hate, and love, although there may be mutual influences.

The point is that words and their standardized meanings in our language play a critical part in shaping the cognitive processing of information that is provided by our senses. Our eyes and ears, plus our senses of touch, smell, and taste, provide us with our initial contacts with the world outside our heads. The sensations that are received by these organs have to be "processed" within our brains so that meanings we will understand can be assigned to them. Those meanings have been learned by each of us as we participated in our language community. The first way in which cognitive processing takes place, then, is in our initial perception of features of our environment.

Perception: Using the pictures in our heads to interpret the world outside.   The words of our language and the meanings associated with them enable us to identify people, objects and situations that we encounter as we constantly apprehend our physical and social world. We refer to this as *perception*. It is the process by which we as individuals *assign meaning to and interpret* what we experience with our senses on an ongoing basis. We engage in perception constantly. We have to, or the world we experience would be a meaningless and confusing jumble.

To illustrate the process and show the importance of language, suppose you are walking along and you suddenly see what appears to be some sort of large bird and hear it making a distinctive sound. For a tiny fraction of a second you are not sure what it is. Clearly you have tentatively classified it in a general way by using the word *bird,* which is stored in your memory, with its associated meanings. That is, you "apprehended it with your senses"—your eyes and ears in this case—and assigned to it a preliminary but very general meaning. At this stage, you have not yet completed the process of perception. You want to narrow down what your senses are revealing to a familiar category of bird that you will understand much better.

Now comes a process of matching and comparing the information your eyes and ears are providing with words and their meanings stored in your memory. Looking more closely, you see that *it looks like a duck* (a named category in your memory). Then you notice that *it walks like a duck* (a feature of that category stored in your memory). Finally, you realize that *it quacks like a duck* (another remembered feature of that category). Aha! You instantly conclude that *it is a duck*. Perception has taken place!

Perception takes place at unbelievable speed—indeed, it is virtually instantaneous in most cases. What were initially just neural impulses sent to your brain from your eyes and ears have swiftly been transformed into a category of meaning that you recognize. The point is that we can perceive a stimulus, such as a duck, because we have the words and their related meanings already stored in our memory, ready to go, to enable us to make this interpretation.

In summary, perception is a critical part of the verbal communication process. We are totally immersed every waking moment in a complex physical and social environment, constantly confronting thousands of objects, people, messages and situations with which we have to deal. Our skills in perception—one of the most essential features of verbal communication—has made this possible because human beings long ago developed language.

Thinking: Using language to analyze situations and decide on actions. A second part of cognitive processing is analyzing what we have perceived and forming an appropriate response. Once we understand what we are perceiving, we can make orderly judgments about it. This is the second important feature of cognitive processing. Perceiving a duck, for example, calls for a different analysis of what to do than perceiving a snake. If we identify the object in our path as a duck, we might just smile and walk on. If we interpret it as a snake, however, we have some immediate thinking, analyses, and decision making to do. Is it a harmless garden critter? Or, is it a dangerous rattlesnake? We sort through that problem (using what we know about the two types of snakes), make a judgment, and choose an appropriate action (running from the

rattler or ignoring the garden variety). Our stored words and their meanings for various categories of snakes and their relationships to possible danger, then, provide what we need to make that judgment. Again, our language enables us to engage in this internal verbal behavior as we process the situation cognitively.

Memory: Using language to store experiences for later recall and retelling. Finally, whatever the bird or the snake turned out to be, we will retain the experience in memory—stored in physical terms as traces within the brain and organized psychologically into a *schema* of what happened, what we thought and how we acted. This will not only permit us to recall the event and recount our adventure to others, but also to formulate an appropriate response if a similar situation is perceived again. Thus, cognitive processing in the form of memory functions is also based on words, meanings, and language.

Language and the Accumulation of Culture

Once human beings gained the capacity to speak and developed language, their ability to invent solutions to problems of living accelerated at a remarkable pace. Within a period of only a few thousand years, people transformed their lifestyle from a precarious existence based on constant wandering around in search of food to a stable existence based on agriculture. Instead of trying to exist on whatever animals that they could kill, or on plants they could find growing wild, they began to raise their own livestock for food and to plant crops to sustain them.

Inventing solutions to problems: The process of innovation. As ways of obtaining a living by using the technology of agriculture were increasingly refined, people moved into *fixed villages*, where they built permanent shelters. It is clear that this remarkable transition took place because they had become physically capable of speech and had begun to develop languages, which in turn enabled them to remember complex ideas, to think, and to invent. Thus, a remarkable period in human existence took place as our prehistoric ancestors developed *Neolithic culture.* (The term *neo* means "new." The other part of the word, *lithic,* refers to "stone." *Neolithic,* then, means "new stone age"—a time of considerable cultural development, but before metals came into use.)

The Neolithic era was a time when remarkable new arts and technologies were invented and slowly accumulated—including agriculture, weaving, clothing, pottery, and the wheel. There was more: The practice of burying the dead with weapons and food indicates that they also developed theories of the nature of life, death, and an afterlife. It was during this period, in other words, that the foundations for the great cultural institutions we know today were developed. With the *family* and the process of educating the young already well established, they added the forerunners of the *political, economic,* and *religious* institutions we now have in our societies. At the same time, progress was slow because these were people who remained in the oral tradition. Their development and ability to pass on solutions to succeeding generations was limited by the capacity of human memory.

Cultural accumulation. For thousands of years after human beings acquired the ability to talk and develop language, each new generation was able to develop and add new solutions to problems of living to those that had already been discovered. New ways of harnessing animal power for plowing and pulling were developed. Then, the ability to capture the wind to move boats, and to use the weight of water to turn wheels for power were discovered. New beliefs were developed, along with new ways to maintain a stable government, to use coins as a medium of exchange, to use a bow and arrow for hunting and defense, and to use the wheel to solve problems of transportation. Slowly but surely, people orally passed on from one generation to the next those solutions already at hand and the new ones that each generation invented. Thus, it was

the ability to speak and to use language that made *cultural accumulation* possible.

This process accelerated greatly when it was freed from the limitations of human memory that characterized societies in the oral tradition. The development of *writing* made it possible to record achievements, rather that relying on people's memories to pass them on. Later, printing and all the rest of the communication media that followed increased the pace. Cultural accumulation today goes forward at a speed that could not have been even remotely imagined thousands of years ago. Even in the lifetime of our most elderly generation living today, such remarkable cultural innovations as the airplane, the automobile, the computer, and the Internet have become commonplace.

Symbolic Interaction: The Key to Developing Mind, Self, and Society

An important *paradigm* (broad theory) that helps in understanding how human beings make use of language and verbal communication to live together in orderly groups and society as a whole is called the "symbolic interaction perspective." Initially developed by Charles Horton Cooley in the late 1800s and early 1900s, it was later elaborated upon by George Herbert Mead and other sociologists. The paradigm explains how people are able to understand both other persons and themselves so that they can relate to each other effectively in human groups.[30] In this sense, symbolic interactionism provides additional insights into what verbal communication does for us both individually and collectively.

Cooley's idea was this: As a baby slowly begins to develop, it begins to interact with other people. At first, the voices, facial expressions, and activities of surrounding adults are only a part of the environment and have no special meaning in themselves. Gradually, however, the baby learns that certain family members are associated with its care, feeding, and comfort. Thus, these beings assume an increasing importance to the baby.

Gradually the child begins to perceive the limits of its own body and to define itself (develop a **self image,** or **self-concept**) as distinct from those other human beings. The word the child learns to label such a distinction becomes important. The social nature of *self-realization* is implied by the word *I*. Once this is learned, it automatically indicates the existence of persons who are "not *I*"—other distinct persons who have to be taken into account. In time, these persons come to be identified by other labels ("momma," "papa," and so on). This provides the beginning of an understanding of a social reality.

As the child matures, it becomes increasingly clear that relating to other people requires an *understanding of their expectations*. If one does not behave according to those expectations—certain rules—rewards may not follow. And indeed, in some cases, punishments may follow. Thus, three things take place in the development process as the child increasingly commands speech and language and engages in symbolic interaction with an ever-enlarging number of people. The first is the maturing cognitive ability to *perceive, think, and remember* through the use of the language that is being learned. A second is the recognition by the child that he or she is a *distinct being* with unique personal characteristics. The third is the understanding that *social behavior is patterned* and one is expected to follow predictable rules.

These three outcomes of engaging in a complex process of symbolic interaction—that is living in a language community and relating to others with speech and language—were characterized by these early sociologists as the development of *mind, self, and society*.[31] Thus, the symbolic interaction paradigm (and its perspective on verbal communication) attempts to explain the foundation for *cognitive functioning,* for *understanding one's self,* and for gaining a command of the *rules and requirements for interacting in groups*.

We have explained in some detail the first of these processes—developing understandings of reality within a language community and how cognitive and processing is influenced by that

The looking-glass self: What reflection does she see of her self image?

language. But what about the other two? That is, how is language important in obtaining an understanding of self? Also, in what way does language serve in acquiring a command of the expectations of others—knowing the patterns and rules of human groups?

The looking-glass self. Cooley provided a very clear answer to the first question—the one about the process of developing a concept of self through a process of symbolic interaction. In an insightful poetic phrase he said this:

> Each to each a looking glass
> Reflects the other that doth pass.[32]

What he meant is that we see *reflections and definitions of ourselves* in the ways that other people react to us. For example, if we walk into a room and people come over, and smile, and say how glad they are to see us, that sends one message—one definition of what we are. If, on the other hand, we walk into the same room and people look the other way, or even get up and leave without saying anything, that sends a quite different definition. Even the number of connections and the interactions we have on social networking sites can provide insight into the way others see us.[33] The reactions of others to our presence, comments, or actions, then, serve as a kind of "social mirror" in which we can see what we are.

Mirrors were called "looking glasses" in Cooley's time, and he called the general idea just expressed the *looking-glass self*. Clearly, then, gaining a concept of what we are, as others see us, and consequently what we come to believe about ourselves, emerges from symbolic interaction, that is communication through language, with others who provide us with their definitions.

Social organization: The rules of human groups. The final feature of human life explained by the symbolic interactionists was *society*—how we learn the patterned expectations of social life. Through the process of verbal communication, the paradigm explains, we learn the *orderly rules for behavior*—the expectations that characterize any human group, ranging from the smallest to the largest. Every group—from the two-person family to the huge corporation or the bureaucratic government agency—has an organization of expectations. These expectations, or rules, bring order, predictability, and stability to the actions of their members. Essentially, there are four features of any such group that provide for predictable relationships within the group.

One feature of the social organization of a group is its *general norms*. Every group has rules that apply to all its members more or less equally. These may deal with such matters as dress codes, modes of greeting, acceptable and unacceptable language or actions, and acceptable behavior for social networking sites. Everyone who is a member of the group is expected to observe these norms.

A second feature of a group's pattern of social organization is the expectations that apply to individuals who play specialized parts within the group. These are the *roles* that are associated with particular activities in the group. In a baseball team, for example, the roles of pitcher, catcher, outfielder, and so on involve all quite different activities. In other groups the specialized roles may be doctor and patient, boss and worker, parent and child, or professor and student. In each case, such specialized activities are understood and defined in terms of the expectations of members as a whole.

A third pattern of social organization is the group's *ranking* arrangement. Some members of any group—even informal ones made up of friends—have more respect, more power, or more authority than others. Some are at the top of the hierarchy and others at the bottom. Most members are somewhere in between. Generally speaking, those who rank high in the pattern receive more rewards. Members must live with these arrangements. They are part of the general social expectations—the social organization—of group life, not only in small groups like families but also in communities and even in society at large.

Finally, all groups have ways of maintaining their stability. This feature of social organization refers to the expectation that those who fail to follow the rules, and deviate in significant ways, risk the application of *social controls*. They can be positive or negative. These controls may be minor in groups of friends—perhaps only amounting to praise as a positive reward or mild verbal criticism for annoying behavior. In families, where parents dominate, allowing or withholding privileges may be a form of control if children do not do well or fail to conform. In the workplace, the control may be a promotion or raise, or more drastically, separation from the group (getting fired). At the most extreme, for violating certain official rules of society, the offending deviant may be executed. Thus, norms, roles, ranks, and controls are the patterns of social organization developed through a process of symbolic interaction. They have been worked out through verbal communication in one form or another for maintaining the stability of human groups.

BOX 2.3   *Talkaholic Scale*

The talkaholic scale measures compulsive communication. Some people are driven to talk. They are highly verbal people and have great difficulty (and often little desire) being quiet in the presence of other people. While these individuals are "high talkers" or "talkaholics," they usually are not the people whom others refer to as one who "talks too much." The term "talks too much" usually is applied to people who are saying things another person doesn't want them to say or who are ineffective communicators. While the term appears to be a quantitative description, it actually is a qualitative reference. Considerable research has determined that the more a person talks (in most cases, unless the person is an incompetent communicator or saying things that are offensive to others), the more positively that person is evaluated by others. They are more likely to be seen as a leader, as being more competent, and generally viewed more positively on a variety of other person perception variables.

Read the following questions and select the answer that corresponds with what you would do in most situations. Do not be concerned if some of the items appear similar. Please use the scale below to rate the degree to which each statement applies to you. Use this key:

5 = Strongly Agree
4 = Agree
3 = Neutral
2 = Disagree
1 = Strongly Disagree

_____ 1. Often I keep quiet when I should talk.
_____ 2. I talk more than I should sometimes.
_____ 3. Often, I talk when I know I should keep quiet.
_____ 4. Sometimes I keep quiet when I know it would be to my advantage to talk.
_____ 5. I am a "talkaholic."
_____ 6. Sometimes I feel compelled to keep quiet.
_____ 7. In general, I talk more than I should.
_____ 8. I am a compulsive talker.
_____ 9. I am not a talker; rarely do I talk in communication situations.
_____ 10. Quite a few people have said I talk too much.
_____ 11. I just can't stop talking too much.
_____ 12. In general, I talk less than I should.
_____ 13. I am not a "talkaholic."
_____ 14. Sometimes I talk when I know it would be to my advantage to keep quiet.
_____ 15. I talk less than I should sometimes.
_____ 16. I am not a compulsive talker.

Scoring: To determine your score on the Talkaholic Scale, complete the following steps:

- Step 1: Add the scores for items 2, 3, 5, 7, 8, 10, 11, and 14.
- Step 2: Add the scores for items 13 and 16.
- Step 3: Complete the following formula: Total Score = 12 + Total from Step 1 – Total from Step 2.

(NOTE: Items 1, 4, 6, 9, 12, and 15 are filler items and are not scored.)

Your final score should be between 10 and 50. Most people score below 30. People who score between 30 and 39 are borderline talkaholics and are able to control their talking most of the time, but sometimes they find themselves in situations where it is difficult to be quiet, even if it would be very much to their advantage not to talk. People with scores above 40 are talkaholics. They are truly compulsive communicators.

Sources: McCroskey, J. C., & Richmond, V. P. (1993). Identifying compulsive communicators: The talkaholic scale. *Communication Research Reports,* 11, 39–52; McCroskey, J. C., & Richmond, V. P. (1995). Correlates of compulsive communication: Quantitative and qualitative characteristics. *Communication Quarterly,* 43, 39–52.

Chapter Review

- Early in the 1900s, a great controversy began about whether or not animals could communicate with language. The value of this controversy was that it brought about enthusiastic efforts to clarify the nature of language and the question of whether only human beings use it. After decades of animal studies, it appears there is a huge gap between the communication abilities of human beings and those of the animals nearest to us on the phylogenetic continuum.

- Human beings require shared language in order to develop normally. If they are denied such an environment, their processes of perception, thought, and memory, along with their social relationships, are impaired.

- Engaging in verbal communication requires that each of us has to command an enormous set of labels for internal and subjective images, interpretations, and experiences that are associated with specific aspects of the world outside our heads. By participating in our language community we learn inner meanings not only for concrete objects that make up the physical world, but also for situations, relationships, activities, and conditions that make up our complex social life. In addition, we learn meanings for ideas that have no physical counterparts and even for things we know do not exist. A broad term for acquiring these processes is the "social construction of reality."

- By using symbols, human beings attach labels to configurations of meaning. Then, by establishing conventions of usage, those same symbols refer to both the object and the meaning. The three ideas—meaning, symbol, and referent—form a triangular system, with each pair stabilized by a convention. The initial choice of a symbol to label a referent and its meaning may be arbitrary, but once consensus is reached regarding the convention, meanings are stabilized.

- Language is composed of thousands of such systems, plus elaborate conventionalized rules for putting symbols together, as in sentences composed of words. The subtlety and complexity of human communication can be appreciated by realizing that just to get by at a simple level requires knowledge of about 5,000 words and their meanings, and an educated person will, on the average, command about 15,000 such meaning systems. Truly able communicators may be able to use up to 30,000. Important structural aspects of language governed by conventions include connotative meanings, grammar, and syntax. These can introduce meanings that are not contained in the conventional usage or that go beyond the meanings of the separate words used in a message.

- The human ability to learn and use language provides the individual with not only a sophisticated means for communicating with others but also the means by which inventions and innovations are achieved and cultural accumulation takes place to constantly enrich human life.

- Engaging in verbal communication is the process by which each person develops the ability to engage in cognitive processing—including perception, thinking, and remembering. It also enables the person to develop self-understanding. Finally, verbal communication—what sociologists call symbolic interaction—has for more than a century been identified as the critical process enabling human beings to develop mind, self, and society.

Key Terms

Notes

1. Pfungst, O. (1907). *Das pferd des Herr von Osten: der Kluge Hans* (Clever Hans: The Horse of Mr. von Osten). Leipzig: Johan Ambrosius Barth.

2. Kellogg, W. N., & Kellogg, L. A. (1967). *The ape and the child: A study of environmental influence upon early behavior.* New York: Hafner. (First published by Whittlesey House in 1933.)

3. Hayes, C. H. (1951). *The ape in our house.* New York: Harper.

4. Geshwind, N. (1970). The organization of language and the brain. *Science, 170,* 940–944.

5. Gardner, T., & Gardner, R. A. (1969). Teaching sign language to a chimpanzee. *Science, 165,* 664–672.

6. Patterson, F., & Linden, E. (1981). *The education of Koko.* New York: Holt, Rinehart, and Winston.

7. Premack, A. J., & Premack, D. (1972). Teaching language to an ape. *Scientific American, 227,* 92–99.

8. One of the first of these experiments is reported in: Rumbaugh, D. M., et al. (1975). Conversations with a chimpanzee in a computer-controlled environment. *Biological Psychiatry, 10,* 627–641.

9. For recent discussions on the controversial issue of animals' ability to use language, see: Marler, P. (1999). How much does a human environment humanize a chimp? *American Anthropologist, 101,* 2, 432–436; Sundberg, M. L. (1996). Toward granting linguistic competence to apes: A review of Savage-Rumbaugh, et al.'s language comprehension in ape and child. *Journal of the Experimental Analysis of Behavior, 65,* 477–492.

10. Gugliotta, G. (April 18, 2002). Suddenly humans age three million years. *The Washington Post,* p. A-03; Moffett, N. (April 18, 2002). Monkey's great-grandpa older than we thought? *Chicago Sun-Times,* p. 10.

11. The family *Hominidae* (humanlike creatures) began to develop as a variation of the order *Primata* (primates) several million years ago. As evolution proceeded, such creatures grew larger and their brain-to-body mass ratio increased. By about 1.8 million years ago they were walking upright. After the genus *Homo* emerged, our ancestors began making tools and using fire. However, cultural development remained at a stone-tool level throughout the Pleistocene period. Modern *Homo sapiens, sapiens,* in the form of *Cro-Magnon,* can be traced back no farther than around 90,000 years. They were the first human beings physiologically capable of using speech and language, which may have been fully developed only as recently as about 35,000 or perhaps 45,000 years ago. It was this communication ability, enabling *Cro-Magnon* to engage in reasoning, organized recall, and the transmission of solutions to complex problems to new generations, that provided the foundation for a rather sudden and increasing elaboration of human culture. By 15,000 years before the present, *Homo sapiens, sapiens* was widely dispersed in Europe, Asia, and Africa, and about 10,000 years ago the great Neolithic era of agriculture and village life began. For a detailed discussion of the fossil record and its implications, see: Lieberman, P. (1984). *The biology and evolution of language.* Cambridge, MA: Harvard University Press.

12. For more information on the development of the mass media, see: Dennis, E., & DeFleur, M. L. (2010). *Understanding media in the digital age*. New York: Allyn & Bacon.

13. Knapp, M., & Hall, J. (2010). *Nonverbal communication in human interaction* (7th ed.). Boston: Wadsworth, Cengage Learning.

14. Goss, B., & O'Hair, D. (1988). *Communicating in interpersonal relationships*. New York: Macmillan.

15. McCrum, R., Cran, W., & MacNeil, R. (1986). *The story of English* (pp. 51–53). New York: Elisabeth Sifton Books, Viking.

16. Ogden, C. K., & Richards, I. K. (1946). *The meaning of meaning*. New York: Harcourt Brace. See also: Adler, R. B., Rosenfeld, L. B., & Towne, N. (1995). *Interplay: The process of interpersonal communication*. New York: Holt, Rinehart, and Winston.

17. McCrum, Cran, & MacNeil, *The story of English*, p. 19.

18. Ibid., pp. 102–103.

19. Schegloff, E. A. (1972). Notes on a conversational practice: Formulating place. In D. N. Sudnow, (Ed.), *Studies in social interaction* (pp. 75–119). New York: Free Press.

20. Hoijer, H. (1964). Cultural implications of some Navajo linguistic categories. In D. Hymes (Ed.), *Language and culture in society: A reader in linguistics and anthropology* (pp. 142–153). New York: Harper and Row.

21. Cherwit, R. A., & Hikins, J. W. (1986). *Communication and knowledge: An investigation in rhetorical epistemology*. Columbia: University of South Carolina.

22. A large body of scholarly writing from such fields as anthropology, sociology, and social psychology support this position. See, for example, DeFleur, M.L., & Ball Rokeach, S. (1989). Stages in the development of human communication, in *Theories of Mass Communication* (3rd ed., pp. 3–45 Longman.)

23. Plato (1945). "Allegory of the Cave." In F. M. Cormford (Trans.), *The Republic of Plato*. London: Oxford University Press. p. 227.

24. For a detailed research report on these issues, see: DeFleur, M. L. & DeFleur, M. H. (2003). *Learning to hate Americans: How the U.S. media shape negative attitudes among teenagers in twelve countries*. Spokane: Marquette Books.

25. Perlmutter, D. D. (September 30, 2001). Why do they hate Americans and America? *The Buffalo News*, p. H5; Why the world loves to hate America: Anti-U.S. sentiment comes in different forms (December 7, 2001). *Financial Times (London)*, p. 23.

26. Grillot, C. (2011, April 11). The C-Section: La.-based reality shows have potential to hurt state's reputation. *The Reveille*. Retrieved from http://www.lsureveille.com

27. Brooks, C. (2009, December 12). Italian Americans and the G word: Embrace or reject? *Time*. Retrieved from http://www.time.com; Brady, J. (2006, February 23). Mormons not laughing about polygamy comedy 'Big Love.' *ABC News*. Retrieved from http://www.abcnews.com

28. Casanto, D. (2008). Who's afraid of the big bad Whorf? Crosslinguistic differences in temporal language and thought. *Language Learning, 58,* 63–79.

29. See: Hoijer H., (1960). The Sapir-Whorf hypothesis. In *Language in culture* (pp. 92–115). Chicago: The University of Chicago Press.

30. See: Cooley, C. H. (1902). *Human nature and the social order*. New York: Charles Scribner's Sons.

31. See: Mead, G. H. (1934) In C. W. Morris, (Ed.), *Mind, self and society: From the standpoint of a behaviorist*. Chicago: University of Chicago Press.

32. Cooley, *Human nature and the social order,* p. 184.

33. Bateman, P., Pike, J., & Butler, B. (2010). To disclose or not: Publicness in social networking sites. *Information Technology & People, 24,* 78–100. doi:10.1108/0959384111110943

Nonverbal Communication: Communicating Without Language

"Action speaks louder than words, but not nearly as often."
Mark Twain

Jerome knew he was late for the interview, and he suspected that Mr. Kim, the personnel director, would be annoyed to be kept waiting. However, Mr. Kim didn't say anything about it, and, after shaking hands and introducing himself, he smiled and said warmly how nice it was to meet Jerome. He invited him to have a seat. Jerome really wanted the job, and he knew he could do the work. All he had to do was explain to this guy how well qualified he was, and he would be in.

They sat facing each other in comfortable leather chairs in Mr. Kim's attractive office. Jerome noticed right away that Mr. Kim was slim and neatly dressed. His conservative blue suit and tasteful maroon tie seemed somehow to suggest competence and dignity. Even his shoes looked expensive. He suddenly felt awkward. I probably should have bought a new suit, Jerome thought, and I should have gotten a haircut, too. He had gained a lot of weight last year, and his coat and trousers were stretched and wrinkled from being too tight. He suddenly realized that he looked shaggy and he should have done something about his overall appearance.

Mr. Kim reached into an expensive-looking leather case and took out a pad and a beautiful gold pen. Then he glanced at an elegant watch and said, "Well, Jerome, let's begin." Jerome cleared his throat several times and squeezed his hands together. Finding it hard to look Mr. Kim directly in the eye, he shifted his gaze from the floor to the ceiling and then glanced quickly at the different objects in the room.

As the personnel director asked various questions, Jerome felt less and less confident. He realized that the interview was not going as well as he had hoped. Even when Jerome talked about his good grades and how much he liked to work with people, Mr. Kim did not seem enthusiastic.

Finally the interview was over. As they were walking toward the door, Mr. Kim explained rather briskly how pleased they were that Jerome had applied. He told him that there were a number of candidates, but that if they decided he was the one they would be in touch right away.

Needless to say, Jerome did not get the job. Obviously, there were a number of things that sent the wrong messages to the personnel director. It wasn't so much what Jerome said in verbal terms that posed a problem, it was the accompanying *nonverbal meanings* interpreted by Mr. Kim that did him in. Such factors as Jerome's lateness, gestures, clothing, and body appearance were not helpful. Mr. Kim's dress, office, and *artifacts* (pen, leather case, and watch) sent other kinds of messages. Thus, the interview illustrates ways in which human communication includes exchanges of both verbal and nonverbal messages.

This chapter examines **nonverbal communication**—how an enormous variety of gestures, postures, tones of voice and many other factors—play a part in human communication. As we will see, they are far more than mere additions to or extensions of what we say. Our nonverbal activities are an inseparable part of the way we communicate.

The Relationship Between Verbal and Nonverbal Communication

Many people are convinced that meanings associated with our actions, facial expressions, and similar nonverbal activities are even more important than what is said.[1] Indeed, some scholars maintain that nonverbally transmitted meanings contribute as much as 90 percent to our interpretation of other people's behavior.[2] That is a considerable exaggeration. Neither the verbal dimension nor the nonverbal dimension of communication should be interpreted without considering the other.

The signs and signals we send as nonverbal communication provide meanings that can alter, amplify, or limit people's understandings of the words we use. However, nonverbal factors are, like our words, a part of the overall human communication process. Thus, an effective command of communication is not possible without understanding how meanings encoded and transmitted nonverbally are part of the process.

Nonverbal communication can be defined as *the deliberate or unintentional use of objects, actions, sounds, time, and space so as to arouse meanings in others.* It is difficult to distinguish neatly between verbal and nonverbal processes. People do not communicate just in one mode or the other, or even rapidly shift back and forth. Their ongoing communication uses both systems at the same time. While speaking words and sentences, all parties in the transaction simultaneously supplement or even modify their meanings with the use of a host of gestures, actions, and other nonverbal cues.

To illustrate, consider the sentence "I love my iPhone!" Each of its words can be pronounced a number of different ways with stress are an important part of the behaviors that human beings use to arouse meanings in others, they do not provide a separate code that has a life of its own. Indeed, they can often be misread to a point where serious consequences follow.

> To assume that you can "read someone like a book" is nonsense. If that was true, poker players couldn't bluff, con artists couldn't dupe, and jurors could easily detect who was lying (and who was not).[4]

Communication scholars note that there are four fundamental ways in which we use nonverbal cues to extend, enrich, or modify our verbal messages to others. Most commonly, we use them to *complement or reinforce* the meanings we intend in our verbal messages. Equally important is the fact that we rely extensively on nonverbal behaviors to *regulate the flow* of our ongoing communication transactions with others. However, nonverbal cues on some occasions can serve as *substitutes for words*. Or, more rarely, they may actually *contradict what we say*.

Complementing Our Verbal Meanings

Almost everything we say verbally is complemented or accompanied by nonverbal actions, expressions, and other behaviors that *supplement, frame, or reinforce* the meanings contained in our talk. As you talk to another person, you may jab the air with your finger for emphasis, extend your palms upward, roll your eyes, tick off points by touching the tips of the fingers one after the other, or shrug your shoulders.

Usually, such actions are subtle or barely noticeable. At times, however, such behavior is done with great enthusiasm. A student may jump up and down, clapping his hands while saying such things as "I got an A in chemistry!" Or, if the student crumples up his paper, throws it on the floor, and says "Damn!" through clenched teeth, such nonverbal cues clearly indicate less enthusiasm. Whatever their form, such

Our gestures, actions, and postures can modify what we say with words. Such nonverbal communication often makes use of objects, actions, vocal sounds, the eyes, space, and time.

and emphases supplied by various tones of voice. If accompanied by specific actions or gestures, the message can take on still other meanings, even though the words remain the same. There is an unlimited number of ways in which a sender can include subtle implications and nuances of meaning in a message while using words. Posture, movement, time sequence, space, eye contact, clothing, gestures, facial expressions, and even odors can all stimulate meanings in a receiver.

Some people mistakenly refer to nonverbal communication as "body language." It has been popularly touted as a means by which the "true" feelings and intentions of people can be read and understood by a shrewd observer armed with knowledge of what nonverbal signs "really mean."[3] Even though nonverbal cues actions are important in that they assist others in understanding the emotional meanings we attach to the message we are transmitting. An important part of learning to communicate and understand the meaning of others is a full understanding of the implications of such complementary cues.[5]

This need to complement or frame our meanings with nonverbal signs and signals runs very deep. It is even done when people can't actually see each other, such as when they talk on the phone. As they speak into the phone, they nod, smile, shrug, and point to supplement what they are saying. Some even make elaborate pointing and body movements to accompany such verbal instructions as "Make a right turn" and "Go to the second light."

Regulating Verbal Interaction

Nonverbal communication is also used to regulate our conversations.[6] Here, the nonverbal cues are not used as part of an encoded message, but as signs and signals making up informal "rules of order" that make conversations orderly.

For example, in ordinary conversation we usually take turns talking. Normally, we wait until the current speaker stops before responding. Then, when we have the floor, others listen until we signal that it is appropriate for someone else to talk. These *turn-taking* rules are intricate, but they are really quite powerful in regulating the flow of conversation. Now try to imagine a conversation among several people where there were no such rules. It would be chaos! No one would know whose turn it was to talk, when to start, when to stop, or when to listen. Individual speakers would be constantly struggling to hold the floor, and everyone would be talking at once.[7]

What are the *turn-yielding* cues that we send to one another to regulate who talks when? Careful observations of people conversing shows that eye contact is one cue.[8] Looking away from a person talking to you and focusing on someone else, for example, tells the speaker

"OK, I listened to you, but now it is the next person's turn." The person who is talking may "sign off" with a shrug, a hand gesture, or simply a change in vocal tone as she winds down. On the other hand, if she wants to continue and someone else tries to take over, she might send the signal "but, but, but," in a kind of stutter that says "Hey, I am not through; I want to say more." Other cues include catches of breath, head turns, eye movements, and gestures. Most of us learn these things as a part of everyday life. A command of such nonverbal cues is an important part of learning to be a good conversationalist.

Substituting Actions for Words

Occasionally we substitute nonverbal messages for words. For example, people commonly use nonverbal gestures or facial expressions rather than words when trying to communicate such emotions as dismay, disgust, frustration, hostility, or love. The facial expressions, gestures or other patterns of behavior that people use in doing this vary from one culture to the next. In the United States, many nonverbal gestures have relatively straightforward meanings that can be translated into direct verbal terms.[9] Conventional gestures that most people understand include the hitchhiker's raised thumb, rotating the first finger around one's ear, sticking out one's tongue, and blowing a kiss. These nonverbal gestures, called **emblems**, have direct verbal translations that are widely understood.[10] Box 3.1 lists some familiar emblems.

Although the meanings of standardized emblems are reasonably clear, other nonverbal substitutes for words can be vague and difficult to read. After an argument with a friend, you might say, "OK, let's forget it," and your friend shrugs. Interpreting nonverbal behavior that does not have clear conventional meanings can be risky. Indeed, the very impreciseness in the link between nonverbal messages and their intended meanings can be a source of serious errors.

BOX 3.1　　*A Closer Look*

Common "Emblems" Used in the United States

Recall that emblems have direct verbal equivalents established by conventions. Can you translate verbally what each of the following emblems supposedly means to many Americans? How many of these do you suppose are interpreted similarly in other societies or cultures?

Grasping your throat with your hand

Shrugging your shoulders while turning your palms upward

Mimicking a talking mouth with rapid finger and thumb movements

Licking a forefinger and marking the air with it

Blowing on your fingertips and then rubbing your nails on your shirt

Pretending to pull up each trouser leg to the knees

Making a telephone with thumb and little finger alongside your cheek

Licking your lips back and forth

Rubbing your thumb across your fingertips over and over again

Pretending to play an imaginary violin

Holding two fingers in the air in the shape of a "V"

Twirling your index finger in the air to make horizontal circles

Nodding your head up and down and from side to side

Cupping your ear and leaning forward

Contradicting Our Verbal Meanings

Although uncommon, nonverbal actions or expressions sometimes openly contradict what we are transmitting verbally. For example, when the husband shouts angrily, "Look! I said I was sorry!" the wife is likely to interpret the nonverbal message as, "I'm not sorry at all; I'm just mad!" Rather than being accidental, this form of nonverbal communication is usually deliberate. People are usually quite aware when they are transmitting or receiving contradictory nonverbal cues. For example, as children, we may have received a stern reprimand or warning communicated in front of others by an authority figure, such as an aunt or a grandparent. But a single wink accompanying such a message and seen only by the child could simply turn the entire meaning around: "What I am saying in words is for public consumption in this situation, but you and I understand privately that my real message is quite different."

As was suggested earlier, some people believe that our nonverbal messages are both *unwitting* and *unintentional*. This leads them to the conclusion that the true meanings of our verbal messages are revealed by nonverbal cues. It would be an interesting world if we could somehow discover a person's true intentions or real message just by careful attention to their nonverbal cues. Poker buffs are particularly fond of this idea. They scrutinize every twitch and eye movement of their competitors in a game to try to divine whether the player is holding a powerful hand or is merely bluffing. At the same time, the ability to show a "poker face" (a total absence of nonverbal cues) is considered essential to the accomplished player. However, as many an impoverished, but wiser, poker player has discovered, making decisions on the basis of such cues can be an uncertain business at best. The really successful poker player telegraphs *disinformation* with the subtle use of nonverbal cues intended to deceive the others.

The detection of lying is another area that focuses on nonverbal cues that somehow "leak" the truth. Some people maintain that it is possible to identify nonverbal gestures, expressions, and postures that indicate when an individual is lying, or is arguing a position counter to her or his beliefs.[11] The best-known form of such detection is the use of a *polygraph* (commonly called a lie detector) to identify activity in the autonomic nervous system that presumably occurs when people are not telling the truth. The assumption is that people have little or no control over such indicators as changes in heart rate, increased electrical conductivity of the skin, and other physiological activities that take place when they lie. The major problem with this assumption is that it does not always hold for many people. Some subjects who are telling the absolute truth blow the needles off the graph, whereas others who are lying through their teeth seem to be able to control their reactions.

The belief that true meanings are revealed by certain types of nonverbal cues may have merit when verbal and nonverbal messages are inconsistent or in conflict. For example, the individual who tells another "I love you," but who at the same time is rummaging through the refrigerator, seems to be saying, "You're okay, but at the moment a sandwich is more important to me." This apparent inconsistency is unlikely to inspire confidence in the verbal message. At the same time, it would not be wise to conclude that the speaker is lying and really does not love the other person; it is possible that the speaker is just hungry.

One of the most interesting ways in which verbal and nonverbal messages can convey different meanings is with the use of *sarcasm*. Adults understand this mode of communication very well and usually have little trouble sorting out the true meaning of a verbal message delivered sarcastically. They recognize that the nonverbal message implied by the sarcastic tones of voice and facial expressions represents a more subtle dimension of meaning. Children, on the other hand, are often relatively unskilled in identifying subtle meanings when sarcastic cues are used in communication. Generally, they are more literal: In a contradictory message where the words say one thing and the nonverbal cues another, children are more likely to believe the verbal.[12]

In summary, then, the relationship between verbal and nonverbal communication is primarily one of *symbiosis*, or mutual dependence. Although we sometimes substitute nonverbal cues for words or even contradict our verbal messages with gestures, facial expressions, and actions, most of the time the two systems complement each other. Box 3.2 summarizes the four major ways we use nonverbal communication.

Interpreting Nonverbal Communication

Although much of our nonverbal communication is subtle, there are occasions when it is loud and clear. For example, students who get restless near the end of a lengthy lecture are experts at sending blatant nonverbal signals. They send unmistakable *leave-taking cues*, shuffling books, putting pens and pencils away, yawning, and transmitting other conspicuous signals that carry meaning. The basic message? "Professor, it is time to stop talking and let me escape."

Communication difficulties arising from inadequate understanding of the nature and importance of nonverbal communication are commonplace. Unless the nonverbal communication is well understood—and used effectively—it is inevitable that we will confuse others and become confused ourselves. For example, most of us have been in situations where we have been truly tired and have yawned while someone was presenting a message that she judged to be very important. Although we might understand completely that the act was involuntary, she will surely read it as "I am bored by you" and will probably feel some resentment.

One reason that speaking is often more effective than writing is that we can include nonverbal cues to enrich and emphasize our meanings. The absence of nonverbal cues in writing can pose problems. For example, in the world of work, a manager who relies solely on e-mail messages may be unable to transmit nonverbally the urgency of what she needs or wants. Consequently, employees receiving the message may glance at it and delete it. Days or weeks later, that manager may be irate at the lack of employee responsiveness. When a fuss is made about the message, the employees may

A Closer Look

Four Major Ways We Use Nonverbal Communication

Nonverbal communication is a very important aspect of the communication process. In fact, much of the meaning that is derived from a verbal message is contingent upon the nonverbal behaviors that accompany it. Exactly how do nonverbal behaviors function in this interpretive process?

1. *Complementing.* When a verbal message is transmitted, it is usually also accompanied by a nonverbal message. In this way, nonverbal behaviors function to reinforce or support the meaning intended in the verbal message.

2. *Regulating.* When we communicate with others, we must follow certain rules, such as when to talk and when to listen. Nonverbal cues, such as eye contact and tone of voice, help to regulate the ongoing flow of conversation.

We call these subtle nonverbal behaviors turn-taking or turn-yielding cues.

3. *Substituting.* Sometimes we can actually substitute or replace spoken words or phrases with simple nonverbal symbols. These nonverbal symbols that take the place of words are known as emblems.

4. *Contradicting.* Nonverbal behaviors can also be used to contradict or undermine a verbal message. A common form of nonverbal contradiction used by adults is sarcasm. We say the words in such a way that our tone of voice, pitch, and rhythm contradict the general meaning of the verbal message. These mixed messages may be difficult for children and (some adults) to decipher.

express surprise at the manager's spontaneous outburst. Thus, the absence of nonverbal cues on even the most basic level of interaction can be problematic at times.

"Things" That Communicate

Other "things" also communicate, including our *body*, the *artifacts* we carrying, and the *clothing* we choose to wear.

Using the Body to Send Messages

Most of the things used to send nonverbal messages are under the sender's control and can be manipulated, modified, selected, or excluded to incorporate intended meanings transmitted to others. An exception is the use of the body itself. Some so-called **body language** can be controlled through various means, but others—those related to age, height, skin color, and perhaps weight—are not subject to voluntary change.

Even so, one's height can carry a nonverbal message. Many short men feel at a disadvantage among their taller peers. In our culture, commanding height among males implies greater authority, leadership qualities, and power. Being short suggests the opposite. Similarly, a woman can be tall and be thought of as glamorous—up to a point. Short women complain that they suffer a special disadvantage in competitive arenas, such as the business world, where those who are taller are taken more seriously.

Skin color further communicates. Among African Americans, particularly prior to changes during recent decades, a longstanding rule was that lighter-skinned individuals had social advantages over those of darker skin. This situation is common in many societies in which

Interpreting nonverbal communication: What "things" are being used to communicate in this photo?

skin colors vary from light to dark, but among those of any race, skin condition can also carry powerful nonverbal messages. Wrinkles, oil, hair, blemishes, and scars typically communicate less socially desirable meanings. The preferred conditions are those that communicate youth, sexual desirability, and good health. An enormous skin-care industry designed to control such messages continues to prosper.

Although it may be tempting to dismiss efforts at body beautification as mere vanity, an abundance of research on the experiences of attractive versus unattractive people shows that being handsome or pretty can have definite advantages.[13] Doors open for physically attractive people that sometimes remain closed for those who are not. It may not be fair, socially just, or acceptable, but in the simplest terms, the majority of U.S. Americans fully believe that "beautiful is good."

Along these lines, one body condition that has long conveyed troublesome meanings in contemporary society is being overweight. Because of the message that excessive weight sends to one's self and others, a large proportion of the U.S. population is dieting, thinking about dieting, or feeling bad because they can't seem to lose weight. Our language contains a long list of epithets (negative terms) for those who are obese. These messages are so powerful that a significant number of people regularly prod themselves into jogging, weight-lifting, dancing, and going to gyms or exercise spas to punish off excess pounds. In more extreme cases, being fat is so feared that individuals undergo liposuction, stomach staples, or deny themselves food to a point of virtual starvation.

Modifying the body in one way or another to make it seem more attractive to self and others has been a feature of human existence since prehistoric times. Tattoos, filing the teeth, extending the lips or ears, and binding the feet to prevent normal growth are all ways that have been used to communicate beauty or status. Some women have silicone surgically inserted to make their breasts look larger and firmer. A growing number of young males take steroids and pump iron to make their muscles bigger. An increasing number of males and females of all ages troop to plastic surgeons to have big noses made smaller, facial skin made tighter, and thighs and bottoms made shapelier. The message of these transformations: "Look at me—I'm young, slim, attractive, and sexy."

We have our hair curled, dyed, razor-cut, streaked, and styled—all to achieve that "natural" look. If we can afford it, we get manicures and pedicures, facial massages, wax applications, or tanning treatments; we apply layers of cosmetics, insert artificial lenses into our eyes, and generally suffer whatever it takes to modify our body so that it will send the messages we desire to others.

The point is that our bodies are available to us as communication devices. Although we can scarcely make ourselves taller or shorter, our bodies are subject to considerable manipulation and change, depending on how far we want to go and what we want to communicate.

Communication with Artifacts

Other things that communicate are the physical objects we possess, or what we call **artifacts**. Such "things" communicate meanings to others about our personal and social attributes. We may want others to believe that we enjoy a social rank of significant status and prestige, or that we belong to special groups. Still others use artifacts to express their individuality by dying their hair green, covering their bodies with tatoos, and piercing their ears, nose, and tongue.

Most commonly, artifacts are used by individuals in our impersonal society to signal their position in the social order. Generally speaking, this translates into messages about personal wealth, status, and power. One of the most obvious ways in which we communicate to others our position in the social order is through the display of things, both large and small, that symbolize *rank*. These include artifacts as obvious and expensive as homes, furniture, and automobiles, and as seemingly insignificant as eyeglasses, earrings, purses, and briefcases. These possessions can communicate to others a great deal about us as individuals concerning where we belong in the social class system; our financial resources; and our tastes, hobbies, interests, and so on.

In the United States, perhaps no single possession communicates more than one's dwelling, including its location and contents. People form impressions based simply on whether the dwelling is large or small, well or poorly furnished, and in a nice neighborhood or on the wrong side of the tracks. At work, an office can become a stage upon which an individual communicates his or her power and status. One kind of message is transmitted by a large and elegant corner office with a nice view, paintings on display and handsome wood furniture. Add an outer office with a secretary and the person's rank goes up even more. In contrast, a small windowless room with metal furniture and linoleum flooring—or even worse, a cubicle with walls that do not reach the ceiling, places the person much lower in the pecking order.

An automobile can also communicate a person's position in the society. Different messages are transmitted by a limousine, a sports car, a minivan, a late-model SUV, and a pickup truck with a gun rack. Such artifacts send loud and clear messages about our financial resources, tastes, and values. What vehicle do you drive? What does your car say about you to others?

Even small artifacts—such as rings, wristwatches, eyeglasses, and briefcases—send messages about our personal qualities. Consider the message sent by a gold fountain pen favored by affluent lawyers (versus the modest ballpoint model that most of us carry). A crucifix or Star of David on a slender gold chain sends a message. Other artifacts that communicate are wedding and engagement rings, alligator handbags (versus knockoffs), leather briefcases, designer sunglasses, and Rolex watches.

In summary, "things" provide us with almost unlimited choices for transmitting messages to other people about meanings we value. That is not to say the interpretations they construct will be the ones we have in mind. Indeed, the very artifacts we regard as signaling high status and good taste may be seen by others as tacky signs of low class and poor judgment. For that reason, the use of artifacts in communicating significant information about ourselves must be approached with care and sensitivity.

Communicating with Clothing

Clothing is another artifact that communicates important meanings.

Dressing to communicate status and power. During the 1400s and 1500s, as the rigid structure of medieval society began to erode somewhat, those in power were concerned about preserving their social ranks. One means of preserving the status quo was specifying by law who could dress in what manner. Both the nobility and the Church backed laws that prescribed *elaborate dress codes,* setting forth what colors, types of cloth, and decorations were allowed at each level and severely limiting what those of lower ranks could wear.

Later, as Western societies moved into modern times, particularly during the late 1800s, ready-made, factory-produced clothing was developed. Early in the 1900s, volume production, low cost, and wide distribution made such clothing available to virtually everyone. This caused great change: As the use of such mass-produced garments spread, status and power could no longer be determined readily on the basis of what people were wearing in public. The shop girl and the heiress, or the banker and the clerk, began to dress rather similarly. Thus, both appearance and styles in clothing became less obvious as overt signs of rank, especially as the designs of the great fashion houses were copied, mass-produced, and marketed through nationwide retail chains.

Communicating with clothing: Which of these job candidates is most likely to be hired? Why does dress matter?

What has happened in more recent times is that very subtle codes of dress have come into use for both men and women. These provide nonverbal cues that enable those in the know to recognize those of "gentility" (presumably of higher social status). Thus, clothing continues to distinguish those who believe themselves to have more refined tastes from those who do not understand or choose to ignore the rules of proper dress.

Many of these codes identify appropriate attire for individuals in positions of power and status in the business and professional world. Working women typically wear a dark business suit, conservative blouse, and plain pumps to command respect. Similarly, men in the business world have dress codes that communicate status, financial means, and good taste (read "high rank").

How much attention should be paid to such rules? Whether you personally think dress codes are important, trivial, or even silly, a significant number of people in our society will make judgments about who you are the basis of what you wear. It is important to keep in mind that those who do feel such dress codes are important are likely to be the ones in charge. Often they are the bosses who have the power to hire, fire, promote, and give raises. Finally, because the way we dress signals rank and power, it influences how we are treated even in the most casual and impersonal encounters, such as when we are customers in stores, banks, or car dealerships.

Dressing to fit in. There is far more to clothing as nonverbal communication than just the dress code idea that we inherited from ancient sources.[14] For one thing, we might dress to be *socially acceptable,* or to "fit in" with others when we engage in certain activities. An obvious case is the uniforms characteristic of some occupations; distinctive uniforms are worn by nurses, police officers, and airline pilots, for instance. However, prevailing dress codes are similar to uniforms in that they identify what one should wear as a member of a particular group. Students do not usually wear formal dress in the classroom, nor does the president of the university wear blue jeans to the graduation ceremony. Appropriate dress can also be important in recreation. Those who play tennis dress differently from those who jog. Such recreations as skiing, sailing, hiking, fly-fishing, riding, and hunting all require different costumes to "fit in."

Although people widely believe that clothes make a difference in social acceptability and popularity, is it really true? Researchers Madelyn Williams and Joanne Eicher found that it is. Their research showed that both popularity and liking are related to the clothes people wear.[15] Even ordinary social events are governed by clothing rules. It is not uncommon to be asked to an informal gathering, such as an outdoor pool party, and be told to "dress casually." On the other hand, sometimes it is difficult to forecast just what that means. A woman, taking the hostess at her word, may arrive at the party dressed in white cotton slacks and a T-shirt. To her mortification, she may discover that all the other guests interpreted "casual" to mean instead silk summer dresses and heels!

Dressing to communicate inner feelings. Clothing is often used to communicate how we feel—or at least how we want others to think we feel. For example, people traditionally wear dark colors at a funeral to communicate that they feel grief and respect for the deceased, whether they do or not. They generally dress in restrained colors to go to church so as to signal their religiosity and concern for the dignity of the service. To demonstrate that they too are just plain folks, politicians campaigning in rural areas commonly wear open-collared shirts with their sleeves rolled up, or farm jackets and feed company caps.

In summary, then, clothing is far more than something we wear for modesty or to keep from getting cold. It is also an extraordinarily complex system of nonverbal communication that can be used to signal what we are as persons, where we are (or would like to be) in the social class structure, that we fit in, and how we feel at a given time.

Nonverbal Sexual Communication in the Workplace

Men and women often have different conceptions of how to interpret nonverbal behavior related to the body as well as various artifacts and clothing in the context of working together. Today women make up 46.5 percent of the labor force in the United States. Differences in the way women and men perceive nonverbal messages can lead to significant misunderstandings.

Many working women today are troubled by nonverbal (or verbal) messages of a sexual nature that make them uncomfortable, afraid, or even unable to continue their employment. These women often maintain that men "just don't get it"—and that even after repeated protests men fail to understand that gestures, actions, hints, and other verbal messages with sexual meanings are *unwelcome* and can cause female workers great distress. On the other hand, when women who feel victimized define those messages as *sexual harassment*, the men involved are often astonished to learn that what they said or did was interpreted as offensive.

There is no misunderstanding about some of the more obvious behaviors, such as misuse of power for sexual advantage, coarse propositions, obscene language, or physical abuse; but sometimes other nonverbal behaviors are

Women now make up 45 percent of the labor force in the United States. Differences in the way women and men interpret nonverbal messages in the workplace can lead to significant misunderstandings. This is especially true for those of a sexual nature.

misunderstood. These include staring, whistling, facial expressions, and gestures often used in flirting. They also include certain kinds of "touching."[16]

How can such misunderstandings occur? Are men simply being immoral when it comes to women in the workplace, or are women being overly sensitive? An alternative explanation is that *neither of these is true*. What may be happening is that, in the workplace, meanings associated with the body, and with various artifacts and types of clothing, are no different than in other walks of life. For example, for working women, remaining slim; using modest amounts of makeup and scent; wearing a nice suit, stockings, high heels, matching accessories; and a flattering hair style may simply be attempts to follow the norms of appropriate dress in the contemporary world. For men, these same features of the body, artifacts, and clothing may send messages of flirtation or availability.

Today, the entertainment products produced by a small number of multinational conglomerates for worldwide distribution emphasize the sexy-woman-interested-in-men portrayal. The fact is that such entertainment *sells,* and produces profits both in the United States and worldwide. For example, motion pictures, designed with younger age categories in mind, often show women willing to have sex on the first date. The reality is quite different, much to the chagrin of males who come to the United States from other countries with such expectations and go on their first dates.[17] Even American men who construct their beliefs about women from media sources may not understand this. The sources for such social constructions are ubiquitous. Television places heavy emphasis on the erotic woman in sitcoms, soap operas, and evening dramas—and much of what we see in advertising.

In summary, misunderstandings concerning both nonverbal and verbal messages of a sexual nature can be confusing. They can seem natural and appropriate to men and objectionable and inappropriate to women. Until traditional men

are able to engage in more sensitive role-taking, sexual communication in the workplace will undoubtedly remain a problem, and confusion over what constitutes sexual harassment will continue.

Actions That Communicate

A number of actions, postures, and activities are part of the nonverbal dimensions of human communication. Among them are facial expressions and gestures, variations in voice, and messages transmitted by eyes. The use of space, touch, and time can also introduce special meanings into ongoing transactions.

Body Movements and Gestures

The study of body movements or how we use gestures, posture, and facial expression to communicate is called *kinesics*.[18] A person's overall body orientation or posture typically communicates interest, liking, and openness. Simply by watching a couple engage in conversation from afar we can guess rather accurately whether or not they are intimate, interested in one another, or strangers who have just met. Some of the indicators are displaying direct, frontal body orientation or close side-by-side seating, open arm gestures (as opposed to folded arms across the chest), and leaning forward. The presence of such postures and movements—along with head-nodding, smiling, and direct eye contact—is a good indicator that the couple is enjoying each other's company a great deal.

Nonverbal gestures are even easier to decipher. Earlier we discussed emblems, noting that they are gestures that have specific conventions of meaning in our culture.[19] Because this is the case, emblems are often used as effective *substitutes for talk*. A good example is simply putting your index finger to your lips, which everyone sharing our culture understands to mean "Shhh" or "Be quiet."

Another category of gestures is *illustrators*—hand and arm movements that demonstrate and reinforce meanings intended by verbal messages. Pointing to your sweater on the chair while explaining "It's lying over there" is an illustrator. Others include stretching your arms over your head to emphasize your level of fatigue, slapping your hand against your head in an effort to recall a thought, punching the air with your fist to accentuate a word or phrase, and using your hands to show length when describing the fish you caught (or the one that got away).

Another category of gestures is *adapters*. These are unintentional hand, arm, leg, or other body movements used to reduce stress or relieve boredom. For example, waiting endlessly for your turn at the doctor's office may elicit such actions as pencil tapping, nail biting, or chewing on eyeglass frames. We may use such adapters excessively when we are anxious or afraid, and they are common among students giving their first speech in front of a class. Many people try to calm themselves by pacing or dancing across the room, twisting their hair, rocking back and forth on their heels, pulling on their ears or nose, or shuffling notecards.

Although these body activities are common, most of us are unaware that we are using them. However, observers are quick to interpret nonverbal adapters as indicators of nervousness, insecurity, or anxiety. In this sense, they can be a problem if not controlled. The last thing we want is for others to perceive us as lacking confidence during such communication situations as job interviews, public presentations, or social engagements.

Nonverbal Uses of the Voice

Our vocal tones often indicate to others that we are happy, sad, confident, nervous, culturally refined, or boorish. The study of such nonverbal uses of the voice is called **vocalics**. We surround the words we use with many kinds of voice-quality cues that contribute significantly to people's judgments about us, and directly or indirectly, to the meanings of our messages. Put simply, *how* you say something can at times be as important as *what* you say.

Nonverbal vocal cues can take many forms: Pitch, tone, rate, volume, and accent patterns in speech all make big differences in how verbal messages are interpreted. For both men and women, voice quality is often associated with suggestions of size, intelligence, and sexuality. For example, if a woman greets a man by saying "Hello," what are the implications when her voice quality is flat and matter-of-fact? Now suppose her voice is breathy and a bit drawn out. Does the subtle meaning change? Of course it does; it sounds sexy, adding an important dimension of meaning to what she said.

Accents are another category of vocalics. These can cause endless problems in misjudging the intelligence, emotions, and personalities of people who speak in ways that seem different and strange to us. For example, people from the Midwest seem to talk through their noses, and such a nasal voice quality may be perceived negatively by listeners from other geographic areas. The same can be true of the Texas drawl, the Boston accent, and the speech patterns heard in the Deep South. Sometimes speakers are assigned characteristics of laziness and ignorance on the basis of their accents.

Speech patterns used by many poor urban Americans may be judged very negatively by the well-educated. Pronunciations characteristic of people raised in some parts of New York City (especially Brooklyn) do not inspire confidence among those from Western states. Regional, racial, and ethnic accents, then, bring with them a curious baggage of positive and negative attributions about the speaker's personality.[20] However, there is absolutely no relationship between any accent and level of intelligence. It is a serious mistake to assume that because a person pronounces words in an unfamiliar way, his or her intelligence is low (or high) or that the individual has any other personality trait.

Not only do we assign personal and social qualities to those who talk differently from the way we do, but we also make judgments about people's *emotions* based on vocalics.[21] Hearing two people in the next room speaking loudly can lead us to assume that they are arguing and angry. We may not be able to understand the words, but the level of hostility often seems unmistakable because of the vocalics.

Research suggests that negative emotions are much more likely to be identified accurately from vocalic cues alone than are positive ones.[22] It appears to be easier to tell if someone is sad, disappointed, or angry from voice tone, level, and pitch than if someone is happy, relieved, or thrilled. Some individuals are more skilled than others in deciphering vocalics to determine how someone feels.[23] Obviously, then, our judgments about emotions based on a person's vocalics are not always accurate.

Eye Contact

Novelists, poets, and songwriters have always been fascinated by eyes. Their works lyrically describe the character traits that different types of eyes supposedly reveal and the subtle messages that eyes presumably can transmit. In such sources one finds a great deal of lore about eyes that are shifty, steely, beady, innocent, or jaded. The idea that we communicate with our eyes, then, is deeply rooted in popular culture. The only problem with such rich descriptions is that they do not seem to have a basis in fact. Nevertheless, we do communicate using our eyes.

A less romantic view of the role of eyes in nonverbal communication is called **oculesics** by communication scholars. The term refers to the study of eye contact and pupil dilation in nonverbal communication. People clearly do use their eyes to indicate their degree of interest, openness, and even arousal as they communicate. Even simple eye contact with another has meaning on some occasions. For example, one of the rules of public address is that speakers are supposed to maintain eye contact with people in their audience.

To illustrate, what assumption do we make when receivers of our message look down or away? Most of us conclude they're not interested in what we have to say. Similarly, teachers, politicians, clergy, and others who make public presentations can become threatened and concerned when the audience fails to meet their gaze. A parent may scold a child, saying, "Look at me when I'm talking to you!" (the kinesics here is usually a finger vigorously shaken at the hapless child). Another example is loss of personal eye contact when you happen to be browsing through a magazine during an exchange with a friend. He or she is likely to ask, "Am I boring you?"

Research on eye contact as communication supports our popular beliefs only up to a point.[24] Even though eye contact with another generally communicates positive feelings toward that person, staring can be interpreted as a sign of hostility or aggression. Keep in mind that eye contact communicates the degree of interest or arousal between persons. Whenever we feel extreme sentiment, whether that sentiment is anger or love, a degree of interest or arousal is triggered. Thus, we are likely to express both emotional extremes through eye gaze, and we have to look to other communicative behaviors to determine the particular emotion that is revealed.

In addition, popular lore has it that the lack of eye contact is a certain clue that someone is lying. So firmly established is this so-called fact that people who suspect another person is lying may demand, "Look me in the eye when you say that." The problem with this idea is that a considerable number of studies on detecting deception have failed to confirm its validity.[25] In truth, most people learn early on to lie quite successfully while steadily holding eye contact with an accuser. As children, most of us were able to fool our parents in this way. Researchers found an average accuracy rate (percentage of correct answers) of only 54 percent—barely above chance—when observers were using nonverbal behavior to judge when people were lying.[26]

The truth is deception is difficult to detect. Those who claim to be able to detect when someone is lying is probably lying about it. With very rare exception, even highly trained deception detectors (like CSI agents!) are accurate only about 50 percent of the time. Becoming a nonverbal communication expert is unlikely to increase your chances of detecting liars from truth-tellers.[27]

Other research reveals that we do gaze at others less when we feel embarrassment, guilt, or sadness.[28] If we feel such emotions, our most common response is to avoid interacting with them. For example, at a dinner party, the last thing you want your host to do is focus undue attention on the fact that you spilled red sauce all over the white linen tablecloth. If you contribute further to your embarrassment by spilling the wine as you try to wipe up the mess with your napkin, you do not appreciate eyes on you at such a time. Similarly, when we experience either guilt or sorrow, we would rather hide than face the open confrontation implied by eye contact.

Many conventions are used in connection with oculesics in nonverbal communication. For example, the rules of eye contact between professor and student in the college classroom are well understood. When the instructor poses a question, students quickly learn to escape from having to provide an answer by avoiding the professor's gaze. They examine their fingernails, glare at their laptops, study the floor, or gape at the ceiling—anything to avoid being singled out and called upon. Equally understood are the rules of flirting with the eyes. Gazing or even repeatedly glancing at someone across a crowded room is likely to result in some kind of response—at best a smile, at worst bored indifference.

Using Space and Distance

Some of the most subtle aspects of nonverbal communication are associated with the use of space and distance or what researchers call **proxemics**. Two uses of space are important in understanding human communication behavior: These are **territoriality** and **personal space**. The term *territoriality* refers to a common tendency that is characteristic of both animals and human beings.[29] That is, many species define some fixed or semifixed space to claim or stake out as their own. When we engage in this behavior, we feel that some territory belongs to us exclusively, but we willingly share other territory with family or friends. Still other territory involves only temporary ownership.

Regardless of the level of exclusivity, we respond to territorial "invasion" as if we have a right to that space. For instance, the most primary form of territory may include your office, your room, your side of the bed, or even your chair. Should others attempt to encroach on your rightful domain, you may feel frustrated, angry, or downright hostile. More public, and thus less exclusive, are forms of territory that provide only temporary ownership, such as a parking spot, a table reserved at a restaurant, or a seat or desk in a particular class. Even though technically we have no rightful claim to such public territories, we may behave as if we actually own that parking spot, table, or seat.

The second proxemic concept, personal space, refers to the *immediate zone* we carry around with us during our daily interactions with others.[30] It is like a bubble that stays with us, contracting and expanding as we move, depending on where we are, what we are doing, and whom we are with. In other words, the degree of personal space we allow with others is determined by the nature of our relationship with them; the topic under discussion; and our gender, age, and cultural background.[31]

Anthropologist Edward T. Hall has identified distinctive zones of personal space that determine or are determined by our interpersonal transactions.[32] The first zone ranges from a distance of zero (touching) to a distance of 18 inches and is called the *intimate zone*. A second ranges from 18 inches to 4 feet to encompass the *casual-personal zone*. Then, 4 to 8 feet constitutes the *socio-consultative zone*. Finally, beyond 8 feet is the *public zone*. Each of these zones tells us something about the nature of the relationship those conversing share. Obviously, the distance between lovers, close friends, or family members during intimate interaction is likely to be limited. When a teacher lectures to a large class, the interaction probably will require space boundaries more typical of the public zone.

Hall's zones have important implications for the study of nonverbal communication. It's very difficult, if not impossible, to talk about intimate topics from a distance of 5 feet or more. Instead, we "move in" to each other when we wish to discuss a secret, share an embarrassing experience, or make very personal comments. Thus, as we move in closer and closer, we imply a change in the meaning and content of our messages.

Both *sex* and *age* are also factors in determining the size of an individual's personal space. Women tend to interact at closer distances with other women than do men with other men. Not surprisingly, mixed-sex dyads (male-female couples) interact at closer distances than do either female-female or male-male pairs. Furthermore, children and adults use space differently. Because people must learn the rules concerning the appropriate distances to maintain in communicating, it is not surprising that young children compose the greatest percentage of "space invaders." They overrun each other's territories and blithely penetrate the distance zones of adults. As they get older, they learn to follow the rules.

Great variability exists from one cultural group to the next as to the rules governing proxemics. For example, compared to those of other societies, people in the United States seem almost paranoid about space. We are a noncontact-oriented people. That is, we avoid spatially close (intimate zone) interactions except with members of our immediate family or with our close friends. Similarly, Asians, Indians, Pakistanis, and northern Europeans (except Germans) are also noncontact people. In contrast, Arabs, Latin Americans, and southern Europeans (particularly male Italians) are identified as more contact oriented.[33] In fact, for many U.S. Americans, attempting to maintain space with Latin or Arabic friends or business acquaintances may seem like a fencing match; as they move forward, the Americans keep moving back.

Differences also exist among African Americans, European Americans, and Hispanics or Latinos. African Americans maintain the closest interaction space and Hispanics the farthest. Research suggests that those variations are more a function of socioeconomic status than of racial or ethnic identification. Shawn Scherer found that such cultural differences were not present when the people interacting were all from the middle class or all from lower strata in the social system.[34]

Some of the more interesting research on territoriality and personal space involves *encroachment,* or space invasion. Experiments on encroachment require a confederate (who is aware of the purpose of the study). The confederate deliberately violates subjects' territories or personal space. The subjects remain unaware that they are in an experiment or of what is about to happen. As the experiment progresses, an observer records each subject's response to the encroachment.

One of the best-known experiments of this kind was pioneered by Robert Sommer.[35] He had confederates approach tables in a library occupied by one other person. Each confederate would sit at the table directly across from the occupant, or right next to him or her, or a few seats away. Observers sitting at nearby tables reported that subjects' reactions to this space invasion were fairly consistent. In almost all cases, victims of the invasion experienced anxiety and then attempted to reduce it by increasing the distance between themselves and the encroacher. Some set up barriers by redistributing their books, book bags, or other materials around them. Some shifted themselves away from the intruder. Only a few defied the invader by glaring. Others gave up and took flight by switching tables or leaving altogether.

Subsequent studies confirm these findings. Almost always, people respond to space invasion in one of two ways—"fight" or "flight." The most common response to encroachment on public or territory occupied temporarily is *flight.*[36] Evidently, people recognize that no one really owns such space. For example, if someone

BOX 3.3   A Closer Look

Techniques to Prevent Territorial Encroachment

Dogs, cats, and other animals are pretty good at staking out their territory by "spraying" the boundaries with their urine. If you've ever moved your dog or cat to a new house or apartment, you've probably had a lot of cleaning to do initially. This is especially true of environments that were inhabited previously by another animal.

In many ways, human beings are little different from animals. Although we seldom stake out our territory with urine, we do construct elaborate fences or walls around our property, post "keep-out" signs on our doors or gates, and sign legal documents of ownership. These are all ways we ward off potential encroachers. Researchers categorize our stakeouts in four ways:

1. *Markers*. We strategically place objects to "mark" our spot, like leaving a sweater on the table to let others in the cafeteria know that the table now belongs to you. Book bags, a partially filled glass or cup, or caps and hats all make excellent markers. Such markers allow us to leave the territory temporarily without worrying that someone else will take over. Curiously, feminine markers (a girl's jacket or a woman's purse) are less likely to ward off invaders than are masculine markers. Why do you suppose that is so?

2. *Labels*. Labels are markers with your name or some other symbol on them. Mothers may label their kids' clothes before the kids leave for college. Checks and credit cards are labeled with your legal name. Signs marked "reserved" communicate to others that the table (or chair or room) is being held for someone else. T-shirts, baseball caps, license plates, and brass door plates use a variety of labels, not only to communicate a slogan but also to identify the owner.

3. *Offensive displays*. Clenching your fists, leaning forward, glaring, and just looking mean are examples of offensive displays. Such displays are very effective at preventing invasion. After all, who would want to mess with Liam Neeson (from *Taken*) or Jason Statham (from *The Mechanic*) when he gives you that look that means business?

4. *Tenure*. By being there first and staying the longest, we can prevent others from taking over the space. One of the authors comes from a family of seven kids and happens to be one of the youngest members. Like all families, they had so-called assigned seats around the table. Now that they are older and living elsewhere, you might expect the seating at homecoming dinners to change. Even with a different table these days, the older siblings still dominate the "best chairs" making it necessary for others to pull up a folding chair! You may have always "slept on that side of the bed," "sat in this chair in the den," or "had the desk closest to the window." As a result, your tenure acts to prevent others from encroachment.

Source: Knapp, M. L., & Hall, J. A. (2009). Nonverbal communication in human interaction (7th ed.). Belmont, CA: Wadsworth.

stands too close to you in an elevator where you are the only other occupant, you are more likely to move over (flight) than you are to complain or to shove the person aside (fight). Nevertheless, some individuals may become agitated and engage in *fight* responses to territorial violations. You may have seen an angry driver yell or even get out of his car when someone took the only parking space available.

Box 3.3 describes a number of strategies people use to prevent encroachment.

Fight responses are more common when invasions occur within primary or exclusive territory. The legal system, police force, and insurance carriers provide services, penalties, and financial restitution to victims of territorial invasion. By such formal means, homeowners are supposed to be protected from thieves, men and women from rapists, authors from plagiarists, and rock bands from overly zealous groupies. Across all these instances, a fight response is expected and typically condoned by our society. Note, however, that (in this sense) fight need not necessarily involve hitting someone or other types of physical force. Fight reactions can range from polite forms of requests ("Would you please move your books to the other end of the table so that I can have the room I need to study?") to enraged commands ("Just what the hell do you think you're doing? Get away from me!"). Whether our response to space invasion is fight or flight, personal space, distance, zones, and territory are very important to all of us.

Touch

Closely related to the use of space in communicating is *touching* when it is used to transmit nonverbal messages. In many ways, the study of touch or **haptics** is a logical extension of proxemics. That is, in order to touch people to convey meaning it is obviously necessary to be very *close* to them. (See Figure 3.1.)

The importance of touching begins early in life. Classic research on animals shows us the importance of touch for infants. Psychologist Harry F. Harlow studied newborn monkeys that had been separated from their mothers and were kept in isolation—and consequently lacked being touched. Harlow discovered that the animals would cling for hours to a wire mesh surrogate (substitute) mother wrapped in soft cloth. Infant monkeys caged with other infant monkeys (who touched each other) survived as well as those that were exposed to the cloth surrogates. Still others, without either a cloth surrogate or other infant monkeys to touch, had clear problems. They developed socially maladaptive behaviors and became violent when caged later with the other monkeys.[37]

Similarly, evidence from human studies indicates that touch plays a vital role in early childhood development.[38] During infancy, touching and stroking seem to satisfy important emotional requirements. In fact, if they are not touched at all, human babies may not even survive. A number of specialists who study early childhood have concluded that there is a relationship between extreme touch deprivation and mortality (chances of dying).[39] Evidence for this conclusion was also obtained from observations made many years ago of infants in orphanages. Some writers argue that the mortality rate of almost 100 percent of infants left in orphanages during the 1800s and the early 1900s, was due primarily to the lack of touch. In those institutions, infants were not picked up, talked to, or cradled. They were just cleaned, fed, and left by themselves. As a result, many died. Those who survived typically became maladjusted or retarded later.[40]

Infants who develop under normal family circumstances are touched very often until they are about two years old. Then, the frequency of touch begins to decrease. Thereafter, people are touched at a decreasing rate throughout life. In fact, senior citizens may be touched very little, or not at all.[41] Despite this withdrawal from touch, however, most people of all ages continue to enjoy both being touched and touching others.

What are the benefits of touch for adults? Perhaps some answers to that question can be seen if we ask, "What happens when we fail to get our needed quota of touch?" A number of correlational studies suggest that *health problems* often arise. For example, a variety of allergies and certain skin diseases are common among those who are deprived of touch.[42] Other research shows that normal speech development may be affected as well.[43] Most important, without the comfort of touch, all of us are likely to experience at least some stress in our daily lives.[44] In particular, during crises we feel greatly comforted and reassured when someone offers both verbal and nonverbal reassurance through touch.

Comfort and reassurance are not the only significant meanings communicated by touch. Depending on the kind of touch employed,

Handshake
agreement

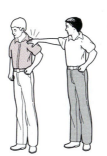
Back-slap
approval

"High-five"
agreement

Forehead kiss
of fondness

Holding hands
in romance

Mutual back-slap
of greeting

Shoulder touch—
friendship

Cheek kiss
as greeting

Cheek pat—
fondness

Arm-in-arm
intimacy

FIGURE 3.1
Using Touch to Communicate
Human beings use touch in a variety of ways to transmit and express various kinds of meanings.

The importance of touch begins early in life and remains throughout our lives. Many meanings can be communicated by touch, including comfort and reassurance.

such actions can communicate dislike or aggression. Poking someone on the chest while making a strong point can arouse hostility. More often than not, however, we consider touch to be positive because it usually communicates attraction or affection. We touch those we like and avoid touching or being touched by those we don't.

In summary, touching can transmit messages intended to arouse many kinds of meanings, ranging from the most tender and significant to those that are offensive or even repulsive. Some people are "touch avoiders" who would never touch a stranger and who feel very uncomfortable with gratuitous pokes, pats, hugs, or kisses. Others are "touch approachers" who just can't seem to wait to get their hands on people.[45]

Time

Have you ever noticed that some people are always late no matter how hard they try to be on time? By the same token, you may know others who are so punctual that they can be downright annoying. The study of the way in which people use time to transmit nonverbal messages is called **chronemics**.

Populations in modern urban industrial societies depend greatly on clocks, watches, and reasonably accurate time in general. In more traditional societies, the position of the sun was the rough regulator of daily routines. Almost all aspects of life proceeded at a slower pace, and schedules were far less compelling. In contemporary societies, such as ours, almost all activities are rather closely regulated by the clock, and people have to be far more conscious of measured time. To appreciate our society's concern with time, count the number of clocks in your home, car, and office, and consider the number of watches you own—and don't forget to include your cell phone!

There are remarkable individual differences in people's tolerances for early or late time schedules. These seem related to a person's biological clock, as is the case with jet lag, but on a more permanent basis. For example, those who are "owls" work best at night and drag around lethargically in the morning. They have difficulty relating to the "sparrows" who wake up early, even without an alarm.[46] Such early birds chatter their way through breakfast and continue to chatter cheerfully to teachers and friends as they arrive for an early morning class. Parking is rarely a problem for them; they are the first into the lot.

Conversely, owls sleep late in the morning if they possibly can. If they absolutely must get up, they may require both a snooze alarm and a wakeup call. Talking at breakfast is out of the question—they just sit glumly with a cup of coffee, trying slowly to get their act together. (Owls never cite breakfast as their favorite meal.) However, owls become more and more functional as the day wears on. About the time the sparrows are at a low, say mid-afternoon, owls are starting to peak.

The study of chronemics encompasses not only our rules, ethical beliefs, and individual personality differences related to time, but also the study of how people actually schedule what they do. In particular, the focus is on what this means to others. For example, what does a host actually mean when he indicates that the party will begin at 7:00 p.m.? Most people understand an invitation to a 7:00 party to mean that it will begin some time between 7:30 and 8:00—a half-hour to an hour later. Their behavior reflects their understanding of that meaning, and they arrive within that time frame. Few hosts are offended if their guests do not arrive promptly at 7:00 p.m.

Consider this: What would be the implications if a guest used the rules of the work ethic and arrived early at the party, say at 6:30 p.m.?

Or, what is the meaning if a guest arrives at 9:45 and then leaves at 10:00? Most people also understand that this informal time frame does not apply to a job interview scheduled precisely for 9:30 a.m. If the interviewee arrives late, as did Jerome in our opening vignette, what meaning does that communicate?

We also share a set of conventions that govern the meaning of time intervals. When friends call and claim they'll be along "in a minute," how long is that? How long is "a while," a "day or so," or "sometime soon"? Such informally specified intervals permit a wide range of actual behaviors—but there are limits. If "in a minute" stretches to several hours, it sends a message that is unlikely to be appreciated.

Misunderstandings concerning time intervals are commonplace because of such imprecise meanings and because of individual variations in actual behavior associated with them. Some people are punctual and take time literally. When they say a "minute" or an "hour," that's exactly what they mean. Others use time flexibly by expanding a second, minute, or hour well beyond limits of courtesy. Regardless of individual differences, however, we tend to judge others' punctuality by our own conception of and value for time. If we are punctual ourselves, we are likely to become upset, or at least concerned, when others fail to adhere to our expectations. If fuzzy definitions of time are more to our liking, we can be taken aback when someone arrives on time or early.

Time orientations are different in other cultures and societies, and this can pose problems in communication. For instance, some societies, like those of the Chinese and Native Americans, place great emphasis on the past. Such societies rely heavily on tradition, and respect the advice and wisdom advanced by their elderly. Present-oriented societies, like those found in the Philippines and many Latin American countries, are said to choose to live for today. In contrast to these past and present preoccupations, most people in the United States reflect a somewhat future-oriented society.[47] Consequently, many Americans share beliefs that tomorrow will bring us greater health, wealth, and happiness. Many middle-class Americans also subscribe to the idea of *postponement of gratification*. This is the idea of working hard today, putting off enjoyment, and saving up for later. This shared future orientation makes it difficult for us to understand those who fail to plan for their future in terms of their careers, family, education, and eventual retirement.

Communication as an Integrated Process

In previous sections of this chapter, the discussion of nonverbal communication has been *analytical*—that is, the process has been picked apart, element by element. The purpose was to explain how each nonverbal usage complements or modifies our verbal messages—showing how meanings are aroused through the "things" we use (our bodies, artifacts, clothing, and so on). We also discussed how our actions (movements and gestures, voice, eyes, touch, and management of space and time) also send messages.

At this point, two notes of caution are warranted. The first is that the tendencies and generalizations that were pointed out are *just that*: That is, they are probabilities greater than chance that people will act in particular ways. They certainly are not ironclad or universal laws of behavior. Thus, even though some forms of nonverbal behavior we have discussed are supported by research, and most make intuitive sense to us, that does not mean everyone always behaves that way. Because this is the case, a particular generalization may fail to match up with our own personal observations or experiences.

The second note of caution is that all the nonverbal uses discussed so far need to be considered as a *system of factors* acting in a simultaneous transaction with one another. Thus, their influences on meanings of both senders and receivers are not element by element. More realistically, they are a kind of *integrated package*. What this means is that when people communicate, they do so as whole persons in a particular context. In a simultaneous way, then, as they transmit verbal messages to one another, they frame their messages by using artifacts, movements, gestures, their voices, and their eyes. While doing those things, they are also managing space and time. It is clear that it is *both* the verbal and the nonverbal systems we use that do the communicating, rather than either one alone. Finally, as we will see in chapters that follow, the additional and very important influences of the *context* will have to be added to this holistic view. Considering all these features and aspects of human communication is necessary to understand the entire process.

The Importance of Nonverbal Immediacy

A practical note can be added to our discussion of nonverbal communication. Viewing human communication as a holistic or integrated process provides insight into ways in which we use nonverbal communication to get others to *like us*—to establish friendships or develop closer relationships with others. Verbal communication is clearly a very important part of that process. At the same time, however, we can achieve and manage our relationships by simultaneously using a number of nonverbal behaviors as part of an overall communication strategy aimed at developing positive relationships with others.[48]

Our use of nonverbal behaviors to get others to like us does not mean that we do so deliberately, in a calculated way or even consciously. Using nonverbal strategies to influence others to perceive us positively can be as unwitting and spontaneous as distancing ourselves from those we find unattractive or unappealing. Recognizing what we do to achieve those relational outcomes is an important part of development of an effective and practical communication strategy. Once we know how to initiate or promote positive outcomes, we are in a better position to exert at least some degree of control over our own behaviors and, eventually, over how others respond to us.

The use of nonverbal signals and other actions that promote physical and psychological closeness with others is called **nonverbal immediacy**.[49] The concept of immediacy is rather complex. It brings together a number of related behaviors that contribute to perceptions of closeness, liking—what psychologists call *affect*. According to Albert Mehrabian and others, the nonverbal immediacy behaviors that, when used together, communicate liking or closeness include smiling, head-nodding, forward-leaning, eye contact, touch, open gestures, and standing close to someone.[50]

Physical closeness with someone can be established using what we have called proxemic, kinesic, and haptic nonverbal behaviors. That is, by moving closer, leaning forward, and increasing our use of touch, we are effectively *decreasing the physical distance* between ourselves and another person.

Psychological closeness is more difficult to describe. Most of us have experienced that condition when we exchanged glances with someone even in the middle of a crowd. In other words, we need not be physically close to be psychologically close with another person. Instead, we might smile, nod our heads affirmatively, and maintain eye contact. Taken together, these particular nonverbal immediacy behaviors all contribute to perceptions of psychological or physical closeness or both.

To understand the importance of immediacy behaviors, we need to consider a modern version of what philosopher Jeremy Bentham (1789) called the "principle of utility." It is a simple idea: Specifically, it maintains that people approach things and others they like or prefer and avoid those they don't like or don't prefer.[51] Mehrabian has applied that principle to his concept of immediacy.[52] According to Bentham's principle, approach/avoidance implies physical as well as psychological and social distance. However, if we find ourselves with someone we dislike, we're not always able to put distance between ourselves and the offensive individual. In fact, we may be in the unenviable position of having to spend an entire evening sitting next to such a person. Unable to rearrange the seating, or otherwise move elsewhere, we are forced to rely on nonverbal

behavior to increase (psychological) distance. We can do this by looking away, frowning, turning our body to the side, or leaning in the opposite direction. By such actions, we are able psychologically to reduce or even avoid contact.

In more positive circumstances we may find ourselves near, but unable to talk meaningfully with, someone we regard as special. The house may be full of guests, or the folks may be staying up late watching TV. In that case, we are likely to initiate or simulate psychological closeness by gazing longingly, sharing smiles, and "accidentally" touching one another.

One of the more fascinating results from research on nonverbal immediacy behaviors is that *immediacy often begets immediacy*. That is, when we engage in nonverbal immediacy behaviors with someone, the probability is high that our target will respond in kind. For example, some individuals laugh in such a contagious way that an entire room can become hysterical. There are some professors who smile, joke, and make eye contact to reduce distance. Usually, the class reciprocates in like manner.

We know that using nonverbal immediacy behaviors is an effective communication strategy in efforts to develop positive relationships with others. Basically, this strategy works because when people engage in immediacy behaviors with us, we often assume that they do so because they like us. When we see that a person apparently likes us, approves of us, and enjoys being with us, we feel like returning those feelings. Clearly, nonverbal immediacy behaviors are hard to resist. For example, even if you have had an argument with your best friend, it's extremely difficult to stay angry or aloof when he or she hugs you and tries to make you laugh. Box 3.4 provides you with an opportunity to assess your own level of immediacy when communicating with others. Check it out.

Applying the Immediacy Principle

We suggested earlier that people usually do not deliberately try to develop nonverbal immediacy in a conscious way. However, there is no

BOX 3.4   *It's Your Turn …*

How Nonverbally Immediate Are You?

The following statements describe the ways some people behave while talking with or to others. Please indicate in the space at the left of each item the degree to which you believe the statement typically applies **TO YOU**. Please use the following 5-point scale:

5 = Very Often
4 = Often
3 = Occasionally
2 = Rarely
1 = Never

_____ 1. I use my hands and arms to gesture while talking to people.

_____ 2. I touch others on the shoulder or arm while talking to them.

_____ 3. I use a monotone or dull voice while talking to people.

_____ 4. I look over or away from others while talking to them.

_____ 5. I move away from others when they touch me while we are talking.

_____ 6. I have a relaxed body position when I talk to people.

_____ 7. I frown while talking to people.

_____ 8. I avoid eye contact while talking to people.

_____ 9. I have a tense body position while talking to people.

_____ 10. I sit close or stand close to people while talking with them.

_____ 11. My voice is monotonous or dull when I talk to people.

_____ 12. I use a variety of vocal expressions when I talk to people.

_____ 13. I gesture when I talk to people.

_____ 14. I am animated when I talk to people.

_____ 15. I have a bland facial expression when I talk to people.

_____ 16. I move closer to people when I talk to them.

_____ 17. I look directly at people while talking to them.

_____ 18. I am stiff when I talk to people.

_____ 19. I have a lot of vocal variety when I talk to people.

_____ 20. I avoid gesturing while I am talking to people.

_____ 21. I lean toward people when I talk to them.

_____ 22. I maintain eye contact with people when I talk to them.

_____ 23. I try not to sit or stand close to people when I talk with them.

_____ 24. I lean away from people when I talk to them.

_____ 25. I smile when I talk to people.

_____ 26. I avoid touching people when I talk to them.

Scoring:

Step 1. Add the scores from the following items: 1, 2, 6, 10, 12, 13, 14, 16, 17, 19, 21, 22, and 25.

Step 2. Add the scores from the following items: 3, 4, 5, 7, 8, 9, 11, 15, 18, 20, 23, 24, and 26.

Total Score = 78 + Sum from Step 1 − Sum from Step 2.

Norms:

Females   Mean = 102.0   S.D. = 10.9
High > 112 Low < 92

Males   Mean = 93.8   S.D. = 10.8
High > 104 Low < 83

Source: Richmond, V. P., McCroskey, J. C., & Johnson, A. D. (2003). Development of the Nonverbal Immediacy Scale (NIS): Measures of self- and other-perceived nonverbal immediacy. *Communication Quarterly*, *51*, 502–515.

reason why that cannot be done. Should you discover that your supervisor or someone else who has authority over you is an ogre and picks on you, you might apply the immediacy principle.

The next time you see him or her, go right up and shake hands. Initiate a conversation; smile a lot; give a lot of strokes, like nodding or laughing at jokes; and maintain eye contact.

BOX 3.5   *Ethical Concerns*

USING NONVERBAL BEHAVIORS RESPONSIBLY

- If you know that by engaging in immediacy behaviors—eye contact, smiling, nodding, and leaning forward—you can get someone to like you, how ethical is it for you to be deliberately immediate with someone who is unaware of what you're doing?
- Could you honestly be immediate with someone you intensely dislike, knowing that you have to somehow get along with this person?

- Assume for a moment that you are the boss—the person with high status, position, and power. Would you require a dress code for your employees? Why or why not? What message does a dress code send?
- If someone compliments you on the cultured pearls you are wearing or the handsome ostrich leather briefcase you are carrying, would you admit that the necklace or briefcase is merely an imitation of the real thing? Why or why not?

It probably will not have an effect right away, but keep it up and changes probably will occur. If all goes well, you may find the individual responding to you in a much friendlier way. If you're still not satisfied with the results, try again; it is very likely that sooner or later the person will come around.

One of the more interesting side effects of this deliberate use of the immediacy principle may reside with you. Over and over, students who have used the strategy report confusion in their own feelings toward the targeted other. They begin to reevaluate their original assessment of the person and tentatively conclude that maybe, just maybe, he or she isn't all that bad.

Before you conclude that using the immediacy principle is the panacea for improving all bad relationships, or for getting everyone to like you, you need to understand the drawbacks of using immediacy behaviors.[53] All too often, people misunderstand nonverbal attempts aimed at eliciting psychological closeness. Some may misperceive our efforts as flirting or even a blatant sexual come-on. Liking is one thing; total intimacy obviously is another. As we saw earlier, if a sexual invitation or an advance is not welcome (as in the workplace), the consequences can be devastating to all parties concerned. Thus, under certain circumstances, attempts at too much immediacy may not be a good idea. Each situation must be assessed carefully.

Another potential problem is that immediacy often results in more, not less, communication with others. If that's what you want, fine. However, once you have initiated immediacy behaviors with someone, you may find it extremely difficult to limit or control the interaction. It is especially difficult if there is a need to terminate it gracefully. For example, it may be essential to initiate immediacy with a client in order to get a sale or close a deal. When the transaction is concluded, however, it's time to move on to other customers. At that point, the client may be unwilling to disengage from an interaction that was positive and reinforcing.

Generally, then, the principle of immediacy—and the nonverbal behaviors composing immediacy—are among the most effective strategies we can use to maximize our effectiveness as communicators. No other single aspect of nonverbal communication has been found to be more closely related to perceptions of liking and approval. When people engage in the immediacy behaviors of approach, they are perceived by others to be more popular, well liked, responsive, and sensitive. Those who behave in opposite ways are likely to be considered aloof, unresponsive, tense, awkward, and insensitive. At the same time, as noted, the principle of nonverbal immediacy has to be applied with careful anticipation of consequences. Box 3.5 discusses some of the ethical considerations involved with immediacy.

Overall, this chapter has shown that nonverbal communication is an extraordinarily complex process. It is not a separate language by which we can read the secret thoughts and intentions of people, but a part of the transaction processes by which people simultaneously arouse meanings in others. If techniques of nonverbal communication are well understood, we can use them responsibly to increase greatly our effectiveness as communicators.

Chapter Review

- Nonverbal communication refers to the deliberate or unintentional use of objects, actions, sounds, time, and space to arouse meanings in others. Nonverbal communication is used to complement our verbal meanings, regulate verbal interaction, and substitute actions for words; at times, it contradicts a person's spoken words.

- Our bodies communicate many kinds of messages, as do the artifacts we possess, including our dwellings and their contents, our cars, the glasses we wear, and the purses or briefcases we carry. Clothing is one of the most meaningful of the artifacts we use to communicate nonverbally. We dress to communicate such meanings as status and power, social acceptability, occupational role, sexual attractiveness, and inner feelings.

- Sexual communication in the workplace has become a widely discussed problem in U.S. society. Some behavior by males is offensive by anyone's interpretations. However, many common forms of nonverbal, or even verbal, communication may be defined as joking and harmless by men whereas they are interpreted as disgusting and sexually threatening by women.

- Actions themselves often communicate. Kinesics, vocalics, oculesics, proxemics, haptics, and chronemics all signal important meanings to others.

- Taken together, many of the actions that we use in nonverbal communication help to establish and maintain closeness with others. These immediacy behaviors include eye contact, touch, leaning forward, nodding, and smiling. In combination, these nonverbal behaviors of approach signal to others, "I like you and I care about you."

Key Terms

nonverbal communication	artifacts	territoriality	nonverbal immediacy
regulate	vocalics	personal space	
emblems	oculesics	haptics	
body language	proxemics	chronemics	

Notes

1. Fast, J. (1970). *Body language.* New York: Evans; Birdwhistell, R. (1955). Background to kinesics. *Etc., 13,* 10–18; Burgoon, J. K., & Walther, J. B. (1990). Nonverbal expectancies and the evaluative consequences of violations. *Human Communication Research, 17,* 232–265.

2. Mehrabian, A., & Farris, S. R. (1967). Influence of attitudes from nonverbal communication

in two channels. *Journal of Consulting Psychology, 31,* 248–252.

3. Argyle, M., Alkema, F., & Gilmour, R. (1971). The communication of friendly and hostile attitudes by verbal and nonverbal signals. *European Journal of Social Psychology, 1,* 385–402; Argyle, M., Sater, V., Nicholson, H., Williams, M., & Burgess, P. (1970). The communication of inferior and superior attitudes by verbal and nonverbal signals. *British Journal of Social and Clinical Psychology, 9,* 221–231; Mehrabian, A., & Wiener, M. (1967). Decoding of inconsistent communications. *Journal of Personality and Social Psychology, 6,* 108–114; Burgoon, J. K., Manusov, V., Mineo, P., & Hale, J. L. (1985). Effects of gaze on hiring, credibility, attraction, and relational message interpretation. *Journal of Nonverbal Behavior, 9,* 133–146.

4. Richmond, V. P., McCroskey, J. C., & Hickson III, M. L. (2012). *Nonverbal behavior in interpersonal relations* (7th ed.). Boston: Allyn & Bacon.

5. Not all complementary framing is done with overt actions and gestures. Sometimes nonverbal cues are included in written or printed verbal messages. This is done not only by using phrasing that permits "reading between the lines" but also by including gesture-like cues. For example, we have all written and received text or e-mail messages with emoticons inserted into the message.

6. Regulators are acts that maintain and regulate the back and forth nature of speaking and listening between two or more people communicating. Ekman, P., & Friesen, W. V. (1969). The repertoire of nonverbal behavior: Categories, origins, usage and coding. *Semiotica, 1,* 49–98.

7. Duncan, S. D., Jr. (1972). Some signals and rules for taking speaking turns in conversations. *Journal of Personality and Social Psychology, 23,* 283–292; Duncan, S. D., Jr. (1974). On the structure of speaker auditor interaction during speaking turns. *Language in Society, 2,* 161–180; Weimann, J. M., & Knapp, M. L. (1975). Turn-taking in conversations. *Journal of Communication, 25,* 75–92.

8. Collier, G. (1985). *Emotional expression* (p. 95). Hillsdale, NJ: Lawrence Erlbaum; Kendon, A. (1967). Some functions of gaze-direction in social interaction. *Acta Psychologia,*
26, 22–63; Exiine, R. V. (1971). Visual interaction: The glance of power and preference. Nebraska Symposium on Motivation (pp. 163–206). Lincoln: University of Nebraska Press; Burkhart, J. C., Weider-Hatfield, D., & Hocking, J. E. (1985). Eye contact contrast effects in the employment interview. *Communication Research Reports, 2,* 5–10.

9. Ekman, P., Friesen, W. V., & Bear, J. (1984). The international language of gestures. *Psychology Today, 18,* 64–69.

10. The use of the term *emblems* to describe nonverbal acts that have direct verbal translations was introduced by: Efron, D. (1941). *Gesture and environment.* New York: King's Crown Press. See also: Ekman, P., & Friesen, W. V. (1969). The repertoire of nonverbal behavior: Categories, origins, usage, and coding. *Semiotica, 1,* 49–98.

11. Riccillo, S. C. (1989). Physiological measurement. In P. Emmert & L. L. Barker (Eds.), *Measurement of communication behavior* (pp. 267–295). New York: Longman.

12. Knapp, M. L., & Hall, J. A. (2009). *Nonverbal communication in human interaction* (7th ed.). Belmont, CA: Wadsworth.

13. Cameron, A., John, O. & Keltner, D. (2001). Who attains social status? Effects of personality and physical attractiveness in social groups. *Journal of Personality and Social Psychology, 81, 1,* 116–132. Berscheid, E., & Walster, E. (1972). Beauty and the best. *Psychology today, 5,* 42–46; Algozzine, R. (1976). What teachers perceive—children receive. *Communication Quarterly, 24,* 41–47; Dion, K., Berscheid, E., & Walster, E. (1972). What is beautiful is good. *Journal of Personality and Social Psychology, 24,* 285–290.

14. Sybers, R., & Roach, M. E. (1962). Clothing and human behavior. *Journal of Home Economics, 54,* 184–187; Rosenfeld, L. B., & Plax, T. G. (1977). Clothing as communication. *Journal of Communication, 27,* 24–31; Taylor, L. C., & Compton, N. H. (1968). Personality correlates of dress conformity. *Journal of Home Economics, 60,* 653–656; and Molloy, J. T. (1975). *Dress for success.* New York: Warner Books.

15. Williams, M. C., & Eicher, J. B. (1966). Teenagers' appearance and social acceptance. *Journal of Home Economics, 58,* 457–461.

16. Lee, J. W., & Guerrero, L. K. (2001). Types of touch in cross-sex relationships between coworkers: Perceptions of relational and emotional messages, inappropriateness, and sexual harassment. *Journal of Applied Communication Research, 29, 3*, 197–220.

17. Interviews by one of the authors with recently arrived males who come to the United States to undertake graduate studies, and who can't wait to date American women, have shown that such first-date behavior is a common expectation, and also a constant source of disappointment when it proves to be untrue.

18. Birdwhistell, R. L. (1970). *Kinesics and context: Essays in body motion communication.* Harmondsworth: Penguin.

19. Ekman, P., & Friesen, W. V. (1948). The repertoire of nonverbal behavior: Categories, origins, usage, and coding, *Semiotica, 1*, 49–98.

20. Addington, D. W. (1968). The relationship of selected vocal characteristics to personality perception. *Speech Monographs, 35*, 492–503; Addington, D. W. (1971). The effects of vocal variations on ratings of source credibility. *Speech Monographs, 37*, 242–247.

21. Soskin, W. F. (1963). Some aspects of communication and interpretation in psychotherapy. Paper presented at the meetings of the American Psychological Association, Cleveland. Cited in Kramer, E. (1963). Judgments of personal characteristics and emotions from nonverbal properties of speech. *Psychological Bulletin, 60*, 408–420.

22. Scherer, K. R., & Oshinsky, J. S. (1977). Cue utilization in emotion attribution from auditory stimuli. *Motivation and Emotion, 1*, 331–346; Wiggets, M. (1982). Judgments of facial expressions of emotions predicted from facial behavior. *Journal of Nonverbal Behavior, 7*, 101–116; Manusov, V. (1990). An application of attribution principles of nonverbal behavior in romantic dyads. *Communication Monographs, 57*, 104–118.

23. Snyder, M. (1974). Self-monitoring of expressive behavior. *Journal of Personality and Social Psychology, 30*, 526–537.

24. Von Cranach, M. (1971). The role of orienting behavior in human interactions. In A. H. Esser (Ed.), *Behavior and environment: The use of space by animals and men* (pp. 217–237). New York: Plenum. Mazur, A., Rosa, E., Faupel, M., Heller, J., Leen, R., & Thurman, B. (1980). Physiological aspects of communication via mutual gaze. *American Journal of Sociology, 6*, 50–74.

25. Ekman, P., & Friesen, W. V. (1948). The repertoire of nonverbal behavior: Categories, origins, usage, and coding. *Semiotica, 1*, 118; Hocking, J. E., Bauchner, J., Kaminski, E. P., & Miller, G. R. (1979). Detecting deceptive communication from verbal, visual, and paralinguistic cues. *Human Communication Research, 6*, 36–46.

26. Bond, C. F. J., & DePaulo, B. M. (2006). Accuracy of deception judgments. *Personality and Social Psychology Review, 10*(3), 214–234. See also: Vrij, A., Edward, K. & Bull, R. (2001). People's insight into their own behaviour and speech while lying. *British Journal of Psychology, 92, 2*, 373–389; Vrij, A., Edward, K. & Bull, R. (2001). Stereotypical verbal and nonverbal responses while deceiving others. *Personality and Social Psychology Bulletin, 27, 7*, 899–909.

27. Richmond, V. P., McCroskey, J. C., & Hickson, III, M. L. (2012). *Nonverbal behavior in interpersonal relations* (7th ed.). Boston: Allyn & Bacon.

28. Costa, M., Dinsbach, W., & Manstead, A. (2001). Social presence, embarrassment, and nonverbal behavior. *Journal of Nonverbal Behavior, 25, 4*, 225–240.

29. For a detailed discussion of the concept of territoriality, see: Altman, I. (1975). *The environment and social behavior.* Monterey, CA: Brooks/Cole.

30. The classic discussion of the idea of personal space is that of: Hall, E. T. (1966). *The hidden dimension.* Garden City, NY: Doubleday.

31. Richmond, V. P., McCroskey, J. C., & Hickson, III, M. L. (2012). *Nonverbal behavior in interpersonal relations* (7th ed.). Boston: Allyn & Bacon.

32. Hall, E. T. (1959). *The silent language.* New York: Doubleday.

33. Watson, O. M. (1970). *Proxemic behavior: A cross-cultural study.* The Hague: Mouton.

34. Scherer, S. E. (1974). Proxemic behavior of primary school children as a function of their socioeconomic class and subculture. *Journal of Personality and Social Psychology, 29*, 800–805.

35. Sommer, R. (1969). *Personal space: The behavioral basis of design*. Englewood Cliffs, NJ: Prentice-Hall.

36. Ibid., p. 291.

37. Harlow, H. F. (1959). Love in monkeys. *Scientific American, 200*, 68–74.

38. Nguyen, T., Hesin, R., & Nguyen, M. (1975). The meanings of touch: Sex differences. *Journal of Communication, 3*, 92–103; Montagu, A. (1971). *Touching: The human significance of the skin*. New York, Harper & Row; Heslin, R., & Alper, T. (1983). Touch: A bonding gesture. In J. M. Wiemann & R. Harrison (Eds.), *Nonverbal Interaction* (pp. 47–75). Beverly Hills, CA: Sage. Thayer, S. (1986). History and strategies of research on social touch. *Journal of Nonverbal Behavior, 10*, 12–28; and Thayer, S. (1988). Close encounters. *Psychology Today, 22*, 30–36.

39. Montagu (1971). *Touching*, p. 75.

40. Adler, R. (2011). *Looking out/looking in* (13th ed.). Belmont, CA: Wadsworth; Burgoon, J. K., Buller, D. B., & Woodall, W. G. (1995). *The unspoken dialogue: An introduction to nonverbal communication* (2nd ed.). Boston: McGraw-Hill.

41. Richmond, McCrosky, and Hickson, *Nonverbal behavior*. See also: Watson, W. H. (1975). The meanings of touch: Geriatic nursing. *Journal of Communication, 25*, 104–112. See also: Lavelli, M., & Fogel, A. (2002). Developmental changes in mother-infant face-to-face communication: Birth to 3 months. *Developmental Psychology, 38*, 2, 288–305.

42. Montagu, A. (1978). *Touching: The human significance of the skin* (2nd ed.). New York: Harper & Row; Fisher, J. D., Rytting, M., & Heslin, R. (1976). Hands touching hands: Affective and evaluative effects of an interpersonal touch. *Sociometry, 39*, 416–421.

43. Despert, J. L. (1941). Emotional aspects of speech and language development. *International Journal of Psychiatry and Neurology, 105*, 193–222; Hill, S. D., & Smith, J. M. (1984). Neonatal responsiveness as a function of maternal contact and obstetrical drugs. *Perceptual and Motor Skills, 58*, 859–866.

44. Richmond, McCroskey, & Hickson, *Nonverbal behavior*. See also: Montagu, (1971). *Touching*.

45. Andersen, P., & Liebowitz, K. (1978). The development and nature of the construct touch avoidance. *Environmental Psychology and Nonverbal Behavior, 3*, 89–106.

46. Richmond, McCroskey, & Hickson, *Nonverbal behavior*.

47. Malendro, L. A., Barker, L., & Barker, D. A. (1989). *Nonverbal communication* (2nd ed.). New York: Random House.

48. See, for example: Rashotte, L. (2002). What does that smile mean? The meaning of nonverbal behavior in social interaction. *Social Psychology Quarterly, 65*, 1, 92–102.

49. Mehrabian, A. (1971). *Silent messages*. Belmont, CA: Wadsworth; Mehrabian, A. (1981). *Silent messages: Implicit communication of emotion and attitudes* (2nd ed.). Belmont, CA: Wadsworth.

50. Mehrabian, A. (1981). *Silent messages*. See also: Andersen, J. F. (1979). The relationship between teacher immediacy and teacher effectiveness. In D. Nimmo (Ed.), *Communication Yearbook, 3*, 543–560. New Brunswick, NJ: Transaction Books; Andersen, P., & Andersen, J. (1982). Nonverbal immediacy in instruction. In L. L. Barker, (Ed), *Communication in the classroom: Original essays* (pp. 98–102). Englewood Cliffs, NJ. Prentice-Hall.

51. See Bentham, J. (1823). *An introduction to the principles of morals and legislation* (rev. ed.). London: W. Pickering. (First published in 1798.)

52. Mehrabian (1981). *Silent messages*, p. 1.

53. Richmond, McCroskey, & Hickson, *Nonverbal behavior*.

The Importance of Listening

Okay, Sara, your breathing is becoming more and more labored," Dr. Luna began. "You need to get in front of this. With your progressive asthma condition, we'll want to upgrade your meds. Understand?"

Coughing, Sara nods quickly.

"Here's how we'll do this. Start with two puffs of QVAR in the morning and two puffs of your inhaler at bedtime. Take two puffs of Albuterol every two or three hours, but only as needed. Whenever your throat begins to get sore, add Serevent twice a day, but only one dosage each time. Before you take the Serevent, use the Albuterol to open up the passageways. Okay?"

This time, Sara's nod is more hesitant. Her eyes seem to grow big.

"When you get a cough or feel stuffed up, add one capsule of Suclor, an antihistamine and decongestant, to your regimen two times a day. And, when you really come down with an attack, add in Prednisone, one tablet per day for seven continuous days. Here are your prescriptions. Have them filled downstairs at the pharmacy. Questions? Look, Sara, it's important that you prevent your asthma from getting worse. You can do that by following this sequence."

Sara returns a blank stare, takes the prescriptions and packs up her things to leave.

Not surprisingly, Sara's adherence to the asthma therapy was less than satisfactory. So many meds, so many different dosages, and a sequence of prescriptions to follow! Too quickly, Sara finds herself in trouble with her asthma—ending up in emergency care.

Sara's failure to comply with her doctor's orders is not unique; fully 25 percent of Americans report a lack of adherence to clinician's treatment recommendations.[1] Patients like Sara who might be feeling sick, tired, depressed, and anxious, may not be especially willing or able to concentrate and process everything the doctor tells them to do.

Perhaps no profession relies on listening skills more than the health care industry.[2] Effective listening is a significant predictor of patient compliance—and satisfaction. Patients report greater satisfaction with their oncologists, for instance, who actively listen when making treatment decisions, they are more willing to carry out prescribed treatments, and they are less likely to file lawsuits against physicians who have good beside manners, which of course, includes empathic listening skills.[3] On the flip side, poor listening skills in the health care profession can be potentially life-threatening. In one study[4] physicians were observed interrupting their patients with the first 18 seconds of the interview. As a result, in most of those visits, the true reasons for the patient's concern were never revealed!

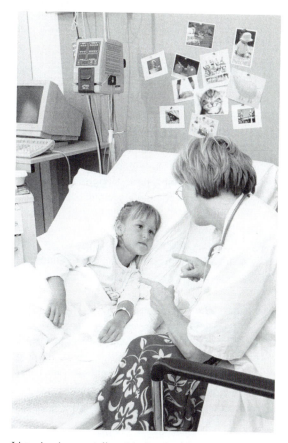

Listening is especially critical to health care. How effectively a physician and patient listen to each other can influence recovery.

Failing to listen can create problems in many settings. A previous chapter explained that many men fail to listen to women in the workplace when the women object to the men's sexual messages; but inadequate listening is not restricted to the work environment. In fact, from time to time, all of us fail to take note of what people are saying, even when they are giving us vital information. Some of us may be like Sara who may be unable to give people our full attention and not even be aware of it. In fact, when employees are asked why they are unhappy in their present positions, most say that they get no respect. They explain that upper-level managers are not listening to them, and that their suggestions and ideas do not seem to matter. Thus, they feel *ignored* and *unappreciated*.[5] (See Box 4.1.)

The fact is, few people are truly competent listeners who are able to grasp all the meanings intended by the source in every message they receive. At the same time, as discussed in both our linear model and the more comprehensive simultaneous transactions model, listening and making accurate interpretations of meanings

FIVE WAYS TO REALLY IRRITATE YOUR EMPLOYEES

Lou Hampton has described five irritating *listening habits* that can bother employees. It is a serious issue because when employees are unhappy they often seek jobs elsewhere. This can pose a real problem for a business because recruiting and training each new employee can cost as much as $13,000. Hampton notes, "A recent survey of 250 business professionals . . . uncovered the five most common listening habits that irritate employees."[1] A boss who employs these listening habits on a daily basis will see employee retention rates drop sharply and costs go up. The following quotations summarize what Hampton sees as the most irritating employer habits:

Irritating Habits

1. *Interrupt your employees when they speak.* "When you interrupt an employee when he or she is speaking, you are taking the focus away from his or her message. Essentially you are telling the person that his or her ideas really don't matter. And there are more important ideas to deal with."

2. *Don't make eye contact with your employees.* "Employees want the reassurance that when they are speaking, you are focusing on them and their ideas. Most people believe that if you are not focusing in a physical manner with eye contact, then there is a good chance that your mind is not focusing as well."

3. *Refuse to give your employees feedback.* "When employees come to you with ideas or problems, they expect you to offer solutions, suggestions and guidance. When you don't respond to their requests or give them feedback in any way, they become confused as to whether you agree or disagree with what they've said."

4. *Ignore your employees to answer the phone.* "Unfortunately, when the phone rings while they are speaking to their employees, the majority of people choose to answer the phone instead of letting their employees finish their thoughts. By doing this, you send your employees the message that the phone takes precedent over their ideas or concerns."

5. *Read the mail or newspaper when your employees are talking.* "[If] you read your mail or other papers while your employee is explaining something to you, you will be missing certain points of the conversation . . . and you [will] make him or her feel unappreciated and unimportant."

[1] Hampton, L. (2001). Five ways to really irritate your employees, *Business Credit, 103*, 5, 20–21.

intended by senders is an essential part of the communication process.

This chapter focuses on the *receiver.* It looks closely at listening as a central part of the human communication process. Not only is effective listening important in developing a theoretical understanding of the basic nature of human communication, but also it is one of the most fundamental, if often overlooked, communication skills.[6]

Why don't we listen to people effectively? At least part of the reason is that we take listening for granted. We assume that *we already know* what listening is all about, and, therefore, there is no need to learn anything more. We also assume that *it is easy* to be a good listener. In fact, many of us probably believe we already have effective listening skills, even when we do not. Both of these assumptions are unwarranted: We cannot take it for granted that our listening skills are already at a maximum, and we certainly cannot assume that effective listening is simple or easy.[7]

It is important to realize that listening is a skill and that, like any skill, it requires learning. What this means is that anyone can learn to become an effective listener. Further, if the foundations of listening skills are understood, anyone can improve his or her ability to sort out more fully the meanings of what is said.

As with many aspects of human communication, listening is a complex process, but, like the other stages in the linear and transactions models, listening is a process that can be analyzed in order to be better understood. Briefly stated, becoming a more effective listener requires us to understand our limitations. It also requires strategic planning for improvement and, above all, systematic practice.

In the sections that follow, we begin with a detailed analysis and description of the listening process. Next, we examine that process from the point of view of good and bad listening. Finally, in a step-by-step fashion, we discuss how each of us can plan to improve our listening skills.

The Listening Process

Social scientists have been attempting systematically to unravel the behaviors involved in the listening process since the 1920s. A considerable body of evidence has accumulated showing the important aspects of that process. Over the past half-century, hundreds of investigators have proposed different definitions of listening. In fact, to list and discuss even the more popular among them would require at least an entire textbook. However, all that is needed for the present discussion is a basic definition that clearly identifies the factors that warrant discussion.

Listening as Behavior

An effective way of understanding listening is to view it as a form of behavior that is a part of the communication process. That implies that, like any form of behavior, it requires active efforts of attention and perception on the part of a person toward whom a message is being directed. In other words, listening is part of the transaction that takes place between people as they communicate. In more formal terms, *listening* can be defined as *an active form of behavior in which individuals attempt to maximize their attention to and comprehension of what is being communicated to them through the use of words, actions, and things by one or more people in their immediate environment.*

One of the problems many people have with listening is that they think of it mainly in terms of using the ears to attend closely to verbal messages. Of course, that is part of the process. In the present analysis, however, listening also refers to monitoring the *nonverbal* and *contextual* aspects of messages. As was discussed in Chapter 3, there is a great variety and subtlety of meanings that can be included in messages by nonverbal means. Thus, in the simultaneous transactions view of human communication, listening includes attending to and interpreting all the ways in which people use words, things, and actions to arouse meanings in their receivers. For this reason, listening is much more than just hearing spoken words.

In our discussions of communication models in Chapter 1, we explained the influence of different *contexts*. We explained that a variety of contexts can add to or modify meanings that are included in a source's verbal and nonverbal messages. For this reason, effective listening requires attention to the contextual aspects of a message as well as its verbal and nonverbal features. These contextual cues can be both complex and diverse and they can have significant influences on interpretation.[8] For example, what we interpret from what people are saying can be very different as we listen to them in familiar and unfamiliar places. This interpretation may vary, depending on whether they are people we know very well or strangers, or whether they are in group situations or are communicating with us one on one. Another kind of context is provided by different media that may be a part of the communication process—a written note, a memo or letter, a telephone call, an e-mail or text, a radio or TV program, and so on. Each of these constitutes a different context, a different communication environment, that has its own influences on the listening experience.[9]

It was also emphasized in previous chapters that what something means to us is based on the accumulation of both indirect and direct experiences we have had during our lifetime.[10] This provides a set of personal internal meaning responses for each of the huge number of symbols, gestures, rules, and so on that make up our language and nonverbal communication. Only when the sender's and the receiver's bases of experience are sufficiently similar can meanings of the parties involved be *parallel,* permitting individuals to share the same interpretations. Therefore, comprehension of a message we receive depends immediately and directly on the existence of parallel meaning experiences. The important point is that these can accurately be produced only by effective listening.

Effective listening is *no accident.* It is not an automated form of behavior that we can engage in without thinking. Although it is true that some aspects of listening are habitual or reflexive, others certainly are not.[11] Therefore, we cannot simply stand when we talk to people and expect that high-quality listening is just going to "happen." To provide for accurate communication, both parties in the transaction need to be actively and consciously involved in attending to and comprehending what is being transmitted by the other, using all the means that we have discussed.

To be effective, then, listening is something that we must deliberately and consciously *manage.* In other words, successfully attending to and comprehending accurately what is communicated to us will be achieved only if it is deliberately set as a key objective—an objective we can achieve if we work hard and systematically. Furthermore, listening is not a part-time pursuit. We must set this objective whenever we communicate with other people.

At the same time, it is possible to listen too intently! It would be impulsive, unreasonable, and even impossible to give our total attention to what is being communicated to us at all times, in all situations, and via all media. This would engulf us in a tidal wave of information with which no normal person could cope. Furthermore, much of it would be either a ghastly bore or a total waste of time. We can all think of situations in which we wouldn't want to involve ourselves intensely in the task of attending to and comprehending whatever information was sent our way. For example, while viewing television, few of us need to focus our attention intensely on every commercial that is broadcast, nor, while surfing online, do we devote highly focused attention to every pop-up advertisement. In other words, an important prerequisite to effective listening is acquiring the skills to be selective and to *discriminate* between what we should pay attention to and what we should not.[12] The importance of being able to listen selectively but effectively is closely linked to the essential objectives or goals of the process.

What We Gain from Effective Listening

Listening serves at least four primary purposes:[13] to *acquire information, to evaluate and screen information,* as it is being *for recreation, and as* a requirement for **social efficacy** (competence in dealing with other people). (See Box 4.2.).

Acquire needed knowledge. Obviously, some message content is important and central to our well-being, whereas other content may be trivial. For example, when a person goes to the doctor to learn the results of a recent test for cancer, AIDS, or another serious illness, obviously the message content is extremely important. In contrast, on hearing that a neighbor's cousin planned to visit, most of us might tune out.

Most message content that we receive is somewhere between these extremes. Much of it has some importance to us. Every student knows, for example, that on those days when, for any number of reasons, it is necessary to miss a class, the lecture content presented will be essential to an upcoming test! When this situation occurs, most people seek out someone

BOX 4.2   A *Closer Look*

The Four Primary Purposes of Listening

1. *Acquire needed information.* In class, at work, or at home, we listen to messages to gain or acquire information we need. Moreover, even if we have been exposed to certain messages before, listening helps to reinforce that information.
2. *Evaluate and screen messages.* If we tried to actively listen to every message we were exposed to, we would certainly experience information overload! Instead, we pick and choose what is important or interesting to us.
3. *Recreation.* Listening can be recreational. Most of us enjoy listening to the radio or watching and listening to the television.
4. *Social efficacy.* In order to win friends and influence others, we need to listen well. It's our social responsibility to pay attention to what others say and participate actively in the conversation. In this way, we are able to better manage our relationships with others and get along at work, at home, and at play.

our lives. For the important ones we can raise our attention to a high level of intensity and listen very closely indeed. To a large extent, then, our ability to *discriminate*, to sort and choose, as we listen will determine the degree to which we can successfully screen what is important from what is trivial.

After screening out what we feel is not important, the second reason people listen is to *evaluate* messages. As previously noted, we are usually on the lookout for specific kinds of messages that are important to us, at least to some degree. However, most of us are exposed to so many people, and to such large numbers of messages every day, that the overload is too much to handle.[14] Indeed, information overload has been cited repeatedly as a major problem by employees in corporate surveys in recent years.[15] We must be able to sort through and evaluate quickly both the relevance and the accuracy of the messages we receive when interacting with others. As indicated earlier, we must be able to discriminate efficiently among the daily flood of transmissions we receive, and select for more intense listening that which is both trustworthy and important to us.

In order to select what is important effectively, we need a set of **criteria** according to which appropriate judgments can be made. These will permit us to evaluate the *source* of incoming messages and the *characteristics* of what is being said against whatever we have selected as standards for judgment. Such criteria are quite personal, but they are based on common sense and past experience, and are not difficult to formulate. Such criteria would normally include ways of deciding whether a source is *credible*, whether what the person is saying is *believable*, and whether what we are receiving is *important* to us in any way.

Such criteria for selective listening provide grounds for judging the degree to which what is being heard is accurate or inaccurate, and therefore unreliable. For example, when a used car salesman solemnly tells you, "This car has only been driven to church on Sundays by a little old lady," is he credible? Are his claims likely

they know in the class to tell them what the professor presented. Here, they will be at the mercy of their informant's ability to listen to, comprehend, and record or remember the information that was discussed. In turn, their own ability to listen will dictate how well they acquire the needed material from their secondary source.

Screen and evaluate messages.   At a low level of importance are all those daily messages that make up minor news and gossip about people, situations, conditions, or events of only limited significance to us. The key here is to develop the ability to monitor the ongoing flow of messages to which we are exposed. In that way, we can sort out that which has true significance in to be true? On the other hand, when the professor says, "We will have a test on Friday, and it will cover chapters 6 through 10 in the text, plus all the material covered in the lectures," common sense tells you to listen closely to this credible source, that the message is important, and that it can be believed.

In summary, effective listening for acquiring and evaluating messages does not occur in a passive or inactive manner. It takes place as we actively receive, interpret, and evaluate both the source and the message against those criteria that we believe to be adequate guides for accepting or rejecting what is said.

Recreation. A great deal of our listening comes under the headings of recreation, amusement, fun, and diversion. We engage in this form of listening when we socialize with relatives or friends, attend concerts, turn on our stereo, view television, or read a novel. In fact, we listen for recreation in most interpersonal situations that are not defined specifically by our need to acquire accurate message content. Recreational listening allows us to interact with people we like for the sole purpose of enjoying one another's company.

At the same time, all recreational listening may not be just fun and games. It all depends on how we define what we are doing. The way we classify a particular listening experience can have a significant influence on what we perceive and how we interpret the incoming message. It may be perfectly harmless just to enjoy much of whatever we are receiving. However, when we define certain types of listening as "simply recreation," it changes how we evaluate the importance and quality of the incoming messages.

In fact, classifying certain kinds of listening as recreational can be dangerous. That is, when we use the term *recreation* we normally think of parallel words like "amusement," "diversion," "entertainment" and "relaxation." Thus, if we are listening in the recreational mode it is unlikely that we will be attentive to certain kinds of information that might have real importance

to us. For example, if a professor regularly provides a lot of entertaining jokes and interesting illustrations during a lecture, the important points of the presentation may well be lost on those students who have defined it as recreation. They will be able to remember the jokes and the amusing examples, but not the essential principles and concepts that were being illustrated. In fact, it is safe to conclude that a great deal of poor listening that goes on in the world results from the tendency to think of the process as recreational.

Social efficacy. The term *social efficacy* means being able to form, manage, and maintain all kinds of social relationships in a positive manner. This implies that success or failure in the vast majority of human encounters depends on how well we are able to listen to what people are communicating by verbal, nonverbal, and contextual means. Human encounters and relationships are found throughout all aspects of daily life—among friends and family, at school, at work, and so on. Learning to listen skillfully in each of these settings can spell the difference between a successful experience and a disappointing failure. In the workplace, for example, promotions and rewards for effective performance may be at stake. Ineffective listening can result in stagnation in a dead-end job.

Thus, in summary, good listening skills are practical tools for developing smooth and comfortable social relationships, including those on which professional success depends.[16] Research shows clearly that an important aspect of any form of work is just "getting along with the people you work around."[17] Outside the workplace, effective listening contributes to success in meeting people, enjoying the company of friends, maintaining family ties, initiating and maintaining a love relationship, and many other similar experiences. Indeed, all these activities depend largely on our ability to hear what people are telling us, to sort out the true meanings of their messages, and to respond in ways that meet their needs.

Actions Required of Effective Listeners

The word *active* was deliberately included in the earlier definition of listening because the degree to which we "actively" listen to someone directly influences our social efficacy.[18] Listening actively implies that we are deliberately aware of our listening behavior and choose listening strategies that make that behavior effective in the four ways described above.

Active versus passive reception. Passive listening is receiving messages without exerting any effort, using any strategy or having any concern about what is being communicated. Depending on the circumstances, there are a number of reasons why some people are passive listeners. Obviously, the causes of passiveness can include complex problems associated with mental and physical illness, but these need not concern us here. Usually, passiveness stems from conditions as basic as boredom, fatigue, disinterest, and apathy. Of the four, the simple lack of interest is probably the most frequent.

People sending us messages are often absolutely sure that what they have to say is both profound and critical to our survival. They expect, and often demand, that we appear to be highly attentive. Typically, we give them what they want: We look and act like we are listening, even though we are not. We look observant, and perhaps nod wisely from time to time, but our minds can be miles away. In some cases, this listening mode is totally justified. The problem is that passive listening can become habitual. If it is used when information important to us is being transmitted, such passive message reception can result in a singularly unsuccessful listening experience.

Active listening, or the active reception of messages, occurs when the receiver makes a substantial effort to maximize attention to, and comprehension of, what is being communicated. When the receiver exercises such effort, the likely result is not only greater attention and comprehension on the part of the receiver, but greater enthusiasm and appreciation on the part of the

Good listeners should look like they are listening. We must look observant and perhaps nod wisely from time to time.

source. There simply is no better prerequisite to high-quality communication than the active reception of messages. It is almost impossible to listen closely without being actively involved in what is being communicated. That kind of feedback motivates the speaker and can make the entire transaction a far better experience than that which occurs when listeners are in a passive mode.

This notion of active listening applies even when a particular encounter ends in disagreement. Whatever the situation, if individuals listen actively, there is a very good chance they will have listened far more carefully to what the other has to say. Once understood, it may be that the differences between points of view are not as great as initially perceived. Effective listening, then, can be a beginning point for *conflict resolution*.[19]

The degree to which we find a person "interesting" will dictate how much effort we exert to listen to what that person has to say. We have a tendency to disregard individuals who, at first glance, appear to be dull or tedious. A major problem is that truly interesting people are in dreadfully short supply. Fortunately, however, almost every person is interesting in some way. One key to becoming an effective listener is to try to look for and isolate at least *one interesting thing* about each individual with whom we interact. In this way, individuals who initially appear terminally boring or totally tiresome can be redefined as worth listening to.

Listening as observable action. Effort and activity when listening are *internal* characteristics. That is, they are factors that operate "in our heads" to influence us as good listeners. Such subjective factors are not observable by others. However, the characteristics of an effective listener can also be inferred by others from observable actions that make us look the part. What are the external and recognizable actions, expressions, and other signs that enable someone to identify a person as a good listener? This is a very important consideration for understanding the relationship between a sender and a receiver.[20]

People easily recognize those who are actively listening to them—in contrast to those who are "tuning them out." They do this by noticing a variety of *signs* or *cues*. If you stop and think for a moment, you can almost close your eyes and see someone you know who is a good listener. He or she has a certain way of reacting to you as you talk. But what are these signs? It is not enough to just say that good listeners "look and act like good listeners."[21] For one thing, good listeners focus their *full concentration* on individuals to whom they are attending, and their bodies nonverbally communicate *receptivity* to what is being said. This is a very subtle nonverbal skill, but people who are concentrating on another's message tend to *lean forward* slightly, with *eyes fixed on the speaker*. Perhaps almost imperceptibly, they

nod in agreement from time to time. The opposite is to stare off in the distance, with eyelids partially closed, perhaps arms crossed, leaning backward, and with a bored look or a slight frown. (See Box 4.3.)

Even a superficial examination of the face of a person engaged in active listening illustrates a variety of distinctive cues. Observable *eye contact*, an alert and *amiable expression*, and an obvious *focus on the source* are all typical of the look of a good listener. In this way, then, part of what it means to be an effective listener is being perceived and classified by others as a good listener on the basis of observable signs and behaviors.[22]

Looking like a good listener contributes to effective listening in at least two important ways: First, when someone is perceived to be a good listener, the person doing the communicating is likely to feel *sympathetic* toward that individual. Accordingly, the sender makes more of an effort to ensure that her or his message will be understood clearly. This is not easy. Making an effort to maximize understanding for the listener involves skill in **adaptation.** Adaptation refers to various ways in which both senders and receivers independently *modify* how they think and behave toward one another. The results of this adjustment (adaptation) include a type of *joint posturing* that contributes to the sharing of meaning.[23] This idea of adaptation will become more relevant in subsequent sections of this chapter. For now it is enough to say that a good listener can influence significantly the amount of effort exerted by a sender simply by *looking like* a good listener.

The second way that looking the part influences effectiveness occurs when a listener initiates a characteristic *pattern of responses* that others can identify. To be viewed as a good listener, a person must exhibit a combination of activities that, taken together, are easily identified and associated with high effort and motivation. What is interesting about doing so is that performing these actions can actually change the listener's own habitual behavior.[24]

To illustrate, if you actually take on the "look" of an effective listener, a real transformation can take place. New effective listening behaviors can displace the poor, ineffective ones. This means that if you successfully exhibit the required look, you not only will *appear* to be a good listener, but you will, in fact, *be a good listener.* Try it out in class. Lean forward, nod your head, make eye contact, and smile appropriately to encourage your teacher to talk. You might be surprised to find that your new appearance is an active listener helps you to become one!

The Listening Encounter

Take a few minutes now to complete the Listening Strengths and Weaknesses Inventory in Box 4.4. What should be clear by now is that listening involves behaviors on the part of both senders and receivers. In other words, as an important aspect of human communication,

listening is a *transactional* process in which all parties are active. Receivers of messages, however, carry most of the burden in accomplishing the actual level of listening effectiveness. Nevertheless, if accuracy of communication is to be high, both senders and receivers participating in an encounter must adapt to one another.

Active attempts to adapt can produce a number of positive outcomes for listeners. For example, adaptation helps to promote and maintain *attention*, which in turn can improve message *comprehension.* When this happens, communication *accuracy* improves. Thus, the meanings encoded into the message by a source are more likely to be interpreted as he or she intends.

Sender-Receiver Reciprocity

Senders and receivers adapt to one another in order to minimize the influence of various "noise" factors that can obstruct understanding of their messages. There are a host of such factors, including language limitations, personality differences, and membership in various social categories (defined by age, gender, race, education, and so on). Mutual adaptation is a means of getting around these potential barriers to accurate and easy communication. However, if this kind of adaptation is to occur, certain responsibilities must be met by both parties. By meeting these obligations, each will be able to communicate more accurately with the other. Thus, the responsibilities of being an adequate sender *merge* with those of performing as an effective listener, and only when these obligations are jointly met can communication accuracy be improved.

Successful adaptation to each other in a communication encounter, then, is a condition of what can be called **sender-receiver reciprocity.**[25] It is a process based on role-taking and feedback, both of which are basic to the simultaneous transactions model discussed in Chapter 1. Feedback, as you recall, provides messages from a receiver back to a source, revealing how the receiver is interpreting and responding to the message being transmitted.

BOX 4.4   *Listening Strengths and Weaknesses Inventory*

Please evaluate your own listening performance on the following behaviors using the scale below. Obviously, you will listen differently in different contexts. Even so, respond to each statement keeping in mind your most typical or usual reaction. When you are finished, have a friend, family member, or colleague who you know well evaluate you using the same assessment. Compare their responses with yours.

Use this 5-point key:

5 = Always
4 = Frequently
3 = Sometimes
2 = Infrequently, and
1 = Never.

_____ 1. I take phone calls and texts during conversations with others.

_____ 2. I look at my cell phone (i.e., to check the time or e-mails) during conversations with others.

_____ 3. I send text messages during conversations with others.

_____ 4. I hold or schedule important and possibly personal or emotional conversations in loud or noisy places.

_____ 5. I have the radio or music on during important conversations.

_____ 6. I constantly take notes during conversations.

_____ 7. I hold conversations from behind physical barriers (e.g., a desk in an office) rather than moving to sit closer to or next to a speaker.

_____ 8. I confirm my understanding of what the speaker is communicating by paraphrasing what the speaker has said.

_____ 9. I use verbal expressions, such as "okay," "oh, I see," "interesting," and "really" to communicate attention and understanding.

_____ 10. I use head nods and facial expressions to indicate that I am listening to a speaker.

_____ 11. I establish and maintain eye contact with a speaker.

_____ 12. I maintain strong posture and avoid slouching during conversations.

_____ 13. I notice changes in a speaker's volume or tone of voice or nonverbal expressions.

_____ 14. I face or sit directly across from a speaker rather than facing away or to the side.

_____ 15. I observe a speaker's posture and body language.

When each of the parties simultaneously engages in both role-taking and feedback, adapting their behavior to each other, they are engaging in sender-receiver reciprocity.

To illustrate, if I begin to talk, you start to listen, which makes me more systematic in my presentation. If you cup your hand behind your ear, I talk louder, which causes you to lower your hand, leading me to speak more softly. If I make a joke, you grin, which makes me smile. If I say something you like, you nod in agreement, which motivates me to provide more positive comments, and so on. Or the interaction may go another way. You may mentally formulate a rebuttal to an argument even as I am presenting it, which leads me to anticipate just such a rebuttal, and, therefore, I systematically incorporate counter arguments into my message.

Such sender-receiver reciprocity can be analyzed by looking at the role-taking activities and feedback signals, and the consequent personal adaptations of each party (separately or jointly) as reciprocity. Reciprocity, in other words, is the combined influences of such behaviors on both parties as they adjust to each other.[26] Thus, adaptation and reciprocity are very similar ideas, but not exactly the same.

Understanding the need for reciprocity helps in understanding the listening responsibilities of both the source and the receiver. In the present

_____ 16. I ask questions to help the speaker clarify and reflect.

_____ 17. I ask if an example from my own experience illustrates the speaker's point.

_____ 18. I use pauses and silence in conversation to allow the speaker to formulate a response.

_____ 19. I ask open-ended questions rather than yes and no questions to elicit more thorough responses from the speaker.

_____ 20. During conversation, I step back and reflect on all communication, verbal and nonverbal, to determine what is really going on.

Scoring:

Step 1. Add the scores from the following items: 1, 2, 3, 4, 5, 6, and 7.

Step 2. Add the scores from the following items: 8, 9, 10, 11, 12, 13, 14, 15, 16, 17, 18, 19, and 20.

Total Score = Sum from Step 2 minus your sum from Step 1.

Interpreting your score: The more positive (and higher) the score, the greater your listening strengths.

Based on these results, respond to each of the following questions:

1. _On which skills did you score the best?_
2. _On which skills did you score the worst?_
3. _On which skills did you rate yourself more highly than the person you chose to provide feedback did? Why do you think this is true?_
4. _How have your strengths in listening skills helped you in your interactions with others, both personal and professional?_
5. _Have your weaknesses in listening skills ever affected your interactions with others, both personal and professional?_
6. _How can you improve your weakest listening skills and continue to improve your strongest ones?_

Source: This inventory was only slightly revised from the original version developed by Hamilton as reported in:

Hamilton, N. W. (2011). Effectiveness requires listening: How to assess and improve listening skills. University of St. Thomas Legal Studies Research Paper No. 11-25. Retrieved from http://papers.ssrn.com/sol3/papers.cfm?abstract_id=1917059

analysis, the focus is on listening, so more attention is given to the responsibilities of receivers. At the same time, the behavior of listening is so closely linked to that of the sender that it is difficult to isolate the responsibilities of one party from the other. (See Box 4.5.)

Responsibilities of senders. As a sender or source of a message, you have several responsibilities:

1. _Know what you want to communicate before you actually say it._ Common observation indicates that much of the content that people communicate is not well thought out.

In fact, poorly structured messages are frequent. This type of message confuses further the already difficult listening process. How can receivers ever be expected to listen effectively if senders are careless in the formulation and preparation of the meanings they try to transmit?

2. _Consider carefully the way your message should be communicated._ The way a message is communicated has a substantial effect on the way it is received. Should it be a formal statement, transmitted seriously, or should it be stated informally, with kidding and joking as a part of the transmission? It is the source's responsibility to select the way of sending a

BOX 4.5 🔍 *A Closer Look*

Listening Responsibilities

Listening effectively does not just happen. Both the sender and the receiver must take on certain responsibilities.

Sender Responsibilities

- Understand as much as possible of what is to be communicated before talking about it.
- Consider carefully the tone and style of delivery that are most appropriate for the message.
- Make sure the message is appropriate for the context or occasion.
- Design the message for the particular targeted receiver or receivers.
- Consider mindfully the possible consequences of the message.

Receiver Responsibilities

- Exercise suitable effort to listen well; some senders and messages require more effort than others.
- Seek out information in the message that is personally relevant.
- Give the sender a fair hearing, even when she or he doesn't come across as being particularly credible.
- Don't overreact to the content of the message or how the sender communicates it.
- Help the sender be successful; look responsive and receptive.

hilarious, but disclosing your losses at work may be interpreted negatively. Clearly, the context controls how a message is interpreted and whether it's listened to at all.

4. Consider who your receivers are when designing your message. Senders who either ignore or are insensitive to the characteristics of their audience use words that their receivers cannot understand, phrasings that are inappropriate, and even words that can arouse audience hostility. Insensitive phrasings and potentially offensive language significantly reduce listening effectiveness.[27]

5. Be mindful of the consequences of your message. An old saying is that you "can't unring the bell." At one time or another, many of us regret having said the wrong thing, and it may not even have been something obviously inappropriate. Such troubling communication seriously limits a receiver's ability to listen.

Responsibilities of receivers. As a receiver of a message, you have several responsibilities:

1. Make an effort to listen. Although effort is important in effective listening, not all messages are worth listening to, so receivers should be discriminating in their efforts to listen. Because we cannot listen with total effort to all the messages sent to us, we must determine from what is initially communicated how important it is for us to make the considerable effort required for effective listening.

2. Provide the sender with feedback. Sources need to know whether their intended message is, in fact, accurately transmitted. Provide feedback with nods, smiles, frowns, gestures, and eye contact. Signal that you understand or fail to understand. Provide verbal feedback as well, such as asking questions, expressing confirmation, or repeating in your own words what was said. In all these ways, you give cues to the sender about the accuracy of the message—as intended.

3. Consider the physical and social context when interpreting a given message. There are a

message that will best help the receiver interpret its full implications and nuances. This point is particularly important when e-mail is used. E-mail is limited to only the words on a page. A phone or face-to-face conversation may be more appropriate for difficult or sensitive message that require feedback and nonverbal cues.

3. Make sure the message is appropriate for the context or occasion. Sharing information about your gambling losses at a party can be number of obvious reasons why where a message is transmitted can shape the way it is received. The contexts within which messages are transmitted and received can alter the way receivers listen. For example, two workers at a job site discussing the solution to a problem will be more attentive listeners than if they were to discuss the same problem in a bar after work. Declarations of undying friendship after the consumption of large amounts of alcohol may not have the same level of accuracy as those made under more sober conditions. As with the other receiver responsibilities, the issue of discrimination is important. To be effective listeners, we need to be able to discriminate competently among various communication contexts.[28]

4. *Give the source a fair hearing.* Messages sent by trustworthy sources are almost universally listened to by receivers. Unfortunately, many of the people with whom we come into contact are not highly credible; how believable we perceive a sender to be can vary substantially. Even so, as a receiver, you are obligated to give all senders a fair hearing. Some sources may be difficult to listen to or fail to contribute substantially to a discussion. Nevertheless, it's a good idea to evaluate the content of a message before dismissing the sender out of hand.

5. *Do not overreact to the message.* Often, receivers forget that an important objective of all communication encounters is to come as close as possible to sharing meaning experiences. Failure to recognize this objective can arouse a variety of ill-advised responses to incoming messages. Inappropriate responses can decrease overall listening effectiveness. For example, if an individual compliments us on our appearance one day, it may be tempting to conclude that he is doing so because of a romantic interest. However, this may be far from the truth. Or, if on another occasion, an individual disagrees with our point of view, we might conclude that she "has it in for us" and is an enemy. Again, we may be way off target. Suspend judgement until you fully appreciate or understand what a person is saying.

Sender-Receiver Similarity

In Chapter 2 it was explained that the use of language in communication is possible only because human beings have an enormous *memory capacity*. Each of us learns, organizes and stores personal meanings and shared symbol-referent customs in elaborate schemas. Thus, we are able to communicate as we do because we have such a high capacity for learning and remembering.

Effective listening depends partly on that same ability to recall previous experience. That is, our ability to listen is based on prior experiences we have had that parallel those of the source of the message. Listening cannot be effective unless we can experience some degree of shared meaning with the individual transmitting the message. This is what is meant by **sender-receiver similarity.** When we attend to and make an effort to comprehend what an individual is saying, we will succeed or fail, depending on whether we are able to construct meanings that are the same as, or at least very similar to, those intended by the source.

Efforts to increase accuracy in communication are widely used in business and industry where the bottom line is cost-effectiveness in the workplace. One corporation, a manufacturer of space satellites and vehicles, avoids the costs of hiring people by creating new work teams out of previously unacquainted employees.[29] Whenever a new item is being considered for inclusion into the company's product line, a group of current employees who have not worked together previously are assigned to the project. This can raise the level of accuracy in their communications about the new product, which can then increase their efficiency and productivity. In this way, the company has the advantage of having employees who are already knowledgeable about the work, even though they have not worked as a team previously.

Essentially, this is a problem in effective listening. Remember that shared experience is one important key to competency in this task. Effective listening skills are an important part of what enables people to work together efficiently and harmoniously as a team. Therefore, in forming such teams it is important to improve listening skills by providing opportunities for team members to share certain kinds of experiences. In particular, they need to get to know one another as individuals so that, in a team situation, they will be able to understand and anticipate how each of the others will assign meaning to the messages they send and receive.

Several approaches to getting employees acquainted very quickly have been tested. In one particular procedure, after the teams are created, provision is made for members to spend the time necessary to get to know one another well enough to be able to work together. This is done by providing for one-on-one interactions between all possible pairs in the team. After spending sufficient time in one encounter, individuals switch and pair up with another member of the team. This activity continues until each member of the work team has had a chance to get acquainted with every other member. Employees communicate with and listen to one another during all these encounters. Because these people have already worked with the company a while and know the general type of work they will be doing, each has had experiences that can contribute to their understanding of what other members will say. They are all members of the local community. They tend to be similar in terms of education; they have a similar income level; they tend to share a common lifestyle; and they have many other characteristics and experiences in common. In short, because of these similar stored experiences they quickly become able to listen effectively to one another.

How does this example from industry increase our understanding of listening skills in general? It shows that listening effectively is easy or difficult depending on the degree to which the sender and receiver *are similar*. For example, two college students can communicate and listen to each other with a relatively high level of accuracy. They can do so even if they are from different schools because they share many common experiences. However, a college student and a person of similar age who went directly from high school to work in a factory will have a much more difficult time listening effectively to each other. Thus, the ability of people sending and receiving messages to recall similar experiences (while listening) influences their understanding. Unfortunately, the listening problems of dissimilar people are not easily solved. Additional listening effort is needed to understand accurately what someone dissimilar to us is saying.

Misconceptions That Impair Listening

In addition to those already discussed, a number of other factors can reduce our listening effectiveness. These include making inaccurate assumptions about what listening requires, plus a number of physical, personal, and even cultural factors that can limit accuracy when listening.

Inaccurate Assumptions about Listening

Ineffective listening may result from having made inaccurate assumptions about the listening process.[30] There are at least four common misconceptions made by poor listeners. These include assuming that listening is *easy*, that it is just a matter of *intelligence*, that it requires *no planning*, and that one who *reads well* can automatically listen effectively.

Listening is easy. Our earlier discussion about recreational listening indicated that thinking about listening as fun or relaxation changes the way we attend to and understand what is being communicated. A common misconception related to this idea is that *all listening is easy*. Certainly, some of the listening we do is in fact easy, but most of it definitely is not. We have indicated repeatedly that effective listening is a complex activity that requires effort. Moreover, good listeners are not born; they are *made*—through hard work. Approaching listening with the assumption that it is effortless, amusement, play, or in any other way just easy is certain to lead to difficulties in interactions with others.

It's just a matter of intelligence. A second common misconception about listening is that all smart people listen well. The conclusion that seems to follow from such an assumption is that "I am smart; therefore, I am already a good listener." Unfortunately, this is not a logical conclusion. Smart people, dumb people, and those in between can be either good or bad listeners.

Listening requires no planning. A popular belief is that because we engage in a great deal of listening every day, we need not plan so that we can do it more effectively. We assume that the large amount of listening we do as part of our routine automatically makes us good listeners. This is totally inaccurate. It is true that all of us engage in a multitude of communication interactions every day, and that whenever we assume the role of a receiver in an interaction, we do something that resembles listening. Unfortunately, most of us neither practice good listening skills nor have the ability to assess the effectiveness of our own listening behavior. What, then, do we actually learn from most of the listening we routinely do on a day-to-day basis? In fact, we learn almost nothing. Effective listening follows from having planned carefully, not just from sheer frequency of doing it.

Read better; listen better. A rather curious but misguided assumption is that by improving our reading ability, we will also improve our listening ability. This idea is founded on the belief that what is acquired in learning one skill automatically transfers to another, even though what is learned is different. This is an interesting idea, but no psychological or educational research has shown that this transfer actually occurs. Certain skills can generalize across a variety of activities, such as being able to run fast, which probably would help in making a touchdown at a football game or winning a foot race—but listening and reading are not based enough on common skills to allow for the same kind of transfer.

Five Barriers to Effective Listening

In addition to the incorrect assumptions just discussed, a number of different types of *barriers* to effective listening need to be considered.[31] The term *barrier* here refers to any condition that can reduce the accuracy in communication. Most of these barriers to effective listening can be grouped into five broad categories. These include *physical conditions* where the communication takes place, *personal problems* that the receiver may have, *cultural differences* between the parties, *prejudices* a listener may have toward the sender and misunderstanding of *connotative meanings*. Earlier, such conditions were referred to as "noise," and it was noted that there were a number of conditions that could reduce accuracy in communication.

Physical conditions. It is surprising how often physical noise can interfere with effective listening. Unfortunately many people tend to ignore such obstacles and assume that they have no influence on the accuracy of their communication. Nothing could be further from the truth. This type of noise interference can come from any number of causes which are often beyond their control. This includes sounds caused by printers, cars and trucks, lawn mowers, dishwashers, aircraft, and any other source that physically blocks our ability to hear. Another type of external barrier is loud voices in the background. These can either distract us or limit our ability to receive messages.

Personal problems. The most obvious personal conditions that pose barriers to good listening are physical ones. Sickness, exhaustion, and discomfort caused by illness all limit our ability to listen effectively. Overindulgence in alcohol or even food can reduce our listening capacity. Also, if we have something on our minds that distract us, such as financial problems, a sick relative or friend, a stressful relationship with a loved one, or a preoccupation with a future event, our ability to listen is affected. We can also be so overextended at work or study that we are unable to concentrate effectively on the communication. Finally, one additional personal issue that can decrease listening effectiveness is *apprehension* about listening to others. Some people experience a high level of "receiver anxiety" when they try to process information from others, and this can interfere with their abilities to receive and interpret what is being said.

Cultural differences.   Many of the problems of ineffective listening are brought about by differences in the cultural backgrounds of the communicating parties. This does not refer only to people from different countries trying to communicate, where languages and ways of life can pose barriers. For example, women who work all day and then find themselves working a "second shift" at home caring for their family complain that their husbands "just don't get it"—even after they repeatedly plea for help. This is a classic case of a cultural barrier to effective listening. In part, this communication failure occurs because of major differences in the cultural worlds of traditional men versus contemporary working women.

Differences in cultural beliefs of this kind occur widely. Individuals from low-income backgrounds may have difficulty in listening to the affluent and well-educated. Management may not listen carefully to the complaints of workers. Those from dominant groups in society may not hear what minority groups are saying. In any complex society with a diverse population, such cultural differences can pose problems. People from different backgrounds often define various features of reality in different ways, which can make it difficult to hear what is being said when communication crosses such lines.

Prejudices.   A fourth set of barriers to effective listening is based on personal **prejudices**. These are a product of cultural differences among various kinds of people in society. Thus, individuals may share with others like themselves negative attitudes toward another specific category of people. Commonly, these prejudices are based on unrealistic beliefs regarding that particular category of people. Common examples are prejudices against minorities, particular religious groups, and LGBT individuals (lesbian, gay, bisexual, and transgendered), or even people have wealth or power. The personal behavior resulting from such beliefs is a tendency to *prejudge* any member of the negatively defined category. Such prejudgments are usually based on **stereotypes**—assumptions that all people in a certain category are alike, regardless of their individual merits.

It is clear that such stereotypes can pose significant barriers to effective listening. They prevent us from perceiving and understanding the actual characteristics, abilities, or intentions of an individual simply because he or she is a member of the negatively defined category. Thus, it doesn't matter what that individual is actually saying; the message is perceived within the framework of the negative beliefs that are the basis of the shared prejudice.

The point here goes beyond common and well-documented prejudices, such as those focusing on race or ethnicity. Those are very obvious. More subtle is the fact that we may have a difficult time listening objectively to someone who is a member of virtually any category if we are convinced that such people lack good judgment or cannot perform effectively in some areas. For example, we may "tune out" individuals who do not have a college education, who have limited income; or who are older, or younger, than we are—assuming that they could not possibly appreciate our concerns and viewpoints. Particularly subtle are prejudices concerning physical attractiveness. We noted in Chapter 3 that many people tend to overrate the competence and capacities of men and women who are unusually handsome or beautiful while seriously underestimating the abilities of those who are unattractive or disabled.

Generally, then, prejudice against categories of people is an especially difficult problem in listening. We explained in Chapter 2 that in all acts of perception we rely on *labeled categories* of the features in our physical and social world. We use labels as concepts to make sense out of the world. We have to do this in order to cope efficiently with aspects of reality we encounter repetitively. However, if we are listening to a person representing a labeled category of people we judge to be negative, our listening is influenced by the schemas of beliefs we have constructed for that entire category. Like the mirrors in amusement parks that distort images, such prejudicial schemas twist the meanings we construct as we process the message. In other words, our beliefs about the entire category in which that person can be classified become part of her or his incoming message. In this way, we construct meanings and interpretations that were never intended by the source of the message.

Connotative meanings. A final category of barriers to effective listening is represented by the connotations we read into messages. Connotative meanings are those personal, subjective, and unshared interpretations we have for certain verbal and nonverbal symbols and signs. Obviously, these are not part of the meanings intended by the source, and when we build them into our interpretations of an incoming message, we impair our listening and reduce the accuracy of the communication. For example, you might remark to your friend, "Professor Jones is *such* an easy grader." Your friend, who knows Professor Jones only too well, recognizes immediately that your real meaning is that the professor is anything but an easy grader.

The influence of connotative meanings on accuracy can be exasperating when either or both senders and receivers associate connotative meanings with the symbols used in a message. Senders may unintentionally use them in encoding messages, while receivers may use them in decoding and interpretation. It is an exasperating problem because it is so hard to detect. We have all come away from encounters feeling that we completely understood and totally agreed with someone, but then later discovered that the other person recalls a completely different version of what was said and what the agreements were. Often, we conclude that the person either has a faulty memory or is deliberately misrepresenting what was said. What we may be experiencing in this situation is an erosion of accuracy in communication due to the very different connotative meanings in the encoding-decoding processes of sender and receiver.

Very little can be done about this influence on listening. Usually, neither party realizes he or she is failing to separate connotative and denotative meanings. However, as listeners, we can be aware of the problem. If we find ourselves in that stressful situation of recalling a communication differently than the other person, we can then search for sources of confusion brought into the encounter by each individual. (See Figure 4.1.)

A Seven-Feature Plan for Strategic Listening

Any person can become a more effective listener by using a systematic plan.[32] This plan is not difficult to understand because its strategy can be based on the factors already discussed in this chapter. Such a plan can be viewed as a *series of steps* we can take to improve both our listening skills and our ability to interpret messages more accurately. The specific activities that can make up such a plan are described below. See Box 4.6.

Be Mindful of Your Self-Talk

Self-talk provides you with a "running commentary" on everything you do and experience. Self-talk is the internal dialogue you engage in throughout your daily activities.[33] As you go through your day, you are constantly thinking

FIGURE 4.1

Barriers to Effective Listening

There are various barriers to effective listening, including personal issues with the listener and context issues, such as where, when, and how the communication is taking place.

about and making sense of your experiences as you encounter them. This inner voice determines how you perceive and respond to every message you hear.

Some self-talk is positive; other self-talk is negative. Some self-talk is reasonable; other self-talk misrepresents reality. Whatever the nature of the self-talk, it influences how you listen, perceive, and process what others say and do.

Positive self-talk will help you listen better than negative self-talk. For example, which of the following statements are more likely to result in greater understanding?

"I can probably learn something from this person."

"I don't like this person; we never agree on anything."

"I always come across as too young and inexperienced to be taken seriously."

"I will work hard to remain open to what this person is telling me."

Once you become aware of the content of your own self-talk, you can begin to control your thoughts when you need to make an effort to listen carefully.

Prepare Yourself to Listen

Effective listening is largely a product of the degree to which senders and receivers have *adapted* to one another to enhance their reciprocity. This second step requires that we be sensitive in relating to others. We must be open to all kinds of sources and receptive to what they are saying.

One way of preparing ourselves for this type of receptivity is to guard against any hidden listening *barriers* and to fulfill those *receiver responsibilities* considered earlier. In effect, we have to be like a runner who is warming up and getting ready for a race. This means preparing ourselves to adapt to the speaker in order to achieve the required level of sender-receiver reciprocity. It also means anticipating the need to

BOX 4.6   *A Closer Look*

Features of a Sound Listening Plan

1. *Be mindful of your self-talk.* Knowing that self-talk influences how you interpret what you hear, you will want to choose positive self-talk. When you do, you are more likely to seek understanding, be open to different points of view, and reduce message distortion.

2. *Prepare to listen.* Prepare yourself to listen by understanding the concept of the sender–receiver reciprocity. This requires that you be open and sensitive to all kinds of sources and to the content of what they are saying.

3. *Control your concentration.* Learn to concentrate actively on what a person is saying. Such concentration rests on the distinction between active and passive listening. Such concentration must be selective, with the greatest effort focused on important messages and least attention on irrelevant ones.

4. *Show alertness and interest.* Appear to be listening even if your attention sometimes wanders from what a speaker is saying. The act of trying to show interest actually results in more effective attention to and understanding of a sender's message.

5. *Search actively for meaning.* Search actively for essential meanings in a sender's message, and summarize them in your own terms. Seek clues to take into account how the sender's background may influence what is being said.

6. *Keep active while listening.* Avoid slipping into a passive manner of receiving, with accompanying daydreaming and distraction. This may require changes in behavior, such as adjusting posture, more active breathing, or other shifts away from a relaxed mode.

7. *Suspend judgment about message and source.* Premature judgments about a person's intentions, qualifications, or actual positions can interfere with what is being said. Therefore, withhold early closure about the real meanings being transmitted, and wait until after the entire message has been heard.

expend effort, to assess the intent of the person transmitting the message, and to understand the implications of the context, as well as recognizing the danger of overreacting.

Control Your Concentration

The third step of planning emphasizes controlling our *level of concentration*. How actively do we concentrate on what others say to us? This idea is related to the earlier discussion of active versus passive listening. Remember, this approach is based on the idea that effective listening is *no accident*. It requires that we deliberately and consciously attend to and try to comprehend what is being communicated to us. At the same time, a good listening plan allows us to maintain a reasonable amount of control over our concentration. As noted earlier, some messages need not be given the same level of attention as others. When a message seems important, however, the time has come to really concentrate.

Show Alertness and Interest

The fourth step in a good plan is to show or demonstrate alertness and interest to a sender when we listen. What good listeners look like was described in earlier sections of this chapter—that is, how they engage in specific kinds of *overt behaviors* that lead senders to believe they are listening to them intently. This does not mean faking an attentive look. However, looking the part does, in fact, improve communication accuracy. Often, senders will try to communicate more effectively when they see that they have a good listener.

What feature of a sound listening plan is best illustrated in this father-son interaction?

Search Actively for Meaning

The fifth step in a listening plan is to provide for *deliberate concentration* on the intended meaning of messages. In this step, we need to develop ways to construct for ourselves the meaning the source intends. This requires that we understand any significant cultural differences between ourselves and the source, as well as grasp how our personal prejudices may distort meanings of messages from people who are different from us. We can engage in a sort of reverse role-taking by trying to understand the purposes of the source's choice of symbols, nonverbal cues, and rules of syntax and grammar. This brings us back to our earlier notion of sender-receiver reciprocity. The point here is that if we are to comprehend messages accurately, we need to look for every clue to what the person is trying to say. Here we take into account the person's characteristics, possible connotative meanings, and implications of the setting or context. If in doubt, we can ask questions, provide feedback, and follow up with requests for further details.

Keep Active while Listening

A sixth part of a good plan is to consider ways that will help us maintain a high level of activity during listening.

Actively maintaining our determination to listen is a little like psyching ourselves up to run a race. Many competitors have lost races because they failed to develop the right mental outlook. Also, a runner must actually be the first to cross the finish line in order to be the winner, not just lead most of the way. In the context of listening, our efforts to attend to and comprehend messages need to last through the *entire encounter*. If listening deteriorates before our interaction is finished, we will likely miss something critical. There are no universally effective approaches to maintaining a high level of listening activity. Each person needs to use his or her own personal resources and determinations to continue listening until a sender has completed transmission of a message.

Suspend Judgment about Message and Source

The final aspect of a good listening plan is to avoid *prejudging* either the source person or the message. It is not easy to separate one's feelings about the person—and the labeled categories he or she represents—from the meanings of the person's message. However, if we can recognize our personal biases, we can take them into account in our listening plan. This kind of deliberate self-assessment helps to identify our problem areas. With this insight, we can limit their influences on our objectivity. See Box 4.7.

EFFECTIVE LISTENING

Suspending judgment until after an entire message has been heard is the ethical responsibility of effective listeners. For example, during the presidential campaigns, it is impossible to evaluate fairly the positions of all candidates on important issues unless the speaker's message is given a fair and objective hearing. In fact, it is *un*ethical to prejudge in these ways. Educated and responsible individuals make an effort to behave ethically when listening to all speakers and to all types of messages.

In overview, this seven-part plan may seem complex. Indeed, it may not be possible to start doing all the activities at the same time. A sensible way to start using the plan is to try to master one or two steps first, and incorporate additional parts later. As progress is made, adding activities will correspondingly improve your listening skills.

Chapter Review

- Effective listening is one of the most important of all communication skills. Fortunately, it is one that we acquire as a result of learning. This means that it can be analyzed, understood, and improved.

- Listening is the process in which individuals actively make the effort to maximize their attention to, and comprehension of, what is being communicated to them. People listen to acquire knowledge, to evaluate incoming messages, and for recreation.

- Learning to listen well is an important part of getting along with others, influencing people, and getting them to think of us in positive terms. Although passive listening is adequate for some recreational activities, a far more active effort is required in social and professional situations. Looking the part—through overt actions, expression, body posture, and eye contact—is an important strategy for becoming an effective listener.

- During the listening encounter, a reciprocity develops between source and listener. The source is responsible for formulating messages clearly, using an appropriate style of transmission, being aware of the influence of context, understanding the unique characteristics of the receiver, and assessing ahead of time the possible consequences of the content. The receiver, on the other hand, is responsible for determining how much effort is needed to listen, assessing the intent, appreciating the implications of the context, and avoiding overreaction. Listening effectiveness is reduced to the extent that people make erroneous assumptions about listening, including the assumption that listening is easy. Moreover, barriers to effective listening arise from five major sources: physical conditions, personal problems, cultural differences, prejudices, and connotative meanings.

- The seven-feature plan for strategic listening outlined in this chapter can help to improve our listening skills.

Key Terms

social efficacy	sender-receiver reciprocity	stereotype
criteria (in listening)	sender-receiver similarity	self-talk
adaptation	prejudice	

Notes

1. Davis, K., Schoenbaum, S. C., Collins, K. S., Tenney, K., Hughes, D. L., & Audet, A. M. (2002). *Room for improvement: Patients report on the quality of their health care.* New York: Commonwealth Fund.

2. Janusik, L. (2002). Listening facts. Retrieved from http://www.paragonresources. com/library/listen.pdf; see also: Listening facts. International Listening Assocation. Retrieved from http://www.listen.org/index.php?option= com_content&view=category&layout=blog&id= 43&Itemid=74.

3. Wanzer, M.B., Booth-Butterfield, M., & Gruber, M.K. (2004). Perceptions of health care providers' communication: Relationships between patient-centered communication and satisfaction. *Health Communication, 16*, 363–384.

4. du Pre, A. (2002). Accomplishing the impossible. Talking about body and soul and mind during a medical visit. *Health Communication, 14*, 1–21.

5. Hampton, L. (2001). Five ways to really irritate your employees. *Business Credit, 103*, 20–22.

6. Bostrom, R. N., & Waldhart, E. S. (1988). Memory models and the measurement of listening. *Communication Education, 37*, 1.

7. Watson, K., & Barker, L. L. (1985). Listening behavior: Definition and measurement. In R. Bostrom (Ed.), *Communication yearbook 8* (pp. 178–197). Beverly Hills, CA: Sage.

8. Rankin, P. T. (1926). *The measurement of the ability to understand spoken language.* Unpublished doctoral dissertation, University of Michigan. University Microfilm Publication No. 4352, 1952.

9. Nichols, R. G. (1948). Factors in listening comprehension. *Communication Monographs, 15*, 154–163; and Nichols, R., & Stevens, L. (1957). *Are you listening?* New York: McGraw-Hill.

10. For complete discussions of the accumulation of experiences see: Baddeley, A. D. (1976). *The psychology of memory.* New York: Basic Books; and DeFleur, M. L., & Plax, T. G. (1980). *Human communication as a biosocial process.* Paper presented to the International Communication Association, Acapulco, Mexico.

11. Goss, B. (1982). Listening as information processing. *Communication Quarterly, 30*, 304–307.

12. Barker, L. L. (1971). *Listening behavior.* Englewood Cliffs, NJ: Prentice-Hall; Meyer, J.,

& Williams, F. (1965). Teaching listening at the secondary level: Some evaluations. *Speech Teacher, 15,* 299–304.

13. Brooks, W. D., & Heath, R. W. (1985). *Speech communication* (5th ed.) 89–90. Dubuque, IA: Brown, W. C. & Weaver, C. H. (1972). *Human listening: Processes and behavior.* Indianapolis: Bobbs-Merrill.

14. Hamilton, C., & Parker, C. (1987). *Communicating for results* (2nd ed. p. 20). Belmont, CA: Wadsworth.

15. Vander Houwen, B. A. (1997). Less talking, more listening. *HR Magazine, 42,* 8, 53.

16. Sarbin, T. R., & Allen, V. L. (1968). Role theory. In G. Lindzey, & E. Aronson, (Eds.), *The handbook of social psychology* (pp. 488–567). Reading, MA: Addison-Wesley.

17. Taylor, A., Rosegrant, T., Meyer, A., & Samples, B. T. (1986). *Communication* (4th ed., pp. 143–145). Englewood Cliffs, NJ: Prentice-Hall.

18. Pearson, J. C., & Nelson, P. E. (1985). *Understanding and sharing* (3rd ed., pp. 57–61). Dubuque, IA: William C. Brown.

19. Folger, J. P., Poole, M., & Stutman, R. (2001). *Working through conflict: Strategies for relationships, groups, and organizations* (4th ed.). Boston: Addison Wesley Longman. See also: Cousins, R.B. (2000). Active listening is more than just hearing. *Supervision, 61,* 9, 14–15; Cohen, C. F. (1999). When managers mediate . . . stuck in the middle with you. *Dispute Resolution Journal. 54,* 3, 65–69.

20. Howell, W. S. (1982). *The empathic communicator.* Belmont, CA: Wadsworth.

21. Mehrabian, A. (1967). Orientation behaviors and nonverbal attitude communication. *Journal of Communication, 16,* 324–332.

22. Samovar, L. A., & Mills, J. (1986). *Oral communication: Messages and responses* (6th ed., pp. 84–85). Dubuque, IA: William C. Brown.

23. DeFleur & Plax, Human communication as a biosocial process.

24. Bandura, A. (1977). *Social learning theory.* Englewood Cliffs, NJ: Prentice-Hall.

25. *Sender-receiver reciprocity* is a contemporary term that communication scholars use for what George Herbert Mead called "interpersonal adjustment" early in this century. See: Mead, G. H. (1934). *Mind, self and society: From the standpoint of a behaviorist* (Charles W. Morris, Ed.). Chicago: University of Chicago Press. See the discussion of interpersonal "adjustment," p. 44.

26. This idea resembles what has been shown in research on how individuals vary in the degree to which they attend to others. This attentiveness has been studied as an aspect of "involvement," "perceptiveness," and "other-oriented perceptiveness." See: Cegala, D. (1981). Interaction involvement: A cognitive dimension of communicative competence. *Communication Education, 30,* 109–121; Cegala, D., Savage, B., Brunner, C., & Conrad, A. (1982). An elaboration of the meaning of interaction involvement: Toward the development of a theoretical concept. *Communication Monographs, 49,* 229–248.

27. For a discussion of which receiver characteristics can affect listening see: Plax, T. G., & Rosenfeld, L. B. (1979). Receiver differences and the comprehension of spoken messages. *Journal of Experimental Education, 48,* 23–28.

28. For a discussion of environmental characteristics that are thought to affect listening, see: Watson, K., & Barker, L. L. (1985). Listening behavior: Definition and measurement. In R. Bostrom (Ed.), *Communication yearbook 8* (p. 185). Beverly Hills, CA: Sage.

29. This example is drawn from the experience of one of the authors, who served as an executive in such a corporation for several years.

30. Brooks, W. D. (1974). *Speech communication* (2nd ed., pp. 80–84). Dubuque, IA: William C. Brown.

31. McIntyre-Birkner, R. & Birkner, L. R. (2001). Overcoming roadblocks to effective learning and communication. *Occupational Hazards, 63,* 4, 12–13; Hansford, B. (1988). *Teachers and classroom communication,* 43–46. Orlando, FL: Harcourt Brace Jovanovich; Watson & Barker, Listening behavior, pp.183–185.

32. Hagevik, S. (1999). Just listening. *Journal of Environmental Health, 62,* 2, 46.

33. Waldeck, J. H., Kearney, P., & Plax, T. G. (2013). *Business and professional communication in the digital age.* Boston, MA: Wadsworth, Cengage Learning.

Chapter 5

Communicating Interpersonally

No, it wasn't love at first sight. Even though Carmen found Philip attractive, she didn't think he was her type. In fact, it was quite some time before she really even noticed him. He was rather quiet and he seemed almost remote from all the others. They had first met at a party, where they had exchanged small talk. Later they were in a class together and they sometimes chatted briefly afterward. Before long they were dating steadily and spending hours talking on the phone, and enjoying their time together.

As the relationship developed, Carmen also found herself disclosing more and more personal information to Philip. She knew that she could trust him to be sympathetic and kind to her about anything she shared with him. She even risked telling him about her fears that she would never be able to measure up to her father's demands and expectations. Always, Philip seemed to understand exactly how she felt about her dad, and about other things that mattered to her.

As time went by, Carmen and Philip began to refer to themselves not so much in terms of "you" and "I," but as "we." Their references to themselves changed to phrases like, "We need to go to the book-store" and "We have to make plans for dinner." As this took place, their friends also began to see them as a couple. When Philip said something like "Jim and Mary invited us to have dinner with them," Carmen couldn't have been more delighted.

It wasn't long after that when Philip asked her to marry him, and they became formally engaged and moved in together. They seemed so happy together, so committed, and so loving. Surely these two would live happily ever after!

But something happened. The first sign was that Philip couldn't get Carmen to commit to a specific wedding date. This seemingly minor issue marked the point when their relationship began to erode. It seemed that Carmen always had some reason for putting off the wedding. She pointed out that, after all, neither of them had yet found a permanent career path, they still were in debt from student loans, and they had a number of problems with their future in-laws to work out. Philip was becoming impatient.

Philip was convinced that Carmen never really wanted to make a commitment. He began to see her as immature and self-centered. She saw him as controlling and vindictive. Some time later, it was clear to both of them that the relationship was over. Philip stayed out later and later with his friends after work, and Carmen made herself scarce when Philip did come home. Finally, Carmen moved out. That was the end of their relationship. Now, they never even see or talk to each other.

The changing relationship between Carmen and Philip illustrates various phases that can characterize *interpersonal communication,* which is the focus of this chapter. The study of interpersonal communication looks at the kinds of messages people use in the stages of the gender relationship that Carmen and Philip passed through. At first, they made *an initial assessment of each other* in a casual encounter. They found each other attractive, and slowly developed an increasingly closer relationship. Then, over time, they *became a couple* by establishing more intimate ties to each other. Later, after they knew each other well, each saw that the relationship was less and less rewarding. It began to erode, leading them to *disengage.* Finally, they *separated permanently* and the relationship was totally finished.

Communicating in an Interpersonal Context

In a general sense, **interpersonal communication** is a process of using language and nonverbal cues to send and receive messages (between individuals) that are intended to arouse particular kinds of meanings. Thus, interpersonal communication incorporates all the verbal and nonverbal concepts and the principles of listening discussed in previous chapters. Although it is no different from other forms of human communication, it is set apart because it focuses specifically on interactions between two people.

This chapter examines interpersonal communication mainly within the context of establishing intimate relationships, which in some cases lead to permanent lives together, but in other cases end in separation. Through such interpersonal communication, emotional relationships are established and maintained. If they work out, they may become the foundation for establishing families—the most basic of all social institutions. If they fail, both the individuals and the society as a whole suffer a loss. For this reason, they are the focus of this chapter.

As you will discover in this chapter, interpersonal relationships, good or bad, do not just happen: As they are being established and as they are failing, they are outcomes of communication exchanges. In both cases, these exchanges can be thoughtfully managed or awkwardly bungled. It is important to realize that such relationships are not static; they are constantly changing. As in the case of Carmen and Philip, they often move from lesser to greater levels of intimacy—or the reverse, from a deeply meaningful and rewarding relationship to one that satisfies neither party and is punishing.

The role of interpersonal communication in the development (or demise) of any given close relationship can be examined within the framework of (1) **engagement**—the process by which people try to move from an initial impersonal relationship to a more personal one, (2) **management**—using communication strategies to maintain valued interpersonal ties, and (3) **disengagement**—making use of communication strategies to withdraw gracefully (or not so gracefully) from a close association with another and remain apart permanently. We begin by discussing the process of interpersonal communication in a *general sense*. What are the major characteristics of this form of human communi-cation, and what does it do for people as they develop close relationships with each other?

Characteristics of Interpersonal Communication

Some theorists argue that interpersonal communication is really a matter of degree and is not restricted by the number of people involved in the exchange.[1] In this book, however, the process of interpersonal communication is dis-cussed in the context of two major background features: First, interpersonal communication takes place in the **dyad**, which is a technical term used by social scientists for *two people in a relatively enduring social relationship*.[2] Second, as the individuals involved come to know each other better, their relationship tends to move

Interpersonal communication is the foundation on which intimate human bonds are developed and maintained over long periods of time.

from *impersonal* to *personal;* that is, they become increasingly close and intimate. With these two features in mind, six key characteristics of interpersonal communication emerge.[3]

Interpersonal communication begins with the self. The term *self* is central to the process of communication.[4] **Self** (sometimes **self-image** or **self-concept**) is a complex idea, but it is not difficult to understand. It can be defined as *that pattern of beliefs, meanings, and understandings each individual develops concerning her or his own personal characteristics, capacities, limitations, and worth as a human being.* In other words, the self consists of our personal conceptions of *who* we are, *what* we are, and *where* we are in the social order. Our position in the social order within our society is determined by how we are classified into categories and on criteria judged broadly as important, such as age, gender, education, income, and ethnic identity. Defined in this way, the self is our personal and subjective configuration of beliefs about how we are classified and evaluated, by ourselves and others, in terms of standards that most people feel are socially important.

The significance of the self-image or self-concept is that who, what, and where we think we are dictates to a large extent how we relate to and communicate with others. Considering our biological, psychological, and social makeup, we bring to our relationships with others complex beliefs about ourselves as human beings. Furthermore, when we communicate with others, we quickly form a set of beliefs (right or wrong) about who, what, and where *those persons* are in the social order. By the same token, those with whom we communicate bring to the process complex self-conceptions of who, what, and where *they themselves* are in terms of important categories and criteria. In addition, they quickly form an image *about us!* In a very real sense, then, we can recognize at least *four images at work* in the process of interpersonal communication. It is a crowded scene, consisting of my self-image, my image of the other, the other's self-image, and the other's image of me.[5]

These four patterns of belief about self and others truly can influence interpersonal relationships. For example, a young marine biologist may believe that she is attractive, hard-working, liberal, intelligent, independent, and self-confident. Another young person, a plumber, may consider himself clever, a bit reckless, hard-working, a born gambler, irresistibly attractive, muscular, and dominating.

Suppose now that by an unusual set of circumstances these two individuals were brought together on a blind date. Although Hollywood might design a scenario whereby the pair overcome their differences and wind up romantically in each other's arms, in the real world these two would have a great deal of difficulty communicating in a way that would bring them closer together.

Previous chapters have shown that people who are very different may or may not have the same set of beliefs about each other that they entertain personally about themselves. These differences can serve as *serious barriers* to effective interpersonal communication. For example, the young woman in our imaginary blind date might form an image of the young man as dull, uneducated, and boring. He, in turn, might put together an image of her as self-absorbed, arrogant, and condescending.

The selves or images of others that we construct, and that we project upon them as we engage in interpersonal communication, are what in ancient times were called **personae,** which means "masks." Masks were often used by actors to indicate the characters being portrayed. Today, we use the term *personality* for much the same purpose—to label the major psychological traits and social characteristics of an individual. Similarly, our "self" image is our imagined "personality."

Although you may never have realized that there can be as many as four distinct personalities or images involved in a conversation between two people, the situation is actually even more complex. After all, when you talk to someone, you cannot help but imagine what that person is thinking about you. In much the same way, the other individual is doing exactly the same thing, putting together an image of what you are probably thinking about him or her. Thus, there are two additional images present during any interpersonal conversation: What you think your image is in the mind of the other person and what that person thinks is the image you have constructed about him or her.[6]

By now it may seem that there is almost an army of images that are present and playing a part in what initially seemed like a simple two-person exchange. It is true that all six personae are involved, and that these images of self and other help shape what is said and what is understood. Fortunately, the process of interpersonal communication takes place so rapidly that most of us ignore these complexities and simply carry on our conversations. At the same time, if you want to gain skill in interpersonal communication, you may want to think closely about these self and other images to help analyze your limitations and develop more effective strategies.

Interpersonal communication is fully transactional. More than in any other context, interpersonal communication is based on our simultaneous transactions model.[7] As communicators, each party uses verbal and nonverbal symbols and other signs to construct messages around his or her intended meanings. At the same time, the receiver brings similar, or possibly different, meanings to the task of receiving and interpreting that message. Information is returned in the form of feedback, and each communicator adjusts by role-taking for the next phase of the process. Thus, each party simultaneously influences the other's behavior while being influenced in return.

Interpersonal communicators share physical proximity. People have to be physically near each other to engage in interpersonal communication. They might talk on the telephone or exchange text messages, but that is mediated communication, and it lacks important elements of the interpersonal process we are discussing. Interpersonal communication takes place with two individuals engaging in face-to-face interaction.

By being in physically close proximity, communicators are able to increase their chances for understanding each other accurately and efficiently. This is accomplished more easily with the accessibility of feedback. When we communicate one on one in physical proximity, we are able to recognize even the most subtle verbal and nonverbal cues that tell us whether or not we're being understood as intended. We can instantly detect eyebrows that suddenly go up, the hint of a frown, eyes that glaze over, tears beginning to form, a jaw that tightens or relaxes, a nose that turns up, a meaningful shift in body position, and other nonverbal cues that provide important feedback.

In interpersonal communication, such subtle and obvious reactions are immediate and frequent, but in other communication contexts, they may not be readily observed. As a result, in the face-to-face situation we are in a better position to adapt to each other's concerns. We can follow up with questions and comments, try to explain our position in another way, pause to let the other person talk, and appreciate the fact that we are able to interact flexibly and competently with one another.

Interpersonal communication is shaped by social roles. When people are engaging in interpersonal communication, what they are saying—that is, the content—can be interpreted only within the context of the roles that define their overall relationship.[8] For example, if we were to witness two men (whose role relationship is not known to us) arguing in the lobby of a hotel, we might attempt to analyze the situation by relying first on the content of the messages exchanged. The verbal content of the messages indicates that the first man wants some money from the second one, but he's refusing to come up with it. Their nonverbal cues seem to indicate that their exchange is intense, serious, and evolving into an argument.

Without knowing anything else about the people involved, we could interpret their exchange as hostile or defensive, depending on the actual words employed by each party. However, to rely on what is said, verbally and nonverbally, is often insufficient for understanding the full meaning of such an argument. We have to understand the *nature of the social relationship* between the two people—the role that each is playing and how their roles are interrelated. For example, the two men could be married or cohabiting. The guy could be the guy's son, one man could be working for the other. The first man could be an undercover agent or police officer and the other one a suspect. Notice how the interpretation of the underlying meaning of the argument changes from one set of such role relationships to another. Both content and relational messages, then, *interact* in determining the meaning of any interpersonal exchange.

Interpersonal communication is uniquely irreversible. There is no way to "erase" a regrettable message the way we erase a Facebook page, unwanted messages on a smartphone, or old photos on an iPad. All too often we find ourselves afflicted with "foot-in-mouth" disease, wishing we could take back the harsh words and labels that hurt someone in the heat of an argument. We can say we're sorry, but unfortunately we cannot make the person forget the unkind words. This "unerasable" feature of many kinds of communication is the case when a judge tells a jury, "You are instructed to disregard what this witness has just said." However, it is unlikely that the testimony will disappear entirely from their memories.

Interpersonal communication is not repeatable. We can all recall a special event with someone that we might wish we could experience again. You may have heard your parents talk sentimentally about how they first met and fell in love. What they said to each other, at least as they recall it, had such special meanings. Others are convinced that their high school or college years, when they communicated in

rewarding ways with their friends, were the best times of their lives. Yet we all know that we cannot go back and relive the exact same communication experiences again. Even if we had one of those wonderful time machines, of which science fiction writers are so fond, we would find ourselves viewing it all with the changed perspectives, altered feelings, and new interpretations that come with later experience. Inevitably, we would communicate differently.

Overall, then, interpersonal communication is in one sense simply one form of the human communication process that was described in Chapter 1. However, it does have the above six characteristics that distinguish it from other forms. The characteristics of interpersonal communication are summarized in Box 5.1.

Reasons for Initiating and Maintaining Relationships

Missing from our analysis of interpersonal communication thus far are the reasons for which people initiate and try to maintain close relationships. Clearly, such relationships require a great deal of time and effort, and they are often accompanied by a great many stresses and emotional costs. Nevertheless, they can also yield very satisfying rewards. In this complex and uniquely human activity there is a kind of **cost–benefit ratio** that results when a person forms and maintains a close personal tie with another individual. For most people, the nature of this ratio influences both the formation and the stability of the relationship.

What are the costs and what are the benefits of this consequence of interpersonal communication? Perhaps the most important answer to this question is that human beings *want and truly need* close personal relationships. Indeed, life can be lonely and shallow without them. Thus, interpersonal communication is the foundation on which intimate human bonds are built. This is true of every kind of close personal relationship. Such interpersonal affiliations characterize the ties between devoted family members, trusting friends, and loving

BOX 5.1   *A Closer Look*

Characteristics of Interpersonal Communication

Interpersonal communication distinguishes itself from other forms of communication by two key features: (1) It takes place within the dyad, and (2) it is the means by which two people move their relationship from impersonal to personal. The following are characteristics of interpersonal communication.

- *Interpersonal communication begins with the self.* Our self-image influences how we relate to others.
- *Interpersonal communication is transactional.* Both individuals simultaneously influence each other's behavior, while being affected in return.
- *Interpersonal communicators share physical proximity.* By being close to each other physically, individuals increase their chances of understanding and being understood.
- *Interpersonal communication is shaped by social roles.* A written transcript of a dialogue is insufficient to show what is truly meant in an interpersonal conversation. Interpreting what each person means is determined in part by the context or the roles that define the relationship.
- *Interpersonal communication is irreversible.* No matter how much you may want to erase a regrettable message, you cannot. Once the message is sent, it's likely to be received and remembered!
- *Interpersonal communication is unrepeatable.* There is no way you can go back and experience the same interpersonal event in exactly the same way. Changed experiences, perceptions, and feelings alter the way we view past exchanges.

members of opposite-sex and same-sex relationships. There are many other kinds of one-on-one human bonds. Some are more intimate than others, but all are important. In each case,

they are founded on effective interpersonal communication. In addition to those already discussed in detail, the list includes such ties as a mutually respectful relationship between employer and employee, professor and student, neighbors, and colleagues at work.

Three broad reasons can be identified for engaging in lasting interpersonal relationships. One is to obtain much needed information about *ourselves*. Another is more pragmatic: Friends, family members, and other intimate associates help us solve a long list of *problems of everyday living* that would be difficult to handle alone. Finally, in terms of *costs and benefits*, we develop close personal relationships with the people whose company and behavior are least costly compared to the benefits that they provide for us. Each of these reasons deserves to be understood in greater detail.

Constructing and maintaining a positive self-image. Earlier in this chapter, we noted that one of the main characteristics of interpersonal communication is that it begins with the self. This was emphasized because it is one of the most significant of the benefits that are derived from interpersonal communication. For example, almost all of us love to tell others what a good person we are, and we especially enjoy hearing others say nice things about us.

Psychologists have understood for a very long time that every clinically normal person wants, needs, and enjoys a positive self-image. If we have to accept a negative one, even on a temporary basis, it is a difficult and miserable experience. To gain a positive self-image, we look early in life for people who will supply us with favorable evaluations of our behavior and characteristics. Although we cannot deliberately choose our family, we can respond coolly toward those family members who do not give us the responses we want and need, and warmly toward those who do. However, we can choose our close friends, and we screen them carefully, often without even thinking about it. That is, from the available pool of individuals we encounter, inevitably we find some who respond

Communicating with others helps us construct and maintain a positive self-image. How do these friends help reinforce positive evaluations of each other?

to us in a positive manner. They are the ones we value. They provide the *benefits*. Others, who are critical or negative can be rejected on the grounds that such unimaginative clods can be discounted as of little worth and deserve to be denied our friendship. Thus, by careful screening, selection, and recruiting, we can build and maintain a satisfying self-image.

At the same time, our friends and associates need the same kind of positive feedback from us. They have their own self-images to construct and maintain. A part of the *cost* in the cost–benefit ratio, then, is that we must make continuing efforts that provide our valued family members, friends, or lovers with supportive and positive evaluations that will fulfill *their* needs.

Such considerations explain in large part why we find *ourselves* to be our favorite, our most engrossing, and our most completely captivating topic. We are anxious to share with others the details of our day—how we cleverly outwitted the professor, received approval from the boss, or put the clerk at the store in her place. We show what noble and long-suffering but clever persons we are when we describe the crowded subway, the unbearable freeway traffic, or the other pressures we have to endure. We offer personal testimony to our intelligence and good taste when we discuss the outstanding dinner we have planned tonight, or our generous intention to pick up the tab at the restaurant. We then look for self-image–fulfilling signs of approval and appreciation.

Of course, we like to hear what happened to the other person too, but if our friend, spouse, lover, or relative talks too long about his or her positive qualities and behavior, we are likely to become bored. We are willing to provide feedback that shows sympathy, approval, subtle applause, or commiseration as needed by the other—up to a point. After all, this is part of the cost we pay for the rewards of the relationship; but soon we will attempt to turn the conversation around again to those topics we feel reflect favorably on us—to those issues and events that best meet *our* needs as topics of discussion.

In summary, then, one of the most important reasons for entering into relationships with others is to learn more about how others perceive and feel about us. However, one of the built-in problems of constructing a self-concept on the basis of evaluations and assessments offered generously by mothers, sweethearts, or good friends is *validity*. That is, such intimate associates are unlikely to offer a dispassionate and balanced system of reality checks. They tell us our new outfit "looks nice," when it is actually frumpy. They say we are "looking better," when we are obviously still suffering from an illness. Their reactions to us are usually positive, and seldom negative. The consequence is that such feedback distorts the self-image we construct. Therefore, if we want to understand ourselves from a more objective perspective, we have to look beyond our immediate circle. The problem there is the reverse. Some whom we encounter will exaggerate our shortcomings or reject us on the basis of trivial criteria.

Either way, we are deeply dependent on the reactions and implied evaluations of others for constructing and maintaining our self-image. Anyone who wants to develop a realistic, if not always flattering, self-concept needs to rely on *many sources*, not just on those who provide positive responses.[9]

Coping with daily problems.   Although we rely heavily on others to help with our self-image, we also need others for many practical reasons. Consider how difficult your life would be without the cooperation of others. If you have ever moved from one apartment to another, you may have counted on your friends' showing up to help pack, lift, and move. In the unlikely event that no one came, you might have found yourself unable to transfer the table from the kitchen onto the truck! Routinely, many of us rely on someone for assistance, such as taking the car in to get it worked on. Rather than waiting around at the shop for hours, we hope to have a friend or family member drive there with us and, when the car is ready, back again to pick it up. In short, we rely heavily on others to help us cope in a pragmatic manner with the realities of day-to-day life.

We are especially dependent on those close to us in times of stress or grief. Our friends and family members serve a **cushioning function.** They supply emotional support when we are anxious or afraid, when tragedy strikes, or even when we are just feeling down. They stand between us and an uncaring world, providing an emotionally safe haven when events beyond our control make life difficult. In many ways, then, both practical and emotional, we need and want their assistance in our efforts to control or adapt to the constraints of our environment.

Maximizing benefits and minimizing costs. This is a very old but very valid idea. In 1789, the British philosopher Jeremy Bentham published *An Introduction to the Principles of Morals and Legislation* in which he developed a complete explanation of human political, social, and personal behavior, called **utilitarianism.**[10] Bentham claimed that people behave according to the *principle of utility,* which simply means that we choose to engage in those behaviors that maximize pleasure and avoid those that result in pain. This idea laid the foundation for more contemporary psychological theories of learning that stressed rewards (pleasure) and punishment (pain) as the basis for everyday, habitual behavior. Today, we no longer believe that Bentham's particular formulation of utilitarianism provides final answers, but it remains the basic framework for what psychologists call a cost–benefit ratio for those punishments and rewards that ultimately guide our actions.

Generally, then, the part played by rewards and punishments in shaping interpersonal relationships remains important. For example, spending a major holiday all alone can be a dismal (even punishing) experience. It is simply more fun, more rewarding, and more pleasurable to share such a time with those we love. Similarly, celebrating a new job, graduation from college, a birthday, winning big in the lottery—all these are events that few people want to experience alone.

For most of us, just being with certain people is rewarding in itself. We simply feel better when we are with those special friends or loved ones. By the same token, we all know people who make us feel bad about ourselves. Whenever we are with them, it turns out to be a punishing experience. In terms of maintaining a positive self-image, we actively avoid spending time with them if we possibly can. It stands to reason, then, that we do not associate frequently, if at all, with those who ridicule us, find us distasteful, or perceive us as unworthy of their affection or attention. A number of research studies support this modern form of utilitarianism.[11]

For all the above reasons—constructing a positive self-image, coping with daily problems, and maximizing pleasure while minimizing pain—we initiate or develop interpersonal relationships with others. We need and want others to like us, talk to us, and share life experiences with us. However, such benefits do not come without cost. Once you decide to enter into a relationship with another person, in order to obtain those advantages in the long run, you must pay a price. At least initially, you will need to follow a number of fairly rigid communication rules that provide self-image building responses for others.

Engagement: The Initial Encounter

What is the process by which two people first meet each other, begin to think that they have a basis for a closer relationship and then go on to develop one that increases to intimacy? Moving from the very first moments in the history of such an encounter to developing a devoted relationship involves a set of relatively regular stages. As this section will explain, the first stage is the *initial assessment* of the person on the basis of physical appearance and his or her opening remarks. Then, if the encounter survives those critical first moments, the next stage is likely to be characterized by **small talk.**

The Critical First Moments

Our first, even momentary, impressions of someone new can influence dramatically our decision to move forward into a relationship. Unfortunately, those initial impressions are often based on *trivial details* about the person we have just met. In fact, the first information we receive about a person usually consists of nonverbal cues—the person's overall physical appearance, clothing, and other "packaging." Yet, it is these initial data that will determine to a considerable degree whether we want to move on to any closer relationship.

If we do decide to continue, the next important information we receive about the candidate comes during the first few minutes of interpersonal exchange. Inevitably, it is based on a relatively superficial and nondisclosing kind of conversation. Nevertheless, both the first impressions we form and what immediately follows can be critical in establishing a new relationship.

When people strike up a conversation with someone new, they rely on well-established routines. These are often called **scripted conversations** because they are like lines rehearsed from a play.[12] Conversations can be classified as scripted if they follow clear, even rigid, rules in certain well-defined situations.

Exchanges of this type are easily illustrated by what we almost always say when we are introduced to someone we do not know. Our initial "Hello" is usually followed by their "How are you?" Most of us understand that we are not expected to answer such questions factually or at any length with a detailed health or personal problem report. The normative reply is "Fine." In reality, you may be feeling rather poorly because you had an accident an hour earlier, or you've been fired from your job, or your dog just died. Still, the expected and usually provided answer is "Fine. How are you?"

Why do this? Why shouldn't we just say whatever we want to say? There are very good reasons for not violating the norms of getting together. First, it is *customary*—meaning predictable and comfortable. Research shows that new acquaintances almost always exchange factual, nonopinionated, and relatively superficial information.[13] Second, few of us are willing to disclose to a new acquaintance any of our deep, personal feelings about sensitive issues. Not knowing the stranger, we cannot trust that she or he will interpret our disclosures in the right way.[14]

Generally, then, initial conversations with others almost always center on safe topics. It is for this reason that in such situations we often find ourselves discussing such trivia as the weather and sports, whereas we scrupulously avoid issues and topics that would disclose more significant attitudes and beliefs. Obviously, there are at least some interesting exceptions to this pattern. Under some circumstances, we may reveal our whole life story to people we have just met and whom we never expect to encounter again! This behavior was illustrated by sociologist Georg Simmel in 1908 in his classic essay, "The Stranger." He explained that when one is with a stranger, such as one sitting next to us on a train (or a plane in modern times), that person is both distant and near at the same time. Under these circumstances such a person can become an instant confidant. The reason is that the stranger is there and available, but at the same time, there is virtually no risk involved in disclosing personal information to a person whom we know we will never see again.[15]

Under most circumstances, however, after the very first moments, if the potential relationship survives beyond initial impressions and early assessments based on the scripted conversation of getting acquainted, it can move to a stage where the messages exchanged by the parties consist of small talk. These are discussions that focus on topics of general interest—ones that have little personal significance or emotional involvement. Although this may sound trivial, it can be a subtle and complex part of establishing a closer relationship. In fact, being able to manage small talk effectively may be one of the most important skills that an individual can develop.

It may seem strange to maintain that small talk may be the most important communication skill we can possibly master! We can say this in all honesty because every dyadic social relationship, to some degree, begins to develop during a stage of small talk. That is, after we form our earliest impressions of a person, we usually get to add additional assessments based on her or his initial small talk. This gives us a somewhat more fully developed image of what that person is like. Without this kind of exchange, we would have a difficult time moving on through the early stages of getting to know the other person. In fact, small talk can be so important in establishing a relationship with a new acquaintance that it should probably be called "big talk."[16]

Despite the importance of small talk, many people claim that they dislike it. We've all heard comments like "I hate small talk; it's so superficial" or "I went to the party and all they did was blab about trivialities." The final putdown of a person in the minds of many is something like "He can go for hours and not say a single meaningful thing!" We could find wide agreement that small talk consists of little more than meaningless chatter. What is missing from such negative interpretations is that small talk serves critical purposes. Beneath its apparent superficiality, small talk can be critical in the development of an interpersonal relationship that is destined to become more meaningful.

Auditioning for friendship.   One function of small talk is to provide what communication researcher Mark Knapp calls an "audition for friendship."[17] Individuals assess one another in an effort to determine whether or not a relationship is worth establishing. Obviously, not all new acquaintances audition well, and in many cases no relationship forms—or it remains purely at the level of small talk. Such an acquaintance-only relationship is likely to die on the vine later.

Controlling self-disclosure. Small talk also allows us to reveal just a bit of who and what we are to others—in a cautious and safe way. We all have at our disposal a variety of *personae* that we can reveal to someone who hardly knows us. We can display our humorous side, our sensitive, or our highly critical side. At the same time, the other person in the interaction is providing us with similar information. In these early stages, we have little more to go on than superficial communication exchanges. Consequently, both individuals involved in the exchange are attempting to reveal limited personal information—while simultaneously struggling to decipher who and what the other really is!

Painless interaction. One of the most useful features of small talk for many of us, when meeting another person for the first time, is that it is easy and relatively painless. It does not require a lot of brain power and it makes few stressful demands on new relationships. As such, small talk can provide a welcome alternative to discussions about more significant topics. This allows us to approach more meaningful dialogue and debates about complex and important themes at our own pace. Good manners dictate that we rarely leap right into heavy discussions with new acquaintances, or even those we know well but haven't encountered for a while. Think about it: The last time you called an old friend you probably initiated the conversation around light and effortless topics. Perhaps you followed the greeting with a brief discussion of the weather, a recent sports event, or a concert you just attended. All of this small talk may have served as a prelude to revealing information of a more important nature—your latest job prospects, progress in school, new friend, recent child, divorce, new car, death in the family and so on.

The feeling-out period associated with small talk has been well documented. What researchers have identified from studies of conversations between new acquaintances is an exchange of very basic biographical data.[18] People in initial encounters tend to reveal simple demographic and biographical information, such as "My name is Melanie" and "I'm from Morgantown, West Virginia." They don't start out with "I'm involved in a messy divorce" or "I just got fired from my job." The simple disclosures are usually reciprocal. Melanie should be able to predict that a new acquaintance will reveal his or her name and hometown. If it is a former friend, he or she might provide basic data on life changes, such as a new child or new job. Importantly, both persons tend to avoid heavier topics because neither wants to risk disclosing their deep feelings about such matters as the abortion controversy or their troublesome health problems.

In summary, then, small talk makes it possible for each party to continue assessing the other, adding to initial impressions formed mainly on the basis of physical appearance. It enables each to begin developing a biographical database from which to round out their first impression of each other. In this way, small talk provides a basis for each person for determining whether or not they would like the relationship to continue. Because small talk serves these functions, it cannot be dismissed as trivial and superficial.

The Skills of Small Talk

Perhaps one reason some people dislike small talk is simply that they lack the specific skills needed to handle this type of encounter well. Some people have no idea what to say after "hello." One source of worry is that what we say will be seen as trite and that others will find our attempts at conversation boring. Worse yet, we may be concerned that we will fail the "audition" and the interesting other will find us unworthy of further contact.

Unfortunately, in spite of its importance, researchers have not produced a body of systematic knowledge concerning the specific skills that comprise successful small talk. No book,

Successful small talk: How does Jon Stewart establish rapport through small talk? What strategies for small talk make him successful?

chapter, or even single study has been published that addresses the details of verbal and nonverbal communication strategies that distinguish effective from ineffective small talk. Nevertheless, the sections below offer some helpful guidelines from the present authors that can be considered in your attempts to evaluate and improve your own small-talk skills.

Maintain eye contact.   As in any form of interpersonal communication, eye contact is important. Indeed, it is mandatory for effectively initiating encounters with new people. As discussed in Chapter 3, eye contact is typically interpreted as a nonverbal sign of *interest*. Most people are pleased and appreciative when someone appears to take great interest in what they have to say. Eye contact provides a clear and standard nonverbal message communicating just that. Consequently, those who are successful at small talk rely heavily on *looking earnestly* at their partner. Note, however, that direct eye contact may be considered rude in some societies with different cultural rules. The Japanese, for example, are taught to avoid staring directly into someone's eyes. Instead, they concentrate on the lower part of the face during a direct conversation. This can pose problems for Americans who do not understand this norm. However, in this society, lack of eye contact may seem to signal a failure to listen closely, or even disinterest.

Be nonverbally immediate.   Other nonverbal cues can signal interest as well. Recall from Chapter 3 that nodding, leaning forward, smiling, and open body positions all suggest interest and liking to the receiver. These actions were described earlier as signs of *nonverbal immediacy*. Using such techniques is one way of establishing physical and psychological *closeness* with your partner, and that is likely to lead to an interpretation of attraction on his or her part.

Remember the other person's name. This is really important, but it is sometimes difficult to do. Shakespeare got it wrong in *Romeo and Juliet*, when he had Juliet ask, "What's in a name?" She went on to claim that names have little importance because "that which we call a rose by any other name would smell as sweet." Maybe that's true with roses, but it does not work well with people. The significance of other persons is diminished if you can't remember their names—and they recognize that. Above all, then, and without fail, be sure to remember and use the other person's name! Our names are so important to us that they are the first pieces of information we deliver about ourselves. People quickly become offended when we misspell, mispronounce, or forget their names. This signals loudly and clearly that we regard them as not worth the effort.

Several strategies can help you remember someone's name. One is to rehearse it quickly several times in your head. Another is say it out loud right away, and frequently, if possible. Writing it down can also be very effective if the situation permits. If you are unable to catch the name when introduced, ask the person to repeat it, or even spell it. In fact, asking the person for the correct spelling can be a good strategy because it implies that the name is important to you. (If the name is Smith or Jones, skip this step!)

Draw out the other person. A great skill to develop in mastering in small talk is to get the other person to talk about himself or herself. People's favorite topic is *themselves*. Capitalize on that insight by asking your small-talk partners a lot of questions about themselves, such as "Where are you from?" "Do you follow sports?" "What brings you here to this event?" (Don't ask "Do you approve of abortion?" or "Don't you think we should eliminate welfare?")

Indicate further interest and *active listening* with follow-up questions. Pursue their responses with directed questions or comments. When your partner indicates that he is from Fargo, North Dakota you can develop the

conversation by asking, "What brings you all the way here?" or "Do you miss Fargo? I'll bet life was different there from how it is here in Long Beach, California." So as not to turn the conversation into an inquisition, you might comment, "I like small towns. In fact, I have grandparents who still live in a small community. I love to visit them because the people there are so friendly." Be sure that your comments and questions evolve either directly or indirectly from what the person just said. Try to avoid random topic switching. If you try that, you'll probably end up talking about what *you're* interested in, as opposed to what the other person wants to talk about.

Keep the discussion light. As was implied earlier, an important rule is to keep the conversation *light*. Should you plunge too quickly into controversial issues early in the relationship, the other individual is likely to feel threatened. No one wants to reveal their deep-seated views on religion or politics, or hear about your latest scrap with your parents and your financial difficulties at this point.

Accentuate the positive. Finally, you are better off making most of your talk *positive*. That means avoiding complaints or criticisms. Even minor complaints—such as the weather is awful, your workload is too heavy, the professors are unfair, or the team is unsuccessful—are commonly perceived as depressing. In particular, commenting negatively about other people in the room, or a mutual acquaintance, can quickly lead to some rather destructive, disagreeable interactions—particularly if your partner finds those same individuals attractive.

Generally, then, mastering the skills of small talk is not all that difficult. (Box 5.2 summarizes the important guidelines.) Once a small-talk conversation has been managed successfully, the next stage in a developing relationship is likely to be more rewarding and more enjoyable. Take a minute now to assess your own small-talk skills by completing the survey in Box 5.3.

Management: Moving Toward and Maintaining Intimacy

Movement toward greater intimacy—close friendship and more intensity in a relationship can be a complex process. The term *intimacy* is often used to imply a sexual relationship. Indeed, many people think, "We have an intimate relationship" means the two are sleeping together. However, this is not always true. People can have sexual relationships without being intimate in the sense discussed in this chapter. A general meaning of the term *intimacy* is the implication of trust and open self-disclosure in communication.

As will be made clear, in the development of an intimate relationship (in the nonsexual sense) much depends on the *rewards* versus the *costs* we think we have gained, or suspect we will gain, from the affiliation.[19] Some theorists claim that we take a kind of mental inventory—perhaps at a less than conscious level—to determine the relative rewards and costs that we can potentially derive from a relationship before we commit ourselves to it. This interpretation is based on a very general sociological paradigm called **exchange theory,** which was originally developed by George Homans to try to explain all forms of human social interaction.[20]

Exchange theorists maintain that we implicitly "count up" the history of rewards received from interacting with a particular other person, weigh that against the history of costs, and then make an estimate of the *worth of the relationship to us.* According to this explanation, when the cost–benefit ratio has been calculated, we make our decision. That is, when the rewards for us outweigh the costs, then the relationship is likely to be continued. Conversely, if we conclude that the relationship is too costly, it is likely that we will not pursue it. That explanation works similarly for both partners. That is, for each the cost–benefit ratio must be favorable or the relationship will not be continued.

Many current theorists believe that this utilitarian, cost–benefit approach to relational

development in its elementary form is oversimplified. That may be the case, but it still has something to offer. Granted, few of us are likely to take this type of systematic inventory regarding each and every person we meet. By the same token, however, we are not likely to be consciously aware that everything we do in a positive or negative way might influence

BOX 5.3   *Assessing Your Small Talk*

Instructions.

The following statements were obtained from actual conversations between strangers. Indicate how frequently you might use these or similar statements in your initial encounters with strangers or new acquaintances. Use the following key:

5 = Extremely Likely
4 = Likely
3 = Maybe/Unsure
2 = Unlikely
1 = Extremely Unlikely

_____ 1. I'm from New York (*insert your state*).
_____ 2. I hate lying in bed at night listening to the clock tick.
_____ 3. I wish my church was more relevant to my life.
_____ 4. I may be stubborn but only because I'm right.
_____ 5. I really liked the movie, *The Help*. I saw it three times.
_____ 6. I go to the ocean (or lake) for relaxation.
_____ 7. I've been married and divorced twice.
_____ 8. I have two cats—-one is named Roxanne and the other, Parker.
_____ 9. I enjoy going to outdoor concerts in the summertime.
_____ 10. Do you celebrate Cinco de Mayo?
_____ 11. I'm forty-five pounds overweight.
_____ 12. How old were you when you had your first sexual encounter?
_____ 13. Have you ever considered fooling around on your partner?
_____ 14. How much money do you make?
_____ 15. Do you own your own home or do you rent?
_____ 16. Have you read the book, *Calico Joe*, by John Grisham?
_____ 17. Are you a Republican or a Democrat?
_____ 18. My name is _____. What's yours?
_____ 19. Do you like to go to tailgate parties?
_____ 20. Where do you like to shop for clothes?

Calculating Your Score:

1. Add your responses to items 2, 3, 4, 7, 11, 12, 13, 14, 15, and 17 = _____.

2. Add your responses to items 1, 5, 6, 8, 9, 10, 16, 18, 19 and 20 = _____.
3. Complete the following formula:
SMALL TALK = 60 – Total from Step 1 = _____.

Then, + Total from Step 2. YOUR TOTAL SCORE = _____.

Interpreting Your Score:

Possible range of scores for the Small Talk Scale: 20–100. (If your own final score does not fall within that range, you made a computational error.)

The ideal score for this Small Talk quiz is 100. The higher the score, the more others will want to continue a conversation with you. Moreover, others will find you interesting, attractive and socially appropriate. Items from Step 2 (1, 5, 6, 8, 9, 10, 16, 18, 19, and 20) are all intended to draw out others or to provide a positive image of yourself to others. In short, these and others statements of this type ensure prolonged interaction with others.

The lower the score, the more likely others will pull away from you and hurry to end the conversation. That is, we would expect to ask questions and provide information that is generally "safe" for ourselves and others. Items from Step 1 (2, 3, 4, 7, 11, 12, 13, 14, 15, and 17) all reflect statements that are potentially risky or unsafe. In addition, several of those statements are worded negatively. Remember: Accentuate the positive! These types of comments or questions can be shared more easily between friends or intimates—-but not between strangers or new acquaintances. Do you understand why?

Source:
A number of these statements were obtained or updated from the following source:
   Berger, C. R., Clatterbuck, G. W., & Shulman, L. S. (1976). Perceptions of information sequencing in relationship development. *Human Communication Research*, 3, 34–39.

the cost–benefit ratio for the other person. Yet, most of us can imagine at least some of the rewards versus costs that are derived from a particular relationship with another person. Furthermore, we can predict some idea of what that ratio might be for that relationship in the future.

Thus, the cost–benefit principle has at least some merit: We know for a fact that most of us prefer to be around individuals who make us feel good. We understand that such people provide us with rewarding experiences as we relate to them. Similarly, we know that we do not like to be around people who make us feel bad. Generally, then, the classic sociological idea of costs versus benefits—the balance of rewards and punishments in an exchange—is still a viable perspective that can predict the fate of a relationship.

Assessing Costs and Benefits

If the exchange concept has merit, it must be reflected in reality. For example, when you examine your current relationships, you should find that most of your good friends, over the long haul, have provided you with greater benefits and rewards than they have costs or punishments. It is not difficult to determine this. Benefits are fairly clear. Good friends probably tell you in many ways (both verbally and nonverbally) that they like you. They may laugh politely at your bad jokes, call you when you are sick or feeling depressed, lend you money when you're broke, and tell you what a great person you are even though others may feel quite differently. To be sure, these same individuals may be burdensome from time to time, and you may not like some of the things you have to do to retain them as friends. Over time, however, it should be clear that you *gain more from these relationships than you lose.*

In lasting interpersonal relationships with friends or family, the individuals involved are likely to have accumulated a kind of *reservoir of rewards* that can be drawn upon in troubled times. It is these rewards that maintain the relationship. True, they have built up a reservoir of costs as well. But keep in mind that the rewards continue to outweigh the costs. This *accumulation process* is critical for managing a relationship. In times of temporary crisis, when costs can be very high, we can turn to that reservoir of rewards to help us through. If it does not exist, the relationship can be in big trouble.

There is, however, an important exception to the preceding principle: We can put up with an incredible amount of costs as long as we can also predict that significant rewards will follow. Social psychologists refer to this as the **principle of delayed gratification.**[21] For example, millions of college students keep their noses firmly pressed to the unpleasant grindstone of boring degree requirements in the expectation that all the work will pay off after graduation. Later, they will work hard in the labor force, anticipating that significant promotions and raises in income will follow.

Applying the principle of delayed gratification to interpersonal relationships, rewards that seem reasonably certain in the future allow us to endure the more immediate costs of continuing the bond with the other person. Such costs may involve financial strain, isolation, career interruptions, or even physical or psychological discomfort. On the other hand, there is no assurance that the principle will hold true over a long period. Consider the often-repeated story of the couple who married very young while they were both still in school. Alas, they couldn't make it financially, so the wife dropped out and took a full-time job. Her reasoning at the time was that her husband would get a good job after graduation and then it would be her turn to finish school. In the meantime, the wife accumulated a lot of costs, fully expecting the husband to deliver to her the rewards of financial solvency, loving gratitude, and other forms of interest on her investment.

In reality, many such couples do not live happily ever after when there is such a high level of balance due. Husbands may resent having to pay off the debt; wives may find that they cannot endure the costs. One party or the other

Good friends self-disclose to one another. Self-disclosure is a key to the development of a relationship.

may find another person more attractive. In such cases, the relationship will likely terminate.

Overall, then, this process of assessing and cataloguing the ratio of rewards and costs in a relationship is important. The outcome appears to determine whether the relationship will move forward or backward—whether it will move toward greater or lesser intimacy. Two individuals moving from casual, impersonal contact to a more meaningful relationship are likely to put a lot of energy into filling each other's reward reservoirs. At the same time, they are likely to avoid adding to each other's costs. However, as the relationship continues, problems can arise that may have a significant influence on its future. One thing that can determine its fate is the degree to which the individuals involved put themselves *at risk* by revealing core information about themselves.

Revealing Core Information about Self

When a particular relationship is rewarding, that is, when the two parties seem to make each other feel good, they usually become more and more trusting. Soon, they find themselves sharing very private information with each other that is usually reserved for only a few individuals that they know very well. Such "core" information involves risks because it requires *disclosure of very personal matters.*[22] This can be a delicate process.

Testing the water with self-disclosure. As we begin this process of mutual **self-disclosure,** we may start cautiously by revealing something about our family or friends that affects us only indirectly. For instance, we might disclose the fact that we were once arrested for driving under the influence. We can dangle that personal skeleton and then wait to see what kind of reaction such a secret will provoke. If our partner responds sympathetically, we might conclude that he or she has passed our test, and perhaps we can reveal more sensitive information. However, if the response is criticism, our partner has failed.

Once a sensitive self-disclosure has been received negatively, we generally keep the other person at a safe distance. We choose not to expose further negative information about ourselves, or our family and friends, because we now have evidence that the person is unlikely to be understanding and supportive. However, if the person passed the test, we have at least an initial confirmation that it is safe to make a more significant self-disclosure or to expose even more sensitive information. Self-disclosure, then, is a key to the development of a relationship.[23]

It all comes down to *trust.* Can we trust the other to respond sensitively to our personal attributes, our secrets, and our deep feelings? Can we be confident that the other will continue to like us after we've disclosed such information about ourselves? If we can answer yes to all the above, with conviction, then we can assume that the relationship will move toward greater intimacy.

This movement toward greater intimacy generally occurs after the initial experimental or test phase of the relationship.[24] Satisfied that the other person will remain sympathetic and supportive, we begin to intensify the relationship. The new partner has similarly established trust; we have also been tested and have passed. In other words, this is a *reciprocal* process. The rule is that, for each party, self-disclosure increases as we tell each other more and more intimate details about ourselves. We begin to reveal not just more positive information, but also more negative information. In this way we risk disclosing information that few others may know.

Labeling the relationship and its consequences. Before long we begin to see that our relationship is taking on a life of its own. We provide many kinds of enduring relationships with labels, such as friends, BFFL, or close friends. This labeling process is important because it attaches specific and culturally shared meanings to the relationship that it did not previously have. Once we have a symbol or label that is in use for a relationship between two people, it greatly changes their own self-conceptions. Suddenly the pronoun *we* becomes far more significant than either *me* or *you*.

Using the label couple brings with it a "baggage" of meanings that play a part in the *perception* and *interpretation* of the two individuals. That, in turn, alters our *responses* to them. They are no longer just two separate and unique persons. They are now a single entity that has to be thought about, responded to, and dealt with socially in a different way.

This change in meaning and behavior by friends, family, and others has many consequences. As noted, it brings different kinds of responses from others. As explained in the discussion of the "looking-glass self" theory, that brings about a reconstruction of the self-images of the individuals who make up the couple. This external social process, along with an increase in self-disclosure, reinforces the movement toward intimacy.

Another consequence is that as we become a two-person dyad, in the eyes of others as well as ourselves, we find that we have established mutually accepted expectations for *relating to each other*. All these new role expectations and normative rules for social relationships as a couple give us guidelines that define how we are supposed to communicate with the other.

At each stage in this movement toward intimacy, the two individuals employ "secret tests" to check out the level of commitment each feels toward the other and about the relationship.[25] For instance, we might test our new partner's commitment by suggesting that it's time to meet the parents—and we all know what that implies! Or, we might mention a chance meeting with a former partner the other day (in hopes that our current partner will become jealous!)[26]

Moving to full disclosure. Assuming that all goes well, the relationship moves on to greater and greater levels of intimacy. Throughout this entire experimenting stage, we take risks by exposing more and more about ourselves. Then we observe carefully how our partner responds to that disclosure. The more consistently our partner responds in a supportive, understanding manner, the more likely we are to *trust* that person—gaining confidence that he or she won't hurt us, no matter what we do or say. In short, once the foundation of trust is established and we reach a state of full disclosure, we have become an *intimate pair*, who are seen as such by ourselves and others.[27] Box 5.4 explains in more detail how "Being Intimate" is code for "Having Sex."

Communicating with an Intimate Other

Once two individuals believe they are in an intimate relationship, a transformation takes place in the way they *talk* and *behave* toward each other. During the process of coming together, pairs develop norms for relating to each other. Some of those normative rules are common to almost any set of intimate communicators. For example, in their study of intimate dyads, researchers Michael Argyle

BOX 5.4   *Ethical Concerns*

Is "Being Intimate" a Code Phrase for "Having Sex"?

All too often people make the mistake of equating intimacy with sexuality. In fact, people typically imply that they are having sex by instead saying, "We have an intimate relationship." Intimacy and sex are not the same thing! Intimacy involves communication: communicating about personal issues—like love, sex, fears, hopes, and dreams—and making yourself vulnerable to each other.

Are couples who are involved in a sexual relationship, then, necessarily *intimate?* Of course not; guppies can have sex! A better question would be to ask, "Are couples who can talk about having sex with each other necessarily intimate?" The answer is probably so!

Movement toward greater intimacy occurs when two individuals are able to communicate their deepest held beliefs, fears, attitudes, anxieties, prejudices, and concerns. When couples are able to take risks and communicate about issues that don't particularly flatter them, that don't project them in the best possible light, they are being intimate. When couples *care* enough to criticize, argue, and share with each other, they are being intimate.

Now then, what does intimacy have to do with hopping into bed or shacking up? Nothing.

and Monika Henderson found that very good friends share several rules such as "Don't nag" and "Don't criticize a friend in public."[28] However, many of the communication norms that develop between intimates are unique to their specific relationship. For example, a couple may develop a communication norm that ensures an easy escape from tedious evening social events. They share an agreement that, when one or the other feels it's time to go home, that person signals the desire to the other by exclaiming, "Well, the dogs need to be fed," or some other phrase serving the same goal. The other quickly agrees, and they then begin the process of leave-taking.

You probably can think of special understandings that you share with an intimate partner concerning what messages are or are not appropriate. Some couples have norms about fighting, such as that they agree never to call each other "ugly" names when they are angry. Others insist on resolving any conflicts before they go to bed at night. You may know couples who avoid any open communication of affection in public—even refusing to hold hands. Whatever they may be, norms tend to be both personal and private to the relationship. Some may be quite explicit and a consequence of negotiations between the partners. Others are implicit and are simply assumed by the two people.

Another characteristic of participants in close relationships is their use of "intimate idioms" and "inside" humor.[29] That is, special friends or lovers generally share words, nonverbal gestures, and private meanings for situations that others may not understand, recognize, or know about. You may have friends who talk *baby talk* to each other when they are alone. Should they slip and reveal that talk in public, others may laugh or feel embarrassed for them. You may know a couple in which one partner calls the other by a *pet name,* such as "Sweetie Pie" or "Honey Bunch," when they are alone. Or, you and your best friend may use a *shared phrase,* such as "That's nice," to signal boredom when they are interacting with outsiders. Another example of an intimate and private dialogue is *inside humor,* in the form of private jokes. It is not uncommon to see a couple crack up over a remark, when no one else thinks it is funny.

In summary, this section traced how movement toward greater intimacy generally occurs. Obviously, although some relationships follow the stages just described, others do not. Some move forward quickly and almost overnight become intimate. Others may take years to reach that stage. Even less predictable is whether or not any given relationship is likely to be successful. Life would be far more comfortable if we could determine our probability of success or failure in the long run before developing an intimate relationship with another person. Unfortunately, many different factors, situations, and events may disrupt any human relationship.

Disengagement: Communicating When Relationships Erode

So far, the focus of this chapter has been relationships in which both partners choose to move toward greater intimacy, and eventually to a stable pattern of companionship or loving affiliation.

When the costs involved in a relationship seem to exceed the benefits, one or both of the partners may decide to disengage, or withdraw. The reasons for this vary widely, but one important factor is what each partner *believes* to be the problem. Some answers to what circumstances lead to disengagement can be found in the study of *alienation* (psychological disaffection) between husbands and wives. Interestingly, individuals tend to avoid responsibility for divorce and instead, attribute the fault to their former spouses.[30] What are the most common reasons given? Women reported infidelity, mental or physical abuse, and alcohol or drug abuse as major factors. In contrast, men reported poor communication or they indicated that they simply did not know the cause for their divorce. Other contributing factors for both husbands and wives included incompatibility, growing apart, and personality issues.

Both members of a couple undergoing disengagement often go through a process of creating their individual interpretations—their own socially constructed realities—of what they believe to be the real causes of the disengagement. These define for them what went wrong, who is to blame, what they were justified in doing, and so forth. These meanings, then, become the basis for their subsequent actions.

Explaining the Reasons for Disengagement

Whenever we finally determine that a friendship, marriage, or any other type of serious intimate relationship is coming to an end, we need to *explain why*—both to ourselves and others. In particular, we feel a need to attribute *blame*. Blame is an important concept in our culture. It provides explanations of human behavior that are easy to understand and that seem to make sense. That is, most people interpret the causes of human behavior within a *good guy–bad guy framework*. It is simple to conclude that bad outcomes are due to bad people (and vice versa). It is too difficult for most people to probe more deeply and to try to understand how human decisions and actions are consequences of complex impersonal forces and factors.[31]

Handling the pressure for an explanation. Even if we try to avoid labeling the other person as the "bad actor," others invariably will ask, "So tell me, why did you two break up?" (Read: What bad things did he or she do?) We can be flippant in our response, but then people think we're being coldhearted and cruel. They may speculate further that we were never really committed to the relationship in the first place. And so it goes. Friends and family need, want, and expect us to give them *an accounting of what went wrong*. Furthermore, not just any interpretation will do—only a certain kind of causal explanation will be met with their approval.[32]

So, for the sake of others as well as ourselves, we have to create an explanation—a believable theory of what went wrong. It has to be one that our friends and family will find acceptable.

Acceptable assignments of blame. One of the first requirements of such a blame story is that our family and friends must believe that somehow, in some way, we were justified in leaving (and were not the guilty party). In other words, we need an explanation in which we are seen as occupying the *moral high ground*. For example, if we "got dumped," we must be careful to spin a tale that does not warrant the other person's leaving!

Ideally, the story we construct should lead us to believe in our own minds, and should compel the sympathetic listener to conclude: "You made a rational decision; and you are definitely better off without such a person!" In other words, we need to convince both ourselves and others that we are still worthy and acceptable candidates for future relational ties.[33] We could be greatly harmed, both personally and socially, if we gave a story in which we assumed blame and identified ourselves as the culprit. By the same token, it may be risky to create a version that blames our partner entirely, because our partner may be making us the villain in his or her version.

Another important requirement for a story explaining a disengagement is that it should reflect a sense of *emotional maturity* and recognition that it takes two to make and to break a relationship. Consequently, a well-crafted story that will be received sympathetically by those we care about ought to include just a little bit of self-blame. It can have a lot of "other-blame," as long as we indicate at least some degree of understanding of our partner's behavior.

Generally, then, a well-designed explanatory story provides an accounting that should satisfy the needs and expectations of others, and—if well constructed—it provides a "true" version of what happened for consumption by friends and family. Also, of course, it is one that we ourselves can firmly believe. Ideally, it lets us accept only a minor part of the blame, but it must assign the lion's share to the other so that we can feel better about our part in the disengagement.

Saying Goodbye

Just as the language of intimate communicators differs significantly from that of new acquaintances or strangers, the language of individuals involved in disengagement reflects a dramatic change. Obviously, couples going through disengagement are unlikely to call each other "sweetheart" or "honey." Commonly, they revert to first names, and once again use some of the more stylized, stereotypic language of strangers. Their conversations become hesitant and awkward as they hold back disclosure. They have trouble sharing their feelings because predictable responses of support are missing.

Couples begin to disengage by a twofold process called **distancing** and **disassociation**.[34] What this means is that in their interpersonal interactions they begin transmitting messages designed to *increase both physical and psychological distance* and to disassociate themselves from their partners.

Establishing social distance between self and other. Messages designed to achieve the goal of distancing can take both verbal and nonverbal forms, but the goal is always the same. For example, one of the simplest and most obvious ways that a person can begin to disengage is by spending more and more time away from the other. He or she may work late at night, take weekend trips to visit friends or relatives without taking the partner along; or go to plays, concerts, or movies with friends. Increased physical distance can also be achieved at home. When one partner is in the living room watching television, the other reads alone in the kitchen. At some point, one partner may continue sleeping in their bedroom, while the other takes to the guest room or the couch.

Psychological distancing can be achieved in many subtle and indirect ways.[35] The partners may look at each other less, touch less, put up such barriers as folded arms, or experience more uncomfortable periods of silence, and they may employ colder vocal tones in exchanges. Psychological distancing can also be accomplished by close control over the content of their messages. That is, as disclosure begins to shut the relationship down, one partner may be unwilling to volunteer a lot of personal information to the other. When this happens, the responses become less supportive and less sympathetic. By any of these strategies and patterns, then, both physical and psychological distance replace the close association that had been developed and maintained earlier. Distancing is a very clear and necessary aspect of the disengagement process.

Disassociation by emphasizing differences.
The term *disassociation* refers to reducing the use of the couple-implying pronoun *we* and reverting to the individualistic *you* and *I*. Unwilling or unable to invest any further interest into the relationship itself, couples are likely to become concerned with their own feelings, costs, and benefits rather than those they shared earlier. Typically, one begins to hear such messages as "You only care what happens to you. What about me?" Where they once referred to "our" furniture and "our" dishes, they now talk about "my" chair and "your" mother's china. Messages about the future become messages about the past.

Throughout the disassociation process, differences rather than similarities are emphasized. Even though such differences may have existed throughout the entire relationship, they are now seen as divisive—and the couple begin to communicate and complain openly, sometimes bitterly, about the differences. The other side of this coin is that discussions centered on common likes, dislikes, and mutual interests are now more limited, or are skipped altogether. Partners experiencing disassociation come to believe that they never really had anything in common with one another. They wonder why they failed to see this before, or, if they remember that they did have commonality earlier, each may conclude that he or she has "developed and grown," while the other has failed to change.

Obviously, neither distancing nor disassociation contributes to relational bonding. To some degree, however, even healthy intimate relationships occasionally experience both of these communication processes. We cannot (and probably should not) spend every waking and sleeping moment with our partner. All of us need personal space, independence, and time away from each other.[36] We cannot (and, again, probably should not) hide or suppress all our likes and dislikes either, simply because our attitudes and beliefs differ from our partner's. Unlike intimate communicators, though, disengagers spend an increasing amount of time and energy avoiding contact and stressing dissimilarities. Whereas intimates talk about togetherness, coupling, and attachment, disengagers frequently communicate separateness, autonomy, and detachment.

Chapter Review

- The study of interpersonal communication looks at the kinds of messages people use when they want to develop close ties to others, when they try to keep valued relationships going, and when they seek to disconnect themselves from attachments that they no longer want.

- As individuals come to know one another better through interpersonal communication, their relationship tends to move from impersonal to personal. That is, they become increasingly close and intimate.

- There are six key characteristics of interpersonal communication: It begins with the "self," it is fully transactional, participants share physical proximity, their messages are shaped by social roles, interpersonal communication is irreversible, and it is unrepeatable.

- Patterns of interpersonal communication change during the different phases of relationship development. During the initial period, people rely on scripted and stereotypic conversational rules. Because all relationships begin with small talk, these communication skills are among the most important we can master.

- To the extent that we find our initial and subsequent encounters with another rewarding and interesting, we are likely to move toward greater intimacy. Much depends on the cost–benefit ratio of rewards versus punishments we think we will gain by going forward in the relationship.

- Communication during the management or intimacy phase of the relationship involves testing the degree to which the other person is open and supportive. This process requires disclosing selected sensitive information about ourselves and waiting to see how the other party responds. Assuming the partner responds positively, we increasingly engage in disclosure. Over time, we negotiate unique rules to govern our relationship, and we generate a unique, private language system for disclosure.

- In terminating a relationship, we have to construct an account of why it went wrong that will satisfy ourselves, our friends, and our relatives. It has to earn us some degree of social credit so that we are still perceived as having the potential for a good relationship in the future. We construct a plausible story that assigns blame to the "bad actor" and puts the best face on the relational disengagement.

- Breaking up a relationship that has yielded warm and satisfying rewards is never easy. Terminating the relationship generally involves both distancing and disassociation: We avoid spending time together and begin the uncoupling process.

Key Terms

interpersonal communication
engagement
management (communication strategy)
disengagement
dyad
self (self-image or self-concept)
personae
cost–benefit ratio
cushioning function

utilitarianism
small talk
scripted (or stereotypic) conversations
exchange theory
principle of delayed gratification
self-disclosure
distancing
disassociation

Notes

1. For a more extensive analysis of the distinctions between the situational and developmental perspectives, as well as in-depth discussion of impersonal and personal relationships, see: Miller, G. R., & Steinberg, M. (1975). *Between people* (pp. 7–29). Chicago: Science Research Associates; Miller, G. R. (1980). Interpersonal communication. In C. L. Bank, (Ed.), *Human communication principles, contexts and skills* (pp. 109–114). New York: St. Martin's.

2. Although it may seem a bit strange, this term specifies rather precisely the idea of two people in a system of repetitive social interaction. It was first brought into the study of human social behavior by the 19th century German sociologist Georg Simmel. See: Simmel, G. (1902). The number of members as determining the sociological form of the group (A. Small, Trans.). *American Journal of Sociology, 8,* 158–196. For a classic discussion of the dyad and dyadic

communication see: Wilmot, W. W. (1979). *Dyadic communication* (2nd ed.). Reading, MA: Addison-Wesley.

3. Pearson, J. C., & Spitzberg, B. (1990). *Interpersonal communication: Concepts, components, and contexts (2nd ed.).* Dubuque, IA: William C. Brown.

4. The term *self* derives from early-20th-century social psychology in which theorists were trying to understand how a person develops personal understandings of his or her social, psychological, and physical characteristics, and the value placed on them by the society. Generally, such understandings were said to be obtained in a process of social interaction with others. See: Charles Horton Cooley's discussion of the "looking-glass self," in: Cooley, C. H. (1902). *Human nature and the social order* (pp. 81–263). New York: Charles Scribner's Sons. For a more recent discussion of the role of the self in interpersonal communication, see: Wood, J. T. (2009). *Communication mosaics: An introduction to the field of speech communication* (Chapter 9) (6th ed.). Boston: Wadsworth/ Cengage; Pearson & Spitzberg, (1990).

5. This self-image and multi-image conception of interpersonal communication was first set forth by Cooley in *Human nature and the social order,* pp. 81–263.

6. In a very general sense, the process of "reading" the reactions of the other was alluded to in Chapter 1 when we discussed role-taking and feedback. The same kind of activity has been called "taking the role of the other" by classic social psychologists in the symbolic interactionist tradition. See: Mead, G. H. (1934). *Mind, self and society: From the standpoint of a social behaviorist* (Charles W. Morris, Ed., p. 254). Chicago: University of Chicago Press.

7. Laing, R. D., Phillipson, H., & Lee, A. R. (1966). *Interpersonal perceptions.* Baltimore: Perennial Library; Waldeck, J. H., Kearney, P., & Plax, T. G. (2013). *Business and professional communication in a digital age.* Boston: Wadsworth/Cengage; West, R., & Turner, L.H. (2009). (2009). *Understanding interpersonal communication: Making choices in changing times* (2nd ed.). Belmont, CA: Wadsworth; DeVito, J. A. (2010). *The interpersonal*

communication book (11th ed.). Upper Saddle River, NJ: Pearson.

8. Bateson, G. (1958). *Naven* (2nd ed.). Stanford, CA: Stanford University Press; Watzlawick, P., Beavin, J. H., & Jackson, D. D. (1967). *Pragmatics of human communication* (pp. 51–54). New York: Norton.

9. For a complete discussion of the importance of the family in interpersonal communication see: Turner, L. H., & West, R. (2006). *Perspectives on family communication* (3rd ed.). New York: McGraw-Hill; Galvin, K. M., Bylund, C. L., & Brommel, B. J. (2011). *Family communication: Cohesion and change* (8th ed.). Boston: Allyn and Bacon.

10. For a summary of utilitarianism, see: (1954). Bentham: Principles of morals and legislation. In W. Ebenstein, *Great political thinkers* (chap. 19, pp. 484–499). New York: Rinehart and Company.

11. Byrne, D. (1971). *The attraction paradigm.* New York: Academic; Byrne, D., & Nelson, D. (1965). Attraction as a linear function of proportion of positive reinforcements. *Journal of Personality and Social Psychology, 1,* 659–663. For a discussion of related research, see: Knapp, M. L., & Vangelisti, A. L. (2009). *Interpersonal communication and human relationships* (6th ed.), (pp. 53-59). Boston: Pearson; DeMaris, A. (2007). The role of relationship inequity in marital disruption. *Journal of Social and Personal Relationships, 24,* 177–195.

12. Originally, a "stereotype" was a rigid cylinder of cast type that fit over a large roller in a newspaper press. Repeatedly, it turned out the same pages of print. Journalist Walter Lippman applied the idea to human thinking and behavior that is rigid and unchanging. See: Lippman, W. (1922). *Public opinion.* New York: Macmillan. The term *stereotype* has been widely used since the 1930s to identify rigid beliefs of a negative sort about a particular category of people. It can also be used to describe communication behavior. See: Knapp & Vangelisti (2009), pp. 146-149.

13. Berger, C. R., Gardner, R. R., Clatterbuck, G. W., & Schulman, L. S. (1976). Perceptions of information sequencing in relationship development. *Human Communication Research, 3,*

29–46; see also Knapp & Vangelisti (2009), pp. 183–187.

14. Rosenfeld, L. B. (1979). Self-disclosure avoidance: Why I am afraid to tell you who I am. *Communication Monographs, 45,* 63–66.

15. Georg Simmel's original essay is contained in: Simmel, G. (1908). *Soziologie.* Leipzig: Dunker and Humbolt. For a summary of the idea in English, see: (1950). The stranger. In K. H. Wolff (Ed. and Trans.), *The sociology of Georg Simmel* (pp. 402–408). New York: Free Press. See also: Knapp & Vangelisti (2009), pp. 262–263.

16. Knapp & Vangelisti (2009), pp. 198–200.

17. Knapp & Vangelisti (2009), pp. 198–200.

18. Knapp & Vangelisti (2009), pp. 200–205; Berger, C.R., & Calabrese, R. J. (1975). Some explorations in initial interaction and beyond: Toward a developmental theory of interpersonal communication. *Human Communication Research,* 1, 99–112.

19. Altman, I., & Taylor, D. A. (1973). *Social penetration: The development of interpersonal relationships.* New York: Holt, Rinehart, and Winston; Thibaut, J. W., & Kelley, H. H. (1952). The social psychology of groups. New York: John Wiley & Sons; Taylor, D., & Altman, I. (1987). Communication in interpersonal relationships: Social penetration processes. In M. Roloff & G. Miller (Eds.), Interpersonal processes: New directions in communication research (pp. 257–277). Newbury Park, CA: Sage.

20. Homans, G. C. (1961). *Social behavior in its elementary forms.* New York: Harcourt, Brace & World. Exchange theory itself was derived from Bentham's utilitarianism.

21. Homans, G. C. (1950). *The human group.* New York: Harcourt Brace Jovanovich; Thibaut, J., & Kelly, H. H. (1959). *The social psychology of groups.* New York: Wiley; Altman & Taylor, *Social penetration,* p. 33.

22. Altman & Taylor, *Social penetration,* 27–29; Knapp & Vangelisti (2009), pp. 252–263.

23. For a comprehensive review of research on self-disclosure, see: Dindia, K. (2002). Self-disclosure research: Knowledge through meta-analysis. In Allen, M., et al. (eds.), *Interpersonal communication research: Advances through meta-analysis* (pp. 169–185). Mahwah, NJ: Lawrence Erlbaum Associates.

24. Knapp & Vangelisti (2009), pp. 252–263.

25. Baxter, L. A., & Wilmot, W. W. (1984). Secret tests: Social strategies for acquiring information about the state of the relationship. *Human Communication Research,*1, 171–202; Duck, S. (1986). *Human relationships: An introduction to social psychology* (p. 50). Beverly Hills: Sage.

26. The use of "secret tests" is also employed in deteriorating relationships. See: Chory-Assad, R. M., & Booth-Butterfield, M. (2001). Secret test use and self-esteem in deteriorating relationships. *Communication Research Reports, 18,* 2, 147–157.

27. Prager, K. J. (1989). Intimacy status and couple communication. *Journal of Social and Personal Relationships, 6,* 435–449.

28. Argyle, M., & Henderson, M. (1984). The rules of friendship. *Journal of social and personal relationships, 1,* 211–238; Duck, *Human relationships,* p. 96.

29. Ibid., p. 95; Knapp & Vangelisti (2009), pp. 305–308.

30. Amato, P.R., & Previti, D. (2003). People's reasons for divorcing: Gender, social class, the life course, and adjustment. *Journal of Family Issues, 24,* 602–626.

31. For an examination of the descriptions people give of current and dissolved relationships see: Hortalsu, N. (1989). Current and dissolved relationships: Descriptive and attributional dimensions and predictors of involvement. *Journal of Social and Personal Relationships, 6,* 373–383.

32. Ibid.

33. La Gaipa, J. J. (1982). Rules and rituals in disengaging from relationships. In S. Duck (Ed.), *Personal relationships 4: Dissolving personal relationships* (pp. 189–210). London & New York: Academic.

34. Ibid.

35. Hess, J. A. (2000). Maintaining nonvoluntary relationships with disliked partners: An investigation into the use of distancing behaviors. *Human Communication Research, 26,* 3, 458–488.

36. Pearson, J. C. (2001). Conflict in our intimate relationships. In W. F. Eadie & P. E. Nelson, (Eds.) *The language of conflict and resolution.* (pp. 47–56) Thousand Oaks, CA: Sage.

Chapter 6

Communicating in Small Groups

Do you remember when you ran for Senior Class President, Pat, and I was your campaign manager?"

"Betty, I'd almost forgotten that. Now that you brought it up, I believe you were the first campaign manager in the history of our high school. You had all of our friends doing jobs to get me elected—painting "Vote for Pat" on the school driveway, hanging banners all over school, creating campaign slogans, and making speeches wherever you could find a crowd."

"Yeah, and Betty got in trouble for it, too. We all had to go back out to the street and wash off the paint the next day," Coleen recalled. "No one really knew WHO did the deed, so the principal had our whole group into her office threatening us with suspension. We all felt guilty, and we felt especially bad for Betty. The principal was always ready to accuse her of anything and everything."

"I'm relieved to this day that we never owned up to it. That's one of things I really like about our friendship," revealed Pat. "We stick to together."

"Yeah, I think we were used to Betty getting us into trouble. She always had these great ideas and could somehow convince us to go along with her," complained Coleen.

"True enough, but you were only too eager to go along. In fact, I think you encouraged me to do it—and then some. You have to admit; your life would have been dull without me in it!"

As the three friends continued to remember their days in high school, they realized how close they remained over the years. They had grown up together in the same town, attending the same schools throughout elementary and high school years. Then they split off and went their separate ways. Pat went off to college, Coleen married and had kids, and Betty became a nurse and eventually married her high school sweetheart. Then, when each had returned home to live in their community, they quickly re-entered their close relationship. They celebrated each other's birthdays, worked out at the same gym, and invited each other to their homes for special dinners.

These three close friends are in a **peer group**—an important kind of small group that is based on close intimate communication and strong emotional ties among its members. Along with the *family*, sociologists refer to it as a **primary group**.[1] These two groups are "primary" in two ways. One is that they are of primary importance early in life, and the other is that they serve very basic needs. Both families and peer groups have existed since prehistoric times, when early human beings led a precarious life. Close bonding between people in families and as peers was essential to survival. They remain essential today. People can exist without corporations, government agencies, schools, factories, or other kinds of larger groups, but they cannot do so without primary groups.

Looking analytically at peer groups, such as the one which Betty, Coleen, and Pat have formed, provides many insights into the importance of small group communication in human life.[2] For example, in the three-person peer group above, communication is completely open.

Every member can communicate with every other member with complete *self-disclosure*.

Sociologists point out that peer groups in early life provide initial training for communication skills. For example, on the playground and among their young friends, children learn how to be polite, what verbal and nonverbal messages make people angry, what amuses them, and what makes them sad. These are valuable lessons in which children develop *skills in role-taking and interpreting feedback*. Children also develop these skills in the context of the family.

As the opening vignette illustrates, primary groups provide *sympathy and emotional support* in times of stress. Their members are *loyal to each other* in the face of outside threats. Over time they build up an accumulation of shared experiences that is the basis of the group's *social cohesion*—the ties members have to each other—the bonds that keep the group together. Both peer groups and the family, then, are primary to human development and human existence.

There are many other kinds of human groups that are very different in their goals and their rules for communication. Each is formed and carried out for different purposes. Whatever its nature and purposes, each type of group constitutes a different *context*. In the simultaneous transactions model developed in previous chapters, context was identified as an important feature that influences communication.

In many respects, human communication in any **group** is based on exactly the same concepts and principles examined in the dyadic contexts discussed in previous chapters. However, communicating with other people in any group is not the same experience as doing so in a face-to-face context consisting of only two persons. It requires different skills, follows different patterns, and has different consequences.

This chapter describes communication patterns and expectations within the context, not only of peers, but also within a variety of different types of small groups. It is important to understand the distinct rules and requirements for communication in each. These shared understandings

When close friends or family members interact, they often share experiences that are both unique to intimate groups and important to their development. For this reason, family and peer groups are often referred to as primary groups.

define *who* can say *what* over *what channel* on *what occasion* for *what purpose.*

The Nature of Human Groups

Just what is a human group? This may seem to be an odd question because all of us have been members of many groups all our lives. Nevertheless, a definitive answer provides the basis for an analytical framework for discussing the communication system that people use in any human group.[3]

Groups versus Social Categories

First of all, a human group is obviously more than one person. Also, the people involved are in some respects similar. However, that is not enough. There are many sets or collections of people who, using those two criteria alone, might seem to be groups—because either they are physically together or they are in some way alike. However, the mere fact that they are spatially near each other, or that they share some common characteristic, *is not a sufficient basis* for calling them a group.

Suppose, for example, that you came upon a dozen or more people who had gathered temporarily on a street corner to gape at an auto wreck that just happened. Later that day, you may have told a friend that you saw a "group" of people looking at an accident. However, in a strict sense, they did not make up a group. They were simply a number of people who happened to be there at the same time and engaged in similar behavior. In fact, they probably did not even know each other and probably dispersed within a few minutes. Strictly speaking, they were not a group, because they did not have any permanent basis for communicating in some regular way. Calling them a *crowd* would be more accurate.

Similarly, in everyday discussion we sometimes refer to some class of people in a population as a "group" because they all share some similar characteristic. An example would be an "ethnic group," such as Hispanics, who come from, or have ancestral origins in, a Spanish-speaking country. In a strict sense, they make up what demographers call a "social category"—a number of people who can be *classified as similar* on the basis of some shared characteristic, in this case their (or their parents') countries of origin. Almost any shared characteristic or set of characteristics can provide the basis for identifying a social category. The idea of social categories is an important one for *demographers*—social scientists who classify people using various criteria in order to study the composition of populations. They classify and analyze people in terms of age, gender, income, educational level, religious affiliation, occupation, and so on. Like the participants in a crowd, the members of such categories do not interact and communicate and probably do not even know each other. In short, they are not groups.

What, then, are the precise criteria or conditions that can be used to decide whether a set of people actually make up a group? The answer is not complicated. The first important consideration is whether the people are collectively pursuing a *common objective* by communicating and interacting together in some sort of coordinated way. People do not come together in groups for no purpose and then act randomly. They seek some goal by collective action that could not be achieved by each member acting alone as an individual.[4] For example, members of a peer group, such as Betty, Pat, and Coleen seek satisfactions that they obtain from each other's company. Those experiences would not be available to isolated individuals who do not communicate with each other. The satisfactions obtained in family life provide another example of a primary group objective. Larger and more complex groups—schools, factories, government agencies, and armed services—also have distinct objectives.

A second important criterion is whether the people in a group have worked out a *stable set of rules and expectations* that define how they are to communicate with each other and how to regulate their behavior to attain their goal. In seeking their shared objective, members of a group have to *coordinate* their actions within a set of understandings that define what is expected on the part of each member, what will not be tolerated, and what will be rewarded by the other members. These understandings define who is to do what; who will have more power, authority, prestige, and rewards; and what will happen to a member who does not do what the other members expect and want. This pattern of definitions and expectations is called the group's *pattern of social organization*. This is a critical feature for understanding communication within the context of any group, regardless of its size and objectives. With all the above in mind, then, a *group* can be defined as *three or more people who repeatedly interact to achieve a shared goal, regulating their conduct and communication within a pattern of social organization.*[5]

Obviously, some groups are small, intimate and informal. Others are the opposite—huge, organized in a very formal and impersonal way, and complex in the different rules for communication and behavior by their members. Nevertheless, each has its objective and each has its pattern of social organization. That pattern of mutual and shared expectations about who can communicate with whom under what circumstances, or behave in what way as a member, is an essential feature of any group that helps understand it as a context.

The Basics of Social Organization

The idea of social organization is essentially a simple and obvious one. At the same time, it can be difficult to "see" such a pattern without observing the members of a group over a period of time to see how they are relating to each other. If such observations can be made, at least four kinds of regularities can be detected in the way they communicate and relate to each other:

- **Norms** that all members of the group are expected to follow
- **Roles** or specialized functions for each member of the group
- **Ranks** or hierarchy that prescribe levels of authority
- **Controls** that members use to reward desired contributions or punish deviations.

A group's pattern of social organization then—whatever its nature, size, and objectives—consists of its **norms, roles, ranks,** and **controls**.[6]

Norms. Rules that every member is expected to follow are called norms. These rules define such matters as when and where the members get together, what kinds of behaviors toward each other imply respect or disrespect, when humor is OK, when to be serious, and so on. In some groups there are dress codes, rules for intergender contacts, rules for use of space and equipment, and so on. In small groups norms are simply understood. In large and formal ones, they may be written out in a formal way in handbooks or other official documents.

Roles. As in a play in the theater, people play different parts in a group. Mother and father act differently than brother and sister. In any group the members have to decide who does what in the group. In peer groups, all the members can act and communicate with the others in a similar way, but often even in this context some members play somewhat different roles from those played by others. In all but the most intimate and informal peer groups, the roles are different, but are linked together in such a way that each makes some contribution to the objectives of the group. This was clear in the older traditional family, where each person did different things for the group as a whole, and even

the kids had their chores and obligations. In certain kinds of more formally organized small "task-oriented" groups (e.g., committees, task forces, juries, or boards) the roles are usually clearly defined. Someone serves as leader and others are members, who may perform different tasks.

Ranks. In virtually any group, large or small, formal or informal, intimate or impersonal, some members have more (or less) of something that is valued. They may have more power, authority, prestige, income, skills, education, or something else. This has to be accepted by the members. In groups where ranks exist, formally or informally, they are a part of the reality that each member must deal with. Acceptance may mean following orders from above, saluting (as in the military), using special titles, wearing different clothing, or just showing respect and deference to those higher in the group.

Controls. Once a group has worked out its pattern of social organization, the rules must be followed. If a member fails to meet the expectations of others, this deviance from the pattern makes it more difficult for the group to meet its goals. For example, in the peer group portrayed in the opening vignette, if Coleen repeatedly failed to show up at the gym or invite the group to dinner, it would be a violation of the norms. Some sort of punishment has to be administered to maintain the rules for communication and behavior. In the case of the peer group it might have consisted of nonverbal gestures, such as a frown, or verbal messages complaining about and denouncing the behavior. In other kinds of groups, negative sanctions can include a low grade, loss of pay, failure to be promoted, or being fired. In extreme situations it may mean life imprisonment or even the death penalty. On the other hand, if a member performs in some positive way above and beyond what members expect, verbal, nonverbal, or material rewards may be used to recognize that contribution. Social controls, then, consist of administration of positive or negative sanctions

BOX 6.1   A *Closer Look*

Social Organization

All human groups have one thing in common. Whether the group is large or small, intimate or impersonal, formal or informal, it has what sociologists call a *pattern of social organization*. This pattern develops because people do not come together to form groups for no reason—or interact with each other randomly to carry on their activities. They do so to pursue collectively some *goal* or objective that they could not achieve while acting alone. To do this they need a shared set of mutual expectations that permit each member to *anticipate* how the others will communicate with and respond to them as they carry on the group's activities. That set of anticipations or expectations consists of four distinct types of rules that define what members are supposed to do and what they can expect of the others under a variety of circumstances. Thus, a human group is organized around its *norms, roles, ranks*, and *controls*.

Norms. All groups have *rules for behavior* that must be observed by every member. These dictate many of the ways all are expected to behave. (Examples are dress codes, time schedules, rules of politeness, modes of greeting, and use of company phones.)

Roles. Like actors in a play, each member of a group performs some *specialized activity* that complements the activities of others and helps achieve the objective. If each member's role is understood and accepted by the others, the members can act effectively as a team. (Examples are father, captain of the team, gang member, foreman, waiter, and supermarket clerk.)

Ranks. Some members play more critical or more honored roles. Others play less important roles. For this reason some members have more authority, power, and prestige, and get greater rewards. Members can be classified on these criteria into *strata* or *levels of ranks*. Those lower are often expected to show deference to, or follow instructions of, those in higher ranks.

Controls. If a member *fails to carry out*, or *deviates from*, the above expectations, the group's goal and stability are threatened and the person will be punished. However, if a member performs positively, above and beyond what is expected, that member will be rewarded. The negative and positive sanctions used constitute the group's system of social control. (Examples are smiles of approval, frowns, verbal compliments, pay raises, getting fired, advancement in rank, grades, fines, jail, and even the death penalty.)

(rewards or punishments) that serve to maintain the pattern of social organization and ensure that the group can achieve its objectives. (See Box 6.1.)

Informal versus Formal Communication

The pattern of communication among our three friends was *informal*. That is, it was spontaneous, unplanned, and clearly not conducted according to any set of officially coded rules.

In following a pattern of **informal communication,** people feel relatively free to say what they want, and they do not constantly worry that their meanings will be misunderstood. This does not mean that there are no rules whatever regarding who can say what to whom on what occasion. Even in the most intimate groups there are understood prohibitions about certain topics or modes of communication. Name calling is out, and references to certain personal or family characteristics may not be acceptable.

When they participate in informal communication, people engage in role-taking and are aware of feedback, as is the case whenever people communicate face to face, but they seldom deliberate ahead of time to assess in detail what a person's response to a routine message is likely to be. Moreover, they do not scrutinize a receiver for subtle or minute feedback signals. They are "laid back" and comfortable with each other. Nevertheless, and in spite of the relaxed way that informal communication proceeds, it is patterned around the mutual expectations that members have of each other. In short, *informal communication* can be defined as *a spontaneous exchange of messages between individuals who feel free to engage in self-disclosure and to discuss whatever topic they wish, using mutually understood noncoded rules.*

In contrast, **formal communication** takes place within a set of official rules, often laid out very specifically in handbooks or other documents. Anyone familiar with life in one of the military services understands formal communication very well. Private Martinez does not greet Major Jones, his or her company commander, with an informal, "Hey, how are you?" He or she stands at attention, salutes, and says something like, "Good morning, Sir (or Ma'am). Private Martinez reporting as ordered." In such a formal system, messages must be couched in highly prescribed forms. Formal titles of address are compulsory. Nonverbal messages (salutes, standing at attention, eye contact) must communicate mutual respect. Slouching posture, sloppy salutes, rumpled clothing, and failure to listen carefully are major transgressions.

There are many systems of coded formal communication that are not as rigid as those used in the military. They are used in such settings as courtrooms, board meetings, and committee deliberations, as well as many other kinds of group settings where a set of coded rules for communicating set the pattern of social organization. The distinction between informal and formal communication is an important one for understanding how communication proceeds in a very large number of groups, both large and small. In this chapter, a number of examples of informal and formal communication in small

groups will be discussed. In summary, then, *formal communication* can be defined as *controlled communication among parties who are allowed or required by the group's coded rules to transmit particular kinds of messages to specific receivers using officially designated rules and restrictions.*

The Consequences of Group Size

How is communication in a group influenced by the number of participants in the process? Communication in a small group is very different from that in a large organization. Even the addition of one person, such as an older adult parent, in a household that previously consisted of a husband and wife, can have a significant influence on the relationship.[7]

The difference between dyadic and group communication is that in the latter a number of *pairs* of participants may be involved at the same time. For example, consider a group with three members. At any given moment one sender may be transmitting a message to a maximum of two receivers. Although the other two may be simultaneously formulating their replies and providing ongoing feedback, the basic linear process is still there, taking place between what looks at first glance like two sender-receiver pairs who are involved in the exchange. However, if one looks more closely, *there are actually three pairs* involved. To be sure, only one person is talking and two listening, but another exchange of influences is taking place between the two receivers. Even though they are not talking to each other at the moment, they are influencing each other in subtle ways, through posture, facial expressions, and other nonverbal signs. In this sense, then, there are in fact three pairs to consider when one person talks to two others. A group of only three, then, has three possible pairs that are to be considered in any act of communication.

What happens when the number of participants is greater than three? How does this influence the communication processes that take place? As will be evident, as the number of such dyads (pairs) grows, it becomes more and more difficult to maintain a full flow of communication among all the members. For example, in our group with only three potential pairs, there would be little difficulty in turn-taking, in reading nonverbal cues, and in understanding potential nuances of connotative meanings. Role-taking would be more difficult than with a single receiver, but it would not be all that complex. Also, each member could recall fairly accurately who said what to whom in prior communication. Generally, then, with three members achieving accuracy in any given exchange would not be difficult.

Now, consider larger groups. Adding only one more person to a group of three doubles the number of pairs to six.[8] This makes turn-taking, role-taking, keeping track of what each person has already said to each of the others, and so on considerably more difficult. A group of 10 has 45 possible pairs, and one with 20 members has a startling 190 potential pairings! Thus, as the number of group members grows, the number of potential pairs engaging in role-taking, feedback, turn-taking, prior communication, and nonverbal communication become geometrically more complicated as size increases linearly.

For these reasons, an optimal size for discussion and making decisions in a small group, with all members participating fully, is pretty small—something like five (with 10 pairs). This brings some diversity of views to the exchanges, but it still permits a relatively full flow of reasonably accurate communication. Although there are no hard-and-fast rules, when a group grows beyond five or so, the dynamics of communication begin to change dramatically.[9] Individual members have an increasingly difficult time communicating fully and accurately in face-to-face dyads to all the others. If the group gets up to, say, 20 or so, some members simply stop trying to participate and sit quietly on the sidelines. Others break up into small cliques, and a few talkers dominate the discussion. Thus, group size can be a critical factor in the way a group functions.

Stages in Group Development

In some groups, the rules for communicating can be designated before members are recruited (for example, formal **decision-making groups,** such as juries). However, many of the **task-oriented groups** discussed previously undergo a *series of stages* after the members first come together. During these stages the rules for communicating are developed by the members during their early encounters, and become stabilized only after a period.[10]

Sociologist Robert F. Bales has been one of the most influential researchers in the study of emerging group communication systems.[11] His classic experiments on "interaction process analysis," conducted during the late 1940s, broke new ground and showed that in an informal group discussion the members of small groups do achieve specialization in the kinds of messages they communicate. Later on, social psychologist Bruce Tuckman came up with four distinct stages that he called *forming, storming, norming,* and *performing.*[12] (See Box 6.2.)

Forming: The Stage of Initial Orientation

When people come together to confront a task or to solve a problem, they face many uncertainties. This is especially true if they do not know one another and are not able to predict how each will respond to what is said. Thus, there is a stage of *orientation*, both toward the task for which the group has been formed and toward one another. Sizing up one another is one of the first things that has to be done in such a task-oriented group. We discussed earlier the concept of *implicit personality*—the process by which individuals who do not really know each other use various salient and other visible characteristics to make judgments about what the others are like. This is exactly what happens in forming a task-oriented group in which the members are not well known to each other. A considerable amount of the early communication involves exchanges designed to determine who responds in what way to what

BOX 6.2   🔍 *A Closer Look*

Tuckman's Four Stages in Group Development

1. *Forming: The stage of initial orientation.* This is the stage of uncertainty: Rules governing communication are tested; norms and roles start to be defined; and members take on particular roles and communicate status, power, and control messages.
2. *Storming: The stage of emerging conflict.* During this stage, orientation activities transform into conflict: Members disagree about power, status, and control roles, and a leader emerges with a particular leadership style.
3. *Norming: The stage of stabilization.* During this stage, conflicts subside: Members finish sizing up one another, and they begin to operate as a group, turning to the task to be accomplished.
4. *Performing: The stage of task achievement.* During this stage, members address the task following a set of stabilizing rules for communicating: Various solutions are examined, and members come together in consensus about the best solution.

Source: Tuckman, B. W. (1950). Development sequences in small groups. *Psychological Bulletin, 63,* 384–399.

kinds of messages. The forming stage, then, is one of uncertainty, probing, implicit personality formation, and trial.

It is in this stage that the rules that will govern communication—the *norms* of how ideas can be expressed and what can be said—begin to be defined. Will a sophisticated vocabulary be the norm? Will they address each other in more formal or informal ways? Is humor acceptable?

Depending on the nature of the group, communication *roles*—specialized parts to be performed by individual members—may also be defined in the forming stage. The need for a group leader may become clear, and some individuals may start to take on that role. Others may try out for the part of "group clown," offering funny anecdotes or jokes. Others may begin to play the part of mediator—the pourer-of-oil-on-troubled-waters—by specializing in the soothing of the feelings of others.

Status and power *ranks* within the group are also clarified during the forming stage. Some members transmit messages intended to define their special expertise. Some, with high status outside the group, will be seen as having more influence than others on what is said. These messages start to identify the levels of prestige that will exist within the group. If these definitions are accepted, the contributions by those group members awarded higher rank will be interpreted as having the most weight. Other group members may be intimidated by these emerging indicators of rank. They may see themselves as low in the system and having less to offer to the discussion.

Communication at this stage also begins to identify the signals of *social control.* Who will transmit messages of reward or punishment, and how will they do this? Will they use verbal ridicule or merely a nonverbal frown or raised eyebrow to transmit meanings of disapproval? Will the others reward a good comment with nonverbal immediacy—eye contact, a smile, a nod—or will they express their approval in verbal terms? Many messages of control are those used more generally by people communicating in other contexts, but some control system will characterize the group, and its dimensions are defined in the forming stage.

Storming: The Stage of Emerging Conflict

The orientation activities of the forming stage shift almost inevitably into one in which *conflict* emerges. Some participants may not accept certain individuals as qualified, of higher rank or competence. Others may construct a negative implicit personality and dislike one or more fellow members. Still others may not want to participate at all, or may want to shift topics, go about achieving the goal in a different way, and so on. Resentments may develop over perceived attempts at social control when negative feelings are aroused as controlling messages are transmitted. Of special importance at this stage is the emergence of a leader and a style of leadership.

Norming: The Stage of Stabilization

After the group has worked its way through whatever conflicts arise, the members will have established the initial images—implicit personalities—they have developed for one another. In addition, they will have achieved definitions of self that are applicable within the group. This brings greater accuracy in role-taking and more predictability in interpreting feedback from verbal and nonverbal messages that are received and returned. At this point, members can move on from the process of sizing one another up and start resolving the conflicts that were generated in the earlier stages. Once they do this, they can deal with the group as a reasonably predictable pattern of social relationships and turn to their task.

Performing: The Stage of Task Achievement

With the group now stabilized, the task for which the participants came together can be addressed fully. Participants at this stage examine various proposed solutions, and they come together in consensus about the one they believe to be best. Not all groups go through these precise stages. Nevertheless, anticipating them can be particularly useful for understanding communication in small groups when participants do not know one another well and have been brought together to accomplish some purpose or goal. Many of the task-oriented groups described in this chapter will undergo some set of similar transitions, and these stages may be found to some degree, even in more formal decision-making groups where communication follows a more structured pattern of social organization.

Informal Communication in Small, Intimate Groups

Not all small groups are alike. We have already discussed the peer group, and we mentioned the family. We noted that both are critical in the lives of all of us and both are contexts in which intimate communication takes place. The factor of intimacy is critical to understanding human relationships within these primary groups and how they develop into intimacy over a period of time. Recall from Chapter 5 ("Communicating Interpersonally") that people sort out and select each other, and then become involved increasingly in self-disclosure and personal communication. In this chapter the approach is also *developmental*, looking at primary groups in terms of the rich functions they serve and the objectives they achieve for their participants.

The messages transmitted and received within both family and peer groups serve as critical sources that provide us with our deepest understandings of other human beings and how to relate to them.[13] It is not always easy to see that communication occurring in such groups has very basic goals. Most people simply carry on their activities within such groups without consciously thinking about them in terms of communication and its consequences. Nevertheless, those consequences are very real and very important—so important that we could not develop as fully functioning members of our community and society without deep involvement in small and intimate groups. More specifically, our family and our closest friends share the goal of shaping our psychological and social development in a variety of ways.

Communicating within the Family

The family is the most basic of all human groups. It is the context within which the first steps toward communication take place. The family is the great teacher of the symbols and rules of meaning that are the foundations of social life. Thus, the family has always been the principal source for learning vocabulary and linking symbols, meanings, and referents so that new members of society could take the first steps in communicating. Today, it is within the family that we sort out and learn the complexities of grammar and syntax.

The acquisition of language allows the child to begin participating in the mainstream culture of larger groups and to start internalizing the beliefs and understandings of the physical, spiritual, and social world. Language acquisition also allows the child to participate in specific specialized cultures with which the family identifies. Thus, the family functions as the primary group in our communication experience.

Learning language in family situations permits us to participate in the entire communication process of a society. Taken together, all these cultural and group influences, plus the learning experiences we acquire as we mature, can be discussed as **socialization.** The term *socialization* refers to those long-term processes of communication within which deliberate or unintended and indirect lessons are internalized, enabling the person to become a unique human being, a functioning member of society, and a participant in its general and unique cultures.[14]

Three aspects of human development are involved in this definition of the socialization process. These are that communication in family situations represents our initial sources of **personality, social expectations,** and **enculturation.** These terms are central to an understanding of both the process and the consequences of communication, especially in small and intimate groups.

Psychologists developed the term *personality* to refer to the individual's enduring organization of meanings, motivations, emotional patterns, orientations, skills, and all other personal attributes that give that individual a unique psychological makeup. Personality, in other words, is composed of *"the individual's distinctive, consistent, patterned methods of relating to the environment."*[15] What this implies

is that each person has a unique psychological make-up. Some people are serious and others are happy-go-lucky. Some are driven to succeed and others are lazy. Some are smart and others are dense. In other words, there is an enormous list of psychological attributes or **personality traits** on which people individually differ.[16] Long before there were psychologists, people commonly identified such individual differences with terms like *stingy, generous, smart,* and *lively,* to describe observable and predictable features of a person's behavior over time. Psychologists have developed many additional and more technical terms, such as *introverted, hyperactive,* and *anal-retentive,* but the idea is the same: People exhibit more or less enduring and predictable patterns of behavior as characteristics of their personalities.

As the above discussion of family communication suggests, personality is not inherited. We must acquire (that is, *learn*) it through our experiences in many kinds of social contexts and situations. The people around us, either directly or via various media, communicate (deliberately or not) a great variety of lessons about what we should think; how we should express our emotions; and what we should value, despise, accept, reject, understand, and so on. This process—including the presentation of lessons, their content, the act of learning, and our resulting personalities—is what is meant by *socialization.*

Socialization is also the source of *social expectations,* that is, our insights into how people expect us to behave in a pattern of social organization of a particular group. Through communicating in social situations, the individual comes to understand the norms, roles, ranks, and controls of various groups. This development of internalized social understandings is one way that socialization makes the individual similar to others. Although this seems contradictory, common sense tells us that all kinds of people, regardless of their individual personality differences, learn to conform to the everyday requirements of social life. By communicating in various social situations and contexts,

How does your family as a group make decisions, and how will those early learning experiences affect your decision making in your own family later?

we learn what others expect us to do in many kinds of groups, sports teams, families, friendship cliques, and so on. Thus, socialization produces both *uniqueness* and *similarity*.

Finally, enculturation also takes place in the socialization process, reducing individuality even further. To be accepted as members of their society, individuals must be keenly aware of that society's way of life—its general or mainstream culture. This includes not only language skills, but also the shared beliefs, emotional orientations, attitudes, values, and every-thing else that make people fit in socially. Overall, enculturation represents a very basic transformation of the individual. As anthropologist Ruth Benedict put it in her classic 1934 analysis *Patterns of Culture,*

> By the time [a child] can talk, he is the little creature of his culture, and by the time he is grown

and able to take part in its activities, its habits are his habits, its beliefs are his beliefs, its impossibilities his impossibilities.[17]

By the same means, children learn the basics of unique specialized cultures in which their families participate. These may involve distinctive languages, values, styles of dress, diets, and many other practices that are different from those of the mainstream culture. These may be associated with race, religion, ethnicity, region, or even socioeconomic level in the society.

In short, the rich communication processes that take place within family situations pro-vide the foundations for our developing mental processes, equipping us to engage in self-communication (thinking, recalling, and reasoning). They also provide our initial exposure to shared social understandings and cultural rules that enable us to engage in goal-oriented activities with other individuals.

Communicating with Peers

As discussed earlier, the family is not the only primary group. *Peer groups* also provide the individual with vital information about the physical and social world. Friends of the same general age and status give us an intimate primary group outside the family. This is very important during early childhood, and peer groups remain critical to our well-being throughout our lives. Through communication in peer groups, individuals improve and maintain their role-taking skills and their ability to interpret feedback.

In the context of young children's groups on street corners, in schoolyards, and on playgrounds, individuals gain deeper understandings of how the messages they initiate influence others and what their friends' responses imply about the meanings they are reconstructing. Their critical skills in message construction, nonverbal communication, and understanding meanings intended by others are sharpened. Thus, by communicating in this peer "society-in-miniature," children learn what words, gestures, and actions make others angry, what causes them to smile or laugh; what brings respect or conveys dishonor; and what establishes one person as a leader or defines another as a follower. These are critical consequences of intimate communication in small groups.

The influence of peer groups does not stop with childhood. During the entire life cycle, people communicate in peer groups to achieve goals they seldom articulate and may never have tried to understand. If asked, their likely reply would be they simply want to enjoy their friends or have fun. Thus, members of such groups communicate among themselves simply for the pleasures that the process provides—the companionship and personal fulfillment that cannot be obtained in other ways. In such groups, communication provides a bonding among members that is its own reward.

Patterns of Communication in Small, Intimate Groups

This section describes the typical rules of informal communication that tend to develop within intimate groups. These rules guide and limit the spontaneous and unrestrained transmissions and receptions of messages that take place among members. The term *informal* means the absence of deliberately designed barriers or constraints—communication that is spontaneous and unrestrained. This is the kind of self-disclosing communication that takes place between good friends, family members on good terms, and friendly work associates.

The fact that informal communication is relatively uninhibited does not mean its social pathways are random. Even in the most intimate groups, rules dictate who can communicate to whom about what. There are always topics that are not to be discussed and times when certain issues are not to be brought up. However, those restraints are simply understood in an unspoken agreement; they are not deliberately designed prior to people entering the group. On the contrary, the members work them out as they go along and revise them as need be.

Communication *norms* are general rules that each member is expected to follow concerning what issues, topics, and modes of transmission are acceptable within the group. For example, few families or even peer groups permit members to discuss gross bodily functions at mealtimes. Sexual experiences and related topics may also be taboo. Even spontaneous and uninhibited primary groups impose a surprising number of limitations on what, how, when, and in what manner specific messages can be transmitted.

A second set of patterned expectations in intimate groups defines individual communication *roles*. That is, what specific person has the right to transmit particular kinds of messages, and who must pay attention to them. One person will usually talk and make decisions about certain areas of concern while another will initiate more messages about other issues. These areas may include such matters as automobiles, food, child rearing, income, and recreation. On the other hand, although one person may initiate more suggestions and proposals, another may be the one who gives final approval.

The roles of husband, wife, child, and even relatives in the contemporary family are more than simply a matter of agreements among members about who will be permitted or expected to say what to whom. Cultural traditions (backed by legal requirements) prepare people, long before marriage and parenthood, for the specialized parts they will be expected to play in the communication patterns of the family. No particular family fits the general model exactly. That is, when unique individuals come together to act out the parts of husband and wife to communicate about family matters, they modify the general model by developing consensus around their own definitions. These, then, become shared within the new group.

In many ways, the role expectations that develop among intimate friends follow parallel patterns to those that characterize the family. All cultures define how friends are expected to communicate with one another, and these serve as general guides for individuals in small groups of close associates. There is vast latitude in the way that one individual can communicate with another in intimate ways. Thus, peer roles have the most flexible of all communication rules found in intimate groups.

Many differences exist in the social *ranks* within intimate groups—hierarchies of authority, power, and privilege. Ranks may not always be easy to detect, but they clearly govern communication within families. Their nature depends on the specialized culture of the specific family involved. One partner may be sternly dominant, constantly transmitting orders, with the other partner feeding back messages of submissiveness. In another, a true partnership may evolve, in which both individuals communicate fully and openly about sharing power, cooperating on household chores, and earning income.

An emerging general model in the United States is the *democratic* pattern, in which the ranks of both adults in the family are the same and each has an equal voice. The children's position is less clear: In some cases they have considerable voice in family affairs; in others, they remain subordinate. In all families, however, some structure of rank has been established that governs their messages.

In friendship groups, the communication rules related to rank tend to be more subtle. People reject the idea that their close friends can order them around. Nevertheless, there is a ranking pattern in every group. Even close friends must make decisions. For example, if all members decide to go to a football game, there is the problem of where they will meet, whose car they will drive, and what they will do afterward. Usually, one individual will suggest a plan and the others will agree to it. This is leadership (higher rank) in a very subtle form. If a party is to be held, there are the questions of location, who will bring what, at what time, and who will be invited. Again, one individual is likely to emerge as the person in control.

Ranking and power in the context of the intimate group of friends also illustrates the broader problem of *authority*. It is in miniature the same problem that Thomas Hobbes wrote about in his *Leviathan* centuries ago.[18] Essentially his idea was that someone has to be in charge. If members of a group refuse to accept the orders, commands, or even suggestions of another member, then chaos and anarchy prevail. It is more convenient to look to a particular individual, in whom the members have confidence, as a source for direction. If a particular individual holds such a position, he or she is informally vested by the members with authority (the principle developed by Hobbes).

The rules for communicating in intimate groups are maintained through process of *social control*. This takes place through the use of *sanctions*—rewards for compliance and punishments for deviance. Sanctions, or control messages, can range from nonverbal signals of approval or disapproval to verbal praise or abuse.

Mainly, however, the communication of controls in intimate groups tends to be subtle.

Communicating to establish or maintain social control in the family can be a complex process. In the traditional family, if measures were needed to control the behavior of an errant child, the father got out the razor strap, took the offender by the ear to the woodshed, and soundly communicated a physical message to the child's posterior. In most families today, however, verbal and nonverbal messages are substituted for woodshed controls and other unacceptable forms of punishment. Instead, parents may use frowns or smiles, scoldings or praise, "grounding," no TV or video games, confinement to room, or other restrictions.

Adult members of families also use special communication categories as rewards and punishments. Simply ignoring another individual, or looking at the person with a stony stare, can arouse meaning. A raised eyebrow, or a glare, can speak volumes under some circumstances. On the other hand, such rewards as pats, strokes, hugs, flowers, candy, and many other kinds of nonverbal communication express approval and elicit emotional responses. Members of families develop sensitive skills at reading the intent and meanings of social control behind such transmissions.

Transmitting social control can be equally subtle in peer groups. Groups of friends do not resort to violence to enforce their rules. Most positive and negative sanctions are expressed in very subtle ways. Whatever modes of communication the group uses—verbal or nonverbal, violent or gentle, subtle or blatant—messages expressing approval and disapproval are the means used to stabilize its communication rules.

Communicating in Task-Oriented Discussion Groups

There is a large number of task-oriented groups in which people are brought together as participants to communicate and get something done.

In each case, they seek to achieve some goal that has been deliberately set as an objective.

Informal versus Formal Discussion Groups

Some task-oriented groups are devoted to *informal discussions* among people who know each other well. One example would be a group of friends who get together to discuss planning a surprise birthday party. Another would be a group of friends who meet at one of their homes for coffee and goodies to try to work out some sort of plan to get the city to do something about the parking problem on their street. The pattern of social organization is not highly structured. The norms, roles, ranks, and controls are not rigid, and any member can chime in at any time with a suggestion or comment.

Other small task-oriented discussion groups are highly structured in that their communication follows a formal pattern of social organization. Examples here would be a jury, a colloquium or a symposium. Such formal discussion groups can be private or public. A private group is illustrated by a business conference within a particular company, where systematic presentations and exchanges of comments take place about confidential policies and problems. In contrast, a public discussion group is a situation in which audiences observe proceedings, or perhaps even participate. Examples are scientific panels or symposia.

An important kind of task-oriented small group is devoted to *reaching consensus* so that a formal decision can be made. Here the pattern of social organization is often laid out in formal documents that prescribe procedures to be carefully followed. Examples are university committees, corporate boards of directors, courtroom trial juries, and permanent councils in religious groups. In this type of group, the goal is to arrive at orderly judgments on the basis of well-regulated discussion. Many of these groups communicate privately, for the purpose of, say, allocating scarce resources, evaluating people's performance, and achieving consensus on the truth of a situation. They usually operate within some large organization or social system. Such groups usually have a highly formalized pattern of social organization, with norms, roles, ranks, and so forth specified in official documents.

Small, Task-Oriented Discussion Groups with Specific Objectives

There are a great many different types of small task-oriented groups that focus on some *specific objective*. Each is different in terms of the kinds of people involved, the goals its members seek to accomplish and the way in which communication proceeds among them. They can also differ in the degree to which their pattern of social organization is formal or informal.

A **round table** is a task-oriented small group in which diverse views on a topic or issue are discussed among a small group of participants.

The members are typically experts or representatives of special interests. In the round table, there is no audience and the participants usually sit in a circle. Communication is usually informal, with limited rules and no formally designated leader.

Another small task-oriented discussion group is the **panel**. In many ways, it resembles the round table, but it is public rather than private. Panel participants tend to be experts or representatives of special interests. The panel is usually coordinated in a formal way by a moderator, and the discussion usually takes place before a live audience. Sometimes questions are taken from the audience after panel members have commented. Panels can be presented to audiences via videoconferencing allowing participants to submit questions. Panels seldom reach firm decisions, but they present

How does a round-table discussion differ from other task-oriented groups?

alternative interpretations and insights, and their discussion may help audience members understand the issues.

A very formal and public small task-oriented group is the **symposium.** This is a discussion group only in a limited sense. Usually a symposium has some unifying theme—a problem or an issue that is being addressed. The participants are typically a small group of experts who are knowledgeable about the theme. They are introduced by a moderator, and each then makes a speech about the theme. The participants seldom talk with one another—even between presentations. Instead, they simply take their turn delivering their views. Sometimes the symposium takes questions from members of the audience afterward. Later, the presentations of the participants are often published as a set of proceedings or a book.

One of the oldest of all small task-oriented groups is the **seminar.** It originated with the ancient Greeks. Plato used this type of group as a teaching format. He and his students strolled through the grounds of his *Academy* and each student took a turn at addressing a central issue or question that was the focus of discussion.[19] The mentor then distilled the important lessons that could be derived from the body of the comments. Seminars remain an important teaching format in higher education, where candidates for doctoral degrees often participate in exchanges that are similar to those used by Plato. Seminars usually have regular meetings over a lengthy period of time, a clear organization, and an intellectual leader who coordinates the discussions of students.

Another small-group discussion format is the **forum.** It combines features of the round table, panel, and symposium. It is a one-time event and somewhat less formal than the panel, round table, or symposium. In the forum, there are usually brief presentations by a small group, each of whose members is introduced by a chairperson. Their presentations are followed by considerable audience participation, again coordinated by the chair. The forum is a favorite format on college campuses because it allows a great deal of audience participation.

A widely used small discussion group context is the **small group conference.** In typical small group conferences, several participants are brought together, usually privately. Their purpose is to share technical information or to discuss some problem in their area of expertise. Such conferences are common in corporations or agencies where solutions to problems can be worked out together. They are also common among professionals such as physicians, lawyers, and engineers. Today, video conferences are commonplace, allowing people to engage in reasonably full and accurate communication at a distance.

Other specialized groups include *buzz groups* or *brainstorming sessions.* Participants—often middle managers or supervisors—review a problem, issue, topic, plan, or policy to see whether the group can come up with a solution or improvement. During the decades following World War II, in industrial settings, another group adopted from the Japanese emerged. In *quality circles,* employees get together periodically in small groups to discuss ways to improve their work. Their suggestions are passed on to management.

Still another is the *focus group,* which is essentially a format in research—particularly of the kind done by the advertising and market research industries. Typically, a small group of consumers is brought together to discuss a new product, or proposed package design, so that the researchers can gain insight into ways to make the product more acceptable and more profitable.[20]

In the treatment of a variety of human problems, the **therapy group** is used by counseling psychologists who try to make people feel better through communication. The goal of the participants is to engage in self-disclosive discussions that will assist members who have personal problems. They might discuss drug addiction, excessive gambling, alcoholism, smoking, loss of a loved one, or abuse of or by one's spouse, to name a few of many possibilities. Participants meet with a coordinator who usually has some special insight into the problem. The underlying assumption is that if people who share a common problem get together and disclose their experiences, thoughts, and feelings, it will help all of them feel better as they gain insight into their difficulty and learn to deal with it more effectively.

Patterns of Communication in Task-Oriented Groups

The rules for communicating in all types of task-oriented groups involve the same concepts of social organization previously identified—norms, roles, ranks, and controls.

Norms. No single set of communication norms governs message transmission across the many kinds of task-oriented groups that exist.

When using an authoritarian style of leadership, the goals, policies, and activities of the group are determined solely by the leader.

The rules for communicating in each context are set by the sociocultural situation—that is, rules are defined broadly by the goal or purpose of the group. In such forms as the round table, panel, and symposium, the norms are usually predesigned, which means that their communication requirements are derived from traditions. When participants are recruited, they are expected to follow those traditional forms. However, each person will bring his or her own personal style and interpretations to those rules. One may joke and be lighthearted, whereas another will be subdued or serious.[21]

Roles. Many kinds of communication roles have been identified in task-oriented groups. A classic analysis of such roles is that of communication scholars Kenneth Benne and Paul Sheats.[22] They proposed three general categories, which depend on what members tend to do repetitively: *task-related* roles (opinion seeker, initiator, or energizer); such as *group building and maintenance (*encourager, harmonizer, and gatekeeper), and, *individual* roles (aggressor, help-seeker, recognition-seeker).

Of particular interest to communication scholars is the role of *leader* in discussion groups. Typically, in the task-oriented type of groups listed above, a leader emerges to take charge and coordinate the group's activities. The questions of how leaders emerge, what kinds of characteristics they have, and what consequences result from their styles are of profound importance.

Classic research suggests that three basic styles of leadership can be found in task-oriented discussion groups: *authoritarian, democratic,* and *laissez-faire.*[23] Box 6.3 will help you assess your leadership style.

In the *authoritarian style,* all goals, policies, and activities of the group are determined solely by the leader, including which members work together. She or he is personal in praise and criticism but tends to remain aloof. This type of leader sets the goal, decides who will do what to get there, and defines the techniques by which success will be achieved.

BOX 6.3   *Assessing Your Leadership Style*

Directions: Listed below are seven pairs of statements about how you might approach leading a small group. After reading each pair of statements, indicate which statement you believe to be of greater importance to you. When reacting to the statements, observe the following ground rules:

1. Do NOT omit any of the items.
2. Never check both of the items.
3. Do not look back and forth through the items; make each item a separate and independent judgement.
4. Only record your first, immediate impression.

For each of the following statements in each pair, which do you place greater importance in your role as group leader?

1. _____ To give everyone a chance to express his/her opinion.
   _____ To know what the group and its membership are doing.
2. _____ To assign members to tasks so more can be accomplished.
   _____ To let members reach a decision all by themselves.
3. _____ To know what the group and its membership are doing.
   _____ To help members see how the discussion is related to the purposes of the group.

4. _____ To assist the group in getting along well together.
   _____ To help the group to what you think is their best answer.
5. _____ To get the job done.
   _____ To let the members reach a decision all by themselves.
6. _____ To know what the group and its members are doing.
   _____ To let the members reach a decision all by themselves.
7. _____ To get the job done.
   _____ To assist the group in getting along well together.
8. _____ To help the members see how the discussion is related to the purposes of the group.
   _____ To assign members to tasks so more can be accomplished.
9. _____ To ask questions that will cause members to do more thinking.
   _____ To get the job done.
10. _____ To let the members reach a decision all by themselves.
   _____ To give new information when you feel the members are ready for it.

Where the *democratic style* is used by the leader, group members discuss prospective policies and then determine them by vote. The leader provides technical advice on how to proceed when needed, but members are free to divide themselves into work teams for specific tasks. The leader is balanced and objective in praise and criticism, tries to be like other members to some degree, but does not do much of the actual work. A democratic leader takes people where they already want to go: He or she helps them determine what that is, the best steps to take to get there, and then coordinates their efforts so that the goal will be achieved.

The leader using the *laissez-faire style* is "laid back" and does little to interfere with the choices or activities of members. The leader lets the group go whatever way it wishes, even if this leads to mistakes. Little visible authority or power is exercised, and the leader does not provide much criticism or reward. All the leader does is answer members' questions and give advice when asked.

In assessing the implications for these styles of leadership in small group discussions, real differences emerge.[24] The bonds between members tend to be stronger in the democratic group because the experience results in greater

Calculating Your Score:

1. For each pair of 10 items, there are two possible responses. One response represents a "democratic" orientation; the other is "autocratic" or authoritarian. Label the democratic responses "D" and the autocratic responses "A" according to the following key:

Item 1: Choice 1 = D Choice 2 = A
Item 2: Choice 1 = A Choice 2 = D
Item 3: Choice 1 = A Choice 2 = D
Item 4: Choice 1 = D Choice 2 = A
Item 5: Choice 1 = A Choice 2 = D
Item 6: Choice 1 = A Choice 2 = D
Item 7: Choice 1 = A Choice 2 = D
Item 8: Choice 1 = D Choice 2 = A
Item 9: Choice 1 = D Choice 2 = A
Item 10: Choice 1 = D Choice 2 = A

2. Next, score a "1" for each "D," and a "0" for each "A." In other words, you get no points for A responses, but 1 point for each D response you made.

3. Finally, add together your total points across all 10 items. Your Total Score = _____.

Interpreting Your Score:

Possible range of scores for the Leadership Scale is: 0–10. (If your own final score does not fall within that range, you made a computational error.)

The higher your score, the more democratic your own group leadership behavior should be. In particular, if your total score was 8 or better, your leadership style is more egalitarian. That is, democratic leaders encourage more group participation, ask for individual input or feedback, and ensure that everyone has an equal opportunity to be heard. Group members feel greater cohesiveness, are more committed toward the group decision, and appreciate working within the group.

Lower scores, 3 or below, reflect more of an autocratic or authoritarian leadership style. If your own score reveals an authoritarian style, you can expect group members to like you less, feel much less satisfaction toward the group, and show less commitment toward the group outcome. On the other hand, authoritarian leaders "get the job done" quickly and efficiently. Authoritarian leaders are more interested in the outcome than they are in people's input or feelings.

Source: This scale was adapted from:
Sargent, F., & Miller, G. R. (1971). Some differences in certain communication behaviors of autocratic and democratic group leaders. *Journal of Communication, 21,* 233–252.

member satisfaction. On the other hand, there is typically less progress toward achieving solutions under this type of leadership. The authoritarian group accomplishes the most in the shortest time, but members tend to achieve their goals in a less original way, and they are less satisfied. The laissez-faire style is less efficient than either of the other two, and it tends to produce the lowest levels of member satisfaction.

What are some of the factors that result in a particular person becoming a leader? There are two answers: One is that the person has *special qualities* or leadership traits. These are personal characteristics that people admire and respect, attributes of personality that are the basis of leadership. This "trait theory" of leadership has been widely studied and seems to be true in many cases.[25] A second answer is that *situations*, rather than personal traits, determine leadership. If this is correct, different types of people (regardless of their individual traits) will be successful leaders in distinctive social circumstances. This interpretation also has merit.

A dramatic leader with a lot of *charisma* (attractive personal traits) may be just what is required in one situation, but entirely inappropriate in another. A different situation may best be served by a technically proficient but relatively inconspicuous individual. Thus, the best explanation for how and why some people become leaders seems to be that commanding personal characteristics do determine leadership in some situations, but in others, technical competence, insight into organizing work, and other factors are important.

Ranks. Because there are so many types of task-oriented groups, one set of observations will not fit all in terms of how social ranks influence communication patterns.[26] In more formally organized groups, such as panels and symposia, members with formal roles of leadership and coordination are obviously in a position to control the flow of messages. Ranking is less clear in discussion groups in which members presumably start on an equal basis.

What often happens is that the person's social position and prestige *outside* the group play a significant part in determining rank within a discussion group. Thus, for example, a physician, a person in a high-prestige occupation, will almost automatically have greater authority in a small discussion group than, say, a dishwasher, or any other person in a low-prestige occupation. Much the same occurs with respect to personal attributes that are ranked by prestige in the community. Thus, in discussion groups, men sometimes appear to have an edge over women, and tall and imposing people may, at first, be listened to with greater conviction than short and small people. In addition, elderly people and people representing ethnic minorities may often be at a disadvantage. Finally, attractive people sometimes are afforded more authority than unattractive people.

Controls. In small discussion groups social controls take many forms. All the principles of communication set forth in earlier chapters govern the expectations of who can say what to whom in a task-oriented group. These expectations are enforced with feedback and with verbal comments and nonverbal signs, just as in any other type of communication. Nodding and smiling can encourage a person to keep talking, whereas sneers, eye rolling, frowns, and slumping can discourage comments. Thus, the group transmits various messages to control the topics of discussion, the performance of roles, and the rankings of the members.

Communicating in Formal Decision-Making Groups

One of the most important and useful small-group discussion formats in our society is that used for formal decision making. The goals of formal decision-making groups are easy to identify, define, and discuss. The manner in which this kind of small group is formed helps to identify its goals: Formal decision-making groups are deliberately constituted to serve decision-making needs of an organization, a community or even the larger society within which they operate.

The members of formal decision-making groups are not selected by chance or for convenience. Usually, their participation is requested, assigned, or even ordered after some sort of screening. A board of directors, a jury, a committee, or a council is usually made up of members who have qualifications related to the goals for which the group is formed.

Goals Pursued in Formal Decision-Making Groups

What kinds of goals are pursued in the context of formal decision-making groups? Essentially, they are all related to making orderly judgments, which fall into four categories: *allocating scarce resources, evaluating performance, formulating or changing policies*, and *weighing evidence to reach the truth*.

Allocating scarce resources. Deciding on who should get resources that are in short supply is a thankless task. All large groups, such as corporations, communities, hospitals, and universities, have to determine who gets what share of their space, time, effort, money, or some other valued commodity. To handle such problems, committees are formed. These small, deliberately designed groups are formally charged with the goal of making recommendations, or reaching final decisions, regarding such matters as approving budget allocations, awarding research grants or prizes, approving loans, providing scholarships, and admitting students to educational programs.

In some organizations, one person is assigned the task of allocating space or upgrading computer technology. In such a system, only a few individuals at the top can command the best, making life difficult for the single decision maker. A convenient solution is to appoint a committee to consider requests for more or better space. Although the decisions reached by such a committee may be identical with those of a single decision maker, at least the claimants can feel that their appeals were examined fairly by qualified individuals.

Such committees don't always achieve such an acceptable outcome. Some groups can act either stupidly or unfairly. However, decisions made by a group have a higher probability of being objective, fair, and intelligent than those made by a single individual.

Evaluating performance. A very difficult task in large organizations is deciding who meets designated standards of performance and to what degree. No issue has more emotional significance than assessing merit—deciding whether people have been doing a good job or a poor job. Such judgments lead to the granting and withholding of salary raises, promotions, titles, or other rewards. In some cases, evaluations can lead to job terminations. Even awarding lesser perquisites—a desirable parking space, access to a special dining room, or a key to a restricted bathroom—can provoke emotional reactions. Consequently, small groups or committees assume this responsibility.

Formulating or changing policy. Establishing or changing the formal rules that guide how organizations do things is another task often assigned to a formal decision-making group. This may involve planning the objectives, strategies, and directions that an organization will take. Powerful policy groups of this type are almost always found at the top of the power structure within large organizations. For example, the armed services have the Joint Chiefs of Staff, and the president has the Cabinet and White House staff of personal advisors. At local levels, every bank, agency, and corporation has a board of directors who are responsible for major decisions, new policies, and changes in direction. A local church will have a committee of lay people who advise the clergy. Even the smallest businesses, if they are incorporated under the laws of most states, must have boards of directors that hold annual meetings.

Weighing evidence to reach the truth. Our society could not operate without groups that weigh facts in order to reach the truth. The trial jury is the most obvious example of a task-oriented group whose goal is to make orderly judgments about guilt or innocence, culpability or lack of responsibility. Coming from an ancient tradition, the use of a small group to weigh evidence and decide guilt or innocence has proved to be efficient over many centuries. Conveniently, truth becomes what a jury says it is—after discussion—even if it is wrong! The jury system is by no means foolproof. However, most people believe that it is the most acceptable of available alternatives. The organization of juries and selection of participants is well understood, but the communication processes by which they reach decisions are less so.

There are other kinds of fact-reviewing and truth-seeking small groups that are formally constituted to reach decisions. Examples are the federally operated Department of Transportation. If there is a major train wreck or an airplane crash, fact-finding experts are assembled. They sift through evidence and attempt to determine the cause of the accident. Other small groups, such as scientific panels, review information concerning new drugs, insecticides, and land use proposals.

Patterns of Communication in Formal Decision-Making Groups

Although there is great variation in the rules for communication in task-oriented discussion groups, the formal decision-making group is another matter. Key features characterize communication rules in this type of context. These features reflect the fact that such groups are typically formed within a larger organization, whose purposes they are designed to serve. As has been explained, small formal groups are necessary for reaching conclusions about resources, performance, policies, proposals, and other matters in all kinds of large contemporary organizations.

The most obvious feature of small decision-making groups is that they are deliberately formed and conducted in such a way that they use carefully defined codes as rules of communication. Thus, in such groups, communication is *formal.*

There are several official versions of coded rules for formal communication, but the most widely used are those developed by Henry Marlyn Roberts, a 19th-century army engineer. Following the Civil War, Roberts was active in civic affairs and presided over debates in a number of nongovernmental groups. At the time, these debates were chaotic because there were no clear rules for discussion and collective decision making, other than those used by official governmental bodies.

Roberts studied the formalized rules for communication used in the British Parliament and the U.S. Congress. He simplified them and produced a short set of guidelines for conducting formal meetings. They seemed to work rather well, and he had them printed up in 1876 under the title *A Pocket Manual of Rules of Order for Deliberative Assemblies.* To meet the growing demand, Roberts sold the rights to a publisher, and it was first marketed in 1896 as *Robert's Rules of Order.* The book quickly became the world's standard, as the "official" rules to be followed in formal decision-making groups. Over more than a century, the work

has been revised many times and has sold more than 3 million copies.[27] Essentially, what *Robert's Rules* provides is a clear pattern of social organization, with norms, roles, ranks, and controls.

Robert's Rules sets forth very clearly a number of *clearly codified norms* that any such group must follow.[28] Some have to do with what constitutes a *quorum*—a sufficient number of members present so that official business can be conducted. Others describe procedures for asking for the *floor,* ways to present proposals. One doesn't say to the group, "Hey, can I talk now?" *Robert's Rules* requires that a plea for the group's attention be phrased as a formal request to have the floor. A member can speak only if recognized by the *chair,* and while he or she speaks, others cannot simply blurt out casual remarks. If they do, they will be ruled *out of order* by the chair, and their comments will be disregarded when discussion of a proposal is allowed. Other norms specify how to call for a vote and ways in which a particular motion can be taken *off the table.*

In decision-making groups using formally coded rules for communicating, *roles* are clearly defined. For example, the role of leader is labeled "the chair." Others in the group can be *delegates* (of some other body) or *representatives* (of some constituency). If the group is very small, they are more likely to be called simply *members.* Formal terms of address related to these roles are deemed appropriate. The chair decides whether proposals for action, or possible solutions to problems, have been communicated to the group in the form of motions. Only after the motion is seconded and the chair indicates that discussion is appropriate can comments or discussion take place. The official rules, then, tightly control both the nature and the flow of messages among people in specific roles.

The *ranks* specifying a hierarchy of power in a formal decision-making group are well defined, and power in the group is not uniformly distributed. At the bottom, below the regular members, is a rank that may include nonvoting members, such as a secretary, who does not participate in debate but is responsible for keeping the *minutes* (an accurate record of all transactions). There may also be a sergeant at arms, whose duties are restricted to controlling unruly members if necessary, although this seldom exists in small groups.

Generally, the largest stratum or level of a group is made up of voting members, and they do have both power and authority. For example, they can offer motions, or amendments to motions, that are persuasive and that capture votes. Through effective presentation of arguments, they can create consensus or conflict regarding a particular issue.

The greatest power is vested in the chair. For example, under formal rules, the chair controls the *agenda*—the topics and issues that will be discussed. The chair can add items to the list, remove or keep off other items, move one item up the list for earlier consideration, or delay discussion or votes on others. Debate can be restricted or extended by the chair, remarks can be ruled out of order, and certain members can be recognized ahead of others. Finally, only the chair has the power to cast the deciding vote in the event of a tie.

Official codes provide ample means for exercising *social control* over members with the use of explicit messages. For example, if a member performs a task for the group particularly well, a *resolution* commending the member may be brought to a vote. If it passes, it is entered into the minutes. On the negative side, critical messages about a motion or a participant's conduct can be offered by an irate member. A member judged to be deviant may be criticized in a specifically worded *motion of censure*, which, if passed by vote, is placed in the official minutes. Beyond this, resignations are sometimes requested. If communication completely breaks down and, for example, a fistfight erupts, a sergeant at arms may have to eject the offenders physically from the meeting. It is not surprising that groups employing integrative conflict management styles tend to make more effective decisions than groups using confrontational methods.[29]

Group Cohesion and Disorganization

The final questions asked in this chapter are: What keeps groups together? What causes them to break down? In every kind of group there are factors that move the participants to maintain their membership and to perform the activities required of them. That binding condition, which is called *group cohesion,* can range from very strong to very weak. As long as the basis of that cohesion is present, members will maintain their memberships and try to achieve whatever goals they are collectively pursuing. If cohesion erodes, the group will begin to break down. Thus, group disorganization often stems from bad communication processes rather than from bad people.

Distinct Bases of Cohesion

Social scientists who study group organization and disorganization have identified four distinct bases of cohesion.[30] The one that is fundamental to intimate groups is **sentiment-based cohesion.** A second, which characterizes the small task-oriented group, is **reward-based cohesion.** A third, called **assignment-based cohesion,** is found in the formal decision-making group. Finally, a fourth variety is *dependency-based cohesion.* This type of cohesion is not typical of small groups but is a condition that is found in large impersonal organizations where a complex division of labor provides interdependency among the system of roles. For that reason, it will be not be discussed here, but will be explained in Chapter 7.[31]

Sentiment-based cohesion in intimate groups. This type of cohesion is based on bonds of affection generated within the group. In a highly cohesive group, the members feel a deep sense of loyalty and obligation to one another. They willingly set aside their personal interests, modify their expectations for the welfare of the group, and are ready to make sacrifices for the other members.[32] In such groups each member is valued not just for a role that he or she can play but as a person. Disruption of the group by illness, death, or other circumstances is a matter of deep emotional concern. Commitment to the group's goals is very strong.

Such powerful cohesion is not universal in small intimate groups. In some, individuals can be tied less deeply to the other members. This can be true in either families or peer groups. In such cases, individuals may value their membership, but they do not feel their bonds so intensely. For this reason, the strength of sentiment-based cohesion varies.

Reward-based cohesion in discussion groups. Discussion groups are seldom held together because of the strong feelings participants have for one another. Here, member satisfaction of a personal nature provides reward-based cohesion. People continue, for instance, in therapy or weight-loss groups because they derive personal rewards by maintaining membership. By participating, they feel better, learn important information, or gain beneficial skills. If there are no such personal rewards, the participants will likely drop out of the group. If people do not want what the group is trying to achieve or if they are getting little out of membership, they will not remain.

Assignment-based cohesion in decision-making groups. People who wind up on the same committee or board of directors are not necessarily bound by strong feelings for one another. In fact, they may be relative strangers or may even actively despise one another. Furthermore, they may see no personal benefit in participation. Yet, it is possible for them to work together effectively to accomplish the group's goals. The reason for this is that these members participate because they have been assigned the task. That is, they have been asked (or ordered) to serve by some authority, they have been voted into membership by a valued constituency, or they must serve for some other valid reason.

Thus, member behavior in small decision-making groups is more likely to be cooperative than disruptive; their members seldom deliberately generate problems. The social control system of the larger organization served by the group carries into the smaller context with powerful influences on its members. People's careers, raises, promotions, and reputations are at stake. Assignment-based cohesion, then, is a condition binding a person to a group based on a willingness to work with others to accomplish goals because that has been defined as the person's duty. At the same time, people who have been assigned to work together in a decision-making group may genuinely come to like one another, and some level of sentiment-based cohesion can develop in such a group. Thus, the two types of cohesion can coexist.

Communication Breakdown and Group Disorganization

The very same factors that produce cohesion in a group can sometimes be sources of confusion and disequilibrium. Whatever the type of group, a loss of cohesion can occur if members are *unclear about its communication norms*. If these have not been effectively understood and shared, or if consensus breaks down about what kinds of messages, topics, or issues are approved and disapproved, **normative confusion** is the result. This can be a serious condition, and it can quickly result in group disorganization. In such a case, individuals lose effective guidelines, conflicts arise, and group disintegration is likely.

Another source of potential disorganization is *unclear role definitions*. Like norms, consensus and shared understandings concerning the communication requirements of the various roles in a group are achieved when members agree on who can appropriately say what to whom in what manner. If these shared understandings are inadequate or unclear, confusion about who should transmit what kinds of messages to whom will result. Whatever the type of group, such role confusion can be a major factor leading to a loss of cohesion.

Failure to gain consensus about the *legitimacy of ranks* is another source of potential disorganization. **Rank ineffectiveness** will exist if members come to believe that the messages transmitted by those in positions of power and authority lack legitimacy or credibility. Under such a condition, group coordination is impossible.

In summary, the very basis of effective control over group communication behavior lies in shared beliefs accepted by group members. Deviating from its pattern of shared expectations—its social organization—will bring disapproval of actions and messages. This can result in hostilities, departures, or rejections. Conforming to the shared expectations will result in approval or even honor. Generally, then, communication breakdown in a group is the reverse side of cohesion. This is an important principle, and it clearly implies that when things go wrong one need not attribute group disorganization to "bad actors" with problem personalities. More likely is confusion in the components of social organization that define acceptable communication.

At the same time, when individual members conform too closely to the group's pattern of social organization and do not tolerate individual differences, it can lead to problems. Communication scholars refer to a phenomenon that they call "groupthink." Obviously, only individual human beings can "think," but the basic idea is that all members of a group may come to think in the same way. They become so much in agreement that they believe that they

are always right about whatever issues come before them. This results in close agreement on issues, a belief in their own invulnerability and superiority. If this does happen, innovation in approaching problems may be lost and the ability of the group to address new problems may deteriorate. (See Box 6.4.)

BOX 6.4   *Ethical Concerns*

Groupthink as Group Breakdown

Group breakdown can also occur because of what the well-known social psychologist Irving Janis describes as *groupthink*. According to Janis, groupthink occurs when the members of a highly cohesive group reach an agreement around the dominant view that emerges during discussion; thus, they think alike, rather than reaching an agreement after members have objectively and honestly evaluated the alternative solutions to a problem. In other words, even though group members start out with different views, they quickly and rather mindlessly change their views so as to correspond with the dominant position that emerges in the group discussion. When this happens, group members are not fulfilling their responsibilities as participants; they are, in fact, behaving unethically.

Source: Janis, I. (1972). *Victims of groupthink.* Boston: Houghton Mifflin; Janis, I. (1982). *Groupthink* (2nd ed.). Boston: Houghton Mifflin.

Chapter Review

- Groups consist of three or more people who repeatedly interact, regulating their conduct within some set of rules for communication and social activity they mutually recognize and follow. People participate in groups in order to accomplish goals they could not achieve by acting alone. Different types of groups provide distinctive communication contexts with unique features.

- The study of groups is divided into two broad classes on the basis of size—small groups and (larger) organizations. Size is essential to understanding the dynamics of communication. As the number of pairs that can be formed in a group grows, it becomes difficult to maintain a full flow of communication. Many communication specialists assert that five members is the optimal size for a small group with all members participating fully.

- Intimate groups, both the family and peer groups of close friends, are sometimes called primary groups because they are earliest in the individual's experience, and they are critically involved in the individual's socialization, enculturation, and personality development.

- Social relationships among group members are controlled by the group's rules of communication. These relationships may be informal or may be formally specified as part of a deliberate design. In many kinds of discussion groups, the rules dictating who can transmit what kinds of messages when and to whom emerge through a series of stages.

- Classic research suggests that three basic styles of leadership can be found in task-oriented discussion groups: the authoritarian, democratic, and laissez-faire styles.

- There are two kinds of factors that result in a particular person becoming a leader. One is that the person has personality characteristics (traits) that people admire and respect. Another is that the situation determines leadership and that different types of people will be successful leaders in distinctive social situations.

- In every kind of group, some set of factors motivates participants to maintain their membership and to perform the activities required of them. Such group cohesion can range from very strong to very weak. As long as cohesion is present, members will try to achieve the goals of the group. If cohesion erodes, the group will break down.

Key Terms

peer group	task-oriented group	forum
primary group	socialization	small group conference
group	personality	therapy group
norms	social expectations	sentiment-based cohesion
roles	enculturation	reward-based cohesion
ranks	personality trait	assignment-based cohesion
controls	round table	normative confusion
informal communication	panel	rank ineffectiveness
formal communication	symposium	
decision-making group	seminar	

Notes

1. The term *primary group* is an old one. It was introduced into the study of communication in groups by Cooley early in the last century. See: Cooley, C. H. (1909). *Social organization* (pp. 23–31). New York: Charles Scribner's.

2. For a classic statement of this function of small and intimate groups, see: Cooley, *Social organization* (pp. 23–31).

3. Homans, G. C. (1950). *The human group* (p. 1). New York: Harcourt, Brace & Jovanovich; Brilhart, J. K. (1978). *Effective group*

discussion (pp. 20–21). Dubuque, IA: William C. Brown; Shaw, M. E. (1981). *Group dynamics: The psychology of small group behavior* (3rd ed.). New York: McGraw-Hill Myers, S. A., & Anderson, C. M. (2008). *The fundamentals of small group communication*. Thousand Oaks, CA: Sage.

4. A number of explanations have been advanced for why people choose to become members of groups. For thoughtful reviews of theories and other relevant issues related to the determinants of such membership, see: Myers & Anderson (2008); Beebe, S. A., & Masterson, J. T. (2011). *Communicating in small groups: Principles and practices* (10th ed.). Boston: Allyn & Bacon; Hirokawa, R. Y., Cathcart, R. S., Samovar, L. A., & Henman, L. D. (2003). *Small group communication: Theory and practice: An anthology* (8th ed.). New York: Oxford University Press.

5. Among communication scholars there is disagreement about whether it takes only two people to form a group, or whether it takes three or more. Sociologists point out that two people can share a common goal; can interact and communicate so as to develop distinct norms common to the two, different roles, different levels of prestige, power, or rewards; and can exercise social controls over each other to stabilize these expectations. Communication scholars prefer to call two people a *dyad*, and to reserve the term *group* for at least three people who engage in such a pattern of social organization.

6. For a detailed discussion of the nature and importance of norms, roles, ranks, and controls in the patterns of social organization in many types of groups, see: DeFleur, M. L., D'Antonio, W. V., & DeFleur, L. B. (1984) Social organization. In *Sociology: Human society*. N.Y.: Random House (pp. 72–104).

7. Bethea, L. S. (2002). The impact of an adult parent on communicative satisfaction and dyadic adjustment in the long-term marital relationship: Adult-children and spouses' retrospective accounts. *Journal of Applied Communi-cation Research, 30*, 2, 107–125.

8. The number of pairs (*p*) in any group of people can be calculated as the number of twos that can be drawn from *n* (the number of members). The formula is $[n \times (n-1)/2]$. If we care to consider combinations of more than two, such as triads or even larger coalitions that can exist in a group, the numbers become astronomical. Here, the algebraic formula is that for combinations, which is typically given as:

$$n\,C\,r = \frac{n\,(n-1)(n-2)\ldots(n-r+1)}{r!}$$

where *n* = the number of people in the group; *r* the number of people in a given coalition of, say, 3, 4, etc.

9. Fay, N., Garrod, S., & Carletta, J. (2000). Group discussion as interactive dialogue or as serial monologue: The influence of group size. *Psychological Science, 11*, 6, 481–486.

10. A classic early study is that of Bales, R. F., & Strodtbeck, F. L. (1951). Phases in group problem-solving. *Journal of Abnormal and Social Psychology, 46*, 485–495. Notable research on group decision development includes: Fisher, B. A. (1970). Decision emergence: Phases in group decision making. *Speech Monographs, 37*, 53–66; Poole, M. S. (1981). Decision development in small groups I: A comparison of two models. *Communication Monographs, 48*, 1–24; Poole, M. S. (1983). Decision development in small groups II: A study of multiple sequences in decision making. *Communication Monographs, 50*, 206–232; Poole, M. S. (1983). Decision development in small groups III: A multiple sequence model of group decision development. *Communication Monographs, 50*, 321–341; Poole, M. S., & Roth, J. (1989). Decision development in small groups IV: A typology of group decision paths. *Human Communication Research, 15*, 323–356; and Poole, M. S., & Roth, J. (1989). Decision development in small groups V: Test of a contingency model. *Human Communication Research, 15*, 549–589.

11. Bales, R. F. (1950). *Interaction process analysis: A method for the study of small groups*. Cambridge, MA: Addison-Wesley.

12. Tuckman, B. W. (1965). Development sequences in small groups. *Psychological Bulletin, 63*, 384–399.

13. For introductory-level overviews of research on communication with family see: Turner, L. H., & West, R. (2006). *Perspectives on family communication* (3rd ed.). New York:

McGraw Hill; Waldeck, J. H., Kearney, P., & Plax, T. G. (in press). *The changing American family. In Social problems*. San Diego, CA: Bridgepoint Education. For a classic theory on child-development within the family, see: Piaget, J. (1954). *The construction of reality in the child*. New York: Basic Books.

14. The term *socialization* was developed by sociologists to identify the process by which a person learns and incorporates into his or her behavior the patterns of social organization of groups in which he or she participates. These may be small and intimate groups, large and formal ones, or others in between. A related term is *enculturation*, which refers to the process by which a person understands, accepts, and incorporates into his or her behavior the features of a culture in which he or she is participating.

15. This is a typical definition. No single definition meets the approval of all social scientists and communication scholars. The present one was derived from a basic version in: Adorno, T. W., Frenkel-Brunswick, E. Levinson, D. J. & Sanford, R. N. (1950). *The authoritarian personality* (p. 5). New York: Harper & Row. See: Houston, J. B., Bee, H., & Rimm, D. C. (1983). *Invitation to psychology* (2nd ed. p. 490). New York: Academic Press. A variety of studies have been published over the years that suggest that an individual's personality influences behavior in groups. See, for example: Beckwith, J., Iverson, M. A., & Render, M. E. (1965). Test anxiety, task relevance of group experience, and change in level of aspiration. *Journal of Personality and Social Psychology, 1,* 579–588; Cartell, R. B., & Strice, G. F. (1960). *The dimensions of groups and their relations to the behavior of members*. Champaign, IL: Institute for Personality and Ability Testing; Haythorn, W. (1953). The influence of individual members on the characteristics of small groups. *Journal of Abnormal and Social Psychology, 48,* 276–284; Mann, R. D. (1959). A review of the relationships between personality and performance in small groups. *Psychological Bulletin, 56,* 241–270; and Plax, T. G., & Rosenfeld, L. B. (1976). Dogmatism and decisions involving risk. *Southern Speech Communication Journal, 41,* 266–277.

16. The seminal work on the nature and origins of personality traits is: Allport, G. W. (1937). *Personality: A psychological interpretation*. New York: Henry Holt. See especially chap. 11, A theory of traits, and chap. 12, The nature of traits, pp. 286–342.

17. Benedict, R. (1934). *Patterns of culture* (pp. 2–3). Boston: Houghton Mifflin.

18. This is, of course, a miniature version of the social contract theory of the origins of roles for behavior (laws), discussed by Thomas Hobbes in the 17th century. See: Hobbes, T. (1950). *The leviathan*. London: J. M. Dent and Sons. (First published 1651.)

19. Plato. (1941). *The Republic of Plato* (F. M. Cornford, Trans.). London: Oxford University Press.

20. For a thorough discussion of focus-group communication, see: Plax, T. G., Kearney, P., Allen, T. H., & Ross, T. (2006). Using focus groups to design a nationwide debt-management educational program. In L. Frey (Ed.), *Facilitating group communication in context: Innovations and applications with natural groups* (pp. 89–108). Cresskill, NJ: Hampton Press. Plax, T. G., & Cecchi, L. F. (1989). Manager decisions based on communication facilitated in focus groups. *Management Communication Quarterly, 2,* 511–535.

21. Robinson, D. T., & Smith, L. (2001). Getting a laugh: Gender, status, and humor in task discussions. *Social Forces, 80,* 1, 123–158.

22. Benne, K. D., & Sheats, P. (1948). Functional roles of group members. *Journal of Social Issues, 4,* 41–49. For reviews of both classic and contemporary studies on group roles, see: Moreland, R. L., & Levine, J. M. (1989). New-comers and old-timers in small groups. In P. B. Paulus (Ed.), *Psychology of group influence* (pp. 143–186). Hillsdale, NJ: Lawrence Erlbaum; Levine, J. M., & Moreland, R. L. (1990). Progress in small group research. In M. R. Rosenzweig & L. W. Porter (Eds.), *Annual review of psychology,* (pp. 585–634). Palo Alto, CA: Annual Reviews; Shaw & Gouran, *Human communication,* pp. 134–136.

23. A classic small-groups study that focused on these styles was done in 1938 under the direction of Kurt Lewin. See: Lippit, R., & White, R. K. (1958). An experimental study of leadership and group life. In E. E. Maccoby, T. M. Newcomb, &

E. L. Hartley (Eds.), *Readings in social psychology* (3rd ed.). New York: Holt. pp. 137–152.

24. For example, see: Stogdill, R. M. (1974). *Handbook of leadership: A survey of theory and research*. New York: Free Press.

25. Fiedler, F. E. (1967). *A theory of leadership effectiveness*. New York: McGraw-Hill.

26. For an excellent review of the classic investigations of personal characteristics and attributes that influence perceptions of social ranking and leadership see: Gibb, C. A. (1969). Leadership. In G. Lindzey, G. & E. Aronson (Eds.), *The handbook of social psychology* (2nd ed., pp. 4, 216–228). Reading, MA: Addison-Wesley. Also, for an excellent discussion of research examining the relationship among physical attractiveness and various social rewards see: Schneider, D. J. (1976). *Social psychology,* (pp. 471–476). Reading, MA: Addison-Wesley.

27. Historical details about this important work were supplied by editors at Scott Foresman and Company, of Glenview, Illinois, where *Robert's rules of order* has been published for many years.

28. See: Roberts, H. (1981). *Robert's rules of order* (rev. ed.). Glenview, IL: Scott, Foresman.

29. Kuhn, T., & Poole, M. S. (2000). Do conflict management styles affect group decision making? *Human Communication Research, 26,* 4, 558–590.

30. These four types of group cohesion were developed by the authors specifically for this chapter. These will not be commonly found in the communication literature.

31. The concept of dependency-based cohesion was derived by the authors from the underlying theory of mechanical versus organic solidarity set forth by Emile Durkheim for describing social solidarity in contrasting types of societies. Our application is not to societies as a whole but to the kinds of groups included in our analysis. See: Durkheim, E. (1947). *The division of labor in society* (G. Simpson, Trans.). New York: Free Press. (First published 1893). Sentiment-based dependency was derived from the contrast between two distinctive types of social bonds that bind people to simple and complex social systems. See: Tonnies, F. (1957). *Gemeinschaft und Gesellschaft* (C. P. Loomis, Trans.). East Lansing: Michigan State University Press. Reward-based and assignment-based cohesion were developed by the authors for this text.

32. The classic study of this type of cohesion was of common soldiers in units of the German army in World War II. The members of such groups were so intensely loyal to one another as peers (but not to Nazi political ideology or to the German high command) that they resisted surrender and fought on even when the odds became hopeless. See: Shills, E. A., & Janowitz, M. (1948). Cohesion and disintegration in the Wehrmacht in World War II. *Public Opinion Quarterly, 12,* 280–315.

Communicating in Organizations

I like working so much, I don't think I'll ever retire," Alex boasted to his friend.

Didi looked genuinely surprised. "You're kidding, right? I don't mind my job so much, what I actually do at work, but my boss makes my job so difficult. I need to work; I need the money, but it would sure make my life easier if I had a different boss."

Now it was Alex's turn to be surprised. "Really? Why does your boss make your life so miserable?"

"She's always on me to do more, more, and then some more. She has no idea what it means to do my kind of work. Her deadlines are unreasonable and undoable. What I do is never enough. How soon I do it is never soon enough. Some days I sit in my office and imagine how wonderful life would be if I was 40 years older and able to bale on this job! Retirement sounds pretty good to me, Alex."

"It's not my manager that's the problem, Didi; it's my co-workers. I work around some really arrogant and condescending people. It's almost as if they go out of their way on some days to make me feel bad about myself. I try to stay away from them. Whole days and weeks go by when I don't have to interact with them. Fortunately, I work with some other folks who are generally supportive. In fact, I've become close friends with one of them. Hank is a great guy."

Alex and Didi recognize that getting along with bosses and co-workers is critical to their overall job satisfaction and success at work.

Research points to human factors as the primary source of employees' dissatisfaction.[1] Work provides you with a salary so that you can pay for food, shelter, and all of life's other necessities and luxuries. Work also gives you a sense of purpose and a feeling that you're contributing to society in some meaningful way. Even though money may motivate and reward hard work, experts agree that money can only do so much. Beyond some threshold of needs being satisfied, money fails to sustain long-term motivation and satisfaction in the workplace. And that is why workplace relationships matter.

Communication within organizations follows both formal and informal channels. Formal channels specify rules for who can say what to whom on what topic. Informal channels, commonly called the "grapevine," include a complex set of passages through which people exchange gossip, rumors, or other unofficial messages by word of mouth.

All modern urban-industrial societies, such as that of the United States and highly developed countries in other parts of the world, are highly dependent on organizations in which people work, study, or serve to carry on their activities. They can be found in business, industry, government, religion, education, the military, and virtually any other sphere of life where important objectives and goals are pursued.

Organizations are critical to the prosperity, well-being, security, and, on occasion, even survival of modern societies.[2] Communication processes within organizations are different from those of other kinds of groups, and they are a critical part of the way that the groups function.[3] This chapter focuses on both formal and informal communication processes within these important groups.

The Nature and Functions of Organizations

An **organization** is a human group in the same sense as small groups discussed in the previous chapter. That is, it is a number of people who have come together to act collectively in order to achieve a goal that they could not attain acting alone as individuals. The term *organizations* is commonly used to label *large* groups that have carefully designed patterns of social organization. These are unlike the small spontaneous primary groups developed as members interact and communicate together.

In organizations the group's norms, roles, ranks, and controls have been thought out and planned deliberately before any people are brought in to carry on whatever activities are required to achieve its goals. That pre-designed pattern of social organization is *formal*—in the sense that it is set forth in documents, such as a table of organization, a reference book for rules and policies and written job descriptions. These provide "official" descriptions of the group's general norms, roles, and ranks, and of the controls that can be used to maintain the pattern.

However, there is a second organization to consider as well. It is the *de facto* one that emerges in practice once people are hired, or are otherwise recruited, to become actual members of the group. Then they have to carry out their day-to-day conduct and communicate with other members about the group's activities. When they do this, an *informal* pattern of social organization emerges. People bring to the organization their own ways of doing things, their unique personalities—attitudes, values, opinions, understandings, and habits. These have profound consequences in shaping their behavior and bring participants to act out the group's pattern of social organization in unique and personal ways. Both formal and informal patterns play key parts in shaping communication within the organization.

As the organization's members engage in their activities, their communication patterns include all the verbal and nonverbal processes, both linear and transactional, that have already been discussed. Both within an organization and within the kinds of small group contexts that were described in the previous chapter, people communicate interpersonally, both formally and informally. However, an organization is *a distinctive communication context in its own right.* That is, it includes forms and processes of communication that are not found in the other contexts previously examined.[4]

As noted, an organization is a human group that has been deliberately designed to achieve a desired objective. Usually, it has a large number of participants, at least compared to the small groups discussed earlier. As indicated in the earlier discussion of the number of possible pairs in a group, it is not possible for a large number of people to engage in interpersonal

communication on a daily basis. Given the size of an organization, such large groups require clear and complex rules that channel or restrict communication in such a way that the activities of the participants can be efficiently coordinated. This coordination is usually handled by a hierarchy of managers who transmit and receive various kinds of messages—upward and downward through the ranks; to and from the various participants; and, in a few situations, laterally from one part of the group to another.

There are many kinds of message transmissions. Some deal with ways in which the organization is related to outsiders—customers, clients, the general public, the political and legal systems, and so on. This chapter is primarily concerned with *internal* communication among workers, supervisors, and managers in the day-to-day operation of any kind of organization, whatever their goals and products happen to be. In this text, *organizational communication* is defined as *the transmission of messages, through both formal and informal channels, of a relatively large, deliberately designed group, resulting in the construction of meanings that influence its members, both as individuals and as a group.* Box 7.1 offers a short "quiz" to test your own organizational communication skills at work: office politics!

Society's Need for Organizations

The basic needs of a population in any society are met by its social institutions. In this sense *institution* does not mean a particular group, like a college or hospital. It means a feature of a society that is "deeply established," or *institutionalized.* Within this meaning, a *social institution* within a society can be defined as *a broad arrangement of closely related cultural elements and organized social activities that are essential to fulfilling a perceived need of the social order.* Those cultural elements may be widely shared beliefs (e.g. "children are valued," "pursuit of profit is good," "democracy is best"). They may also be laws or other cultural rules, practices, values, or beliefs. They also include the groups that are necessary to carry on activities that fulfill the society's needs.

Although this definition may seem complex and technical, it can be illustrated easily. For example, the *educational* institution is one of the five basic ones that exist in every society—without exception. (Box 7.2 gives an overview of social institutions.) That is, organized social life requires that members born into the society be systematically introduced to its ways and requirements. In traditional societies, without formal schools, that task is usually assigned to parents or other relatives. These individuals are responsible for teaching children the skills they need as well as the rules for socially acceptable behavior. In our society today, some of those functions are still under the domain of the family, but many educational aspects are now handled by organizations, such as schools, churches, and even recreational organizations (such as the Girl Scouts and Big Brothers/Big Sisters).

In each institution a variety of groups may be developed to achieve the general goal of meeting a basic societal need. For example, in the religious institution there are many systems of beliefs, denominations, and so forth that serve this need. Some may involve great cathedrals or mosques, organized congregations, holy scriptures, and complex rituals. Others may include shamans, magic spells, or the sacrifice of animals. Nevertheless, whatever their nature, they are part of the overall religious institution of their society.

All societies have five basic social institutions. In addition to the *educational* institution discussed above, the institution of *government* provides the order, predictability, and security that we need in social life. The *religious institution* meets our need to understand and try to influence the supernatural. The *economic institution* handles the production and distribution of goods and services. Finally, the *family*—the oldest and most fundamental institution of

all—regulates the bearing and rearing of children within responsible and stable groups. In modern urban societies, there are many other institutions in addition to the basic five. Examples of today's newer institutions are medicine, science, spectator sports, and the mass or new media.

Against that background, the relationship among societal needs, social institutions, and organizations becomes clearer. It is easy to see this relationship with respect to the economic institution. Business enterprises, industries, banking, and commercial establishments that meet our economic needs are obviously structured around organizations. However, this is also true of other social institutions. Education, for example, is not just a matter of individuals learning how to read and the ways of their society. Our educational needs are satisfied by a complex list of beliefs, values, laws, groups, and their activities that provide educational services to millions of members of our society.

One reason for emphasizing the relationship between societal needs and social institutions is that scholars who specialize in the study of organizational communication typically have been more narrowly focused. They have been preoccupied with assisting management in solving problems of worker control and productivity in business and industrial environments. Although this chapter addresses that issue because it is a traditional concern of the discipline, and is undoubtedly important, there is more involved in understanding organizational communication. Thus, several perspectives are presented that apply to all organizations, regardless of their location within a particular social institution.

Bureaucracy as a Theory of Formal Social Organization

The basic organizing theory of organizations is *bureaucracy*. It is a special way of defining the social organization of a complex group—such

BOX 7.1 *What's Your Office Politics IQ?*

Be very wary of the prospective employer who tells you "we have no politics here." Every organization has politics; but some members might be in denial or lack an understanding of how those politics might actually enhance performance and structure. There simply isn't a workplace in existence where fostering positive relationships with a variety of people isn't helpful in getting things done.

For many people, office politics is synonymous with drama, game-playing, manipulation, and stepping on others in order to succeed. But, really, politics can be viewed in a very different way—as an opportunity for success. Think of politics not as backstabbing or cunning, but as a way of understanding how the big machine of your organization works, and becoming a moving part. Don't think of politics as exploiting your relationships with important people; rather, view those relationships as strategic pieces in a puzzle that you must solve in order to be successful. Now that you've learned more about what office politics are or should be, take the following quiz. For each scenario, choose the best available behavioral response.

1. You've developed a new initiative that should streamline the sales inventory process for your company. Your co-workers often complain that new inventory is often ordered too late and that customers are often left waiting. So you expected that your proposed solution would be well received. However, the response has been lukewarm. What do you do?
    a. Cave. Out of embarrassment, pretend like you were never really that invested in your idea anyway.
    b. Listen. Ask for specific objections and concrete evidence why your proposal may not work. Use this information to tweak your idea. Bring it back and continue to work with your team until the plan seems feasible.
    c. Just move ahead with your plan. You don't really need anyone's support, anyway.

2. You overhear your boss's private phone conversation about her daughter's persistent eating disorder. What do you do?
    a. Try to forget you even heard the private conversation. Everyone has family problems, and it's none of your business, or anyone else's at work.
    b. Spread the news among your co-workers.
    c. Talk to her about it and offer your support.

3. Your manager has relaxed the dress code for the summer months. What do you do?
    a. Just continue to wear whatever you want. Pushing the envelope is a sign of a creative achiever.
    b. Show up wearing your usual formal professional attire anyway. Can't hurt to look the part of a successful person.
    c. Read the policy and act accordingly. Enjoy being comfortable while it's hot outside!

4. Which of the following best describes your evening and weekend technology habits?
    a. Send as many e-mails late at night or on weekends as you can, especially to your

as the kinds of organizations discussed in this chapter. Unfortunately, the term has a number of negative connotations, such as red tape, mindless rules, and bumbling inefficiency. However, the technical meaning of bureaucracy is quite different. *Bureaucracy* is defined as *a deliberately designed plan of the goals, norms, roles, ranks, and controls in an organization.*

Simply put, it is these features that control an organization's patterns of formal communication, and they will provide a framework for the discussion in this chapter.

The need for bureaucratic organization arises for two reasons—group size and the complexity of the tasks a group must pursue to achieve its goals. Recall from Chapter 6 boss. Let her know that you're an over-achiever.

b. Periodically check your e-mail for anything urgent, or when you know a time-sensitive project is under way. But, overall, you try to maintain sensible work-home boundaries.

c. Never look at work e-mail from home. That's my time, and my boss can't dictate what I do with it.

5. A colleague has just pitched a marketing campaign that you believe has some major flaws. What do you do?

a. Praise your colleague effusively to his face, but privately let others know that you had nothing to do with the proposal as a way of covering your behind.

b. Aggressively let your colleague know how lousy the idea is, and badmouth him to others so that they are sure not to support the idea.

c. Be clear, respectful, and honest in your objections. Provide evidence and constructive criticism. Offer your support in enhancing the plan and executing it once approved.

Key:

"Grade" your responses using this key:
Item #1: B
Item #2: A
Item #3: C
Item #4: B
Item #5: C

Interpreting Your Score:

If you answered correctly 4 or higher, then you selected the "right" answer for the majority of the items in the quiz. You have the foundation to be a "clean" political player—not a dirty one. You've internalized the ideas that political situations can be win-win and are always handled with diplomacy and competent communication.

A score below 4 reveals some problems. Check to see which items you didn't answer correctly. The other options represent fairly "dirty" ways to engage in office politics: brown-nosing, and blatant disrespect for the political environment and those operating within it. Forming insincere alliances, paying inauthentic compliments, and sacrificing your own values and ethics to go along with the crowd (or a single person) will never help you develop long-term success.

Alternatively, just deciding not to play politics at all is a mistake. Blatant disregard for policies, norms, and others' opinions and feelings are all surefire ways to lose the battle, and eventually, your job.

Source: This "quiz" was adapted from: Waldeck, J. H., Kearney, P., & Plax, T. G. (2013). *Business and professional communication in the digital age* (Module 9). Boston: Wadsworth, Cengage Learning.

that as the number of members in a group increases, it rapidly becomes very difficult to maintain face-to-face communication. This means that frequent communication cannot take place among all members of a group larger than, say, about 20. Clearly specified and restricted channels of communication must be defined, if only to avoid having workers spend the entire day just trying to greet one another!

One of the critical features of a design for an effective organization, then, is provision for a formal communication network that will both *maintain cohesion* and make it possible for the group to *attain its goals*. In the sections that follow, we look closely at the nature

BOX 7.2 🔍 *A Closer Look*

Basic Social Institutions

- *Educational institutions.* Introduce young people to and teach them about the ways and requirements of society.
- *Government institutions.* Render an order, predictability, and security in society.
- *Religious institutions.* Help people understand and try to influence the supernatural.
- *Economic institutions.* Handle the production and distribution of goods and services for a society.
- *The family.* The oldest and most fundamental institution, handles the bearing and rearing of children.

In modern urban societies, there are other institutions, such as medicine, science, spectator sports, and the mass or new media.

BOX 7.3 🔍 *A Closer Look*

Weber's Four Principles of Bureaucracy

In articulating his theory of bureaucracy, the German born scientist Max Weber described four principles that should be inherent within a well-designed bureaucratic organization in a modern industrial society.

1. *Fixed rules.* Norms or rules within an organization should be grounded and concrete. These rules should be easy to follow and easy to learn. The rules should stay the same (remain fixed) for every individual within the organization.
2. *Division of labor.* Official rules and regulations concerning the duties of individuals holding various positions in an organization should be written out. These rules should be adhered to as a means of creating the most productive environment possible.
3. *Hierarchy of power and authority.* An established chain of command should be included in a well-run organization. Superior–subordinate relationships define who has power and authority over certain duties or individuals or both.
4. *Universal system of sanctions.* Workers' competence and performance levels in the organization should be the deciding factor as to whether they are promoted, demoted, given a raise, or fired. The criteria for this system should be fixed and applicable to all individuals within the organization.

of bureaucracy because in the sense defined it helps in understanding formal communication within a large and complex group.

Max Weber's Classical Theory of Bureaucracy

Although organizations have been with us since ancient times, the systematic study of the basic principles of their design did not begin until early in the twentieth century. A complex theory of bureaucratic organization was developed by Max Weber, a German social scientist.[5] (Box 7.3 describes Weber's four principles of bureaucracy.)

Weber developed his theory of bureaucracy to help clarify the broad societal changes that he saw resulting from the Industrial Revolution that had been taking place all during the 1800s. The underlying change was a movement away from traditional forms of society, in which relatively homogeneous and overwhelmingly rural societies were held together by cohesion based on sentiment, shared values, and beliefs.

The emerging urban-industrial society was quite different in that it was far more heterogeneous and impersonal; the new society was made up of many different kinds of people who did not have meaningful social ties to one another and who did not share the same set of values and beliefs. Nevertheless, they were able to live and work together in a coherent social order. Weber believed that one reason they were able to do so was that they made effective use of formal bureaucratic organization.

The Emergence of "Rational" Society

Weber began his analysis by asking an important question: If a population is heterogeneous and impersonal, how is the social order held together? That is, what is the basis of *social cohesion* in society itself? Weber believed that it was an outcome of the urban-industrial society's trend toward "rationality." Increasingly, he saw, the new society was developing around *thoughtfully designed organizations* that provided for the needs of their populations. He found two factors underlying this trend: society's increasing ability to design organizations along rational lines and an increasing understanding of the nature of the leadership that made such organizations work.

Weber wanted to understand the *basis of leadership* in the emerging rational order. This led him to an analysis of **authority** and the exercise of power in different types of societies. Understanding leadership in society as a whole and in its organizations, he felt, would provide an important clue to the basis of social cohesion. In earlier times, authority was often based on *tradition* and in some societies, on *charisma*. In urban-industrial societies, however, authority tended to be based on *legal-rational organizational designs*.

Tradition. The idea of tradition as a source for the leaders' authority is evident at almost all levels in many earlier societies. At the family level, the traditional power exercised by the father was virtually absolute. He had the undisputed, legitimate right to approve or disapprove of the actions of all family members. Similarly, the local lord of the manor had the (tradition-based) legitimate authority to assign work to serfs and peasants and to decide whether they could live on his lands. At the top of the society, the political sovereign's power was based solidly on tradition. An example is the Japanese society's traditional beliefs about the divine origins of the emperor. This was also the case among monarchies in other parts of the world.

Charisma. A second source of legitimate power can come from **charismatic authority,** based on the personal qualities of the individual exercising power. Weber maintained that in such situations authority is grounded in charisma—a personal magnetism or charm that arouses feelings of loyalty or support in others. For example, throughout history, strong personalities have emerged in many parts of the world. They brought together emotionally devoted followers into a remarkably cohesive whole. Powerful military leaders have often done this. To his followers, Genghis Khan seemed to possess extraordinary personal qualities. During World War II, this personal type of authority was characterized by Adolf Hitler in Germany and Benito Mussolini in Italy. Later, this type of charismatic leadership was characterized by Mahatma Gandhi in India and by the Ayatollah Khomeini in Iran.

Legal-rational. Weber saw, however, that neither tradition nor charisma accounted for leadership legitimacy and authority in modern urban-industrial societies. Here, the exercise of power is far more likely to be based on **legal-rational authority.** That is, leaders in the (bureaucratic) organizations that provide for institutional needs are usually selected or appointed not by tradition or for their charisma, but because they possess technical managerial skills, and they are permitted to exercise power within a limited sphere that is narrowly defined by official definitions and rulings.

Weber's Principles

Weber set forth a number of basic principles that should be present in the operation of a well-designed bureaucratic organization. Because his description is too complex to be presented in full, the focus here is on the central factors with which Weber was concerned. These help in understanding the nature of formalized channels of communication in bureaucratically organized groups.[6]

1. *Fixed rules.* This principle requires stable and explicit norms for all forms of behavior (including communication) that apply equally to everyone and that can be readily learned and followed. Today, such norms would include standards for relationships between male and female workers, between ethnic groups, and so forth.

2. *A rationally defined division of labor.* This principle requires that each position within the organization be mapped out in a formal (written) job description. The jurisdiction and official duties of the individual carrying out the specialized tasks of such positions should be set forth in official rules, laws, and regulations. These govern not only the exact activities to be performed but also what messages the person occupying the position can transmit to whom about what.

3. *A clear and graded hierarchy of power and authority.* This principle requires a chain of command in which the ranking system is formally set forth in an official plan. This shows that every worker has a supervisor, and every supervisor has specified subordinates. The official rules state who has authority to transmit what orders to whom, who must comply, who must communicate reports to whom, and so on.

4. *A fixed and universalistic system of sanctions.* This principle requires that workers be hired, promoted, rewarded, reprimanded, or fired solely on the basis of their competence and performance. The criteria should be made explicit and equally applicable to all (universalistic). That is, everyone should be judged by clear and uniform standards, and personal factors such as likes or dislikes, family ties, or, today, such factors as race, age, gender, and ethnicity should not influence the exercise of social controls. Such a system requires clear and accountable communication and records of all decisions concerning those rewarded or punished and the reasons on which such decisions were based.[7]

Although Weber was the pioneer in the systematic study of bureaucracy, scholars now publish thousands of research studies concerning many aspects of organizational design every year, especially from fields related to management.[8] As a result, a massive body of knowledge has accumulated about the relationship between types of organizations, various strategies of management, and the kinds of communication problems they engender. In fact, so many different approaches, theories, and perspectives have been advanced that one scholar, Harold Koontz, has characterized the situation as the "management theory jungle."[9] Because it is impossible to cover such a body of knowledge in the present chapter, the next section provides a brief outline of several alternative ways of looking at organizations.

Management's Designs for Organizational Communication

As previously noted, the study of organizational communication today focuses heavily on problems of management and the design of production-oriented groups. This is perfectly understandable because factories, corporations, and other work-related organizations are at the heart of the economic institution in our industrial society. Communication within such groups has significant consequences for the society.

This section reviews four distinct theories of how communication is managed in work-related organizations. Each was originally developed as a means of promoting efficiency, raising productivity, and increasing output. Of course, these goals are critical to higher returns on investment—a deeply approved value in a capitalistic society. Thus, today's study of organizational communication is preoccupied with designs for the flow of messages and influences by which management can achieve more output from themselves and their employees.

The theories considered here were developed during the past two centuries. For simplicity, these can be called *human use theories* (developed between the early 1800s and the late 1920s), *human relations theories* (dominant from the early 1930s until the 1960s), and *human resources theories* (begun in the 1960s and still of interest today). More contemporary approaches such as *systems theories* are also included.

Human Use Perspectives

In the first decades of the Industrial Revolution, those who established and managed factories or other organizations had little to guide their communication with employees but their intuition, prior experience, and common sense. They often made serious mistakes. They did not understand the social and psychological nature of workers or how workers could be motivated to produce more by effective messages. Additionally, managers did not view workers as sensitive human beings, but as *resources to be used,* along with machinery, and to be exploited much in the same way as are raw materials.

This kind of thinking was at the heart of the **human use perspective.** In fact, early in the 19th century, some owners and managers considered using slaves to work in the newly established factories, but public sentiment was against it. About the only other example of an efficient use of labor was the armed services. In the armed forces of the time, common soldiers or sailors were controlled in large part by violence; they could be flogged, clapped in irons, or even shot if they disobeyed orders, failed to do their job, or talked back to their superiors.

Communication within 19th-century organizations often seemed like military commands. Orders were given, and they were not to be questioned. Workers were often bullied into high levels of performance. Iron-fisted fore-men drove them with blows and kicks. Low-performing workers were threatened with being fired. With no alternatives for earning a living, this meant disaster for their entire families.

Another human use perspective was based on what Weber referred to as "rationality." It focused exclusively on a *formula for wages.* In 1776, just as the Industrial Revolution was

about to begin, Adam Smith published his *An Inquiry into the Nature and Causes of the Wealth of Nations*—one of the most influential books ever written and the foundation from which modern capitalism developed.[10]

During the early decades of the Industrial Revolution, Smith's ideas dominated thinking about management-worker communication. In particular, it was his ideas about the relationship between wages and the demand for labor that shaped the thinking of managers about the use and control of workers. Smith had maintained that if labor was scarce, higher wages would have to be paid—but a labor glut would permit them to be lower. Generally, he maintained, wages in balance with performance provide the proper return for work. Thus, wage level is not to be set based on humanitarian considerations, but solely on the demand for and the supply of labor, plus considerations of individual productivity. With little understanding of human nature as we know it today, wages were thought to be virtually the only means available to motivate employees. Thus, it was assumed that if ways to earn more money could be communicated to workers, they would rationally decide to work harder. It was an idea entirely consistent with the times.

Early in the 1800s, then, the major form by which managers communicated to motivate messages to workers was through **wage incentive systems.** Piecework formulas were developed so that wages were tied to personal output. That is, earnings for a worker in a production shop were determined by the number of units the individual produced in a given time period. Production norms (such as pieces produced by the worker per hour) were established for a standard day's work, and bonuses were added as motivating controls to stimulate workers to exceed those norms.

By the end of the 1800s, this approach to job design and to social control on the factory floor was in wide use. However, it had many problems. For one thing, workers hated it. They had discovered that if they increased the pace of their work—producing more per hour to receive bonuses—management would simply raise the norm to force their wages back down. Indeed that often happened. Then, they had to work harder than ever just to get the same wages as before. As a result, workers developed ways to undermine the piecework formulas to keep the norms down.

During the late part of the 1800s, Frederick W. Taylor developed a startling refinement of the human use approach for controlling workers. It came to be called **scientific management.** Taylor started his career as an apprentice patternmaker and machinist in a Philadelphia foundry. He gradually worked his way up and became a chief engineer in a large steel mill.[11] He began to make careful studies of conditions of work in the mill, and he was appalled at the inefficiency he found. Poorly qualified and ill-trained workers were left to figure out for themselves how to perform their jobs. The wage incentive formulas in use caused workers to restrict their output (which he called "systematic soldiering") to prevent management from raising workload norms.

Taylor decided to make detailed observations of how each worker actually performed his individual task in the mill. Taking careful notes and using a stopwatch, he painstakingly timed the various movements workers made while performing such mundane tasks as shoveling coal and lifting blocks of pig iron. As a result of his studies, Taylor was able to get workers to simplify, standardize, and control how they performed their tasks. Taylor rearranged work stations, controlled rest periods, and redesigned the flow of work through the mill. As a result of his innovations, the workers were less fatigued at the end of the day. In addition, they were able to increase their pay by an astonishing 60 percent! Furthermore, their increased efficiency raised the profit margins of the mill significantly.

It was with these *time and motion studies,* plus Taylor's other innovations, that scientific management was born. Essentially, it was a system for managing an organization by communicating rules to workers concerning how to perform their tasks, wage incentives, the flow of work, and patterns of authority. These ideas

made Taylor famous.[12] He went on to develop his theories more elaborately, and by the beginnings of the 1900s, his principles of scientific management had been widely applied throughout the industrial world.

Unfortunately, Taylor's humane approach was not always followed by those who adopted his scientific management strategies for creating efficiency. Workers were often regarded as little more than mechanical cogs in the machine. Many were shamelessly manipulated and dehumanized as the drive to boost efficiency and maximize profits surged. During the Great Depression years, Taylor's open communication system between workers and managers was abandoned. However, even today, many of the innovations introduced by Taylor remain in use.

Still another important organizational design was embodied in what was later called the *universal principles of management.* These ideas were developed by theorist Henri Fayol, a French engineer and manager of a large mining enterprise. In 1919, Fayol published an important book setting forth his version of such universal principles.[13] He did not publish his book until he was 75 years old, and it reflects his many years as an experienced, practical administrator.

The most important contribution of Fayol was the *organization chart.* Such a chart communicates graphically the chain of authority and command and thereby the flow of formal messages. (Figure 7.1 illustrates such a chart.) It is especially helpful in understanding the vertical flow of communication—up and down the organization. Fayol maintained that communication between supervisors and their subordinates should be easy and uninhibited, but it should also be restricted to the tasks or operations related to the work being done.

Furthermore, in normal operations, it was essential for communication to follow rigidly the channels mapped out in the organization chart. At the same time, he recognized that during times of crisis it might be necessary and helpful to bridge or bypass those formal channels. Thus, "Fayol's bridge" idea provided for the rapid transmission of vital messages when they

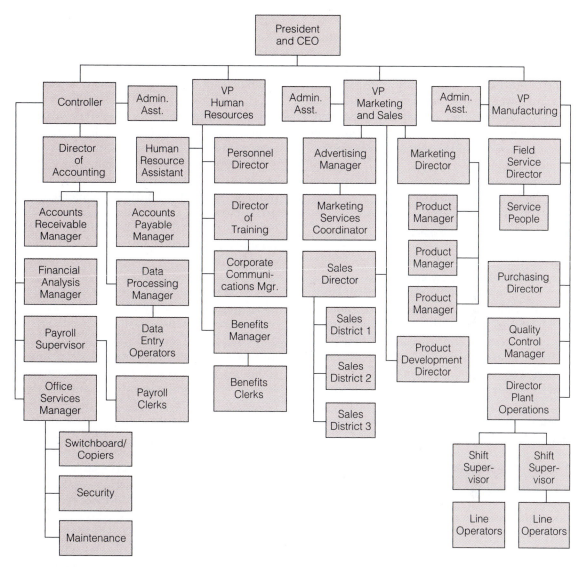

FIGURE 7.1

Organization Chart

An important feature of an organization chart is the graphic display of the links of power and authority in the group from top to bottom. It is also a map of the formal channels of communication, indicating clearly who must report to whom as well as who will give or receive orders from whom.

were critically needed. However, this was necessarily an informal communication process. In recent times, this bridging process has recurred as an advocated idea in the federal government of the United States. A failure of communication by and between federal agencies, such as the FBI and CIA, was cited by some authorities as a critical factor that made it possible for terrorists to bring down the World Trade Center buildings on September 11, 2001.[14]

The work of Taylor and of Fayol added to Weber's classic bureaucratic theory in focusing attention on the essential nature of deliberate rational planning in the design of formal communication systems in organizations. Their norms, roles, ranking patterns, and systems of control (governing who should transmit what to whom) were not left to chance, spontaneous development, tradition, or common sense. People could work best in achieving their goals in organizations only if the activities and communication channels of every one of their members were deliberately defined. Few would quarrel with that generalization today.

Human Relations Perspectives

During the first two decades of the 1900s, American industry grew enormously. During the 1920s, for example, cheap immigrant labor, raw materials, abundant capital, weak unions, and seemingly insatiable markets brought manufacturers great prosperity. At that time, scientific management was in vogue. Business leaders were determined to maximize production by standardizing, organizing, and controlling all aspects of work—materials, space, pay incentives, and any other factor that would achieve top efficiency and profits.

The Hawthorne studies and their legacy. It was in the context of this search for ways to maximize production that a number of scientific management experiments began in 1924. They were conducted in Cicero, Illinois, at the Hawthorne Plant of the Western Electric Company.[15] These large-scale experiments were a joint effort between the huge Western Electric Company and the National Academy of Sciences. They have become classics in the study of organizational communication because they radically revised the thinking about how people communicate at work.[16]

One group of experiments in the series accidentally resulted in insights into the communication process. Researchers began by focusing on the effects of *illumination* on worker output. In the tradition of scientific management, their purpose was to see if some particular level of light-

ing would promote greater worker efficiency. As it turned out, the illumination studies serendipitously had significant implications for understanding important aspects of organizational communication, and they touched off a sweeping change in management philosophy. It was a shift from the perspectives of scientific management to what came to be called the **human relations perspective.**

Strangely enough, the illumination experiments were total failures—at least from the point of view of scientific management experts. However, their seemingly inexplicable outcomes provided the major evidence that the personal and social characteristics of workers *as individual human beings* are often critical factors in the work process.

The scientific management perspective had regarded assembly-line workers as basically interchangeable—easily replaced parts or units that merely needed to be controlled and motivated by communicating to them simple economic incentives, or by other measurable factors. The illumination experiments were based on that perspective. The industrial engineers conducting the studies were convinced that output per worker was closely related to the *level of lighting* in the workplace—that is, the more light, the more work—at least within limits. They began by gathering *baseline data*. They recorded the output of three sections of women workers in the plant who were assembling telephone equipment. The women were fully aware of the nature of the experiments. They had been told that efforts were being made to find the best level of illumination to make their work easier and more efficient. Because pay was tied to productivity via a piece-rate system, this seemed fine to the workers.

After the initial baseline output levels were determined, the engineers began to vary systematically the level of lighting in the work areas, always keeping track of levels of worker output. During one week, they would increase the level of lighting slightly. The next week, they would lower it a bit or greatly increase the illumination. Finally, they would return to the very low level of lighting from which they had started. They maintained each of these conditions over a sufficient time period so that they were able to obtain accurate measures of per worker productivity. The engineers confidently expected that production per worker would increase with level of illumination, at least up to a point.

Oddly, however, every time the level of lighting was changed, *output per worker went up*—regardless of whether the illumination was increased or decreased. No matter what the condition, the workers just kept on getting more productive. Baffled by this, the engineers gradually lowered the lighting to a level where the workers could barely see what they were doing. Even this did not slow their productivity! At that point, the engineers threw up their hands and declared the experiments a total loss.

What they had failed to account for was that the workers had their *personal feelings and shared beliefs* about the experiments. The workers had informally discussed the situation among themselves, and generally they liked the idea that management was concerned about them. They thought it was fine that management had sent the nice engineers to experiment and find the best level of illumination so that they could do their work better and make more money. They were happy that management was treating them in a special way and excited at being part of an important experiment. The women had talked it over and had decided to do a good job all the time, so that the experiments would be a success.[17] Those positive feelings motivated them to increase output, even when the lights were low.[18]

Given those understandings about human relations on the job, management set out to design new ways to increase worker efficiency. What they had to do now was to find messages that would motivate, encourage, and foster performance by taking advantage of factors in individual personality and human relationships.

This is the human relations perspective in a nutshell! Styles of supervision changed. New efforts were made to promote high morale and loyalty to the organization. Ways in which workers could obtain personal satisfaction and subjective fulfillment while working had to be built into the design of work organizations. Overall, the new gospel was that it was the responsibility of managers to design work environments in organizations that would produce high job satisfaction. The assumption was that such satisfaction would lead to high work performance.

In reality, sometimes the human relations perspective worked and sometimes it didn't. Although it was more humane than earlier ones, the human relations approach to organizational management could not universally guarantee worker efficiency. However, the human relations theories did make it clear that social ties existing among workers and their patterns of informal communication were critical factors in tying the worker to the organization.

In summary, the early theories of Weber, Taylor, Fayol, and others were fine as far as they went. However, they were incomplete. They made it clear that the de facto organization was made up of some combination of the deliberately designed bureaucratic rules and the spontaneous peer group communication that emerged as people worked with one another on the job. Human beings at work develop complex networks of likes, dislikes, friendships, and animosities. These provide the basis of deeply established channels of informal communication that have nothing to do with the organization chart. The discovery of the importance of informal communication within the larger organization, then, was largely a result of the rather curious Hawthorne experiments. The study of informal networking and the kinds of communication that occur within this part of the organization thus came to be pursued with vigor by communication scientists and management specialists alike.

The decline of the human relations perspective. Overall, the human relations perspective remained the dominant one until the 1960s. However, managers slowly lost much of their initial enthusiasm for its principles because it was extremely hard to implement. Furthermore, in some cases it produced unforeseen and often undesirable consequences. For example, in practice it proved to be difficult to communicate freely with rank-and-file employees, and supervisors who tried to be caring and sympathetic to workers were sometimes seen as weak and indecisive by both workers and higher-level managers.

One requirement of the perspective—involving workers in decision making, policy formation, and power sharing—proved to be particularly difficult. People who lack expertise often make bad decisions. Effective policy making demands solid knowledge and experience, and it is not for amateurs. Furthermore, those who have status and power seldom want to share it with those lower in rank. These are central activities of management, jealously guarded by those with driving ambition. They are often the center of political upheavals in organizations, such as when competition for promotion becomes keen. Involving rank-and-file workers in such activities often created an uproar of unwanted tensions and conflicts.

Human Resources Perspectives

Although it is not widely known in the United States, some of the fundamental principles of industrial production that helped Japan to develop a strong economy following World War II were not invented by the Japanese. These principles were taught to the Japanese at the time by an American, W. Edwards Deming—a statistician and management consultant. Deming had developed a complex philosophy of industrial production that stressed *quality* above all else.

At the close of World War II, Japanese industries were in shambles—virtually bombed out of existence. But President Harry Truman and other American leaders decided that rather than punishing the nation for its misdeeds, they would develop a reliable ally against the Soviet Union that had emerged as a new threat. This was to be done by assisting the Japanese in rebuilding their lost industrial base. Deming was brought to Japan to help train postwar managers in techniques that would establish a solid manufacturing basis for the rebuilt economy.

Deming insisted that the best way to ensure a strong place for Japan in the postwar industrial world was get them to produce goods of maximum quality. That was a drastic change from prewar Japan, when the emphasis was on cheap goods of low quality. With his objective in mind, Deming taught Japanese industrialists to emphasize the production of goods manufactured *to the highest possible standards*. He provided them with a very clear program as to how to achieve this goal from a technical point of view. He believed fully that because they were, so to speak, starting from scratch, the Japanese could become a major industrial power within a relatively short time. To say that he was right is to understate the situation. By the 1960s, Japan was well on the way to becoming one of the world's foremost economic powers.

Perhaps no one was more surprised at their success than the Japanese. They listened politely to Deming, and, equally politely, they followed his program. The end result was the incredible rise of postwar Japan as an industrial power producing goods known for their high quality. Today, Japanese automobiles, electronic consumer goods, and other products retain that reputation. As one Japanese executive wrote in his diary in 1950:

> Here was this tall American telling us that we would be an important force in five years if we listened to him. We really didn't believe him, but in order not to lose face, we did what he told us, *and it worked!*[19]

In terms of organizational communication, by 1970, it was clear that Japan was doing something different in its design of production-oriented organizations. The Japanese had not only adopted Deming's guidelines regarding statistical bases for quality control and management, but they had also developed production organizations with patterns of communication that were very different from those used in the Western world.[20]

Essentially, Japan had implemented a **human resources perspective** in their design of organizations. It was a management theory based on the belief that bonds of loyalty and attitudes of dedication to work can be created among employees by selective patterns of management–worker communication. The Japanese implemented this perspective in a way that was totally consistent with their culture and equally consistent with the principles of management brought to them by Deming. For example, until recent times, many Japanese workers were virtually assured of lifetime employment in the same firm, and they were promoted solely on the basis of seniority. This was clearly contrary to Weber's principles, but it eliminated cutthroat competition among employees that could threaten the goals of the larger group. For example, in such a system, managers would have no reason to feel threatened by competent and successful subordinates. Those subordinates could communicate their ideas, which could then be incorporated into production processes.

Things have changed in Japan today. Lifetime employment in many organizations can no longer be counted on. Other nations have become industrialized, and an increase in the number of global multinational corporations has added to an intensely competitive environment. However, Japan's unique perspective on organizational communication and management style allowed it to overcome the devastated position in the industrial world that it started from at the close of World War II, and to do it swiftly and dramatically.

Even now, because Japan's population is racially and ethnically homogeneous, there are fewer barriers to communication than are typical in the multicultural United States. Senior members of a Japanese firm listen to and understand ideas suggested by those lower in the organization's hierarchy, which also makes training and indoctrination easier. Also, bonds are created between workers and management that would be more difficult to establish in a racially and culturally diverse labor force.

The Japanese realized that workers on the line have insights and a grasp of the production process that cannot be understood by executives far removed from day-to-day operations. For that reason, they created small groups of workers called *quality control circles*. These are composed of individuals from particular units right on the line whose members all face the same production task. In industries where they are used, they meet weekly as discussion groups and are coordinated by their supervisor. Their objective is to find ways in which their particular assembly work can be done more efficiently and at a higher level of quality. Their solutions are taken very seriously by management, and, if implemented, the group earns cash bonuses and awards.

The Japanese strategy was also tried in the United States, but was never particularly successful. It was quite different from the U.S. tradition, where jobs were usually designed by remote experts and where worker suggestions were often unwelcome. Under such conditions, workers seldom care about quality because they have no personal stake in the outcome. The Japanese quality control circles, on the other hand, effectively make use of human resources—the insights, talents, skills, and loyalties of workers—to improve efficiency of production and to maintain high standards in products. In other words, the channels of communication between workers and management are deliberately kept flexible and open, and workers' messages come through loud and clear.

In summary, the human resources approach is related to the human relations theory, but there are important differences. In particular, the human resources approach sees employees as a major potential resource for the organization in terms of talent, energy, dedication, and pride in work. If the ideas of these human resources can be communicated effectively and incorporated into the manufacturing process, the result will be both efficiency in production and high quality in products. The task of management, then, is to design a system that minimizes communication barriers and leads to high performance by workers while maximizing factors that motivate them to work at a high level of quality.

Contemporary Perspectives

The search for models of organizational effectiveness did not end with human resources perspectives, however. Organizational theorists and practitioners recognized that classical and humanistic theories, such as those already described in this chapter, failed to consider the *effect of the environment* upon the organization. Thus, more contemporary perspectives such as *systems theory* were developed to acknowledge the interrelationship of different components, both within and outside, of the organization that have an impact on the organization.

Systems theory, derived in part from ideas developed in the field of botany, views the organization as similar to a living organism, composed of multiple subsystems working together to achieve balance or *homeostasis*. The subsystems of an organism, and the subsystems or parts of an organization, are related and function in similar ways. If one part of the organism breaks down, for example, the rest of the system is directly affected. In like manner, if one person in an organization fails to complete his or her work, the entire organization can suffer. Thus, the organization is a system of *mutually dependent parts.*

In addition to the interdependency of its parts, systems theorists emphasize the *synergy* of the organization. This means that the combined abilities and knowledge of organizational members is greater than the sum of the efforts of individuals working alone. In other words, members of the system who work together also learn together, and they are more effective and creative because of their interactions with each other.[21]

However, in order to maintain balance and "health," the organization must also consider the *outside environment*, which has a strong influence on its operation. This includes all political, economic, social, and legal or regulatory factors or institutions that may have a positive or negative impact upon the organization. Previous theories did not recognize the environment as a factor in the effectiveness of workers or the organization.

Finally, systems theory emphasizes the critical importance of *communication* within the organization. Communication is a central focus of the organization, rather than just a means for controlling the behavior of workers. In other words, communication is the "glue" that holds all the subsystems together, enabling them to function in sync with each other and with the environment in which the organization operates.

In recent years, managers and theorists have focused more closely on the degree of change in the modern workplace. With heavy reliance on computer systems and electronic methods for sending and retrieving information, organizations face more challenges as they seek ways to manage and process the massive amount of information they receive and process. Organizations must constantly adapt to changing technologies and global competition. Thus, it is clear that newer theories will continue to be developed to reflect the changing nature of the world in which people communicate and work together to achieve common goals. (See Box 7.4.)

The Flow of Messages in Large Organizations

One of the most important of all the kinds of behavior constrained by an organizational design is *formal communication*. That is, an important function of the social plan of any organization is to direct the way that messages flow through the system. As we have already noted, formal communication takes place only within a set of carefully defined rules between certain designated parties. Several other features could be added to that definition: Its messages concern only a range of topics *relevant* to the organization; they are transmitted and received via *prescribed media*; and their purpose is to *accomplish goals* set by the organizational design. That rules out all forms of personal messages transmitted for reasons other than the official business of the organization. A simple

BOX 7.4 🔍 *Workplace Perspective*

Ten Easy Rules for Managing Your Manager

The key to a successful working experience is to understand some basic rules for managing your manager better than he or she manages you. It is important to establish a relationship of mutual respect and confidence between you and your boss. Your manager needs to know you as a decent and hard-working employee. Here are some basic rules offered by Guy Browning:

Rule 1: *Do your job without bothering your boss.* A good employee does not need to be managed. Develop your own solutions that get the job done the way the boss wants it.

Rule 2: *Inform the boss before doing it—not afterward.* Keep your boss "in the loop" by regular informal communication about what you are doing—but don't be pesky and overdo it.

Rule 3: *Unleash the power of gratuitous flattery.* Bosses are people and they like to be told what a good job they are doing. Flatter selectively. Do not overdo it or be too obvious.

Rule 4: *Ask the boss for wisdom.* Ask bosses for specific advice and make them believe they have helped, even if you already know what they tell you. It makes a boss feel good.

Rule 5: *Help your boss to do his or her job.* Remember that someone is evaluating your boss and that anything you do to make your boss look good will be appreciated.

Rule 6: *Go to your boss with solutions, not problems.* Do this and you will be seen as making positive contributions, not as a source of annoying problems to be solved.

Rule 7: *Do more than is required of you.* Relieving the boss of some task makes his or her life easier and expands your area of responsibility—and improves your evaluation.

Rule 8: *Treat the boss like a colleague and a sensitive human being.* This does not mean trying to become a pal, but it does mean making the boss feel better and less like a formal manager.

Rule 9: *Never undercut your boss with negative comments to fellow workers.* You may feel that such criticism is justified, but it is unwise and it may get back to him or her.

Rule 10: *Always invite your boss to office-related gatherings of fellow workers.* Bosses like to think they are appreciated and can mix easily with their employees, even if they can't.

Source: This list is based on Browning, G. (January 10, 2002). How to manage your manager, *People Management, 8,* 102.

---

way of describing formal communication in an organization is to say that *the design for the content, transmission, and reception of messages dictates who can say what, to be received by whom, about specific kinds of topics, by communicating with what medium, in order to achieve specified types of goals.*

Because official channels of formal communication are so tightly controlled and restrained, and because they can be used for only a limited range of topics, more flexible and open channels for informal communication develop. People working in groups need to communicate in a variety of ways about a host of issues and topics. For that reason, the **grapevine** and other similar informal systems and networks also develop and are used to convey a great many messages to and among large numbers of people about a variety of topics without noticeable restrictions on their transmission.

Formal Communication through Official Channels

Four issues need to be considered in describing the flow of official messages through an organization. One is the nature of the channels themselves—*who* is allowed or required

How does the configuration of this room influence the formality of communication? How do you think messages are delivered and received in this organizational environment?

to communicate *with whom*. The second concerns the kinds of *topics* that make up most of the message content. The third is the *quality* of communication. Finally, it is important to understand the *consequences* of both the restrictions and the limitations on accuracy produced by the formal communication system.

Vertical transmission. As can be seen in almost any organization chart, the hierarchical structure almost automatically implies **vertical transmission.** That is, in a group with clearly graded levels of power and authority, communication must by definition flow either up or down in the system. If messages follow the design, employees at the bottom in a given unit communicate formally only with their supervisors. Those supervisors, in turn, communicate formally only with the individuals who command their particular division, and so on up to higher-level officials and ultimately to the top. No one is supposed to short-circuit these channels and leak important messages between categories or across lines of authority.

Message content in formal communication. The message content that flows upward and downward through formal channels in almost all organizations is remarkably similar. What kinds of messages flow *upward* in a formal communication system? In most organizations, most messages deal with the following four categories of content:

1. *Routine operational messages.* A large part of the upward flow of messages consists of technical details about materials needed, inventory completed, personnel issues,

accounting data, cost estimates, and the like. These provide the day-to-day data used by managers to make routine decisions.

2. *Assessments by experts.* These are messages regarding the best ways to accomplish certain kinds of goals or to do particular kinds of work. Employees at or near the bottom often have precisely the skills, knowledge, and experience that supervisors need to understand when preparing proposals or designing work roles. Consequently, this type of content is sent up the line.

3. *Feedback on completion of tasks.* Reports on how well orders were carried out and on what results were obtained provide important insights needed at the top. Such details can be provided only in the form of reports that are initiated at the lower levels where the work is actually performed.

4. *Reports on problems.* Decision makers at the top must have full knowledge about problems encountered either within or outside the organization. These messages provide vital input so that policies can be changed to minimize such problems. Top management makes many decisions. The quality of those decisions depends on the accuracy and timeliness of the message content that moves up the system.

Looking at vertical transmission from the other direction, what are the categories of messages that flow *downward* in the formal system? Again, these messages generally fall into one of the following four basic categories of message content:

1. *Routine operational messages.* This is the counterpart to the first category of upward–flowing information.

2. *Specific orders and instructions.* These focus on particular individuals, concerning matters such as new job assignments, promotions, and staffing changes. They also include instructions concerning the production or processing of particular services or products (for example, how many are to be ready by what time).

3. *Operating guidelines.* These are generally messages on long-term matters. They may concern ways to perform particular kinds of work, how to allocate space for specific functions, means to incorporate certain materials, how to package finished products, or ways to handle the clients in a particular order.

4. *Policy-shift directives.* These messages usually concern relatively broad changes in the way of doing things. They represent shifts in the goals of an organization, in its organizational plan, or in the general way in which work will be handled. For example, a shift from a paper-based to a computerized accounting system, with consequent personnel changes, could be a policy-shift directive.

Messages moving within the formal channels are often critically important both to the people who send them and to those who receive them. People's jobs can depend on the kinds of messages they receive in the way of orders, assessments, reports, and instructions. Their rewards can be linked to how accurately they interpret the meanings that the messages are intended to convey. Indeed, improving such communication is a key factor in the motivation of employees.

Given this high level of importance, it would seem to follow that people would make few mistakes, either as senders or as receivers, in constructing or interpreting official organizational communication; but the fact is that errors are common. What, then, are some of the factors that can contribute to a loss of accuracy, misunderstanding, and other limitations on the degree to which the meanings aroused by such formal communication are similar in senders and receivers?

Accuracy versus distortion up and down the line. As messages move upward and downward, a number of factors tend to distort the meanings that are encoded and decoded by those involved in the chain of transmission.

Viewed within both the linear and simultaneous transactions models (see Chapter 1), policymakers, managers, and supervisors at every level have the problem of *effective role-taking*. That is, they must encode their messages in such a way that, when they are transmitted downward, their content will be both understood as intended and influential in shaping the behavior of the persons they are supervising. If either of these goals is not achieved, the messages are ineffective. There are many reasons to anticipate that role-taking problems will be encountered. Furthermore, managers and supervisors face the challenge of effectively interpreting feedback—interpreting the real meanings of messages that originate with subordinates and that may have undergone change as they traveled upward.

To begin to understand how such a formal system can fail to provide for accurate communication, consider the fact that it is human beings who formulate the messages that move up and down the line and human beings who receive those transmissions and try to interpret their meanings. Unfortunately, no human being is a perfect sender or receiver, and many factors can distort and limit the paralleling of meaning between communicating parties. This is as true in the organizational setting as it is in any other communication context. In fact, given the significance of work and career to those involved, such factors may operate in this context with particular force!

Consider, for example, what can happen to formal messages that move up through an organization's hierarchy. (Box 7.5 summarizes how messages can be distorted as they move upward in an organization.) Such messages may not be interpreted correctly because they have been:

1. *Condensed*. Messages tend to grow shorter and more concise as they move up from one level to another. For example, a written report explaining a mechanical breakdown or a complex personnel matter is likely to be a much briefer version when it lands on the desk of the chief executive officer than it was when formulated several levels below by an immediate supervisor. Even the phrase *to brief* (an executive) implies that subordinates supply condensed versions of what has actually taken place.

BOX 7.5 🔍 *A Closer Look*

Messages Can Be Distorted as They Move Up the Line

1. Messages may be *condensed* as they move from one level in an organization to another.
2. Messages may be selectively *simplified* as they move from one level to another.
3. Messages may be recast in familiar terms, into *standardized* words and phrases, as they move from one level to another.
4. Messages may be rewritten to make people look good, or *idealized*, as they move from one level to another.
5. Messages may be combined with other information, *synthesized*, as they move from one level to another.

2. *Simplified*. This is a counterpart to condensing a message. Details are selectively deleted from complex reports. They are then organized around the most salient details. Often this transforms the content into simplified categories, such as "good," "bad," "all," or "none," whereas this was not the case in reality. This represents a loss of richness of detail that, although seeming to clarify the issue, actually deprives the original message of subtle interpretations. It may also exaggerate mild situations or conditions at the bottom into more glaring problems when they reach the top.

3. *Standardized*. Messages are couched in standard terms familiar within the organization's jargon. The original events may be of such a nature that the official language does not describe them accurately. For example, a soldier who, despite his or her best efforts, was unable to get back to base on time (for example, canceled flight) may be classified in official jargon as AWOL (absent without official leave). Unfortunately, this implies a deliberate moral transgression (which was not the intention) that should be punished. Thus, meaning is changed.

Attention to formal communication may lapse for any number of reasons.

4. *Idealized.* A message transmitted to a higher level may be rephrased to cast the sender in the best possible light. People want their supervisors to believe that they acted wisely and within organizational guidelines. Thus, they may leave out certain details and modify others almost unwittingly so as to idealize their own behavior.

5. *Synthesized.* The transmitted message may be combined with additional details to form a more understandable overall picture, even when the added meanings were never part of the original event. For example, a report on an individual who behaved unusually may have included a comment that the person was in the care of a psychiatrist several years earlier. This fact may have had no bearing on the incident, but it could obviously introduce distortions in the interpretations made by those above.

Messages coming *down* the line can also undergo characteristic changes, and their intentions may be undermined. The factors that

BOX 7.6 🔍 *A Closer Look*

Messages Can Be Distorted as They Move Down the Line

1. Messages may have *selective exposure* because receivers misplace them, lose them, or only read one part of the message.
2. Some messages receive *selective attention and listening.* They may be distorted because the receivers are distracted or their listening deteriorates for one reason or another.
3. Messages may be *selectively received* because receivers' physiological factors reshape what receivers hope for, want, fear, or like.
4. Messages may be *selectively retained and recalled* because receivers tend to remember what they want to remember and to repress what seems stressful, punishing, or difficult to interpret.
5. Messages may be processed with a degree of accuracy but they may be *selectively acted on.* The actions may be postponed for a variety of distorting circumstances.
6. Messages may be distorted because individuals at different points during transmission have *vocabulary differences;* they may not share the same meanings for important words or phrases.

may produce such a result are the same general communication factors that limit the degree to which senders and receivers achieve completely parallel meanings or the degree to which messages modify the behavior of receivers. (Box 7.6 lists these distortion factors.) Formal messages from supervisors may not be interpreted correctly for any of the following reasons:

1. *Selective exposure.* Messages may not be read or heard for a variety of reasons, including fatigue or just plain circumstance. Messages get misfiled, misplaced, and accidentally thrown away.

2. *Selective attention and listening.* Even if a person hears a message in full, attention may wander and listening may deteriorate. Busy people may be distracted by others, and attention to a formal communication may lapse. People are often surprised when they reread a message and find meanings in it that they simply did not notice the first time.

3. *Selective perception.* It has been shown repeatedly that the psychological process of organizing incoming message symbols into associated meanings is a complex activity that is fundamental to the communication process. Assigning meaning to formal messages in an organization follows the same general principles set forth in earlier chapters. In addition, formal messages coming down from high places are a particularly important kind of transmission that may have implications for a person's welfare. Therefore, perception and interpretation take place within a system of personal attitudes, beliefs, values, and expectations that may influence reconstructed meanings. To a considerable extent, those psychological factors may reshape the interpretation to fit with what the receiver hopes, wants, fears, or likes.

Along those lines, a message's meaning may be transformed by a receiver to minimize a potential threat; this is commonly referred to as a perceptual defense. Another transformation of meaning may occur because of perceptual set, whereby a receiver expects a particular meaning to be implied in a message. Although these are subtle psychological reactions, selective perception does operate to modify the meanings received, even via channels of formal communication that have been carefully designed to minimize misinterpretations.

4. *Selective retention and recall.* No one's memory is perfect. Receivers tend to remember complex meanings in important messages in very selective ways. This process involves reshaping message symbols to fit the interpretation of a particular receiver's hopes, wants, fears, or likes, in very selective ways. For example, people tend to remember good or rewarding parts of a message and to repress (unconsciously forget) those parts that seem stressful, punishing, or difficult. For this reason, a message coming down the line may be well understood at the time of reading, but later it may be remembered in a distorted way.

5. *Selective action.* Even if a message is perceived and interpreted accurately and remembered fully, it may not be acted on as requested or ordered. Circumstances may require that some of the ordered actions be postponed, modified, or ignored. Subordinates quickly learn how to sidestep or avoid difficult or unrewarding actions requested by supervisors, or how to develop logical reasons why the orders cannot be followed as specified.

6. *Vocabulary differences.* Well-educated managers and less educated employees may not have the same vocabulary, or they may not have the same meanings for words that they do share. Furthermore, in a multicultural society, language usages may vary among people who come from different social categories. These factors may distort interpretations of a message due to the different ways that people establish conventions linking words, realities, and subjective meanings.

Informal Communication in Organizational Contexts

Not only is the actual organization made up of its deliberately designed structure, but also it includes the social ties among the many small and intimate groups of peers found in any large group. Thus, messages flow not only through the official channels prescribed for formal communication but also through informal grapevines—complex social pathways in a network of intimate groups.

The use of the term *grapevine* can be traced back to the 1860s during the Civil War. Because battle fronts moved frequently, the telegraph wires that were used by the army were loosely strung from tree to tree across battlefields, similar to grapevines. Because the wires needed to be hung quickly, and little effort was given to the care with which they were installed, the messages transmitted over them were often garbled, leading to misinterpretation and inaccurate communication. In time, rumors or unofficial commands were said to have been heard "via the grapevine." The grapevine has been part of organizational culture ever since.[22]

Social constructions of meaning. It is through such networks that rumors are passed on, gossip is exchanged, and word-of-mouth diffusion of important news is transmitted. In many ways, the fate of an organization may depend on message content within this network and how well it works. If communication through the grapevine continuously contains meanings defining management as negative, uncaring, callous, or exploitive to workers, then these are the socially constructed meanings about management that workers will share. This sharing validates such meanings—gives them social legitimacy. Individuals use these meanings to build or rebuild their personal beliefs about the organization. If this happens, a very different organizational culture may develop from the one desired by the organization. For such reasons, studies of informal communication within organizational grapevines can be very important.

Capacity, flexibility, and speed. Generally speaking, informal communication networks within an organization convey a great number and variety of messages on a day-to-day basis— possibly exceeding the number carried in the formal channels. These networks are very flexible, which is exactly the opposite of the channels for formal communication. In the informal process, messages flow by word of mouth, phone, computer, and texts. They move without restriction, both up and down the ranks and horizontally within a given stratum. Certain centers for the exchange of messages facilitate the process. These include restrooms, coffee machines or water coolers, the cafeteria or lunchroom, and the parking lot. Indeed, any point or place where employees frequently encounter one another or get together can serve as a message center. Furthermore, people call one another at home and continue the process after working hours.

Because of these conditions of few barriers, many channels, and virtually no restrictions on content, informal communication can flow very swiftly to surprisingly large numbers of people. In this sense, it is a very efficient form of communication in that it can bring messages and meanings about a variety of topics to a large number of participants in a relatively short time. "Cybergossip" (gossip by computer) has made the grapevine an even faster means of communication.

The messages, rumors, and gossip that travel through the grapevine can have a dramatic impact upon the organization. However, these messages also have consequences for those who initiate them. Informal communication can enhance or detract from the influence an individual has in the workplace depending on the nature of the communication.[23]

Distortion of Messages in the "Grapevine"

The accuracy of an organizational grapevine can be very low. This is not always the case, however, especially with very short messages (such as "The boss has just quit" or "Sonja has been promoted"). Nevertheless, for more complex messages, a number of specific patterns of distortion have been found by social scientists studying word-of-mouth communication as it occurs in a variety of contexts.

Two general patterns of distortion characterize the spread of rumors, the movement of news reports from one person to another, and almost any similar interpersonal transmissions of verbal messages. These two patterns will be described separately, but in reality they tend to occur together in the same setting when a particular message is transmitted by word of mouth along an interpersonal grapevine:. the **embedding pattern**[24] and the **compounding pattern**.[25]

The embedding pattern. The embedding pattern refers to a particular set of distortions in a message that may occur when it is transmitted orally from one person to the next in a kind of serial pattern. That is, a person learns firsthand about some event or condition and then passes on a message about it by word of mouth. The receiver lacks access to whatever realities prompted the first person to formulate the story but passes on a new version of the message to a third. From there it continues in a chain of tellers and retellers, none of whom have actually seen or heard the facts that were the basis of the original account.

Such a system is typical of what often happens along a grapevine, and it invites several kinds of distortions. A considerable amount of research has identified three specific forms of distortion that often characterize the content of a message as it moves along a chain of tellers and retellers. These are **leveling, sharpening, and assimilation.**

Leveling refers to a general shortening of the original account, rumor, or story. As it travels from one person to the next, limitations of attention, perception, and memory (much like those discussed in distortions of formal communication) quickly reduce the message to fewer words and ideas. If the original account is relatively long, it can lose as much as half of its detail as it is retold by the first person in the chain. The second will forget additional details and pass on a still shorter account. The story or rumor continues to shrink in number of words and details as it passes on through additional individuals until only a short (leveled) version remains. This brief version is then passed along more or less intact as it continues to move from one person to another.

Sharpening is the counterpart of leveling. As the story or account shrinks, it becomes organized around its more central or salient details. The version becomes increasingly concise until it is only a summary of the original message. This is a result of the way human beings construct meanings and store them in memory. Inevitably, this results in loss of detail, and con-sequent distortions creep in as the message is successively repackaged into briefer and briefer versions.

Assimilation is a process by which the message is reshaped by the psychological characteristics and culturally learned habits of the person who hears it. This is what most people call distortion, in that meanings are changed and the story undergoes transformations in content. These transformations can be substantial. They occur because of selective perception, memory, and recall based on individual attitudes, values, and other personality factors. They also occur because of cultural tendencies to think about topics in characteristic ways. To illustrate, a man and a woman who are married, but not to each other, can be reported as having been seen in a lengthy and private conversation. The next person, with romantic orientations, may interpret this as a possibly passionate encounter. A third, using cultural definitions of male–female relationships as potentially implying intimacy, speaks of the couple as lovers, and a juicy scandal sweeps the organization.

Through leveling, sharpening, and assimilation, then, the embedding process can produce many unexpected and unusual changes in the content of a message as it moves by informal word-of-mouth communication through the grapevine of an organization.

The compounding pattern. The second major pattern of distortion is what DeFleur has called the compounding pattern.[26] When a message transmitted along a grapevine is of especially high interest to a group, it can move very swiftly and can undergo a pattern of distortion that is quite different from that described by the embedding process. A substantial body of research has revealed a pattern whereby an original message passed by informal communication in a grapevine gains additional details and interpretations that were never part of the original. This tends to happen under two conditions: first, if the original message is relatively brief and, second, if it is of a threatening or disturbing nature.

To illustrate, assume that a short rumor is transmitted along the grapevine to the effect that the factory will be closed and everyone will be laid off. Such a tension-producing message is likely to travel through the informal network very swiftly. However, as it moves along, individuals are likely to add elements that they believe are relevant and that help explain what is happening. One may have heard that some government agency was planning an investigation. Another may have heard that accountants were seen working overtime. These elements could be compounded into the idea that the factory was going to close and all would lose their jobs because the owners were going bankrupt as a result of someone mismanaging the funds. On this basis, the story could grow even more with the retelling. Speculation would arise as to who would be fired first, when the closing would take place, and what benefits would or would not be provided for those let go. Further, rumors could circulate about who mismanaged (embezzled?) the funds and who is being investigated.

In reality, the embedding and the compounding patterns tend to work together in the actual transmission of rumors through a grapevine. A story can grow one day and shrink the next. It can be shortened, assimilated, and compounded at the same time. No single pattern characterizes the flow of messages in a process of informal communication in an organizational grapevine. What can be said with certainty is that messages transmitted in this manner are very likely to result in reconstructions of meaning by receivers.

Implications for Managers

As the previous discussion indicates, the grapevine is not all *pinot noir*. Informal communication networks suffer many problems such as the inaccuracy of the content that is passed along and misinterpretation by those at the receiving end. Another potential problem is the threat of legal action arising from false information that is passed along in the workplace. In recent years, lawsuits for defamation, fraud, invasion of privacy, emotional distress, harassment, and discrimination have resulted from grapevine inaccuracies.

Yet, the grapevine can also be an asset to an organization. Although some managers try to silence the grapevine in order to avoid problems, management communication scholar Patricia Karathanos recommends instead that certain ground rules be followed to promote a "healthy" environment in which the grapevine operates. These include the following:

1. *Accept that the grapevine exists and don't try to eliminate it.* Although it has the potential to create problems, it can also be used to benefit the organization.

2. *Acknowledge the fact that the grapevine should generally remain unrestrained.* When managers try to systematically thwart or take control of it, the grapevine can loose its effectiveness.

3. *Do not underestimate the power of the grapevine or its importance to the organization.* Ignoring the grapevine can do more harm than good, as many managers have learned the hard way.

4. *Make use of the grapevine, rather than remaining a passive observer.* Monitor the content of the grapevine, so that false information can be corrected before damage is done. Used this way, it can serve as an early warning system for the organization. Indeed, managers often use the grapevine to send "trial baloons" or to test new plans or ideas and get employee reactions before final decisions are made.

5. *Maintain all formal communication channels in the organization.* The grapevine is not a substitute for formal communication; the idea here is to use the grapevine as an effective supplement.

6. *Remind and encourage organization members to question and assess the accuracy of grapevine messages before responding to them.* This will help keep the grapevine from becoming a facilitator of false rumors that can seriously damage the organization.[27]

Consequences of Organizational Communication

Communication processes in organizations are extraordinarily complex. Both formal and informal communication provide the basis for different forms of social organization and pathways for the flow of messages.[28] This rich flow has at least two major consequences: The first is the development of a unique or specialized organizational culture and the second is the development and maintenance of two kinds of cohesion that binds the members of the group to the whole.

Specialized organizational cultures. Every human group has a culture. As explained in Chapter 8, specialized cultures are those beliefs, attitudes, values, and patterns of behavior shared within some segment of a society that distinguish it from the general culture of the society. Within each organization, an internal culture develops that is unique to that particular group. Thus, IBM, your college or university, and the U.S. Army all have specialized internal cultures that are different from that of any other category or group. Similarly, each government agency, church, prison, and bank has its own specialized internal culture. It includes all the physical objects, attitudes, values, beliefs, sentiments, rules, and special language produced and shared by its members.

Moreover, within any organization, there are many mini- or microcultures. These are highly localized versions of unique cultures that are developed by particular branches or divisions—or even small groups of peers and friends.

Unique organizational cultures develop from two basic sources: One is the official organization as it functions with its carefully defined channels of formal communication; the other is the informal network from which many individual microcultures at all levels of the organization develop. In some organizations, the group's overall internal culture may support the organization and help it achieve its goals. In others, conflicting microcultures can become the basis of serious conflict.

Cultures in conflict. Recall the earlier discussion on the vertical nature of the formal channels of communication in large organizations. In a typical production-oriented industrial organization, then, within the engineering division, formal messages flow up and down the line. They do the same within the manufacturing division and within the sales division. However, few formal messages cross these boundaries. Engineers seldom communicate extensively with sales specialists, who in turn seldom communicate with those who manufacture the product. This results in three separate communication structures that foster unique cultures within the three divisions. Thus, engineers, sales personnel, and manufacturing specialists develop and use their own languages and habits of perception. Within each of these separate cultures, people share distinctive attitudes, values, and beliefs that are not the same as those of the other divisions.

There is always a danger that these differences among unique cultures within a diverse organization will interfere with overall communication, that the language of one may become incomprehensible to the others. These are barriers to effective communication, even of the formal type, and the degree to which the group can achieve its goals is limited.

Such cultural differences can become a basis for *conflict*. Remember, even small groups of work associates can develop a microculture. A small group on the day shift, and an equally small group on the night shift, who do exactly the same work on the same machines, may have different microcultures. One may share favorable views toward management whereas the other views management negatively. In such circumstances, one group has been known to quietly sabotage the other.

Organizational cohesion. If some form of cohesion did not exist within an organization, there would be no way to keep its members performing the often unpleasant tasks needed to accomplish its goals. We saw earlier that various management-oriented approaches have tried to find policies and strategies to enhance motivation to keep workers performing at a high level of efficiency. These approaches were based on the necessity of providing personal goal satisfaction to maintain the loyalty and dedication of individual group members.

Organizational cohesion is different from personal satisfactions, such as one might derive from a good salary, a secure job, or high status. It is also different from that which keeps other kinds of groups together. For example, earlier it was discussed that it is sentiment-based cohesion that binds members to small intimate groups, such as families and peers. However, it is reward-based cohesion that characterizes discussion groups and assignment-based cohesion that operates in small, formal decision-making groups.

Cohesion in an organization is not easily explained by any of these types. Such a group is kept together as an organized whole by what is correctly called *dependency-based cohesion.*[29] This type of cohesion is a product of the complex division of labor that produces a strong pattern of dependencies among individuals (and even units) within an organization. To illustrate, workers on the assembly line depend on clerks in the payroll division who process their wages into a check. In turn, those clerks would have nothing to do if it were not for such workers. In the same manner, every person performing a task in the entire division of labor produces a product or service on which others depend. Such people may not even know each other—or if they do they may dislike each other. Nevertheless, they are in a relationship of mutual task dependency that holds the overall group together so that it can function as a unit.

What coordinates the activities within this division of interdependent labor is formal communication. For example, the payroll department would have no idea how much workers should be paid without formally communicated data regarding pay scale, hours worked, and so on, for each individual. Similarly, throughout the system, a flow of formal communication provides vital instructions that coordinate subgroups and individuals performing specialized tasks within the structure.

Generally, then, formal communication is the basis on which dependency-based cohesion is established and maintained. That was true at the time the pyramids were built, and it remains true today. If that formal communication becomes disrupted, distorted, or even delayed, serious consequences follow. Realistically, however, we must look at all four types of cohesion to explain fully what holds an organization together, enables individual members to satisfy their needs, and makes it possible for the group to attain its collective goals. That is, the bonds that link members to the whole in the de facto organization are based on a combination of sentiment-based cohesion within small groups of work associates, reward-based cohesion in more temporary groups, assignment-based cohesion among members of decision-making groups, and dependency-based cohesion that is a product of interrelated tasks in the overall structure. Throughout, however, communication in all its various forms holds the organizational system together.

Chapter Review

- An organization is a relatively large human group whose pattern of social organization has been rationally designed to achieve a desired objective. Any large group requires complex rules for communication so that the activities of its participants can be effectively coordinated. This is usually handled by a hierarchy of managers who transmit and receive messages, upward and downward, to and from the rank and file and, more rarely, laterally among themselves.

- Bureaucracy is a theory of social organization used in designing the goals, norms, roles, ranks, and controls in an organization. While some denounce its negative features, it is the impersonal rules of bureaucratic theory that define the basic ways in which people communicate and relate to each other in large groups with formal patterns of formal organization.

- Leadership in organizations is based on what Max Weber called legal-rational authority. Such leaders are usually selected because they possess technical managerial skills, and they are permitted to exercise power within a limited sphere that is narrowly defined by official definitions and rulings.

- Four general theories that focus on strategies of organizational design, management, and communication have been developed during the past two centuries: *human use, human relations,* and *human resources* and *systems theory.* Each incorporates very different systems of communication between workers and management in organization.

- Formal communication takes place only between clearly designated parties; it concerns a restricted range of organization-relevant topics; and messages are transmitted and received via prescribed media. In short, formal communication dictates *who* can say *what* to be received by *whom* about specific *topics* making use of what *medium.*

- Messages flow not only through the official channels prescribed for formal communication but through grapevines as well. Two general types of distortion have been found—the embedding pattern and the compounding pattern—that characterize the spread of informal messages through grapevines.

- A specialized internal culture can be found within any organization. Members of the group share language patterns, beliefs and orientations that set it apart from other similar groups. Furthermore, within the organization microcultures can develop in various units and divisions or even among small groups of work associates. These unique cultures can support an organization, or they can be the basis of serious conflicts.

- The bonds that link members in an organization are based on a combination of sentiment, reward, assignment, and dependency-based cohesion that is a product of task interdependencies in the overall structure.

Key Terms

organization	scientific management	compounding pattern
authority	human relations perspective	leveling
charismatic authority	human resources perspective	sharpening
legal-rational authority	grapevine	assimilation
human use perspective	vertical transmission	organizational cohesion
wage incentive system	embedding pattern	

Notes

1. Muzio, E. G., Fisher, D. J., & Thomas, E. (2008). Four secrets to liking your work: You may not need to quit to get the job you want. Upper Saddle River, NJ: *Financial Times Press.* Retrieved from http://www.ftpress.com/store/product.aspx?isbn=0132344459.

2. In earlier times of war, the survival of a society was largely a matter of the strength and

bravery of individual armed men who fought each other in hand-to-hand combat. In modern times, individual bravery is still important, but wars are won or lost on the basis of production of military equipment, technology, and supplies that support armed forces. That was the case in World War I. It was true in World War II, when the Manhattan Project (a gigantic complex of organizations) provided the means to end the war with Japan. It clearly remains the case today as organizations produce the advanced technology that determines the outcome of conflicts.

3. For excellent elementary discussions of the importance of groups and communication in organizations, see: Goodall, H. L., Jr. (1990). *Small group communication in organizations* (2nd ed., pp. 1–21). Dubuque, IA: William C. Brown; Richmond, V. P., & McCroskey, J. C. (1990). *Communication in organizations* (pp. 1–10). Edina, MN: Bellwether. Also, for more advanced discussions see: Jablin, F. M., Putnam, L. L., Roberts, K. H., & Porter, L. W. (Eds). (1987). *Handbook of organizational communication.* Newbury Park, CA: Sage; Jablin, F. M., & Sussman, L. (1983). Organizational group communication: A review of the literature and model of the process. In Greenbaum, H. H., Falcione, R. L., & Hellweg, S. A. (Eds.), *Organizational communication: Abstracts, analysis and overview* (Vol. 8, pp. 11–50). Beverly Hills, CA: Sage.

4. For excellent discussions of both the historical roots and the distinctive aspects of organizational communication, see: Miller, K. (2011). *Organizational communication: Approaches and processes* (6th ed.). Boston: Wadsworth; Modaff, D.P., Butler, J.A., & DeWine, S. (2011). *Organizational communication: Foundations, challenges, and misunderstandings* (3rd ed.). Boston: Allyn & Bacon; Shockley-Zalabak, P.S. (2009). *Fundamentals of organizational communication: Knowledge, sensitivity, skills, values* (8th ed.). Boston: Allyn & Bacon.

5. See: Weber, M. (1947). Wirtschaft und gesellschaft, Part I of which has been translated by Henderson, A. M., & Parsons, T. (1947). *The theory of social and economic organization.* New York: Oxford University Press. A good secondary source is Gerth, H. H., & Mills, C. W. (Eds.

and Trans.). (1946). *From Max Weber: Essays in sociology.* New York: Oxford University Press.

6. Weber's analysis of the nature of bureaucracy was not focused exclusively on problems of communication. In fact, it dealt more centrally with components of formally prescribed social organization (which, of course, depend on well-defined channels of communication). For purposes of this text, we have adapted his analysis to emphasize communication issues.

7. This list is a composite drawn from: Henderson & Parsons, *Theory of social organization,* pp. 333–336. See also Gerth & Mills, *From Max Weber,* pp. 196–204.

8. Kreitner, R. (1983). *Management* (p. 38). Boston: Houghton Mifflin.

9. Koontz, H. (1961). The management theory jungle. *Academy of Management Journal, 4,* 174–188.

10. Smith, A. (1976). *An inquiry into the nature and causes of the wealth of nations.* Chicago: University of Chicago Press. (First published 1776.)

11. Copely, F. B. (1923). *Frederick W. Taylor: Father of scientific management* (p. 3). New York: Harper & Brothers.

12. See: Taylor, F. W. (1919). *Principles of scientific management.* New York: Harper & Row.

13. Fayol, H. (1949). *Administration industrielle generale.* Translated by C. Storrs as: *General and industrial management.* London: Isaac Pitman & Sons.

14. Flynn, K. (January 30, 2002). A nation challenged: Emergency policy; a focus on communication failures. *The New York Times,* section A, p. 11; Downes, L. (June 4, 2002). Connect government stovepipes. *USA Today,* p. 13A.

15. Mayo, E. (1966). *Human problems of an industrial civilization.* New York: Viking. (First published 1933.)

16. The entire series of the Hawthorne studies are discussed in detail in: Roethlisberger, J., & Dickson, W. J. (1939). *Management and the worker.* Cambridge, MA: Harvard University Press.

17. This type of outcome, in which the experiment itself fosters motivations and behavior among subjects that can interfere with

the results, came to be called the "Hawthorne effect." It is a standard research hazard to which social scientists are alert when they study human behavior in experimental settings.

18. Our account of these experiments is necessarily a simplified one. In later years they became more controversial than our discussion would make it seem. Various *post hoc* interpretations have been offered in later years about why the results were obtained and what they really mean. Some of these are quite different from those offered in the original reports. See, for example: Carey, A. (1967). The Hawthorne studies: A radical critique. *American Sociological Review, 32,* 403–416; Frank, R., Kaul, J. (1978). The Hawthorne experiments: First statistical interpretation. *American Sociological Review, 43,* 623–643.

19. Roth, J. (1985). The stuff that quality is made of. *Industrial Management, 9, 7,* 18–19.

20. McMillan, C. J. (Spring 1982). From quality control to quality management: Lessons from Japan. *Business Quarterly, 32.*

21. Bertalanffy, L. von (1950). An outline of general system theory. *The British Journal for the Philosophy of Science,* 1 (2), 134–165.

22. Karathanos, P., & Auriemmo, A. (1999). Care and feeding of the organizational grapevine. *Industrial Management, 41, 2,* 26–30.

23. Kurland, N. B., & Pelled, L. H. (2000). Passing the word: Toward a model of gossip and power in the workplace. *The Academy of Management Review, 25, 2,* 428–438.

24. The seminal study is that of: Allport, G. W., & Postman, I. (1947). *The psychology of rumor.* New York: Henry Holt.

25. For a summary of classic studies on these issues, see: DeFleur, M. L. (1962). Mass communication and the study of rumor. *Sociological Inquiry, 32, 1,* 51–70.

26. This concept as a description of message distortion in rumor transmission was introduced by DeFleur, M. L. (1962). Mass communication and the study of rumor. *Sociological Inquiry, 33,* pp. 51–70.

27. Karathanos & Auriemmo, Care and feeding of the organizational grapevine.

28. For additional discussions of formal and informal communication see: Shockley-Zalabak, P. (2009); Miller, K. (2011); Kreps, G. I. (1990). *Organizational communication* (2nd ed., pp. 195–221). White Plains, NY: Longman.).

29. This is a version of what Emile Durkheim called "organic solidarity" in his classic analysis: (1947). *The division of labor in society* (G. Simpson, Trans.). New York: Free Press. (Originally published 1893.)

Chapter 8

Communicating
Between Cultures

The Boeing 747 touched down at Chicago's O'Hare and slowly taxied to the gate to unload its passengers. It had been a long flight from Seoul, South Korea, and Yu-Jin Park was very glad that it was over.

With plans to attend Northwestern University, Yu-Jin was anxious to try out his English-speaking skills. He had studied the complex language for a number of years—first at the high school level and then for four years at the university in Seoul.

Yu-Jin knew that his Korean name might be difficult for native English speakers, so he had chosen a new one: "Eugene."

After clearing customs and immigration, Yu-Jin headed for the door marked "Ground Transportation." No problem there. He understood the meaning and knew that there would be taxies available—as there are at any airport in the world. All he had to do was tell the driver the address where he would be staying.

Yu-Jin entered the taxi and then politely asked the driver to take him to his cousin's address, which he carefully read from a card so he would say it right.

For a long time the driver didn't say a word.

Finally, the driver turned to Yu-Jin and asked, "How do you like them Cubs?"

Yu-Jin was puzzled by the question. He was not quite sure of the meaning of "cubs." Whipping out his electronic translator, he quickly typed in "c-u-b-s." Instantly he saw the Korean translation on the screen: "The immature offspring of certain animals, such as lions and bears."

Ah, thought Yu-Jin, I can answer that question.

"Oh yes," he replied, "they are animals. I like them," he replied.

"Yeah, you're right," said the driver. "They really are animals. I get disgusted with them, too.

"Don't worry," said the driver, "when they play tomorrow afternoon, the Reds are going to slaughter 'em."

Yu-Jin was not at all sure that he heard that right. He worried that perhaps he did not understand the term "reds." He thought it meant a color. To check he quickly used his translator and keyed in "r-e-d-s." The Korean meaning instantly came up: "A colloquial term often used to refer to communists." He knew a great deal about communists. They ruled North Korea.

Somewhat puzzled Yu-Jin replied, "Well, such a slaughter would be unfortunate. I hope that it can be prevented."

The driver nodded, relying, "Yeah, you're right. Let's hope that it isn't a real bloodbath."

As the cab pulled up in front of the apartment building, Yu-Jin felt that he had handled his first conversation with an American quite well. Still, it did seem bizarre. He wondered why the Americans would allow such innocent animals at play to be killed by communists. Oh well, he thought, such animal sacrifices are probably just some sort of local custom.

The cab driver thought, nice kid. Seems to be from China or Japan, but he really knows a lot about American baseball.

Why is **intercultural communication** important, and worthy of close study? A major reason is that the American society has greater diversity than virtually any other and it is very important that we all get along. Our society is one where, over nearly four centuries, starting in 1620, people came together from many places of origin and slowly had to learn to live together, even though they have always been of different religions, races, and specialized ways of life. In contrast, in many other parts of the world, people cannot seem to tolerate each other. They do not easily mix, or they even engage in massacres, holocausts, "ethnic cleansings," and endless wars against each other. In contrast, the United States remains a stable society in which many kinds of people coexist—with tensions and prejudices, to be sure, but with remarkable overall tolerance and accommodation in comparison with countries torn with hatred, brutality, and violence.

This chapter discusses the nature of **culture**, both in terms of **general culture** (sometimes called "mainstream culture"), such as the culture of an entire nation, and **specialized cultures**, such as the cultures that exist among different **social categories** of people in the society (important examples are people who share particular ethnic, racial, or religious backgrounds; people of male or female gender, distinctive socioeconomic classes, occupations, and sexual orientations; and people with physical challenges). In particular, this chapter analyzes the features of the *specialized cultures* among examples of such categories that can pose barriers to effective interpersonal and group communication. It suggests guidelines as to how these can be dealt with in interpersonal and group contexts so that people who are different can relate to each other in more effective ways. (See Box 8.1.)

BOX 8.1   *A Closer Look*

The Meaning of the Term *Culture*

Culture in a basic sense consists of the ways in which a society, group, or other category of people *solve problems* in approved and acceptable manners. Some problems are solved with tools and other forms of *material culture*. This began with the earliest human beings who made tools from stone. Later people developed clothing, shelters, pottery, and other artifacts. Eventually the need for reliable supplies of food was solved by the development of agriculture. Material culture accumulated over the course of eons; artifacts spread from one society to another and material culture became increasingly complex. This process continues today, as advanced societies develop more and more complex technologies (computers, aircraft, weapons, and objects of daily living) that solve problems.

Another category of culture is *symbolic*—that is, language-based. When the evolution of physical changes in the human body made speech possible, languages were developed to solve problems of communication. Language also made possible the accumulation, spread, and sharing of beliefs about the nature of social and physical reality. As advances were made through the development of writing, print, and eventually the complex media of today, the storing of ideas was freed from dependence on memory alone to pass on solutions from one generation to the next. Today the process continues with huge amounts of knowledge stored and accessible in many forms.

Finally, another category of culture is *normative*. This consists of a body of shared rules and beliefs about how people should behave as they relate to each other and conduct their daily activities. Such rules for behavior are embedded in a system of *values*, which are shared conceptions of what is right or wrong, permissible or not, punished or rewarded. Each society, category, or group may hold different versions of these norms and values.

The Nature of Culture

The term *culture* was first introduced into the social sciences in 1871 by anthropologist Edward B. Tylor, who said, "Culture . . . is that complex whole which includes knowledge, belief, art, law, morals, custom, and any other habits acquired by man [and woman] as a member of society." Tylor's rather broad definition of culture is still basically correct today, but a more modern definition would be this: *Culture refers to the total of all material, social and symbolic creations that a society's members have incorporated into their overall design for living.*

One key to understanding the nature of culture is to emphasize the difference between a *society*—a large and complex group of people carrying on a common life—and their *culture*, which they produce and practice. In other words, a culture is not a group of people. It is the things they use, the beliefs they share, and the distinctive rules or patterns of behavior they follow. In this sense, culture is the social heritage of a society—all the solutions to problems of living that are handed down from one generation to the next.

Seen from this perspective, *culture* is an umbrella term—a very broad and inclusive concept covering many things that people use, say, think, and do. Two types or categories of culture fit under that umbrella here in the United States: The first is the *general* or mainstream culture, which brings a certain uniformity to the ways of life of people living in a diverse society. The second category is *specialized* cultures (sometimes called "co-cultures"), or the unique ways of life that characterize an

When people communicate interculturally, messages are exchanged between people of different cultures under conditions in which their backgrounds influence or change the process in a significant way.

such as science, sports, and the military.[1] These institutions broadly define the ways such activities are carried on within the society, with many variations among specific segments of the population. The general culture also includes the principal *language* in use, widely shared *beliefs,* the material *artifacts* and *technologies* that people employ (airplanes, refrigerators, computers, spoons, wristwatches, and all the rest), plus the *values* to which most people subscribe. For example, almost all of us living by the rules of the American culture obey the nation's laws; rely on automobiles for transportation; buy things in supermarkets and shopping malls with U.S. currency; watch television; and live in homes furnished with tables, chairs, beds, and so on. As Americans, we also value children, condemn crime, wear customary clothing, and generally live out our lives in and around the major social institutions of our society.

enormous number of social categories within a complex society (such as ours).

General Culture

To the extent that people of a society share a more or less similar material culture and live together within a common set of major social institutions—even though there may be many diverse social categories among them—they participate in a *general* or mainstream culture. It is this basic culture that enables all of us to coexist within a larger, single society and to communicate with one another in relatively predictable ways. It holds society together in a functioning system regardless of where our parents or grandparents came from, the color of our skin, or the first or second language we speak.

In a diverse society, such as ours, **general culture** includes the basic design of what social scientists call the society's principal *social institutions* (family, economic, political, educational, and religious). There are also others,

Specialized Cultures

A second and equally important set of cultures are those that provide ways of life for members of social categories that are in some way unique or different from the general society. Examples would be those who are rich. Their way of life, artifacts, and shared beliefs, as well as many other features of what they own, do, and believe, is different from that of the poor. In each of these categories, people carry on *specialized cultures.*

These are "cultures within cultures."[2] They are unique ways of life, including material artifacts, language, values, shared beliefs, and ways of speaking that characterize people in particular social categories, such as those classified by occupation, racial, ethnic, and religious affiliations, social classes, regions of the country, and sexual orientation. Examples include Latinos, Muslims, the very wealthy, vegetarians, Midwesterners, lesbians, men, first-year college students, factory workers, marines, and prison inmates.

Actually, specialized cultures *in miniature* exist in every family, corporation, school, police department, hospital and other group within our society. In each the participants must learn how that specialized culture defines the social and behavioral expectations of the group—its way of life and the pattern of social organization discussed in earlier chapters.

In many ways this factor of specialization is the bottom line of diversity. It is a consequence of the fact that each social category—and even each small group—has its own different pattern of culture. Distinctive patterns of beliefs, attitudes, language, and norms for behavior set the members of each such group apart from others in society. At the same time, however, the group members all participate in the general culture along with everyone else.

It is socialization within the general culture—learning its ways and its requirements—that *makes all of us similar;* but it is socialization within the specialized and miniature cultures of the social categories and groups to which we each belong that *makes each of us different.* This is the source of the unique personality each person develops.[3] Unique socialization within a cluster of specialized cultures is what brings one individual to *think,* and on occasion, to *act* differently from another. For example, an individual might identify herself as an Asian American (one specialized culture), a woman (another specialized culture), an attorney (a third), a vegetarian (a fourth), and a Catholic (a fifth). The amount of influence those specialized cultures have on the individual depends on a number of factors. For example, being a woman may not be one of her more dominant identities for most of her interactions with others. However, being a woman may become an important part of how she thinks of herself and how others see her in many communication exchanges.

For some people, the general culture defines much of what they believe, think, and do—especially among those whose families have been in the society for generations. Others, whose ancestral origins in another society are more recent, may enjoy retaining distinct identities of a specialized ethnic culture. Importantly,

the general culture ensures that all the various categories and groups with specialized cultures in the United States are not completely separate entities. They interact and overlap. With disparate specialized cultures in contact with one another, some assimilation and accommodation is inevitable. Consequently, we have learned to borrow from or imitate one another; to observe one another's holidays and eat one another's foods, to adopt one another's specific words and phrases, and to adjust to one another's customs and traditions. The result is a mix and match of diversity coming together.[4] Things that were originally unique to one specialized culture (tacos, sushi, soccer, specific fashions) may, over time, become part of the ever-evolving general culture.

Our cultural diversity is greater than that of any other nation in history. People from every nation on earth have immigrated to this country. No other nation can boast of the special contributions that each of our immigrant categories brought to this country. However, even though we are a nation of diversity, and a nation striving for justice, equality, and harmony among all people, we often fall short of that goal.

In the year 2010, the number of foreign-born residents in the United States reached the *highest level in history.*[5] According to the results of the 2010 census, the estimated foreign-born population climbed to 37.6 million or or about 12.7 percent of the total population. Our immigrant population has doubled in the last 20 years, and nearly tripled in the last 30.[6] The census results also showed that almost half of the foreign-born residents were from Latin America, especially Mexico and Central America.[7] Many others came from Asia, but only 12 percent came from Europe—a significant change from many previous decades when the majority of immigrants listed a European country as their place of birth.

These recent arrivals settled mainly in California, New York, Florida, Texas, New Jersey, and Illinois. These states combined accounted for 65 percent of the total. However, California led the nation with 27 percent of foreign-born residents.[8] Recent census data and projections reveal that a number of states, including California, Hawaii, New Mexico, and Texas are characterized as minority majorities; that is, the combined population of any and all groups that are non-hispanic, non-whites is greater than 50 percent.[9]

Importantly, the immigrant cultures brought to the United States remain with us. Even third and fourth generations can find influences on their lives that are derived from the ethnic, religious, or racial origins of their ancestors. Thus, although we in the United States are Americans, we are not all alike. We truly live in a multicultural society where cultural divisions often create special problems in communicating accurately and effectively. To assume, then, that all people will, and should, behave and communicate in the same way ignores our rich cultural mix. This chapter attempts to sensitize us to unique demands of specialized cultures that make a difference in how we communicate.

Dealing with Diversity

How has the United States coped with the diversity of its population? Initially, our country was committed to a **melting pot policy**—an attempt to reduce cultural differences between people as quickly as possible and to assimilate them into the general culture. The logic behind that policy was that, if strong "tribal"-type groups developed in the country, they would soon make efforts to separate themselves into politically independent entities. That was, in fact, a real and understandable risk. It had happened earlier, in the South during the Civil War and in Louisiana and Texas, where separate governments came into existence.

It was the schools that led the melting pot effort. They were used to transform the children of immigrants from "foreigners" to "Americans" as fully and as soon as possible. In the early part of the twentieth century, the nation's goal was to *eradicate the differences* among people and thereby to eliminate language, social, political, and economic problems. Everyone was required to learn English and adopt the basic general American culture.

It worked! The nation remained together even though millions of people from other countries poured in during the 1800s and the early 1900s. Later, and in more recent times, the melting pot policy has come under criticism on the grounds that it did not respect people's ways of life. Furthermore, it often produced many problems for immigrant families—especially between children, who assimilated rapidly, and their parents, who retained their culture of origin.

The melting pot policy has also been criticized for producing a majority-is-superior viewpoint. That is, any culture outside the majority was expected to assimilate or conform to the majority—certainly not the other way around. A quick look at the numbers of each ethnic category in the United States reveals that the majority who immigrated were primarily from European countries. It is for this reason that most white Americans in the United States are called *European Americans* by some scholars (as opposed to African Americans, Native Americans, etc.).

Originally, the word **majority** was intended to refer to the actual numbers of those most numerous in the population. Later it came to have connotations, including dominant, superior, and more powerful. In comparison with the majority, then, all so-called **minority** cultures were regarded as somehow less significant, less dominant, and less important. This view has by no means vanished. It may not be acceptable to many, but in a factual sense, there has been a long tradition, which remains an ethnocentric tendency today, for some people in the United States to regard themselves and their way of life as superior, while looking down on that of others.[10]

While the melting pot policy did prevent political breaks from the union, and it did very effectively help develop a general American culture, it did not completely eradicate cultural differences among immigrant people. In communities across our country, people whose ancestors came from one "old country" or another continue to keep alive many of the traditions and feelings of identity that the policy was intended to remove. Even people who are several generations removed from their immigrant ancestors still feel the influences of their cultural roots.

On the other hand, it is also true that after several generations have passed, many Americans no longer feel a connection to the land of their ancestors. In other words, with the passage of time and increased assimilation into the general American culture, many believe that they and their families have "become" American.

In addition, many of the specialized cultures of those groups who came to this nation earlier have disappeared or are doing so now. For example, a study of 80 older Issei women (Japanese women who had immigrated from Japan to the United States) was completed back in 1957. It showed that the women of the immigrant generation maintained an essentially Japanese way of life—in language, relating to their husbands and children, diet, recreation, religion, and many other ways. About half of their Nissei daughters (second generation) had married men outside their ethnic group (mainly white Americans). Additional studies showed that by the third generation, the Japanese language was no longer in use by such women. Their daily routines were typically American. Their physical characteristics had changed due to the biological mixing. In every other respect they had both amalgamated (biologically) and assimilated (culturally) into the mainstream of American culture. Much the same process is occurring among those who came to the United States from Cuba, Mexico, the Caribbean, and elsewhere in recent decades. As each generation matures, then, features of their original immigrant culture disappear to be replaced by those more common in the general American culture.[11]

Today, our nation embraces a policy of **cultural pluralism,** which means that we try to tolerate and accept our differences; maintain a strong sense of diversity; and, at the same time, remain a unified nation committed to similar democratic ideals. Within the context of cultural pluralism, we recognize that although we remain diverse, citizens of all backgrounds share a general American culture that enables us to carry on our day-to-day activities and relate to one another in fairly predictable ways. In a mature multicultural society with a strong political system, complete assimilation is no longer needed.

Excessive Ethnocentrism

Regardless of how long they or their ancestors have been living in the United States, most U.S. citizens are proud to be Americans. When faced with outside threats or aggression, Americans are very patriotic and loyal to their country. Indeed, many have died defending their country against brutal aggressors who were bent on destroying it. There is no doubt that pride in country, loyalty, and patriotism are beneficial. Still, in the extreme, such beliefs can be problematic if they are used to exclude or dominate others' valued cultural orientations. The sense of pride that teaches us to value our way of life can also teach us that we are somehow superior to all others. The point is that cultural pluralism depends on **cultural inclusion**—a commitment to acknowledge, respect, and (when possible) defer to others who may think, feel, and behave differently from ourselves. In contrast, **cultural exclusion** is a condition that ignores our inherent diversity and imposes a singular view of all other people—one that insists that there is only one right way to think and act.

A term for such an attitude is **ethnocentrism**—from the Greek word *ethnos,* meaning "the people." This attitude is often at the root of cultural exclusion. People like to think of their particular group as the "insiders," and everyone else as "outsiders," who are not as acceptable. Such distinctions between "in-groups" and "out-groups" are sometimes harmless.[12] Indeed, some level of ethnocentrism can be helpful to a society or to a particular group if patriotism or pride is needed to meet an emergency. Take a moment now to assess your own degree of ethnocentrism by completing the survey in Box 8.2.

BOX 8.2   *Are You Ethnocentric?*

Instructions:

We all hold stereotypes. This questionnaire assesses some of your own stereotypes about your and others' membership in particular specialized cultures. Complete these five steps *in order*:

Step 1: Think of one specialized culture of which you are a member (for example, female, Muslim, student, or Latina)—but only select ONE.

Step 2: Think of another specialized culture to which you don't belong (for example, male, Jewish, professor, Middle Eastern American)—but again, only select ONE.

Step 3: In the column labeled "My Culture," check five descriptive adjectives you think apply to your group.

Step 4: In the column labeled "Another Culture," check five adjectives you think apply to that group.

Step 5: Go back through the list of adjectives and rate each adjective you selected in terms of how favorable a quality you think it is. Use this scale:

5 = very favorable
4 = moderately favorable
3 = neither favorable or unfavorable
2 = moderately unfavorable
1 = very unfavorable

Put these ratings in the final column labeled "Favorableness Ratings."

My Culture	Another Culture	Descriptive Adjective	Favorableness Rating (5 – 1)
		Intelligent	
		Materialistic	
		Ambitious	
		Industrious	
		Deceitful	
		Conservative	
		Practical	
		Shrewd	
		Arrogant	
		Aggressive	
		Sophisticated	
		Conceited	
		Neat	
		Alert	
		Impulsive	
		Stubborn	
		Conventional	
		Progressive	
		Sly	
		Tradition-Loving	
		Pleasure-Loving	

Calculating Your Score:

The adjectives you checked reflect the stereotypes you hold about your own and another cultural group. Add the numbers for the two groups separately. Enter the two scores in the blanks below. Each score should range from a low of 5 to a high of 25. The higher the score, the more favorable the stereotype.

My culture = _____   Another culture = _____

Interpreting Your Score:

Compare your two scores, and consider what they say about your own degree of ethnocentrism.

Answer these questions:

- In what ways are you ethnocentric? To what extent do you think your stereotypes about another person's culture are real or grounded in truth?
- Do you think your stereotypes about your own culture generally reflect the way everyone really is who belongs to that group? Why or why not?
- Are stereotypes ever favorable? Why do you think so?
- Can so-called favorable stereotypes ever be a problem for members in that group? Why?

Source: Adapted from Gudykunst, W. B. (1991). *Bridging differences: Effective intergroup communication* (p. 75). Newbury Park, CA: Sage.

But rampant ethnocentrism is sometimes found in a more troublesome and exaggerated form called **chauvinism,** which can be defined as a condition of "boastful and truculent group self-assertion."[13] Chauvinism has in some cases in the past been particularly ugly and dangerous when people came to believe not only that their group is superior but also that they had a right to exploit, suppress, or even eliminate others whom they defined as less worthy. Such self-righteous and exaggerated ethnocentrism has been at the heart of many forms of truly dreadful human abuse throughout the world.[14] These include religious and ethnic wars, slavery, forcing women to serve as sexual servers for an army, and the concentration camps of World War II.

Cultural Relativity

An important way to view cultures without being judgmental is to use the principle of **cultural relativity,** a perspective that recognizes and accepts the idea that other people do things differently. This principle embodies the idea that what works for a group is right and correct from their point of view—even though it may be different from our own. For example, many of us would enthusiastically endorse the general American way of life as the most desirable, but if we were to ask people living in, say, South Korea, Iceland, or Maylasia, we would find that they do not agree and would argue that their own ways are just as desirable. Similarly, we might find people practicing different specialized cultures within the United States disagreeing over standards to live by; for example, consider some of the different attitudes of Catholics and Protestants, women and men, teenagers and senior citizens, and rural farmers and city dwellers. Looking at other groups of people within the perspective of relativity can help us understand how people can approach specific aspects of life in very different ways. Such understanding is the foundation for accepting them as people like ourselves.

At the same time, common sense must prevail. Few in the United States would have been willing to accept with comfort the culture of the Taliban, the Muslim fundamentalists who took power in Afghanistan in 1996 after the Soviets left. While they brought a rigid sense of order to that war-devastated country, their beliefs and practices were brutal. Ritual punishments and arbitrary, immediate flogging and other measures administered by gun- and whip-wielding youths were commonplace. Scholars have described the treatment of women by the Taliban as "the most systematic repression of women in history."[15] Special laws against women left them destitute, terrorized, without medical care, and physically and mentally ill. In addition, no woman could leave her home without the company of a male relative. Every woman had to wear a *burka* (a sacklike garment that covers the entire body, with only a small screen in front of the face out of which the woman can peer). No girl was allowed to go to school. Punishments for transgressions were severe. The Taliban "moral police" beat women with sticks in public for minor transgressions such as showing an ankle. All males were forbidden to shave. Listening to popular music, watching TV, and going to the movies were strictly forbidden. Finally, when the Taliban were found to support terrorist groups, such as the ones that attacked the World Trade Center on September 11, 2001, Americans had had enough. Cultural relativism did not prevail and armed forces were sent to root them out.

In a similar way, contemporary neo-Nazis, wanting to restore a society like that of Hitler, would not be acceptable to Americans. Or, a group like the Ku Klux Klan—with its negative definitions of African Americans, and its cultural practices of intimidating victims, burning crosses, and wearing white robes and hoods—would be difficult to accept using the principle of cultural relativity. Nevertheless, and again within a perspective of common sense, differences in cultural practices and beliefs that do not harm people need to be interpreted within that principle. Thus, cultural relativity does not mean that one must accept *any* form of behavior simply because some group practices it.

The excesses of pogroms, "ethnic cleansing," and oppression that exist in many societies could never, and should never, be acceptable to us.

The Influence of Culture on Communication

Culture and communication are inseparable. Anthropologist Edward T. Hall argues that *culture is communication and that communication is culture.*[16] He explains that the way we communicate—how our beliefs influence what we say, the language system we use, and the gestures we employ—are all preset for us by the culture we acquire. In other words, how we relate verbally and nonverbally to others is learned from the culture in which we grow up. In the same way, how we dress; our use of time; the odors we savor (and the ones we abhor); the distances we use to interact with others; and when, where, and with whom we maintain eye contact all are dictated, to a large extent, by the culture of our particular society or group.

In other ways, communication style speaks volumes about a person's specialized cultures. For example, Chinese Americans tend to be indirect and to understate their own accomplishments and successes. They learn to speak "humbly." European Americans, in contrast, learn to be "assertive" and to show pride in what they are able to do. Nonverbally, we might find some Latinos and Latinas and some African Americans associating direct and prolonged eye contact with status and power. Among them, looking directly and steadily at the eyes of someone of higher status is a sign of disrespect. It is not difficult to understand, then, that communication and culture are inseparable.

Intercultural Communication Defined

The increasing awareness that cultural backgrounds are central to understanding communication has been coupled with dramatic economic, political, and social needs to communicate internationally. Thus, researchers have urgently tried to discover those factors that "make a difference" in our efforts to communicate accurately and efficiently with others who are different.

Probably the single most significant lesson learned so far is that knowing someone's language *does not* ensure understanding. In fact, effective intercultural communication requires much more than learning, say, how to speak Spanish, French, German, Russian, or any other language. It requires an understanding and appreciation of the cultures that permeate the interaction. We all know of foreign visitors who are quite competent English speakers (some understand our grammar better than we do!) who violate our culturally defined norms dramatically. They may "invade our space" or arrive inexcusably late for an appointment or a dinner engagement—the sort of deviation that speaks volumes about their lack of understanding.

Similarly, some Americans traveling abroad have earned a reputation for being boorish because they did not recognize; accommodate to; and, at times, respect the rules of other people's cultures. For example, Americans sometimes blunder when they jump too quickly to a first-name basis with the English or French, ignore the strict dietary rules of a devout Hindu, or heartily slap a Taiwanese business person on the back.[17] Similar problems occur here in the United States when we violate one of the norms defined by a person's specialized culture.

We can define *intercultural communication* as *an exchange of messages that takes place between people of different social categories under conditions in which the cultures of those categories influence or change the process in some significant way.* In other words, a transaction classified as intercultural communication takes place between people whose culture-based perceptions and interpretations of verbal and nonverbal symbols are different enough to influence in different ways the meanings involved in the communication event.

In spite of these problems and considerations, the need to practice cultural relativism, to try

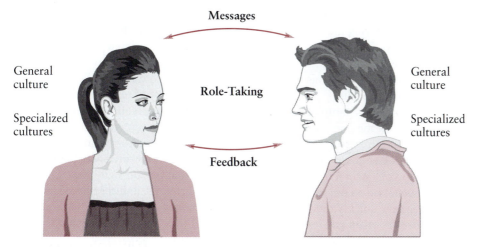

FIGURE 8.1

Intercultural Communication

Intercultural communication involves all of the factors of communication, with the influence of general cultures and specialized cultures that communicators bring to the exchange.

to get along with other kinds of people within our own society, and to accept them fully even though they are different from ourselves has never been more important. Following the end of the Cold War, the United States became locked in intense international competition in world markets, which has a powerful effect on us all. If we cannot meet that competition, our standard of living and general way of life will deteriorate.

Principles of Intercultural Communication

What do we need to know about intercultural communication that will help us relate to one another better? (Figure 8.1 illustrates the factors involved in intercultural communication.)

At least five factors should be acknowledged:

- *A person can belong to several specialized cultures, and the number of such affiliations can vary for an individual.* A man might identify himself as a business executive, a member of the upper middle class, and a Vietnam War veteran. He might further identify himself as a New Yorker and a Mormon.

Each of these terms is a label for his participation in specific specialized cultures.

- *Being a participant in a specific culture is both self and other defined.* Others may not know of, or may refuse to recognize, your identification with a particular culture. By the same token, they may assume incorrectly that, and act as though, you are a part of others. That is, you may think of yourself as independent politically, but others may regard you as a liberal Democrat or a conservative Republican. Or, consider a woman who denies the charge that she is a feminist, but others continue to claim that she is, and further, they respond to her as if she were. Remember the principle of the social construction of reality and W. I. Thomas's dictum: *If people believe something to be true they will act as though it is true.*

- *Any given specific culture can emerge to dominate a person's beliefs sufficiently to influence or alter a message exchange.* Whether or not a particular culture emerges and dominates the interaction depends primarily on the context and the parties involved.

For example, being a male may not be one of your more dominant identities during most of your interactions with others. However, there are occasions, and there are individuals, who can trigger that identification. If this happens, being a male can substantially change an ongoing interaction. For example, your male cultural identification may not be important to you when you are discussing the weather, your workload, or your reading preferences—particularly in your interactions with good friends, other men, and so on; but you probably will discover very quickly the special meaning of that identity when you have conversations with guys who are fans of particular sports teams, or when you find yourself among a group of mothers discussing problems of infant and child care.

- *The greater the number of similar cultures an individual brings to a conversation with others in an exchange, the higher the potential for accurate communication.* Recall that we expect others who share our background and cultural experiences to think as we do; behave as we do; and more important, construct meanings as we do. If this is indeed the case, people can communicate more accurately. Sometimes this does not work because we can have mistaken interpretations of cultural overlap. For example, just because two individuals are of a particular racial origin does not necessarily mean that both identify themselves as participating in the same specialized culture. Some may reject such a self-identity, preferring to distance themselves from the category, particularly if membership is associated with negative stereotypes and prejudice.

- *The greater the number of shared cultures individuals bring to a conversation, the greater their feelings of attraction and comfort while communicating.* We know that persons who think of themselves as holding similar beliefs, attitudes, and values are likely to find each other compatible and even attractive. The old saying "Opposites

attract" has been overshadowed by a greater traditional saying: "Birds of a feather flock together." Recognizing that culture has a dramatic influence on the way we think and act, we are likely to welcome those who share some features of our identity. Discovering that another person you have just met grew up in your hometown, is of the same religion, and has ancestors who immigrated from the same country increases your attraction toward that person significantly. These shared backgrounds, and the shared specialized cultures they imply, reduce your uncertainty about initiating a relationship.

These principles of intercultural communication, then, emphasize the importance of searching for shared identities we can use in communication with others. But what happens when there is no such overlap, and two people have virtually nothing in common? Obviously, disparate cultural backgrounds might interfere with efficient and accurate interaction; but, given the multiculturalism of the United States, we need to know how to communicate interculturally with people in our own backyards—whether they are like us or not.

Features of Culture That Make a Difference

The need to get along with people of all specialized cultures within our own society, to accept them fully, and to be able to communicate with them with a high degree of accuracy has never been more important. There is an abundance of different specialized cultures in our society of great diversity. Obviously, we all live within the general American culture prevailing in the United States. However, if we think about our own gender, profession, and family history for a moment, most of us can clearly identify with several specialized cultures that influence in some fashion how we communicate with others. In this way, we all bring something different to our multicultural society and to the communication situations we face.

What we bring from our specialized cultures are different (and sometimes opposing) values or ways of viewing the world that can influence how we construct, transmit, receive and interpret messages. Researchers have found four cultural features that make a difference in how we relate to one another. They refer to these as: (1) **individualism** *and* **collectivism**, (2) *high and low* **context**, (3) *high and low* **power distance**, and (4) **masculinity** *and* **femininity**. Each of these terms represents extreme ends of a continuum that illustrates different values or ways of viewing the world. As you will see, no cultural group or individual actually is at those extremes— most are somewhere in between. Each of these continua need explanation. (See Figure 8.2.)

Individualism and Collectivism

The first of these continua—a cultural feature that seems to make a difference in how we communicate—indicates whether a particular culture views the world from an individualistic or a collectivistic orientation. To clarify, a culture with an orientation toward *individualism* places a high value on people who can speak or stand up for themselves and not have to depend on others beyond their immediate family. People who view the world this way like to think of themselves as "rugged individualists" who can "stand on their own two feet" and take care of themselves. Such people work hard to remain emotionally independent of any particular social, organizational, or institutional affiliation. Individualists emphasize the "I" when they speak, not the "we." This type of culture promotes personal initiative, independence, individual expression, and privacy.[18] General cultures of societies around the world that can be described as highly individualistic include Australia, Great Britain, New Zealand, and Canada. In the United States, African Americans and European Americans (in particular, male European Americans) tend to represent such an individualistic orientation.

At the other extreme of this value continuum is *collectivism*. This cultural feature is characterized by close-knit and familylike groups of people who clearly define themselves as part of a particular in-group. Others are considered outsiders. Individuals belonging to the in-group (relatives, clans, organizations) are required to look after one another in virtually every situation and context. In-group membership means not competing with others in the in-group. Collaboration and respect are required. In exchange for such loyalty, the group offers support, care, and protection. Collectivists emphasize the "we" when speaking, rather than the "I." Predominantly collectivistic cultures are Japan, Pakistan, Colombia, Venezuela, Taiwan, and Peru. In the United States, Middle Eastern Americans, Latinos and Latinas, Asian Americans, Native Americans, and many females in other specialized cultures tend to value this orientation over individualism.

High and Low Context

A second world view that governs how people from different cultures relate to one another is context.[19] In this continuum, *context* has to do with whether what is communicated is inherent in the setting and simply "understood" by the people involved (high context) or whether the bulk of information must be communicated *overtly* through the spoken exchange of messages (low context). In contrast, *low context* implies that individuals tend to be verbally explicit, precise, and accurate. They do not assume that others will be able to figure out what they mean without a lot of help.

People communicating in a low-context culture have trouble understanding one another unless every effort is made to be as explicit and clear as possible. When relating a story or explaining how to do something, low-context communicators are likely to provide a lot of background information, nonessential details, examples, and other data. If insufficient information is provided, low-context receivers will ask questions and demand even more details. Vagueness and ambiguity are simply not tolerated.

Individualistic	←————————————————————→	Collectivistic
African Americans Euroamericans		Asian Americans Latinos/Latinas Middle Eastern Americans Native Americans
Males		Females

	Moderate context	
Low context ←—————	African Americans Latinos/Latinas	—————→ High context
Euroamericans		Asian Americans Middle Eastern Americans Native Americans
Males		Females

Low power distance	←————————————————————→	High power distance
African Americans Euroamericans		Asian Americans Latinos/Latinas Middle Eastern Americans Native Americans
Females		Males

Masculine	←————————————————————→	Feminine

African Americans
Asian Americans (Japanese Americans)
Euroamericans
Latinos/Latinas (Mexican Americans)
		Asian Americans
		  (Chinese Americans and
		  Taiwanese Americans)
		Latinos/Latinas
		  (Chilean Americans,
		  Peruvian Americans, and
		  Spanish Americans)
		Middle Eastern Americans
		Native Americans
		Scandinavian Americans

Males		Females

FIGURE 8.2

Value Orientations of U.S. Ethnic and Gender Cultures

Each of the ethnic and gender cultures described in this chapter can be placed on continua representing the four different cultural features. An individual's ethnic and gender cultures may differ in their orientations. The amount of influence a particular orientation has depends on the individual and the context: In some situations, ethnic background may be the dominant factor influencing communication style; in others, gender or another cultural identity may be the more important factor.

High-context cultural groups, on the other hand, are more verbally *implicit*. They don't need to be so explicit because much is taken for granted or assumed. High-context cultural groups tend to be more indirect and subtle, and to rely more on nonverbal cues in communicating with one another. Interactions between two people who have been married for a long time provide an example. Over the years, they have come to know each other so well that they sometimes complete each other's sentences. They "just know" how the other will respond in a given situation; and they do not always feel a pressing need to talk in order to understand each other.

In other words, high-context cultures rely a great deal on *what is not said* and depend less on what is actually said in the explicit message. They look for meaning from the physical setting itself, or from the implied demands of the situation. As a result, they often talk in "verbal shorthand" simply because they already have a good idea of what each means. Recognizing that not everything needs to be spelled out in conversation, high-context speakers rely more on innuendo, ambiguity, equivocal messages, and implication. Rather than on telling someone what and how to think, high-context communicators merely suggest or offer alternatives.

Societies around the world that are more low context in their cultural orientation are Germany, Sweden, and England. High-context cultures include Japan, China, and Korea.[20] Here in the United States, Asian Americans, Native Americans, and Middle Eastern Americans can be characterized as high context. Latinos and Latinas and African Americans tend to be more moderate in their contextual orientation, with European Americans characterized by the lowest context.

High and Low Power Distance

How societies with different cultures distribute power, rank, and status among their members—their power-distance preference—is a third factor that influences the way people communicate. Although some cultures allow for, encourage, and even legislate as much equal status, rank, and power among individuals as possible, others greatly value status differences and social hierarchies.

As a feature of their general culture, Americans tend to value equality as a way of life. In the official and widely accepted view, no one is inherently superior or inferior to anyone else. Most Americans believe they can speak to virtually whomever they want, about almost any topic, in practically any style of delivery, and in any public or private situation without having to consider very carefully the other person's power, rank, or status. U.S. citizens can use Facebook or e-mail to direct questions to say, the president or other prominent elected officials. They can follow along on Twitter for the latest observations from say, entertainers such as Alec Baldwin or Carrie Underwood. Such familiar interactions would be unheard of in other parts of the world. In fact, outside of showing a minimum level of respect for others, Americans have few cultural restrictions or sanctions on the way they communicate with other people. Similar cultures with regard to low power-distance preferences are Austria, Denmark, Israel, New Zealand, and Ireland.[21]

Other cultures, such as those of Mexico, the Philippines, Venezuela, and India, place a high value on social status, birth order, and occupational and political rankings.[22] In these societies with high power-distance cultures, people tend to have less access to and less direct communication with individuals of higher status, and they are less likely to question authority figures. They tend to accept the actions of high-ranking individuals, often without question or justification. Vietnamese-American children, for instance, are expected to obey their parents without question or debate. In contrast, African-American children are often rewarded for being assertive and challenging their parents' points of view. Your own culture's view toward power and status may similarly influence how willing or reluctant you are to engage in the following:

1. Disagree with a professor during class (even when you know the professor is wrong).

2. Ask questions in class.

3. Interrupt your boss at work.

4. Call your instructor by her or his first name.

5. Question your boss's evaluation of your performance.

6. File a grievance at work.

7. Marry someone your parents disapprove of.

8. Drop by your professor's office just to say hello.

In the United States, specialized cultures that are likely to represent a high power-distance orientation can be found among Asian Americans; Latinos; Native Americans; and, to a lesser extent, Middle Eastern Americans. A low power-distance preference is more characteristic of African American and European Americans (especially females).

Masculinity and Femininity

The fourth discriminating cultural factor is a continuum that concerns the extent to which cultures are traditionally more masculine or more feminine in their orientation. *Masculinity* in this regard refers to the degree to which a culture values and encourages assertiveness—sometimes illustrated as achievement, success, ambition, and competitiveness. *Femininity*, on the other hand, is evident in a peoples' preference for nurturance—often defined as friendliness, affection, compassion, and general social support.[23]

In more masculine-dominated cultures, sex roles are clearly differentiated; males are supposed to be aggressive and females passive. Personal achievement and competitiveness is highly valued in masculine cultures; relational concerns are secondary. Winning is more important than how you play the game.

Ambition is a highly desirable personal quality; so is being a good provider for the family. At the other extreme, more feminine-dominated cultures deemphasize strictly defined role definitions. Sex roles are more flexible, and equality between the sexes is likely.

In feminine cultures, social and personal relationships are highly valued; being a good father and mother, husband and wife, sister and brother, and son and daughter are very important relational roles. More than achieving, winning, or accomplishing some instrumental goal, getting along, cooperating, and collaborating are more likely to be recognized and rewarded. Being a good person and showing sympathy and concern for unfortunate others are culturally valued qualities. Feminine cultures emphasize the more intrinsic, almost altruistic aspects of life.

Masculine and feminine orientations permeate how we communicate. Highly masculine communicators are likely to emphasize their credibility and expertise, to prefer objective facts and data, and to come across forcefully and directly. At the other extreme, highly feminine communicators strive to connect with their receivers by building rapport and empathy, seeking support for their views, and appealing to others' feelings and personal experiences.

Countries identified as masculine in their cultural orientation are Austria, Italy, Japan, and Mexico. Included among the more feminine cultures are Chile, Norway, Portugal, and Thailand.[24] In comparison to others, the general culture prevailing in the United States tends to be slightly more masculine than feminine in its orientation. Within the United States there are many specialized cultures representing the more masculine orientation. These include a number of specific Asian American cultures (particularly among Japanese Americans), African Americans, some Latino groups (especially Mexican Americans), and European Americans (particularly males). Feminine cultures in the United States can be found among Native Americans, certain Scandinavian American groups, Middle Eastern Americans, and some Latino groups (especially those of Chilean, Peruvian, and Spanish ancestry). Box 8.3 summarizes the cultural features that make a difference in how we communicate.

Unique Styles of Communication Common in Specialized Cultures

Each of the four cultural features discussed in the previous section influences how people from different specialized cultures relate to one another. Each feature makes a difference in how we communicate with people from our own cultural background as well as react to others whose cultures are different from our own. When we understand why other people communicate or behave as they do, we can begin to accept and understand our own pluralistic society.

People in the United States have come to take pride in their specialized cultural identities and to accept the importance of all such cultural groups. However, coexisting and communicating comfortably within that cultural diversity is not easy. The challenge, then, is to acquire enough information about other people's specialized cultures to be able to communicate in ways that show respect for them and to adapt to their differences.

Before turning to a discussion of particular styles, however, there are two cautionary notes to keep in mind: First, we must *never* assume that just because a person is a member of a given social category, he or she will necessarily assume all its cultural characteristics. In other words, the danger of identifying patterns of unique cultural characteristics is the very human tendency of *stereotyping* all individuals who affiliate with that pattern. For example, just because Cuban Americans tend to value social contact with friends and family more than with others, we cannot assume that all people of this background share this equally. In other words, there is diversity *within* social categories of similar people as well as *between* them. So, we must be open to exceptions and individual variations at all times.

Second, we need to keep in mind our almost inescapable tendency to be ethnocentric. As the unique characteristics of each specialized culture are described, we need to keep in mind the principle of cultural relativity: We all do things differently. What works for another group is all right for them (within the commonsense limits we have discussed)—even if it differs from our way.

To illustrate how even sophisticated people can be surprisingly ethnocentric, one of the authors of this text had the following experience. Pat Kearney comes from a small farming community in the Midwest. Its specialized culture actively promotes hunting for game birds, rabbits, and, occasionally, deer. Currently, she lives in a very urban environment in southern California, but her family continues to send as special delicacies pheasants and wild rabbits they have hunted themselves. On one very special occasion, Pat invited her city friends to a dinner of baked rabbit. Much to her dismay, they refused to eat the "little bunnies" that had been hunted down, terrorized, and murdered!

The point is, our own cultural background may bring many surprises when we spend time with people unlike ourselves. To prevent problems, we must recognize that we are all ethnocentric to some degree and inclined to judge people by our own cultural standards. We should also remember that our goal is to communicate accurately and efficiently with others who are not like us. Consequently, we need to try to understand why other groups of people behave as they do.

What are the principal specialized cultures in the United States? Recent census data reveal that the people grouped under the heading Whites make up the largest group in the United States (72.4 percent). Persons of Hispanic or Latino origin make up the second largest group (16.3 percent), followed closely by Blacks or African Americans (12.6 percent). Asian Americans constitute the fourth largest group (4.8 percent), followed by American Indian and Alaska Native persons (0.9 percent). Middle Eastern Americans constitute the sixth largest

BOX 8.3   *A Closer Look*

Cultural Features Affecting Communication

Individualism

Place high value on those who stand up for themselves.

Rugged individualists who stand alone and do not depend on others.

Work hard to be emotionally independent.

Emphasize "I" when they speak.

Promote individual initiative, achievement, competition.

High Context

What is communicated is implied or simply understood.

Nonverbal communication is more important than verbal.

Information is indirect and subtle.

Communicators rely on innuendo and implication—suggest rather than demand.

High Power Distance

Value status differences and social hierarchies.

Less access to and communication with those of higher status.

Expected to obey parents and leaders without question.

More formal and distant.

Avoid confrontation; listen agreeably.

Masculinity

Value assertiveness, competitiveness, and success.

Ambition an important personal quality.

Winning is more important than how you play the game.

Emphasize personal credibility and expertise.

Important to be forceful and direct.

---

group, although census data do not differentiate this group from non-Hispanic Whites. The final pair of specialized cultures examined in this section overlap all the ethnic cultures just listed: females (50.7 percent) and males (49.3 percent).[25]

European Americans

This chapter uses the label "European American" to refer to individuals residing in the United States whose common cultural heritage is primarily from European; other labels that are sometimes used include "Euroamerican," "white," and "Anglo."

Although European Americans are a large, diverse, and frequently misrepresented group of people, they tend to illustrate a number of unique communication patterns that distinguish them from other specialized cultures. But, note that European Americans consist of a hetereogeneous group that include the Irish, French, Polish, Germans, English, Russians, and Scandinavians. And within each of these groups, are cultures represented by profession, sexual orientation, political preference, region, religion, and more. Even so, some commonalities exist across most individuals who identify themselves most clearly with the European American culture.

So, what are the common characteristics that distinguish the communication styles of this large and heterogeneous category from other kinds of communicators in the United States?[26] To begin with, European Americans tend not

Collectivism

Define themselves as members of a group.

Members of the in-group take care of one another.

Virtues are collaboration, respect, and loyalty.

In exchange for loyalty, group offers support and protection.

Emphasize "we" when they speak.

Low Context

What is communicated is explicit and overt.

Verbal communication more important than nonverbal.

Word choice is important—must be precise and accurate.

Communicators spell out everything, including what to think and how to feel.

Low Power Distance

Value equality; no one inherently superior or inferior.

Speak to whomever they want about almost any topic.

Children are encouraged to question and challenge authority.

Considered a "right" to confront, ask questions, or disagree.

Accessible, approachable, and unassuming.

Femininity

Value interpersonal connections and nurturance.

Sex roles are more flexible; equality between sexes is preferred.

Getting along, cooperating, and collaborating are important communication skills.

Strive to build support through empathy and rapport.

Valued qualities are being a good person and showing concern and sympathy for unfortunate others.

---

to communicate readily about highly personal topics—they simply do not disclose a lot of personal information. Although this tendency may be more descriptive of males than females, it is often illustrated in conversations between strangers, casual acquaintances, or business associates. That is, when European Americans first meet someone, they normally engage in a period of small talk about uneventful or unimportant issues, such as the weather, sports, a TV program, a type of automobile, a particular restaurant, or a product in the grocery store. They avoid discussions about more substantive topics, such as financial matters, personal earnings, religion, politics, and sexual behavior.

The nature of communication exchanges between European Americans also distinguishes them from people with other specialized cultures. European Americans do not tend to speak with one another for a very long time. Their public presentations are generally short, and they tend to be impatient with people who talk a lot. There is little formalized ceremony or ritual in exchanges between European Americans. Because equality is valued, they are careful to take turns when they talk. They also tend to avoid arguing in public when they communicate with one another, believing that intense arguments in public are rude. When they do argue in public, they strive to remain noticeably calm, objective, and unemotional or rational.

European Americans tend not to get very involved with one another when they communicate. Once again, this is probably more true of men than women. Also, European Americans tend to avoid close involvement with a lot of different people, reserving their involvement with a few close friends and family. Most of their initial interactions with strangers, acquaintances, or business associates occur on a surface level. When they do communicate with one another, they often want to know what the objective of the conversation is and how long it will take.

In terms of the cultural features that were discussed earlier, European Americans rank high in individualism, low in context and power, and high in masculinity. Based on these features, then, we can assume that they tend to be ambitious and competitive, and that they value and appreciate assertive, outspoken communication behavior. They generally value individual over group achievement, believe in equality, and minimize status differences. Such Americans also rely more on explicit than implicit information when they communicate. That is, they rely more on verbal than nonverbal messages. This overwhelming preference for verbal communication is revealed in their preoccupation with *facts* and *evidence* as opposed to emotional appeals. Composure is a sign of credibility, they believe. Losing control of emotion and extreme displays of emotion are signs of weakness.

Overall, then, a large number of European Americans can be characterized as communicators who are self-oriented and who may appear to be cold, distant, impatient, unemotional, rational, exact, nondisclosive, and uninvolved. Obviously, there are many individual differences and not every European American fits these descriptions exactly. Similarly, not every Latino and Latina or African American will fit the descriptions to be developed below either. However, it is also important to note that each of us is typically the last to know what we are like as communicators—especially in terms of how we appear to others from different cultural groups.

Latinos and Latinas

The second largest ethnic category in the United States is made up of people whose surnames or cultural origins can be traced through their family background to a Spanish-speaking Latin American country or to Spain itself.[27] A number of designations are used to identify people in this social category, including Hispanic, Chicano or Chicana, Mexican American, and Latino (or, for females, Latina). All are regularly used synonymously in the United States. As is the case when referring to any of the categories of people described in this chapter, we must be able to distinguish among these labels if we are to communicate respect and adjust to the unique characteristics associated with this specialized culture. Researchers Ron Lustig and Jolene Koester effectively distinguish among these alternative labels:

> *Hispanic* derives from the prevalent use of the Spanish language, but many shy away from this term because it tends to homogenize all groups of people who have Spanish surnames and who use the Spanish language. *Chicano* (or *Chicana*) refers to the "multiple-heritage experience of Mexicans in the United States" and speaks to a political and social consciousness of the Mexican American. Specific terms such as *Mexican American* or *Cuban American* are preferred by those who *wish* to acknowledge their cultural roots in a particular national heritage while simultaneously emphasizing their pride in being U.S. Americans. Finally, *Latino* (or *Latina*) is a cultural and linguistic term. As Juan Gonzales, Jr., suggests, *Latino* includes "all groups in the Americas that share the Spanish language, culture and traditions."[28]

Taking the lead from Lustig and Koester, this text refers to this broad and varied category of people as "Latinos" or "Latinos and Latinas."

Latinos show a great deal of expression when they communicate. To the Latino, a person's manner of expression is often more important than what the person says. Socializing and being friendly are very important to typical Latinos.[29] Arguing or disagreeing in public is considered rude and disrespectful. Instead, Latinos like to appear agreeable and courteous. They like to talk; visit; and establish an amiable, cheerful climate or speaking environment. These characteristic communication styles may (and often do) frustrate traditional European American businesspeople who are often preoccupied with *time;* that is, they want their Latino or Latina associate to get down to business. For Latinos, however, showing concern for one another and chatting to show that they care are precursors to doing business. Demonstrating diplomacy, tact, and respect for one another is essential.

As communicators, Latinos are highly expressive, compelling, and intense. Like African Americans, they enjoy telling a good story, often relying on metaphors or parables. More important than the story itself, however, is the telling of it, using graphic, vivid expressions. Latinos are likely to be responsive and agreeable when others talk. They are unlikely to challenge an individual publicly, even when they think she or he is wrong; instead, they prefer to show respect.

In terms of world view orientation, Latinos are collectivistic, moderate in context, and very high in power distance. Some Latino cultures are highly masculine in orientation (Mexican American), whereas others are more feminine (Chilean American, Peruvian American and Spanish American). Consequently, Latinos prefer relating with in-groups, are very loyal to family and friends, place a high premium on smooth and pleasant social and business relationships, avoid conflict, and enjoy small talk. Moreover, they value conformity, obedience, and respect for authority. Latinos are a "contact culture"; that is, they stand closer to one another and engage in more physical contact than others might find comfortable. Even though the stereotyped perceptions of male "machismo" have not been fully documented, traditional sex roles are strongly encouraged. Whereas men are expected to be husbands, fathers, and providers and to be responsible and brave, women are expected to be protected, to stay closer to home, and to nurture and support their families.[30]

Latino communication can be characterized as amiable, expressive, dramatic, friendly, cheerful, and extroverted. Once again, we caution against assuming that all Latinos behave according to these generalizations. These characterizations are merely guidelines for the decisions we make in our attempts to relate effectively with one another.

African Americans

Citizens whose ancestral origins were in Africa represent the third largest category of people in the United States. The designation "African American" acknowledges both their ancestral origins and the influence of African societies on their cultural heritage. Although it has become popular, the term *African American* is not accepted by the entire membership of this social category.[31] A significant number still refer to themselves as "blacks," or as *Afro-Americans.*[32]

African American communication behaviors, like those that characterize other specialized cultures, are unique enough to differentiate them from others. The African American style of communicating tends to be highly intense, expressive, distinctive, forceful, assertive, and openly emotional. How people connect and share with each other—how they use wit, humor, intelligence, touch, and other characteristics—is of primary importance to this group.[33]

African American audiences are also known to employ "call-response patterns" as positive feedback to public speakers. (Call-response patterns are active audiences responses to a speaker, such as "I hear you" and "Damn straight!") African Americans are open and expressive and let speakers know that they are actively listening and giving their approval and support.[34]

African Americans tend to be highly individualistic, more moderate in context, low in power distance, and high in masculinity. In other words, most value competition and personal distinctiveness, and trust their emotions and feelings—but also appreciate the power of the spoken word. They also tend to be highly intense and assertive. African Americans appreciate the use of examples and personal testimony or stories when arguing a point, and they have a keen sense of justice.[35] More generally, the style of speaking and communicating of a large number of African Americans can be characterized as active, expressive, colorful, emotional, often humorous, nonverbal (as opposed to verbal), and, overall, positive in outlook.

Once again, "one size does not fit all." It would be a mistake to assume that all African Americans communicate in these ways at all times. As with the European Americans described previously, and all the others that follow, the African American culture comprises all kinds of people who think and behave in very different ways.

Asian Americans

"Asian American" is a broad label that includes a number of very different specialized cultures. These consist of people whose ancestral and cultural roots are in China, Japan, Taiwan, Korea, Singapore, Thailand, and Vietnam or in other countries with predominantly Asian populations. Despite substantial differences among their cultures of origin, research shows that, in a broad sense, Asian Americans share certain communication patterns that differ from those of other U.S. cultures.

More than any other cultural feature, *collectivism* dominates the world view of Asian Americans.[36] First-generation Asian Americans—more than those of second and third generations—are likely to value collaboration, conformity, loyalty, and acceptance of, acquiescence to, or even deference to *authority*. Power, rank, and status differentials are valued and highly respected. These cultural values contrast sharply with the dominant values of the African American and European American cultures we examined. In those, the values emphasized are personal achievement, resistance or even rejection of authority, disapproval of status differences, and approval of competition, independence, freedom, and individual thought and opinions. Not coincidentally, then, we find that with increased contact with the general American culture, all specialized cultures derived from immigration become less extreme as each generation passes.

Many Asian Americans may hesitate to voice their opinions or express what they truly think, simply because it is customary to show deference to persons of authority, higher status, or greater age.[37] Moreover, Asian Americans as a group tend to be more sensitive to the feelings of others and, thus, unwilling to directly challenge a person's beliefs or attitudes or give unsolicited advice. Instead, they may be more likely to disagree or offer advice in some indirect and highly tactful manner.[38] Engaging in assertive behavior or self-disclosure with people outside their family is unlikely. Self-restraint is important to Asian Americans. Thus, being polite and tactful is a key characteristic of these communicators.

As members of a high-context culture, Asian Americans tend to mask their emotions nonverbally when they communicate. Many Asian Americans are restrained in their nonverbal behavior and will not engage in direct eye contact, nodding, smiling, or gesturing when talking or listening. It is easy for others, who use openly expressive communication styles—African Americans and Latinos for instance—to misinterpret the reserved manner of Japanese or Chinese Americans as signs of boredom, inattentiveness, or even passive aggressiveness.

As an illustration of how confusion can occur, one sensitive student of intercultural communication related the following incident: While at work, he observed his European American supervisor become increasingly frustrated toward an Asian American employee. The problem arose during an information-giving session in which the supervisor was explaining to the employee how to proceed on a particular job. Instead of looking directly at the supervisor and occasionally providing some nonverbal feedback (a nod, a smile, or an "Uh huh"), she continued to look down and away, waiting respectfully for the supervisor to finish his "lecture." The supervisor totally misinterpreted her response. If the student observer hadn't interfered and explained to the supervisor the communication style the employee was bringing to the encounter from her cultural community, she might have lost her job.

Family honor is another important part of the Asian American collectivistic orientation. One's personal achievements bring honor to the entire family, while one's failures bring shame and dishonor. Evidence of this orientation can sometimes be seen in the classroom. Asian American students have a reputation for working hard to achieve high grades. They do so not just for self-satisfaction but, importantly, for the honor of their family. To fail a course can mean letting one's family down, and bringing disgrace. Among European Americans, on the other hand, the individual is likely to take (or be granted) personal credit for her or his successes and, at the same time, be forced to take responsibility for personal failures.

As communicators, we might expect Asian Americans to be much less flamboyant and outgoing than either Latinos or African Americans. Compared to the others that have been discussed so far, Asian Americans are likely to be constrained in both their manner and their words. Their communication style is simple and restrained, with little or no dramatic, illustrative facial expressions or gestures. They tend to be more indirect in their approach, preferring their listeners to provide their own interpretations and draw their own conclusions. Asian Americans often come across as *good listeners:* In public situations, they can be counted on to be quietly reserved, polite, and pleasant. They are unlikely to ask questions or publicly to challenge another's point of view.

In summary, Asian Americans are highly collectivistic and high in both power and context. However, they are not easily classified on the masculinity-femininity continuum. Japanese Americans tend to be high in masculinity (assertive, ambitious, achievement oriented), but other Asian Americans tend to be much less so—particularly Chinese and Taiwanese Americans. All of these cultural orientations influence the way the broad category of Asian Americans communicate. As a result, they can be characterized as implicit, understated, deferential, quiet and somewhat withdrawn, courteous, inexpressive, harmonious, sincere, and always respectful.

Native Americans

Ambiguity has long surrounded both what constitutes *membership* and what is the most appropriate label to use in talking about this complex category of Americans. Locke effectively explains the chronology or these ambiguities and provides the rationale for the appropriateness of the label "Native American" as used in this book.

> Historically, the name *Indian* was used, followed by *American Indian* and, more recently, *Native American*. The Bureau of Indian Affairs (BIA) (1988) defines a Native American as one who is a registered or enrolled member of a tribe or whose blood quantum is one-fourth or more, genealogically derived. Hirschfelder (1982) reports that one Native American law center has assembled 52 legal definitions of Native Americans. The U.S. Census Bureau, on the other hand, records anyone who claims native identity as Native American. Although there appears to be no consensus as to the most appropriate term, *Native American* is used here because it connotes both the heritage of the original inhabitants of this continent and the group's status as United States citizens.[39]

Native Americans, like the other categories of citizens described in this chapter, represent a number of tribes, nations, pueblos, and unique individuals that are not easily classified or characterized. Although they are diverse, Native Americans use a number of identifiable cultural patterns. As in the Asian American specialized culture, collectivism is highly valued; cooperation, harmony, and getting along are the expectations in interactions with one another. Unless personal competition benefits the entire group, and the situation is clearly defined as competitive (as in an athletic event), it is an undesirable human characteristic.[40] Among the Pueblo nations, such as the Zuni of New Mexico, the traditional culture restricts anyone who tries to outdo others by striving for personal power or success.[41] This restriction on competition can pose significant problems for Native Americans who attempt to assimilate into other specialized cultures. In a competitive business world, for example, traditional Native Americans may have a hard time competing for jobs, dollars, and power. On the other hand, they may be successful working in businesses that depend on team players who can work harmoniously to get the job done.

Given the high-context nature of their cultures, Native Americans also avoid sustained and direct eye contact when speaking. Both the Hopi and the Navajo define direct eye contact as offensive. In fact, staring can be interpreted as a form of aggression.[42] Moreover, the Hopi tend to be restrained in their nonverbal facial expressiveness; their communication exchanges tend to be more implicit than explicit. Compared to other moderate- or low-context cultures (such as Latinos, European Americans, and African Americans), Native Americans are observably less dramatic and less animated in the way they normally communicate with others.[43]

Although their nonverbal behaviors may not be all that expressive and obvious to others outside their specialized culture, these cues are a vital means for relating. With the exception of Cherokee, written language was virtually nonexistent before Native Americans were forced to interact with White settlers. Over the years, Native Americans have taken pride in passing on their traditions and customs through oral myths, legends, and stories. "One can learn much by 'listening' to what Native Americans are expressing through body language, eye movements, silence, and tone of voice."[44]

Characteristic of high-context cultures, Native Americans learn from early childhood to communicate in more indirect ways. To illustrate, let's look for a moment at the Laguna, another Pueblo people of central New Mexico, whose children enjoy a rather unique relationship with their parents.[45] When Laguna children misbehave, their parents seldom punish them—and they seldom need to. When a child does misbehave, the parents turn to a unique and indirect way of communicating social control. They instruct the child that the *cha-be-u* (chah-bey-oo)—dreadful beings said to come from Mexico—will come for them.

Actually, the *cha-be-u* are enacted by two members of the tribe, who dress in fearsome costumes and ride into the village on horses for the occasion. Their task is to punish those children who have seriously misbehaved—or at least to scare them so that their behavior will improve. In the case of younger children, the *cha-be-u* appear at the door of the home and ask whether a naughty child lives there. The parents admit that their child has misbehaved and will not obey them. The *cha-be-u* then say that they are going to take the child with them, away from the parents and the village, to a very bad place. The child, of course, is terrified. The parents then have a change of heart and plead with the *cha-be-u* to leave the child with them.[46]

Not only does the *cha-be-u* method of communicating discipline result in well-behaved children for the most part, it also preserves a warm parent-child relationship. Laguna children fail to associate punishment with their parents; instead, they see their parents pleading on their behalf. In other cultures, parents *are* the punishers in that they communicate discipline directly. Indeed, a conversation among European American parents about disciplining children ("Spare the rod; spoil the child") and the associative guilt after applying punishment ("It hurts me more than it hurts you") would probably shock and repel a Laguna parent.

The analysis of cultural features that influence the way Native Americans communicate suggests that they can be characterized as a high-context culture and are, thus, indirect, quiet, understated, inexpressive, nonassertive, and even somewhat withdrawn. Also, because they are collectivistic, Native Americans are group- and family-oriented, noncompetitive (except under special circumstances), publicly agreeable (privately, they may disagree), and cooperative. In terms of power distance orientation, Native Americans respect the elderly: With age comes experience; with experience comes knowledge. They also believe in harmony and balance with nature—showing great respect for all living things. Finally, Native Americans can be characterized as more feminine than masculine in their value orientation. The family is of utmost importance, and interpersonal relationships are more valued than personal success or ambition. Native Americans also tend to be wary of material wealth and the collection of material possessions.[47]

In summary, as communicators, Native Americans tend to express themselves similarly to the way Asian Americans do. Their nonverbal gestures and body movements are likely to be restrained or subdued. They appreciate a good story, relying heavily on myths and legends that have been passed on for generations. They are likely to suggest rather than insist on a particular way of thinking or behaving. Native Americans often appear agreeable and accommodating. Saving face or maintaining the dignity of self and others is important to them. They "are keenly sensitive to being singled out for public disapproval, laughter, or ostracism."[48] Consequently, Native Americans are likely to be publicly polite and receptive to other communicators—whether or not they agree with or like them.

Middle Eastern Americans

Middle Eastern Americans form another category of citizens that has substantial representation in the United States. People from Egypt, Lebanon, Jordan, Armenia, Iran, Iraq, Syria, and numerous other Middle Eastern countries have long made the United States their home. Although these Americans operate in every social, political, and industrial sector of our society, they maintain many traditional aspects of their cultures as well. Despite their assimilation into the general culture, some of their behaviors continue to differ noticeably from the social and cultural practices of the majority. Similar to the traditions of Native Americans, they communicate as a predominantly oral culture. For centuries in the Middle East, people relied on tribal storytellers to serve as the record keepers of

significant events, recording history and passing it on orally generation after generation.[49]

Today in the Middle East, this oral tradition continues, but the storytellers are now called "poets." Poetry is an essential part of contemporary Middle Eastern culture. Poets often interpret political and social events; thus, poets influence what opinions people hold and how they respond to events.[50] Because of this, poets are held in very high esteem in Middle Eastern countries.[51]

The oral tradition of the Middle East has influenced the way people from this part of the world define public discourse more generally. Middle Easterners view public speaking as a highly valued activity. Much of their public discourse relies heavily on religious references; it's not at all unusual for Muslims to quote extensively from the Koran or for Jews to quote from the Torah.[52] Their style of speaking is highly emotional, and they rely heavily on the rhythm of language and the sounds of words as they compose their messages. Both the content and the logical presentation of ideas is secondary. In her handbook for Westerners, Margaret Nydell sums up the speech mannerisms of Arab communicators:

> Arabs talk a lot, repeat themselves, shout when excited, and make extensive use of gestures. They punctuate their conversations with oaths (such as "I swear by God") to emphasize what they say, and they exaggerate for effect. Foreigners sometimes wonder if they are involved in a discussion or an argument. If you speak softly and make your statements only once, Arabs may wonder if you really mean what you are saying. People will ask, "Do you really mean that?" or "Is that true?" —not that they do not believe you, but they need repetition and a few emphatic "yeses" to be reassured.[53]

Middle Eastern Americans are less likely than European Americans to believe that the future can be controlled. Because they tend to be more retrospective than prospective about life, what happens in the past concerns them more than what will happen in the future. Thus, Middle Eastern Americans view speaking primarily as a way of relating, rather than controlling. Speaking eloquently holds particular appeal to them. They might communicate to express formal generosity to someone or to maintain their cultural pride, honor, and personal self-respect.[54]

Like African Americans and Latinos, then, Middle Eastern Americans tend to be dramatic, demonstrative communicators. They frequently speak to evoke an emotional effect as opposed to communicating a specific message. In other words, they don't always say exactly what they mean. When communicating within their high-context culture, Middle Eastern Americans insinuate or imply, expecting others to know or understand what they mean. Their arguments rely more on subjective personal experience than on objective data. Middle Eastern Americans also tend to be collectivistic, somewhat high in power distance, and marginally feminine in their value orientations. They are very sensitive to others' perceptions of them. As a proud people, they make every effort to be perceived positively in all social and political situations.[55]

Females and Males

Whether we belong to one of the foregoing specialized cultures or not, we all identify with a particular *gender category*. Being either male or female is more than a biological condition of the body. It also means that, as a product of socialization into our society, enculturation into its general culture, plus into the specialized cultures characteristic of our particular gender, we hold unique world views directly related to our sexual classification. Whatever their conditions during childhood or adolescence, females and males learn during their entire lives to think and behave in particular ways. If you are a male, you have learned in a variety of ways to act the way males in our society are expected to act. The same is true for females. When males and females do not behave in expected gender-appropriate ways, they are responded to negatively. Growing up as a male implies being a member of the male culture, and growing up as a female means being a member of the female culture. The question here is: How

does membership in a particular gender culture influence how we communicate?

The same four cultural features we have already discussed, which significantly influence how different categories of people communicate, can help us understand the communication styles of females and males. Across the many cultures present in the United States, certain tendencies define women's value orientations that differ from men's. Obviously, these value orientations are dominated or mediated in part by each individual's other memberships and affiliations, along with other factors.

Even so, when compared to men, women tend to be different in how they communicate. They tend to be collectivistic, high context, low power, and feminine in their orientation. As a result, we might expect women to place a high priority on personal relationships, particularly family and friends. Providing support, showing compassion, and nurturing others are important personal and social qualities. To achieve symmetry or equality, women often reveal parallel experiences to show others "I felt that way, too" or "The same thing happened to me." Moreover, because they value being polite and showing respect and courtesy toward others, they often avoid being condescending or critical.[56]

Women also tend to be sensitive and indirect in their communication transactions. In contrast, men tend to be individualistic, low context, high power, and masculine. Consequently, we might expect men to prioritize individual success and achievements, to appreciate competition, to assert themselves and challenge others, and to control or dominate interactions.

To some extent, research findings support the influence of such value preferences.[57] Women's talk is perceived as being deferential and polite; men's speech as forceful and assertive. Women use more qualifiers than men, words such as maybe and perhaps. They introduce their questions with phrases such as "This may be trivial to ask, but. . . ." Women further rely on verbal fillers during silent, awkward moments: "OK," "Well," "Sure," and "You know." Women use tag questions two to three times more often

What problems does this couple have communicating? How does gender-based socialization influence their interactions?

than men: "It's a beautiful day, *isn't it?*" Women are also more likely than men to insert intensifiers into their speech; instead of "That's pretty," women are more likely to say, "That's so pretty."

Nonverbally, women use more facial expressions than men, and they initiate and return smiles more often (even when they're not happy). They also rely on more eye contact to communicate. Men tend to talk more loudly than women, at a lower pitch, and with less tonal variation. Men also use more sweeping hand and arm gestures when they speak, tap their feet more than women, and take up more physical space. Whereas men usually sit with their legs apart and seem to expand when they sit on a chair, women hold their knees together and seem to contract.[58]

One of the myths that is often perpetuated between the genders is that women talk more than men. Contrary to popular belief, no single study supports that claim. In fact, there appears to be no difference between how much females and males talk; however, in most contexts (but particularly so in male-female conversations), males are more likely to decide what is talked about and for how long! Also, when men talk, they tend to be more absolute, directive, and authoritative than women.[59]

These differences between male and female communication styles have led some researchers to label men's talk as "powerful" and female talk as "powerless."[60] Unfortunately, such nonegalitarian labels can have devastating effects on women in politics, at work, at home, and in virtually any social context. For example, research indicates that women communicators who use numerous intensifiers, qualifiers, verbal fillers, and tag questions are often perceived negatively—by both men and women.[61] Listeners tend to interpret such verbal cues as indicators of uncertainty, a lack of knowledge (or intelligence), and a limited ability to influence others. Alternatively, it has been suggested that the tentative quality of female speech reflects women's desire to create equality and to invite others to participate in conversation.[62]

What is also disturbing for many women is that research finds that women are negatively perceived when they use these verbal cues, but that men (when they use the same tag questions and qualifiers) are often perceived as polite and receiver oriented.[63] At the same time, however, women's communication style is also rated as more attractive, more polite, and closer to the ideal than men's.[64] Although the female communication style is preferred, a double standard is applied when it is used by women; that is, women who use this style are less likely than men to be seen having authority, credibility, and control.

Communicating Successfully in Intercultural Contexts

Even in the best of circumstances, most of us are not completely successful multicultural communicators. The success of our multicultural encounters depends to a large extent on our approach. What follows is a set of guidelines for achieving or maximizing our success.

1. *Recognize that every individual has emotions, needs, and feelings that are as sensitive as yours.* Never make the mistake of believing that people who differ from you, in one or in many ways, are less sensitive or even less worthy of your respect. Their eyes look out on the same reality as yours, and although their particular culture may cause them to respond to it differently, their perceptions and interpretations are as valuable as yours.

2. *Try to understand the cultural norms of the person with whom you communicate.* Recall that culture, by definition, prescribes rules not only for communicating but also for virtually all human behaviors. To maximize the success of our multicultural communication,

then, we need as much understanding of their culture as possible when we interact with people from backgrounds and orientations that are different from our own.

3. *Respect the customs and traditions of others.* Remember the principle of cultural relativity, which asserts that people practicing every specialized culture we have discussed in detail in this chapter have worked out solutions for the problems encountered in day-to-day living. For these people, their solutions define the correct ways of thinking, believing, and behaving. Although certain behavior may seem unrealistic, inappropriate, or even unappealing, we can appreciate that it is proper and satisfying to other kinds of people. Every effort should be made, therefore, to respect the customs and traditions of others.

4. *Listen actively in a communication encounter with others from a different culture.* Effective listening is crucial to the success of any communication encounter and even more so when the exchange involves more than one culture. In fact, multicultural differences only further confound the difficulty of achieving fidelity in communication. The skills of effective listening are more important than ever in multicultural exchanges (see Chapter 4).

5. *Learn to cope with uncertainty.* A predictable and normal response to encountering people from different cultures is uncertainty.[65] As a result, our level of anxiety is aroused. How we handle such uncertainty and the associated anxiety is crucial to determining the relative success of our multicultural communication experiences. The key is to monitor and control our overt reactions. By accepting that we are going to experience some degree of uncertainty, we can more easily suspend judgment and thereby open ourselves to accepting and understanding differences between ourselves and others.

6. *Avoid stereotyping people who are different from you.* Negative labeling and stereotyping not only have long histories but also are alive and well in today's multicultural society. Unfortunately, the meanings aroused by such

labels strongly influence the way individuals in different social categories are perceived, understood, evaluated, accepted, or rejected. Stereotyping people who are culturally different from us in negative ways obviously exacerbates our efforts to communicate. To avoid this, we should check very carefully all labels we use to designate others. Are the labels derogatory? Do they in any way humiliate or belittle others? Then, determine what labels (if any) the people use to describe themselves; that is, discover what labels, if any, are acceptable from their perspective. Finally, make every effort to avoid negative sterotypic thinking; instead, seek understanding beyond simple and obvious categories.

7. *Be aware of your own ethnocentrism.* Most Americans would state with conviction that their way of life is the best. That may be true—for us. We tend to be ethnocentric in much the same way as we label and stereotype. Excessive ethnocentrism can be both dangerous and counterproductive to communicating multiculturally. Accept that we are all ethnocentric to some extent—and that this can be positive—but recognize that ethnocentrism in multicultural communication can at times significantly reduce the chances of successful interaction.

Overall, these seven guidelines (summarized in Box 8.4) offer practical advice with which to approach multicultural communication. Viewing them as a set of interrelated suggestions is the most productive way to consider their application, as the issues they address overlap in one or more ways.

Tips for Successful Intercultural Communication

Successful multicultural communication results when all individuals involved are satisfied with the process and the consequences of their encounter. How do you know when successful communication occurs? Briefly, all communicators will want to pursue their conversation further. Also, they will seek future opportunities to interact with one another. And, when asked, communicators will report positive, satisfied feelings about their exchange. But this is no simple task. How do we go about becoming a successful multicultural communicator?

1. Recognize that every individual has emotions, needs, and feelings that are as sensitive as yours.
2. Try to understand the cultural norms of the person with whom you communicate.
3. Respect the customs and traditions of others.
4. Listen actively in a co-cultural communication encounter.
5. Learn to cope with uncertainty.
6. Avoid stereotyping people who are different from you.
7. Be aware of your own ethnocentrism.

Chapter Review

- Culture influences how we think, feel, and behave. Because of the cultural diversity of the United States, nowhere is there a greater potential for inaccurate communication and misunderstanding. Cultural pluralism depends on cultural inclusion—

a commitment to acknowledge, respect, and adapt to others who are different from us.

- Culture and communication are inseparable. The way we communicate, what we believe, what we say, the language choices we use, and the nonverbal signals we employ are all a function of the culture we acquire. How we speak and relate nonverbally to others is learned from the culture in which we grow up.

- Some cultural identities are more important than others. In a communication encounter, the greater the number of cultures the participants share, the greater the accuracy of their messages and the more satisfied they are with their exchange.

- Researchers have found four cultural features that make a difference in how we relate with one another: individualism and collectivism, high and low context, high and low power distance, and masculinity and femininity. Each of these cultural features represents different values or ways of viewing the world.

- This chapter reviews the cultural orientations and communication styles of the six largest ethnic and racial categories in the United States—European Americans, Latinos, African Americans, Asian Americans, Native Americans, and Middle Eastern Americans—as well as the important differences between the communication styles used by women and men.

- Successful intercultural communication is an exchange of messages in which all individuals in an encounter are satisfied with the process and the consequences. This chapter offers guidelines to help you communicate interculturally.

Key Terms

intercultural communication	melting pot policy	cultural exclusion	collectivism
culture	majority	ethnocentrism	context
general culture	minority	chauvinism	power distance
specialized culture	cultural pluralism	cultural relativity	masculinity
social category	cultural inclusion	individualism	femininity

Notes

1. Generally, these are a set of broad and complex patterns of deeply established beliefs, practices, traditions, customs and other social forms within the culture by which a society achieves important goals (e.g., economic activity, family relationships, political systems, religious beliefs, and the education of the young). Complex societies also have a number of other goals—military, scientific, welfare, and so on.

2. There is a lively debate among communication scholars about what such specialized cultures should be called. The name *subcultures* (meaning a culture within a larger culture) was the term used initially by anthropologists and sociologists when, many years ago, they began to study different lifestyles that existed among unique social categories in the society—such as among convicts in prison, those practicing specific occupations, prostitutes, confidence men, college and university professors, commercial fishermen, and police officers (among many others). Later, some scholars worried that the prefix "sub" implied inferiority, especially when racial and ethnic categories were the focus. They advocated the use of *co-cultures* instead. A problem with using *co-culture* is that it is hard for many ordinary people to regard professional criminals, the drug trade, prostitutes, and others who are held in legitimate disrespect as having cultures (beliefs and practices) that are "equal" in value and in their contribution to society, to the cultures of law-abiding groups. To avoid this problem, the nonjudgmental term *specialized cultures* is used throughout this book.

3. See, for example: Triandis, H. C., & Suh, E. M. (2002). Cultural influences on personality. *Annual Review of Psychology, 53,* 133–160.

4. Samovar, L. A., Porter, R. E., & McDaniel, E. R. (2009). *Communication between cultures* (7th ed.). Boston: Wadsworth/Cengage.

5. U.S. Census Bureau (2010). U.S.A. Quick Facts. Retrieved from http://quickfacts.census.gov/qfd/states/00000.html; and www.census.gov/compendia/statab/2012/tables/12s0041.pdf

6. Camarota, S. A. (2011, October). A record-setting decade for immigration: 2000–2010. Center for Immigration Studies. Retrieved from www.cis.org/2000-2010-record-setting-decade-of-immigration

7. U.S. Census Bureau (2010). U.S.A. Quick Facts. Retrieved from http://quickfacts.census.gov/qfd/states/00000.html; and www.census.gov/compendia/statab/2012/tables/12s0041.pdf

8. Camarota, S. A. (2011, October). A record-setting decade for immigration: 2000–2010. Center for Immigration Studies. Retrieved from www.cis.org/2000-2010-record-setting-decade-of-immigration

9. Minority babies set to become majority in 2010 (2010, March 10). Life on MSNBC.com. Retrieved from www.msnbc.msn.com/id/35793316/ns/us_news-life/t/minority-babies-set-become-majority/; Minorities expected to be majority in 2050 (2008, August 13). CNN U.S. Retrieved from http://articles.cnn.com/2008-08-13/us/census.minorities_1_hispanic-population-census-bureau-white-population?_s=PM:US

10. Sumner, W. G. (1906). *Folkways* (pp. 28–30). Boston: Ginn.

11. DeFleur, M. L., & Cho, C. S. (1957). Assimilation of Japanese women in an American city. *Social Problems, 4,* 3, 244–257.

12. Sumner, *Folkways,* p. 27. See also: Brewer, M. B. (1999). The psychology of prejudice: Ingroup love or outgroup hate? *The Journal of Social Issues, 55,* 3, 429–444.

13. Ibid, p. 30

14. See, for example: Okafor, T. (2001). Ethnocentrism in Africa. *UN Chronicle, 38,* 2, 30–31.

15. Schulz, J. J., & Schulz, L. (1999). The darkest of ages: Afghan women under the Taliban. *Journal of Peace Psychology, 5,* 3, 237–254.

16. Hall, E. T. (1959). *The silent language.* New York: Doubleday, p. 37.

17. Axtell, R. E. (1990). *Do's and taboos of hosting international visitors* (pp. 6–7). New York: Wiley; Martin, J. S., & Chaney, L. H. (2012). *Global business etiquette: A guide to international communication and customs* (2nd ed). Santa Barbara, CA: ABC-CLIO.

18. Samovar, Porter, & McDaniel (2009).

19. Hall, E. T. (1976). *Beyond culture.* New York: Anchor Books/Doubleday.

20. Samovar, Porter, & McDaniel (2009).

21. Hofstede, G. (1984). *Culture's consequences. International differences in work-related values.* Beverly Hills, CA: Sage. See also: Samovar, Porter, & McDaniel (2009).

22. Hofstede, G. (1984). *Culture's consequences: International differences in work-related values.* Beverly Hills, CA: Sage.

23. Dodd, C. H. (1991). *Dynamics of intercultural communication.* (3rd ed., pp. 73–74). Dubuque, IA: William C. Brown. See also: Hofstede, *Culture's consequences,* pp. 89–191.

24. Samovar & Porter, *Communication between cultures,* p. 95.

25. U.S. Census Bureau (2010). USA Quick Facts. Retrieved from http://quickfacts.census.gov/qfd/states/00000.html

26. Athen, G. (1988). *American ways: A guide for foreigners in the United States.* Yarmouth, ME: Intercultural Press; Park, Y. S., & Kim, B. S. K. (2008). Asian and European American cultural values and communication styles among Asian American and European American college students. *Cultural Diversity and Ethnic Minority Psychology, 14,* 47–56.

27. Marin, G., & Marin, B. V. (1991). *Research with Hispanic populations: Increasing multicultural understanding* (p. 21). Newbury Park, CA: Sage.

28. Lustig, M. W., & Koester, J. (1993). *Intercultural competence:* Interpersonal communication across cultures (p. 21). New York: Harper Collins.

29. Collier, M. J. (1988). A comparison of conversations among and between domestic cultural groups: How intra-and intercultural competencies vary. *Communication Quarterly, 36,* 122–144.

30. Marin & Marin, *Research with Hispanic populations*.

31. Hecht, M. L., Collier, M. J., & Ribeau, S. A. (1993). *African American communication: Ethnic identity and cultural interpretation* (p. 74). Newbury Park, CA: Sage; Hecht, M. L., Jackson, R. L., & Ribeau, S. (2003). *African American communication: Exploring identity and culture* (2nd ed). Mahwah, NJ: Erlbaum.

32. Lustig & Koester, *Intercultural competence*, p. 21.

33. Hecht, Collier, & Ribeau, *African American communication*, p. 97.

34. Hecht, Collier, & Ribeau, *African American communication*, pp. 102–103; Kochman, T. (1981). *Black and white styles in conflict* (pp. 130–132). Chicago: University of Chicago Press.

35. Locke, D. C. (1992). *Increasing multicultural understanding: A comprehensive model* (p. 26). Newbury Park, CA: Sage.

36. Gudykunst, W. B. (1991). *Bridging differences: Effective intergroup communication* (pp. 45–49). Newbury Park, CA: Sage. See also: Hofstede, *Culture's consequences*; Hofstede, G., & Bond, J. (1984). Hofstede's culture dimensions. *Journal of Cross-Cultural Psychology, 1, 15*, 417–433.

37. Locke, *Increasing multicultural understanding*.

38. Ting-Toomey, S. (1988). Intercultural conflict styles: A face-negotiation theory. In Y. Y. Kim & W. B. Gudykunst (Eds.), *Theories of intercultural communication* (pp. 213–235). Newbury Park, CA; Sage.

39. Locke, *Increasing multicultural understanding*, pp. 46–47. See also: Bureau of Indian Affairs. (1988). *American Indians today*. Washington, DC: Author; Hirschfelder, A. (1982). *Happy may I work: American Indians and Alaska natives today*. New York: Scribner's.

40. Bennett, C. I. (1990). *Comprehensive multicultural education* (2nd ed., pp. 164–165). Boston: MA: Allyn & Bacon.

41. DeFleur, M. L., D'Antonio, W. V., & DeFleur, L. B. (1981). *Sociology: Human society* (3rd ed., p. 92). Glenview, IL: Scott, Foresman.

42. Samovar, L. A., & Porter, R. E. (1995). *Communication between cultures* (p. 195). Belmont, CA: Wadsworth.

43. Ibid., p. 193.

44. Locke, *Increasing multicultural understanding*, p. 50.

45. DeFleur, D'Antonio, & DeFleur, *Sociology*, pp. 146–147.

46. Ibid, p. 147.

47. Locke, *Increasing multicultural understanding*.

48. Dutton, B. P. (1983). *American Indians of the Southwest* (p. 13). Albuquerque: University of New Mexico Press.

49. Hamod, H. S. (1963). Arab and Moslem rhetorical theory. *Central States Speech Journal, 14*, 97–102.

50. Almaney, A. J., & Alwan, A. J. (1982). *Communicating with the Arabs: A handbook for the business executive*. Prospect Heights, IL: Waveland.

51. Anderson, J. W. (1991). A comparison of Arab and American conceptions of "effective persuasion." In Samovar, L. A., & Porter, R. E. (Eds.), *Intercultural communication: A reader* (6th ed.), pp. 96–106. Belmont, CA: Wadsworth.

52. Ibid., p. 98.

53. Nydell, M. K. (1987). *Understanding Arabs: A guide for Westerners* (p. 104). Yarmouth, ME: Intercultural Press.

54. Ibid.

55. Condon, J. C., & Yousef, F. S. (1975). *An introduction to intercultural communication* (pp. 159–162). New York: Macmillan.

56. Wood, J. T. (1994). *Gendered lives: Communication, gender, and culture* (p. 140). Belmont, CA: Wadsworth.

57. For a review of that research, see: Mulac, A., Bradac, J. J., & Gibbons, P. (2001). Empirical support for the gender-as-culture hypothesis: An intercultural analysis of male/female language differences. *Human Communication Research, 27, 1*, 121–152; Ivy, D. K., & Backlund, P. (1994). *Exploring gender speak: Personal effectiveness in gender communication*. New York: McGraw-Hill; Pearson, J. C., Turner, L. H., & Todd-Mancillas, W. (1991). *Gender and communication* (pp. 111–115). Dubuque, IA: William C. Brown; and Wood, *Gendered lives*.

58. Pearson, Turner, & Todd-Mancillas, *Gender and communication;* Wood, *Gendered lives.*

59. Pearson, Turner, & Todd-Mancillas, *Gender and communication;* Wood, *Gendered lives.*

60. Lakoff, R. (1975). *Language and women's place.* New York: Harper & Row; Lakoff, R. (1973). Language and woman's place. *Language in Society, 2,* 45–80.

61. Bradley, P. H. (1981). The folk-linguistics of women's speech: An empirical examination. *Communication Monographs, 48,* 73–90.

62. Wood, *Gendered lives,* p. 143.

63. Bradley, The folk-linguistics of women's speech.

64. Mulac, A., & Lundell, T. L. (1986). Linguistic contributors to the gender-linked language effect. *Journal of Language and Social Psychology, 5,* 81–101.

65. Gudykunst, W. B. (1985). The influence of cultural similarity, type of relationship, and self-monitoring on uncertainty reduction processes. *Communication Monographs, 52,* 203–217.

Chapter 9

Presenting Yourself Effectively

Howie, I think I have a problem with my boss. I don't think he likes me."

"Why do you care, Audrey, whether your boss likes you or not? Are you worried about losing your job?"

"Not really. It would just be a lot easier to go to work each day if I thought my boss liked me, respected me, and defined what I do as important."

"Why do you suppose he doesn't like you? Maybe you're just being a little paranoid."

"No, Howie. I don't think I am. My boss never responds to any messages I leave him, and he doesn't even bother to return my phone calls."

"If that's true, Audrey, why do you suppose he feels that way?"

"I don't know. I work hard. And yet, he complains that I am high maintenance. He told one of my colleagues that I ask too many questions, but I need direction. He said I don't follow through on my responsibilities, but that's not true at all. I just don't do each and every task the way he would do them. He tries to micro-manage me—which I hate. It always seems like he's looking over my shoulder. But when I need help, he's just never around."

"Well, if you're right and his impression of you is wrong, you have your work cut out for you. From my experience, it is very hard to get someone to change their impressions of you. You have to wonder how the boss reached these conclusions about you in the first place."

Howie is right to question what Audrey might have said or done to contribute to her boss's negative impression of her. Impressions are not created in a vacuum; instead, they are based on a whole host of verbal and nonverbal behaviors that communicate specific messages. What you say and how you say it influences how others form impressions of you. The problem is that most of these impressions are created quickly and with very little information to base them on. Once created, these impressions become very difficult, if not impossible, to change.

Audrey is also right to worry that her boss's impression is an inaccurate one. People act on impressions or what they believe to be true about others. Knowing that her boss perceives her to be high maintenance, Audrey is unlikely to receive the respect, acknowledgment, and sense of importance that she wants and maybe even deserves. First impressions are important in just about every situation—when you meet someone you might want to date, when you make a presentation in class, and when you interview for a job. This chapter will answer four major questions: First, *how* do people form impressions of others when they are meeting them for the first time? Second, how can you influence the first impressions others form *about you?* Third, what specifically can be communicated, both verbally and nonverbally to make the impressions others form about you *more favorable?* Finally, what can be done to change *unfavorable impressions* that people already have about you?

The Impressions You Make in Initial Encounters

Presentation of self is the strategy of creating and sending *verbal and nonverbal messages to other people about the kind of person you are.* As you talk, dress, or act in various ways, you communicate meanings about your personal qualities. In doing so, you present descriptions and definitions about your inner nature to others. From these messages, others construct interpretations, understandings, and impressions about what you are really like. It works both ways, of course. As others form impressions about you during your initial encounters with them, you will be doing the same about them. It is, as you will see, an inescapable form of human behavior.

In your initial encounters, you do not always try or plan to get other individuals to evaluate you in some particular way. However, if you want to do so, it is certainly possible. You can plan a communication strategy and transmit verbal and nonverbal messages that are deliberately designed to create a particular set of impressions. Sociologist Erving Goffman referred to this process as **impression management.**[1] In this chapter, impression management refers to *effective* self-presentation. Messages can be said to be "effective" insofar as they cause others to evaluate you in ways you desire.

There is little doubt that what an individual says and does during an initial encounter leaves lasting impressions in the minds of others. In other words, the verbal and nonverbal messages you transmit as you are getting to know someone can strongly influence what that person comes to believe about you. Those early impressions may be very difficult to change. For these reasons, presentation of self can be a serious business on which both personal and social success can depend.

What Research Tells Us about Initial Impressions

To develop a greater understanding of the relationship between initial encounters and person perception, some of the classic experiments on how people form impressions of others provide important insights. A brief review of the principles discovered in early research can show you how to improve your ability to manage your impressions—that is, to present yourself effectively to others.

The principle of rapid impression formation. Of the pioneering research on impression formation, the work of Solomon Asch in the 1940s was the most significant.[2] At the time, Asch was conducting experiments to try to find out how a person quickly infers personality traits and attributes concerning another individual when all he or she has is a limited amount of known characteristics. (Obviously, this is related to the idea of forming impressions of a person one has just met.) The point here is this: You must make some sort of assessment—even though these are guesses or assumptions—about people you have just met if you want to talk to them. You can't relate to another human being where everything about that person is just a *blank*. Each new person has some things you notice right away, and you use these to make assumptions about what that person is like, and how she or he will respond to what you say.

It was this issue that prompted Asch to conduct his classic experiments focused directly on the problem of examining how a person forms first impressions of other people. They were simple experiments but they revealed provocative findings. In the typical investigation he conducted, each participant or subject received a list of descriptive words said to characterize a target person—an individual whom the subject had never actually met. All the subject had about that person was the list of words said to describe the otherwise unknown individual. Then, after reviewing the words, each subject was asked to write a paragraph describing her or his first impressions of what that person was like. Following that, each subject was given a second list of descriptive terms and asked to indicate those terms each felt would *also* be likely to characterize the person each had already described in the previous paragraph. Each did so, thereby revealing in greater detail the overall impressions of the new person.

Thus, in this second step, Asch was able to gather each subject's early impressions of the target person formed on the basis of the very limited descriptions (by the words) supplied in the first step. Because early impressions in real life are formulated during initial meetings, this simple experiment was like the real impression-forming process. Asch found that subjects quickly formed surprisingly elaborate impressions of the target person after receiving only very limited descriptions of that individual.

In another of Asch's classic experiments, additional aspects of the process were shown. Again, subjects were provided with lists of descriptive terms and asked to form an impression of a target person. This time, however, the list of words described the unknown person quite positively as intelligent, skillful, industrious, determined, practical, and cautious. Next, each of the subjects was asked to write a paragraph describing the target person. After these paragraphs were completed, the subjects were again asked to assess that same individual, but in terms of four additional attributes: generous, happy, good-natured, and important. The results of this experiment were striking. Table 9.1 provides the findings. Look at the column titled "Trait List A." The point is that if the target was thought to have one set of favorable qualities, subjects believed that he or she had other favorable ones, too.

The principle of the salient characteristic. In a similar experiment, Asch inserted the descriptive word *warm* in the middle of his first list of characteristics—the words used by the subjects to write their descriptive paragraphs. What happened was that the subjects' initial impressions of the target person were *favorably influenced* by the word *warm*. This is shown in Table 9.1 under the column labeled "Trait List B." Clearly, adding a single known **salient characteristic**—a feature of the person that stands out ("warm" in this case)—sharply altered initial impressions of the target person.

	Impression Formation in Asch's Experiments	
TABLE 9.1		

Trait List A	Trait List B	Trait List C
Intelligent	Intelligent	Intelligent
Skillful	Skillful	Skillful
Industrious	Industrious	Industrious
	Warm	*Cold*
Determined	Determined	Determined
Practical	Practical	Practical
Cautious	Cautious	Cautious

Attribute	Percentage of Subjects Indicating That Attribute Is Characteristic of Person Described by Trait List		
Generous	55%	91%	8%
Happy	71	90	34
Good-natured	69	94	17
Important	88	88	99

Source: Asch, S. E. (1946). Forming impressions of personalities. *Journal of Personality and Social Psychology, 41,* 258–290.

Asch was interested in whether this substantial change in impressions would occur with an emotionally negative quality as well. Therefore, he did still another experiment using the same procedures, but this time he substituted the unfavorable word *cold* in place of *warm*. What happened was that the favorability of the final ratings of the target dropped sharply. This can be seen in Table 9.1 under the column labeled "Trait List C." Thus, this final experiment strongly confirmed the principle of the salient characteristic.

Asch concluded that the words *warm* and *cold* had served as strong focuses of attention for the subjects. That is, these emotionally meaningful terms did indeed become salient characteristics around which the subjects organized their overall impressions of the target person. The more neutral words, used in the first step to describe target persons, implied a positive general impression of temperament and social acceptability; but when the more powerful words *warm* and *cold* were introduced, the resulting impressions were restructured considerably.

Although these were experiments in an artificial setting, the results of Asch's research provided guidelines that could be studied in more realistic settings. In that way, they provided valuable insights into how people seemed to form impressions of others. The findings implied that when individuals meet a stranger they quickly bring together a kind of initial configuration of impressions of that person on the basis of what limited characteristics they can observe. In addition, a single bit of significant information—a salient characteristic—can alter that impression considerably.

Asch's ideas were followed up by many scholars and it became clear that the principles of rapid formation and salient characteristics operate in real life. When we meet someone who seems to have many attractive qualities, our initial pattern of impressions is positive. Then, a single additional revelation suddenly changes the picture drastically. Such a salient characteristic might be that the person is an ex-convict, uses drugs, or was fired from his or her job for sexual misconduct. Upon fitting that into the configuration, our impressions may switch immediately to a negative or less favorable pattern.

The principle of labels as shaping perception.
Those who study various kinds of deviant behavior—activities that depart from the norms of society—have extensively discussed the salient characteristic phenomenon. They have observed it not just through experiments with words but also through observations of the way people in real life respond to individuals who break accepted moral norms. They call this principle **labeling theory**.[3] It is in many ways an extension of the Asch principle. For example, if you learn that your neighbor's child, little Johnny, who is your son Eddie's friend, was brought home by the police after a local merchant complained that he had swiped candy bars in his store, Johnny has suddenly become a "problem child," or worse, maybe even a "criminal." Such labels identify new salient characteristics that bring with them emotionally charged meanings.[4]

In our language culture, labels such as "criminal" or "thief" are associated with firearms, muggings, early drug and alcohol use, and the like. Perhaps little Johnny had never done anything bad before, and never will again. However, his 10-second act of shoplifting has now labeled him in a very serious way. Although this is no doubt unfair, after hearing that Johnny has become a "criminal," you forbid your son Eddie to play with him ever again.

The basic idea, then, is that one critical piece of information about a person can communicate a powerful message. Labels are often the means that communicate such messages, regardless of whether the interpretation they bring is right or wrong. Any negative label—such as "former mental patient," "suspected sex offender," "unfair professor," "cheater," or "plagiarist"—can have a dramatic influence on the impressions people form. The label is like a magnet: It brings a baggage of cultural meanings commonly associated with it, whether deserved or not.

The principle of implicit personality formation.
During the 1950s and 1960s, social scientists continued to use the investigative methods developed by Asch. They followed up on his study of the strong influence of a salient characteristic on people's overall impressions of others.[5] In a line of investigation called **implicit personality theory**, researchers tried to determine just how people combine different kinds of visible features attributed to a person into an overall configuration of beliefs about that person. They were concerned with how people put together their early patterns of impressions about a person, quickly making a set of assumptions about the nature of the person on the basis of what they know up to that point. They were also concerned with the way in which some readily observable (salient) characteristic comes to be seen as more important or central and how other attributes are interpreted as less essential. In other words, how do people construct an assumed personality for someone they have just met, and, on the basis of limited data, project it onto a person to form a pattern of initial impressions?

Recall that the general meaning of the term *personality* was discussed in Chapter 7. The term refers to a pattern of psychological attributes that makes each individual different and that those traits are thought to shape the individual's responses to his or her physical and social world. Thus, the reason we form impressions of another person, constructing our interpretations of his or her implicit personality, is that we are trying to predict in our own minds how that person will behave toward us and others. As noted earlier, we literally *have to do this*. We cannot communicate with a total blank.

An investigation by John Wishner clearly illustrates implicit personality research.[6] He reasoned that when we are responding to a target person, the central characteristics "warm" and "cold" would have the greatest influence on those personal characteristics that were most related to the personality traits they imply. It is a complex idea, but to illustrate, the characteristic "strong" is not particularly related to either "warm" or "cold." In contrast, the attribute "friendly" is definitely related to "warm."

How does this salient characteristic influence your perception of this woman? What are other salient characteristics that affect your evaluation of others?

That is, "warm" and "friendly" as attributes of a person fit together very well, but "cold" and "friendly" do not. Thus, adding "warm" to the list of terms describing a person should raise estimates of *friendliness,* whereas adding "cold" could be expected to reduce them.

Wishner tested this reasoning by having a group of college students rate their professors on a list of personal characteristics. Then the terms *warm* and *cold* were added, as in the Asch experiments. An examination of the students' evaluations of their professors showed that the characteristics that were most strongly affected when "warm" or "cold" was added were those traits in the list that the students perceived to be *most highly related* to the general ideas of "warm" and "cold." Also important, the results indicated that for characteristics that were not related, impressions of the target person were not influenced.

What Wishner's results imply is that the overall pattern of impressions of a particular individual can be *predicted* from the relationship between the list of characteristics that the target person is first thought to possess. What this means is that people construct a relatively *well-organized* pattern of what they think is important about someone on the basis of very few facts. Furthermore, certain kinds of characteristics have a truly powerful influence on the implicit personality that is projected onto the target person. This is important because that quickly constructed personality will strongly influence both the subsequent evaluations of and the actions toward that person.

Is what has been found in these experiments closely related to what happens in reality? The answer is yes. The findings of studies like those of Asch and Wishner are consistent with extensive observations of people in everyday life. It may not be particularly comforting to realize that certain of your own personal salient characteristics will be observed very quickly by people when they first meet you. They will then use these characteristics as the central features of a rather elaborate set of assumptions about your nature and probable behavior. Those salient characteristics may be visible indicators of racial, ethnic, or cultural differences. Or they may be mannerisms, speech patterns, labels, tatoos, hair length, or some other prominent and visible feature.[7] Salient characteristics may also include the firmness of a handshake during a job interview,[8] or any attractive or unattractive features that you possess.[9] Such characteristics may even include whether or not you exercise regularly.[10]

You might wonder what your salient characteristics are. Are they flattering or demeaning? Furthermore, what kind of implicit personality do others project onto you on the basis of a few central attributes? Is it one that truly represents you, or is it some grossly distorted image of you? Above all, can you control or manage the kind of personality assumptions that others make about you?

Before turning directly to specific ways in which self-presentation can be managed more effectively, we need to review several additional features of initial encounters that can pose problems when meeting people for the first time.

Problems in Initial Encounters

It is important to look closely at three additional considerations that influence the process of getting to know one another. The *difficulties* inherent in meeting someone for the first time; the *number of people* present in an initial encounter; and the context or setting in which people meet can all play a significant role in determining people's success in their presentations of self and the impressions they make in initial encounters.

Common difficulties when meeting people for the first time.   If you were to worry about all the potential problems that can come up when you initially meet someone you might never want to go through it again.[11] More realistically, it is possible to learn to handle effectively the most common difficulties associated with initial encounters. Consider the following list of common problems that are encountered when people meet for the first time:

- Finding things in common with strangers.
- Finding things to say to strangers.
- Not knowing how to say things appropriately.
- Meeting people you just don't like.
- Meeting people who just don't like you.
- Adjusting to language differences.
- Adjusting to different backgrounds or experiences.
- One- or two-way communication apprehension.
- Feeling generally awkward.

- Feeling self-conscious.
- Feeling alienated from others.
- Worrying about saying the wrong thing.

Suppose these potential difficulties arise in the context of a worst case first meeting. The scene is a party: Cynthia and Bill have just been introduced. Bill is from a small town in Texas, and Cynthia comes from Chicago. Both are new to the area, and both really want to make some friends. Each is anxious to make a positive first impression. During the first few moments of their meeting, they both react positively and are even physically attracted to each other. Each sees the other as about the same age, obviously intelligent, and about right in height; and they even have the same hair and skin color. Neither has bad breath, dirty fingernails, a detectable body odor, or any other salient characteristic around which an unfavorable implicit personality can be instantly organized. So far, so good! All things considered, Cynthia and Bill should be able to get along just fine. So, rather than politely disengaging and moving on, each decides to try to carry on a friendly conversation—engaging in effective self-presentation and hoping that it might lead to a pleasant outcome.

Unfortunately, as the conversation begins, things begin to go downhill. The first problem they encounter is that they actually don't seem to have much of anything in common. They really do come from very different cultural backgrounds—rural Texas versus big-city Chicago. They have difficulty in finding things to say to each other, and there are a lot of long and noticeable pauses in their conversation. The more difficult the meeting becomes for each, the more frustrated they are by the whole situation. Yet they do not give up. Each continues to try to find out things about the other. Both ask questions and probe as best they can, but it doesn't work. The encounter is falling on its face.

After a few more uncomfortable moments, it becomes apparent that they are both being very careful about how they are communicating with each other for fear of saying the wrong thing and being misunderstood. Neither Cynthia nor

Bill wants to prejudge the other—and each is obviously trying to avoid not being liked.

The more they talk, the more they discover that they come from very different worlds and have had totally different experiences. They even seem to be using language differently. It sounds as if they are both speaking English, but the words that each is using appear to be arousing different meanings for the other. Each has to explain and apologize for meanings that were not intended. Cynthia's language was acquired both in her family and in schools typical of a sophisticated and well-educated urban class. Bill's language is from a ranch culture in rural Texas.

By this time, each has constructed a pattern of impressions about the other. This now strongly influences how they speak and act. To Bill, Cynthia seems to be a sophisticated city girl—maybe "stuck up"—and accustomed to having a lot of boyfriends. He is afraid she will think he is just a dull country boy. To Cynthia, Bill seems very polite and sincere but a bit old-fashioned and shy. She is afraid to say anything that will seem like she is putting him down.

It has become clear that both are apprehensive. Moreover, their apprehensiveness seems to be accentuated by having to communicate with a total stranger. In other words, each feels awkward and self-conscious. So, the more they try to talk to each other, and the harder they try to get together, the worse they feel.

At this point, things are not looking good. It is obvious to each that there will be no lasting relationship between them. In fact, after about 20 minutes both Cynthia and Bill decide to give up. Their conversation just sort of dries up, and the noisy confusion of the party allows them to drift apart physically. It should be obvious from this vignette that Cynthia's and Bill's chances for a second meeting, let alone a lasting relationship, are near zero. In fact, nearly every problem in the list of difficulties occurred. At the same time, both had very good intentions; both sincerely wanted to make an effective and positive presentation of self; however, things just happened that derailed what started as a promising encounter.

Often, things "just happen" in many of our sincere efforts to communicate a good first impression to others. The bottom line of all this is that presenting ourselves effectively is a difficult job. It is not easy to communicate our preferred pattern of positive first impressions.

Returning to Cynthia and Bill, a fair question to ask about this first meeting would be, What (if anything) would have been different if more than the two of them had been present? That is, what happens to the process of getting to know others when more than two individuals are involved in an initial encounter? In particular, how would this influence both the presentation of self and the resulting formation of impressions? Would it have helped the situation or made things worse?

The effects of meeting one person or several. Many initial encounters involve more than two people. Examples are students and teachers walking into their classroom for the first time, a new employee going into an office full of people on the first day of work, or indeed any situation where people meet in groups.

The influence of group size was discussed in Chapters 6 and 7. As opposed to two-person dynamics, what happens in a group situation is very different. Additional potential difficulties are typically involved.[12] This is not to say that all group encounters are negative; in some ways, they can be easier. However, the inclusion of additional individuals can influence perceptions, evaluations, and the exchange of messages.

First, consider some of the typical problems that arise when more than two people meet:

- Fragmenting participation and focuses of attention.
- The problem of "you can't please everybody."
- Individual differences that create difficulties.
- Perceptions of favoritism.
- Speaking generally versus specifically to one person.

- Coalitions among pairs.
- Conversational intrusions and interruptions.

With this list in mind, reconsider the scene with Cynthia and Bill. This time assume that they encounter each other not alone but in a trio that includes Peggy. They have all just been introduced at the party. In such a situation, the energies and focuses of attention will be spread across three people rather than just two.

In the new scene, Cynthia and Bill are introduced along with Peggy, who is about the same age. During the first moments of appraisal, all three look each other over and reach the same conclusions. Initially, each is impressed favorably, and all is "go" for trying to get to know one another better. Therefore, each thinks that it is a good idea to try to engage in favorable presentations of self, just on the chance that a meaningful, long-term, friendly relationship might develop.

So, there they stand in a trio, surrounded by other people at the party. Just as Bill begins to open the conversation by asking Cynthia where she is from, Peggy interrupts and asks Bill's opinion about last night's football game, a topic about which she seems quite enthusiastic. After they spend a few moments listening to his negative opinions about spectator sports, Cynthia tries to present a positive self-image to Bill by telling him of her impressions of a recent symphony performance she attended.

Before Bill can explain that he isn't into classical music, but likes country and western, Peggy begins explaining her devotion to a local rock group. It is clear that Peggy's tastes are quite different. Both Bill and Cynthia now seem somewhat bored. They begin looking around the room to see what other possibly interesting people there might be at the party. However, they decide to try once again to learn more about each other. They begin discussing what restaurants each knows in the area. Peggy, who was initially somewhat taken with Bill, now senses that he has less interest in her than in Cynthia. She feels a bit slighted, with just a twinge of jealousy. At this point, she asks Bill if he would mind getting her a fresh drink. Bill, whose mother tried to teach him to be a gentleman, agrees to do so. He leaves the trio to go to the bar. When he returns with the drink, Cynthia is gone. She is now talking animatedly with another guy in the far corner of the room. Bill is disappointed and feels that he has been rejected. He decides he doesn't like the party and soon leaves.

This account illustrates several of the limitations inherent in trying to communicate positive impressions of self in conversations that involve more than two people. First, it is difficult to maintain a central focus on getting to know someone when a third person introduces topics that derail such an effort. In Bill's case, with two individuals interested in him, he could not be equally pleasing to both. Furthermore, it seemed that none of them had the same tastes. In such a situation, Cynthia and Bill could not concentrate fully on personal matters but had to discuss general topics (football, restaurants, music), rather than each other. In spite of all these difficulties, there was at least the beginnings of a dyad within the trio, sometimes called a "coalition of the triad" into an obvious pair interested in each other.[13] Peggy, who was left out, perceived that to be favoritism and took action to disrupt it. Thus, with all the interruptions and intrusions, Bill and Cynthia never did get to know each other, and each went their separate ways.

Could anything have been done to improve the chances that what took place between Bill and Cynthia would have resulted in a more positive outcome? For example, if they had met in a different place, would the dynamics of the initial meeting have been altered and would the outcome of their encounter have been different?

Meeting in familiar versus unfamiliar places. The idea that where you meet people can influence the outcome of a meeting is scarcely new.[14] However, when this idea is linked to implicit personality theory, it becomes meaningful in terms of understanding what factors influence effective self-presentation.

Generally, people are more at ease in familiar surroundings.[15] The importance of location is that the physical surroundings where a person meets others can have a dramatic effect on how capable and *confident* the person feels during that meeting. When manifested in behavior, those feelings can serve as salient characteristics that help observers organize the pattern of personality traits they project onto the individual. Thus, persons who are seen as at ease, capable, and confident are also perceived more positively overall than those who are thought to be inept and nervous. In addition, observers may make judgments about the personality of an individual they are meeting based on the physical environment or setting—a room or office, for example—that the individual occupies.[16] In these direct ways, then, physical settings can help or hinder the outcome of self-presentation.

To illustrate this principle, consider once again the initial encounter between Cynthia and Bill, but this time in terms of a different location and without the troublesome Peggy present. Previously, the initial meeting occurred in the unfamiliar context of a party—a place in which neither was particularly at ease. Suppose now that Cynthia and Bill had just met in a quiet lounge at the dorm where both were living. In such familiar physical surroundings, they would have had something in common from the very start of their encounter. Clearly, this would have made it easier for them to find out the many other things they had in common. In this way, their concern about liking or not being liked by the other would have been far less significant. In all likelihood, neither would have been as guarded, and they would have had a basis for more easily dealing with their differences. Factors like their regionally associated languages would have become less central.

Unfortunately, people cannot always count on meeting others on familiar ground. When they do, however, it provides a sense of assurance about having successfully negotiated a complex social context. In other words, a familiar meeting place often has associated memories of previously successful self-presentations.

The lessons learned from those efforts greatly aid communicating favorable impressions in the same surroundings the next time the need arises.

Presenting Yourself in Encounters That Really Matter

Thus far, this chapter has highlighted factors that are pertinent to getting to know other people and forming first impressions. It has concentrated on essential issues that can enhance or limit the effectiveness of a person's presentation of self to others. From what has been discussed, it is safe to assume that people tend quickly to form impressions of others based on a limited amount of information. Moreover, some salient characteristic often has a strong influence on that overall pattern of impressions. Also, the number of people present can make a difference, and, finally, physical settings are another factor in the formation of first impressions.

These principles provide a good basis from which to develop practical strategies for the effective presentation of self. The next task, therefore, is to move from a review of what researchers have concluded from experiments and real-life observations to a consideration of what is actually needed on an everyday basis to achieve the goal of managing people's impressions.

Goals in Initial Encounters

Meetings can be either intentional or accidental. They can be organized as either very structured or completely open-ended. As discussed previously, the social situation that you happen to be in defines the purpose of meeting people for the first time. That purpose might be a job interview, getting to know someone that you have just noticed in a crowded room, getting acquainted with the parents of a close friend, or giving a talk before a group. Whatever the nature of the encounter, having a clear idea of why the meeting has been initiated can help in the selection of strategies, content, and style of delivery. In particular, in those meetings that can have an effect on your future, understanding every aspect of impression management in self-presentation can be truly important.

Many people fail to realize how important it is to map out a *deliberate strategy of self-presentation* before an important meeting. Others sense the value of planning but feel that first meetings should be spontaneous and fall together naturally. However, if the encounter is a critical one, planning in advance for self-presentation can lead to a more favorable outcome.

Obviously, in many social situations where you meet people little is at stake. Going to the supermarket and meeting the checkout clerk or dealing with a server in a restaurant is hardly an occasion that calls for strategic consideration of effective self-presentation. Similarly, when you are among people close to you—peers and family—you can indeed just be yourself and let it all fall together as it will. However, it is crucial to approach those encounters that really count with a thoughtfully formulated plan.

Developing a strategy for initiating and engaging in a social encounter is not as difficult as it may sound: First, before the encounter takes place, you must clarify for yourself the *goals* to be achieved as a result of your presentation of self. Second, you must focus attention on setting the stage to accomplish those goals. This means selecting strategies of self-presentation ahead of time that are most likely to accomplish those objectives.

What are the goals to be achieved in an important encounter? If you want the outcome to be favorable, there are three. Each is an important part of the self-presentation process, and the strategies you use to achieve them are all related to gaining greater control over the outcome. You plan ahead to achieve effective control over at least three outcomes:

1. The *earliest impressions* formed during initial moments of the contact. Recall the previous discussion of the critical nature of

the first qualities others attribute to you. You need to ensure that some salient characteristic that can turn people off right away does not immediately spoil your identity.

2. The *expanding configuration* of impressions organized as your presentation of self unfolds. This is a result of systematic impression management, and it needs to be done with grace and style so as to produce a positive image of your qualities in the minds of observers.

3. The *lasting pattern* of impressions that the other party takes away. This is the bottom line—the fairly permanent implicit personality that observers attribute to you. It is the most important goal of all.

A very effective way to gain control over these outcomes is to know your objective ahead of time. Simply ask yourself, "What is it that I really want out of this meeting?" The answer may be obvious, like getting the job. Or it may be something very different, such as entry into a particular social group, an experience with a member of the opposite sex, wanting to be assertive, or perhaps even getting paroled.[17] In any case, knowing clearly what you want in the first step makes that goal easier to attain.

Defining the goal of an encounter ahead of time contributes to the design of the self-presentation strategy needed to attain it. Goal clarification, in other words, helps you identify the impressions that are most likely to contribute to success. Stated more simply, knowing what you want helps identify what it is that people need to believe about you.

Preselecting the Impressions You Want to Make

In some first meetings, what you really want and how you want to be perceived may be virtually the same thing. For example, if you are running for public office and will be speaking to groups of potential voters, you will want the audience to feel positively enough about you to cast their vote in your direction, and to convince others to do the same. As you can see, what you really want (to get elected) and how you want to be perceived (to be liked) are closely linked.

It is important, then, to communicate those *characteristics that count* in the situation so that they will be quickly and unmistakably perceived and understood by those on the receiving end. We see politicians do this all the time. A candidate will don a farmer's cap and an informal jacket and use a country folks speech style when addressing a rural audience. The next day, when speaking to a group of bankers, the same candidate will be dressed in a conservative suit and will use a different vocabulary. Still later it will be hard hat, blue shirt, and macho talk when making a speech to factory hands.

Few of us need to go to such lengths in our personal presentations of self, but the principle is there. Strategies can be used in a more subtle way to preselect certain kinds of impressions that we want to create so as to achieve our goals. As discussed later, this can be done through selection of clothing, vocabulary, message content, demeanor, and many other alternatives.

There are two major reasons why preselection of qualities that can create positive impressions is not particularly difficult. The first is that *everyone has many positive qualities*. Each of us— no matter what our gender, race, ethnic identity, cultural background, age, body shape, educational background, and so on—has a long list of favorable characteristics that will be of genuine interest to others. The real task is to understand those attributes and to demonstrate them in appropriate ways through verbal and nonverbal communication. At the same time, pitfalls do exist. All of us have dull, unimportant, and undistinguished characteristics that if arbitrarily communicated in the wrong situation can be boring or interpreted negatively. An important part of the task of effective self-presentation is to minimize such potentially negative influences.

The second feature of the process of meeting someone for the first time that works in favor of creating positive impressions is the fact that most people *tend to like* other people. Unless there is something obvious that quickly turns them off, the cards are stacked for, rather than against us, and a favorable impression is likely at the outset in most encounters. The real trick is to identify and maximize the influence of your positive features and to minimize those potentially troublesome salient characteristics that are so important in initial impression formation.

From the principles of salient characteristics and implicit personality we know that first impressions tend to be lasting. However, lasting or not, it is difficult to explain just how people immediately pick out some particular characteristic from an individual's presentation of self that they decide is salient and then organize other attributes or qualities around that factor. It is this, the universal tendency to perceive selectively, that is at the heart of impression formation.

The significance of selective perception. The term *perception*, explained in Chapters 1 and 2, refers to making sense of, that is attaching meaning to, some aspect of reality that has been apprehended by the senses. Perception is an important part of forming impressions of other people, and there are easily understood reasons why it is inevitably a selective activity. We all have different memories of meanings linked to signs, signals, and symbols, and even to human characteristics stored in our memories from our lifetime of experience. No one's associated meanings for those stimuli are exactly like those of anyone else. Thus, no one's stored meanings used to interpret a particular thing or event are an exact duplicate of those of others. What happens is that when you search your memory traces and schemas for an interpretation of something you see or hear, you cannot avoid putting your own personal stamp of meaning on it. This is the basis of **selective perception.**

Selective perception is heavily influenced by what we like and dislike. This occurs because people have a stable organization of **predispositions**—probabilities of behavior that lead us to approve of some things and disapprove of others. These are shaped by our attitudes, values, opinions, preferences, and so on.

These predispositions modify our perceptions and interpretations of things that we experience, because they lead us to like some stimuli and dislike others.

Even our ever-changing emotions and needs can alter the way we interpret something we see or hear at a particular moment. For example, when you are angry or afraid, things don't seem the same as they do when you are happy and relaxed. Or you see some things differently when you are hungry, like a big juicy piece of apple pie, as compared to seeing the same piece just after having finished a huge Thanksgiving dinner. Thus, people perceive and experience the world through their own internalized meanings, dispositions, emotional states, and needs. *Selective perception,* then, refers to *the unique way people interpret and assign meaning to what they observe.*

The importance of selective perception for present purposes is that it will always happen. It is a fundamental part of person perception that always takes place in initial encounters. It is also the basis for the selection of a salient characteristic around which an observer can create a complex initial set of impressions about what another person is really like. It may not be easy to detect when another person is perceiving you in some selective way, but you can be totally certain that it will take place.

Knowing the consequences of selective perception, and that it is inevitable, it is obviously very important to try to control it. This may be easier said than done. However, one good way to influence the way others perceive you is to *plan ahead* by organizing a flexible preliminary game plan. This will go a long way toward limiting a display of negative salient characteristics. By the same token, presenting positive ones is an obvious part of such a strategy.

Developing a preliminary plan. Strategies of effective self-presentation are not hard to identify. They consist of using such nonverbal forms of communication as clothing, mannerisms, gestures, posture, and demeanor, plus verbal messages with specific content delivered with a particular style and level of vocabulary. The problem here is that the best combination can be difficult to identify. Furthermore, you can never be sure exactly what people might pick out as salient characteristics. In one context, shaggy hair, sloppy clothing, and scruffy shoes, plus a laid-back speaking style sprinkled with four-letter words, might be a basis for negative selective perception (as in a group of conservative business people). In another context, a tailored suit, neatly trimmed hair, well-polished shoes, plus a sophisticated vocabulary and a well-organized speaking style, might make exactly the wrong impression (for example, among a group of construction workers).

Clearly, clothing plays an important role in impression formation and can affect one's ability to obtain a good job. Clothing worn by a job applicant may be an indicator of status, power, and ability, and may determine the outcome of the interview. As a recent study indicates, clothing is especially critical for poor women who lack the financial resources necessary to enhance their appearance with appropriate job-related clothing. In the past few years, a number of programs have been designed to provide clothing to poor women entering the workforce and to recognize the unique challenges they face.[18]

How do you know in a general way which strategies to use so that personal characteristics might be perceived selectively in ways you desire? Perhaps the best guide is common sense. Do not do, say, or otherwise communicate, either verbally or nonverbally, anything that those whom you are meeting might perceive selectively and use as the basis of their negative implicit personality for you.

Although one single checklist cannot be used as a game plan for all people in all situations, certain principles can be used in preselecting the kind of impression that you want to create during a particular initial encounter. For example, examine the guidelines in Box 9.1.

You need to be very deliberate in your preencounter planning—specific in the selection of the self-defining characteristics you decide to present and intentional in the strategies you plan

BOX 9.1   *A Closer Look*

Principles for Preselecting Initial Impressions

1. Analyze the people to whom you are making a self-presentation. Understand the standards they will probably use in judging you.
2. Analyze the physical setting where the encounter will take place. Understand the factors in that environment that might be important in your self-presentation.
3. Never intentionally misrepresent yourself. People can spot a phony very quickly. The discovery of even a minor untruth will backfire into a negative salient characteristic!
4. Use all available communication channels to get your positive qualities across. This means both verbal and nonverbal messages that communicate your positive characteristics.
5. Analyze feedback messages of a subtle nature. Use them to shift strategies if necessary or to follow up on ones that seem successful.

effective role-taking and to have a pretty good idea about how they are going to interpret your presentation and how they are likely to respond to you.

Fortunately, there are many role-taking guidelines that have emerged from research and common experience for making educated guesses about people. Furthermore, most of us have already learned to make certain assumptions about how and why people from different categories in society will think and behave. Although these can sometimes prove to be wrong, they are certainly better than mere guesses. Nevertheless, social scientists have studied not only how people think others are likely to behave in certain situations but also the causes to which they attribute such behavior.

Attributing motives to others.   An important part of the study of person perception is what social scientists call the **attribution process**. This process refers to *the selection and*

to use. Your presentation must be honestly communicated, while focusing attention away from anything that might result in negative evaluations. Careful assessment of the people, the situation, the available channels of communication, and the nature of feedback transmitted during the encounter is far more likely to result in an effective self-presentation than a strategy that consists of just letting things proceed naturally.

Assessing the People You Meet

The central factor in any encounter is the *people.* All the planning in the world will make no difference unless it is done in conjunction with an understanding of the individuals to whom you will be presenting yourself. You must have enough knowledge about them to engage in

What attributions might you make about this person? How would those attributions change if you knew he was really a police officer, a research scientist, or a teacher?

BOX 9.2   *A Closer Look*

The Attribution Process

When you first meet someone, you experience a certain degree of uncertainty about that individual. In order to reduce that uncertainty, you tend to categorize or stereotype that person. In this way, you create an environment that offers you some degree of predictability concerning the other person's behavior. Your categorizing involves attributing the causes of a person's behavior to internal and external factors. By attributing causes in this way, you feel that you can anticipate how and why that person is likely to react to you. The attribution process can be summed up as follows:

1. You meet someone new and face some degree of uncertainty regarding how the person will behave.
2. In an attempt to establish some degree of predictability concerning the person's behavior, you place the person in social categories or stereotypes.
3. The categories in which you place the person are based on internal and external clues. Internal clues are those within the person, such as their attitudes and beliefs. External clues are based on circumstances outside the person, such as social norms and rules.
4. In order to predict how a person will behave and understand that behavior, you attribute their behavior to salient internal or external clues.

As an example of the attribution process, suppose you work at a retail store and have mistakenly given a customer too much change. The woman who made the purchase realizes she is holding more money than she should be and gives the excess change back. Based on external clues—such as her clothing and the context of the situation—and internal clues—such as her honesty—you attribute her behavior of returning the money to her being a nice, caring, and honest person.

---

assignment to another person of various personal qualities, conditions, or dispositions that we believe are the causes of or influences on some aspect of that person's behavior.[19] The attribution process is explained most clearly in what is called "attribution theory." According to attribution theory, making assumptions about other people's behavior is a normal human process—people do it all the time. That is, people make attributions whenever they try to understand why someone is behaving in a particular way. According to the eminent psychologist Fritz Heider, people act like naive psychologists when trying to figure out why someone acted in a specific way. They draw inferences about the cause of someone's actions. Moreover, the inclination to draw inferences about others' behavior involves several steps (described in Box 9.2).

Some attributed causes or influences are seen as *internal* to the person (for example, attitudes, values, and motivations). Other influences are seen as *external* to the person (such as requirements of norms or roles or other aspects of group organization).[20]

The attribution process is related to the idea of implicit personality discussed earlier. The difference is that, in an encounter in which attributions are made about causes of a particular form of behavior, you are not considering the entire personality. You are concerned only with selective characteristics that can explain why you think a person will engage in a particular action. For example, you may assign (attribute to) the other person the specific traits of being mean and malicious if you believe the individual will be likely to refuse you a raise or a promotion.

Thus, when you assess people, you are making inferences about them in two ways: (1) how they are likely to react to you and (2) why that probably will be the case. In so doing, you base your predictions on either *internal factors* that you believe will influence their action (personality traits) or *external conditions* (norms, roles, social controls) that you see as limiting or shaping what they will do. Either way makes you feel better because it makes their behavior more predictable.

Remember the earlier discussion of the ways in which personality traits are attributed to others in initial encounters. Recall that as part of the communication transaction, others form their assumptions about what we are like during the early part of an encounter. The point now is that, in an additional transaction, you also form impressions of what they are like—all before anything happens. But how can you make judgments about either internal personality traits or external influences on action? One way is to examine the **social categories** to which the individuals belong; another is to grasp the social constraints (norms, roles, and so on) within which they are performing.

Typical behavior as a basis for attribution. You cannot invent attributions about probable behavior or its causes out of thin air. One source of information that can be used for attributions about other people is their *membership in significant social categories* (such as males, children, educated people, working class, farmers). Often, people in such categories are said to be characterized by certain predictable *regularities* in their behavior. These are generalizations about behavior considered typical of people from particular walks of life. For example, if you want to make a good impression on an elderly person who has little schooling and a low income, your initial small talk with that individual probably would not be based on the merits of the local symphony orchestra or a particularly good year for French wines. You could be wrong, of course, but it would seem safer to discuss alarming increases

in the cost of medical services or possibly the local baseball team.

As a normal part of living in a complex society, people learn to make such predictions on the basis of typical interests of people in specific social categories. However, there are certain dangers in such forecasts. As discussed in Chapter 2, rigidly held assumptions, categorical attributions, and unfounded forecasts become *stereotypes*—especially if they attribute socially undesirable qualities to the target category. Still, there are topics of interest typically associated with people of a particular age, occupation, gender, region, social class, religion, ethnic and racial identity, and so on. Knowing the category memberships of individuals to whom you will make a presentation of self, then, provides at least some information for making attributions about their tastes, beliefs, values, attitudes—and therefore their probable behavior.

Socially imposed conditions as a basis for attribution. External to the individual, but very influential on behavior, are social norms, roles, and ranks that dictate at particular times how the individual has to evaluate and respond to your self-presentation, regardless of inner feelings and attitudes. For example, a person who is acting as a recruiter for a company may be all business in such an encounter. The same person would be different at a cocktail party with peers or at home with the family. Similarly, people in positions of power and authority have to think and act according to the mandates of those positions at times. If they did not, they would lose their jobs. Response to your self-presentation, then, may be strongly influenced by social organization factors, stemming from the demands of externally imposed constraints, as well as by a person's inner psychological traits.

What, then, are some practical techniques for assessing others so that you can understand how and why they will respond to your verbal and nonverbal communication? The following list includes seven simple and effective steps to help you gather personal information about others and to reduce uncertainties about their probable reactions and behavior:

- Observe people to identify any obvious verbal or nonverbal behavior that communicates psychological characteristics (attitudes, intelligence, emotions).

- Observe people interacting to see how they respond to one another (aggressively, politely, formally, warmly).

- Ask questions about your potential audience in advance if possible, to understand as much as you can about who they are and where they come from, both geographically and socially.

- Compare the people with individuals you know. If they seem alike, they may think and behave similarly.

- Gather information about social category membership (education, occupation, age, race, ethnicity, religion) that can provide clues to probable normative behavior.

- Review the social constraints on these people at the time of the encounter, or other requirements they have to meet, and assess what they require them to do.

- Review everything you have learned and try to put together a composite—an organized prediction—of how they will respond to various aspects of your self-presentation and why.

In review, note that there are several steps in the development of a sound design for self-presentation. First, consider carefully what you want to achieve in a first meeting. Second, you must preselect the impressions you want people to perceive. Third, you need to analyze the information you have about the individuals to whom you will be presenting yourself. Fourth, anticipate how they will react to verbal and nonverbal messages that communicate your characteristics. The final step is to consider, choose, and incorporate the actual techniques and strategies that you will use to create the impressions you prefer. A successful plan means that you communicate well-designed messages through all available channels in such a way that the people receiving them immediately begin to like you.

Getting People to Like You

In recent years, social scientists have done extensive research on strategies that people use to try to get others to like them. A more precise and widely used term for that process is **affinity seeking**.[21] A number of affinity-seeking strategies have been reported by researchers. For example, students often use specific strategies to get their teachers to like them, such as observing the rules of conversation in a classroom or completing additional course requirements. Teachers, on the other hand, also use affinity-seeking strategies, such as listening closely, treating a student with equality or trustworthiness.[22]

Affinity-seeking strategies. The search for effective affinity-seeking strategies has turned out to be unbelievably complex. The problem is that there are literally dozens of strategies that seem to work, at least sometimes. To provide an idea of how complex this process can be, Box 9.3 identifies 25 affinity-seeking strategies.[23]

Although this may seem like a large number of possible strategies for getting people to like you, the situation gets much more complex because each participant can use more than one strategy from the list. Two, three, or more strategies may be combined. If so, the number of available patterns of strategies has to be added to the original 25. Taking each of these two at a time, and then three at a time, then four, and so on, the number of all possible combinations adds up to a staggering number—over 40 million combinations. This is the same issue of combinations of two taken from a larger number that we discussed in Chapter 7—where organizations include huge numbers of pairs of people.

It is clear, then, that there is no shortage of strategies and huge numbers of combinations of strategies can be used to get people to like you. The question is, in the face of this abundance, which strategy to select.

Selecting strategies to use. It is not possible to set forth a simple set of rules for the selection of strategies. Certainly, no single strategy is appropriate for everyone. A particular person's selection of a strategy, or some combination of strategies, must be based in part on that person's gender, cultural identity, personal preferences, and familiarity with the situation, plus a combination of personality characteristics. Your own selection and eventual use of any of the available strategies needs to occur in combination with all the other issues relevant to planning for self-presentation. That is, the effectiveness of a decision to employ a particular strategy or set of strategies within a unique social context depends in large part on your knowing what you want, how you want to be perceived, and as much as possible about the people to whom you will be presenting yourself.

For example, assume that Tushita, a local real estate agent, has several houses to sell. She has scheduled a meeting this afternoon at the local real estate office with a young married couple interested in purchasing their first home. Tushita's objective for this first meeting is the successful initiation of a relationship with the couple that will lead to their purchase of a house. After assessing the situation, she believes that the best way to maximize the chances of meeting her objective is to communicate as quickly as possible the impression to the couple that she is a very honest and credible business person.

Considering the time available, Tushita has gathered as much information about the couple's social categories as possible. She knows that the young man and woman (1) are in their mid-20s, (2) both have college degrees, (3) do not have children, and (4) together make just over $100,000 a year. With this information, Tushita can choose from the impressive number of available affinity-seeking strategies listed in Box 9.3. To be realistic, she needs to consider whether she can reasonably employ some of them in this particular context. Additionally, she must consider whether she has the ability to communicate a given strategy effectively.

After evaluating all these issues, Tushita decides that her best alternative is to go with a combination of five strategies from the box. Her selections are *nonverbal immediacy, reward association, similarity, supportiveness,* and *trustworthiness.* There are, of course, others that might work. However, she has concluded from her planning and evaluation activities that she might risk reducing her chances of communicating a positive impression if she attempts to employ too many.

Deciding What to Say

At this point, the time for background data-gathering and preliminary planning is over. Now you must decide very specifically what you intend to say in your self-presentation. This is in many ways the most critical point of any encounter. It is here that sitting and thinking about what you want to do stops and actual performance begins. You need to move easily from plan to performance without a hitch. What are some of the guidelines for making this transition?

One pitfall to avoid is getting to the point of communicating with someone for the first time and then saying nothing like what you had intended to say. A very effective way to minimize either having nothing to say or saying the wrong thing in initial encounters is to begin with a topic that you know a lot about. In fact, it is a good idea to select a subject that you know better than anyone else. What is that topic? What you are most qualified to talk about (are you ready for this?) is *yourself!* Furthermore, it is a most suitable subject matter for beginning a self-presentation. Almost by definition **self-disclosure** (revealing information about yourself) is an important part of what goes on in any self-presentation.

Self-Disclosure in Initial Encounters

The issue here is the idea that disclosure of information about yourself dictates both how others will perceive you initially and how they will formulate impressions about you.

BOX 9.3   *A Closer Look*

Affinity-Seeking Strategies

- *Altruism.* The affinity-seeker strives to be of assistance to the target in whatever she or he is currently doing. Example: The affinity-seeker is generally available to run errands for the target.
- *Assume control.* The affinity-seeker presents him- or herself as someone who is in control over whatever is going on. Example: The affinity-seeker takes charge of the activities engaged in by the target and her- or himself.
- *Assume equality.* The affinity-seeker strikes a posture of social equality with the target. Example: The affinity-seeker avoids one-up games and behaving snobbishly.
- *Comfortable self.* The affinity-seeker acts comfortable and relaxed in settings shared with the target. Example: The affinity-seeker ignores annoying environmental distractions, seeking to convey a "nothing bothers me" impression.
- *Concede control.* The affinity-seeker allows the target to assume control over relational activities. Example: The affinity-seeker permits the target to plan a weekend the two will share.
- *Conversational rule-keeping.* The affinity-seeker adheres closely to cultural rules for polite, cooperative interaction with the target. Example: The affinity-seeker acts interested and involved in conversations with the target.
- *Dynamism.* The affinity-seeker presents her- or himself as an active, enthusiastic person. Example: The affinity-seeker is lively and animated in the presence of the target.
- *Elicit other's disclosure.* The affinity-seeker encourages the target to talk by reinforcing the target's conversational contributions. Example: The affinity-seeker queries the target about the target's opinions regarding a significant personal issue.
- *Facilitate enjoyment.* The affinity-seeker tries to maximize the positiveness of relational encounters with the target. Example: The affinity-seeker enthusiastically participates in an activity that the target is known to enjoy.
- *Inclusion of other.* The affinity-seeker includes the target in the affinity-seeker's social group. Example: The affinity-seeker plans a party for the target at which numbers of the affinity-seeker's friends are guests.
- *Influence perceptions of closeness.* The affinity-seeker engages in behaviors that cause the target to perceive the relationship as closer than it actually has been. Example: The affinity-seeker uses nicknames and talks about "we," rather than "you and I," when discussing their relationship with the target.
- *Listening.* The affinity-seeker listens actively and attentively to the target. Example: The affinity-seeker asks the target for frequent clarification and elaboration and verbally recalls the things the target has said.
- *Nonverbal immediacy.* The affinity-seeker signals interests in the target through various nonverbal cues. Example: The affinity-seeker smiles frequently at the target.

However, self-disclosure does not mean gushing on about intimate details about your life. That is not an effective strategy.

The actual content of your self-disclosure will depend on both the depth and the breadth of what you communicate about yourself.[24] The *depth* of self-disclosure refers to the degree of intimacy of what you say about yourself. *Breadth* refers to the amount of personal information you communicate. Appropriately, deciding what to say about yourself in a particular situation is tied to all your planning decisions and, in that way, to the overall development of your design for self-presentation. That is, as

- *Openness.* The affinity-seeker discloses personal information to the target. Example: The affinity-seeker reveals the some social insecurity or fear to the target.
- *Optimism.* The affinity-seeker presents him- or herself to the target as a positive person. Example: The affinity-seeker focuses on positive comments and favorable evaluations when discussing mutual acquaintances with the target.
- *Personal autonomy.* The affinity-seeker presents her- or himself to the target as an independent, free-thinking person. Example: The affinity-seeker demonstrates a willingness to express disagreement with the target about personal and social attitudes.
- *Physical attractiveness.* The affinity-seeker tries to look and dress as attractively as possible in the presence of the target. Example: The affinity-seeker always engages in careful grooming before interacting with the target.
- *Present interesting self.* The affinity-seeker presents her- or himself to the target as someone who would be interesting to know. Example: The affinity-seeker discreetly drops the names of impressive interesting acquaintances in the presence of the target.
- *Reward association.* The affinity-seeker presents her- or himself in such a way that the target perceives the affinity-seeker can reward the target for associating with him or her. Example: The affinity-seeker showers the target with gifts.
- *Self-concept confirmation.* The affinity-seeker demonstrates respect for the target and helps the target to feel good about her- or himself. Example: The affinity-seeker compliments the target frequently.
- *Self-inclusion.* The affinity-seeker arranges the environment so as to come into frequent contact with the target. Example: The affinity-seeker plans to have drinks at the same time and place as the target.
- *Sensitivity.* The affinity-seeker acts in a warm, empathic manner toward the target. Example: The affinity-seeker sympathizes with the target regarding a personal problem the target is experiencing.
- *Similarity.* The affinity-seeker seeks to convince the target that the two of them share many similar tastes and attitudes. Example: The affinity-seeker often points out things to the target that the two of them have in common.
- *Supportiveness.* The affinity-seeker supports the target in the latter's social encounters. Example: The affinity-seeker sides with the target in a disagreement the target is having with a third party.
- *Trustworthiness.* The affinity-seeker presents her- or himself to the target as an honest, reliable person. Example: The affinity-seeker consistently fulfills commitments made to the target.

Source: This information was originally reported in Bell, R. A., & Daly, J. A. (1984). The affinity-seeking function of communication. *Communication Monographs, 51,* 91–115.

you consider what it is about yourself that you should incorporate into your presentation, you must keep in mind your objective for the meeting, how you want others to perceive you, what you know about the individuals with whom you will be communicating, and what you have selected as your affinity-seeking strategies.

In light of the above, let's go back to the real estate example to illustrate what is involved in appropriate self-disclosure. Because Tushita—the agent—and the young couple had never met before, it would be inappropriate for the realtor to present either intimate details or vast amounts of personal information in this initial

BOX 9.4   *Self-Disclosure Test*

Psychology Today's "Self-Disclosure Test"

25 questions, 15 minutes

"Are you the type of person who is comfortable confiding in people, or do you keep tight-lipped? Although being able to open up to others is essential to developing a deeper connection, if we bare our soul at the drop of a hat we can put ourselves in a vulnerable position. Self-disclosure and communication skills overall are important components of any healthy relationship. Find out whether your tendency (or inability) to reveal personal information is helping or hindering these relationships with this self disclosure test.

"Read each scenario carefully and indicate which option best applies to you. There may be some questions describing situations that you

perhaps feel are not relevant. In such cases, select the answer you would most likely choose if you ever found yourself in similar circumstances. In order to receive the most accurate results, please answer as truthfully as possible.

"After finishing the test, you will receive a Snapshot Report with an introduction, a graph and a personalized interpretation for one of your test scores. You will then have the option to purchase the full results" (*Psychology Today's* online self-disclosure test).

Use this link: http://psychologytoday.tests. psychtests.com/take_test.php?idRegTest=1610

Source: Psychology Today's Self-Disclosure Test. Retrieved from http://psychologytoday.tests.psychtests. com/take_test.php?idRegTest=1610

encounter. When strangers provide intense self-disclosure, it tends to make their listeners feel very uncomfortable. Consider for a moment how you would feel if a real estate agent you had never met before disclosed a lot of intimate information, such as personal finances, sexual interests, and life history. Obviously, disclosures of such breadth and depth would be inappropriate.

What would be more acceptable in Tushita's situation would be the disclosure that she and her spouse, Rashad had made a similar choice when they purchased their first home. Then she could further indicate that they had felt terribly uneasy with this first purchase, but that later they saw it had been a wise decision. In other words, two additional admissions of personal information would appropriately follow from the disclosure of the agent's similar family decision. First, information about the uneasy feelings could be disclosed—obviously similar to what had been disclosed by the young couple. Second, information about the long-term wisdom of the choice could be disclosed. This definitely would be perceived as supportive of

the clients' decision to buy a house. Any other topics would need to be carefully prescreened before being disclosed.

There are good reasons for being cautious what you say about yourself during self-disclosure in an initial encounter. Because of the factor of selective perception, early disclosures communicated to strangers are highly susceptible to misinterpretation. Also, elaborate attributions are made to people on the basis of very limited information. Thus, the risks are especially high during the early phases of an encounter. Putting this idea a little differently, it should be remembered that self-disclosing information that is other than what is obvious, likely to be misinterpreted, or too intense and revealing for strangers is both undesirable and highly risky. For these reasons, effective self-disclosure aimed at creating positive impressions must be provided carefully, gradually, and systematically. (In order to "test" your own effectiveness at self-disclosure, take the online test referenced in Box 9.4. When you've completed the questions, submit your answers for scoring and interpretation. You may be surprised.)

BOX 9.5   *A Closer Look*

Why Does Dexter Morgan Seem So Likable?

The basic idea that there are specific strategies that can be used to get people to like you has not escaped the world of television entertainment. For example, the writers who prepare the popular TV show *Dexter* faced a difficult job. The character in the show is Dexter Morgan, played by Michael C. Hall, who is a blood spatter pattern analyst for the Miami police department. While working to solve murder crimes, he also moonlights as a serial killer for all those offenders who might have otherwise "gotten away" with murder! By any set of rational criteria, Dexter is not exactly a nice person. His activities at night can only be objectively described as horrifying, immoral, unethical, and illegal. Yet, somehow, the writers for the program have made this serial murderer seem human and lovable. How did they do it? Essentially, they have Dexter act out a number of impression-management techniques, such as those listed in Box 9.3 (Affinity-Seeking Strategies). To many in the audience he comes across as likable, warm, brotherly, and caring. In many ways, he appears to be a decent man who is loyal to his friends, supportive of his family, and concerned about his little boy. Indeed, those affinity-seeking depictions in his on-screen behavior may be an important element in making the show so popular.

Dexter Morgan (actor Michael C. Hall) from Showtime's critically acclaimed series, *Dexter*.

Box 9.5 illustrates how a variety of impression-management strategies can be used with even the most unlikely individuals.

Talking with People You Have Just Met

Looking at the process more specifically, there are several kinds of messages that offer opportunities for self-disclosure in initial encounters.[25] They are divided here into *greetings, small talk,* and a broad category referred to as the *main topic* of the encounter.

Greetings. These messages include all the salutations that are employed when individuals recognize and acknowledge one another. They can be verbal, nonverbal, or both. Regardless of which of these you employ, the specific salutation you communicate to others at a first meeting can have important implications for how you are perceived from that point on. Thus, even your greeting can influence receptivity to what you say later.[26]

For example, assume that you are going to meet for the first time a group of individuals with whom you hope to maintain a very formal and long-term professional relationship. Greeting this group with a "Hi there. How ya doin?" is likely to be less helpful than a simple "Good morning." In fact, employing the "Hi there.

How ya doin?" salutation with such a group would almost certainly lead them to form a negative impression of you. As a general rule, then, initial salutations must be considered very carefully.

Small talk. In addition to choosing a greeting, small talk, which was discussed in Chapter 5, typically has an important place in your presentation of self. Remember that what makes small talk important is that individuals getting together for the first time can maintain distance and do not have to discuss immediately topics that they are not ready to talk about.

Consider the possible small talk that could have occurred between Tushita, the realtor, and the young couple to whom she was showing a house. In addition to the self-disclosure that Tushita engaged in, a number of totally unimportant topics could have been introduced and discussed. Engaging in small talk while showing the couple neighborhoods and homes would create a more relaxed climate. Moreover, such small talk could contribute to the impression that Tushita was a nice person from whom to buy a home.

Generally, then, introducing small talk on such casual topics as the weather, the quality of a local restaurant, the recent football game, or whatever fits the occasion can stimulate relaxed discussion. Important business issues can be inserted gradually and naturally into the encounter. The only caution is that small talk must be perceived as sincere and believable as well as spontaneous.

Changing to the main topic. If the occasion is informal, there will be no main topic to discuss. That is, when people are at parties or in other social gatherings, self-presentations typically do not extend beyond greetings, small talk, and perhaps a limited amount of self-disclosure. In contrast, in a formal encounter (such as an interview, a sales presentation, or a committee meeting), the stages are different. After greetings and a certain amount of small talk, the participants must get down to business and communicate about the subject matter that brought them together in the first place.

However, there are several kinds of formal situations, and the stages of the encounter differ in each. For example, one common situation is the initial meeting with the primary objective of presenting information to an audience. Although the individual delivering the information does make a presentation of self to members of the audience, it occurs as a secondary activity. Examples of this type of situation include lectures, informative talks, narrations, and public reading of factual material. In these situations, audience attention may be devoted more to the specific subject matter than to the individual presenting the information.

Another common situation occurs when an individual is presenting a message to one or more others and it is that person's specific interpretation of a situation that is the concern of the audience. Examples would be a witness giving testimony at a trial, a job applicant responding to questions during an interview, an expert presenting a personal analysis to a decision-making group, or a student explaining to a professor why he missed the final examination and should be excused. In these situations, almost everything that is transmitted is used to assess the presenter. In other words, the presentation of self is much more relevant to the audience than are the specifics of the message. It is not uncommon for the members of an audience in this type of situation to hang on every word of the speaker. Here, **credibility** can be a critical factor. That is, the information that is communicated may be judged within a framework of important dimensions— as valuable or worthless, critical or trivial, true or false—depending on the presenter's perceived sincerity and honesty as evaluated by the audience. Thus, perceived personal credibility can have a strong influence on the interpretation of the main topic under discussion.

In overview, whatever the specifics of the situation, an effective strategy for talking with new people begins with a greeting that is appropriate to the situation and the audience. Next, the right amount and kind of small talk is used to put people at ease. This provides an opportunity for beginning a planned, subtle self-presentation. Above all, personal credibility must remain high or subsequent efforts to present ideas about the main topic will be discounted and the entire encounter will fail.

Changing Negative Impressions

Sooner or later, you will have to confront someone's old and lingering impression of you, which unfortunately may be based on earlier unfavorable attributions. In other words, someone may still be evaluating you in a negative way from an earlier encounter. How can the strategies, techniques, and analyses described in this chapter be used to change such old impressions?

Changing someone's entrenched convictions about a person is a formidable task. However, there are a number of similarities between the steps needed to do this and those required to communicate a new impression. Even so, working back through each of the areas discussed so far would only partially undo someone's negative impression of you.

It is much more difficult to change a person's previously formed impression because there are more steps involved in changing an impression than in creating a new one. The individual has to *erase the existing impression* and then *recreate a new one* by effective communication of fresh messages while disregarding older, well-remembered, and entirely workable views of you as a person. That is a complex task.

To aid in understanding why it is difficult to make the transition, recall two principles learned earlier in this chapter from the Asch experiments on person perception: (1) People quickly form impressions of others when they meet them for the first time; (2) people formulate those impressions on the basis of a limited amount of data.

It should not be surprising that these two principles are so important. People have to adapt to those they have just met in these ways. That is, when you encounter someone new, you must immediately use a kind of filter for selectively perceiving the target person. You must be ready to respond to that person in an appropriate way from the beginning. Therefore, you have to make quick attributions and assumptions about the individual. However, in doing so, errors are likely. Because each human being is immensely complex, it is not possible to take in and understand every aspect of a person all at once. You have to work first with incomplete data (which can lead to inaccurate impressions). Nevertheless, you project onto that person a general framework of attributions as quickly as possible. These enable you to respond in what you think is an appropriate manner.

Thus, right or wrong, you quickly form impressions on the basis of the first indicators that you perceive. These tend to become entrenched right away because once you have formed an initial impression about a particular person, you have reduced your uncertainty regarding how you should relate to that person. Reducing uncertainty makes you feel more comfortable. From then on, any attempt to change your framework for selective perception will threaten to bring back that uncertainty and resulting discomfort. Therefore, the energy and inconvenience required to abandon an existing impression and create a very different one will be resisted. Nevertheless, people who entertain older negative impressions about you can be retrained, although it is not easy.

The Inflexible Nature of Preexisting Impressions

A plan to extinguish a preexisting impression begins with an understanding of the way that people make attributions about themselves. This process differs from the way other people attribute personality characteristics to you. Specifically, conclusions derived from research indicate that when you engage in an activity you perceive as unacceptable to others, you tend to attribute the causes of that behavior to external forces beyond your control, rather than to your own internal preferences and desires, which you can control. However, when other people observe you engaging in that unacceptable activity, they make just the opposite attribution: They tend to believe that you have deliberately chosen this course of action because of internal motivations. In other words, in interpreting the causes of your own behavior that is judged unacceptable by others, you feel you are driven by outside forces, but others believe you deliberately choose to be bad.

This fascinating difference between how you see yourself and how others see you is particularly relevant to attempts to change the impressions others have of you. For example, if you meet someone who has been told by another person (who claims to know you) that you are untrustworthy, then your new acquaintance will have a preexisting negative impression of you coming into a first encounter. In fact, that person is very likely to perceive you negatively and to make biased and unfavorable attributions about the causes of your actions. In short, you have a problem.

What can you do to change such an impression? The first thing would be to begin planning what you are going to say and how you are going to say it. The basic goal is to suppress the existing impression and help the target individual in rebuilding a new one that includes greater credibility and more favorable attributions to you. Objectively speaking, your preparation in this instance would follow the same sequence of activities that was described for all self-presentations. However, because the purpose of the presentation would be to change rather than to create an impression, the specifics of your plan would have to be different.

Attributions concerning behavior are a function of three factors: the distinctiveness of the behavior, its consistency over time, and the consensus regarding the behavior among attending persons.[27] Research done on such factors has uncovered what is called the *principle of covarying attribution*. This is a kind of general rule, and it goes like this: If a person engages in a repetitive pattern of behavior, observers will attribute the behavior to either an internal or an external cause with which it seems to be consistently related over time. For example, suppose you are excited about having been accepted at

a particular university (distinctive behavior) and you continue to be so over a period of time (consistency). Now assume that all your friends are not the least bit positive about that university; in fact, they are uniformly negative (consensus). Under these conditions, an attribution concerning the causes of your behavior is likely, and it will be made directly to you. That is, you probably would be perceived as *lacking good judgment*—an internal cause. If, however, under different circumstances, where you are fascinated with the idea of attending this particular university and all your friends believe it to be a good one, an attribution probably would be made to a different cause of your behavior, namely, to *the high quality of the university*— an external cause.

These conclusions offer a possible strategy for attempting to change the impressions people have of you by altering their attributions. Let's return to the problem of the person who has a preexisting impression of you as *untrustworthy*. You now design a strategy that will communicate effectively to that person that your behavior was, in fact, acceptable to many people (consensus); that such acceptance has been in effect for a long period of time (consistency); and that such a behavior pattern (distinctive) is typically expected of people in similar circumstances; that is, it is externally caused. If the self-presentation is effective, the initial unfavorable impression of you might begin to change.

Overcoming Resistance to Change

It was suggested earlier that people tend to resist attempts to modify existing impressions of an individual. In fact, it is difficult for people who have constructed internal meanings for almost any object or situation to shift to new ones. There are clear reasons why this is the case, and they are embedded deeply in the psychological processes people use to cope with the complexities of their physical and social environment.

Specifically, all people, everywhere, construct "pictures in their heads"—meanings for various aspects of the world they live in. They do this in a process of communication with others.[28] Those constructions include their meanings, impressions, and interpretations not only of physical objects and situations but of specific individuals as well, such as each of us.

Generally, attempts aimed at restructuring constructed realities of others will inevitably be resisted. One typical situation in which there is likely to be strong resistance to change is when a person has privately formed a negative first impression of you. Another case would be a long-term negative impression passed on by a trusted third party. The outcome of either of these situations is that you will be consistently and selectively perceived negatively. What do you do?

Because long-term habits of meaning can be so deeply established, the first question to consider is whether it is realistically possible to change another's impression of you. Second, is it worth the effort? There are going to be situations where the effort involved in changing someone's impression greatly outweighs the value associated with any change. If that seems to be the case, don't even try! In addition, there will be occasions when a negative impression is so sturdy that it is virtually impossible to change. Again, don't even try. Part of being successful at presenting self is learning to evaluate effectively such costs versus benefits.

Constructing New Realities

Let's assume that you feel change is possible and worth the considerable effort. You have decided to move ahead. The process of reconstructing a person's impressions and attributions by self-presentation should begin by careful consideration of the objectives. Obviously, if you are being perceived in a negative way, your overall goal is to change it to a positive one. But what beyond that? Do you have specific kinds of personal qualities of which you want that person to be aware? Furthermore, what are effective strategies for successfully communicating them so as to alter the person's existing impression?

Remember from Chapter 2 that the specific reality people perceive for any particular object is made up of subjective or internal meanings aroused by the perception of that object (or by a symbol that stands for that object). In the case of human beings, such realities are constructed from the variety of experiences the person has with the other individual. Finally, this present chapter shows that early experiences are especially influential in forming that construction of reality.

Given all of that, the task of restructuring is to communicate unmistakably favorable (distinctive) meanings that are shared by others (consensus). This needs to be done *over and over* (consistency) without belaboring the message. By actions and comments, skillfully communicated, you can show that others regard you favorably, respect your judgment, believe you to be trustworthy, and so on.

In addition, another person's impression of you may lack depth. You may have additional distinctive characteristics that can simply be added to what that person already thinks he or she knows. For example, if you are active in charities, play the piano, have a special hobby, care for a cockatoo, or have other positive qualities, communicating this new knowledge may improve the impression another entertains. If such information can be linked to the interests of the target person, so much the better; it may open new channels of communication that can be used to displace or at least minimize the unfavorable impressions that already exist.

To achieve such change, you have both verbal and nonverbal communication at your disposal. The meanings associated with words, gestures, and actions are the bricks and boards with which you can assist people in constructing new realities. The use of verbal and nonverbal communication for the restructuring of realities to achieve a positive impression follows the same general sequence of design activities outlined in previous sections. Note again that self-presentations must not be false or misleading. Phony presentations are a sure route to disaster. Being perceived as honest and truthful in self-presentation contributes to being perceived as ethical and having personal credibility.

The final caution regarding the effective use of verbal and nonverbal symbols and signs when presenting self to others is to communicate only that which contributes to the creation of a supportive climate for interaction. In many ways, that is the most important principle and the hardest lesson of all. Because you are human, you are emotional; when people make you mad, you feel a normal need to express your feelings in no uncertain terms. However, it is a losing game that can bring only unfavorable consequences. Defensive or hostile words and phrases fired off in the heat of the moment cannot be withdrawn or erased. Achieving thoughtful control over emotional responses is the factor that most clearly sets apart the person who is in complete control of self-presentation from those who are content to just let it fall together naturally.

Chapter Review

- The process of presenting yourself effectively is based on communicating, verbally and nonverbally, favorable meanings of your personal qualities. The goal is to help others form as positive an impression of you as you can.

- People make elaborate inferences about others on the basis of relatively little information. Salient characteristics become particularly important in constructing an impression of what another individual is really like. In fact, with limited data, you put together an organized implicit personality that you think can predict the behavior of the individual you have just met.

- Labels are an important part of implicit personality construction. If you have a convenient label—"compulsive," "pothead," "jock," or whatever—you will load onto the person all the meanings such terms carry. These meanings may be incorrect and quite unfair, but they provide guidelines for action that may seem at the time to be based on realities.

- One of the problems in self-presentation is selective perception. People tend to attribute unacceptable behavior to your personal shortcomings and praiseworthy behavior to causes beyond your control. Thus, it's important to plan ahead—to decide what to say and how much to self-disclose. Saying too much too quickly may be counterproductive.

- Changing impressions that people already have of you is very difficult. It is possible to change their impressions, but at times it may not be worth the effort. If such a change is necessary, you must first deal with people's natural resistance to change. This means being prepared to keep your emotions under control and carefully constructing the new impression you wish to create.

Key Terms

presentation of self	implicit personality theory	social categories
impression management	selective perception	affinity-seeking
salient characteristic	predispositions	self-disclosure
labeling theory	attribution process	credibility

Notes

1. Goffman, E. (1956). *The presentation of self in everyday life.* Edinburgh: Social Sciences Research Centre. For an excellent discussion of impression management, see: Giles, H., & Street, R. L., Jr. (1985). Communication characteristics and behavior. In M. L. Knapp & G. R. Miller (Eds.). *Handbook of interpersonal communication* (pp. 205–262). Beverly Hills, CA: Sage.

2. Asch, S. E. (1946). Forming impressions of personalities. *Journal of Personality and Social Psychology, 41,* 258–290.

3. See: Becker, H. S. (1973). Labeling theory reconsidered. In H. S. Becker (Ed.), *Outsiders: Studies in the sociology of deviance* (2nd ed.). New York: Free Press. A classic in this field is: Goffman, E. (1963). *Stigma: Notes on the management of spoiled identity.* Englewood Cliffs, NJ: Prentice-Hall.

4. The salient characteristic and the labeling principles are also closely related to the concept of *stereotype.* Insensitive people still use pejorative labels to "keep down" categories of people, some of whom have a salient characteristic, such as skin color or some other visible feature. Prejudiced people try to dominate such a category of people by using a slang label in such a way that negative meanings are uniformly associated with all its members of the category.

5. Hays, W. L. (1958). An approach to the study of trait implication and trait similarity. In R. Tagiuri & L. Petrullo (Eds.), *Person perception and interpersonal behavior.* Stanford, CA: Stanford University Press; Bruner, J. S., Shapiro, D., & Tagiuri, R. (1958). The meaning of traits in isolation and in combination. In Tagiuri & Petrullo (Eds.), *Person perception;* Wishner, J. (1960). Reanalysis of impressions of personality. *Psychological Review, 67,* 96–112; and Crockett, W. H., & Friedman, P. (1986). Theoretical explorations of the processes of initial interactions. *Western Journal of Speech Communication, 44,* 86–92.

6. Wishner, Reanalysis of impressions of initial interactions.

7. Diabase, W., & Hjelle, L. (1968). Body-image stereotypes and body-type preferences among male college students. *Perceptual and Motor Skills, 27,* 1143–1146; Secord, P. (1958). Facial features and inference processes in interpersonal perception. In Tagiuri & Petrullo, *Person perception, p. 300–315;* Verinis, J., Roll, S. (1970). Primary and secondary male characteristics; the hairiness and large penis stereotypes. *Psychological Reports, 26,* 123–126. For an excellent general discussion of the characteristics influencing impression formation, see: Burgoon, J. K., Buller, D. B., & Woodall, W. G. (1995). *Nonverbal communication: The unspoken dialogue.* New York: McGraw Hill.

8. Chaplin, W. F., Phillips, J. B., & Brown, J. D. (2000). Handshaking, gender, personality, and first impressions. *Journal of Personality and Social Psychology, 79, 1,* 110–117.

9. Jackson, L. A., Hunter, J. E., & Hodge, C. N. (1995). Physical attractiveness and intellectual competence: A meta-analytic review. *Social Psychology Quarterly, 58,* 108–122.

10. Martin, K. A., Sinden, A. R., & Fleming, J. C. (2000). Inactivity may be hazardous to your image: The effects of exercise participation on impression formation. *Journal of Sport and Exercise Psychology, 22, 4,* 283–291.

11. For a complete discussion of the many difficulties of getting to know others, see: Duck, S. (2007). *Human relationships* (4th ed). Thousand Oaks, CA: Sage.

12. Hackman, M. Z., & Johnson, C. E. (2009). Leadership: A communication perspective (5th ed.), pp. 201–202. Long Grove, IL: Waveland.

13. Sociologist Georg Simmel originated this idea that a three person group generally reduces to a pair and a third party. See for instance: Mills, T.M. (1954). The coalition pattern in three person groups. *American Sociological Review, 19,* 657–667.

14. Goffman. *Stigma,* pp.106–140.

15. Knapp, M. L., & Vangelisti, A. L. (2009). Interpersonal communication and human relationships (6th ed.). Boston: Allyn and Bacon.

16. Gosling, S. D., Ko, S. J., & Mannarelli, T. (2002). A room with a cue: Personality judgments based on offices and bedrooms. *Journal of Personality and Social Psychology, 82, 3,* 379–398.

17. Ibid., 84–87.

18. Turner Bowkar, D. M. (2001). How can you pull yourself up by your bootstraps, if you don't have boots? Work-related clothing for poor women. *The Journal of Social Issues, 57, 2,* 311–322.

19. An excellent introduction to this area of study is provided by: Shaver, K. G. (1975). *An introduction to attribution processes.* Cambridge, MA: Winthrop.

20. Attribution theory was originally proposed in: Heider, F. (1958). *The psychology of interpersonal relations.* New York: Wiley. It was refined by: Kelley, H. H. (1973). The process of causal attribution. *American Psychologist, 28,* 107–128. For reviews of the accumulated research, see: Kelley, H. H., & Michela, J. L. (1980). Attribution theory and research. *Annual Review of Psychology, 31,* 457–503. Also, see: Harvey, J. H., & Weary, G. (1984). Current issues in attribution theory and research. *Annual Review of Psychology, 35,* 427–460.

21. Bell, R. A., & Daly, J. A. (1984). The affinity-seeking function of communication. *Communication Monographs, 51,* 91–115.

22. Wanzer, M. B. (1998). An exploratory investigation of student and teacher perceptions of student-generated affinity-seeking behaviors. *Communication Education, 47, 4,* 373–382; Prisbell, M. (1994). Students' perceptions of teachers' use of affinity-seeking and its relationship to teachers' competence. *Perceptual and Motor Skills, 78,* 641–642.

23. Ibid.

24. For several excellent examples of contemporary research and writing on self-disclosure, see: Bochner, A. P. (1982). On the efficacy of openness in close relationships. In M. Burgoon (Ed.), *Communication yearbook 5* (pp. 109–124). New Brunswick, NJ: Transaction; Bradac, J. J., Tardy, C. H., & Hosman, L. A. (1980). Disclosure styles and a hint at their genesis. *Human Communication Research, 6,* 228–238; Pearce, W. B., & Sharp, S. M. (1973). Self-disclosing communication. *Journal of Communication, 23,* 409–425; Rosenfeld, L. B. (1979). Self-disclosure avoidance: Why I am afraid to tell you who I am. *Communication Monographs, 46,* 63–74; Wheeless, L. R. (1978). A follow-up study of the relationship among trust, disclosure, and interpersonal solidarity. *Human Communication Research, 4,* 143–157.

25. Dindia, K. (2002). Self-disclosure research: Knowledge through meta-analysis. In M. Allen et al., eds., *Interpersonal communication research: Advances through meta-analysis* (pp. 169–185). Mahwah, NJ: Lawrence Erlbaum; Goldsmith, D. J., & Baxter, L. A. (1996). Constituting relationships in talk: A taxonomy of speech events in social and personal relationships. *Human Communication Research, 23,* 87–114.

26. Krivnos, P. D., & Knapp, M. L. (1975). Initiating communication: What do you say when you say hello? *Central States Speech Journal, 26,* 115–125; Nofsinger, R. E. (1975). The demand ticket: A conversational device for getting the floor. *Speech Monographs, 42,* 1–9; Schegloff, E. A. (1972). Sequencing in conversational openings. In E. J. Gumperz & D. Hymes (Eds.), *Sociolinguistics: The ethnography of communication* (pp. 346–380). New York: Holt, Rinehart, and Winston.

27. Kelley, H. H. (1973). *Causal schemata and the attribution process.* Morristown, NJ: General Learning Press; also: Kelley, H. H. (1973). The processes of causal attribution. *American Psychologist, 28,* 102–128; Kelley & Michela, Attribution theory, pp. 457–503; and Harvey & Weary, Current issues, pp. 427–460.

28. For a detailed review of scholarly writings (from Plato to the present) and various contemporary theories about the process by which people construct meaningful and shared interpretations of reality, see: DeFleur, M. L., & Rokeach, S. B. (1989). Mass communication and the construction of meaning. In DeFleur, M. L., & Rokeach, S. B. *Theories of mass communication* (5th ed., pp. 228–271). White Plains, NY: Longman.

Chapter 10

Overcoming Communication Apprehension

Karina sat outside the paneled boardroom waiting for her turn to make a presentation. Having just been promoted to assistant manager of the transportation department, she knew that she had a lot riding on the report she was about to make. In her previous position, she had never been invited to make a presentation to the board of directors, and she was very nervous. She felt especially apprehensive about her ability to speak fluently before the important and powerful board. She knew that they would be evaluating her and, if she blew it, her career might well be over before it really got started.

Her anxiety had been growing over the last few weeks. It began when her boss had first asked her to make the presentation. Since that moment she had spent every night and weekend preparing. She just knew that she might make mistakes. She had gathered all the information that she would need and had outlined her presentation in at least five different ways. She had tried to practice it more than 10 times. Her poor boyfriend Alvin was nearly bored to death.

This was the moment of truth. Despite all her preparations, Karina began to experience a sense of panic as she sat waiting. She began to feel a hard knot in the pit of her stomach. Her hands started to tremble and her mouth was dry. She felt a sudden urge to bite her fingernails.

At some point in our lives, most of us have had a counterpart of Karina's experience. Even polished and accomplished communicators never quite get over a sense of nervousness and *communication apprehension* about getting up to speak in front of a bunch of strangers. Anxiety and nervousness about communicating in a public setting are common and unavoidable; in fact, they are the primary factors that interfere with effective public speaking performances.

Note that it was not that Karina lacked the necessary skills. She had a good report prepared and she knew her subject well. She was an intelligent woman and had dressed well for the occasion. She had never had any formal training in public speaking, but contrary to popular opinion, research reveals that all the skills training in the world may contribute only minimally to effectiveness as a speaker.[1] Furthermore, practice does not always make perfect. Performing over and over again may help some to communicate more effectively, but others may actually get worse.

What is important is one's emotional state before and during a presentation. This may have little to do with training or skills. In fact, the results of over 200 separate studies reveal that a person's ability to perform well while speaking to a group is closely related to a condition called **communication apprehension.**[2]

Communication apprehension is a condition closely associated with *public* speaking; however, it can occur under other conditions, while talking to strangers or during a job interview. In contrast, communicating within family members and close friends is seldom a problem for people. After all, those people are safe. We trust our friends and family to support us, encourage us, and generally make us feel good about ourselves. We don't share that same trust with people we do not know. We have no reason to believe that an audience of strangers will understand and sympathize if we forget part of what we were going to say, generally look stupid, and are forced to sit down in embarrassment. We have no reason to believe that any audience will easily overlook our "uhs" and

"ums" and "you knows" as we stumble through our presentation. Clearly, then, we have *very good reason to feel apprehensive* whenever we consider communicating with strangers.

Many people are convinced that competent communicators are just born with the right performance skills, or that speaking comes naturally for some. There are no grounds for such a belief. A large body of research underscores the need to reduce people's fears of addressing audiences.[3] For example, skills training is likely to aggravate some people's anxieties and actually make their condition worse.[4] These people, unable to perform competently in front of a group, are exposed over and over again to their own failures. It doesn't take too many trials before they learn to *expect* failure. This expectation only increases their fears about trying to do it again. Even if such people are able to acquire all the necessary skills to give a good talk, anxieties about communicating before an audience can continue to interfere with competent performance.

This chapter has been designed to help you cope with the communication apprehension and anxieties we all feel under a variety of circumstances. For example, apprehension can arise when we interact with people we don't know very well, or when we have to engage in small talk, handle conflict, justify our employment in an interview, work productively in a small group, give a briefing, or simply participate in class discussions. All these situations can provoke anxiety.

Communication Apprehension as a Common Reaction

Communication apprehension refers to *fear or anxiety associated with either real or anticipated communication encounters.*[5] Note that communication apprehension does not have to coincide with the actual speaking encounter; it can occur ahead of time, simply in anticipation of having to speak. Take yourself, for example. Your grade in a course may be contingent, in part, on your participation in class discussion. Just knowing that you will have to talk before the group may trigger enough anxiety to inhibit your ability to ask or answer questions. Similarly, anticipating the social demands of a dinner at the home of your new boss may stimulate communication apprehension long before you arrive. In other words, anxiety about communicating is a condition that can occur either prior to or during any particular encounter.

Some specialists regard communication apprehension as a special kind of shyness.[6] However, the two are not really the same. Reasons for shyness can vary greatly. Some shy people may lack communication skills. Others may have the necessary skills to communicate effectively, but may simply enjoy being unobtrusive or reflective. Certainly it is not true that all shy individuals experience communication apprehension. Looking at the population as a whole, about 40 percent report being shy, whereas only a little over 20 percent experience a truly significant degree of communication apprehension.[7] Therefore, about half of the people who are shy appear to be satisfied with avoiding interaction with others. The remainder, however, are probably shy because of some degree of fear about communicating. This is especially likely among those who lack communication skills. A kind of circular pattern can often be seen in the behavior of many shy people. It begins with a person being shy, which creates anxiety, which reduces communication skills, which results in increased shyness, and so on.

The circular link between shyness and apprehension can manifest itself in many ways: Because such individuals are not good at small talk, they become anxious about engaging in it. Also, because they are not skilled at speaking eloquently in front of a group, they become fearful of doing it. Similarly, because they are not good at asking for dates, they become apprehensive about that. Then, because of limited experience, they become even more shy as time goes on.

Others just dread communicating, not because of any skill deficiency, but simply because they are afraid of the act itself. Even thinking about it ahead of time brings on fear.[8] People who are afraid to communicate may actually avoid interacting, even when it's in their own best interest to do so. For example, they are unlikely to approach a boss to ask for a raise, although they know they deserve more money. They may avoid answering a professor's question in class even when they know the answer. In both instances, such individuals may know how to perform the required behavior—that is, they can utter the words necessary to request the raise, or they can comprehend and respond to the professor's demand; however, their emotional reactions to the situation often prevent them from doing so.

To understand further the nature of communication apprehension, it is necessary to differentiate between two categories of people in which this condition is present. The first is *apprehensive individuals* who, regardless of the situation, almost always feel anxious about relating to others. The second is people who have had *apprehensive experiences* that have incited fears about communicating. Both categories are widely found. But, although apprehensive people are troubled with a continual and pervasive condition, individuals who have had apprehensive experiences often suffer more temporary anxieties.

Individuals High and Low in Apprehension

Apprehensive people fear communicating with almost anyone in any kind of situation. McCroskey labels this type of relatively stable and predictable fear "traitlike."[9] Recall that the term **trait** refers broadly to "*any* [personality] *characteristic in which one individual differs from another in a relatively permanent and consistent way.*"[10] Each of us has literally thousands of personality traits—such as stingy, sweet, creative, loyal, and humorous. Evidence of such traits is observable in a person's patterns of behavior over time. Similarly, over time, individuals can acquire a trait of being *highly apprehensive about communicating* across situations.

Social scientists do not assume that personality traits have genetic origins. That is, we do not *inherit* traits, we *acquire* (learn) them over a long period of time.[11] In terms of the trait of communication apprehension, then, we learn from our past experiences to be generally anxious (or nonanxious) while communicating. Because of its learned nature, such trait apprehension can be reduced by training.[12]

Personality traits are not rigid. Individuals characterized by a particular trait may or may not exhibit the behavior in every instance. For example, a person who is generally honest or jovial may not be like that in every circumstance. The same is true of people with the communication apprehension trait. Much depends on the *context* and the nature of the *other party*. For example, individuals who are high in communication apprehension report little or no anxiety in the context of interacting with their best friends or with family. They may even be comfortable communicating with a specific professor or employer. Thus, they are fully aware that they experience anxiety under some circumstances. Overall, however, persons high in the apprehension trait usually try to avoid most communication situations.[13]

At the other extreme are people who actively seek out others and talk easily and sometimes endlessly. Some talk so much that it is hard to get a word in edgewise. These individuals are classified as *very low* in the apprehension trait. In our society, being low in communication apprehension can have great advantages—as long as it is not too low. For the most part, we tend to approve of those who can give a good interview, entertain a crowd, or meet new acquaintances with finesse and charm. In contrast to the chronically apprehensive, who avoid communication encounters, those low in the trait seek them out. For example, a person low in communication apprehension will look forward to attending a party where he or she may not know anyone. On the other hand, a person high in this trait would dread such a situation.

A number of studies reveal that persons with little fear of communication tend to talk more,

to date a greater variety of individuals, to choose occupations that demand more social contact, to communicate more assertively, and to engage in more self-disclosure than do those who are more fearful.[14] In contrast, the accumulated research shows that apprehensive people tend to be withdrawn, to engage in steady dating (versus playing the field), to select careers that allow them to work apart from others, to agree with the opinions of others (rather than express a dissenting point of view), and to be reluctant to reveal much information about themselves.

Although people who are high or low in communication apprehension represent the ends of the continuum, most people can be categorized as *moderately apprehensive*. In other words, having some fear of communicating is normal. About 20 percent of the population fall

Sometimes our anxieties about communicating with others are revealed in the oddest of ways.

into the high category, and roughly the same percent are at the other end of the scale. This means that the remaining 60 percent—the majority—is in between.[15]

This in-between category experiences apprehension only when a particular situation arouses discomfort. For example, it is normal for most people to experience some level of apprehension in situations where their behavior is being *evaluated*. When people recognize that what they say and how they say it will make a difference in how some significant person (such as a prospective employer) views them, it is entirely normal for them to feel some anxiety or fear. Furthermore, it is highly likely that everyone experiences some *stage fright* before or during any kind of presentation. If a speaker is ill prepared, or believes that the audience will be hostile, this fear probably will (and should) increase.

Experiencing Communication Apprehension

There is probably no one who has not at one time or another temporarily experienced communication apprehension. The situations that trigger it vary greatly. Some people feel anxious even when they have to talk on the phone or leave a voice mail. For others, it is particular individuals who trigger apprehension, such as a person conducting a job or promotion interview—or a special friend's parents. If you take your pulse and it is rapid when you approach your boss for a raise, meet your future in-laws, or ask someone special for a first date, you may be such a person.

When people's apprehensions are temporarily provoked (even for low or moderately apprehensive individuals), they are likely to respond just as high apprehensives do—they will avoid apprehension-producing situations. Thus, whether apprehension is a function of some enduring personality trait, or is based on an experience producing temporary apprehension, the ability to communicate suffers in similar ways.

Causes of Communication Apprehension

Trying to explain why we develop fears that interfere with our ability to communicate competently is no simple task. Recent thinking focuses on biological antecedents to our communication fears and anxieties. Genetics, we've discovered, play a vital role in how we relate and communicate with others. While the role of genetics may be substantial, they are not all that controllable. Thus, we look instead to other environmental factors that can be managed.[16] Sometimes those answers can be found *within the immediate context* of communication, and other times they are deeply ingrained *within the individual* who continuously experiences communication apprehension.

Contextual Sources of Anxiety

Certain situations as well as certain individuals can lead us to be apprehensive. Sometimes there are good and logical reasons for concern. For example, if we are driving at 70 miles per hour in a 45-miles-per-hour zone and a police car with flashing red and blue lights and a siren pulls up quickly behind us, adrenaline will undoubtedly flow! In such a situation, we have real cause for anxiety.

At other times, however, we feel distress even when the situation does not realistically call for such feelings. Also, we often misinterpret the context: We believe there's reason for concern when, in fact, there really are no objective grounds for worry. An example of how our imagination can mislead us is provided by the following (actual) experience of a former student.

Terry developed a severe case of communication apprehension when his girlfriend Jill announced that she had planned for him to meet her parents. Jill explained that her mom and dad were looking forward to meeting him. She knew that her parents were loving, sensitive, and warm individuals. Clearly, Terry had no basis in reality for fearing a meeting with Jill's folks. However, even though Terry was normally a personable and outgoing young man, his initial meeting with Jill's mom and dad revealed quite another side to his character. It was almost like a Dr. Jekyll and Mr. Hyde situation. At their first encounter, he seemed withdrawn; he mumbled responses to their questions; he spilled coffee on his pants and then retreated to the bathroom where he stayed for a long time. Jill was embarrassed (and furious). Afterward, Terry justified his behavior by arguing that he suffered great apprehension about the whole encounter. However, Jill contended that he distorted the situation and misread the entire context.

Both were correct. Understandably, Terry and Jill interpreted the situation differently. Each defined the meeting with Jill's parents from her or his own perspective. Jill believed that a meeting with her parents would be enjoyable. Terry, however, believed there was good reason to be nervous because he worried that they might judge him unworthy of their daughter.

Whatever the contextual cues, factual or imaginary, a major principle of human behavior is that people behave according to their own personal and subjective *definition of the situation* That is, they react to *what they believe is real*.[17] And what people believe about the context influences how they communicate. Researchers have identified a number of contextual factors that heighten our apprehension and affect our ability to communicate effectively.[18] Included in the list are: *unfamiliar or dissimilar others, novel or formal occasions, subordinate status,* conspicuousness or excessive *attention from others,* undergoing *evaluation,* and previous repeated *failure*.[19] (Box 10.1 overviews these contextual causes of communication apprehension.)

Communicating with people you don't know or who are not like you.   It is always easier to talk to people you know as opposed to those who are unfamiliar. Initiating conversation with strangers can in itself be anxiety-producing. In such an encounter, where do you start? What do you say to people you don't know?

BOX 10.1   *A Closer Look*

Contextual Causes of Communication Apprehension

Sometimes there are good reasons for us to be apprehensive. The context or situation itself may cause us to feel tense and anxious. Consider the following factors:

- *Communicating with unfamiliar or dissimilar others.* Strangers or mere acquaintances may cause us to feel some uncertainty and anxiety. At the same time, people who seem different from us, who don't share our beliefs and attitudes, are likely to make us feel a little anxious.
- *Novel or formal situations.* It's difficult to predict what to say or how to behave in new circumstances or in situations that require following a particular set of rules.
- *Subordinate rank.* People of higher status may make us feel nervous and self-conscious when we try to speak.
- *Conspicuous and excessive attention.* If we feel that we have become the center of attention, we are likely to be anxious when its our turn to talk.
- *Undergoing evaluation.* If we feel that someone is scrutinizing us, evaluating our performance, we typically feel anxious when we try to present our point of view.
- *Repeated failure.* If we know that we have performed poorly in the past, we will be worried that we will fail again the next time we try to do it—whether its giving a speech, relating a story, telling a joke, or giving a toast.

Correspondingly, people who are different from you may generate anxious moments. If you have ever interacted with someone who dropped out of high school and who resents college students as "obnoxious" who always "look down" on others, then you know how difficult it can be to try to communicate.

Or imagine a conversation between two people who hold opposing views on a controversial and emotional topic like abortion, gun control, or capital punishment. These individuals are likely to be hard pressed to find common ground in order to communicate constructively with each other about such topics.

Communicating in formal or unfamiliar situations. Novel, formal, or unfamiliar occasions tend to trigger communication apprehension because they are filled with uncertainty. Predictability is a very important factor in social interaction. The nature of your relationship and the context itself allow you to anticipate correctly what people will say, do, and expect of you. This helps you to know what to say and do. When you can't make such predictions, you begin to worry. A good example of the consequences of an unfamiliar situation was your very first date. No doubt, you felt much anxiety about what to say, what to wear, and what to do (or not do). Similarly, your first day at college, the first day on your new job all presented you with uncertainty. Communication apprehension tends to be very high in such unfamiliar and relatively unpredictable situations.

Truly formal situations—such as elegant dinners, elaborate weddings, and funerals, or other important ceremonies—are also likely to induce uncertainty and apprehension. Recognizing that such events require you to behave correctly, you may feel uncomfortable because you are not familiar with the etiquette others expect you to follow. Or, you may not know how to behave casually in a rented tuxedo or a long formal gown. Again, the factor of unpredictability raises apprehension.

Communicating with people of higher status or rank. Certain kinds of situations define people's status and rank. Many of those situations underscore your own lower status compared to others. For example, attending a dinner party at your boss's home may remind you of where you fit into the power structure—making you self-conscious about your behavior in the presence of those who control your destiny. Communication apprehension is likely to follow.

Communicating when you are suddenly the center of attention. More than any other aspect of a public speaking situation, *conspicuousness*—the belief that all eyes are riveted on you, scrutinizing everything about you—can induce communication apprehension. This can happen in any occasion when you become the center of attention. Perhaps you've felt self-conscious when a professor used your work as an example to the class of what to do, or worse, what not to do!

Similarly, *excessive* attention from others may give rise to communication apprehension. For example, you are likely to feel uncomfortable when a counselor seems determined to have you reveal private and confidential information. You may find it difficult to communicate in such circumstances. Another example is the discomfort you feel when someone *monopolizes all of your time* at a party. You may wish the person would go away or that you were somewhere else. Most of us like *some* moderate level of attention from others but are ill at ease when someone wants to peer at us through a microscope.

Communicating when you are being evaluated. Being evaluated is almost certain to bring on communication anxiety. In situations where you know that your supervisor at work—or your professor in class—is appraising you on the basis of an oral performance, you are likely to become anxious. Even though you might do well without the scrutiny, the idea that you're being evaluated heightens apprehension about what you say or do. Students often report that when they practice their speeches at home, they experience no problems. However, as soon as they see the professor with that grade book, they get nervous, forget their lines, and generally perform poorly.

Communicating when you have repeatedly failed before. Finally, memories of previous failures in identical or similar situations are a common source of apprehension. For instance, if the last 12 times you tried to arrange a date with someone attractive, only to be repeatedly turned down, it may be distressing to ask for the 13th time, to say the least. Or, if you know from past experience that every time you have asked for a raise, the boss has listened impatiently and then flatly denied your request, you might well be nervous and reluctant about going in and asking one more time.

Most of us can readily identify with such contextual sources of communication distress. We all have found ourselves in circumstances that seemed to provoke a degree of temporary or transitory apprehension. They are relatively easy to understand and explain. However, the problem becomes more complex when one attempts to identify causes of communication apprehension as *a persistent personality trait*.[20]

Learning to Be Apprehensive

People whose apprehension is a stable personality trait tend to distort their interpretations of the contextual factors discussed above. They selectively perceive events around them and interpret them differently from the ways those who are not usually apprehensive interpret similar events. For example, those high in apprehension sometimes perceive a situation to be more novel or more formal than it really is; or they may feel very conspicuous and feel convinced that everyone noticed a mistake they made and is laughing at them. Even if we try to persuade them otherwise, they don't buy it. Unfortunately, those with a high apprehension trait engage in so much self-monitoring that they can be oblivious to reality or to the way other people interpret the context.

Where does such a personal condition come from? As we mentioned previously, communication apprehension is likely to be rooted, to a large degree, in a person's genetic makeup. Even so, an individual's apprehension level can be reduced or increased through the process of learning or socialization.[21] There are two related ideas that must be understood. One is

learning—a process by which a person's behavior and knowledge is shaped by experience. Learning can take place with no one around. People have personal experiences from which they acquire a greater understanding of their environment, even though no one else is present. Such learning can also occur through observation of other people doing something. The term *socialization* refers more specifically to a particular kind of learning that takes place within a social and cultural environment, such as a family, peer group, society, workplace, or school. Here, the expectations of those in that environment shape what the person learns.

Long-term socialization. Trait apprehension is a function of long-term socialization. To illustrate, it will help to compare the socialization process that produces communication apprehension to that which produces fear of going to the dentist. In our society, fear and dread—supposedly caused by pain and suffering—are indelibly associated with dentists. Children understand this early and well—even if they have never gone to a dentist. Any child can tell you that it is a dreadful experience to be avoided! They have learned this from cartoons, old movies, lore in the street, jokes heard from others, and tales told by earlier generations. The fact is, however, that going to the dentist today is virtually painless. It may be inconvenient, perhaps uncomfortable, and certainly expensive, but it is hardly an experience that leaves every person visiting a dentist racked with pain and suffering. In short, this is a culturally shared construction of meaning that people learn for "going to the dentist" through a process of socialization, rather than from personal experience with objective reality. In a similar way, some people acquire convictions about the terrors of "speaking before a group," even if they have never done so.

The importance of learning and unlearning. The good news is that anything that is learned can be unlearned. Although there may be little hope that people's apprehension can be totally eliminated, with systematic training they may be able to unlearn *at least some* of the negative beliefs that promote communication anxiety. In other words, with adequate training, new beliefs, attitudes, meanings, and behaviors can be acquired that will make it easier for shy and apprehensive people to communicate more comfortably. Such approaches to relearning have been successful in reducing fear of flying, improving sexual adequacy, reducing smoking, and minimizing fear of snakes.

To gain a perspective that may help reduce excessive fears of communicating, we need to look at how learning takes place. Two theories of learning are particularly relevant to communication apprehension: **social learning theory** and **reinforcement learning theory.**[22]

Social learning theory. Acquiring a habit, idea or trait or some other pattern of behavior by seeing it performed by others is often explained by *social learning theory* (sometimes called "observational" learning). This theory was developed originally by psychologist Albert Bandura.[23] As the name suggests, this theory explains how individuals learn, not by performing actions themselves, but by observing how other people cope with similar problems.

Essentially, social learning theory explains that we begin learning to be high or low in communication apprehension by observing the behavior of people who are important as *models* in our lives. When we were young children, our parents and siblings served as our primary models of how to behave. When we entered school, friends and teachers probably became significant models as well. As Bandura and others have illustrated, we often learn how to do something by seeing how others do it. We watch another person perform an activity—such as smoking—and then, under certain circumstances, we imitate that performance. We do this all the time with many forms of behavior. For example, from our earliest years, we learn to talk and respond to others appropriately by copying many of the verbal and nonverbal patterns of others—especially those we admire and want to emulate. Looking to the behavior of other people is the main source from which we find out what our family, friends, and society at large expect of us. From the beginning, they serve as our models, and we emulate them.

The key to this modeling approach is trying out the observed behavior. We're more likely to do that when we perceive that the model is *rewarded* for engaging in that behavior. In other words, it is not enough just to imitate. Any new form of behavior copied from another has to be *useful* to us in some way. If it seems so, we may try it out. Then, as a result of such trials we may or may not adopt the new behavior as part of our own habit patterns. What leads us to adopt it more permanently is when the modeled behavior does actually help us cope with a problem. If it does so successfully, we experience a personal reward (that is, "it worked, and the problem was handled"). Removing a problem and feeling relief can in itself be a reward.

Learning specialists refer broadly to the consequences of such rewarding experiences as *reinforcement*, which can be defined as an increase in the probability that we will respond in that particular way again when confronted with the same circumstances. By this means, the response is learned—it becomes "habitual"—a lasting part of our overall behavioral patterns. On the other hand, if adopting the modeled behavior results in a bad or punishing experience, it is very unlikely we will make it a permanent part of our behavior.

Not only do we copy actual or overt behaviors in this manner, we are also good imitators of our models' fears and anxieties. Some people learn to fear spiders, snakes, or mice simply by observing the anxiety of a parent shrieking at the sight of them. For example, an actual instance of such modeling occurred in the following way. When Kerry was in third grade, her teacher owned a pet tarantula named Precious. The pet became Kerry's favorite. Despite that early positive experience with Precious, Kerry, now a grown woman, shakes in fear every time she faces even the tiniest spider. What happened? Observational learning played a key part. Over the years, she was exposed to the repeated hysterics of her mother every time an uninvited spider, or any bug, entered the house. Her parent served as a model, and, in spite of her earlier comfort with the creatures, Kerry acquired her pattern of reacting with fear to the stimulus of a spider. Her mother was someone she wanted to be like, and emulating her was rewarding. That reward "reinforced" the bug-fear connection.

Similarly, children pick up on the subtle and obvious cues of their parents', siblings', or peers' anxieties about communicating.[24] Exposed at an early age to a number of important models who appear to be uncomfortable in communication situations, any of us might have been unintentionally socialized to be high in apprehension.

Reinforcement learning theory.   While social learning theory is an attractive explanation that seems to make sense, it fails in one important respect: It does not explain fully why one individual raised in a particular set of circumstances acquires a communication apprehension trait whereas another, reared in exactly those same circumstances, does not. We know, for instance, that a child who is high in communication apprehension may grow up in the same family that also produces another child who is low in such anxiety. Presumably each has been exposed to the same behavioral models by the parents. Therefore, social learning theory may explain the problems of one but not the other. Furthermore, we know that children can be low in apprehension about communicating even when both parents (as models) are highly apprehensive. The same is true in reverse. Thus, whereas the modeling perspective may provide a reasonable account of why apprehension results in some people, it fails in others.

An alternative explanation that does not have the preceding shortcoming is *reinforcement learning theory*. (See Box 10.2.) According to this explanation, individuals try out a number of behaviors by chance in some cases, or in others for some different reason. These initial trials are followed by some sort of *consequence*. If the consequence is positive, that is rewarding (and thereby reinforcing), then the behavior has a chance of becoming part of the individual's more permanent repertoire, to be repeated in similar circumstances.[25] If this happens over and over, a connection is established—that is, learning has occurred. Should the initial consequence be punishing, however, the behavior is likely to be dropped and replaced with some other response. Assuming that we prefer positive consequences to our behavior, reinforcement learning theory explains why some of us enjoy social situations that require communication, whereas others avoid them. More than any other explanation of communication apprehension, this perspective has been fairly consistently confirmed by research.[26] Basically, then, reinforcement theory can be used to explain how people high in communication apprehension have been punished for their communication, whereas those low in apprehension have been rewarded.

However, an important question is this: Why does the individual try out a new response in the first place? One answer to that question is provided by what are called *operant* versions of reinforcement theory. Essentially, this view holds that *chance* plays a part. The individual may need to cope with some sort of problem. To do so, he or she randomly tries out many potential solutions—similar to trial and error— and finally gets it right. In fact, hitting on a form of behavior that reduces the problem and thereby produces rewards need not be the result of a conscious decision. The individual may simply have unwittingly engaged in a form of activity that produced a rewarding experience. That response pattern then is reinforced and has a higher probability of being repeated. If rewards continue when the behavior takes place, it becomes a permanent habit pattern, perhaps without the individual even realizing what has happened.[27]

BOX 10.2   🔍 *A Closer Look*

Social Learning Theory versus Reinforcement Theory

Communication scholars explain how individuals acquire communication apprehension with one of two theories. These theories are reviewed here.

Social Learning Theory

This theory, originally developed by Albert Bandura, was first used to explain how children learn, based on observing other people's behaviors, fears, and anxieties. Here, it is used to explain how we learn to be more or less apprehensive when we communicate.

1. We begin by observing how our role models (parents, siblings, teachers) respond to communication situations. For example, is our role model assertive or passive? Does she appear tense or relaxed? Does he apparently enjoy talking or not?

2. If our role model is rewarded for communicating and if we determine that what our role model does is useful to us in some way, then we will try it out ourselves. For example, is she rewarded for communicating that way? Does he get punished?

3. When we try out the new behavior ourselves, we are more likely to adopt it as our own if we get rewarded. If punished, however, we will likely discontinue that behavior. For example, if we try to be assertive ourselves (a rewarded behavior for the role model), and we find that we get what we want as a result (a reward), we will continue to be assertive. On the other hand, if we are punished for our attempts to be assertive, we will abandon it and opt for another way.

Reinforcement Theory

This theory is based on the notion of trial and error. That is, we try out a number of different behaviors (not just those we've observed our role models use) in response to particular situations.

1. We begin by encountering a novel situation. We're not sure what to do or how to act. For example, we see an attractive individual that we would like to ask out. What do we say? What do we do?

2. So, we try out different responses to the situation. To continue with our dating example, we have a number of options available: We could wait to see if the person asks us out; we could see if the person is available Saturday night; or we could simply ask the person to go out.

3. If we are rewarded for our trial (received reinforcement), then it's likely we'll adopt this behavior and use it again. Let's assume then, that our target decides to accept our direct invitation to go out. Thus, we'll try that particular approach again the next time we see an attractive individual we want to go out with.

4. However, if we are either punished or ignored for our trial, then it's likely we'll drop this behavior and, thus, try out an alternative response. In our dating example, we could have received a punishing response ("Are you kidding? I wouldn't go out with you!") or the individual could have ignored our request altogether and kept walking. Either response is sufficient to keep us from trying the direct approach the next time.

The resiliency factor. Despite our learning histories, many of us have encountered negative consequences to our communication behavior at one time or another, and yet, we have not become crippled by communication apprehension. Fortunately, most of us are psychologically *resilient* enough to not let a failure or two shape our behavior permanently. We simply try again to gain positive consequences. This **resiliency factor** is a product of our socialization and reinforcement history, which suggests that we can usually expect our communication to be well received. As a result, when an occasional performance goes wrong, we are able to chalk it up as an unusual event—a mistake.

Those already high in apprehension do not share this resiliency. For them, success is not expected. Failure or punishment is. Such individuals have learned to expect failure or punishment when they talk. A history of punishment for talking prompts those high in apprehension to avoid the behavior that typically results in negative consequences. Thus, fear of communicating and the expectation of negative consequences have become a deeply established personality trait.

The consequences of inconsistency. A follow-up of reinforcement theory suggests that some individuals may experience inconsistent consequences to their behavior. If a youngster is rewarded for talking *sometimes,* but punished at *other* times, the child is likely to develop high communication apprehension. Irregular or inconsistent consequences for behavior over time can induce a condition of **personal anomie**—a feeling of anxiety or distress arising from confusion concerning the social expectations of others. This can be a serious condition, and it has even been linked to increased probability of suicide.[28] In the present discussion of communication apprehension, if we cannot accurately make reliable predictions about what will happen to us—whether we will be rewarded or punished when we communicate—we probably will develop fears and anxieties about it and stop communicating altogether.

Another source of anxiety is the *no-win situation.* For instance, we may always say the wrong thing. Suppose we greet the next-door neighbor saying, "Good morning," and then she grumbles and claims that it isn't. Then, the next morning, we change strategy and declare, "We've seen better days than this one." She then argues that we should appreciate what we have. After a few such attempts we choose to ignore her altogether. She then tells other neighbors that we are cold and unfriendly. This no-win situation, like the repeated-failures condition, is likely to make us feel very apprehensive in subsequent encounters with that neighbor. We are helpless to initiate a successful communication. Should this experience occur often in other contexts and with other individuals, it becomes apparent that **learned helplessness** would be aroused in almost all of our attempts to communicate with others.[29]

By the time we are adults, we have confronted and learned from a number of communication experiences that eventually result in different levels of communication apprehension. Those of us who share a history of positive reinforcement for communicating are probably moderate to low in our apprehensions. Although we may occasionally suffer from anxiety in a specific situation, as a rule we tend to be comfortable with people and enjoy talking with them and to them. Conversely, those who have experienced a very different history of socialization—with punishment or unpredictable consequences tied to attempts to communicate—are likely to be chronically apprehensive about approaching any communication task.

Consequences of High and Low Communication Apprehension

Suffering from high anxiety about public speaking is not the only consequence of being chronically apprehensive. Over 100 research studies demonstrate that individuals high in apprehension are evaluated differently by others than those low in apprehension.[30] The consequences of these assessments can be seen throughout individuals' lives. Those who are low in apprehension are evaluated positively, whereas those who are high are regarded negatively in a variety of ways.[31] These assessments can have profound and long-term consequences. One of the earliest arenas for such evaluation occurs in the classroom and on the school playground. When it comes to communicating with others, how apprehensive are you? Complete the self-assessment in Box 10.3.

In the Classroom

The social dynamics of the classroom (in all school levels) have been intensively studied in the search for understanding of the causes and consequences of communication apprehension.[32] One important aspect of the classroom context is the way in which teachers evaluate individuals. The consequences of evaluations in the classroom can be illustrated by comparing two boys: Jerry, who is low in communication apprehension, and Richard, who is high in communication apprehension. We will assume that the two are actually fraternal twins, who were separated at birth and raised in similar middle-class homes in different cities. Neither is aware of the other. While these are two fictional people, they represent composites of individuals whose experiences have been closely studied.[33] These composites will seem familiar because we all know people who fit each of these profiles.

Jerry and Richard are both 14 years of age, and are both healthy and active. They both like sports, girls, pizza, and rock stars (not necessarily in that order). Jerry is outgoing and popular, and is captain of the soccer team. Richard is more of a loner. He reads a lot, and checks his e-mail on the computer before school every morning. Jerry is rarely, if ever, apprehensive about talking to anyone about anything. Richard seldom initiates conversations with others at school.

There is a striking difference in the ways teachers respond to Jerry and Richard. Their responses favor Jerry, who is low in communication apprehension. Teachers perceive Jerry to be a better student than Richard, even though the two are intellectual equals and have identical grades and IQ scores.

The patterns of communication affect the ways teachers respond to Jerry and Richard. In class, Jerry raises his hand and volunteers to talk frequently. Teachers call on Jerry more often than on Richard. Teachers also initiate informal conversations with Jerry much more often than with Richard.

When teachers ask Jerry a question and he doesn't know the answer, they assume the question is too hard or unclear and give hints to assist him. When the same thing happens with Richard, teachers assume that he doesn't know the answer because he's not too bright, and they move on to another student. Teachers interpret Jerry's ease in communicating as a sign of an enthused, dedicated, and delightful student. Richard's quietness is construed as detachment, indifference, or even apathy toward school.

Clearly, students like Jerry, who are low in communication apprehension, are more likely to be seen as ones who do well in school, despite the fact that teachers often give them extra help and attention. Students like Richard, who are high in communication apprehension, have their work cut out for them. Teachers regularly underestimate their intelligence and misinterpret their quietness as an attitude problem. This discriminatory behavior magnifies communication apprehension by punishing or ignoring students high in apprehension.

In Social Encounters

Richard and Jerry are now 19 years old and both are in college. Richard and Jerry's differing levels of communication apprehension continue to affect their lives, both in the college classroom and in interpersonal relationships. For example, Jerry goes out frequently, and he enjoys seeing a number of different women. Most women find him attractive, affable, and exciting. Richard's experience is quite different. Few women notice him when he's in the same room with them. Like most people high in apprehension, Richard appears to hide or physically contract when others are around. He dates one person regularly, but he would like to go out with others. Sometimes people interpret his high-apprehension behavior to mean that he is cold and distant.

Interpersonal opportunities are much greater for individuals like Jerry, who are low in communication apprehension. Such individuals seem approachable and fun to be with. They are affinity-seekers and give the appearance of being good listeners in conversations. They ask and answer questions; and they are generally

BOX 10.3 *Personal Report of Communication Apprehension-24 (CA)*

Instructions: This instrument is composed of 24 statements concerning your feelings about communication with other people. Please indicate in the space provided the degree to which each statement applies to you by marking whether you:

5 = Strongly Disagree
4 = Disagree
3 = Undecided
2 = Agree
1 = Strongly Agree

There are no right or wrong answers. Many of the statements are similar to other statements. Do not be concerned about this. Work quickly, just record your first impression.

____ 1. I dislike participating in group discussions.
____ 2. Generally, I am comfortable while participating in a group discussion.
____ 3. I am tense and nervous while participating in group discussions.
____ 4. I like to get involved in group discussions.
____ 5. Engaging in a group discussion with new people makes me tense and nervous.
____ 6. I am calm and relaxed while participating in group discussions.
____ 7. Generally, I am nervous when I have to participate in a meeting.
____ 8. Usually I am calm and relaxed while participating in meetings.
____ 9. I am very calm and relaxed when I am called upon to express an opinion at a meeting.
____ 10. I am afraid to express myself at meetings.
____ 11. Communicating at meetings usually makes me uncomfortable.
____ 12. I am very relaxed when answering questions at a meeting.
____ 13. While participating in a conversation with a new acquaintance, I feel very nervous.
____ 14. I have no fear of speaking up in conversation.
____ 15. Ordinarily I am very tense and nervous in conversations.
____ 16. Ordinarily I am very calm and relaxed in conversations.
____ 17. While conversing with a new acquaintance, I feel very relaxed.
____ 18. I'm afraid to speak up in conversations.
____ 19. I have no fear of giving a speech.
____ 20. Certain parts of my body feel very tense and rigid while giving a speech.
____ 21. I feel relaxed while giving a speech.
____ 22. My thoughts become confused and jumbled when I am giving a speech.

perceived as being friendly and personable. People with high communication apprehension, like Richard, give off the wrong signals. They often send a message of avoidance: They look away, respond only when spoken to, and rarely ask questions about another person with whom they may be talking. As a result, people with high apprehension are perceived as being disinterested and unfriendly—even though they may really want companionship.

At Work

After graduating from college, both Richard and Jerry looked for jobs. Jerry applied for career opportunities in public relations (his major), whereas Richard considered jobs in data analysis and computer software development (he majored in computer information systems). Obviously, the communication demands of these career paths differ dramatically: Jerry's choice required him to interact regularly with corporate clients, whereas Richard will have limited interaction with others.

When you consider your own major and the career decisions you have made thus far, do these decisions reflect positive or negative feelings about communication? People low in communication apprehension are more likely to choose careers in speech communication,

_____ 23. I face the prospect of giving a speech with confidence.

_____ 24. While giving a speech I get so nervous, I forget facts I really know.

Calculating Your Score:

The PRCA-24 allows you to compute both an overall, total apprehension score as well as 4 different subscores which measure your apprehension toward 4 familiar contexts: talking in groups, meetings, dyads, and public situations.

Group =   18 + scores for items 2, 4, and 6 – scores for items 1, 3, and 5.
          YOUR GROUP SCORE = _____.

Meeting = 18 + scores for items 8, 9, and 12 – scores for items 7, 10, and 11.
          YOUR MEETING SCORE = _____.

Dyadic = 18 + scores for items 14, 16, and 17 – scores for items 13, 15, and 18.
          YOUR DYADIC SCORE = _____.

Public = 18 + scores for items 19, 21, and 23 – scores for items 20, 22, and 24.
          YOUR PUBLIC SCORE = _____.

Intepreting Your Score:

Overall Communication Apprehension (CA) = Simply add your subscores together: Group + Meeting + Dyadic + Public.
YOUR TOTAL CA SCORE = _____.

Possible range of scores: 24–120. (If your own overall CA score does not fall within that range, you made a computational error).

High CAs (scores higher than 83) are characterized as low talkers, shy, withdrawn, fearful, tense, and nervous. Low CAs (scores lower than 55) talk a lot, seem to enjoy the company of others, are more immediate with people, and occasionally communicate even when others would rather they wouldn't. Most people score between 55 and 83 and are considered moderately apprehensive. They know there are times when they should talk and times when they should not. Moderates are apprehensive during important job interviews, but feel little or no tension at all when talking to acquaintances over the telephone.

Source: McCroskey, James C. (1982). *Introduction to rhetorical communication* (4th ed.). Englewood Cliffs, NJ: Prentice Hall. Also available in more recent editions of this book published by Allyn & Bacon.

theater, journalism, advertising, and public relations. Those high in communication apprehension are more likely to choose careers in accounting, computer science, pharmacy, and engineering.

The situation of applying for a job clearly illustrates how communication apprehension can affect the impressions people form in the workplace.[34] All things being equal, those who communicate easily generally make a better first impression in job interviews than those who are more anxious. Employers would be more likely to perceive Jerry as being sociable, competent, responsible, and having leadership potential. Richard would more likely be perceived as being uncommunicative, restrained, aloof, and tense.

In Lifelong Careers

If we look in on Richard and Jerry seven years after graduation, we find Jerry in management and Richard still working at a lower career level. Those low in communication apprehension are promoted significantly more often than those who continue to be fearful and nervous about communicating. Those who communicate comfortably are apparently able to alert their bosses to their achievements and to assert their needs. Those reluctant to communicate

Low communication apprehensives are confident at work. Employers are likely to perceive them as sociable, competent, responsible, and having leadership potential.

may hesitate to tell others about their successes; they are more likely to wait for a promotion to come to them.

In terms of job satisfaction, Jerry is more satisfied with his work than Richard.[35] This may be a reflection of reality—that is, those low in apprehension report significantly more satisfaction than their high-apprehension counterparts simply because their jobs are more rewarding. After all, Jerry's job probably pays more, includes greater work variety, and provides more flexibility than Richard's lower-ranking position.

To summarize, the impressions that people construct on the basis of someone's apprehension about communicating can easily lead us to conclude that the world of the "easy talker" is much more positive than that of the person who is shy and timid. In some ways it is. Overall, people who are more or less permanently apprehensive about communicating appear to be less likely to succeed in academic pursuits,

social relationships, and career opportunities. In contrast, those who are not particularly anxious seem to get more of what they want because they are perceived as being competent, sociable, popular, hard-working, attractive, responsible, and more qualified for leadership roles.

Remember, however, that the descriptions of Richard and Jerry represent tendencies documented by research, not ironclad laws. In other words, they are *generalizations* with many exceptions. There are children high in communication apprehension who do well academically. As adults, many such people establish long-term successful marriages and friendships and have rewarding and high-paying jobs. No one would deny the successes of Microsoft leader Bill Gates and Mr. Apple himself, Steve Jobs—two examples of highly apprehensive communicators. In contrast, there are people with low communication apprehension who have trouble finishing college, getting a date, or holding down a job for long. Being shy and somewhat uncommunicative need not limit your social and professional options. For one thing is possible to change if desired. Interestingly, the majority of people who are apprehensive about communicating have learned to live with this tendency and see no need to change.

Dealing with Stage Fright

At one time or another, everyone has to make a presentation before a group. Communication apprehension while preparing for or delivering a speech is commonly called **stage fright.** In fact, few people have never experienced it.[36] Stage fright is *normal.* Almost all professional performers complain about feeling nervous before they address an audience. It's no simple feat to march up onto a stage with all eyes on us, and then to speak fluently and meaningfully.

To understand stage fright, two of its potential causes need to be examined: the *apprehension-producing event* itself and *your own level of communication apprehension.* Contrary to what you might think, it's not a good idea to rid yourself completely of stage fright. Like unpleasant medicine, in limited doses it can serve you well!

The Contributions of the Context

Like other aspects of communication, stage fright is partially a product of the context in which the activity takes place; public speaking is done in a *physical place,* in a *social setting,* and among people in particular *social relationships.* Each of these contextual factors can contribute to the speaker's temporary communication apprehension. In addition, speaking before a group is characterized by the contextual sources of anxiety as noted earlier such as *unfamiliar others, formal occasions, conspicuousness,* and *evaluations.* It is little wonder, then, that this kind of communication generates anxiety.

Are these sources of apprehension real or only imagined? They are very real! Giving a talk places us in a formal situation with unfamiliar others where we are conspicuous and being evaluated. Every audience rates a public speaking event much the same way they judge ball games, phone apps, or movies. Because most public events are culturally defined as entertainment, people expect speakers to be amusing or at least informative and interesting. The audience's expectations seem to increase as a function of how much money, time, and effort is involved in attending the presentation—making everyone a critic.

The Contributions of the Speaker

Recall that people with high communication apprehension are likely to magnify the stress factors in almost any situation. Even though we all recognize the conspicuous situation of the public speaker and the evaluation involved in the event, people who are chronically apprehensive negatively interpret the situation, perceiving that the people in the audience are strangers and that their presentation will be judged harshly.

As much as possible, those high in communication apprehension avoid speaking before an audience. Such people would not voluntarily enroll in anything like a public speaking class. If their university requires such a class, these students may enroll, drop the class, and enroll again. Sometimes they do not muster the courage to enroll in the class until the last term of their final year in college, and, in fact, there are students who have never graduated simply because they were unable to complete that one required course.

In contrast, easy talkers typically enjoy public speaking courses, and, despite stage fright, they learn to perform quite well. For such individuals, and indeed for those who are moderately apprehensive, stage fright can be controlled. By practicing skills, they learn to channel their apprehension toward the event in productive ways. For these people, a certain amount of stage fright generates motivation—enough drive so that they can excel on stage.

Systematic desensitization: The way to cope with anxiety-producing situations is to ease back and relax.

Reducing Communication Apprehension

No one has to go through life avoiding events that require him or her to communicate. Anyone can learn to cope with stage fright and even modify a communication apprehension trait. Strong evidence indicates that even those who are truly anxious can be moved to a moderate level where their apprehensions can be managed. If so, they can gain enough confidence to communicate with others effectively in both public and private settings.

A number of methods have been touted as potential cures for communication anxieties. This chapter considers only three that appear to be effective. These are *systematic desensitization, cognitive restructuring,* and *skills training.* There are many other techniques in use, such as hypnosis, group counseling, and psychoanalysis. Although these may have merit, they can be very costly, and none is as successful as the

three discussed here. Today, most colleges and universities offer at least two of these techniques as part of training in public speaking. After reviewing each, you may want to consider examining one that is available to you.

Systematic Desensitization

The process of **systematic desensitization (SD)** is the most widely used of all treatment programs for communication apprehension. Systematic desensitization, developed in the early 1950s, is a form of treatment used to reduce many kinds of fears, including fears of flying, heights, driving, and so on, as well as communication apprehension.

In the mid-1960s, research began on the effects of SD on public speaking anxiety. Experimenters repeatedly found that the procedure significantly reduced students' fears about communicating. In 1972, an SD program was initiated for students at Illinois State University. It included published guidelines that others have used to initiate similar

FIGURE 10.1

Sequence of Communication Situations for Systematic Desensitization
In systematic desensitization, the individual learns to associate relaxation, rather than tension, with increasingly stressful speaking situations.

High Apprehension

Giving a speech
Participating in a class discussion
Standing in front of class without talking
Asking a question during class
Working on a group project
Talking with an instructor after class
Talking with a friend

Low Apprehension

treatment programs at universities and high schools across the country.[37]

Systematic desensitization focuses on *physical responses* to apprehension. We all become tense and tighten our muscles when we are anxious. It is an involuntary response. If we have reason to be fearful, our bodies automatically react to prepare for action—whether or not physical action is required to deal with the source of the anxiety. Systematic desensitization works on the principle that if an alternative response—muscle relaxation—can be substituted for tension and stress, then people can learn to cope with anxiety-producing situations, including communication situations.

So, the big message of SD is *relax!* "Well," you say, "that's easier said than done. How can anyone ease back and relax when they have a speech to perform?" The fact is, it can't be done without learning how to do it. In SD treatment programs, individuals are actually taught *how* to relax. They learn to tense and then relax each of their muscles and to control their breathing so that, on cue, they can let go as they exhale. In this treatment program, then, the trainee becomes conscious of physical tensions and practices releasing that tension on command.

The next phase of SD introduces the anxiety-producing conditions for which the training is all about. In the case of communication apprehension, students are exposed gradually to a sequence of communication situations.

Figure 10.1 illustrates a hierarchy of communication situations commonly used in SD training, ranging from most apprehensive (giving a speech) to least apprehensive (talking with a friend).

At first, situations are presented that arouse relatively little apprehension. For example, while in a relaxed state, subjects are asked to imagine themselves talking on the phone to their best friend. Next, to increase the level of potential stress, they may be asked to visualize themselves working on a group project or going out to dinner with someone new. In later stages of the program, people are asked to visualize situations that would have produced a lot of stress before the therapy began, such as presenting a speech or being interviewed on television. By the time they get to this level, individuals have developed their relaxation techniques to a point where they can handle the situation. Over time, individuals learn to associate *relaxation*, not *tension*, with the increasing demands of each successive communication situation.

In addition to its obvious success rate, SD is cost effective. Each session lasts about an hour, and the entire program only requires about five to seven sessions. Research shows that if students are exposed to SD at the same time they are enrolled in public speaking classes where they learn specific skills, they are more likely to finish the course, perform competently, and report feeling less apprehensive about communicating.

Cognitive Restructuring

Whereas systematic desensitization focuses on muscle tension—the physiological effects of our apprehension—**cognitive restructuring** centers on (as the name suggests) our thought processes. It examines the individual's interpretations of the anxiety-producing situation itself. Again, this is a general therapy system and is not restricted to communication anxieties. Nevertheless, it is used to reduce temporary or chronic communication apprehension.

Proponents of this method argue that people label certain situations inappropriately and that they often evaluate events as being more negative than they actually are.[38] These negative evaluations are based primarily on specific irrational beliefs that underlie a lot of their emotions.[39] Three irrational beliefs that individuals commonly entertain can be summed up in the following statements:

- Everyone must love me all the time or I am a bad person.
- I must be competent or successful in all situations or I am a bad person.
- When life is not the way I want, it is awful and upsetting.

Cognitive restructuring focuses on changing these kinds of beliefs. The role of the therapist is to help individuals understand the basis for their anxieties. When irrational beliefs are exposed, the therapist challenges them, questioning each and arguing logically against them all. Then the therapist offers rational alternatives to replace those that have been discredited. In this way, troublesome beliefs are restructured or removed, and new convictions are established.

When cognitive restructuring is applied to communication apprehension, five major steps are involved. Let's look at how each of these steps is applied to fears about public speaking.

In the *first* step in cognitive restructuring, called the "introduction," the basic principles involved in cognitive restructuring are explained. The trainer (or therapist) explains that apprehension about public speaking is learned and that anything that has been learned can be unlearned and replaced with new ideas and behavior. Apprehension can be reduced significantly when people become aware of their irrational beliefs or negative thoughts about public speaking.

The *second* step requires that subjects identify negative self-statements that inhibit their speaking performances. These are derogatory convictions that anxious people often say (to themselves) about the situation or their activities in that situation. Individuals are asked to consider three separate occasions for saying (silently) those negative statements—before, during, and after the speech. Step 2 in Box 10.4 lists some sample negative self-statements. Do you recognize any that you might use? What are others you may have said to yourself?

In the *third* step, each of these statements is then analyzed for errors in logic. (Notice the logic errors in step 3 in Box 10.4 that undermine or disable each negative self-statement identified.) Cognitive restructuring aims to show individuals that they have been rehearsing an entire monologue of irrational negative self statements that typically form the basis for a kind of self-fulfilling prophecy: Believing that they are failing, they wind up doing so. It is no wonder their attempts at public speaking have been so frightening and frustrating up to this point.

In the *fourth* step, individuals learn a new set of coping statements to communicate to themselves. The therapist helps them generate these alternative statements and substitute them for the previous list of negative ones. Once again, the coping statements are generated for use before, during, and after the communication event (see step 4 of Box 10.4). The trainer encourages everyone to replace their entire repertoire of negative expectancies and evaluations with positive, self-directed statements. Rather than emphasizing the negative aspects of their performances, they learn to attend to the positives.

Finally, the *fifth* step of cognitive restructuring requires that individuals practice the new coping statements. The trainer points out that given the number of years the individuals have been rehearsing negative self-statements, they

BOX 10.4   *A Closer Look*

Cognitive Restructuring

What are the steps in cognitive restructuring? These four steps are outlined here:

Step 1: Introduction

The principles of cognitive restructuring are explained to the participants. The trainer explains that individuals' apprehensions and fears about public speaking are learned and can be unlearned.

Step 2: Identify Negative Self-Statements	Step 3: Identify Errors in Logic	Step 4: Learn New Coping Statements
Before Speech		
• My topic is so boring. Why did I pick it?	• Topics are inherently boring. I will make this one interesting.	• I chose my topic carefully. People in my audience will be interested in it.
• I know I'll forget my second major point.	• I have a notecard with all my major points listed.	• I've rehearsed my speech over and over. I'll remember all my main points.
• No one will like me or my speech.	• People generally like me; they'll like what I have to say, too.	• My audience will love me—and they'll love my speech, too.
During Speech		
• I can see that no one likes what I'm saying.	• I'm overgeneralizing; of course, someone will like it.	• Most of my audience is interested; they appreciate what I'm saying.
• My hands are all sweaty. Everyone can see how nervous I am.	• Sure, they're sweating, but no one will even notice.	• I am a little nervous: no one seems to notice it but me.
• They don't think I'm funny. I'm doomed!	• Not everyone will die of laughter, but I'm sure I can get most of them to smile.	• Nearly everyone in the audience laughed or grinned when I delivered that funny line.
After Speech		
• I blew it.	• I did it, didn't it? I gave my speech.	• I did a good job. I did a great job!
• I can't do it again.	• Of course I can. That's why I'm taking this course—to learn how to give a speech.	• I'm looking forward to my next speech so I can do an even better job.
• I was as bad as I thought I was going to be.	• The truth is, I'm never as bad as I imagine I'm going to be. I didn't throw up; I didn't fall down; and I'm still alive.	• I did very well—better than I expected.

Step 5: Practice

This final step is often overlooked, and yet it can't be more important! Individuals must rehearse over and over the positive self-statements that they generated in step 4. In this way, participants are more likely to recall positive rather than negative statements when they need them most—during apprehensive moments.

should not realistically expect to replace them immediately with positive ones. Old habits are hard to break. A whole new tool kit of coping statements has to be developed, memorized, and made available for immediate recall when the occasion demands. Eventually, these coping statements become automatic and help subjects reduce communication anxieties. This kind of automated behavior is common in such physical tasks as driving, typing, reading, and playing tennis, in which, over time, we have learned not to monitor every move we make. Our responses to communication situations can also be reduced to this level by appropriate cognitive restructuring. (See Box 10.5)

Like SD, cognitive restructuring has a record of success in dealing with communication apprehension. Over and over again, we find that people's apprehensions toward communicating are reduced significantly with this technique. The emphasis of the treatment program, however, should be on the coping statements themselves and the practice of those statements, rather than understanding the principles. Mere insight into the negative self-statements is insufficient and can even serve to increase anxieties simply by giving excessive attention to the problem rather than to the solution.

Skills Training

The third method of reducing communication apprehension, **skills training,** differs sharply from the other treatment techniques. Rather than assuming our apprehensions lead to problems in communicating successfully with others, skills training reverses the causal sequence. It assumes that people's skills limitations in communicating influence their apprehension levels. That is, proponents of this technique argue that a primary cause of fears of communicating is a deficit in skills. Gerald Phillips, the leading proponent for this mode of treatment, reasons that some people develop apprehensions partly because they find themselves inept in communication situations.[40] In other words,

Implications of Communication Apprehension

Research clearly shows that people who are highly apprehensive about communicating are often perceived in negative ways. Because they avoid, rather than approach, communication situations, people attribute to them other qualities that seem unfair and unwarranted. Not knowing them, others often perceive those who are highly apprehensive about communicating as aloof, disinterested, uninvolved, and unappreciative.

Who is obligated to change here? Should high apprehensives become less so and learn to approach others, to talk, and to participate more actively in social, school, and work situations? Or should the rest of us become more aware of our prejudices and learn to perceive them more accurately?

Finally, what is so great about being a good talker? Don't we already have too much talking with too little thinking? Do you know individuals low in communication apprehension who should learn to be a little more apprehensive and thus more cautious when they speak?

they have good and sufficient reasons for feeling anxious: They just do not know how to communicate effectively. Once they learn how to perform successfully, their apprehensions will be reduced. Thus, training programs based on these assumptions are designed to teach appropriate and effective communication skills.

When skills training is used to help reduce public speaking anxieties, the usual approach is to expose speakers first to lectures, readings, and discussions of important public speaking concepts and principles. This exposure is typically followed by some form of rehearsal or performance of the principles studied. Speakers are encouraged to practice their new communication behaviors in front of an audience. Practice is seen as the key to success.

Early in this chapter it was maintained that practice does not always make perfect, yet the popular skills training method holds that it does. There is little doubt that training in skills can result in learning more effective techniques and strategies for communicating in various settings. However, the degree to which it specifically reduces apprehension is another matter. The fact is, there is less agreement on this issue, and research evidence on the effects of skills training on apprehension remains equivocal. There are many clear instances where, with specific training, amateur speakers have learned the requisite communication skills to become effective—and thus less anxious—public speakers.[41] If your own anxiety about public speaking stems from not knowing how to prepare and deliver a speech, skills training should help reduce your apprehension a great deal.

Nevertheless, there are people who have learned exactly how to perform the necessary public speaking skills, but whose apprehension continues to interfere with their ability to give a talk. The source of their apprehension, then, is not a deficit in skills but some other anxiety producing cause. In other words, skills training sometimes reduces apprehension and sometimes it doesn't. Compared to SD and cognitive restructuring, skills training alone is probably the least effective approach to reducing apprehension. A recent evaluation of all of these methods reveals that a combination of all three is more effective than any single treatment.[42]

Chapter Review

- Some individuals suffer from a chronic communication apprehension trait; others tend to be low in that apprehension. Those high in apprehension are often shy and withdrawn; they seek occupations that demand little interaction with others, and they prefer quiet evenings at home with family and friends. In contrast, people who are low in communication apprehension are likely to be open and talkative, to choose careers that require interaction with the public, and to look forward to parties and large get-togethers.

- For many people, apprehension is only temporary. Contextual factors that can temporarily affect our ability to communicate include unfamiliarity, dissimilarity, novelty, formality, subordinate status, conspicuousness, excessive attention from others, evaluation, and previous failure.

- Those who are chronically apprehensive differ in their socialization and learning histories from those who are not. According to social learning theory, individuals who are truly apprehensive acquired their anxieties by adopting the fears and behaviors of models that were significant to them in their early social development. Reinforcement theory explains apprehension by suggesting that those high in the trait may have tried a variety of responses in social encounters that failed or were not reinforced.

- People respond differently to individuals who are characteristically high in communication apprehension. Apprehensive people are often regarded as aloof, disinterested, and uncaring. These negative impressions influence their experiences in academic, social, and work situations. In contrast, people low in communication anxiety are perceived as friendly, industrious, and warm, which gives them advantages in the classroom, at work, and in social life.

- A number of treatment programs are available to reduce communication apprehension. The most successful programs include systematic desensitization (SD), cognitive restructuring, and skills training. The SD method reduces communication apprehension through muscle relaxation techniques. Cognitive restructuring changes or modifies beliefs about the particular communication event and substitutes positive self-statements for negative ones. Skills training recommends instruction and practice in communication skills.

Key Terms

communication apprehension
trait (personality)
social learning theory
reinforcement learning theory

resiliency factor
anomie (personal)
learned helplessness
stage fright

systematic desensitization (SD)
cognitive restructuring
skills training

Notes

1. A number of studies indicate that skills training alone fails to reduce fears about communicating. If these fears aren't addressed and alleviated, performance may continue to suffer. See: Dwyer, K. K. (2000). The multidimensional model: Teaching students to self-manage high communication apprehension by self-selecting treatments. *Communication education, 49,* 72–71. For a more detailed review of relevant research, see: Bourhis, J., Allen, M., & Bauman, I. (2006). Communication apprehension: Issues to consider in the classroom. In B. M. Gayle, R. W. Preiss, N. Burrell, & M. Allen (Eds.), *Classroom communication and instructional processes: Advances through meta-analysis* (pp. 211–227). Mahwah, NJ: Erlbaum. Allen, M., Hunter, J. E., & Donahue, W. A. (1989). Meta-analysis of self-report data on the effectiveness of public speaking anxiety treatment techniques. *Communication education, 38,* 54–76.

2. For a comprehensive review of studies, see: Daly, J. A., & McCroskey, J. C. (Eds.). (1997). *Avoiding communication: Shyness, reticence and communication apprehension,* 2nd ed. Cresskill, NJ: Hampton Press.

3. Ibid.

4. Ibid., pp. 13–38.

5. McCroskey, J. C. (1977). Oral communication apprehension: A summary of recent theory and research. *Human communication research,* 4, 78–96; McCroskey, J. C. (1982). Oral communication apprehension: A reconceptualization. In M. Burgoon (Ed.), *Communication yearbook* 6 (pp. 136–170). Beverly Hills, CA: Sage.

6. McCroskey, 1982, Oral communication, pp. 142–143; McCroskey, J. C., Richmond, V. P., & Stewart, R. A. (1986). *One on one: The foundations of interpersonal communication* (pp. 41–42). Englewood Cliffs, NJ: Prentice-Hall.

7. Duck, S. (1986). *Human relations: An introduction to social psychology* (p. 19). Beverly Hills, CA: Sage; McCroskey, Richmond, & Stewart, *One on one,* pp. 41, 48.

8. McCroskey makes a distinction between communication competence (knowing and understanding the appropriate behaviors to engage in) and communication performance or skill (being able to adequately perform those behaviors). He argues that even competent communicators can be apprehensive about interacting with others. For a more intensive explanation of this distinction, see: McCroskey, J. C. (1984). The communication apprehension perspective. In Daly & McCroskey, *Avoiding communication,* pp. 13–38.

9. Ibid., pp. 14–22; McCroskey, Richmond, Stewart, *One on one,* pp. 49–58.

10. Hilgard, E. R., Atkinson, R. C., & Atkinson, R. L. (1975). *Introduction to psychology,* 6th ed., p. 368. New York: Harcourt Brace Jovanovich.

11. The seminal work on the nature and origins of personality traits is: Allport, G. W. (1937). *Personality: A psychological interpretation*. New York: Henry Holt. See especially chap. 11, A theory of traits, and chap. 12, The nature of traits, pp. 286–342.

12. See, for example: Rumbough, T.B. (2000). The effects of impromptu speech exercises in reducing trait and situational communication apprehension. *New Jersey Journal of Communication 7*, 2, 206–215.

13. McCroskey, 1982, Oral communication, p. 164; McCroskey, Richmond, & Stewart, *One on one*, pp. 58–63.

14. Between 1970 and 1980 alone, over 200 reported studies examined the causes and effects of communication apprehension and related constructs. For extensive reviews of these, see: McCroskey, 1982, Oral communication, pp. 136–170; Richmond, V. P. (1984). Implications of quietness: Some facts and speculations. In Daly & McCroskey, *Avoiding communication*, pp. 145–156. In addition, a bibliographic listing of relevant studies is available in: Payne, S. K., & Richmond, V. P. (1984). A bibliography of related research and theory. In Daly & McCroskey, *Avoiding communication*, pp. 247–294.

15. McCroskey, Richmond, & Stewart, *One on one*, pp. 49–50.

16. McCroskey, J. C., & Richmond, V. P. (2006). Understanding the audience: Students' communication traits. In T. P. Mottet, V. P. Richmond, & J. C. McCroskey (Eds.), *Handbook of instructional communication: Rhetorical and relational perspectives* (pp. 51–66). New York: Allyn and Bacon.

17. This concept had its roots more than two millennia ago in Plato's "Allegory of the Cave," set forth in his *Republic*. In more modern form it was developed as a specific principle of human behavior by W. I. Thomas (1923) in *The unadjusted girl*. New York: The Social Science Research Council. A summary can be found in Coser, L. A., and Rosenberg, B. (1964) *Sociological theory: A book of readings* (2nd ed., pp. 233–235). New York: Macmillan.

18. For a discussion of alternative interpretations of the causes of communication apprehension, see: Beatty, M. J., & Friedland, M. H.

(1990). Public speaking state anxiety as a function of selected situational and dispositional variables. *Communication Education, 38,* 142–147; and Beatty, M. J., Balfantz, G. L., & Kuwabara, A. Y. (1989). Trait-like qualities of selected variables assumed to be transient causes of performance state anxiety. *Communication Education, 38,* 277–289.

19. Buss, A. H. (1980). *Self-consciousness and social anxiety*. San Francisco: Freeman; McCroskey, Richmond, & Stewart, *One on one*, pp. 56–58.

20. Many approaches and explanations have been advanced to account for the origin of communicator traits. This focus of research has produced a number of models of the origins of communication apprehension. For example, see: Beatty, M. J., & Valencic, K. M. (2000). Context-based apprehension versus planning demands: A communibiological analysis of anticipatory public speaking anxiety. *Communication Education, 49,* 1, 58–71.

21. For a general explanation of the principles of operant conditioning or reinforcement theory, see: Skinner, B. F. (1957). *Verbal behavior*. New York: Appleton, Century Crofts.

22. For a brief but comprehensive review of the origins and nature of learning theories and their relationship to both socialization and communication, see: DeFleur, M. L., & Ball-Rokeach, S. (1989). *Theories of mass communication* (5th ed., pp. 174–181, 212–219). White Plains, NY: Longman.

23. Bandura, A. (1977). *Social learning theory*. Englewood Cliffs, NJ: Prentice-Hall.

24. Beatty, M. J., Plax, T. G., & Kearney, P. (1985). Reinforcement vs. modeling theory in the development of communication apprehension: A retrospective analysis. *Communication Research Reports, 2,* 80–85.

25. For a general explanation of the principles of operant conditioning or reinforcement theory, see: Skinner, B. F. (1957). *Verbal behavior*. New York: Appleton-Century-Crofts. For a discussion linking reinforcement theory to the development of communication apprehension more specifically, see: McCroskey, *Communication apprehension perspective*, pp. 22–30; McCroskey, 1982, *Oral communication*, pp. 153–155.

26. Beatty, Plax, & Kearney, Reinforcement vs. modeling, pp. 80–85; Daly, J. A., & Friedrich, G. (1981). The development of communication apprehension: A retrospective analysis of contributory correlations. *Communication Quarterly, 29,* 243–255.

27. One of the problems of such operant explanations is that they give little credit to the rational abilities of human beings to engage in analysis, planning, insight, and other thought processes. As we have explained in earlier chapters, human beings are able to use language as a basis for such rational and analytic mental activity. Psychologists, seeking universal laws of learning that apply to all organisms, have generally been reluctant to bring uniquely human mental processes into their learning theories.

28. The term *anomie* was first introduced into the analysis of social life by Emile Durkheim at the end of the 19th century. See: Durkheim, E. (1951). *Suicide: A study of sociology* (J. A. Spaulding, Trans., and G. Simpson, Eds.). New York: Free Press. (First published in French in 1897.)

29. Early research on learned helplessness examined dogs' responses after inconsistent or random rewards and punishments were applied to their behaviors. After trying out a variety of behaviors, the dogs eventually gave up responding altogether and, instead, retreated to a corner. See: Seligman, M. F. (1975). *Helplessness: On depression, development and death.* San Francisco: Freeman. For a more intensive application of learned helplessness to communicate apprehension development, see: McCroskey, Communication apprehension perspective, pp. 26–30.

30. Daly, J. A., & Stafford, L. (1984). Correlates and consequences of social communicative anxiety. In Daly & McCroskey, *Avoiding communication,* pp. 125–144; Payne & Richmond, *A bibliography,* pp. 247–294; Richmond, Communication apprehension perspective, pp. 145–156.

31. McCroskey, Richmond, & Stewart, *One on one,* pp. 63–66.

32. See, for example: Myers, S.A., & Rocca, K. A. (2001). Perceived instructor argumentativeness and verbal aggressiveness in the college classroom: Effects on student perceptions of climate, apprehension and state motivation. *Western Journal of Communication, 65,* 2, 113–137.

33. Payne & Richmond, *A bibliography,* pp. 297–294.

34. Ayers, J., et al, (1998). Communication apprehension and employment interviews. *Communication Education, 47,* 1, 1–17.

35. For a review of the research that examines the impact of communication apprehension on job satisfaction and other work-related variables, see: Richmond, V. P. (1984). Implications of quietness: Some facts and speculations. In Daly & McCroskey, *Avoiding communication,* pp. 153–155.

36. Bippus, A. M., & Daly, J. A. (1999). What do people think causes stage fright? Naive attributions about the reasons for public speaking anxiety, *Communication Education, 48,* 1, 63–72.

37. McCroskey, J. C. (1972). The implementation of a large-scale program of systematic desensitization for communication apprehension. *Speech teacher, 21,* 255–264.

38. Fremouw, W. J. (1984). Cognitive-behavioral therapies for modification of communication apprehension. In Daly & McCroskey, *Avoiding communication,* p. 210. For a more detailed description of the steps involved in cognitive restructuring, see: Fremouw, W. J., & Scott, M. D. (1979). Cognitive restructuring: An alternative method for the treatment of communication apprehension. *Communication Education, 28,* 129–133.

39. See, for example: Messman, S. J. & Jones-Corley, J. (2001). Effects of communication environment, immediacy, and communication apprehension on cognitive and affective learn-ing. *Communication Monographs, 68,* 2, 184–200.

40. Phillips, G. M. (1977). Rhetoritherapy versus the medical model: Dealing with reticence. *Communication Education, 26,* 34–43; see also the review by: Kelly, L. (1984). Social skills training as a mode of treatment for social communication problems. In Daly & McCroskey, *Avoiding communication,* pp.189–207.

41. Kelly, Social skills, pp. 201–205.

42. For analyses comparing the effectiveness of the three methods in treating public speaking anxiety, see: Bourhis, Allen, & Bauman (2006); Allen, Hunter, & Donahue, Meta-analysis on public speaking anxiety treatment.

Influencing Others

Tyler Clementi, a freshman at Rutgers University, was having sex with his lover while his roommate secretly watched by web cam from next door. Shortly thereafter, his roommate Dharum Ravi was arrested, facing 10 years in prison for bias intimidation and invasion of privacy.

Weigh in: What do you think? What do you suppose motivated Ravi to do this? Was this really a criminal act or just a college prank?

Now what if the prosecuting attorney told you that Clementi's lover was an older man?

Weigh in: How might this additional information change your mind? Would you find Ravi guilty of a hate crime? Do you think Ravi was homophobic? How would you know?

Now what if you learned that shortly after Clementi discovered the web peeping, he committed suicide by jumping off the George Washington Bridge?

Weigh in: Would you find Ravi guilty now? Would you increase the severity of his punishment?

What if the defense team called to the stand 10 different college students and friends of the family— all of whom denied ever hearing Ravi make any derogatory comments about gays? And what if Ravi himself testified that what he did was childish, immature, and irresponsible—but not hateful?

Weigh in: Now what do you think?

The jury convicted Ravi, but the sentence was reduced to 30 days in jail, three years probation, 300 hours of community service, counseling, and a $10,000 fine.

Check out these two web links for the full story:

http://www.nydailynews.com/news/crime/spying-tyler-clementi-roommate-texted-pal-gays-article-1.1033292

http://abcnews.go.com/US/rutgers-trial-dharun-ravi-sentenced-30-days-jail/story?id=16394014

Few of us will have to persuade a jury that a defendant is innocent or guilty of a serious crime. Yet, the process of getting other people to accept our ideas and conclusions, or get them to reach decisions and take actions that we desire is something central to all of our lives. Obviously, it is very important to understand this kind of communication. Sometimes we are like a lawyer, trying to influence others whose decisions are important to us. At other times, we are like members of the jury, being bombarded by claims and counterclaims as we try to sort out the truth. In both cases, whether we like it or not, we are participants in the process of *persuasion*.

This chapter examines that process—influencing others using various strategies of communication. How does influence take place? What are the various kinds of messages that can be used to modify how people think, feel, or act? What are some of the barriers encountered in persuading others to change? And what strategies do people use to resist influence attempts?

The Importance of Persuasion in Everyday Life

One of the most frequent tasks we face daily is to try to influence people's ideas, feelings, or actions. In addition, we constantly receive other peoples' messages aimed at modifying our thinking or conduct. Almost from the time we get up in the morning until we retire at night, people, groups, and agencies try to get us to attend to messages urging us to buy some commercial product, favor a particular political candidate, support a cause, modify our health practices, donate to a charity, or change some other way that we think and act. Such efforts impinge on us from the worlds of advertising, politics, education, religion, and health care, to mention only a few sources.

In other words, persuasion is one of the most ubiquitous communication processes in modern life—so pervasive, in fact, that people have to develop "mental calluses"—to learn how to ignore and resist most such efforts. But some forms of such communication are beneficial. Persuasion for a variety of purposes is so critical to many of our social institutions that we could not continue our contemporary way of life without it. Politicians use it in their campaigns for reelection and to establish support for legislative policies. Persuasion also plays a key role in religion, education, and public health. We encounter persuasive messages every time we view TV, listen to the radio, surf the Internet, read a newspaper, or glance through a magazine. In almost every face-to-face encounter, people initiate communication for the purpose of modifying the beliefs, attitudes, or behavior of someone else, including a friend, neighbor, boss, professor, or family member.

Person-to-Person Persuasion

The persuasion that occurs in everyday social interaction is a complex communication process. In a single day, we might need to coax a friend into loaning us a few dollars, convince our parents that they should not be concerned with our low grade in chemistry, talk our way out of a speeding ticket, and persuade an instructor to let us into a closed class. At first glance, the goals involved in these influence attempts, and the persuasive communication process required to achieve them, all seem quite different. On closer analysis, it becomes clear that they all have a great deal in common.

To look more closely at person-to-person persuasion, let's examine a situation in which an individual constructs and presents messages to another person in an attempt to achieve influence, and in which the second party responds by changing views, feelings, or actions.

Tony was upset with the D he got on his history test. He knew that he didn't do well on essay exams. However, he felt that his answer to the question about the factors that brought about World War I contained all the major points. He decided to make an appointment to try to persuade Professor Cheng to change his grade to a C. He knew he could be pretty convincing and felt it was worth a try.

Tony appeared at Professor Cheng's office at the appointed time. He was dressed neatly and had rehearsed all the points and arguments he was going to use to present his case. He felt he had a good chance. When she smiled and invited him to sit down and explain what he had in mind, his spirits rose.

He began his presentation by claiming that she really had not read his answer to the one question carefully enough. (He knew this was a form of aggression but thought it would place him in a strong position and her on the defensive.) Then, to soften the attack, Tony outlined how really interested he was in the subject matter of her course and how much he enjoyed her lectures. (This, he knew, was flattery, but he thought most people liked it.) He then explained with great sincerity how hard he had studied for the examination. (This, he believed, would arouse her sympathy.) Tony concluded by explaining to Professor Cheng how badly he needed the grade. He pointed out that, because of personal problems he had earlier, his overall GPA was quite low and that he was working hard to raise it. If she did not give him a C for the course, he might have to leave school. (This, Tony felt, would make her feel guilty.)

Professor Cheng listened carefully and then went over his written answer to the test question. She asked him to show her how he had addressed each of the major issues. She also asked a few questions, all of which were about the specific content of his answers. Then, for a time, she just sat there, looking at him a little strangely and drumming her fingers on her desk. Tony felt a growing fear that his effort to persuade her had bombed. But then, to his surprise, she said, "Well, Tony, I see that you really did include all five of the major points in your answer. I think that you have a good case, and I will give you an additional five points on your grade for the examination."

Tony could hardly contain himself; he left her office grinning. "It worked," he said to himself. "She really is a sucker for a sob story. I laid on aggression, flattery, sympathy, and guilt and got her to change the grade. Wow, what a tear-jerker! I should have gotten an Academy Award."

As Tony was leaving, Professor Cheng thought, "What a con artist! He thought I would fall for his baloney about his burning interest in the course and how much he enjoys my lectures. His heart-wrenching story about how hard he had studied and how he might have to leave school was too much. I really had to try not to laugh." Professor Cheng smiled to herself and thought, "In spite of all his B.S., the fact is that his answer really was more complete than I first thought, and it did merit an additional five points."

Did persuasion take place? Clearly, the grade was changed, and Tony's effort was successful in that sense. Yet, somehow it doesn't seem that Tony's messages really *caused* Professor Cheng to comply with his goal. There are, in fact, two different interpretations of what actually happened during the encounter: One is that Tony's cleverly constructed appeals based on interest, admiration, hard work, and deep need swayed Professor Cheng to comply. The other is that she was unmoved by Tony's appeals and that she had actually persuaded herself to make the change because of the factual content of his test answer. Which of these interpretations is correct *depends on how one defines persuasion*. In fact, the major lesson to be derived from the little drama is that there are two ways to go in formulating a definition. Persuasion can be viewed either as a one-way, that is linear, process or as an interactive exchange between the parties.

Linear versus Transactional Views of Persuasion

Earlier in this century, when research on the process first started, persuasion was something that one person "did to" another. Later, researchers began to realize that every person brings to every act of communication (whether persuasive or not) all the personal attributes that were described in previous chapters. They saw that these attributes play a critical part in forming the meanings people construct in response to an incoming message. These two views of the persuasion process are obviously very different: One is a linear "magic bullet" interpretation, whereas the other is consistent with the simultaneous transactions model.

Persuasion as "magic bullets." In this view, the message transmitted by the sender in the persuasion process is seen as "aimed at" the person selected as the "target." The components of the message are designed as persuasive verbal projectiles—striking the receiver and having an effect. That is, a source organizes a message with clever words, arguments, and appeals, then aims these at the person to be persuaded. Once the bullets arrive, the receiver undergoes the alterations desired by the source. Thus, the message organization and appeals are what cause a change of belief, attitude, or behavior. In this perspective, the change of grade made by Professor Cheng would be seen as a direct result of Tony's clever transmission of messages with meanings of aggression, flattery, sympathy, and guilt.

Persuasion as transactional communication. A second interpretation of the way in which persuasion works is based on the other view of what happened between Tony and Professor

An older method of persuasion used simple messages that worked like "magic bullets." This poster, from World War I, was thought to be very effective in persuading young men and women to volunteer for military service. Would it have convinced you?

Cheng. That is, he presented his messages, including all his carefully constructed appeals and arguments, and she listened carefully to what he was saying. However, in the end, she herself decided to make the change that Tony desired. She did not do so because of his clever magic bullets but because of her own decisions about the meaning of the situation and the response she should give.

This interpretation of persuasion indicates that the receiver of the message plays as active a part in achieving whatever changes take place as does the source or sender. It requires that persuasion be defined as a *transaction* that occurs between two parties, rather than simply as a one-way action of one individual firing verbal bullets at another.

Most communication scholars now subscribe to this transactional view of the persuasion process. Because of the importance of persuasion, and the power inherent in the ability to influence others, researchers continue to search for understanding as to how the process takes place. Every aspect or factor in the process has been considered, even such things as the nasality of a voice and how it affects persuasion.[1] Other studies have investigated the "third-person" effect, or the degree to which an individual believes that he or she is less susceptible to persuasive communications than other people.[2] However, the heaviest emphasis in the search remains on the so-called tools of persuasion—just the right kinds of symbols, images, and combinations of words that can arouse emotions, shape beliefs, sway attitudes, and change actions as the receivers of the message play their part in the transaction.

The fact is, this kind of persuasion can work! Messages have been designed to which people have responded with great enthusiasm. This persuasion strategy has led large numbers of people at various times to buy things, vote for people, or take other actions that someone has wanted.[3] Sometimes, however, the strategy fails, and when it does no one is quite sure why. Nevertheless, given the potential power at stake, it is little wonder the search for the "magic bullets" that will work—the effective appeals, message organizations, and other persuasive tactics continues with great enthusiasm.

A Formal Definition of Persuasion

In bringing these many ideas together, persuasion can be defined in a way that is entirely consistent with the two models of human communication; that is, although linear processes are involved, both parties engage in simultaneous transactions and play active parts.

What makes persuasion distinct from other communication transactions is that change takes place in the person interpreting the message. That change may be precisely what the originator of the message intended, or it may

not, depending on the way the interpretation is constructed. However, if the desired change is in fact achieved, **persuasion** can be defined as *a communicative transaction in which a source constructs and transmits messages designed to influence a receiver's constructions of meanings in ways that will lead to change (desired by the source) in the receiver's beliefs, attitudes, or behavior*. If the attempt fails, the message is then just another piece of the vast communication clutter all of us experience every day.

As this definition implies, messages from a source can be very important, even though persuasion is a transactional process. A sender's messages can bring facts, arouse feelings, and present logical arguments that lead receivers to form new conclusions. Sometimes they do not, and even if they do, they may not do so in ways intended by the sender. However, if no transaction takes place, no change will occur. In the example of Tony and Professor Cheng, a transaction did take place that resulted in a change. Without a visit from Tony, she never would have awarded him additional points. Even though his linear-type message structure and appeals fell flat, she did review the situation and raise his grade, and in that limited sense it was a consequence of the transaction.

Alternative Methods for Achieving Influence

It is not difficult to understand why people try to persuade others: They want them to comply with or conform to some desired change that is the objective of the persuasive attempt. Achieving compliance or conformity means getting someone to hold certain beliefs, have particular feelings, or engage in specific actions that seem desirable to the person originating the message. By looking at several important kinds of situations, it is possible to see how people modify their ideas, feelings, or actual behavior as a result of persuasive communication. (Box 11.1 overviews reasons for people's compliance with persuasion.)

BOX 11.1

Why People Comply with Persuasive Messages

- People comply because a coercive message forces compliance.
- People comply because group expectations influence compliance.
- People comply because a persuasive message changes the way people think.

Coercion

The term **coercion** refers to compelling others to do something, or restraining them from action, by threatening them with undesirable consequences. Many kinds of goals are pursued by using the threat of force and bodily harm to alter behavior. At one extreme is the threatening statement of the mugger, who, with knife at throat, simply says, "Give me what I want or I will kill you!" That message, of course, can be very persuasive! In fact, this type of persuasion fits the magic bullet definition very well. The statements of the sending person directly and immediately cause the receiver to behave in the manner demanded.

At the same time, coercive messages that threaten force or bodily harm to modify another's behavior do not really fit with most people's idea of persuasion. The process implies a much more subtle communication in which the individual is led to make changes by some kind of clever message. For that reason, no further discussion is included regarding physical coercion as a form of persuasion by which one person controls another's behavior.

Social Expectations

The organizing factors of all kinds of human social behavior (including communication) in group settings are the kinds of shared rules referred to in Chapter 8 as norms, roles, ranks, and controls. These general concepts are the heart of the sociocultural persuasion that is based on clarifying **social expectations.** (Simply put, group members are expected to follow the rules.) The key here is that persuasive messages can define the kind of behavior that is permitted and expected, or discouraged and even punished, by members of a group. Such messages can be very effective in getting people to conform. This social expectations approach to persuasion is widely used in our multicultural society for the purpose of getting people from all backgrounds to behave according to some set of social rules.

Of particular importance is that such sociocultural persuasion can be an effective strategy in getting people to change their behavior in relatively difficult ways. People value their memberships in groups and want to be accepted by others. For this reason, the compelling nature of social expectations can sometimes bring about changes in people's behavior that probably would not occur as a result of lectures, pleas, appeals, or other conventional persuasive strategies. For example, people who urgently feel the need to lose weight often go to commercial groups that specialize in persuading people to drop pounds. Part of their process is to get such individuals on a weight-reduction diet and perhaps into some form of exercise. The task of convincing them to follow such rules is a classic exercise in sociocultural persuasion. It works something like the following:

> Lois has been seriously overweight for a number of years. She hates being fat and has tried many kinds of exercises and diets. Most importantly, she understands that being overweight can have serious consequences for her health. Numerous people have lectured her about her weight and have tried to get her to reduce. Over the years she lost a few pounds from time to time, but they always seemed to come back. As something of a last resort, Lois decided to go to Pounds Ltd., an organization specializing in helping people with weight reduction. She listened to their sales pitch, read their literature, and with the tantalizing vision of a slim figure to come, she paid her

(rather substantial) fee. She started preparing her meals according to the plan and ate them without cheating, even though at first they left her hungry and unsatisfied.

A few days later, at her first Pounds Ltd. group meeting, Lois had to get on a scale and be weighed by one of the counselors. She was embarrassed when the trim young counselor said that she tipped the scales at 183 pounds. She was told that her weight would be recorded again next week. Then the counselors and clients held a group discussion of different problems people were having in managing their eating. As part of the meeting, each person's weight was revealed to the others. For each participant, a history of where they had started was summarized along with details about their present weight. Those who were success stories were vigorously applauded. Even those who were still new to the program but who had lost a pound or two were given a round of applause. Those who had gained were given encouragement and sympathy—along with looks of pity, she thought.

In the weeks that followed, Lois had mixed feelings about the program. She did meet some nice people who were struggling with her same problems. She also admired those who had been fat and were now trim. It gave her hope. However, it was humiliating to have her weight revealed publicly. Most of all, she was in constant fear that she would not lose weight during the week and that she would be the object of pity when her weekly weigh-in was announced.

As the weeks turned to months, however, Lois did lose weight. Within four weeks she was down to 170; in six months she weighed 150. She stayed with the program and finally broke the 130 mark in 16 months. She began to feel better and be asked out on dates. She had become accustomed to the smaller meals and felt that she soon would get down to a normal weight for her height. Perhaps the most helpful thing about the program was the people she had met and their joint determination to get rid of their excess pounds.

What are the factors of persuasion here? Clearly, losing a lot of weight is a difficult goal and a long-range process. Equally clearly, motivating a person to do that takes far more than persuasive pep talks or lecturing by those in charge of the program. One key factor in this situation is the negative evaluation (norm) existing in society concerning being fat. That shared belief in its negative assessment was most significant in getting Lois into Pounds Ltd. in the first place. Once she was participating, however, the functioning of the group itself played a central part in persuading her to continue. One factor was the *norm* constantly apparent within the group— defining weight loss as beneficial and approved, and weight gain as harmful and deviant.

In addition, messages concerning *role definitions* within the group centered on personal responsibility for adherence to the diet and on continued weight reduction. When this role is played according to expectation, the applause received from the others is a well-appreciated social reward—a form of *social control*. Another social control is that failing to lose, or gaining on the weekly weight report, results in a significant negative sanction. Those who have achieved substantial weight loss are *ranked* much higher in prestige within the group than those who have yet to do so. They receive messages of deference and are envied for their accomplishment. Along with all these factors, there is the additional reward of forming friendships with others who are trying to cope with a similar problem.

Thus, the process of sociocultural persuasion based on social expectations is far more than simply a sender formulating a persuasive message and a receiver constructing some kind of meaning that will influence action. It is a complex process in which norms, roles, ranks, and social controls all play a part in defining what is acceptable versus what is deviant behavior.

Cognitive Reorganization

The commonsense view of how behavior is determined and how it can be changed goes something like this: We all have a mental organization of understandings, attitudes, feelings,

How does the use of language in this ad reconstruct what smoking means to you?

beliefs, and preferences. This cognitive organization is what guides our decisions about acting. In other words, it is commonly assumed that mind controls action. From this assumption it follows that if mental organization (feelings, attitudes, and beliefs) can be changed—by gaining the attention of receivers to persuasive messages—then overt behavior will correspondingly be changed.

Although that is not a bad way of thinking about certain kinds of persuasion, the language is old-fashioned. Today these "mental" phenomena are discussed with greater precision in terms of *cognitive functioning*. This term broadly refers to what used to be called thinking, interpreting, and knowing. The related term, *cognitive organization*, refers to the structure or patterning of one's beliefs, attitudes, and values, as they exist "in our heads," so to speak. A third

term, *cognitive processing*, refers to the way we perceive, interpret, remember, and recall some event, message, or situation as we observe it.

Cognitive organization (or structure) is important in discussing persuasion because many communication scholars assume that persuasive messages can alter the components of that organization. They believe that carefully designed messages can change the way people think, believe, or feel about a topic. They assume that if such changes are achieved, they will alter the way they act toward the object of the communication. This has also long been an assumption made by advertisers.[4] Stated simply, this approach, which can be called the **psychodynamic strategy**, rests on the assumption that the route to achieving behavioral change lies in achieving **cognitive reorganization**. Sometimes it works, but sometimes it does not.

Constructing or reconstructing meanings. One important way in which cognitive organization can be influenced is by providing people with meanings for objects, situations, and events that they have to interpret and to which they must react or respond. This is most easily accomplished when the phenomena are unfamiliar. Through the clever use of symbols, message senders can sometimes get receivers to accept their desired meanings. Then, when those same receivers are called on to act toward whatever is at stake, those meanings can have an influence in determining what they will do.

Just how cleverly people can influence the meanings of others can be illustrated by referencing an important historical event that took place back in 1989. It was a year of political turmoil and upheaval all over the world, but some of the most remarkable episodes were the massive demonstrations that occurred in the People's Republic of China as many thousands of people congregated and demonstrated in Tiananmen Square in Beijing.

Those demonstrations were protests over corruption and misconduct by officials in the Chinese government. The students who led the protests were demanding certain reforms of the existing system. They were certainly not advocating that the existing Chinese government based on communism be replaced by democratic institutions, modeled by the United States. At the same time, those student leaders urgently wanted international attention focused on their cause—particularly U.S. attention. They were afraid (with ample justification) that without this scrutiny from abroad the Chinese leadership would put down their demonstrations with military force, which has long been a traditional Chinese solution.

What did they do? Because leaders among the Chinese students understood very well the cognitive organization of the average U.S. citizen, they supplied the American public with a substantial number of televised symbols and images. They wanted to make sure that what the Americans saw on their TV sets would be completely familiar and acceptable. What they did was use a meaning-construction strategy designed to attract and hold the attention of Americans and to gain their sympathetic support.

To understand the strategy they used more fully, it must be kept in mind that the entire upheaval was, as previously indicated, a *Chinese* event. Its causes and solutions were firmly rooted in the problems and the system of that country. However, by carefully selecting and presenting symbols that had *powerful connotative meanings* for Americans, they were able to redefine it into terms that had special significance for the people of the United States.

How did they do this? They accomplished this goal by focusing on slogans, sayings, expressions, and symbols that are at the heart of American democratic values. Then they made sure these were presented to the American public by television, newspapers, and magazines that were trying to show what was going on in Beijing. For example, many signs and banners with slogans in English were paraded before television cameras, who obligingly focused on them. These placards and banners displayed messages with which Americans are deeply familiar—such as "Give me liberty or give me death!"—which is not exactly an ancient Chinese saying. Students were shown reciting the Declaration of Independence, or talking about the importance of "freedom of the press," along with other American favorites. A big statue was built—called the Goddess of Democracy. It was carefully modeled after the Statue of Liberty and it was conveniently located where the television cameras couldn't miss it. Thus, a barrage of Fourth of July Americanisms were used to give the events in Tiananmen Square a special connotative meaning for Americans who tuned in.

The fact is that those American icons have little meaning for the average Chinese citizen. Indeed, the vast majority neither understand English nor know anything about the history of the American Revolution. Few would recognize the Declaration of Independence if they heard it in their own language. These *Americana* had little to do with the cause of eliminating corruption in the Chinese government or the proposed reforms in the communist system—the issues that actually brought on the demonstrations in the first place.[5]

Although the demonstrations in Beijing ended in tragedy, crushed by the Chinese military, the purpose in using this example is not intended to be a criticism of either the demonstrations or the Chinese students involved. It was a very clever thing to do, and it clearly accomplished its objectives. Americans were genuinely sympathetic with those who led the protests and were deeply disturbed when they were put down by the Chinese authorities with a great deal of bloodshed. The purpose in citing the events at Tiananmen Square is simply that it provides a clear example of the meaning-construction strategy for redefining an event in terms that can be understood and approved by those to whom the messages were directed.

These same strategies of meaning construction and redefinition can be very effective at any level of communication and within and across different cultural groups. Watching YouTube videos can show how something like a car can be given new meanings of glamor, power, and sexiness by persuasive advertising. Observation of the tactics of an effective trial lawyer can show how a body of factual evidence can be given new meanings by questioning selectively, raising doubts, suggesting alternative interpretations, and so on. This is not to imply here that this strategy is based on untruths or deception. Rather, it is a process of establishing, extending, substituting, and stabilizing *meanings* that are associated with particular words, concepts, events, or situations.[6] (Box 11.2 reviews the process of cognitive reorganization.)

Shaping or altering beliefs. One of the most important parts of our cognitive structure (the way things are organized in our heads) are our beliefs. The term **beliefs** is so fundamental that it is not easily defined. In terms of the present discussion, a belief is a kind of statement of truth that an individual accepts about some object, situation, or event.

The Process of Cognitive Reorganization

- Establish new meanings for particular objects, situations, and events.
- Extend old meanings for particular objects, situations, and events.
- Substitute new meanings for currently held meanings.
- Stabilize (or reinforce) currently held meanings.

Each of us has thousands of such truth statements in memory, such as "the world is round," "the sun rises in the east," and "water runs downhill." But, for many objects or situations we have no statements. One strategy that is widely used in persuasion is to provide people with *preshaped* beliefs about events, issues, or situations where they have not yet formed any. Or, if they have, the strategy focuses on *modifying* the beliefs they already have but hold only slightly.

Some beliefs are simply factual—like the three examples listed above. They do not involve any kind of judgment (positive or negative) or imply any kind of emotional orientation on the part of the person holding the belief. Other beliefs have an evaluative or emotional quality that implies such feelings as like, dislike, acceptance, rejection, approval, or disapproval. For example, it is one thing to believe that San Francisco is a *large* city. It is and that is factually correct. Such a statement of truth about San Francisco implies no evaluative judgment. However, it is quite another thing to believe that San Francisco is a *beautiful* city. This kind of belief does have an affective component. It is a statement of truth, to be sure, at least for the person holding the belief. More important, it reveals a positive affective orientation toward that particular city.

The psychodynamic strategy of shaping or altering beliefs focuses mainly on affective truth

Most people have a positive attitude toward voting. Why, then, are voter turnout rates so low?

Walter Lippman stated the principle in a much simpler way: The "pictures in our heads," he said, guide our actions toward things in "the world outside."[8]

That principle—that beliefs guide action—is amply illustrated thousands of times every day. People regularly punish others whom they believe to have violated the acceptable norms. Fistfights break out when one individual believes that another has insulted or ridiculed him, even if that was not the other's intent. Even more serious, every year some police officer regularly shoots an innocent person when he or she believes that the individual is going for a gun. In each of these cases, reality is not the basis of action; it is their *beliefs about reality.*

This link between beliefs and behavior provides the foundation for one of the most important assumptions underlying the entire field of persuasive communication: It is assumed that *persuasive messages can be designed to alter people's beliefs*—factual or affective—at least under some circumstances. If the messages do indeed achieve that objective, and people do modify their beliefs, then it follows that their actions may also change.

Does such a persuasion strategy work? The answer is a hesitant yes, but only sometimes. Successful persuasion can often be an indirect, cumulative process that occurs over a long period of time. It seldom works dramatically in a quick and immediate sense (like a magic bullet). Traditionally, in the social sciences, changing people's beliefs has been seen as a *learning process.*[9] Thus, belief changes have been brought about by lectures and exposure to training films, by group discussions, by asking people to read different kinds of materials, by having them listen to presentations, or by viewing material on video. Through any of these forms of communication, beliefs can be changed, but not easily.

Creating or modifying attitudes.   Most research on persuasion has focused not on factual beliefs, but on affective or emotional beliefs that are called **attitudes.** The term *attitude* is very old, and it predates all the social sciences.

statements because they are closely linked to the kinds of actions often sought in persuasion—that is, accepting or rejecting something or acting positively or negatively toward it in some other way. Note that people who hold beliefs rarely make the distinction between factual and affective beliefs in their own minds. Believing that San Francisco is beautiful becomes as valid and compelling to them as the more objectively verifiable fact that the city is large.

The reason that altering beliefs is so often sought as a goal of psychodynamic persuasion is that beliefs—both factual and affective—guide our actions. More than 2,000 years ago, Plato, in his "Allegory of the Cave," showed that if people believe a situation to be real, they will act as though it is real.[7] In the 1920s,

It was adopted about a century ago by the social sciences from previous meanings. The word came into the English language during the early 1700s. Originally, it derived from the Latin words *aptitudinem* and *aptus*. When it became a part of both French and Italian during the 15th century, it was as an important term in the world of art and design meaning the *physical positioning* of an object in space. In England, in the 1830s, it became associated with the positioning of the mind. However, it did not become an important concept in the behavioral sciences until 1918, when it was used in its present form by W. I. Thomas and Florian Znaniecki to denote a person's affective or emotional beliefs about an object that bring about particular forms of action toward that same object.[10]

Today, the term *attitude* is perhaps the most widely used concept in the social sciences, and it has been studied in research for nearly a century. Unfortunately, during that long period it has been defined in dozens of different ways, providing many different interpretations of the term's meaning.[11] However, these controversies can be avoided by dealing with it in a way that is completely consistent with the previous discussion of beliefs and their relationship to behavior.

First, reject the notion that an attitude is some mysterious force that lies latent in your psyche and that becomes activated only when forming intentions to act. That is too complicated. A much simpler approach is to view attitudes as an extension of what has already been analyzed in the way of *beliefs*. That is, an attitude can be thought of as a package or configuration of beliefs of an evaluative or affective nature that a person has about some "object."

An attitude may be held about many kinds of "objects." An example would be a particular category of people. These evaluative beliefs about that object will be related to one another. For example, Nancy believes that politicians are undesirable; she probably will also think that they are unethical, insensitive, and immoral. Alternatively, if Nancy believes that medical doctors are competent, she probably also finds them smart, skillful, hard-working, and trustworthy. Thus, Nancy has an interrelated set of affective beliefs about these two attitude objects. When confronted with individual members of that category of people, either directly or indirectly, Nancy uses those affective beliefs to shape her thoughts or actions toward them.

How closely do people's actions match their beliefs? If one has a negative attitude toward some category of people, will that person act unfavorably toward the individuals in the category? The answer is "not always." Common sense tells us that our behavior seldom takes place in a social vacuum. Whatever or whoever is present in a situation can influence our behavior, regardless of our inner feelings. For example, we may feel negatively toward dogs; but if we are among friends who own and love dogs, we may refrain from saying or doing anything that we know they would resent. Thus, although our negative attitude can increase the probability (the chances) that we will act negatively toward the object, various factors in our immediate situation can greatly reduce that probability.

In the previous section, careful attention was given to the meaning of the term *belief* because it is so central to the meaning of attitude. Affective beliefs, as explained, are "truths" that people embrace—implying such feelings as good/bad, like/dislike, acceptance/avoidance, and approval/disapproval.

The attitude object (that we think about, evaluate, and respond to) can be almost anything. However, it is usually thought of as *general* rather than specific. That is, it is a broad topic or issue, as opposed to a narrowly focused concern. Examples are categories of people (like those who are addicted to drugs or those who litter beaches), policies (capital punishment or disarmament), practices (abortion or child abuse), or issues (animal rights or welfare reform). Social scientists do not normally use the term *attitude* for people's affective beliefs about very specific objects (like left-handed saxophone players who have blue eyes, or brown dogs with long ears).

Two additional features of an attitude must be a part of a formal definition. One of them is that attitudes are presumed to be a *relatively enduring* (long-lasting) part of a person's cognitive structure. Many are learned early in life, and they remain as a permanent part of the individual's psychological makeup. What this implies, of course, is that they are not easy to change. The second feature of attitudes is the assumption that they play a significant part in *shaping or determining actions* toward whatever is the object. This follows logically from the widely accepted principle that was set forth earlier—that beliefs shape actions. That is, if attitudes are interrelated organizations of beliefs, they should also provide a basis for influencing the ways we act—in a manner consistent with those beliefs. With these features in mind, *attitude* can be defined in a more formal way as *a relatively enduring organization of affective beliefs about some broad object (such as a policy, social category of people, or situation) that increases the probability that an individual will respond to that object in a manner consistent with those beliefs.*[12]

Where do attitudes come from? They are learned. Like beliefs of any kind, our attitudes are developed through experience. From the experiences we have with objects, people, and situations, we acquire complex patterns of interrelated affective beliefs that define our liking or disliking of those things. For example, we can develop a negative attitude toward the elderly by having a number of negative experiences with older people. These can then influence our behavior toward senior citizens.

As was suggested, when people talk about influencing others by using persuasive communication, they are typically talking about changing attitudes. It seems self-evident to many people that if a person's attitude toward a particular topic or object is changed, then corresponding changes in behavior will also take place. Not so fast!

The relationship between attitudes and behavior. Research on the relationship between attitudes and behaviors has been extensive.[13] For decades, researchers have continued to probe the question of whether or not attitudes are related to behavior.[14] They generally agree that in most real-life situations, attitudes fail to directly predict what people actually do.[15]

Why, then, does such strong interest in this particular psychodynamic strategy continue? The answer is that the relationship between attitudes and behavior is not yet fully understood, and it is far too early to dismiss changing attitudes as a means of bringing about changes in behavior. A far better alternative is to ask what are the conditions under which attitudes and behavior are related, and what factors reduce or enhance this relationship? Social scientists first faced the reality of inconsistencies between attitudes and behaviors in the 1930s when an early study challenged the assumption of a direct relationship.[16] Prior to that a direct relationship was almost universally assumed.[17] However, investigations of the degree of correspondence between attitudes and behavior have shown that any number of situations can have an influence on that relationship. That is, if some factors are present, the link between attitudes and behavior may be strong indeed. If other factors are in the situation, the relationship may be weak or even nonexistent. The probability of acting in accord with one's attitude depends on the presence or absence of several limiting and facilitating factors.

There are three considerations that must be understood about the relationship between attitudes toward a topic and the probability of consistent behavior toward that same topic. Each must be considered in any communication strategy designed to change people's attitudes and subsequent behaviors. These three considerations are topic importance, social pressures, and action constraints.[18] (See Box 11.3.)

One reason that attitude change may not necessarily lead directly to corresponding behavior change is that the topic may not be sufficiently important to the person. Some topics for which we hold attitudes simply have very little influence on what we actually do. If a topic is not of much importance to us, our attitude

BOX 11.3 🔍 *A Closer Look*

Three Issues in the Relationship between Attitudes and Actions

1. The more important a topic is to people and the more it has consequences for them, the more likely the attitude toward the topic will influence subsequent action.
2. The more pervasive the social pressures are in a given situation, the more likely people will conform to those pressures. In highly public situations in which pressures prevail, and unless the action in question is already consistent with the attitude toward that action, people are likely to conform to the social pressures of the situation rather than behave in accordance with the attitude.
3. The more people face nonsocial constraints—inconvenience of the act, potential financial loss, physical difficulty of the act, lack of opportunity to act, or lack of competence to engage in the act—the less likely that behavior will occur.

toward it is not likely to be strongly held. In other words, it is relatively easy for someone to get us to change our attitudes toward topics that have no real consequences in our lives. Such topics could include political issues like programs for farm parity supports, campaign finance reform, or federal regulation regarding tariffs. Typically, young adults do not hold deeply entrenched views about such issues, and they seldom resist changing attitudes toward them. Furthermore, whatever their attitudes on such topics, they may have no relationship to their behavior if ever confronted with a need to act in some relevant way.

On the other hand, a variety of topics can be truly significant and consequential for a person. It is unlikely that behavior toward them will be easily changed by exposure to a few persuasive messages. For example, people are often deeply committed to their positions on such matters as

abortion, organic foods, capital punishment, using animals in experiments, and smoking.

For many people, the beliefs they hold about such topics are deeply entrenched. If this is the case, both their attitudes and behavior toward such topics are very difficult to change by any means. People work out their configuration of affective beliefs about such matters after long experience, and those patterns of convictions remain very durable. Having a firm attitudinal position on a controversial issue makes life easier. This is because decisions concerning the topic are uncomplicated. When such topics come up, people can simply respond with behavior consistent with their strongly held attitudes. There is no need to work it all out over and over again, with endless considerations of new facts and new appeals for change. In that sense, then, an entrenched and well-defined attitude toward a personally significant topic is efficient in providing immediate guidelines for action.

Another critical factor in shaping our overt and visible behavior is the pattern of **social pressures** we encounter in the situation of action. These are our needs and desires to comply with social rules for behavior that are expected by others whose approval we seek. What we say and what we do are usually observable by other people. The context of our actions then almost always includes rules for social behavior. (Remember how that worked in the example about overweight Lois and Pounds Ltd.) Thus, while attitudes are invisible inside our heads, overt behavior is visible and subject to scrutiny by others. This poses a set of social pressures on us that can cause attitudes and behavior toward the same topic to be very different (inconsistent).

Generally, then, the relationship between attitudes and behavior is unpredictable if that action takes place in a group context. If we know that the people in that context hold the same attitude and expect corresponding behavior, then there probably will be a close relationship. However, if people whose opinions we value would be appalled by our behavior if it were consistent with our privately held (but contrary) attitude, then it is entirely unlikely that the two will correspond.

Suppose that Jim, for example, a college senior, came from a conservative business-owning family who share a longstanding anti-union tradition. As a result of family discussions at home, Jim has held anti-union attitudes since childhood. Sandra, Jim's girlfriend, comes from a family of card-carrying union members. Jim is really taken with Sandra, and he wants to make sure that her family likes him. One day Sandra's father invites Jim to accompany him to a union meeting. What will happen? One scenario would be that Jim's attitude would guide his behavior and he would decline. Another would be that social pressures would prevail; Jim would accept the invitation, Sandra would be pleased, and he would avoid a strained relationship with her parents. In other words, it would be difficult to predict whether his attitude and behavior would be consistent.

Each of us faces a diversity of such social pressures daily. They come from social expectations at work, at school, in family relationships, and so on. Regardless of our feelings, we may or may not act in accordance with our attitudes. The importance of the topic may carry the day, but social pressures in the context of action can have a strong influence on our behavior.

Many **nonsocial constraints** can also influence our actions. That is, there can be occasions when people are inclined to act in accordance with their attitudes, and there are no social pressures to inhibit such behavior, but their actions do not correspond with their attitudes. One simple reason is that a number of physical and personal difficulties interfere with the action. They may be too busy or too lazy. Or, the act may be inconvenient, perhaps requiring traveling a long distance to perform it. The behavior may involve potential financial loss. There may be risks or unwanted trade-offs. The act may be physically difficult to perform. There may be no real opportunity, or the person may lack competence to engage in the behavior. Action constraints of this type can sharply reduce the consistency between attitude and action.

Understanding Resistance and Yielding

Attempts to change our beliefs, our attitudes, or our actions are everywhere. We live in a society in which we are constantly the targets of an almost unlimited number of message sources who seek to control our behavior in some way. Think about it. Every day we face an army of persuaders who are determined to alter our lives. They include public health officials encouraging individuals to stop smoking, get more exercise, eat more nutritious foods, and adopt a healthy lifestyle. The persuaders also include advertisers seeking to change the products we buy, politicians trying to shape our voting intentions, charities soliciting contributions to worthy causes, professors trying to improve our minds, and religious leaders wanting to shape the ways we believe about and relate to the supernatural. It would be totally impossible to comply to everything they want us to believe or do. We absolutely must develop personal strategies that enable us to *resist change*.

Resistance as Reaction to Persuasion Attempts

How do we go about resisting change? In spite of the importance of the topic, published research focusing directly on resistance to change is limited. Furthermore, the information that is available explaining people's universal tendency to resist change is only indirectly related to the issue of persuasion. One particular perspective, however, is Jack Brehm's theory of **psychological reactance.** This theory provides valuable insights into the universal inclination to resist change.[19] (See Box 11.4.)

Psychological reactance occurs when people are motivated to rebel when their established beliefs, attitudes, or habits of behavior are threatened by persuasion. Consequently, those who demand compliance from us may actually increase our determination to resist persuasion—causing a reaction against the

BOX 11.4   A Closer Look

Brehm's Theory of Psychological Reactance

When someone tries to persuade us to do something, or to change our attitudes and beliefs, we are resistant to that change. Our resistance to change follows from our desire to remain in control over the way we think and the way we act. If someone tries to persuade us differently, we are likely to tune that person out or to develop a strong negative feeling for the person. Social psychologist Jack Brehm calls this type of resistance to change psychological reactance. Brehm's theory of psychological reactance can be summed up as follows:

1. Throughout the course of our life, we develop various attitudes and beliefs.
2. Because we like to be in control of our lives, we are resistant to attempts to change us. We do not like others telling us what to do or what to think.
3. When someone tries to convince us to change our beliefs, or tries to alter our behavior, we are likely to resist that person and his or her message.
4. The overall resistance to change is known as psychological reactance.

attempt. Brehm expresses this idea by suggesting that the person who is the target of the influence attempt feels that "he can do what he wants, that he does not have to do what he doesn't want, and that at least in regard to the freedom in question, he is the sole director of his own behavior."[20]

Thus, our need to be in control, plus our strong desire for a stable and balanced life, provides the foundation for reactance. As adults, we expect and like the freedom to choose what we think and to control most of our own behaviors. This expectation of freedom, the importance of that freedom, and many other closely related issues all motivate us to resist particular influence attempts.[21]

Brehm's perspective is a useful one for several reasons. First, it makes intuitive sense. Think about how you react to the endless pop-ups of commercials on the Internet, pushing products that advertisers want you to buy. You probably use controls to shut them off or try not to look and listen. We do generally react negatively to people who openly attempt to get us to do things we don't want to do. We don't like to believe that we are being talked into doing something against our better judgment. Moreover, because we are bombarded with such a daily barrage of messages attempting to change us, we have to develop a "thick skin"—a strong tendency to resist—just to get through the day.

A second reason why Brehm's explanation has merit is that it complements our previous explanations of the nature of beliefs and attitudes, including the position of the relatively unpredictable relationship between attitudes and behavior. Brehm's perspective strengthens an important part of that discussion. Although the previous explanation focused on social and nonsocial factors, Brehm's theory adds a psychological perspective to our understanding of attitude and behavior inconsistency by noting people's *universal tendency to resist changing their behavior* as a result of exposure to persuasive communication.

Finally, Brehm's explanation serves as a useful point of departure for discussing additional areas that are important in learning how to communicate in ways that will influence people. Specifically, before considering how a variety of available communication strategies can be used, it is necessary to consider the nature of resistance to change through persuasion.

Types of Resistance

Discussions of resistance to persuasion often characterize any kind of opposition to persuasion as negative or even destructive.[22] Furthermore, the idea of people resisting to only a

What type of resistance is a protest? What issues would cause you to resist?

limited degree has seldom been addressed. This is unfortunate because viewing resistance as essentially "destructive" limits our ability to understand those who resist to some degree, but who do not entirely reject, influence attempts. Obviously, some kinds of resistance are entirely justified and serve constructive purposes. Thus, it is more realistic to maintain that there are essentially two types of resistance—*destructive* and *constructive*—and to assume that people resist in *varying degrees*.[23]

Destructive resistance. In its maximum form, **destructive resistance** is characterized as disagreeable, negative, subversive, or rebellious behavior. From this perspective, resistance is *misbehavior*—disobedience or corruption of authority. This type of resistance clearly illustrates contempt for an authority figure or for authority itself. That is, people who resist the requests and influence attempts of legitimate authorities, for no other reason than that they are authorities, are, in fact, destructive.

For example, if a manager directs an employee to engage in a legitimate work task (that does not involve immoral or illegitimate behavior) and the employee refuses to comply, the employee is being *destructively resistant*. In this situation, the employee is being openly disobedient and is undermining the manager's rational-legal authority. The fact that it is a designated superior who is making the assignment legitimizes the request and requires the employee to comply. In such a case, the employee's destructive resistance contributes nothing to a situation.

Constructive resistance. There are numerous ways in which **constructive resistance**—refusing to comply when the behavior being solicited is against ethical norms—can contribute to a situation. For example, in the well-known psychological experiments of Stanley Milgram, participants were ordered to administer what they thought were dangerous levels of electric shocks to other individuals. (The participants believed that were administering strong shocks to others, but the people being "shocked" were pretending to be in pain by shouting and screaming.) Many who read the reports of these experiments were surprised that only a few individuals resisted their orders.[24] Similar real-life situations arise on some occasions in the armed forces during wartime, when soldiers are unethically ordered to kill civilians. Some refuse. Unfortunately some do not. Refusing to engage in such behavior, despite orders to comply, provides an example of constructive resistance.

In normal daily activities, the boundaries between constructive and destructive resistance can be very murky indeed. What seems constructive to one group may be interpreted as destructive by another. For example, members of certain fundamentalist religious groups refuse to consult physicians when a family member becomes ill. They hold deep convictions that prayer will provide healing and that turning to conventional medicine amounts to a rejection of their faith. From a legal standpoint, such resistance can be a violation of law. Some see such resistance as destructive and unacceptable when lives are at stake. Others, however, see that society needs to respect religious convictions and make provision for such resistance.

The debate about what is constructive or destructive may never be settled. Today, some people feel morally compelled to resist laws supported by the majority of society that they deem improper. One example is the animal rights groups that break into laboratories to free animals used in medical research. Another example is activists who block the entrances of abortion clinics even though they know they will be arrested for their resistance. These individuals believe they are engaging in constructive resistance. Others in society see their behavior as destructive resistance to legitimate norms and laws.

Two important implications follow from the previous discussion: *First,* and most obvious, is that when trying to persuade people to change their views or behavior, it is almost certain that resistance will be encountered. This implies that provision must be made for reducing that resistance if at all possible. *Second,* to develop a strategy for reducing resistance, it is important to understand whether, from the resister's standpoint, it is seen as constructive. If this is the case, persuasion may be difficult or virtually impossible because constructive resistance is often based on deep commitments to ethical, moral, and culturally based positions. Such beliefs are particularly difficult to overcome. For example, it would not be an easy task to persuade an animal rights advocate that research on animals is essential to human health, or an anti-abortion advocate that undergoing the procedure is acceptable for any reason. Thus,

viewing resistance as constructive *from the subjective viewpoint of the person to be persuaded* changes the way we think about it, and it certainly has a bearing on the strategies that might be used to circumvent it.

Types of Yielding

There are many occasions when people either consciously or unconsciously need to submit to influence. That is, there are a variety of circumstances in which we might want to yield in a particular situation when someone is attempting to influence our beliefs, attitudes, and behaviors. In a now-classic article, the social psychologist Herbert Kelman described three common and frequently overlapping types of yielding: *compliance, identification,* and *internalization.*[25]

Compliance. Kelman's first type of yielding is consistent with the previous discussion of compliance. It refers to yielding publicly or observably to an influence attempt—but, in this case, privately refusing to accept the change. A number of questions arise in discussions of this kind of **compliance.** First, why would anyone publicly *appear* to change while not having some corresponding private change in his or her own mind? The answer is that we frequently find ourselves in situations in which it is better to "go along to get along." That is, it is more expedient or useful not to challenge what is being said by an individual or a group than it is to speak out in opposition or to resist.

It is for that reason that many people simply comply in situations like this, either to receive a reward or to avoid being punished. For example, suppose you are driving on the highway and a police officer drives up alongside and directs you to slow down. Even though you are not exceeding the posted speed limit, you slow down. The issue here is that you accept being influenced because this individual controls certain punishments that can be imposed (such as a ticket). When the police officer is down the road and out of sight, however, you are likely to resume your original speed. Compliance in this situation is solely public or observable; it lasts only as long as the influencing agent is visibly present. Compliance as a form of yielding, then, is based on our expectation of *gaining rewards or avoiding punishment*.[26]

Identification.   Kelman's second type of yielding to influence, **identification**, occurs because of our desire to emulate or imitate a particular individual or group. Yielding of this type is based on our wish to gain satisfaction in *being like* some individual or group that we want to imitate or that we admire. For example, suppose that you became acquainted with a man you would like to have as a close friend. After all, you feel good about yourself when you are around him, and he has a positive influence on your behavior in ways that please you very much. In other words, you admire, and want to be like (identify with) this individual.

Now suppose that this person you admire is zealously committed to consuming only organic or free-range foods—an issue that you find faddish, expensive, and foolish. Your new friend frequently attempts to get you to accept his position. Although your natural inclination is to resist change, based on what has been described, it is likely that you will yield to his attempts to influence you. You will become more positive toward organic foods. This probably would not come all at once, but if your relationship with this individual continued to develop in a rewarding way, you probably would eventually yield. Why do you end up yielding in these kinds of circumstances? The answer is that there are *rewards* in having this individual as your close friend and in feeling that you are like this person. He makes you feel good about yourself, and that, in itself, is very rewarding.

Internalization.   Kelman's third type of yielding indicates that we do so because it is personally rewarding or useful. But more important, people yield in this manner so as to be *consistent with their values*. The term *value*

refers to whatever an individual deeply believes to be important in life. Thus, values (like attitudes) are configurations or interrelated sets of affective beliefs. Unlike attitudes, however, they do not have clear-cut objects. Furthermore, they are much more general because they are goals or end-states that people seek, rather than objects. To illustrate, a person may value (seek as a major goal) such end-states as a moral life, happiness, freedom, service to others, power, or even wealth. Such broad and general objectives help to determine many of an individual's attitudes and beliefs as well as actions.[27]

The basis of Kelman's **internalization** as a type of yielding is how much intrinsic value a specific change actually provides for the person. It is no simple task to influence people to internalize a change. They must have an incentive; that is, making the change must be worthwhile for them. This type of yielding is the result of a rational decision to do so because the change fits into the individual's system of values. In this way, such change is interpreted as consistent with the person's innermost convictions of what is important in life.

Traditional Communication Strategies for Influencing People

The result of most of our attempts to influence people won't extend over a long period. However, even immediate or short-term influence encounters can and should be handled as if we intend to develop a long-term relationship. That is, to make any influence attempt successful, we must approach the encounter as we would approach the development of a lasting relationship.

This long-term perspective is critical. Regardless of the cultural or ethnic groups to which we belong, all of us like to feel special, attended to, and cared about. It is impossible to create the impression that you care about people you want to influence unless you sincerely approach your encounters with them as if you would like to develop a lasting relationship. Convincing people that you care in this way contributes to the style and affect of your influence attempt.

In addition to the influence processes and changes already discussed, several specific communication strategies can contribute to the success of attempts to influence people. These strategies, which have been researched for many years, focus on characteristics of *receivers, messages,* and *sources* of persuasive messages.

Understanding Characteristics of Receivers

Persuasion strategies require some knowledge of the receiver targeted for change. If an individual is identified as possessing a particular attribute or a set of characteristics, then that knowledge can be part of a planned communication strategy. Any person possesses a number of identifiable attributes that make them more or less susceptible to influence attempts. These include *gender differences* and certain *personality characteristics.*

Gender differences. One of the more widely investigated (and most controversial) of the attributes related to susceptibility is whether a person is male or female. Investigators have studied the effect of gender on susceptibility for many years. Early studies supported the assumption that females were more easily influenced than males.[28] By the late 1970s, however, researchers had concluded no major gender differences in susceptibility to persuasion. Contemporary investigations indicate that certain features of traditional male and female specialized cultures probably do affect the degree to which they are susceptible to influence. Attributes like emotionalism, expressiveness, and assertiveness that were part of the definitions of traditional male and female roles in decades past do seem to be related to susceptibility to persuasion. Overall, however, no assumption should be made that either males or females are easier to persuade.

Personality characteristics. Many researchers have investigated whether differences in personality characteristics are related to susceptibility to persuasion. One particular study provides insights into the specific receiver personality characteristics that affect their susceptibility.[29]

As an initial step in the research, college students completed an extensive battery of personality tests. Their attitudes toward several topics of communication were also assessed. Later, on a different occasion, the investigators asked randomly selected groups of these same students to engage in a "counter-attitudinal activity." This required them to act as if they actually believed in one or more of the originally assessed communication topics. Attitudes toward these topics were assessed again at the end of this second session. Analyses of the results enabled the researchers to define *receiver personality profiles* of students who showed high and low levels of yielding. The results indicated that high and low amounts of change were clearly tied to particular receiver personality profiles. Specifically, large amounts of change occurred with receivers who were *obliging, changeable, dependent, and unstable.* Minimum change occurred among those who were *aggressive, unchanging, forceful, efficient, and well informed.*

What is the importance of these findings? If the person seeking to persuade another understands the personality structure of the target individual, and if it includes the first list above, persuasion may succeed. If the target person is like the second list, success is less likely.

Features of Effective Messages

As noted earlier, for decades researchers have tried to discover the magic keys (words, appeals, message structures) that can be used to influence people. Of all the potential keys examined in thousands of studies, only a few come even close to working that way.

With this caveat in mind, there are several keys to changing people that have shown at least some results in research. These keys are more accurately called *features of effective messages* that have persuaded people, at least in experiments and other kinds of studies. Keep in mind that the degree to which these can be incorporated into real-life influence attempts outside experimental settings is not clear.

Message "sidedness." Some of the earliest and most meaningful examinations of communication strategies were conducted in the 1950s by social psychologists Carl Hovland, Irving Janis, and Harold Kelley.[30] One of the factors they studied was called **message sidedness**. Specifically, this concerns whether to use a message that presents *only one side* of a persuasive argument, to *include both sides,* or to use both sides and *refute the opposing arguments* as well. Results from a number of studies seemed to show that the strategy of using the two-sided message, which refutes the other's position, worked best.[31]

Message order of presentation. A substantial amount of research has examined whether the first side of an argument that is presented, or the most recent side, carries the most influence. This is often referred to as **message ordering**, or the *primacy-recency* question. That is, is it more persuasive to put the arguments favoring a position early in a message, or does more change result when arguments are inserted at the end of the message? The safest recommendation concerning this persuasion strategy is that no universal law of primacy-recency has been uncovered, and one's choice should depend on the conditions that exist at the time of the influence attempt.[32]

Fear appeals. One of the more intriguing communication strategies involves the use of fear-arousing appeals to influence change. Results of many studies remain contradictory. The original research examining the effectiveness of this strategy indicated that large amounts of change are produced with *weak* fear appeals and that little or no change results from *strong* appeals that arouse high levels of fear.[33] More recent fear-appeal studies suggest that the

opposite is the case.[34] That is, strong fear appeals do work, producing more persuasive influences than weak appeals. The explanation of this seeming contradiction may be that there is a point at which too much fear in a message causes people to avoid or disregard the message, or to do both.[35] Further research reveals that fear alone doesn't work unless the message includes a realistic, feasible way to reduce the danger.[36]

Behavior-alteration techniques. This refers not to a single persuasion strategy, but to a set of message techniques. Each of these techniques is represented by a set of messages of a particular kind. For example, one of these techniques is called "reward from behavior." It includes messages such as "You will enjoy it," "You will get a reward if you do," "It will make you happy," "It will help you," and "You will benefit if you do it." Investigations of these techniques indicate that using several behavior-alteration procedures may sometimes be effective in motivating a person to yield in a particular influence attempt.[37]

Recent research indicates that the **behavior-alteration techniques** are more appropriately categorized into two general types—*prosocial* and *antisocial*. For example, the "reward for behavior" technique is an example of the prosocial type. A technique called "punishment from behavior" is a good illustration of the antisocial type. Messages using this antisocial type include "You will lose if you don't," "You will be punished if you don't," "You will be unhappy if you don't," and "You will be hurt if you don't." Again, there are no solid rules to use as guidelines concerning which of these techniques will succeed or fail in a given persuasion attempt.

Nonverbal cues. Recall from Chapter 3 that nonverbal immediacy refers to such behaviors as smiling, nodding, leaning forward, eye contact, and standing close to someone. Also recall that the effects of immediacy are based on the *principle of utility.* In brief, we tend to approach people we like both physically and psychologically, and we tend to avoid behaving in these ways toward people we don't like. People understand this, and, therefore, signals of nonverbal immediacy can be an effective form of persuasive communication. Clearly, nonverbal messages of all kinds can exert significant influence on the persuasive process.[38]

Credibility of the Source

In its simplest form, **credibility** refers to how believable or knowledgeable others perceive a source to be.[39] This simple definition says two very important things: First and most critical, credibility is something that is *perceived*—that is, it is in the eye of the beholder. Thus, a man may think that he is a highly credible person, but if others don't think so, he is not.

The second issue implied by the definition is that to be credible we must be both *knowledgeable* and *believable*. After many years of investigating source credibility, researchers have come to define it as a combination of three separate dimensions: *expertise, trustworthiness,* and *goodwill*. For us to get people to perceive us as credible sources, and thus use it as a communication strategy, we need to understand each of these dimensions and how they fit together.

The three dimensions of credibility can be explained very simply. The first, expertise, refers to how knowledgeable or competent, a source is thought to be in a given content area. If others perceive that you know what you're talking about, they will find you credible. The second, *trustworthiness,* refers to whether people believe us to be honest or truthful. Perceived liars or evasive communicators simply do not come across as credible. The third dimension of credibility is goodwill or how caring the source is perceived to be. Goodwill communicators seem to have our best interests at heart; they come across as understanding, responsive, and empathetic.

Taken together, these three dimensions influence people's perceptions of credibility. Box 11.5 provides a list of descriptors that researchers currently use to assess credibility. See if you can identity those adjectives that reflect each of the dimensions of the construct. If you are successful at getting people to see you in these ways, you will likely be seen as a believable or credible person. If that can be done, you might be effective at changing a person's beliefs, attitudes or behavior.[40] In fact, that conclusion has been suggested by a considerable body of research.[41]

The Elaboration Likelihood Model of Persuasion

Psychologists Richard Petty and John Cacioppo, who have studied the process of persuasion extensively, have developed a complex theory that brings together many of the factors and considerations that have been discussed in this chapter. They have labeled their theory the **elaboration likelihood model** of persuasion (ELM).[42] The term **elaboration** refers to the perceptual and cognitive processes by which a person receives and carefully considers the meaning of a persuasive message, the appeals for change that it contains and other features of its content. The idea of *likelihood* refers to the chances or probability that some change will take place in a person's attitude (and related behavior) as a result of receiving, considering and understanding the persuasive message. Essentially, the ELM begins with the proposition that people are motivated to hold "correct" attitudes. That is, attitudes that are consistent with those held by people they regard as important in their social environment. For example, if our peers, other friends, and family all hold negative attitudes toward the death penalty, it is unlikely that we will have positive attitudes toward that form of punishment. A second proposition states that if a person receives a message designed to persuade him or her to hold a particular or different view about some issue or topic, the amount of "issue-relevant elaboration"—defined as the extent to which a person thinks about or considers the relevant arguments or appeals in the message—will vary with the message and the situation.

BOX 11.5 | *Assessing Source Credibility*

Source credibility refers to the receiver's perception of another's expertise, trustworthiness, and goodwill. Given the definition of each of these factors in your book, label each of the following adjectives as potential descriptors of each dimension.

E = Expertise
T = Trustworthiness
G = Goodwill

_____ Intelligent
_____ Trained
_____ Cares about me
_____ Honest
_____ Has my interests at heart
_____ Trustworthy
_____ Expert
_____ Not self-centered; receiver-oriented
_____ Concerned with me
_____ Honorable
_____ Informed
_____ Moral
_____ Competent

_____ Ethical
_____ Sensitive
_____ Bright
_____ Genuine
_____ Understanding

To what extent do you find these descriptors adequate or sufficient for characterizing expertise, trustworthiness, or goodwill? For example, should educational attainment and experience also be included as descriptors of expertise? Why or why not?

What additional adjectives can you think of for each factor?

At one time, researchers argued that someone's composure and dynamic personality (extroversion) also made a difference in perceptions of credibility. What do you think?

Source: These descriptors are taken from the actual measure of source credibility developed by McCroskey, J. C., & Teven, J. J. (1999). Goodwill: A reexamination of the construct and its measurement. *Communication Monographs, 66,* 90–103.

The next consideration is whether the message and topic are "relevant" to the person. Many of the persuasive messages we all receive are not. For example, we constantly see advertisements about products that have no place in our lives, or attempts to convert our views to positions on topics we have no interest in. These are not relevant. On the other hand, if our college administration tries to persuade us that a huge increase in tuition is a really great idea, we would probably see that as very relevant. We would be strongly motivated to try and understand why they are saying that, and what the consequences to us might be. In ELM terms, we would engage in issue-relevant elaboration.

Assuming that the individual finds a persuasive message both relevant to his or her interests and is motivated to consider it carefully, close attention will then be paid to whatever appeals or persuasive arguments have been placed within it. On the other hand, if the message is about something not relevant, the person is less likely to process or think carefully about it. Instead, the receiver will use a variety of peripheral cues as guides to making a quick decision to accept or reject the message. Such cues may include the credibility, attractiveness, or status of the speaker, or the number (rather than the type) of arguments presented. Even if the message is accepted, any attitude change that may take place is likely to be weak and temporary. (This is the **peripheral route** to persuasion indicated in Figure 11.1.)

However, if a person does indeed have the capacity and interest to process the message carefully, considering the appeals in some detail, and if a good case is made for a change in thinking, he may be persuaded to alter his attitude toward the position advocated in the message. (This is the **central route** shown in Figure 11.1.) Indeed, if that is the case, and if the appeals have an influence on the person's thinking, an enduring change in attitude toward

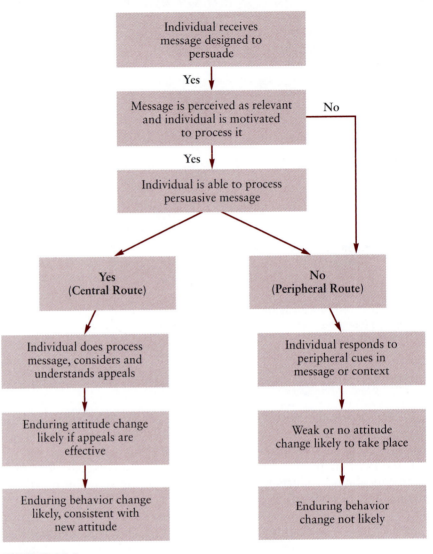

FIGURE 11.1
Elaboration Likelihood Model of Persuasion

the topic or issue is likely to result. This change may be in a positive or a negative direction, depending on the topic and the appeals. As a result of exposure to the persuasive message, and the mental elaborations described, the person may now have a favorable or an unfavorable attitude toward the topic or issue at stake.

The model also assumes that if a person undergoes a change in attitude as a result of receiving a persuasive message (the central route), then it is likely that his or her behavior will undergo a corresponding change (which is an assumption not always supported by empirical evidence).

Thus, the model emphasizes two distinct types of persuasion. For those messages that are relevant and important to us, we will be motivated to think about the issues involved, and we will consider the merits and the strength of the arguments or appeals (the central route). Under these circumstances, the theory predicts, the attitude change that may result is likely to be strong, enduring, and predictive of behavior.

However, we can't scrutinize in depth every message that is presented to us. So we often use a "mental filter" to allow messages that aren't significant to us to pass through with little processing or consideration (elaboration). Instead, we will use simple cues to make a decision, rather than analyze the information that is presented (the peripheral route). Under these circumstances, any attitude change that may result is likely to be weak, temporary, and less predictive of behavior.

The ELM then, is an attempt to bring together a number of the complex factors, considerations and psychological processes that are involved in achieving attitude change through the use of persuasive messages. In that sense, it represents another way of understanding how people can be influenced through communication.

Chapter Review

- In modern society, numerous individuals, groups, and agencies constantly try to influence people's ideas, feelings, or actions. At one time, persuasion was seen as something that one person "did to" another, following the linear magic bullet model. Now we know that influence is determined by both sources and receivers, following the simultaneous transactions model.

- Compliance falls into three categories: coercion, in which people may have little choice but to change their behavior; sociocultural expectations, using persuasive messages; and cognitive reorganization, in which people change the way they think or feel about the topic of persuasive messages.

- The attitudes we hold and the actions we engage in are seldom consistent. Although an attitude can increase the probability that we will act consistently, other more immediate social factors can greatly reduce that probability.

- Human beings are universally resistant to change, making persuasion especially difficult. Psychological reactance to persuasion occurs because of our need to be in control, plus our strong desire for a stable and balanced life. As adults we expect and like the freedom to choose and control most of our own behaviors.

- Desire for this freedom, and many other closely related issues, motivate us to resist influence.

- There are two types of resistance—destructive and constructive. Extreme destructive resistance is characterized as disagreeable, negative, subversive, or rebellious behavior, clearly illustrating contempt for authority. In contrast, constructive resistance can be positive, especially when the behavior solicited is against ethical norms.

- There are three types of yielding: compliance, identification, and internalization. Compliance refers to yielding publicly to an influence attempt, but without actually changing privately. *Identification* is yielding to the influence of another due to desire to emulate a particular individual or group. Internalization is yielding because it is personally rewarding or useful.

- All persuasion strategies require knowledge of the receiver, including personal characteristics that make people either more or less susceptible to persuasion.

- Five features of messages have been widely studied as possible keys to persuasion: message sidedness, message ordering, fear appeals, behavior-alteration techniques, and nonverbal cues of immediacy.

- Source credibility refers to whether a receiver believes the originator of the message can be trusted or believed. Researchers define credibility as a combination of five dimensions: competence, trustworthiness, extroversion, composure, and sociability.

- The Elaboration Likelihood Model (ELM) represents an attempt to bring together a complex set of factors and variables that explain how a person may or may not be influenced to change his or her attitude toward a topic or issue. If the topic is relevant, and the appeals effective, such change will take place as a result of "elaboration"—and will presumably be followed by corresponding behavior change. If these factors are different, enduring behavior change is unlikely.

Key Terms

persuasion	nonsocial constraints	message ordering
coercion	psychological reactance	behavior-alteration techniques
social expectations	destructive resistance	credibility (of a source)
psychodynamic strategy	constructive resistance	elaboration likelihood model
cognitive reorganization	compliance	elaboration
belief	identification	peripheral route
attitude	internalization	central route
social pressures	message sidedness	

Notes

1. Bloom, K., Zajac, D. J., & Titus, J. (1999). The influence of nasality of voice on sex-stereotyped perceptions. *Journal of Nonverbal Behavior, 23*, 4, 271–281.

2. See, for example: Henriksen, L., & Flora, J. A. (1999). Third-person perception and children: Perceived impact of pro- and anti-smoking ads. *Communication Research, 26*, 6, 643–665.

3. A classic example is the case of Kate Smith, a popular singer and radio personality of the 1940s, who sold $39 million worth of war bonds during an 18-hour marathon radio broadcast. See: Merton, R. K. (1946). *Mass persuasion: The social psychology of a war bond drive.* New York: Harper & Brothers.

4. Advertisers who strive to sell products with the use of persuasion communications mastered this formula decades ago. They call it the "learn, feel, do" approach. As far as they are concerned, it is not particularly effective. See: Jones, J. P. (1986). *What's in a name? Advertising and the concept of brands* (p. 141). Lexington, MA: Heath.

5. This example was drawn from a seminar paper: Ordman, L. (Fall 1989). On money and meaning in the popular press. Prepared for a graduate course, Syracuse University, Syracuse, NY.

6. Originally formulated by Melvin DeFleur and Timothy Plax as an explanation of certain kinds of effects of mass communication, meaning theory is equally applicable to persuasion at an interpersonal and group level. See: Lowery, S., & DeFleur, M. (1983). *Milestones in mass communication research* (pp. 28–30, 383–385). New York: Longman.

7. Cornford, F. M. (Trans. and Ed.). (1941). *The Republic of Plato* (pp. 227–231). London: Oxford University Press.

8. Lippmann, W. (1922). The world outside and the pictures in our heads. *Public opinion* (chap. 1, pp. 1–19). New York: Macmillan.

9. A large earlier literature is summarized in: Hovland, C. I., Janis, I., & Kelley, H. H. (1953). *Communication and persuasion.* New Haven, CT: Yale University Press.

10. Thomas, W. I., & Znaniecki, F. F. (1927). *The Polish peasant in Europe and America* (Vol. 1). New York: Knopf. (First published in 1918.)

11. DeFleur, M. L., & Westie, F. R. (1963). Attitude as a scientific concept. *Social Forces, 42,* 17–31. See also: Fishbein, M., & Azien, O. (1975). *Belief, attitude, intention, and behavior* (pp. 5–13). Reading, MA: Addison-Wesley; Bettinghaus, F. P., & Cody, M. J. (1987). *Persuasive communication* (4th ed., pp. 6–10). New York: Holt, Rinehart, and Winston.

12. This definition is derived from: Rokeach, M. (1973). *Beliefs, attitudes and values* (p. 122). San Francisco: Jossey-Bass.

13. Seibold, D. R. (1975). Communication research and the attitude-verbal report-overt behavior relationship: A critique and theoretic reformulation. *Human Communication Research, 2,* 3–32; Cushman, D. P., & McPhee, R. D., eds. (1980). *Message-attitude-behavior relationship: Theory, methodology, and application.* New York: Academic; Cooper, J., & Croyle, R.T. (1984). Attitudes and attitude change. In Rosenzweig, M. R., & Porter, L. W. (Eds.), *Annual review of psychology* (Vol. 35, pp. 395–460). Palo Alto, CA: Annual Reviews.

14. Ibid.

15. Ibid.

16. LaPiere, R. T. (1934). Attitudes versus actions. *Social Forces, 13,* 230–237.

17. DeFleur, M. L., & Westie, F. R. (1958). Attitudes and overt acts. *American Sociological Review, 23,* 667–673.

18. Plax, T. G., & DeFleur, M. L. (1980). *Communication, attitudes, and behavior: An axiomatic theory with implications for persuasion research.* Paper presented to the Western Speech Communication Association, Portland, OR.

19. Brehm, J. W. (1966). *A theory of psychological reactance.* New York: Academic.

20. Ibid., p. 9.

21. Most explanations of why people resist change follow from discussions of the human need for a comfortable, stable, and balanced life. In U.S. society, middle-class children are told from early childhood that if they engage in the right forms of preparation, a comfortable lifestyle will follow. In other words, if they work hard, go to school, get good grades, get a good job, and save their money, they will have stability, balance, and thus happiness in their lives; they will achieve the American Dream. We are taught to make achieving this lifestyle one of our highest priorities, and to do so we must attain control across a diversity of activities. Our natural and common reaction to threats to such control, with their possible suspensions of personal freedom, is to resist both change and attempts to get us to comply.

22. Burroughs, N. F., Kearney, P., & Plax, T. G. (1989). Compliance-resistance in the college classroom. *Communication Education, 38,* 214–229.

23. Ibid.

24. Milgram, S. (1963). Behavioral study of obedience. *Journal of Abnormal and Social Psychology, 67,* 371–378.

25. Kelman, H. C. (1961). Processes of opinion change. *Public Opinion Quarterly, 25,* 58–78.

26. Wood, W. (2000). Attitude change: Persuasion and social influence. Rosenzweig, M. R., & Porter, L. W. (Eds.), *Annual review of psychology* (Vol. 51, pp. 539–570). Palo Alto, CA: Annual Review.

27. The most frequently cited treatment of values is Rokeach, *Beliefs.* For other interesting discussions of values see: Oskamp, S. (1977). *Attitudes and opinions* (p. 13). Englewood Cliffs, NJ: Prentice-Hall; Simmons, H. W. (1976). *Persuasion: Understanding, practice, and analysis* (p. 20). Reading, MA: Addison-Wesley.

28. For a discussion of the early research on this topic see: Cronkhite, G. (1969). *Persuasion: Speech and behavioral exchange.* Indianapolis: Bobbs-Merrill. A large number of subsequent research studies have probed this issue, but the findings have been inconsistent. Some studies indicate that women are more susceptible; other studies suggest that men are more susceptible; and yet other research reveals no differences between the two. More likely, biological sex has no impact on susceptibility to influence; instead, gender-based socialization and status affect susceptibility.

29. Plax, T. G., & Rosenfeld, L. B. (1977). Antecedent of change in males and females. *Psychological Reports, 41,* 811–824. For additional examples of research examining

personal characteristics and persuasion see: Boster, F. J., & Stiff, J. B. (1984). Compliance-gaining message selection behavior. *Human Communication Research, 10,* 539–556; Hunter, J. H., Gerbing, D. W., & Boster, F. J. (1982). Machiavellian beliefs and personality: Construct invalidity of the Machiavellian dimension. *Journal of Personality and Social Psychology, 43,* 1293–1305. Also, for a review of research on locus of control and persuasion, see: Miller, L. C., Cody, M. J., & McLaughlin, M. L. (1994). Situations and goals as fundamental constructs in interpersonal communication research. In M. L. Knapp & G. R. Miller (Eds.), *Handbook of interpersonal communication* (2nd ed.), (pp. 162–198). Thousand Oaks, CA: Sage.

30. Hovland, C. I., Janis, I. L., & Kelley, H. H. (1953). *Communication and persuasion.* New Haven, CT: Yale University Press.

31. Allen, M., Hale, J., Mongeau, P., Berkowitz-Stafford, S., Stafford, S., Shanahan, W., Agee, P., Dillon, K., Dickson, R., & Ray, C. (1990). Testing a model of message-sidedness: Three replications. *Communication Monographs, 57,* 275–291.

32. Hovland, C. I., Mandel, W., Campbell, E. H., Brock, T., Luchins, A. S., Cohen, A. E., McGuire, W. J., Janis, I. L., Feierabend, R. L., & Anderson, N. H. (1957). *The order of presentation in persuasion.* New Haven, CT: Yale University Press.

33. Janis, I. L., & Feshbach, S. (1953). Effects of fear arousing communications. *Journal of Abnormal and Social Psychology, 48,* 78–92.

34. See, for example: Kraus, S., El-assal, E., and DeFleur, M. L. (1966). Fear-threat appeals in mass communication: An apparent contradiction. *Speech Monographs, 23,* 23–29. Also: Higbee, K. L. (1969). Fifteen years of fear arousal: Research on threat appeals: 1953–1968. *Psychological Bulletin, 72,* 426–444.

35. McGuire, W., J. (1968). Personality and susceptibility to social influence. In E. E. Borgatta & W. W. Lambert (Eds.), *Handbook of personality theory and research* (pp. 1130–1187). Chicago: Rand McNally.

36. Witte, K. (1992). Putting the fear back into fear appeals: The extended parallel process model. *Communication Monographs, 52,* 329–349; Witte, K. (1994). Fear control and danger control: A test of the extended parallel process model (EPPM). *Communication Monographs, 61,* 113–134.

37. Kearney, P., Plax, T. G., Richmond, V. P., & McCroskey, J. C. (1984). Power in the classroom IV; Teacher communication techniques as alternatives to discipline. In R. Bostrom (Ed.), *Communication yearbook 8* (pp. 724–746). Beverly Hills, CA: Sage. For an excellent review of the research on compliance-gaining, see: Seibold, D. R., Cantrill, J. G., & Meyers, R. A. (1994). Communication and interpersonal influence. In M. L. Knapp & G. R. Miller (Eds.), *Handbook of interpersonal communication* (2nd. ed.), (pp. 542–588). Thousand Oaks, CA: Sage.

38. Ifert, D. E., & Gibbons, C. A. (1999). Look at me when I'm influencing you: Nonverbal messages and persuasion. *New Jersey Journal of Communication, 7, 2,* 171–179.

39. McCroskey, J. C., & Young, T. J. (1981). Ethos and credibility: The construct and its measurement after three decades. *Central States Speech Journal, 32,* 24–34; McCroskey, J. C., & Teven, J. J. (1999). Goodwill: A reexamination of the construct and its measurement. *Communication Monographs, 66,* 90–103; Frymier, A. B., & Nadler, M. K. (2010). *Persuasion: Integrating theory, research, and practice* (2nd ed., pp. 213–239), Dubuque, IA: Kendall Hunt.

40. Plax, T. G., & Rosenfeld, L. B. (1980). Individual differences in the credibility and attitude change relationship. *Journal of Social Psychology, 111,* 79–89.

41. Bettinghaus & Cody, *Persuasive communication,* pp. 84–94; Frymier, A. B., & Nadler, M. K. (2010). *Persuasion: Integrating theory, research, and practice* (2nd ed., pp. 213–239), Dubuque, IA: Kendall Hunt.

42. Petty, R.E., & Cacioppo, J. T. (1986). The elaboration likelihood model of persuasion. In L. Berkowitz (Ed.), *Advances in experimental social psychology* (Vol. 19, pp. 123–205). For an excellent overview of the theory, see also: Frymier, A. B., & Nadler, M. K. (2010). *Persuasion: Integrating theory, research, and practice* (2nd ed., pp. 213–239), Dubuque, IA: Kendall Hunt.

Coping with Conflict

F rank is upset. This is the fourth time he's been asked to work late because his co-worker Ebony had child-care responsibilities. He couldn't help it that he didn't have children and she did. "She should have known that kids get sick," Frank groused. "She needs to find a way to deal with that—instead of assuming that the rest of us would fill in for her and do her job!"

Like a number of other workers without children, Frank is showing signs of discontent over the family-friendly policies that pervade his workplace. "Look, I know that working parents have special demands put on them," he concedes to himself, "but I feel I'm being taken advantage of. Ebony and the other parents around here get all kinds of special benefits that I don't. They get to select vacation days during the summer and holidays when their kids are home; they get priority for shift assignments; the company gives them more perks—like generous family health care plans, parental leave, and child-care assistance. I don't get special perks because I'm single and child-free! Sometimes these parents even bring their children to work, expecting the rest of us to keep an eye on them—like we're the babysitters!"

"Ebony!" Frank barked. "This is the last time I'm covering for you. You're going to have to make some other arrangements."

"I wish I could, Frank, but what can I do? I am a mother, and my daughter comes first!"

Conflict is just as normal as any other routine exchange, and people frequently experience disagreements over many issues. Conflict can also produce positive consequences as people understand ways to handle their differences and make compromises.

At that retort, Ebony quickly puts on her coat and hurries out the door to drive over to the elementary school where her sick child is waiting. "I hate it that Frank has to fill in again for me at work," she muses, "but what can I do? Didi needs her mother when she is ill. She gets these asthma attacks every once in a while, and I have to take her to the doctor. Once her breathing became so bad that she had to go to the emergency room!" She presses down harder on the accelerator to get to Didi.

Like many other working parents, Ebony is often torn between her job and her family. She needs the financial security a job offers; and she likes her career choice. "Too many companies," she argues to herself, "offer no accommodation for working parents. When the kids get sick, enjoy workweek holidays from school, and come home every day early to an empty house, parents need to be there. What job allows us to do that? I fight every day for companies to see that parents have special challenges, and we need greater flexibility so that we can meet those challenges." Shaking her head, she mutters aloud, "Frank doesn't get it; he doesn't understand—and unless he has children himself, he'll never appreciate what I'm going through."

Perhaps the conflict between Frank and Ebony sounds unusual—the kind of thing that rarely occurs between intelligent people. After all, employees are adults, and they must surely think and act like mature individuals. Almost anyone can disagree from time to time, but intelligent people should be able to resolve any issue that comes up, right? Wrong! We all get angry when we perceive a threat to something we value. We try to protect ourselves and to stop the person who is representing the threat. Sometimes we might even want to get back at anyone who tries to take something away from us that we feel is ours. The result is often an *unresolvable conflict.*

Why does this happen? For one thing, it is a standard psychological principle that, regardless of what is at stake, we all respond to frustration with *aggression.*[1] Hostility between people can occur anywhere, and for a variety of reasons. *Conflict* occurs between people in all sorts of relationships—between strangers, friends, and lovers; between employees and employers; between spouses, and relatives; between teachers and students; and between parents and children Conflict is both widespread and normal. Sooner or later, we all get mad at someone. Conflict can develop between people in almost any relationship. In fact, the scenario of Frank and Ebony as employees could be rewritten into a description of Frank and Ebony as husband and wife, as close friends, as landlord and tenant, or as professor and student.

The Major Characteristics of Conflict

One of the first characteristics of conflict to recognize is that it can range from trivial to brutal. However, this chapter is not concerned with violent conflicts, such as gang wars, police shoot-outs, or barroom brawls. The concern here is with people's everyday conflicts, those that occur in the family, at work, among neighbors, or at school—the type illustrated by what happened between Frank and Ebony.

These kinds of conflicts are normal and as typically American as apple pie, motherhood, and the flag. Actually, certain forms of conflict are an established and approved part of our culture. That is not to say that as a general culture we blindly approve of violent or destructive behavior. However, ours is a complex society made up of many groups and categories, with distinctive specialized cultures and agendas. People are often in competition for power, privilege, and other scarce resources. This inevitably generates struggles—conflicts—among various segments of the society. Thus, Americans often see themselves in a "we versus they" perspective. Examples are management versus labor, rich versus poor, males versus females, one racial or ethnic group versus another, farmers versus city dwellers, or old versus young.[2]

A second major characteristic of conflict can best be understood within this cultural perspective: That is, within limits, to be a fighter is commonly regarded as a good thing by U.S. standards. To shrink from conflict is widely regarded as bad. People who typically go out of their way to dodge conflicts are sometimes described with pejorative terms, such as wimpy, spineless, and weak. The mainstream U.S. culture, then, often supports a culturally approved readiness to engage in conflict, as long as it does not escalate to physical violence.[3]

There are other cultural roots of our readiness to engage in conflict. In many ways, this orientation is an extension of our cultural mandates to *succeed in life.* Middle-class children in both the dominant and many minority groups are taught early on that, to be happy and worthwhile, they must be successful. In childhood this means winning in various settings, ranging from sports contests to spelling bees. Later, it means making it by acquiring impressive material possessions and achieving upward mobility in a career. Thus, getting ahead is an important value to many Americans, particularly among the middle class and perhaps the majority.

Getting ahead inescapably means getting ahead of *someone else.* Thus, we share a conflict perspective on the so-called American

Dream (of upward mobility). To act in ways consistent with this aspect of our culture, then, we literally must engage in a lifetime of competitive conflicts. To please ourselves and others, we compete at home, at school, on the job, and in any other situation that lends itself to rivalry. Thus, our tendencies to be competitive and to engage in conflict are deeply embedded in our way of life. They are part of our mainstream cultural traditions, and they inevitably become a central part of our personalities as we participate and are socialized within that culture.

Formulating a More Precise Definition

Although the idea of conflict may seem simple enough in a commonsense way, there is surprising disagreement among experts about exactly what kinds of states, situations, and behaviors should be called conflict. Consequently there are a variety of definitions of conflict, each stressing a different meaning. Unfortunately, most are either narrowly linked to a specific scientific research project or quite complicated and technical. Thus, few existing definitions fit the present general discussion. For the purposes of this text, then, **conflict** is defined as *a dispute in which different values result in claims to rewards or resources that are in limited supply, and in which the main objective of the people engaged in the process is either to neutralize or to eliminate their opponent's prospects to win what is at stake.*[4]

This definition may seem complex, but it systematically sets forth the essential features of conflict: It notes the *object* around which conflict develops, the *goals* of the participants (to win, and to keep the other from doing so), and the *nature of their relationship* (as one of controversy). These are important features that need to be included in a workable definition.

In many ways, this definition asserts a kind of *economic model* of the causes of conflict. This is only one way to look at the causes of conflict, but it does provide a good beginning because it shows that conflicts develop over some *commodity* (reward or resource) that all

the participants desire but that not all can have. If a commodity is valued, and if it is possible for only a few people to have it, the commodity will appear to them to have *great worth*. This sets the stage for strong competition to attain it. The struggle can be over any commodity—anything people want: money, power, authority, prestige, immediate access to the boss, or an office with a nice view. The scarcity of the reward or resource valued in the specific situation serves as an important beginning point for the development of conflict.

These principles are inherent in the Frank and Ebony example. Their conflict represents one of the most common types found in the workplace—competition for rewards and resources. The conflict began when Ebony became pregnant; took maternity leave (that was rightfully hers); and occasionally left work early, came in late, or took entire days off to take care of her family. Frank believed that Ebony took advantage of the "system," and used her child as an excuse to avoid the more difficult assignments. In his mind, the company bent over backward to accommodate her without simultaneously offering him any of those same perks. They even had a baby shower for her at work where he was expected to bring a gift! To Frank, Ebony represented a threat to his status at work. All too frequently, in his mind, Ebony was perceived as special and he was not.

Was Frank's interpretation irrational? Perhaps. But we each define our own interpretation, of reality, and as explained in previous chapters, they become the facts on which we base our actions and decisions.

For Ebony, a very different set of facts was operating. She knew that being a mother was her number one responsibility. No work assignment, even this one, should come at the expense of her child. At one point, she tried to explain to Frank that she understood that he was having to pick up a lot of the slack when she had to leave work. But he should understand that she would do that for him, too, if the situation was reversed. She could tell that he wasn't at all satisfied with her offer.

Other cultural norms surround the goals and objectives of those in conflict. These norms define limits on how we go about winning—that is, neutralizing or even eliminating the chances of the opponent to capture the commodity. It is not acceptable in our society to damage, destroy, or discredit our opponent in a destructive way. Our mainstream culture requires that we follow certain ethical standards.

These seemingly conflicting cultural definitions are not incompatible. There are ways to neutralize one's competition in a conflict while remaining ethical and constructive. That is, the opponent does not have to be destroyed and end up with absolutely nothing. In some situations, and ideally in *all* situations, each of the parties in a process of conflict can and should benefit in some way when it is resolved.

Getting what we want, then, simply means that in a conflict we compete with someone in an ethical manner—and in the end gain at least some advantage (from our perspective). This implies getting a share of whatever value, reward, or resource is at stake, but in a way that allows both parties to gain something through the resolution of the conflict.[5]

These points about the process and meaning of "winning" are extremely important. Opponents in a conflict need not even be cold and distant; in fact, they can compete vigorously and remain friends. For example, friends and family members frequently train for and compete in activities ranging from athletic events to courtroom trials. Co-workers often spend time in conflicts that lead to formulating the best approach to such activities as marketing, employee relations, labor negotiations, hiring, and so on. Viewed in these ways, conflicts are not inherently negative or adverse. In fact, conflicts can range along a continuum from positive to neutral to negative.

Consequences of Conflict

Conflicts are not, inherently, either productive or destructive. What is important is *how people behave* during a conflict and especially the specific *consequences* of the process. Moreover, it is the people who initiate and engage in a conflict who determine whether it will ultimately be productive or destructive; their specific personalities influence the kinds of outcomes that result from all forms of human interaction. Conflict is no exception.

Conflicts produce unproductive, negative, or even destructive outcomes when the participants enter the process with negative attitudes or hostile feelings toward their opponent. As previously noted, these directly arouse needs for *aggression*. Therefore, as one might expect, conflicts that start on a negative note often end up that way. Fortunately, most of us are not normally antagonistic toward other people. Unless provoked, we seldom go out of our way to be hostile toward one another. Because we aren't naturally antagonistic, most of our conflicts start out innocently. In some cases, however, things "just happen" and a conflict begins and escalates.

Conflicts that produce bad feelings and destructive results tend to be those that get out of hand. One of the opponents gets hot under the collar, or the other gets angry, and the encounter deteriorates into ugliness and hostility.

Examples of conflicts that often end unproductively are those centering on divorce, child custody, job termination, disputes between family members over an inheritance, and union-management impasses. These frequently lead to bitterness; alienation; sabotage on the job; or even, in some cases, physical violence. In these kinds of cases, all the parties involved lose even if they win, because of the negative consequences they face, whatever the outcome.

Conflicts that have bad or unproductive consequences for the people involved seldom start out in a dramatically negative way. Often, the initial events are minor, and the early exchanges seem little more than mild disagreements. In fact, what occurs between people during the early stages of a conflict can, and often does, dictate what happens later in the encounter, as well as its ultimate consequences. In particular, what happens initially usually determines

An uncontrolled escalation of conflict results in bitterness, alienation, sabotage, and in some cases, violence.

whether a conflict will escalate or deescalate, becoming unproductive or productive for the people involved.

It is important to keep in mind that the uncontrolled escalation of a competitive encounter can change an apparently minor disagreement into something resembling World War III. Part of learning to handle confrontations effectively is acquiring the ability to distinguish between potentially good and bad conflicts *during their early stages*. Thus, we need to learn to recognize the symptoms of disagreements that potentially lead to escalating and unproductive conflicts. This is not always easy, but there are several obvious identifiers of potentially good and bad conflicts. One class of such identifiers is the characteristics of the people in the encounter. People who are likely to engage in unproductive conflicts are the easiest to spot. (See Box 12.1.)

Specifically, individuals likely to escalate a conflict and cause it to have unproductive outcomes often show signs of stress, even during the early stages. Such signs can include a conspicuous loss of energy or dedication; rapid conversation; noticeable anxiety; and various forms of compulsive behavior, such as overeating, excessive consumption of alcohol, or drug abuse. If an unproductive conflict persists over a long period, other symptoms are likely to be evident. These might include spending inappropriate amounts of time and resources to undermine an opponent at the expense of getting important work done.[6]

There are a variety of additional identifiable indicators of unproductive conflicts as well. The effects of conflict on individuals tend to vary, both by person and by particular situation. It is important to be able to recognize the

BOX 12.1   *A Closer Look*

Observable Indicators of Unproductive and Productive Conflict

Unproductive Indicators

Decrease in dedication.

Anxiety and energy loss.

Rapid speech or conversation.

Excessive or compulsive behaviors.

Attempts to sabotage or undermine.

Productive Indicators

Friendly conversation.

Open discussion and deliberation.

Productive problem solving.

Creativity and innovation.

Careful and critical analysis.

negative signs of either a useful and positive conflict or one leading to counterproductivity. If we recognize these signs in time, it may be possible to redirect a degenerating communication encounter into one that yields productive consequences.

Productive conflicts can be identified by a different set of signs. The most important are the participants' characteristics and actions. The most obvious include friendly conversation between the opponents. At the nonverbal level, the signs are smiles versus frowns, friendly versus threatening gestures, and the distance at which the opponents have positioned themselves during their encounter.

Most of the constructive signs are very obvious. Yet, typically, people who witness a productive conflict tend to see the encounter as negative because people are committed to the idea that all conflicts are somehow destructive. As explained earlier, such a narrow interpretation is both incorrect and unfortunate. Certain types of conflicts can result in positive

consequences that far outweigh the potential drawbacks.

For example, two individuals working together on the design for a product's sales campaign with a profit potential are likely to engage in conflicts. Disagreements will inevitably occur over issues pertinent to the potential effectiveness of the campaign. These may focus on which media to use, how to phrase the advertising copy, what colors are best, what meanings to imply, whether personal endorsements are worthwhile, and so on. In such a case, some level of disagreement is a normal part of a productive working relationship.

Conflicts of this kind amount to a forum for deliberating on and discussing important professional ideas. Depending on the profession, the result of such a conflict can be a thorough and critical analysis leading to a variety of ways to solve problems more effectively. Those solutions may be innovative legal strategies, more accurate medical diagnoses, more efficient production techniques, or (among students) more effective presentations in classes. Constructive conflicts of this type are common in almost all educational, professional, and business environments.

Conflicts can be productive in *any* setting where people communicate with one another. For example, conflicts of varying intensity constantly arise between husbands and wives. Most couples find some mutually acceptable means of dealing with such disputes—they have to if they are to continue their relationship over time. These solutions range from the congenial settlement of long-term disagreements to the mutual definition of acceptable ways to communicate during heated discussions over sensitive issues. Thus, constructive conflict and negotiation can be beneficial for couples because it signals a commitment to the relationship.[7] To illustrate this point, consider some typical and potentially productive conflicts that were observed between a couple.

Gabe and Janna met their first year in college. By their second year, they had moved in together. Soon enough, they found that living together involved a variety of problems, which, if not handled constructively, could affect the stability of their relationship. They hadn't anticipated having conflicts over money, household chores, friends, privacy, or pets—to list just a few of the issues that caused trouble during the early years of their relationship. It seemed as if almost every issue they dealt with provided a basis for disagreement. They often didn't understand why they were so frequently at odds with each other.

Ironically, before Gabe and Janna moved in together, they seemed to agree on almost everything of importance. They truly believed that they had considered and worked through all the potentially rough spots in their relationship. They were sure that they were completely compatible, and that they agreed on everything important. Both assumed that they would marry one day.

Clearly, any number of things happen to couples that can contribute to the occurrence of conflict. For example, research has identified three primary tensions that can lead to conflict for couples. First, they will experience differing needs for *independence,* and changes in these needs are highly likely to produce conflict. Another source of potential conflict is each individual's need for *expression.* Each must learn to balance the need to state personal views with remaining open to the other's views. Finally, *change* is also a source of tension, as the couple balances the need for predictability and novelty in their relationship.[8]

Thus, it is in the first few years of a relationship that people are particularly likely to experience conflicts. During this period, failures to resolve conflicts often have negative outcomes. Statistics on divorce, for instance, show that breakups are most likely within the first 10 years. If the marriage survives this critical early period, it is likely to last much longer.[9]

The truly critical issue is how the couple will handle their conflicts. In large part, the success or failure of their relationship hangs on that issue. If they allow minor disagreements over the problems that arise to escalate into negative and unproductive conflicts, they will soon be making

arrangements to move on—separately and alone. If they can deal with their disagreements, and keep their conflicts from escalating, they are more likely to continue their lives together.

Fortunately, when conflicts occur, many couples try to direct their discussions toward productive outcomes, which is just what is required. Obviously, the actual nature of the effort depends largely on the specific causes of each conflict; however, it also depends greatly on the probable reactions of the people involved in the encounter. It is important, then, to consider the common ways in which people deal with conflict.

Common Causes of Conflict

It is important to understand some of the common *causes* of conflicts. Recall that conflict was defined earlier within an economic perspective. The definition stressed that conflicts arise when there is a scarcity of some reward over which competition has developed. This is still a good explanation, but two other major causes can also play a part in generating conflicts between people. One is obvious, consisting of the *meanings* constructed by each party for the messages transmitted and received during a process of communication. The other cause is more subtle. It consists of *contextual factors*—physical settings, sociocultural situations, and social relationships in which people communicate.

Misunderstood Meanings as a Primary Cause

To say that the meanings people construct during processes of communication can be a primary cause of conflict is to state the obvious. Unless people communicate with each other, there is no way for them either to initiate or to engage in conflict. In this sense, the meanings aroused as people disagree, become competitive, or get angry are—as logicians say—a "necessary" but not "sufficient" condition. Conflicts of all types are in some way an

Unless the resolution of a conflict is approached constructively and rationally, it will quickly escalate and become impossible to resolve.

one who was defensive and hurt. When that happened, both Frank and Ebony began communicating messages with negative, malicious, and hateful meanings about each other to others at work. Thus, from the beginning, the meanings constructed by each party from the messages transmitted served to define, maintain, and escalate their conflict.

Generally, then, problems of meaning are at the heart of virtually any conflict. Stated more systematically, the *constructions of meaning* by communicating parties assume a primary instrumental role in generating and escalating conflicts. Also, messages transmitted and interpreted by senders and receivers who are in the process of conflict development are likely to be of *low accuracy*. These two conditions work together as central causal factors in producing and intensifying controversies.

Contextual Factors That Can Generate Conflict

Although, as the previous section indicates, misinterpretations of meanings may be primary causes of conflicts between people, other conditions typically seem to the participants to be the real causes. In particular, many people in a conflict come to believe that their opponent's flawed personality is responsible for what occurs. In fact, this is almost universal. To the participants in a conflict, it seems obvious that bad people cause bad relationships.

To those outside the conflict, this is not at all obvious. It usually seems to observers that both parties are decent people and that their conflict must be the result of other factors. In most cases, this is far closer to the truth. The flawed-personality explanation seldom holds up.

A very different set of factors that contribute to the generation of conflict can be found in the *context* within which communication takes place. Here, as the general transactions model suggests, both the sociocultural situation in which the communicators are involved and the social relationships that exist between

outgrowth of human communication.[10] By the same reasoning, it is our ability to communicate fully and effectively that enables us to resolve conflicts. Ironically, then, although communication skills enable us to show aggression and hostility toward each other, it is precisely these same skills that provide the foundation for peaceful resolution of conflicts.

Returning to the opening discussion of what happened between Frank and Ebony, their conflict started with her pregnancy leave and, in her absence, his increased workload. Every time Ebony attempted to clarify the meaning of her parental priorities to Frank, he became increasingly hostile. Eventually, what Frank provided in the way of feedback to Ebony made her change from an empathetic co-worker to them play parts in shaping the meanings they construct as they communicate. The physical setting may also play a part, but it is these two contextual features that contribute most significantly to the generation or escalation of a conflict, regardless of the personalities involved.

The sociocultural situation. It is not difficult to see how the sociocultural situation in which people pursue goals can be a factor in generating conflict. In the conflict that developed and escalated between Frank and Ebony, both parties were in a work situation. In that feature of their context, both were dedicated to the same overall group goals: doing a good job in carrying out their work assignments. However, each had very different personal goals. Frank believed that everyone should do his or her fair share in accomplishing the group's goals. He felt strongly that he was doing more than his share. Although Ebony sympathized with Frank's position, she thought the company should handle the problem—not her. After all, she had her own personal goals of balancing work and family to pursue. This kind of situation—where all the parties are basically good people, but all are convinced that they are in the right in pursuing their own goals—is almost certain to generate conflict.

Counterparts to Frank and Ebony's situation are common in daily life. Every family in which a husband and wife both have jobs to which each is dedicated has many potential sources of conflict. Personal goals, work goals, and family goals can produce an unstable mix. Two common goal conflicts come easily to mind: (1) If either relational partner has a great opportunity for advancement, but it requires moving to another city, which individual should sacrifice his or her career goals? (2) If the partner's job requires evening and weekend work to be successful, should the other partner complain or make sacrifices to help achieve that goal?

Even achieving the routine domestic goal of living together as a family provides bases for conflict. For example, whose job is it to do the shopping, run the vacuum cleaner, look after the cars, make the beds in the morning, do the laundry, feed the cat, cook the meals, clean up the kitchen, and take out the garbage? Each of these may seem to be a minor assignment, but each poses the potential for a disagreement that can escalate into conflict.

Social expectations. The way in which expected patterns of social relationships are a basic feature of a communication context was discussed at length in Chapter 5. The basic social rules for behavior in human groups—norms, roles, ranks, and controls—provide powerful definitions concerning who can legitimately communicate what kinds of messages to whom within a particular social situation. Misunderstandings or misinterpretations of those expectations are often at the heart of breakdowns and difficulties in groups; serious problems of group disintegration can develop when there is confusion concerning any of those rules and expectations.

In precisely the same way, conflicts can arise. That is, conflicts among members of a group tend to occur when inaccuracies in communication lead to normative confusion, unclear definitions of roles, inadequate understanding of the rules of power and authority (social ranks), and ineffective messages of social control.

How difficulties with such rules can contribute to a conflict can be illustrated by referring again to Ebony and Frank. The social relationships between them in the workplace were defined by a large number of norms, role definitions, considerations of social ranking, and social controls. These placed many demands on them—dictating both their overall behavior in the group and the kinds of messages each could transmit to others. These rules were shaped by a number of policies, decisions, practices, and company politics.[11] Like all employees, Ebony and Frank constantly had to deal with these complexities and consider them when formulating messages and making decisions.

Frank had to follow a compelling norm demanding that he satisfy the boss by doing a good job, in spite of the frequent absences of his co-worker. At the same time, he had to cope with a different norm that required him recognize the importance of Ebony's parental responsibilities. It was not possible to comply with both norms—a situation of *anomie,* a contradiction and confusion of norms.

Another confusion that contributed to their conflict was the conflicting role definitions that prevailed. Specifically, Frank was convinced that he was supposed to do what his job description stated. Such descriptions communicate clear, formal definitions of an employee's rights, duties, and responsibilities. However, recent family-friendly company policies confused the situation by allowing Ebony to leave work when her child was sick—communicating a different set of rights, duties, and responsibilities to both parties. Job descriptions (and even temporary assignments) of work roles indicate what employees are supposed to do (or not do) if they are to perform their work satisfactorily. Workers can experience confusion when their roles are not clear or when they conflict with those of others.

In many respects, then, the expectations prevailing in Frank and Ebony's work situation forced both of them into a no-win situation. Both were caught in a turmoil of confusing and even conflicting definitions of norms and roles created by the company.

In the situation that developed, therefore, their supervisor must bear a special responsibility. An effective leader understands social expectations defining relationships and takes steps to head off conflicts before they begin by appropriate communication. Instead of explaining to both Frank and Ebony ahead of time valid reasons for the policy and providing some means of temporary compensation to Frank for his efforts, the supervisor let a serious conflict develop. If anyone was most responsible for the messy situation that developed, it was neither Ebony or Frank. It was the boss.

Generally, then, the social settings within which people communicate can be major factors in generating or escalating conflicts. Potentials for their development arise out of the general sociocultural situation (work, family, and so on) within which people interact, and especially when confusions and contradictions exist in the rules and expectations defining their social relationships. Although conflicts can arise because of personality clashes, few are due solely to the bad actions of bad people.

Personal Styles of Coping with Conflict

Much human behavior is relatively predictable because it follows patterns of action and reaction deeply established by the rules and expectations of our culture. This is certainly true of reactions to conflict. That is, it is possible to predict with some degree of accuracy how people will try to deal with various kinds of conflict situations. These can be described in terms of what communication researchers refer to as *personal conflict styles.*[12]

Although the idea of common coping styles to deal with conflict has been examined in a number of ways, the discussion here will focus on an assessment and classification system devised by Ralph Kilmann and Kenneth Thomas.[13] According to these investigators, one's personal style of handling conflicts is based on the need to meet two interconnected yet competing objectives: *concern for self* and *concern for the opponent.* Although these appear to be different goals, they actually overlap in terms of the way we make decisions about coping with confrontations. Kilmann and Thomas maintain that this struggle over goals is a reflection of our underlying desire to be either competitive or cooperative in dealing with opponents in a conflict situation.

Our resolution of these two interdependent goals in a specific situation represents our predictable style of reacting to all kinds of conflicts. This formulation allows for the assessment of five distinct **conflict styles** based on competition, collaboration, compromise, avoidance, and accommodation. These five coping strategies point directly to alternative ways in which conflicts are typically handled. (See Box 12.2.)

BOX 12.2   A Closer Look

Kilmann and Thomas's Coping Strategies for Conflict

1. *The competitive style.* Characteristic of strongly competitive people who view all conflicts as win-lose events; they believe that winning is their only goal and that having a concern for their opponent is both unnecessary and unimportant.
2. *The collaborative style.* Characteristics of individuals who not only are seeking personal goals in a conflict situation but also care about their opponents' objectives.
3. *The compromising style.* Characteristic of people who fall somewhere between the competitive and cooperative styles. Their behavior in conflicts is sometimes incorrectly interpreted as giving in.
4. *The avoidance style.* People with this style do not expect to attain personal goals, nor are they sympathetic to their opponents' goals. They refuse to engage in conflict. Avoiders stay away from situations where conflicts are likely to arise.
5. *The accommodating style.* This is the opposite of the competitive style. Such individuals are passive; they forgo trying to reach their personal goal, opting to let their opponents reach their goals.

The Competitive Style

Although the term *conflict* is generally defined to mean some sort of competition over something of importance, certain people are so predictably and strongly competitive that they can be described as fitting this style. What are such people like? Strongly competitive people narrowly view all conflicts as win-lose events. They believe that winning is their only goal and that having a concern for their opponent is both unnecessary and unimportant. Highly competitive people would agree with statements like "Once I get going in a heated discussion,

I am unable to stop" and "I like the exhilaration of engaging in disagreements and conflicts." In short, such people are commonly very aggressive in the way they react to conflicts.[14]

Individuals who clearly illustrate a **competitive style** are often found in jobs or professions where this style may be an advantage, such as courtroom lawyers, police interrogators, labor leaders, salespeople, or people doing other types of work in which conflicts are defined as strictly win-lose encounters. For example, in labor-management negotiation meetings, where demands are being made by representatives from both sides, every issue is defined as a win-lose conflict. Opponents on both sides predictably act as if they are doing battle to their last breath. In some respects, such competitive behavior is often seen as acceptable in negotiation sessions for union contracts because they have become a tradition, but these same behaviors can be far less productive in other conflict situations. However, they are typical of highly competitive individuals who tend to use this style as a means of resolving their disputes.

The Collaborative Style

Another common style of coping with conflict is based on collaboration, which literally means working jointly or willingly in cooperation with an opponent. The **collaborative style** is characteristic of people who not only are seeking their own goals in a conflict situation but also have a sincere concern for their opponents. People who use this style would endorse statements like "When I get in a conflict with someone, I try very hard to find mutually acceptable solutions," or "I like to assert myself, but I also like to cooperate with others." These kinds of statements communicate that the person is trying to find alternative solutions to conflict that will maximize reaching goals for both participants.

An example of collaborative styles of conflict would be two members of a study group who have a conflict over whether each chapter in their textbook should be outlined and summarized as a study aid. Each disagrees with the

Some people avoid conflict by trying not to step on each other's toes.

other's position on the need for the outline. However, both parties feel that their personal objective in studying together is to get a better grade on the next test (self-goal). At the same time, they believe that by working together both parties can score higher than by studying alone (opponent's goals). Thus, in an attempt to maintain a productive relationship, they resolve their disagreements and work collaboratively toward a shared interpretation of what should be done.

The Compromising Style

A third common and predictable way of coping with conflict is based on compromise. This means reaching agreement by making mutual concessions. People who use a **compromising style** fall between competitive and cooperative styles on the coping strategies continuum. The behavior of compromisers in conflicts is sometimes incorrectly interpreted by observers as "giving in."[15] Individuals using this style would agree with statements like "I accept the fact that I can't always get my way," "I am thankful to get part of what I asked for," and "I know I am going into a conflict where I will have to give a little."

An example of a person using this style would be an individual who is brought in as a third party to help resolve a conflict. Neither of the protagonists is willing to reach an agreement,

and all efforts to resolve their differences thus far have resulted in increased hostility. Finally, they agree to seek help. Typically, third parties in such mediation efforts try to get the participants to compromise. There really are no alternatives to getting each party to move toward a middle-ground position so that each of the opponents makes equal compromises.

The Avoidance Style

The typical coping style of individuals who are passive, subservient, and acquiescent in conflicts is avoidance. People using an **avoidance style** do not expect to attain personal goals from the conflict, and they are not sympathetic to their opponents' goals. They just want to escape from the whole confrontation. Thus, they generally remain idle and refuse to engage in what we would normally expect from people in a conflict. Avoiders simply stay away from situations where conflicts are likely to occur. If they are in a conversation that is beginning to sound like a disagreement that might lead to a conflict, they find some way to remove themselves from confrontation.

Conflict avoiders are easily recognized. Many are highly apprehensive individuals. Some are even reclusive people who fear all interaction with others. For example, people with high levels of communication apprehension experience fear and anxiety when they have to talk with others in a variety of social contexts. If they are communicating in a situation that might lead to conflict, they will either excuse themselves or find some reason to change the topic of discussion. They will not make any effort to pursue their side of a position on an issue.

At the same time, people use avoidance for other reasons. Many times conflicts break out among one's fellow workers, associates, relatives, or friends. Often, taking part in such confrontations has no payoff for an individual. Indeed, it can easily result in significant losses. It may be far better to stand on the sidelines and watch the fight, rather than join the fray for no personal benefit. Although this is also a form of avoidance, it is a mature and thoughtful strategy that does not imply negative, apprehensive personality characteristics.

The Accommodating Style

People who use an **accommodating style** give in to their opponents. Thus, accommodators are the opposite of competitors. They tend to be passive in that they forgo trying to reach their personal goal, preferring to let their opponents reach their objectives. Moreover, accommodators typically go along with the position argued by the majority of the individuals in the conflict. In other words, they exhibit no resistance and make every effort to yield to their opponents' decisions.

Examples of accommodators in conflicts are those who never want to be the leader of a group, those who commonly defer to authority, and those who place a higher value on relationships than on being decision makers. Arguing with accommodators is very difficult: They simply will not engage in much disagreement over anything. Even if they initially take a position on a particular issue, they will push the point only to a limited extent. Their primary objective in all conflict situations is to conform to the majority position of their opponents.

Although each of the above styles may be used exclusively by some people, it is more likely that a particular person will *shift among these various styles,* depending on the nature of the conflict and the characteristics of the people involved. On any given day, an individual may choose to compete vigorously with one person, collaborate with someone else, and compromise with still a third. The same individual may avoid a particular conflict but accommodate in another. It all depends on the circumstances and on whether the conflict is with a loved one, a stranger, a person in a lower status position, a boss, or a child.

These conflict styles offer different models for us to apply to try to defuse, escalate, or ignore a particular conflict. This implies, of course, that we are capable of shifting from one style to another. If this is not the case, and if we do tend to use one strategy to the exclusion of the others, at least understanding our likely reaction to conflict situations can be helpful. Specifically, such understanding provides us with important information about ourselves that can help us in selecting conflicts in which we really want to engage. In this way, we can better assess which conflicts are likely to be productive for us and which strategy we want to use in managing our conflict relationships. Take a minute now to complete the self assessment in Box 12.3 to determine your own tendency to appreciate (or avoid) a good argument!

Successful Conflict Negotiation

Now that we have seen some of the more salient causes of conflicts and the different strategies people use to cope with them, the remaining question in this chapter is, How do people successfully negotiate conflicts when they occur? Answering this question begins by defining the term **negotiation**. Then, clear-cut principles and guidelines for negotiating many kinds of conflicts will be presented.[16]

Understanding Negotiation

In a basic sense, *negotiation* refers to *a continuing set of transactions in which proposed solutions are communicated back and forth between opponents for the goal of reaching agreement on ways to resolve a conflict.* The basis of negotiation is carefully planned communication with the goal of the mutual construction of similar meanings between opponents. Thus, communication plays two parts in conflicts: Just as it is a primary cause of conflict, it is also the principal means by which opponents negotiate conflicts.

The effective resolution of a conflict cannot begin until all the individuals involved agree on two basic principles: First, both parties must seriously propose and consider alternative solutions, and second, they must agree to reach an agreement as an end-product at some point. All the discussion in the world will not result in a successful resolution if the people involved do not agree that they want to air their grievances and try to resolve their differences. In fact, what usually occurs when opponents in a conflict are not serious about negotiating is further escalation of the controversy.

Guidelines for Negotiation

Over several decades, a group of researchers at Harvard University studied extensively the process of conflict negotiation. The result of these efforts has been the identification of a number of specific guidelines concerning *the most feasible way to negotiate conflicts through the use of carefully planned communication.*[17] Their program has been widely recognized as one of the most effective approaches to conflict resolution. The section that follows is directly derived from that program, with a review of the basic features of the researchers' suggested guidelines and illustrations for using them.

Part of the popularity of this approach has to do with its demonstrated applicability. That is, it provides a practical and effective way to negotiate conflicts by using a specific set of guidelines for planned communication. The method, called *principled negotiation,* is designed to help people get what they want from others in every conceivable type of conflict—from the simplest to the most complex—and to do so within an ethical framework, which is very important. For example, principled negotiation has been used successfully in a variety of legal situations (including sticky divorce cases), union contracts, and a host of political and organizational conflicts, from local to international levels.

These recommendations boil down to eight points, which, if applied correctly, lead to successful negotiation and thus conflict resolution. (See Box 12.4.) Each point is a kind of rule of thumb as to what should and should not be done. Each guideline is discussed and then applied to Ebony and Frank case.

Don't bargain over positions. People trying to negotiate should not attempt to bargain over, to explain, or to justify the different positions they hold on the issue of disagreement. Conflicts are seldom if ever negotiated when people try to bargain solely over their opinions on a particular issue. If each party in a conflict takes a strong position on an issue, and if the positions are far apart, there is simply no way for negotiation to occur. People are never going to reach an agreement over an issue if they stubbornly maintain very different views. Moreover, trying to defend very different positions on an issue can only contribute to opponents' greater and more heated separation on that issue.

Recall a similar stalemate over positions in Frank and Ebony's case. Ebony approached Frank several times in an attempt to explain and justify her position regarding her need to leave work to care for her family. She wanted to stress that it wasn't her fault and that she was simply doing what any parent would and should do. Frank, on the other hand, wasn't buying that interpretation, and he wanted to defend his position that she was taking advantage of the system every time her kid had a sniffle and, thus, shirking her work responsibilities.

The result was an early collapse of the relationship. Her bargaining attempts increased Frank's hostility toward her. Moreover, because Ebony was frustrated in her bargaining effort, she ended up as antagonistic toward Frank as he was toward her. As long as they narrowly stuck to their initial positions, no concessions could be made.

Separate the people from the problem. This rule stresses the need to get the participants to look beyond personal characteristics and suspected motives to see the nature of the problem itself. That is, what led up to the conflict? What is at stake for both parties? How might it have happened to anyone in the same social situation and set of relationships? This makes a great deal of sense. Individuals engaged in conflicts often tend to build up more and more antagonism toward each other. The results of such antagonism

BOX 12.3   *Argumentativeness Scale (ARG)*

We know that people have different ways of approaching conflict, ranging from competitiveness to avoidance. Moreover, we know that some of us are more skilled at arguing than others—and when they are, they are more likely to approach arguing differently from others who are less skillful. Turns out, what we're good at, we also typically enjoy. Thus, if you enjoy engaging in a good argument, then you are also probably pretty good at it. Take a minute now to complete this questionnaire and then calculate your Argumentative (ARG) score immediately afterward.

Directions: This questionnaire contains statements about arguing *controversial issues*. Indicate how often each statement is true for you personally by placing the appropriate number in the blank to the left of the statement. Use the following options:

    5 = Almost always true for you
    4 = Often true
    3 = Occasionally true
    2 = Rarely true
    1 = Almost never true for you.

____ 1. While in an argument, I worry that the person I am arguing with will form a negative impression of me.

____ 2. Arguing over controversial issues improves my intelligence.

____ 3. I enjoy avoiding arguments.

____ 4. I am energetic and enthusiastic when I argue.

____ 5. Once I finish an argument I promise myself that I will not get into another.

____ 6. Arguing with a person creates more problems for me than it solves.

____ 7. I have a pleasant, good feeling when I win a point in an argument.

____ 8. When I finish arguing with someone I feel nervous and upset.

____ 9. I enjoy a good argument over a controversial issue.

____ 10. I get an unpleasant feeling when I realize I am about to get into an argument.

____ 11. I enjoy defending my point of view on an issue.

____ 12. I am happy when I keep an argument from happening.

____ 13. I do not like to miss the opportunity to argue a controversial issue.

---

typically include rampant misunderstanding, counterproductive communication, and irrational or overly emotional reactions.

This was clearly the case between Ebony and Frank. Each of them failed to separate the person they were dealing with from the problem. In fact, Frank and Ebony saw each other as the problem. As long as they continued to approach their conflict in this fashion, no negotiation could occur. The more Frank and Ebony associated the issue of their conflict with their beliefs about the personal motives and characteristics of the other, the more they became each other's enemy. They forgot that they were working in the same organization; they forgot that they shared the same basic business goals. Their conflict became a personal vendetta—a search for ways to punish the other as a bad person.

Separating people and their personalities from the problems that cause conflicts reinforces that it is the relationships between the people that are most important. If people take the position that their relationships must remain constructive if at all possible, their opponents will change how they perceive, think about, and communicate with them. Thus, the participants are less likely to overreact emotionally to what they say and do to each other. What occurs when opponents separate people from problems is an increased willingness to negotiate compromises and solutions that may be acceptable to all.

_____ 14. I prefer being with people who rarely disagree with me.

_____ 15. I consider an argument an exciting intellectual challenge.

_____ 16. I find myself unable to think of effective points during an argument.

_____ 17. I feel refreshed and satisfied after an argument on a controversial issue.

_____ 18. I have the ability to do well in an argument.

_____ 19. I try to avoid getting into arguments.

_____ 20. I feel excitement when I expect that a conversation I am in is leading to an argument.

Calculating Your Score:

1. Add your responses to items 1, 3, 5, 6, 8, 10, 12, 14, 16, and 19 = _____.
2. Add your responses to items 2, 4, 7, 9, 11, 13, 15, 17, 18, and 20 = _____.
3. Complete the following formula:
   60 – Total from Step 1 = _____.
   Total from Step 1 + Total from Step 2.
   YOUR TOTAL SCORE = _____.

Interpreting Your Score:

Possible range of scores for ARG: 20–100. (If your own final ARG score does not fall within that range, you made a computational error.)

The average score or midpoint for the ARG is around 60. If your score falls below 50, you are among those who are low in argumentativeness or what we call, "avoiders." Avoiders try to keep arguments from happening and generally feel relieved when an argument is over. When compelled to argue, low ARGs experience unpleasant feelings before, during and after the argument. If your score falls above 70, you are classified as high in argumentativeness, or what we call, "approachers." Approachers find arguing an exciting intellectual challenge, a competitive event. High ARGs feel invigorated, satisfied and delighted after an argument—even if they did not win. If you scored between 50 and 70, you are "moderate" in your argumentativeness orientation. Moderate ARGs neither like nor dislike arguing. In order for them to argue, they must feel that either there is something to gain or the probability of winning is high.

Source: Infante, D. A., & Rancer, A. S. (1982). A conceptualization and measure of argumentativeness. _Journal of Personality Assessment,_ 46, 72–80.

Focus on interests, not positions. This guideline recalls the first principle: the recommendation that opponents refrain from bargaining over positions. Instead, opponents should focus on interests, looking beyond their positions to the personal goals and needs that must be served for each party. That is, in all conflicts, opponents take positions because of the personal interests at stake. In Ebony and Frank's case, Frank's primary concern was to ensure that he wasn't taken advantage of at work. Ebony's primary interest was to balance her work and family obligations responsibly.

If Frank and Ebony had focused on their primary interests and dealt directly with what was at stake, they might have been able to negotiate their conflict themselves. They could have explained their interests, discussed alternative ways to solve their dilemma, and sought help and support from their manager. For example, Ebony could have worked with Frank by offering to come in on a weekend to make up the work she was unable to do. Alternatively, Frank could have suggested that she take work home to be completed.

Invent options for mutual gain. An important part of resolving a conflict is to get to a point where each party gets something he or she values out of the process. One of the many incorrect assumptions that we make that can lead to an escalating conflict is that there is room for only

BOX 12.4   🔍 *A Closer Look*

Eight Recommendations for Principled Negotiation

1. *Don't bargain over positions.* Never bargain over the different positions people hold on the issue of disagreement. Trying to defend different positions contributes to more disagreement.

2. *Separate the people from the problem.* Look beyond the personal characteristics and suspected motives of the people involved to what actually led up to the conflict.

3. *Focus on interests, not positions.* Look beyond individual positions to the goals and needs of each of the participants.

4. *Invent options for mutual gain.* It is not true that there is only room for one winner. Opponents should try to invent options of mutual gain.

5. *Insist on using objective criteria.* Begin negotiation by setting mutually agreed-upon rules within which to discuss potential solutions.

6. *Develop the best alternative.* Know ahead of time exactly what the bottom line will be to resolve the conflict.

7. *Cope with resistance to negotiation.* Don't attack the position the resistant opponents are advocating. Deal with what is compelling them to be resistant. Minimize the time spent defending ideas; ask for criticism and advice from opponents. Ask questions and pause for answers.

8. *Deflect dirty tricks.* Recognize a dirty trick; raise the issue candidly, question the appropriateness of using the trick, and negotiate over it.

one winner. This is by no means always true; as indicated earlier in the chapter, people engaged in conflict do not have to be enemies. Remember also that conflicts, if handled properly, can actually be beneficial to everyone involved.

To illustrate, if Frank and Ebony had not acted as if there was only one solution to their disagreement, a variety of other possible outcomes could have been considered. From the start, the position of each was "It's my way or no way." Making the assumption that there is only one possible solution precludes negotiation.[18] The opposite is assuming that there are alternative ways to resolve the problem so that everyone can gain. This is an important foundation for successful negotiation. If both Ebony and Frank had been open to communicating about options for mutual gain, they would have been able to negotiate their conflict.

Insist on using objective criteria. Remember that, in negotiation, it is important to have mutually agreed-upon rules within which to communicate about potential solutions. Establishing shared criteria for evaluating proposals from one side or the other is part of that process. If this is not done, opponents in the heat of an intense conflict typically impose subjective criteria when they are evaluating proposed solutions. The phrase *subjective criteria* refers to personal or private standards for making such evaluations—standards not necessarily shared by others.

Subjective criteria seem fair *only to the person using them.* Objective criteria seem appropriate to *most people.* When subjective criteria are used, conflicts escalate because they often seem unfair to the other party. Employing an agreed-upon set of objective criteria that both parties regard as fair provides an important basis for successful negotiation.

Using subjective standards will almost always lead to such evaluations as "Your proposal is totally unfair to me" and, in response, "You are unwilling to make any concessions." These judgments are oriented toward only one side's feelings and interests. A more effective approach is for opponents to develop a mutually agreed-upon set of objective criteria before negotiation even starts.

Neither Frank nor Ebony even considered employing objective criteria for evaluating their positions in the conflict. If they had mutually generated a set of objective criteria when their conflict first started, they could have handled the disagreement much more rationally. Also, if they had taken the time to do this, they would have been able to reach an agreement.

Develop the best alternative. Even when people follow the five previous guidelines, things can go wrong. In this case, several other strategies need to be addressed to reach a successful negotiation. One important strategy is for each person to develop an acceptable fallback position in case the negotiated outcome is not entirely satisfactory. In other words, it is wise to have in mind an acceptable alternative to what is considered the most desirable negotiated agreement.

This alternative refers to knowing ahead of time exactly what is acceptable as a resolution to a particular conflict. It is the bottom line by which a particular conflict can be resolved. It has to be a realistic position. It may not be the most desirable option, but one that could be agreed to if all else fails. When a party to a conflict has such a position already in mind, he or she is in a much better position to ask for concessions from the opponent.

If both Ebony and Frank had gone into their disagreement with a solid grasp of their own best alternative to a negotiated resolution, the composition of their conflict would have been very different. For example, several "best" alternatives for Frank could have been compensation for overtime/overload, more reasonable, extended deadlines for his added responsibilities, or even some assistance from others in the office. By developing an acceptable alternative to his already held position (i.e., Ebony must stay at work and do her job), Frank might have been able to gain some concessions from Ebony. Similarly, Ebony needed to develop her own best alternative for a negotiated agreement. Rather than insisting that Frank must simply adjust to her parental demands, she should have a fallback position. She might have offered to come in early or leave late.

Cope with resistance to negotiation. We all run into people who simply stonewall all attempts to negotiate a conflict. This can bring things to a permanent halt. We must be prepared to cope with such a situation without abandoning the negotiation process. Fortunately, most people, even when in a resistant mood, can be persuaded to communicate and even to negotiate if it is done in the right way. It can be a complex and difficult task, but there are several ways it can be approached.

First, never attack the position a resistant opponent is advocating.[19] Look beyond the position to the personal values and interests that are motivating the individual on the issue. It is these that are leading to his or her unwillingness to change. By dealing directly with what is driving the resistance, it is much easier to weaken it. Proposed solutions can be based on those same values and interests. People have a difficult time resisting proposed solutions that are consistent with their own needs and orientations.

Second, minimize the time spent defending your own ideas during conflict, and solicit criticism and counsel from your opponent. This disarming tactic seems to work especially well. When given the opportunity, people can rarely resist the chance to criticize and give advice. This, of course, changes their perspectives on the issues at stake.

Third, ask questions and pause for answers. This promotes a transactional process—a rather simple and obvious idea based on the analyses of verbal and nonverbal communication in the early chapters. It is an important tactic for lowering resistance to negotiation because it opens and promotes communication, which in turn provides a basis for proposing mutually acceptable criteria, different perspectives, alternative solutions, and so forth.

Promoting a transactional process would have helped greatly in Frank and Ebony's conflict. Specifically, if during Ebony's initial attempts to communicate with Frank, she had resisted attempts to justify leaving work, and instead, solicited his council on how to handle the work problem she had created, he might have responded differently. This is not to say that Ebony was at fault for Frank's early resistance; but if she had minimized the time spent defending herself, Frank might have been willing to offer suggestions that would have brokered a quick solution.

Deflect dirty tricks. Many conflicts are characterized by dirty tricks that opponents often play on each other.[20] These can include using deception, inventing phony facts, invoking ambiguous authority, creating stress, employing retribution, and making personal attacks. (See Box 12.5.) This final guideline is based on three steps to follow when an opponent appears to be employing a dirty trick: (1) "recognize the tactic," (2) "raise the issue explicitly," and (3) "question the tactic's legitimacy and desirability—negotiate over it."[21] These three steps can sometimes deflect further dirty tricks.

BOX 12.5   *Ethical Concerns*

Dirty Tricks

- Dominating the conversation to prevent others from verbalizing their own opinions.
- Eliciting comments that are intended for later use to embarrass or harm.
- Tactically employing knowledge about someone's vulnerabilities to gain an unfair advantage.
- Storing up numerous gripes to bewilder others by unloading them all at once.
- Presenting irrelevant or trivial issues and arguments in an attempt to gain advantage.

Source: Ross, R. S. & Ross, M. G. (1982). *Relating and interacting* (pp. 77, 138–141). Englewood Cliffs, NJ: Prentice-Hall.

Chapter Review

- Every human conflict represents a unique and complex process. However, each of us can determine the kinds of outcomes we get from the conflicts in our lives.
- Conflict is a large part of our culture. Many conflicts result from our shared cultural orientations regarding competition and getting ahead.
- Conflicts are not inherently negative; many can have positive consequences. People determine how productive or unproductive their conflicts will be. Some people tend to be highly competitive; others are collaborative. Some are compromising or accommodating; others attempt to avoid conflict at any cost. Finally, some people shift from one style to another as the occasion demands.

- The primary cause of conflict is problems in communication. However, context can serve as the basis of conflict as well. Both the specific situation in which we pursue goals and the social relationships that prevail in that situation can cause conflicts between people.
- The Harvard group's recommendations for negotiating conflict include suggestions concerning bargaining over positions, separating people from the problem, focusing on interests rather than positions, inventing options for mutual gain, using objective criteria for assessing issues, developing a bottom-line position for settling a conflict, coping with resistance to negotiation, and handling dirty tricks.

Key Terms

conflict	competitive style	compromising style	accommodating style
conflict style	collaborative style	avoidance style	negotiation

Notes

1. Berkowitz, L. (1964). Aggressive cues in aggressive behavior and hostility catharsis. *Psychological Review, 71*, 104–122; Berkowitz, L. (1965). The concept of aggressive drive: Some additional considerations. In L. Berkowitz (Ed.), *Advances in experimental social psychology* (vol. 2, pp. 301–329). New York: Academic.

2. DeFleur, M. L., D'Antonio, W. V., & DeFleur, L. B. (1981). *Sociology: Human society* (3rd ed., pp. 93–94). Glenview, IL: Scott, Foresman.

3. At least some Americans stress the opposite—to avoid standing out or being pushy. Native American groups, such as the Hopi and the Pueblo groups of New Mexico, share a strong orientation toward maintaining harmony and avoiding actions that imply one is trying to rise above others.

4. This definition is similar to Lewis Coser's. See: Coser, L. (1956). *The functions of social conflict* (p. 8). New York: Free Press.

5. A similar discussion of conflict is offered in: Jandt, F. E. (1985). *Win-win negotiating: Turning conflict into agreement*. New York: Wiley.

6. Ibid., p. 101.

7. Booth, A., Crouter, A. C., & Clements, M. (Eds.). (2001). *Couples in conflict*. Mahwah, NJ: Lawrence Erlbaum.

8. Pearson, J. C. (2001). Conflict in our intimate relationships. In W. F. Eadie, & P. E. Nelson, (Eds.). *The language of conflict and resolution* (pp. 47–56). Thousand Oaks, CA: Sage.

9. Rollins, B. C., & Feldman, H. (1970). Marital satisfaction over the life cycle. *Journal of Marriage and the Family, 32*, 20–28.

10. Ibid., p. 10.

11. Koehler, J. W., Anatol, K.W. E., & Appelbaum, R. L. (1976). *Organizational communication: Behavioral perspectives* (p. 241). New York: Holt, Rinehart, and Winston.

12. Wilmot, W. W., and Hocker, J. (2010). *Interpersonal conflict* (8th ed.). New York: McGraw Hill; Cai, D. A., & Fink, E. L. (2002). Conflict style differences between individuals and collectivists. *Communication Monographs, 69*, 1, 67–87.

13. Kilmann, R., & Thomas, K. (1975). Interpersonal conflict-handling behavior as reflections of Jungian personality dimensions. *Psychological Reports, 37*, 971–980.

14. Wilmot & Hocker, *Interpersonal conflict*.

15. Ibid.

16. Fisher, R., Ury, W., & Patton, B. (2011). *Getting to yes: Negotiating agreement without giving in*. New York: Penguin.

17. This definition is similar to Fisher and Ury's position. See: Fisher & Ury, *Getting to yes*.

18. Ibid.

19. Ibid.

20. Ibid. For the indirect and informal ways subordinates use to "get even," see: Fortado, B. (2001). The metamorphosis of workplace conflict. *Human Relations, 54*, 9, 1189–1221.

21. Fisher & Ury, *Getting to yes*, p. 135.

Chapter

13

Using Media to Communicate Interpersonally

Margaret knew that it was going to be a busy day. She was Vice President of Human Resources for Grover Industries, and an important part of her job was to oversee all personnel actions. In plain English, this meant making final decisions regarding hiring, firing, and promoting for her division, as well as representing the corporation in settling grievances with the union and so on. Grover Industries was a large organization, with over 8,000 employees.

She began with the stack of memoranda on her desk from supervisors who had interviewed prospective applicants, whose cases had been passed on to her for final approval. The cover memo for the first application was from Phyllis, a mid-level manager in accounting, explaining the qualifications of one applicant. Margaret was annoyed that the memo from Phyllis rambled on and was poorly organized.

Before making a final decision about each applicant, Margaret "Googled" each person, and reviewed his or her profile on LinkedIn and Facebook. She even looked up the "Klout Score," a measure of influence and activity on social networks, for one potential hire who would monitor the company's social network presence. Of course, she reviewed each background check reported by their security firm. Finally, Margaret carefully composed letters offering positions to those who had been selected. Such letters had to be done carefully, with accurate details of the salary and benefits and a clear explanation of the nature of the position and the duties for which the new hire would be responsible.

Once the letters were completed, Margaret turned to the long list of telephone calls she had to make. Even though she made dozens of phone calls a day, she did not think the telephone was an effective medium for explaining important ideas or complex situations. Role-taking by phone was difficult with strangers, and feedback was limited. Moreover, many people used the phone thoughtlessly.

Between tasks, she turned to her e-mail. She screened the list of incoming messages and answered those she felt were most important, forwarding some to an assistant to deal with. She shook her head when she saw some of the messages with poor composition and errors in spelling and grammar. "People should learn," Margaret said to herself, "to prepare their messages more carefully."

Late that afternoon, she logged onto a website and learned about an important upcoming meeting of human resource professionals. "Great," she thought, "I'll mark my calendar." She then reviewed Grover's website and updated some information.

Before wrapping things up for the day, Margaret used Skype for a prearranged videoconference with four personnel managers in the other cities with Grover Industries plants. "This is really an effective way to discuss common problems," Margaret thought. "Just a few years ago, we would have had to travel to some centrally located city and take a whole day to get done what we just accomplished in less than an hour." Finally, as she was leaving her office,

she sent a text message to her husband, reminding him of their dinner plans for the evening.

Using media to communicate directly and effectively with other people may seem simple and easy. However, there are a great many ways that mistakes and unwanted negative impressions can be made.[1] Furthermore, in spite of the growing use and reliance upon new media technologies for communication, effective writing and speaking skills when using media are still essential. Such skills are critical for landing a good job and then advancing up the ranks. People with poor spelling and incorrect grammar are easily spotted, as are poor speaking styles. Such individuals are the least likely to be hired, are the most likely to be stuck in dead-end jobs, and may be among the first to be fired.

This chapter examines the interpersonal communication process as it takes place using a number of different media, from traditional written letters and memos to electronic systems that instantly move information. Significant differences exist between face-to-face communication and mediated communication. The chapter also shows that the widespread adoption of any new communication technology affects the social, economic, and cultural lives of those using it.

Face-to-Face versus Mediated Communication

Chapter 1 discusses human communication as a process that may be conceptualized in both linear and transactional terms. As explained, the linear model indicates that a source person begins with some purpose or goal that can be achieved with a message. The source then selects a pattern of symbols to represent intended meanings. Those same initial stages characterize any linear form of communication, whether media are involved or not. Once the message has been formulated, the transmission stage requires that the distance (and in some cases time) between the message sender and the intended receiver be overcome. Obviously, media are used both to increase the distance the message can travel and reduce the amount of time the transmission requires.

What do such media actually do? In terms of the analysis in Chapter 1, they simply transport "information" from one place to another. Examples of *information* are the sound waves produced by human vocal cords or the variations in light patterns that travel between a person sending a written message and a receiver who reads and interprets the symbols. Information, then, is a set of physical events. It can range from simple agitations of air molecules, or variations in light patterns, to high-frequency radio waves relayed through space by satellites.

Whatever the means of information transmission, in the final stages of the communicative act the physical stimuli are perceived by a human being and reconstructed into symbols. That is, one or more receivers interpret them within their own frameworks of meaning. Those interpretations may or may not match those hoped for by the sender. Accuracy in communication is attained only if the decoded meanings of the receiver correspond to those intended by the sender. It is with those functions in mind that the actual role of media and the difference they make in the communication process will be examined.

Why Media Matter

A **medium** can be defined simply. It is *a device that moves information over distance (or through time) so that people who are apart can communicate.* The simplest medium that might be imagined is a children's toy, consisting of a wire stretched between two tin cans. When the message sender shouts into his or her tin can, the bottom of the can acts as a diaphragm and sends vibrations (information) along the wire. The bottom of the can at the other end vibrates sympathetically and reproduces the sound, which is then interpreted by the receiver.

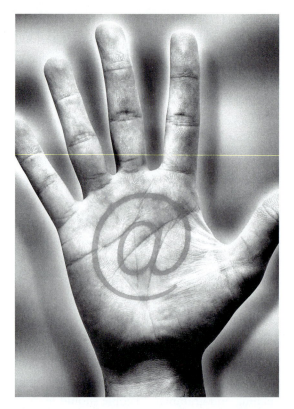

The Internet has become the major source for transmission of information in the digital age. However, effective writing and speaking skills are still essential for effective communication.

Although it doesn't really work all that well, the communication principles are there. Like the tin cans and the wire, all the media that are used today are designed to move information across distance, whether they are traditional handwritten letters or sophisticated digital technologies.

A key question to ask is whether the process of moving information across distance by using a medium *alters the correspondence* in some way between the meanings intended by the sender and those constructed by the receiver. As this section will indicate, the answer is a definite yes. Each medium places its own demands on both the sender and the receiver. As will be seen, mediated communication is both similar to, but different from, face-to-face communication. Some media alter the process greatly. Others do so only minimally.

The major similarity between mediated and face-to-face communication is that there are people at each end—just as in the example of the tin cans and the wire. There is a source person transmitting. That source has to formulate a message at one end so that a receiver (or receivers) can interpret it at the other. If the medium requires writing, the process is complicated by the rules, skills, and requirements of written expression. So it is with other media. Each has its own requirements. Thus, contemporary media systems—such as cellular telephones and computers linked by satellite relays—continue to make use of the basic features of human communication—verbal and written symbols based on language, nonverbal cues and signals, transactional constructions of meaning, and all the rest, but they add additional features as well. Thus, despite the similarities in the underlying principles of all forms of human communication, there are also important differences. Some involve the social relationships that link face-to-face senders and receivers versus mediated communicators. Others involve the technical features of the media themselves.

Media limit effective role-taking. One difference in the social relationship between sender and receiver when media are used is the limit on role-taking. This activity on the part of the message sender is especially critical in face-to-face communication. As explained in Chapter 1, the sender mentally plays the part of the receiver (assuming his or her role) to try to predict how that person will interpret and respond to particular kinds of messages. If the sender knows the receiver well and can anticipate subtle ways in which he or she will interpret a given message, there can be very effective role-taking.

Role-taking can be accomplished reasonably well with some media, such as private and confidential letters between people who know each other intimately. However, it is far less possible to anticipate others' responses in many of the communication contexts where media are used.

For example, when a typical internal memo is sent by e-mail to all employees in an organization, it is simply not possible to forecast the potential reactions of each person reading the message. Even when friends text or talk by phone, role-taking can be less than complete. The sender cannot anticipate exactly how the receiver will react as the message is read.[2]

Media limit the adequacy of feedback. A second problem in using media centers on the process of feedback. Here, more depends on the nature of the medium than on the existing relationship between the communicating parties. For example, in a phone conversation, at least some immediate feedback is possible. Nonverbal cues such as voice tones, long pauses, audible yawns, or laughing convey to the speaker the manner in which his or her message is being received. However, some cues that would be visible in a face-to-face situation cannot be observed. One never knows in a phone conversation—even one with an intimate friend—whether that person is smiling, frowning, slumped down looking bored, or listening intently with an enthusiastic expression (unless both are using FaceTime on their iPhones while talking). Thus, most conversations via phone are not as rich in nonverbal feedback as one in which the two parties can see each other.

Thus, in most instances, accuracy in communication is automatically reduced by limitations imposed by the use of a medium. For this reason, face-to-face communication is the mode of choice for those who want to get a valid understanding of others' feelings or views or who are trying to gain their cooperation, sell them something, or otherwise influence them. Nothing beats face-to-face communication when accuracy is desired or influence is an important goal. That is true whether it is a conversation among peers, an interview, a personally presented sales pitch, or a talk before a group.

Despite these disadvantages, mediated communication is critical to us all and has long been a part of civilized life. Throughout history, increasingly sophisticated media have been used—from carvings on stone, to systems using computers, and satellites—to preserve information over time or to send it over longer distances at an ever-faster pace.

Using media to develop relationships. Early research on computer-mediated communication (CMC) often presented a bleak picture. For example, one of the first studies of the social and psychological effects of Internet use found that people who spent even a few hours a week online experienced higher levels of depression and loneliness than those who did not. In addition, participants in the study reported a decline in their interaction with family members and friends. The researchers hypothesized that relationships developed over distances without face-to-face contact did not provide the psychological support to maintain satisfying relationships. In other words, such relationships were shallow and caused participants to feel less connected to others.[3]

As a result of this and other research, communication theorists were skeptical of the ability to develop close relationships online. They assumed that the lack of nonverbal and social context cues, especially in early text-only messages, limited the usefulness of CMC for building relationships. However, a communication professor, Joseph Walther, proposed an alternative theory in which he claimed users adapt to the limitations of computer-mediated communication and are able to develop close relationships. Walther's theory, **social information processing theory (SIP)**, acknowledges that nonverbal cues such as facial expression, tone of voice, appearance, gestures, touch, etc., are missing from computer-mediated communication. However, users find other cues instead. The theory makes the following points:[4]

1. When individuals are motivated to develop relationships, they form impressions from any cue system that is available. Thus, CMC users can create mental impressions of what others are like based entirely on the verbal content of an online message. These

impressions help to determine if the individuals will continue to develop a relationship.

2. The exchange of social information through text-based computer-mediated communication takes place at a slower rate than face-to-face communication. As a result, impression formation takes longer to accomplish. Yet, given sufficient time, it does take place.

SIP theory states that individuals are creative and able communicators who can convey warmth, affection and emotion even in the absence of nonverbal cues. How is this achieved? Individuals use praise, statements of affection, self-disclosure, compliments even when disagreeing, more frequent responses, and other verbal behaviors.

In fact, Walther claims that there are times in which computer-mediated communication may result in a higher quality of communication than face-to-face communication. Through the use of selective self-presentation, people who communicate online have the opportunity to make a positive impression by writing about their most positive personal characteristics and accomplishments without contradiction from others. They can avoid revealing those aspects that they feel are less positive. Receivers, in turn, will attribute an idealized image of the sender from this small amount of information. In addition, computer-mediated communication allows the sender to plan and edit the message, knowing the receiver will tend to the message at a convenient time—actions that are not always possible with spontaneous face-to-face communication.

Of course, newer forms of computer-mediated communication are now in use, including social networking sites such as Facebook, LinkedIn, Pinterest, and many others. Social networking sites differ from text-only CMC not only because such sites include photos and links to other content, but also because users create a personal profile, build a network of contacts, and add information to the profiles of other users. In other words, social networking sites have information controlled by the owner of the profile, and information contributed by others that is not directly under the control of the owner of the profile. This is important because outsiders may trust and give more weight to the content of friends' comments, or wall posts, when assessing the credibility of the profile owner. Walther refers to this as the warranting value of information, or the perceived validity of information presented online.

The theory is not without limitations or criticism. For example, some studies suggest that online relationships can form just as quickly as when people meet face-to-face, which contradicts one of the major ideas of the theory. However, social information processing theory is a useful theory that cautions us not to assume automatically that strong relationships can't be developed online.

How Communication Technologies Change Our Lives

The current revolution in communication processes is more than a change in the gadgets we use or the speed of transmission of messages. Throughout human existence, new media have always altered people's personal and social lives. When papyrus replaced stone, the portability of the new medium allowed empires to extend their boundaries. When Johannes Gutenberg's press made hand-copied manuscripts obsolete, large-scale production of books resulted in the rapid spread of new ideas in science, religion, economics, and politics. Those ideas altered the entire nature of society. Thus, the transition to new communication technologies has always had both personal and social consequences.

The reason for these changes is that new technologies alter the communication process itself. This is because each new medium (1) imposes its own special requirements on the ways in which messages are formulated, (2) governs the speed and convenience with which message transmission takes place, and (3) influences the ways in which receivers reconstruct meaning from what is sent to them.

The ways in which new communication technologies influence both the communication process and the people who use them can be well illustrated by noting the changes that took place during the 19th century after the introduction of the now-venerable telegraph. That new technology (at the time) made it possible to send words at a mind-boggling 186,000 miles per second—literally the speed of light. Before 1844, when practical telegraphy started, the fastest way of moving a message was by swift horse or by train, which could reach the then-frightening speed of about 40 miles per hour.

The telegraph was adopted very rapidly. The first message, "What hath God wrought?" was sent in 1844 along a copper wire between Washington, DC, and Baltimore. Within a mere three years, New York had been linked by wire to New Orleans, nearly 2,000 miles away, and a network of the magic wires connected every major city in the United States.[5]

How did this new medium change the communication process? For one thing, a message via telegram took on distinctive meanings for both sender and receiver that other forms of communication did not have. The implication was one of *urgency* and *importance*. When families received a message sent to them via the wires, they knew that it probably meant emergency or crisis. Telegrams brought news of illness or death, making the opening of the envelope a stressful event. For business and commerce, the great increase in speed provided by the wires enabled the stock market to develop, and the nation's economic activity accelerated greatly. Changes also took place in communication within the military as well as in the government as a whole.

Communicating by wire had broad and subtle effects on the entire society. For one thing, it greatly expanded the consciousness of U.S. citizens concerning events far away. Prior to the telegraph, newspapers concentrated mainly on events in local communities. There was some national and international coverage, but it was often delayed and limited. In the spring of 1848, the Associated Press (AP) was formed for the purpose of transmitting news stories over the magnetic wires.[6] A single reporter could send copy to many papers on the system at the same time. Within a decade the AP had expanded nationwide, and even the smallest newspapers got a daily flood of wire stories from outside their local area, reporting relatively trivial happenings such as fires, robberies, and murders.

When local papers published these accounts, many critics were offended; they thought the press was encouraging crime and should serve a more noble purpose. (Many still think this today.) Moreover, the wire services provided stories for both liberal and conservative newspapers. Reporters had to develop a style that was not supposed to be rejected by either group. It was out of this requirement that objective journalism developed—a way of reporting that did not editorialize (take sides) in its stories.

Thus, the introduction of the telegraph as a new medium of communication was far more than just a technological advance. It brought about significant changes in both interpersonal and mass communication that touched the lives of every citizen. It altered the functioning of our most basic institutions and changed the way people thought about their society.

What lessons can be drawn by this brief look at the development of the telegraph as a new medium? We are now living in a period of accelerating change in communication media that will bring about consequences even more sweeping than those of the 19th century. During the 21st century, our ability to communicate with one another has grown to a degree that has never before been experienced. We already have satellite-based digital phones that can be carried in our pockets—phones that can contact anyone in the world who also has a telephone. Hundreds of television channels are now available and more will come. More sophisticated computers and social networks will expand the offerings on the Internet. Although it is difficult to forecast the specific ways in which these media will influence us, both individually and collectively, it is certain that our ways of communicating will become different

from the way they are now. Inevitably, these changes will influence us personally, socially, and culturally. Test your approach to the use of new technology by taking the "Communication Technology Avoidance" self-assessment at the end of the chapter. (See Box 13.4.)

Communicating Using Traditional Written Media

Written communication has been around for thousands of years and will continue to be used in both traditional and innovative media that will be developed in the future. The present chapter does not address such traditional print media as books, magazines, and newspapers (they will be discussed in the next chapter). The focus here is on written communications that originate with a single individual who wants to transmit a message to one other person, a small group, or even a larger number of people. In particular, this kind of written communication takes place when people write personal or business letters or send memoranda in the workplace. Later sections include written communication that makes use of technologically sophisticated media.

Letters

Writing effectively is a complex skill that can be acquired only by experience.[7] Nevertheless, letters remain the medium of choice for many kinds of message transmissions. These include private correspondence between friends or family members as well as various messages from individuals to organizations, between officials in different organizations, and from organizations to outsiders.

In an organizational context, letters remain of critical importance. Composing a concise and readable letter is one of the most important job skills that one can master. Letters are sent for a host of purposes including to advise customers and clients, request donations, solicit business, ask for voters' support, respond to specific inquiries, provide notification, build goodwill, and accept or reject applicants.

People have been exchanging letters since writing began, and until very recently, this was the only way that people could communicate at a distance.

The great problem of letters in earlier times was, of course, just getting them to their destinations. The process was neither reliable nor cheap. Mainly it was the rich and powerful who sent letters. In the United States until about 1850 it was very costly to use the mails, and they were dreadfully undependable. Although Congress established an official postal service as early as 1790, it was not until the mid-19th century that a reliable and inexpensive system became fully operational, making use of improved roads, trains, and steamship lines.

How well can letters achieve that complete and accurate communication discussed at a theoretical level in Chapter 1? What factors reduce accuracy conveyed in a letter, compared to one transmitted face-to-face in a verbal and nonverbal context? On the other hand, are there features of this medium that give it an edge in certain situations? (See Box 13.1.)

Advantages. One nice feature of traditional (hard-copy) letters is that they are not based on a complex technology, and they are truly portable. All the letter sender needs is a pen or pencil, writing paper, an envelope, and a stamp. After delivery, letters can be carried easily and read almost anywhere.

Letters are especially important in work settings, because letters can be saved or placed in a file—as official documents. In business correspondence, a distinct advantage of letters over either conversations or phone calls is that they imply the recipient should do something—make a decision, take some action, or at least send a written reply. Oral communication often lacks this implication of required action. Conversations can accidentally—or conveniently—be forgotten. The same is true of the content of phone calls, which leave no permanent trace. Letters, however, are physical objects, and they sit there on the desk

---

---

or the computer of the receiver, reminding the receiver that they need to be dealt with.

Another positive feature of letters is that they can be composed thoughtfully at the writer's own convenience and pace. In writing to a loved one, words and phrases can be selected with care. The same is true of business or official communication, where the words used can have significant legal implications. In private exchanges, a letter can be carried in a pocket, saved as a treasured memento, and read or reread at one's own pace. In these ways, letters as a medium share a distinct advantage over face-to-face communication, in which one can regret irretrievable messages formulated and transmitted in haste.

Finally, letters sent through the U.S. mails have one clear advantage: They are *private*. Strict federal laws forbid tampering with a person's mail or even the mailbox. Although these laws do not totally deter a highly motivated snoop, they certainly reduce people's temptation to take a quick look at another person's letters. As will be explained, other media—such as e-mail—lack these legal protections. Publicized messages sent by unprotected media can have embarrassing and sometimes disastrous consequences.

Disadvantages. Composing a letter thoughtfully—getting each phrase and sentence in a logical sequence and spelling every word correctly—can be a demanding task. For many people, these steps seem like a lot of bother, and it is far easier just to pick up the phone and call or quickly knock out an e-mail message.

There is no doubt that writing a good letter requires skill with word selection, spelling, syntax, and grammar. Even if the intended receiver is a loved one or close friend, drafting a letter requires creative composition. Many of today's employees lack these skills, which is a significant handicap.

Although there are complex rules for good letter writing that cannot be reviewed adequately here, some basic guidelines can help in the preparation of any business letter:

- *General features.* Business correspondence requires *meticulously correct grammar, spelling, and punctuation.* Such letters must meet the highest possible standards of neatness, and most should be written or transmitted on formal letterhead stationery that identifies the source of the communication.

- *Format.* There are a variety of acceptable business letter formats for positioning the address, the salutation, the body of the letter, and the signature. To some degree, these are a matter of personal preference, although many organizations insist on a common style. A host of manuals and stylebooks set forth various business letter formats in use today.[8]

- *Appropriate message.* A number of considerations are involved in formulating effective messages for business and professional purposes. The appropriate strategy depends above all on the writer's goal. Such goals can range from applying for a job to persuading a receiver to buy a product. Some letters bring happy news about promotions and raises; others bring unwelcome news

about denials, refusals, and unfavorable decisions.

Whatever their purpose, effective letters express sincerity and concern, and they are readable and concise. They not only emphasize the main points in the message, but also have some pleasantries. Letters, especially those bringing bad news, must be couched in diplomatic terms.

Memoranda

A **memorandum** is similar to a letter in that it is a document sent to one or more receivers. However, it has important features that are different from those of letters. For one thing, it serves a relatively restricted purpose.[9] The memorandum (or "memo" for short) is a widely used medium for communication among members of an organization, particularly when a permanent record is desired. There are some organizations that use memos to communicate with people outside the group, but memos are seldom used for communication between friends, family members, or other private parties.

The memorandum is a very "stylized" medium. That means it follows a very standardized form that has evolved for internal organizational communication over many decades. Some organizations even supply preprinted forms for convenience, and users can just enter the information on the form that they want to transmit. Minor variations exist, but generally a memorandum follows the form shown in Figure 13.1.

Within organizations, this medium is used for a number of purposes. One is **vertical communication**—up and down the levels in an organization. Supervisors send messages to subordinates. Subordinates use memos to transmit requests or to send reports up the line. Memoranda also flow between divisions in an organization. At times the CEO will send a memo to everyone in the entire organization if the message is important to all.

Advantages. As the Latin origins of the name suggest, one of the most important features of

+---+
| |
| **Memorandum** |
| |
| TO: (receiver's name) |
| FROM: (sender's name) |
| DATE: (month, day, and year) |
| SUBJECT: (concise statement of topic) |
| |
| |
| |
| (The body of the message goes here, |
| seldom exceeding one |
| 8 1/2 × 11-inch page.) |
| |
+---+

FIGURE 13.1

Memorandum Format
The typical memorandum format includes "To,"
"From," "Date," and "Subject" headings, as well as
the body of the message.

memoranda is that they *leave a memory,* that is,
a "paper (or electronic) trail," in an organization. Memoranda, like letters, are documents
that can be placed in a file. Such files often develop around sensitive transactions. (An example would be performance evaluations of
specific individuals for purposes of granting or
withholding salary or promotion.) Memos are
the proof that certain communications took
place, such as warnings about incompetence or
sexual harassment. Thus, memoranda are often
used later, in hearings or legal cases, when there
are disputes about what happened earlier. For
this reason, even though it is quicker and more
convenient to call or to send a quick note via
e-mail, the memorandum is a more formal type
of communication that effectively preserves
messages through time.

Most memoranda are concise. This makes
them convenient for both senders, who need
not compose a long message, and receivers,
who do not have to plow through long documents. A rule of thumb is that the memo's message should fit on a single page; if this is not
possible, the rule says, send the message another way.

Disadvantages.   Although memoranda serve
important purposes in an organization, they do
have a number of limitations. For one thing,
they lack legal protection. Further, they suffer
from the same limitations on role-taking and
immediate feedback as do other media.

Even if memoranda are marked "Confidential," there are no legal sanctions to protect
their privacy. In other words, memoranda lack
the official protections and deterrents applicable to letters sent through the U.S. mail.

Certain kinds of memoranda tend to be
given little attention or ignored. This can be
particularly true for those that are addressed to
collective receivers like "Staff," or "All Personnel." They may actually contain very important
information. However, this address is so impersonal that the memos may be seen as another
form of junk mail, and receivers may either
throw them away after a quick glance or not
read them at all.

Finally, memoranda suffer from numerous
role-taking and feedback limitations. Because
they need to be concise and to be formulated in
official language, memos may contain unnatural and sometimes awkward wordings. This is
especially true of memoranda that are sent to
many people at different levels and in different
areas in an organization. The differing abilities and resources with which receivers bring to
the task of constructing interpretations of the
memo's meaning can significantly reduce the
accuracy of the communication.

Despite these disadvantages, however, the
memorandum remains an important medium
in organizational communication. In particular,
because it has the advantage of being a memory
record, it will not be easily replaced.

Communicating by Telephone and Related Media

The basic instrument and technology by which we telephone one another was invented in 1875 (and patented the following year) by Alexander Graham Bell.[10] And, despite the incredible growth and remarkable changes in telephone technology, when we use this medium we still use the basic principles that he developed. The telephone, like the telegraph before it, had a powerful influence on the communication process during the 19th century and introduced great changes in our culture.[11] Today, not only are we very frequent telephone talkers, but our worldwide system has made other media possible. Long-distance and oceanic telephone lines and satellite-based systems carry media, such as computer networks and teleconferencing worldwide.[12]

Telephone

In 2003, only 3 percent of U.S. households used only a wireless cellular (or mobile) phone for calls, while 43 percent used only a fixed "landline" phone. In 2008, however, the number of cell phone only users surpassed the number of landline only users for the first time as many households eliminated their landlines. By the end of 2009, one of every four American homes (24.5 percent) had only wireless telephones. In addition, one of every seven homes (14.9 percent) had a landline but received all or almost all of their calls on wireless phones. Those most likely to live in a household with only wireless telephones include young adults aged 25–29 and adults living in poverty. Approximately 2 percent of U.S. households live without any telephone service.[13] (See Figure 13.2.) The rate of growth for cell phone adoption and use is estimated to be the fastest of any electronic medium in history, including radio, television, VCRs, and compact disc players.[14]

Thus, telephones continue to be, and will remain, one of our most important interpersonal communication media.

We all use telephones so often that they are taken for granted. Americans make in excess of an astonishing 800 million telephone calls a day. This means more than three calls per day for each member of our population. One of the unique features of this type of interpersonal communication is that we seldom take the time to plan a telephone message before we start talking. We simply grab the phone, dial the number, and begin. However, there is a reasonably well-understood etiquette used by thoughtful senders and receivers.

As it was true of the telephone more than a century ago, the explosion in cell phone use is having both personal and social consequences. For example, some experts claim, "downtime" is becoming a thing of the past. Air travelers kill time between flights dialing business contacts and friends. Commuters caught in traffic make office calls from behind the wheel. Parents can keep a tighter "leash" on the whereabouts of their children. The use of cell phones is pervasive; on the street, at the theater, during meetings, in restaurants, at the mall—even in restrooms. Emergencies can be reported in seconds rather than minutes, potentially saving lives. At the same time, however, studies have linked cell phone use by motorists to as many as 1.5 million accidents every year. Thirty-five states and the District of Columbia have banned texting while driving, while nine states and DC bar the use of handheld cell phones except during emergencies. More and more businesses are fighting lawsuits filed by those who claim they were injured in accidents caused by employees talking on company cell phones.[15]

Clearly, cell phones have erased communication boundaries to enable conversation anywhere and anytime. According to many people, however, they have created another problem: *wireless boorishness.*[16] Complaints and anger over the inappropriate or discourteous use of cell phones by others are increasing. In addition, the use of cell phones with built-in digital cameras has created unique problems. These devices have triggering fears that they can be widely abused as "spy cams," causing some

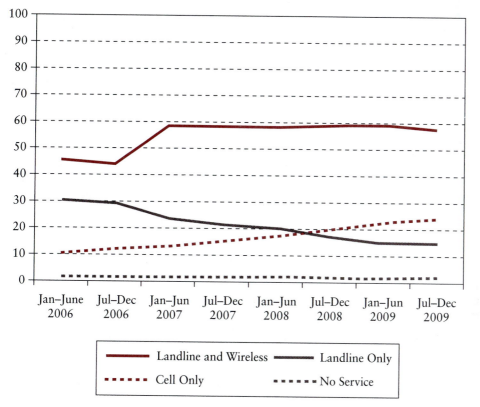

FIGURE 13.2

Household Telephone Status, 2006–2009

Source: CDC, National Health Interview Survey: http://www.cdc.gov/nchs/data/nhis/earlyrelease/wireless201005_tables.htm#T1

health clubs to ban these camera phones from locker rooms where voyeurs can snap compromising photos of patrons.[17] However, along with the complaints of inappropriate use of cell phones came a plea for the development of an etiquette for cell phone use. (See Box 13.2.) Norms of behavior include the following:

- *Don't be a cell phone "hotshot."* No one is impressed with how many calls you receive, or your personal (and loud) ring tone. Just because it is possible to receive a call anywhere doesn't mean you should. No one wants to hear the intimate details of your conversations; this can be a problem, especially for people who are seated next to you. Whenever possible, move away from others to answer your calls.

- *Don't yell.* Using a cell phone like a megaphone is distracting and annoying to others.

- *Accept the limits of the technology.* When cell connections disintegrate, call back after finding a stronger signal or a land line. Shouting over the static will not improve the reception.

- *Avoid answering a cell phone during a business meeting.* It sends the message that the intruder on the cell phone is more important than the client next to you. It may also cost you business. Turn your cell phone off *before* the meeting, or switch it to "vibrate" mode. If you know a call is coming, and it is absolutely *necessary* to take the call, forewarn others of the call and the fact that you must take it. Even then, take the phone outside the

BOX 13.2   🔍 *A Closer Look*

Do's and Don'ts for Cell Phone Users

Always do the following:

- Turn off the phone before entering such settings as a movie theater, classroom, church, or concert hall.
- If you forget to do this, turn it off instantly if it rings in such a setting.
- Turn off the ringer and keep the phone on vibrate mode when you are in crowded public areas.
- Speak as softly as possible when others are present so that they need not share your call.
- Show respect for others near you by limiting the length of your call.

Never do the following:

- Display or use your cell phone conspicuously to impress other people.
- Place your phone between you and someone else when dining or doing business. To do so implies that any caller is more important than the person you are with.
- Discuss private and personal issues in public settings where others can hear.
- Approach a rude cell phone user with anger. Don't respond to rudeness with rudeness.

Source: Based on the recommendations of Carol Page, a promoter of cell phone etiquette. *The Boston Globe*, July 26, 2003.

meeting to someplace private and quiet. Don't use your cell phone during meetings for other purposes, such as reading or answering your e-mail messages or texting.

- *Do not answer a cell phone, or even allow one to ring, during public events.* This includes religious ceremonies, concerts, symphonies, speeches, or other presentations. Always exercise good judgment and consideration of others.

Text messages. Overall, 83 percent of U.S. adults own cell phones, and most of these adults (73 percent) send and receive text messages. In a recent survey, 31 percent of adults who regularly text said they prefer sending and receiving text messages to talking on the phone. By far, young adults are the most avid users of text messaging. Cell owners between the ages of 18 and 24 exchange an average of 109.5 messages during a typical day, which amounts to a total of more than 3,200 texts per month. In comparison, older adults typically send or receive about 10 texts daily.[18] Although text messaging (also called SMS, for short message service) is fast and efficient, remember that some mobile phone plans require subscribers to pay a premium for text messaging. This means you want to use text messaging effectively and courteously. Here are a few tips for doing so:[19]

- Keep text messages brief and informal. Do not use text messaging to discuss important or sensitive topics.

- Avoid abbreviations and slang when texting for business purposes. Although it is common to use abbreviations such as "u" for "you" when texting friends, it is best to avoid doing so when texting supervisors, clients, etc.

- Consider others' usage habits and schedules. Just because you are awake and have your cell phone near you doesn't mean your recipient will appreciate a text message from you any time of the day or night. Remember there are times when people cannot (or should not) respond to a text message immediately.

- Be considerate of those around you. Don't compose and send text messages while having a face-to-face conversation with someone else.

- Don't text during meetings. In most cases, texting during a meeting or presentation is considered as rude and unacceptable as taking a voice call. If you are expecting an urgent message, inform the meeting facilitator or presenter ahead of time.

How public should cell phone conversations be? How private is your cell call?

Communicating by Computer

Much as the telegraph and then the telephone have had dramatic impacts on our society, today's computers have in many ways revolutionized communication. This revolution, which is still taking place with breathtaking speed, has already brought about remarkable modifications in the ways people relate to one another.

Background

Communication by computer in homes and businesses is a comparatively recent development. The machines began as esoteric devices that could be used only by highly trained technicians. Today, the widespread use of computers is influencing the way we work, the way we communicate with others, and the way we spend our leisure hours.

Although early forms were used as far back as World War II, computers before about 1960 were large, difficult to use, very expensive, and (by today's standards) severely limited in capacity. A large computer in the 1950s might have had as much 4K RAM (random access memory). That means a temporary working memory of only about 4,000 letters, numbers, or other characters. Also, before 1960 there was nothing like the word-processing software we know today. A computer accepted only cumbersome decks of cards with holes punched in them, which the machine read one by one. It then processed the information and printed out the results on paper, because there was no monitor on which to view information. Although such machines represented a great leap forward, and calculated numerical data swiftly, each could be used by only one person at a time. Because they were not connected to any other computers, they had no communication applications.

In 1960 Digital Equipment Corporation made a significant advance in computer hardware by developing the first commercially available *interactive* computer. This meant that it allowed what a person was typing on a keyboard to be displayed on a screen as it entered the computer's working memory. Then a software program written by Dan Murphy at Massachusetts Institute of Technology (MIT) allowed people to write and edit programs on a screen *before* they were run. This was truly a great advance. Murphy's program was the forerunner of today's word-processing software.[20] Soon, scientists and engineers began working on the idea of *linking* several computers in different locations (via long-distance telephone lines).

Out of this need to transmit information to others effectively via computer came the first **computer network**. By the late 1960s, a small community of computer scientists—backed by the U.S. Defense Department's Advanced Research Projects Agency (ARPA)—came together to determine how scientists and engineers could communicate and share technical data quickly and easily, even if they were widely dispersed.[21] They designed a system by which computers could be linked by long-distance phone lines. With several universities linked in this way—via a computer network—rapid communication between researchers became possible, allowing faster scientific advances.

Only one additional step was needed to create a new medium of communication: This was how to *package* information electronically for efficient transmission. Paul Baron of the Rand Corporation found the solution. He realized that digital messages (where each letter or character is coded into a distinct pattern of electronic impulses) could be sent in "packets" over phone lines by one computer to another. In this way, the network would be an efficient communication medium. In 1968 a group of scientists began to design the network.

The original ARPA net was very slow by today's standards, but at the time it seemed blazingly fast and a marvel of technology. It was designed to use smaller computers to handle the phone connections and larger, more sophisticated ones to pass along the messages. All were linked through a network of dedicated phone lines. In 1969 the first ARPA net site was installed at UCLA. By 1970, facilities were completed at Harvard and MIT in Boston.

Today people use a vast system of computer networks to communicate back and forth across the nation at speeds vastly faster than the original system. They can transmit complex information in a few seconds that would have taken days or even weeks in the pre-computer-network age. Furthermore, people do not have to be sophisticated about computers to use such systems.

Of significance to most people using computers for communication purposes is the Internet. It was originally designed during the Cold War as a secure system of communication for military and government purposes. Even in the event of an attack on key U.S. cities, military and government officials could still communicate because the system could not easily be damaged. The reason was that it was like a spiderweb. It was a network of networks. Connecting links among the networks form a weblike system, and although large parts of the system might be destroyed, messages could still get through, following the remaining connected lines.

Today's Internet has expanded enormously. It is a huge cooperative venture that links millions of host computers in local networks around the world. The Internet's size is difficult to specify as it continues to grow at a rapid rate. Sometimes called the information superhighway, this vast system of linked smaller networks provides worldwide access to e-mail, surfing, topical searches, information websites, databases, and many other information resources. On the World Wide Web can be found an almost unlimited number of interactive multimedia displays with audio and video messages, advertisements, and entertainment. Many thousands of websites display information—websites ranging from simple home pages of individuals to sophisticated presentations by corporations, government agencies, colleges and universities, charitable groups, and virtually any other source imaginable.

In a somewhat different way, many corporations and other groups have developed *intranets*—local area networks (LANs) that function like the Internet but that only serve their members. These networks, which are not open to the public, are used to distribute e-mail and other information to those within the system. Intranets usually consist of a set of linked desktop computers and a server—a computer that coordinates them. Intranet systems allow individuals at work stations to send and receive e-mail and to share programs, software, data files, storage space, and expensive equipment. Composing and sending e-mail on an intranet is no different from doing the same on the larger Internet.

The following sections briefly review three specific functions for communicating by computers: using e-mail, social networking sites, and *teleconferencing*. Although there are many other uses for computers, these require the user's active involvement. These computer communication functions represent mediated interpersonal communication in that the individual plays a significant role as a sender—deciding what a message should contain, designing its style, assessing its likely influence on its receiver, and so on. Thus, the same steps that were outlined in Chapter 1 in the discussion of the basic linear model are followed when communicating by computer.

E-Mail

Although networks originated to make it easier for scientists to communicate, they are now almost universally used for business and personal correspondence. One of the most commonly used applications is **e-mail** (electronic mail)—messages sent from one person's computer to another's by combining word-processing software with nearly instantaneous transmission.

Advantages. E-mail allows people to send messages that are transmitted almost instantly to the receiver's electronic address. The source's computer sends electronically coded "information" along the network directly to the recipient's computer. The receiver can see the message on the screen and respond immediately if he or she is "online." If not, the message is stored in the receiving computer's memory so that it can be called up later. Messages can be sent instantly to a single receiver, to several receivers, or to an entire local area network. E-mail can be sent through gateways to receivers in other networks or to receivers in other countries via international connections.

Obviously, e-mail has great advantages. It is incredibly fast and efficient, which by itself justifies its cost for many organizations. E-mail can significantly reduce the time required to make decisions, which can increase profits and efficiency in operations.

Disadvantages. One disadvantage of e-mail is that, in most systems, if the receiver's terminal is off, the message simply reaches its electronic destination and sits there, until the receiver connects to the server or computer. Thus, the sender is at the mercy of the receiver's schedule for reviewing e-mail messages.

Another problem with e-mail is that it is not private. Sometimes an e-mail address belongs to a group of people, rather than just one person. It is not always clear whether a particular computer address belongs to an individual or to several people. This means that one ought to think twice before transmitting highly sensitive or potentially embarrassing information.

Another limitation is snooping. Never, ever, assume that your e-mail is private. There are no legal protections, such as the ones that protect letters delivered by the postal system. If an employer owns the computer at work, he or she can gain access to your e-mail. There have been many instances where personal and private computer messages were found by an employer.

E-mail norms. As in all forms of communication, e-mail provides clues about the person sending the message. That is, even when communicated by an electronic medium, message content and style play a part in the presentation of self by which receivers form opinions about the personal qualities of the sender. Thus, application of the principles of accurate communication, along with those of effective self-presentation, provide *e-mail norms* or "netiquette."[22] For computer transmitted messages generally, a set of *do's* and *don'ts* has been developed for the use of e-mail. Box 13.3 provides a number of norms that are important when relying on electronic communication.

E-mail users ignore e-mail norms at their peril. One of the troublesome features of e-mail as it is typically used on college and university campuses is that students and professors do not always share the same expectations when using this medium. For example, many students transmit e-mail messages to their professors and expect answers right away—during evening hours, on weekends, holidays, or even during the summer when classes are not in session. The professor may view answering a long list of e-mails as something that is appropriate only during working hours—to be accomplished along with other tasks that have to be done when she or he is actually on the job. Professors who receive truly long lists of e-mails daily have a special problem. Messages from the professor back to the student can seem short, abrupt, and even unfriendly—simply because the sender has to deal with so many.[23]

There is also a question of what kinds of messages are appropriate for e-mail and what are not. Some students demand detailed explanations of how the professor arrived at their grades for a particular test or for the entire course. Professors may view such demands as inappropriate. Matters of grades are best discussed in person during office hours.

Overall, research shows that students have three primary reasons for using e-mail with their professors. First, there are *personal and social reasons,* such as to get to know the professor better and to show interest in a course, to continue discussions started in class, to discuss personal issues, and even to impress the professor. Second, students also use e-mail for *procedural*

BOX 13.3   *Workplace Perspective*

E-MAIL NORMS OR NETIQUETTE

- *Don't SHOUT.* Messages typed in all uppercase letters are hard to read and can be irritating. Use upper- and lowercase letters as in a regular letter.
- *Use the subject line.* Users often search for messages based on key words in the subject line. Make sure the subject line is relevant to the topic.
- *Remember that your e-mail may not be private.*
- *Remember that a given e-mail address may be used by more than one person.* Sometimes a whole group of people will have access to all messages.
- *Consider the tone of what you write.* Humor and sarcasm are not easily conveyed through e-mail.
- *Don't flame.* Do not respond in anger. Always think before composing an e-mail message.
- *Don't e-mail anything you would not want your boss or your mother to see.*
- *Use correct spelling and grammar.* Follow the same rules for e-mail messages that you would use for composing a letter. Too often, cryptic messages result in confusion and error.
- *Keep your messages brief.* Avoid long dissertations. Individuals may have many messages to retrieve, and reading long messages may be burdensome.
- *Avoid cluttering someone's e-mail.* Don't send unnecessary attachments, large files, jokes, and other trivia to others.

or clarification reasons, such as to clarify material from a lecture, or for guidance on an assignment. Third, students send e-mail to their professors for *reasons of efficiency*—because they don't want to waste the professor's time (or theirs) and know the professor will check for messages when it is convenient. Besides these primary reasons, students sometimes use e-mail because they want to avoid speaking to the teacher by phone or in person.[24]

Role-taking and feedback are always a problem with electronic mail messages. In other words, *nonverbal cues are very limited* in the technological environment of a message sent by computer. Without those cues, words can be misunderstood.

Addressing messages correctly is essential. The potential embarrassment of incorrect addressing is limited only by your imagination. For example, one man sent an e-mail to his girlfriend that contained explicit sexual references. However, he goofed on the address, and his message was sent to a distribution list of several hundred names—everyone who worked in their large company. Their relationship did not survive the embarrassment.

Correct spelling and punctuation are as important in e-mail as they are in letters and memos. Some e-mail users thoughtlessly assume that it is acceptable to use abbreviated writing styles. For example, consider the following (actual) e-mail message:

> peggy we need to schedule mtg 2day or 2morrow let me know what times u are free. need to know what u want to discuss so I can put on agenda for mtg.

Such cryptic messages may be understood in some cases, but they may imply that the receiver is not important enough for the sender to have to bother with correct grammar and spelling. That in itself is a message.

The very speed of electronic messages can also create problems. Because of the ease of e-mail, message originators may quickly type and send what might be regretted only a few minutes later. For example, someone may compose a quick and nasty note about an unpleasant experience, perhaps using ill-advised epithets or four-letter words, and then reflexively press a key to send it. A few moments later, the sender may feel quite differently.

Finally, e-mail should be brief and to the point. Some people like to forward to others jokes, clever stories, or interesting trivia that they run across while surfing the Net. Keep in mind, however, that many e-mail users rely on the system primarily for business, not social, reasons. As a result, they may have many messages to retrieve, read, and respond to each day. Lengthy messages should be avoided unless it is certain that they will be appreciated.

Teleconferencing

Both the telephone and broadcast media offer opportunities for **teleconferencing.** The term comes from the Greek word *tele,* meaning "at a distance." Today, it refers to the use of several different media systems to overcome distance and to link people so that they can conduct meetings. Thus, telecommunication is relevant to the discussion of small group communication (Chapter 7) because it enables participants to communicate in ways that approximate face-to-face discussion.

There are a number of ways to accomplish this goal, and some are far more effective than others. The medium used can vary greatly in complexity and richness of verbal and nonverbal exchanges. The more the medium is able to duplicate the conditions of face-to-face exchanges, the greater its effectiveness and its cost. The traditional ways of conducting a conference at a distance include *audioconferencing*—or in more elaborate systems, using television cameras, receivers, and even satellite transmissions so that people can see one another on screens. More recently, personal computers linked through the Internet have provided a system for teleconferencing that has many advantages.

Audioconferencing

An older and more familiar form of teleconferencing is **audioconferencing.** Anyone who has arranged for a conference call, in which people at several locations use telephones to engage in a group discussion, has experienced a simple form of audioconferencing. More formal audioconferences often take place in special rooms, one at each site, with participants seated around tables communicating via telephone lines. Such rooms are usually equipped with speakers and microphones for high-quality voice transmission.

For some purposes, audioconferences may be used instead of face-to-face meetings. These conferences have some clear advantages over alternatives, such as comparative costs and time. Telephone charges are much less expensive than travel costs; furthermore, audioconferences can be arranged on short notice, allowing people to get together faster, and with less disruption to work schedules, than would be the case in face-to-face meetings.

On the other hand, audioconferences suffer all the limitations of other forms of telephone communication. Recall from Chapter 3 the discussion on the use of both actions and artifacts to arouse meanings in others. In an audioconference, there are no visual nonverbal signals.

The ability to "read" the audience, so as to engage in effective role-takng, is also limited, as is the availability of immediate visual feedback. Even if the participants know one another well, and can anticipate how their messages will be received, and can detect feedback signals from voice tones and pauses, role-taking and feedback are still more difficult than in a face-to-face situation.

Despite these limitations, audioconferences provide a comparatively inexpensive and flexible system for permitting people to engage in group discussion.

Videoconferencing

An effective form of teleconferencing is accomplished with the use of television technology. In its most sophisticated version, **videoconferencing** brings together studios, videocameras, interactive satellite transmission, and television receivers. An example can be observed on public television stations. Their broadcasts frequently present several individuals discussing a current issue. Although one or two participants may be in the TV studio with the moderator, others are brought in by satellite from distant cities. Their faces appear on screens in such a way that it almost seems as if they are in the same room.

Many businesses find videoconferencing to be efficient if they frequently require conferences between colleagues and clients. It is much cheaper to conduct these meetings via videoconferencing than to bring people from distant locations together face-to-face.

The primary advantage of the videoconference over the other technologies is that it provides richer messages with both verbal and nonverbal elements. People can both see and hear one another in approximately the same way that they would if they were in the same room. This allows relatively effective role-taking, feedback, and the use of nonverbal cues. Another advantage of videoconferencing is that people can see various graphics, film clips, or displays of physical objects. For example, if a new product is under discussion, it can be shown on screen. In medical videoconferencing, delicate surgery can be shown in a way that may be even more visible to viewers, because of special camera effects, than if they were right in the operating room. The video conference, then, is an effective system when the issues under discussion are time sensitive, when interaction is important, and when the discussion can be significantly enhanced by video.

On the other hand, videoconferencing can be expensive. Equipment—including special cameras, satellite modems plus uplinks and downlinks, special rooms, lights, complex receivers, and transmitters—and trained technicians may be needed.

In addition, seeing another person on a TV screen is not the same as face-to-face contact. For example, immediately after the terrorist attack on the World Trade Center on September 11, 2001, the use of video teleconferencing spiked upward. It seemed like a safe alternative to bringing executives and specialists together by flying them to face-to-face meetings. Indeed, the *Boston Globe* reported that by the beginning of 2002 the stocks of companies that make the necessary equipment, surged on Wall Street.[25] After a period of time, however, the spike in the use of videoconferencing decreased. The reason was (according to a number of business executives) that clients and colleagues who needed to get together preferred face-to-face contact. Seeing and listening to each other via a two-dimensional screen is just not the same. The bottom line here is that new technologies are useful and often efficient. However, they do not always replace the firm handshake, the direct eye contact, and the warm smile that are so important in many kinds of business activities that require interpersonal communication.

By far the most efficient form of videoconferencing today is accomplished through the use of desktop computers linked to the Internet and using special software such as Skype. Skype, a voice-over Internet protocol service and software application, allows users to communicate with others by voice, video, and instant messaging over the Internet. Participants sitting at their desktop computers hear one another as they speak and see each other on their screen. This is the least costly form of teleconferencing—with the possible exception of simple audioconferencing (which provides no video of the other people).

Using the voice and video capacities of modern computers has simplified the teleconference greatly. A Skype videoconference requires little or no advance preparation, no technicians to operate complex equipment, and no need for people to leave their offices or workstations.

There are limitations to the Internet conference, with the main problem being in the technology itself. At this point, only so much information can be carried at high speeds (limited "bandwidth"). This restricts the number of video frames per second that can be transmitted and downloaded to the host computer. As a result, the video seen on a computer screen may be jerky. Sometimes audio transmissions are downloaded slowly. Nevertheless, for many applications, Internet teleconferencing may be entirely suitable.

Whatever the limitations, however, one thing is clear: Internet teleconferencing technology is undergoing rapid development. In the years ahead, as computers continue to develop—and as the software for Internet conferencing evolves—this technology will continue to have important consequences for the way people relate to one another.

Social Media

Social media include social network sites, social news sites, and blogs. Social network sites (SNS) are defined as "web-based services that allow individuals to (1) construct a public or semi-public profile within a bounded system, (2) articulate a list of other users with whom they share a connection, and (3) view and traverse their list of connections and those made by others within the system."[26] Since their introduction, social network sites such as Facebook, Twitter, and LinkedIn have attracted millions of users who have integrated these sites into all aspects of their lives. Although sites such as Facebook and Twitter were created for social communication, they are now used for business and professional purposes as well. Other sites, such as LinkedIn, were created for professionals to promote themselves and connect with other professionals.

Using the preceding definition, one of the first social network sites was SixDegrees.com, which began in 1997. SixDegrees.com allowed users to create profiles, list their friends and, later, surf the list of friends. Although the site attracted millions of users, it failed to become a sustainable business and closed in 2000. Many users complained that there was little to do after accepting friend requests.

From 1997 to 2001, a number of sites were started that allowed users to create personal, professional, and dating profiles. For example, Ryze.com was launched in 2001 to help users

Social media are changing how we communicate. Since their introduction, social network sites such as Facebook, Twitter, and LinkedIn have attracted millions of users who have integrated these sites into all aspects of their lives.

leverage their business networks, but never gained popularity. Friendster was introduced in 2002 to compete with Match.com, a profitable dating site. However, as Friendster's popularity grew, the site's servers and databases could not handle the rapid growth, and the site failed regularly. Many sites during these early years failed because of technical difficulties or a lack of trust between the users and the site.

Another wave of social network sites began in 2003. In fact, so many new sites were launched that critic Clay Shirky called them YASNS ("Yet Another Social Networking Service"). In addition, websites that focused on media sharing began adding SNS features and becoming social network sites themselves, such as Flickr (photo sharing) and YouTube (video sharing). MySpace was started in 2003 to compete with sites such as Friendster. After rumors began that Friendster would change to a fee-based system, users posted messages encouraging everyone to join other

social network sites such as MySpace. Friendster lost the trust of its users. Thus, MySpace was able to grow rapidly by attracting the disgruntled adopters of Friendster. In addition, MySpace differentiated itself by allowing users to personalize their pages and adding features based on user demand.

Unlike previous social network sites, Facebook was designed for college networks only. Facebook, which began in 2004 at Harvard University, required users to have a harvard.edu e-mail address. When other universities joined Facebook, the new users had to have university e-mail addresses associated with those institutions. This contributed to users' perceptions of the site as an intimate, private community. Then, in 2005, Facebook expanded to include high school students, professionals in corporate networks, and others.

The success of social network sites such as Facebook signaled a change in the organization

FIGURE 13.3

Adult Internet Users Who Use Social
Networking Sites, 2005–2011

Source: Pew Internet & American Life Project,
http://www.pewinternet.org/Reports/2011/
Social-Networking-Sites/Report/Part-1.aspx

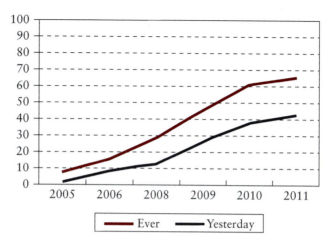

of online communities. A feature of social network sites that distinguishes them from other websites is that they are primarily organized around *people*, rather than topics or interests. Social network sites are *personal networks*, with the individual at the center of his or her own community.[27]

Overall, 65 percent of adult Internet users say they use a social network site (see Figure 13.3). Facebook alone has more than 800 million active users (see Figure 13.4). On average, the typical Facebook user has 130 friends and likes 80 pages. Also, 13 percent of online adults use the status update service, Twitter. One hour of

video is uploaded to YouTube every second.[28] We could go on . . .

Clearly, social media are changing how we communicate. This, in turn, has an impact on our behavior and our relationships with others. We are sharing more information about ourselves than ever before (often with people we barely know), including age, political views, academic and employment history, interests, relationship status, and sexual orientation. Even the profile photo you select says a lot about how you view yourself and how you would like others to see you. Is it formal or casual? Are you alone, with friends or your spouse . . . or with your dog?

FIGURE 13.4

Number of Active Facebook Users,
2005–2011

Source: Facebook.com

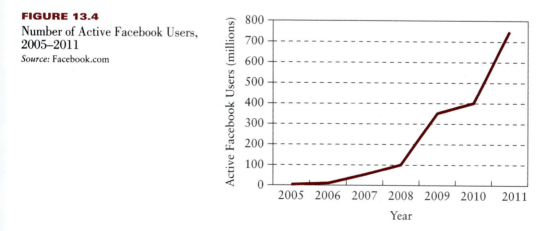

BOX 13.4 *Communication Technology Avoidance*

Directions. We are interested in your orientation toward using various types of high tech media in your daily life. Listed below are 10 pairs of statements. Read each pair and place a mark beside the media choice that best reflects your own personal preference for using that particular medium or technology.

Never check both of the items. Do not look back and forth through the items; make each item a separate and independent judgment. Your first impression, your immediate preference for each medium is what we want.

Again, which of the following communication media in each pair do you prefer to use in your own life?

1. ____ Use a DVR (digital video recorder) to record and play back programs.
   ____ Rely on a DVD or VCR player to play programs or movies.

2. ____ Call using a mobile or cell phone.
   ____ Call using a landline.

3. ____ Send e-mail messages.
   ____ Send phone texts.

4. ____ Download and read an e-book.
   ____ Mail order and read a hard-copy book.

5. ____ Leave a text message.
   ____ Leave a voice mail message.

6. ____ Follow celebrity news on Twitter.
   ____ Follow celebrity news on TV or in magazines.

7. ____ Access and search the online library.
   ____ Go to the library.

8. ____ Use a FAX machine to send a business letter.
   ____ Rely on a scanner and e-mail to send a business letter.

9. ____ Post pictures on Facebook for friends and family.
   ____ Attach pictures to e-mail to send to friends and family.

10. ____ Rely on videoconferencing or Skype to talk to several people at the same time.
    ____ Arrange a conference call to talk to several people at the same time.

Calculating Your Score:

1. For each pair of 10 items, there are two possible responses. One response represents an "avoidance" of communication technology;

Given the number of people who may view your profile, including employers, how you portray and manage your public identity is important. This is especially true as new communication technologies increasingly erode the boundaries between our personal and professional lives.

The keys to effective communication online are the same as offline. According to social media experts, this includes *trust* and *authenticity*, as well as courtesy and consideration of others.[29] Here are a few tips for successful social networking:

- *Use different profiles or accounts for your personal and business connections.*

Remember that business and pleasure don't always mix, and some information that you share with close friends may be considered too personal and unnecessary by your business contacts.

- *Save one-on-one conversations for other media.* Don't use Twitter or your Facebook wall for private conversations that are strictly between you and another individual. Send an e-mail or a text message instead.

- *Don't send invitations to play games or for other timewasters to your business contacts.* Your business contacts will not the other is an "approach" orientation toward the use of high tech media. In every case, the second option represents the more "avoidant" response.

2. Score a 1 for every avoidant option you selected (option 2) = _____.
3. Finally, add together your total points across all 10 items = _____.

Interpreting Your Score:

The possible range of scores for the Communication Technology Avoidance scale is 0–10. (If your own final score does not fall within that range, you made a computational error.)

The higher the score, the more avoidant you are toward the use of new media. There may be a number of reasons you may wish to employ low tech over high tech media, but one important reason is typically because people are afraid of change. After all, calling someone on the phone has worked perfectly for us for a very long time; why switch over to text? Secondly, as avoiders, we may experience anxiety about trying out the new technology because we fear evaluation from others. That is, we assume others already know how to use it (like using Skype or iTunes), and we fear revealing to others that we do not know

how to use it ourselves! Third, we may think we'll damage or break the technology (such as a computer). Just because the technology appears more complicated, we often assume that it is also more fragile.

Low scorers on the Communication Technology Avoidance Scale, particularly those with scores of 2 or below, approach the use of technology with anticipation and enthusiasm. They look forward to their use because they are sure the new technology offers advantages, such as speed, simplicity, and convenience. Approachers are anxious to try out the new media and be on top of all the latest advances in communication technology.

A word of caution: Communication Technology Approachers are not necessarily those who are also media literate. Approachers may boast of owning the new technology, but may fail to learn how to use all their phone or tablet apps; have trouble changing the message on their voice mail; have difficulty entering new software onto their computers; or never learn how to use iCloud or other Internet storage systems. Whereas approach/avoidance reflects a personal orientation or preference, communication literacy or media competency requires skill!

appreciate it, and you will be viewed as unprofessional.

- *Use your own name and photo.* Use your own photo, not your dog or cat, etc. Don't use your profile as a blatant promotion for a company.
- *Check out those who want to follow you or be your friend.* Remember that you may be judged by the company you keep.
- *Always think about the consequences of what you post.* Personal attacks, negative comments, unflattering photos, etc., can cause problems for the intended target as well as for you.

- *Keep your address books private.* Don't allow your social network site to access and send invitations for various purposes to your entire address book.
- *Compose your posts, updates, or tweets carefully.* Be sure to check grammar and spelling before you send.
- *Don't post anything you wouldn't want your current or future boss or clients to read.* Everything you do online makes an impression, and others will draw conclusions about you as a result.
- *Don't post when you are overly tired, angry, or upset.*

Chapter Review

- We are living in an age of swiftly changing and developing communication technology. Mediated communication differs from face-to-face communication. Some elements of the communication process are absent or severely curtailed when people use media, including opportunities for role-taking and the availability of feedback.

- Each new medium alters the communication process itself—by imposing special requirements on the ways in which messages are formulated, by controlling the speed and convenience with which messages are transmitted or recorded, and by influencing the ways in which receivers reconstruct meanings from the messages they receive.

- Letters and memoranda are the traditional media for many communication needs. Both letters and memos have specific advantages and disadvantages.

- Telephones (landlines and mobile phones) continue to be among the most widely used media in our society.

- Electronic e-mail is typed into the sender's computer, sent over a network, and recorded by the receiver's computer to be read on screen later. Over the Internet, people can exchange messages rapidly worldwide.

- Teleconferencing helps to overcome distance and link people in ways that approximate face-to-face meetings. There are audioconferences with telephone systems and videoconferences that closely approximate the conditions of a face-to-face meeting.

- Social media include social network sites, social news sites, and blogs. Social network sites (SNS) are web-based services that allow individuals to construct a public or semi-public profile within a bounded system, list other users with whom they share a connection, and view and use their list of connections and those made by others within the system for various purposes.

Key Terms

medium
social information processing (SIP) theory
memorandum

vertical communication
computer network
e-mail
teleconferencing

audioconferencing
videoconferencing

Notes

1. Ramirez, A., Jr. (2002). Information-seeking strategies, uncertainty and computer-mediated communication. *Human Communication Research, 28,* 2, 213–228.

2. Hancock, J. T., & Dunham, P. J. (2001). Impression formation in computer-mediated communication revisited: an analysis of the breadth and intensity of impressions. *Communication Research, 28,* 3, 325–347.

3. Harmon, A. (1998), August 30). A sad, lonely world is discovered in cyberspace, surprising researchers. *The New York Times,* p. A1.

4. Walther, J. B., Anderson, J. F., & Park, D. W. (1994). Interpersonal effects in computer-mediated interaction: A meta-analysis of social and antisocial communication. *Communication Research, 21,* 460–487. doi:10.1177/009365094021004002; Walther, J. B. (2007). Selective self-presentation in computer-mediated communication: Hyperpersonal dimensions of technology, language, and cognition. *Computers in Human Behavior, 23,* 2538–2557. doi: 10.1016/j.chb.2006.05.002; Griffin, E. (2012). *A first look at communication theory.* New York: McGraw-Hill.

5. Czitron, D. J. (1982). *Media and the American mind* (p. 6). Chapel Hill: University of North Carolina Press. This book offers valuable insights into the social and cultural impact of three new media after they arrived: the telegraph, motion pictures, and radio.

6. Stephens, M. (1988). *History of news* (p. 259). New York: Viking.

7. Chenoweth, N. A., & Hayes, J. R. (2001). Fluency in writing: Generating text in L1 and L2. *Written Communication, 18,* 1, 80–98.

8. For an extended treatment of the art of writing effective business and professional letters, see: Treece, M. (1986). *Communication for business and the professions* (pp. 50–101). Boston: Allyn & Bacon.

9. The word *memorandum* derives from the Latin *memor,* which means "with a good memory." Two spellings for the plural of *memorandum* are widely used. One is the Latin *memoranda* and the other is an English-language version, formed by simply adding an "s" to make *memorandums.*

10. For a detailed history of the early years of the telephone see: Casson, H. N. (1910). *The history of the telephone.* Chicago: McClurg & Co.

11. de Sola Pool, L. (1977). *The social impact of the telephone.* Cambridge, MA: MIT Press.

12. Increasingly such systems are based on wireless technologies. The use of traditional long-distance lines will be declining sharply in the decades ahead. See: Vanston, L. K., & Hodges, R. I. (1998). *Wireless vs wireline for voice services: Forecasts and impacts* (3rd ed.). Austin, TX: Technology Futures.

13. Blumberg, S. J., & Luke, J. V. (2010, May). *Wireless substitution: Early release of estimates from the National Health Interview Survey, July-December 2009.* National Center for Health Statistics. Retrieved from http://www.cdc.gov/nchs/nhis.htm

14. Lollar, M. (September 15, 2002). Is it time to cell out? For many, wireless service replacing old land phones altogether. *The Commercial Appeal* (Memphis, TN), p. D1.

15. Lowy, J. (2011, December 14). Ban urged on phones, texting by drivers. *The Advocate,* pp. A1, A8.

16. Crowley, M.. (December 20, 2002). Experts say cell phone users must relearn manners. *Las Vegas Review-Journal.*

17. Howe, P. (November 8, 2003). Camera phones roiling gyms. *The Boston Globe,* p. A1.

18. Smith, A. (2011, September 19). *Americans and text messaging.* The Pew Research Center's Internet & American Life Project. Retrieved from http://www.pewinternet.org/Reports/2011/Cell-Phone-Texting-2011.aspx

19. Waldeck, J., Kearney, P. & Plax, T. (2013). *Business & professional communication in a digital age.* Boston: Wadsworth.

20. Markoff, J. (December 16, 1990). Digital fetes the "germ" that began a revolution. *The New York Times,* p. 11.

21. This brief history of the development of networks is based on: Markoff, J. (September 2, 1990). Creating a giant computer highway. *The New York Times,* sec. 3, p. 1.

22. Anderson, A. (1988). The etiquette of electronic mail. *Perspective, 12,* 3, 1–5.

23. See: Young, J. R. (June 11, 2002). Online education's drawbacks include misunderstood e-mail messages, panelists say. *The Chronicle of Higher Education.* Available: http://chronicle.com/free/2002/06/2002061101u.htm.

24. Waldeck, J. H., Kearney, P., & Plax, T. G. (2001). Teacher e-mail message strategies and students' willingness to communicate online. *Journal of Applied Communication Research, 29,* 1, 54–70.

25. Howe, P. (September 16, 2002). Farewell to face-to-face. *The Boston Globe,* p. C-1.

26. Boyd, D. M., & Ellison, N. B. (2008). Social network sites: Definition, history and scholarship. *Journal of Computer-Mediated Communication, 13,* 210–30. doi: 10.1111/j.1083-6101.2007.00393.x

27. Ibid.

28. Madden, M., & Zickuhr (2011, August 11). 65% of online adults use social networking sites. *Pew Reports.* Retrieved from http://www.pewinternet.org/Reports/2011/Social-Networking-Sites.aspx; Smith, A. (2011, June 1). Twitter Update 2011. *Pew Reports.* Retrieved from http://www.pewinternet.org/Reports/2011/Twitter-Update-2011.aspx

29. Business etiquette tips for social media: 12 tips from Georgia business etiquette expert Lydia Ramsey (2011, September 7). *PR Newswire.* Retrieved from http://www.marketwatch.com

Chapter 14

Understanding Mass Communication

Emily reached over to shut off the radio alarm. The music was hard rock, which she loved because it helped to wake her up! She didn't feel like facing the rat race this Monday morning. After her shower, she clicked on the TV to catch the *Today Show* while she dressed. She followed the chatter and the commercials as she fixed a light breakfast. Then she turned to The Weather Channel to see what Mother Nature had planned for the day. Rain was predicted, so she took her umbrella.

Driving to work wasn't too bad. Emily tuned to a local radio news station to find out about any traffic tie-ups, and then changed to an FM station that played classical music. That was just the thing to ease the stress of driving—even the ads were subdued.

As she passed through the lobby of her office building, Emily picked up the morning paper at the newsstand. Although she received news updates throughout the day on her iPhone, she still liked to read the newspaper. She enjoyed reading about the love problems of others, so during her coffee break she would read her favorite advice column. She read at least some of the news and did the crossword puzzle. She also needed to look at the classified ads to see if she could find an apartment closer to work. Sometimes she read the comics too—a habit left over from childhood.

On her way to lunch, Emily bought her favorite fashion magazine; she liked being up on the latest styles, cosmetics, and diet plans. She would glance through it during her afternoon break and then take it home to read. Also she had seen a very attractive actress on TV wearing a dress she liked; she wanted to buy one just like it.

During the drive home, she listened to a radio talk show on which a political candidate discussed the merits of her new plan for improving health insurance in the country. Emily liked what she heard and decided she would cast her vote in the next election.

Emily ate dinner while she scanned the news apps on her iPad. First, CNN, then she checked Flipboard for tech and lifestyle news. However, she didn't have much time because her boyfriend, Everett, was picking her up at 6:45. She had picked out a movie she wanted to see after watching the preview on Fandango and reading the reviews.

After the movie and a snack, Everett drove her home. They talked about the movie, which had included a lot of violence. They wondered if this bothered anybody.

Even though it was getting late, Emily decided to do some surfing on the Internet. Using her iPad, she found what she was looking for—a website that offered an interesting vacation package in Cancun, Mexico. After requesting information, she went to bed. She wasn't really sleepy, so she turned on the TV and caught the last few minutes of a talk show. A bespectacled communication professor was claiming that we have become a media-saturated society and that all of us are heavily *dependent* on mass communications. "What a nerd," Emily thought. "Media dependent, indeed!" She muttered, "I'm completely independent, and I'm not influenced by mass communications."

We live in a society saturated by mass communication but seldom realize how dependent we are on mass media. What are some ways in which the media influence your daily decisions and actions?

Like Emily, we all live in a society saturated by mass communications. We seldom realize how dependent we actually are on mass media. Yet, because of this **dependency**, the media influence our decisions and actions on a daily basis.[1] Many discussions of the effects of the media focus on violence and sexual depictions, but media influences extend far beyond these two issues.[2]

Today, we are bombarded almost constantly by messages aimed at influencing what we do or think about. We are targets for mass communicators who want us to purchase, vote, donate, adopt, support, or otherwise behave in ways they desire. Even the entertainment offered by media poses lessons about what we should look like, how we should live, what we should like and dislike, and how we should relate to other people.

The question is, where did all these media come from, and why do we allow them to operate as they do? How do people cope with this daily tidal wave of mass media messages? Do the media directly influence us or do they affect us in ways that are unintended and maybe even unnoticed? These are some of the questions that will be addressed in this chapter.

In order to understand these issues, then, the chapter begins its analysis of mass communications by tracing briefly the development of each major medium in our society—print, broadcast, film, and digital. The section that follows will provide an overall view of mass communication as a *process*. This will help to explain why our media continuously deliver the kinds of messages that they do. The chapter also examines how people cope with their daily deluge of information. It shows that, as the 21st century began, American media were serving a multitude of purposes for a multitude of different kinds of audiences, and, in turn, were having a multitude of influences.

Social and Cultural Factors That Have Shaped Our Media

What is mass communication and what are mass media? Where did they come from? What was there about the American society that shaped their technologies, their present patterns of ownership, their audiences, and their ways of operating? To answer these questions, a necessary first step is to review the accumulation of communication technologies and the cultural heritage that have influenced the ways in which our media have evolved in the setting of the United States.

We will offer a formal definition in a later section, but simply put, mass communication can be thought of as a *process* that in many respects is similar to the one described by the analytical linear model discussed in Chapter 1. That is, sources (professional communicators) select and encode messages that are transmitted widely and rapidly over distance (by media) to arouse intended meanings in large numbers of people who receive them.

Our mass media came into being only as new technologies for communicating over time and distance allowed them to develop. While the technologies of print, broadcast, computer networks, and film are basically the same for the media used in many countries, each system of mass communication came to be organized and regulated in different ways. These technologies changed cultures as they were used in different systems of mass communication. It is important, then, to look briefly at the development of media technologies and the influences on social life that they produced.

The Influences of New Communication Technologies

At various points in time—some of them in the distant past—new technologies of communication were developed. These developments were the foundation of *drastic changes in human culture*. An illustration is the beginning of writing. Human beings began to be able to speak and use language, much as we know it today, somewhere around 45,000 years ago. However, a new technology began to arrive about 15,000 years back when ancient people (the Cro-Magnon) painted beautiful representations of animals on the ceilings and walls of caves.[3] Such representations were the only way they had to preserve ideas graphically over time. Not much changed for thousands of years. Then, about 7,000 to 6,000 years ago (between 5000 and 4000 B.C.) people in various regions of what we now call the Middle East began to record messages by scratching crude pictures of ideas on rock slabs.[4] Crude though it was, making marks on rocks to express meanings was a new technology. Those who saw these simple *pictographs* were able to interpret the intended meanings of the person who made them. Within a few centuries, however, hundreds of *stylized* (that is, simplified) **pictographs,** with specific meanings for each, were *standardized* to form the earliest writing systems.[5] Independently, the Chinese and (later) the Mayans of Central America also developed complex systems of writing.

With this new technology available, people could record and later recover ideas without relying on human memory. It was even possible to understand ideas from people who were dead—which gave writing a special significance. When true writing began, it had profound consequences for human civilization. Recorded speech was a great advance over mere talking and gesturing. One of its consequences was that writing made possible great advances in science, medicine, law, philosophy, and many other forms of knowledge. Early on, it was used mainly by the political and religious elite. This was another factor that gave writing a special significance.

About 1700 B.C., another great advance was made in communication technology. Alphabetic writing began. The basic idea was that very simple symbols were developed to represent *sounds* rather than whole ideas.[6] This greatly simplified writing and made it possible for much larger numbers of people to master its skills. Although alphabets were developed in many regions, our current system was first standardized by the Ionian Greeks about 500 B.C. It was then refined by the Romans, from whom it passed to Europeans and eventually to settlers of the New World. As you read this text, you are using a communication technology that was first developed nearly 4,000 years ago.

The term *medium* (plural *media*) refers to any system of surfaces or devices that is used to transport some form of stimulus (that can be detected by human senses) over distance. For example, we project our human voice by noises we make. These move across space to our listener in the form of physical *information*—in this case sound waves. Print relies on variations and patterns in light waves that we receive and recognize as letters and words. Other forms of information conquer space and distance as electrical impulses along a wire, or electromagnetic pulses, such as those in radio and television broadcasts. All move or store information that human beings can detect and then interpret within their learned language or visual cultures.

As noted, the first medium was stone. It was very effective for preserving messages through time, but it was not easy to move around. Later, clay tablets baked in fire were used—a little easier to move, but still cumbersome. In time, *portable* media were developed to overcome this problem. Early ones were **parchment, vellum,** and **papyrus.** Papyrus was made by the Egyptians from interwoven slices of a tall reed growing along the Nile. When squashed together, pressed, and dried, it produced a paper-like surface. Because papyrus was scarce, the skins of sheep (parchment) and calves (vellum) also came into use.

Such portable media made it possible to transmit messages swiftly by horsemen and boats, permitting military and political leaders to administer large territories much more effectively. Indeed, some scholars maintain that great empires, such as those of China and Rome, could never have been established and maintained without portable media.[7]

As empires and other complex religious and political systems developed, archives and libraries of "books" (rolled-up scrolls of papyrus and parchment) became increasingly important. These were developed to standardize systems of law, disseminate religious interpretations, preserve government records, foster commerce, and accumulate knowledge. The Romans developed the book in the form we know today, with cut pages bound at the left, writing on both sides of the page, and thin boards on the ends. They also standardized sentence structure, paragraphs, and punctuation. Books in this form, then, became an established idea well over 2000 years ago.[8] Again, new communication technologies advanced the human condition.

Eventually, merchants began to produce hand-copied books. By about the 13th century, they were producing many kinds of books on portable media for sale to scholars and students in the new universities, and for others who were literate. By this time, paper was used to supplement parchment and vellum. Papermaking from rags had been invented by the Chinese; the process was adopted by the Arabs shortly after 700 A.D., and the Moors brought papermaking to Spain. After about 1200 A.D., it had spread throughout Europe.[9] It was a great new medium. Once more, a new technology added to ways in which human beings could communicate.

In 1455, Johannes Gutenberg, an obscure goldsmith in Mainz (Germany) was able to print 200 elegant and identical copies of the Bible. He had experimented for more than 20 years with ways to cast letters in metal, arrange them line by line in trays, and use a special press to imprint multiple copies of a page. But before Gutenberg could get the pages of his Bible bound and sold, he was taken to court over a loan. He was stripped of the completed pages of his Bible, his inventions, and his shop; his work was sold and the profits were confiscated. He died blind and in poverty a few years later.[10]

The printing press was an astounding new technology that brought a great revolution in human communication. At the time, Gutenberg feared that his new system would not catch on. However, by the time Columbus reached the New World, only 37 years later, the printing press and movable type had spread throughout Europe and millions of copies of books had been printed.[11]

The importance of the press was that it made books widely available to people in their own languages. Printed books spread religious interpretations, new ideas about government, scientific discoveries, and many other topics throughout the world. Those ideas changed the course of history. The great Protestant Reformation, the rise of democracy, and the development of modern science were made possible because books became available in languages many people could read.

It is clear, then, that human communication—beyond the spoken word—is tightly linked to *technology*. As new media and related technologies come into use, patterns of communication change. More and more people are able to communicate with greater ease and efficiency to ever larger numbers of others. This makes communication—and especially mediated communication—more central to their lives. Thus, as the future unfolds, this relationship between technology and communication will continue to be important. Mass media will become increasingly sophisticated and available and will continue the process of transforming human life.

The Development of Media in the United States

Today, the mass media in the United States reach large and diverse audiences through point-to-multipoint dissemination of messages. Traditionally included among these media are books, newspapers, magazines, film (and videotape or DVD extensions), radio, and television (either network or cable and satellite). Today, the Internet, with its World Wide Web, is also a mass medium in some applications.

Books.   The first book printed in the American colonies was a religious work called *The Whole Book of Psalms*. It came off a press at Harvard College in 1640, the first to operate in the colonies.[12] (However, a press was established in Mexico in 1539, and books were being produced there almost a century before the Pilgrims arrived in the New World in 1620.)

By the 1840s, statewide mandatory and free (tax-supported) *public education* began in the 1830s. After Massachusetts established such a system, other states soon followed. Thus, as the century progressed, and especially after the Civil War, books became a major mass medium. Libraries were established in virtually every community; books were the foundation of education, and the ideas expressed in them shaped the culture.

Today, books are still our most respected medium. In fact, book reading is more popular than at any time since World War II. More books have been printed and sold in recent decades than during any period of our history. Overall, the outlook for book publishing remains positive.

Many books have had a powerful influence on history. Obvious examples are Adam Smith's *The Nature and Causes of the Wealth of Nations* (1776), providing the foundation of modern capitalism, and Karl Marx's *Das Kapital* (1844), which became the intellectual base of 20th-century communism. The influence of books continued. Harriet Beecher Stowe's *Uncle Tom's Cabin* (1852) shaped the ideas of American abolitionists. After World War II, Rachel Carson's *Silent Spring* was a source for the early environmental movement, Michael Harrington's *The Other Americans* stimulated efforts to redress the problems of our nation's elderly poor, and Betty Friedan's *The Feminine Mystique* played a key role in establishing the feminist movement. In short, books have long been and will remain a major medium in our culture.

Books have distinctive characteristics that set them apart from other media. For example, since books take longer to produce, they are less timely than other print media such as newspapers and magazines. In addition, books are made to last longer than other print media, which results in more in-depth exploration and development of topics or ideas. Finally, like movies, they are not heavily supported by advertising and profits are earned by their sale.

However, a transition is taking place in the ways in which books are produced, distributed, sold, and read. Specifically, the Internet is increasingly used as a source for downloading books from vendors, and special devices for reading books in digital form, such as the Kindle and Nook, are selling well. Readers also can download books on other platforms, including smartphones and tablet computers. Although many have predicted the demise of books in printed form in the very near future, it appears likely that, for the time being, print and digital books will continue to coexist in the marketplace, and bookstores and libraries will handle both forms.

Newspapers. The earliest versions of newspapers were the *corantos* that appeared in England early in the 1600s. They provided mainly commercial information. By 1665, a regularly published newspaper, *The Oxford Gazette* (later published as *The London Gazette*), was established, and it survived into the present century. Like virtually all newspapers of the time, *The Gazette* was controlled by the Crown, but it had the characteristics of a true newspaper: It was published regularly (twice a week) and was produced by a mechanical printing press. Available to the public (for a price), it contained news of general interest (as opposed to specialized topics, such as religion or commerce) and was readable by those with ordinary literacy. Its reports were timely, and it was stable over time.[13]

The development of the American **colonial press** was influenced by a number of social and cultural factors, including the nature and distribution of the population, the growth of commerce (creating a need for news of shipping and advertising), and increasingly strained relationships with England.

Because of low literacy, uncertain financing, and suppression by the British Crown, newspapers were difficult to establish and maintain in the Colonies. In 1690 Benjamin Harris published a four-page paper called *Publik Occurances Both Foreign and Domestick*. It caused an uproar, and its first issue was also its last! Harris succeeded in insulting the King of France, Native American allies of the British, and the governor of Massachusetts. The paper was immediately banned.

A number of other printers tried newspaper publishing in the early decades of the 1700s with mixed success. Most ran into the problem of "prior restraint," meaning that the Crown's representatives insisted on approving the content of the papers before publication. A number of printers refused and wound up in jail. It was this policy that instigated the belief in **freedom of the press** among American colonists.

One of the most significant events in the long struggle to establish freedom of the press began in 1733. John Peter Zenger published the first issue of the *New York Weekly Journal*. He ran articles that were openly critical of Governor

William Cosby. Soon he was sent to jail and charged with "seditious libel" (criticism of the Crown). By common law standards of the time, he was guilty because he had published the articles and the law did not recognize truth as a defense.

Zenger was brought to trial in 1734, where he was defended by Andrew Hamilton, a distinguished lawyer. In a stunning upset, a jury acquitted Zenger—even though he had clearly violated the Crown's laws. The trial strengthened the people's belief that the press should be allowed to criticize government. A few decades later, that principle would be incorporated in the first of the amendments to our Constitution that make up the Bill of Rights.

Newspapers before 1800 were very different from those we know today. They were smaller (about 10 by 14 inches) and shorter—on average only about four pages. They were very expensive. Their content was designed for well-educated readers, and they were usually highly partisan (advocating a particular political point of view).

Early in the 1800s, the new technology of steam was applied to printing. The Hoe rotary press of 1830 could produce an astonishing 4,000 sheets an hour, printed on both sides. That invention made modern newspapers possible in the sense of large numbers of copies printed cheaply. In September 1833, a curious little newspaper called the *New York Sun* appeared on the streets of New York. Its publisher, Benjamin Day, was experimenting with a totally new approach. The *Sun* offered exciting stories of local events, with an emphasis on crime, human interest, accidents, and humorous happenings (real or otherwise).

There were three major differences between the *Sun* and earlier papers. The first was that it was aimed at ordinary people, not an educated elite. The second was that Day's plan was to recover his costs and make a profit by selling his newspaper for only a penny. By this means, he hoped to boost circulation hugely, which Day knew would appeal to advertisers who wanted to get their messages to the largest number of readers possible. Because he had so many

readers, Day was able to charge very high rates for advertising space. He was able to recover the cost of production and make a substantial profit.

The third difference between the *Sun* and earlier papers was in the *system for distribution*. Instead of mailing his paper, Day devised a system for selling copies to newsboys for 67 cents per 100. They could hawk them in the streets to make 33 cents per 100 sold. Regular routes were soon established, and the system worked.

The *New York Sun* was an instant success, launching the era of the **penny press**. Within weeks, it was selling 8,000 copies a day. Within three years, its daily circulation was over 30,000. Day's experiment resulted in the newspaper as we know it today.

With the invention of the telegraph, another new communication technology, the Associated Press began distributing stories by wire to subscribing papers in 1848. By the time of the Civil War, railroads and regularly scheduled steamboat service on inland waters made it possible for large numbers of citizens to receive a daily newspaper. Daily newspaper usage grew steadily from the mid-19th century until the early decades of the 1900s. They reached their peak about the time of World War 1.

A major trend in modern newspapers is in *patterns of ownership*. Mainly as a result of declining circulations, about 75 percent of all daily newspapers in the United States are now owned by chains. In 1920, a mere 31 chains owned an average of 5 newspapers each. Today, Gannett, the largest newspaper company, owns 90 daily newspapers, including *USA Today*. Concentration of ownership had reduced the number of dailies from a high of about 2,400 in 1910 to 1,387 in 2009.[14] Figure 14.1 shows the pattern of the declining number of daily newspapers from 1940 to 2009.

Another major trend is that on a per capita basis *newspaper use continues to decline*. In 1910, households in the United States subscribed on average to 1.36 newspapers per day (many received both a morning and an afternoon paper). Today, that has dropped below

0.62 per household. Still, newspapers remain a substantial mass medium. More than 51 million copies are sold every day, and newspaper websites average more than 111 million unique visitors monthly.[15]

One of the reasons for the survival of newspapers is that they serve a variety of functions not served by other media. These include detailed analyses of local news and in-depth coverage of national and international events. In addition, printed newspapers are portable with no equipment or software necessary to read them. They are accessible and cost-effective.

Today, however, newspapers face major challenges. Some critics have suggested that newspapers are a dying medium. Indeed, some newspapers have ended their print editions in recent years and now publish only online. Although newspapers have long survived the introduction of other media—radio, television and cable—never before have newspapers faced so much competition. There are now tens of thousands of Internet "newspapers" and news services competing for advertisers and readers. Newspapers' two major sources of revenue—sales of copies through home subscriptions and newsstands and advertising revenue—have declined significantly. In response, news organizations have been building their online offerings and developing new digital products and new revenue streams. For example, advertising revenue has grown in a number of areas, including from ads targeted to smartphones, tablets, and social network sites that seek to drive people to newspaper websites. The circulation of the Sunday edition, with its coupon-heavy inserts, has held steady and remains profitable. However, print advertising revenue continues to decline faster than online ad revenue is growing. In 2011, print losses were greater than digital gains by 10 to 1.

Also in 2011, newspapers such as The *New York Times* began the use of pay walls for digital content. A number of other daily newspapers began to experiment with variations of the "metered model," which allows free viewing of a limited number of articles but requires a monthly fee for unlimited access. Overall, most newspapers remain profitable, but profit margins are razor-thin. Pay systems help maintain the idea that users should pay for valued content, which is expensive to produce, regardless of the platform on which it is distributed. This change is unlikely to have a major financial impact immediately but will likely help newspaper organizations make the transition from print to digital platforms in the years ahead.[16]

Magazines. Magazine publication began in Europe, where concentrations of literate, urbane, and affluent people took a keen interest in social and political affairs. Thus, magazines started as *media of politics*. The first magazine to be published in English was *The Review,* which appeared in London in 1704. Its publisher was Daniel Defoe (who later wrote *Robinson Crusoe*). It contained essays on politics, manners, and morals intended to influence the opinions of its readers. It caught on quickly and soon had imitators.[17] By the mid-1700s, the magazine was an established medium. It made a profit from subscriptions and advertising, and its readers were well educated and affluent. It was not a medium for the masses.

Experiments with magazines in the United States were unsuccessful at first.[18] Unlike Europe, with its great urban concentrations of elites, the United States had only a few small cities and a widely dispersed population, most of whom were poor and had limited reading skills. Even more of a problem for early magazines was the quality of postal services: Until the 1850s, mail delivery was uncertain and very expensive. After that, the postal system in the United States provided relatively cheap and reliable delivery of magazines. Once those barriers were removed, the magazine industry began to flourish: The American population was expanding and becoming increasingly urbanized. More people were literate, subscription costs dropped, and magazines for virtually every interest and taste became available.

During the early 20th century, general interest magazines had circulations in the millions. Their readers were like contemporary television

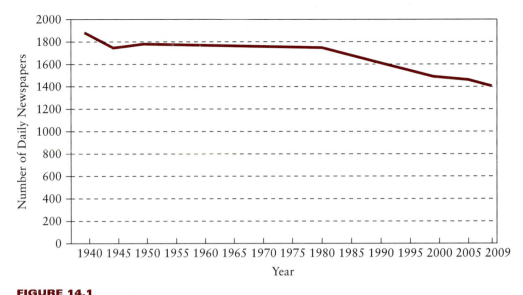

FIGURE 14.1

Number of U.S. Daily Newspapers, 1940–2009
Source: Pew Research Center's Project for Excellence in Journalism

audiences in that they were from diverse social classes and backgrounds. Some magazines—such as *The Saturday Evening Post,* and the *Ladies Home Journal*—came out monthly; others were weeklies. All carried a mixture of short stories, serious articles, humorous pieces, and serialized fiction. They were an ideal medium for advertisers who wanted to reach a broad spectrum of consumers across the nation to promote mass-produced products like cosmetics, automobiles, and soft drinks.

After about 1960, when television had become almost universally adopted, virtually all of the great general circulation magazines began to fail as the new medium took away their advertising income. Television could reach more people more rapidly than magazines, and on the basis of per-person exposure to an advertising message, TV was far cheaper. One by one, the magazines that had been so successful stopped publication.

For a time it appeared that the magazine was finished as a mass medium. Then, magazines found a new format and new audiences to serve and came back stronger than ever. The key was

content specialization. Although there are still several very popular general interest magazines with circulations over 10 million a month, most are much smaller and aimed at specific categories of consumers.

Today, thousands of small magazines are published for readers with some *specialized interest*—for instance, photography, home decorating, boating, painting, cooking, horses or any one of literally hundreds of other topics. These specialized publications are an effective medium for advertisers with products that relate to a particular age category, hobby, or other topic. In fact, there are over 15,000 periodicals of different kinds currently in circulation.

Magazines remain a major mass medium. They survey the political and economic landscape, often delivering *information, entertainment, and analysis* ahead of other media. They *correlate* events in society by interpreting trends and movements and linking isolated facts and events. They also serve many other information and entertainment needs. However, many of the challenges facing newspapers today also are confronting magazines. Increasingly, magazines are posting content online, and some magazines have ended their print editions. Furthermore, through the use of search engines and social network sites such as Facebook and YouTube, individuals can create their own specialized magazines. The end of magazines has been predicted many times in the past. However, for the foreseeable future, most analysts think magazines will continue to exist in paper form or online because their specialized interests have wide appeal.

Motion pictures. Two of our modern media provide what we commonly think of as motion pictures—film and television (including cable and DVDs). The Internet may also be included in this category insofar as it distributes video entertainment.

Although, as a mass medium, the movies were a 20th century phenomenon, they have a long technological history.[19] Even the first motion pictures required an understanding of optical principles of *lenses;* techniques for *projection of shadow images;* the functioning of *human vision,* which perceives an illusion of motion from a series of still pictures; the *chemistry of photography;* and mechanical techniques for photographing and projecting *rapid sequences of still pictures.*[20] Other matters involved in making the movies a mass medium included paying for and making a *profit* from their production and distribution, and defining *limits* on what they could portray to the public.

The movies became a mass medium to entertain the public during the first decade of the 20th century.[21] Inexpensive and crude movie houses (called nickelodeons) were established in cities to exhibit to unsophisticated audiences the short films produced by the fledgling industry. They were very successful, and by 1910 they had spread to most major U.S. cities and were grossing more than $90 million a year.

Beginning in the 1920s, movie theaters became more elaborate. Films became longer and more sophisticated as producers and exhibitors sought larger markets among the middle class. One factor boosting films produced in the United States

was that World War I shut down the movie industry in Europe. This gave American films a global marketing advantage that they still enjoy. In 1927 sound was added to the film, and movies emerged as one of the nation's leading forms of recreation. Figure 14.2 shows the number of admissions per person to movie theaters in the U.S. and Canada from 2001 to 2010.

In terms of box office receipts, movies had a *Golden Age* during the 1930s. One reason was that they had no competitors. For a modest ticket price, an entire family could go to the movies and see a film about 90 minutes in length, along with special features, like a newsreel and a cartoon. The movies were made to order for the difficult economic times of the 1930s, and motion picture attendance reached all-time highs during the Great Depression.

By 1950, theater attendance began to drop. As the decade increased, box office receipts plunged. The problem was that television was gaining acceptance, and people were simply staying home to view whatever came on their sets. Slowly, the deeply established habit of going to the movies often declined. Neighborhood theaters closed, drive-ins disappeared, and exhibitors shifted to malls where they could operate multiple screens. The number of films produced dropped sharply from over 300 per year between 1931 and 1942 to less than 150 per year since 1980.

In recent decades, movie audiences have changed as well. They are now mainly teenagers with leisure time, plus young dating couples. Few people today attend movies as a family. Older people seldom go to the movies. To adapt to their tastes, films now emphasize themes that appeal to younger age groups—fast action, vulgar language, and sexual depictions. Although Americans are now spending more dollars than ever to attend films, this trend mainly reflects the increasing cost of admission. Thus, films shown in theaters are attracting a smaller proportion of the household entertainment dollar than ever before.

Are movies headed for oblivion? Not at all. Although the traditional form of viewing movies

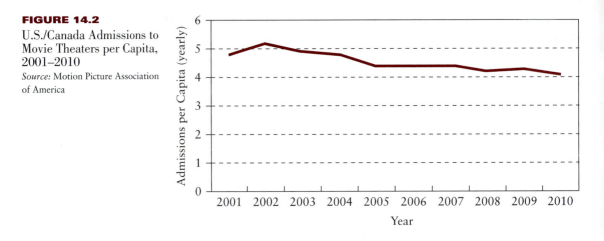

FIGURE 14.2

U.S./Canada Admissions to Movie Theaters per Capita, 2001–2010

Source: Motion Picture Association of America

in theaters has obviously declined greatly, movies are being seen in other ways. The industry has survived and prospered by adapting to new technologies in movie delivery. Movies are produced for broadcast and cable television, and the industry has benefited from distribution systems such as Netflix and other services that allow viewers to download movies. The industry has adapted to every new platform of the digital age, including iPads, smartphones, websites, video-on-demand, and others. There are apps and websites for the motion picture companies, for movies, and for actors. Thus, the movie industry is harnessing digital technologies to its advantage. The industry labor force is holding steady, even though the number who work in traditional motion picture theaters is declining.[22]

In addition, foreign markets continue to be a very important source of revenue. Most countries in the world lack local production facilities and import their films. Thus, motion pictures as a medium will continue to be financially healthy.

Radio and television. Although radio and television are very different media, they share a history of technological, social, and economic development.[23] Television is a child of radio in many respects. As it emerged as a separate household medium, many program formats and stars of the radio industry were simply adopted into television. These included the basic

legal provisions of the Federal Communications Act and related legislation, advertising support, regular programming, a star system, and many categories of content (sports, daytime serials, evening drama). For that reason it is possible to discuss these media together from a common technological, economic, and cultural base and then to indicate how they developed into two distinct media.

With the arrival of the telegraph, incredibly swift, long-distance communication became possible. Prior to the development of the telegraph, the fastest a message could be moved was at the speed of a train (about 45 miles per hour at the time). With Samuel Morse's invention, all that changed.

In 1887 a German scientist, Heinrich Hertz, developed devices that could generate and detect curious *invisible magnetic waves* (what Hertz called "radiations") that traveled through the air from one side of his laboratory to the other. Within a few years many people were experimenting with these curious phenomena. Guglielmo Marconi, a wealthy young man in Italy, succeeded in turning the radiated waves on and off to produce the *dots and dashes of Morse code.* This allowed him to send and receive messages by a wireless telegraph. Marconi patented his device and improved it to the point where it could span huge distances. By the beginning of the 1900s he had sent a signal across the Atlantic Ocean.

A number of important inventions followed quickly—the vacuum tube, systems for transmitting and receiving on specific frequencies, and circuits that greatly increased the quality of performance. By 1906, the *radio telephone* became a reality when the human voice was first heard over the airwaves on ships along the Atlantic seaboard.

Despite these impressive inventions, radio did not become a household medium until the early 1920s. By then its technology was developed sufficiently that simple sets for home use were being manufactured and eagerly bought by the public—even though there were no regularly scheduled programs for them to listen to.

Radio station KDKA in Pittsburgh was the first to begin regularly scheduled broadcasting.[24] It went on the air on November 2, 1920, with a historic broadcast of the returns of the Warren Harding presidential election (with information from a nearby newspaper received by telephone).

The early 1920s were a chaotic time for the new medium. People eagerly bought sets, and hundreds of unregulated new transmitters went on the air, often broadcasting on the same frequencies as existing stations. It was a chaos of sound. Both the public and the new industry cried out for help from a reluctant federal government. Temporary measures were taken, but it was not until Congress passed the *Federal Communications Act of 1934* that the frequency assignments and power levels of transmitters were finally controlled by licenses. This legislation established the principle that *the airwaves belong to the people* and that they can be used only with their government's permission.

Meanwhile, radio became a mass medium delivering regular broadcasts into American homes. Financing the transmissions was accomplished with advertising. Time was sold to those who wanted to publicize their products over the airwaves. Although people resisted this at first, the money made it possible to hire popular performers and to transmit plays, sports, religious programs, concerts, dance music, and other content that would have been impossible without such funds.

Radio quickly became a truly massive medium. By 1935, set ownership in American homes was at the saturation level. By 1970 it exceeded an impressive five sets per household. Figure 14.3 shows the growth of radio ownership from 1920 to 2010.

Radio prospered from the mid-1930s to about the mid-1950s, largely because it had no rival on the airwaves. Major networks brought an enormous variety of programming to the nation. Radio became a much-appreciated source of free home entertainment, especially during the Depression, when a third of the labor force was unemployed.

Radio served well as a news source, and by 1940 worldwide systems permitted direct broadcasts from virtually every part of the globe. After World War II broke out in Europe, dramatic broadcasts were received from London. Then, on Sunday, December 7, 1941, the nation learned that the Japanese had bombed Pearl Harbor. It was radio's single most dramatic day, and its messages unified what had been a divided United States. On September 11, 2001, television played a similar dramatic role.

Meanwhile, in 1933, a new kind of radio was patented by Edwin Armstrong. He termed it FM, for *frequency modulation*. Unlike the prevailing *amplitude modulation (AM)* systems, it was virtually static-free. Ultimately, it came into use for radio stations specializing in music and for carrying the audio signals of television. Today, most radio listeners tune into FM stations, and the use of AM system is in slow decline. The digital age has provided several new options for listeners, including satellite radio, Internet radio, high-definition (HD) radio, and radio programming on mobile phones. Listeners can download podcasts or post comments on the blogs of their favorite DJs at the station's website. At the same time, digital technology allows stations to track listeners and embed more ads. Thus, radio remains a versatile and adaptive medium.

Television is an extension of the technology of radio. It began with experiments on ways to

FIGURE 14.3

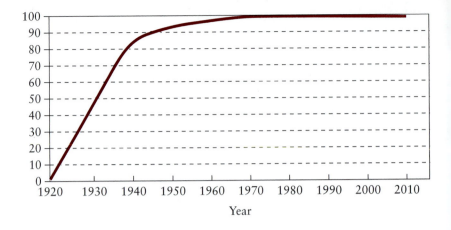

Percent of Households
with Radio Receivers,
1920–2010

Source: U.S. Census Bureau,
*Statistical Abstracts of the
United States*

send pictures over the air via radio waves. The basic technology of television was being developed during the time that radio was becoming a mass medium.[25] At first, mechanical systems of whirling (Nipkow) disks seemed promising. The disks had little holes punched in them that let through lines of reflected light as they swept across a surface. Sensitive receivers detected the light and transformed it into radio transmissions. In a reverse system, a picture could be crudely reproduced at the receiving end.

In 1922, far more efficient electronic circuits were designed, based on a cathode ray tube oscilloscope and electronic sweeping. The first to be patented was the work of Philo Farnsworth, an unusual high school boy who lived in remote Rigsby, Idaho. Farnsworth astounded his high school teacher with sophisticated diagrams for an electronic system of television transmission and reception. In 1927 he moved to California and succeeded in transmitting and receiving moving pictures.

Early TV broadcasts began before World War II. A transmitter had been built on top of the Empire State Building, and a few broadcasts had begun, but the war intervened. Once the war was over, television stations went on the air in a number of cities. The Federal Communications Commission (FCC) slowed down television's growth between 1948 and 1952. No new transmitters were licensed during those years so as to allow the development of a system of frequency

and power allocations that would avoid the chaos of early radio. After the "freeze" was lifted, the sale of sets and the construction of transmitters soared. Within a decade, 90 percent of U.S. homes had a television receiver. As Figure 14.4 shows, the new medium was adopted very rapidly, and within only a few years most of the families in the U.S. had a TV set at home. Recently, however, the number of homes in the United States with television sets has dropped. In 2011, the Nielsen Company reported that 96.7 percent of American households own television sets, a decline of about two percent from the previous year. One reason for the decline is that some young people, who are more comfortable using laptops than remote controls, are choosing not to buy TV sets when they graduate from college or enter the workforce, at least not at first. Instead, they prefer to view programs and movies on their laptops or other devices. Another reason may be due to the economic recession, during which fewer low-income households are replacing old sets when they no longer function with new digital sets.[26]

For over five decades, television has been the dominant medium in American society. Cable systems now deliver TV signals to well over two-thirds of the nation's households. New ways of delivering television signals and programming have grown rapidly. Systems for receiving direct broadcasts from satellites (DBS)

FIGURE 14.4

Percent of Households with Television Receivers, 1950–2010

Source: http://www.nytimes.com/2011/05/03/business/media/03television.html?_r=1&pagewanted=print

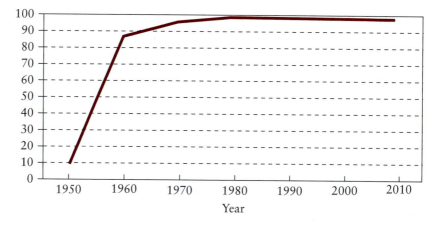

have been adopted. Such signals now reach virtually every part of the country to be received via a small dish about the size of a dinner plate in the attic or on the roof. Another delivery system uses fiberoptic cable instead of copper wire to deliver signals to homes.

One of the most significant changes occurred on February 17, 2009. On that date, conventional over-the-air analog broadcasting came to an end, and a new era of digital broadcasting was fully in place. For the consumer, this meant improved pictures and sound with high-definition television, along with interactive functions. For broadcasters, the change resulted in increased channel capacity and changes in production, distribution, and transmission.

But there are additional advantages. For example, TiVo and other digital recording devices allow viewers to determine their own viewing schedules. Mobile technologies allow viewers to see programs on hand-held devices such as smartphones and iPads, as well as online. Internet sites such as Hulu retrieve programming for viewing on a home computer or smartphone at the viewer's convenience. However, these changes have also resulted in a decrease in the number of viewers for broadcast television. Increasingly, television, cable, and satellite platforms are merging with digital, on-demand, and Internet platforms. Further changes are ahead as this innovative industry continues to evolve.

However dazzling the new technologies, in some ways *not much will change.* The content that comes over the new systems will be will be much the same as we have today—sports, formula serials, staged wrestling, movies, cartoons, news, religious broadcasts, home shopping, and all the rest—and, of course, advertising. This is because the content must be tailored to the tastes of the audience in order to attract a large number of viewers to maximize profits from advertising. That is unlikely to change greatly.

Another major change in television viewing has resulted from the same competitive forces that brought intense specialization to the magazine industry. "Splintering" or "narrowcasting" has become clearly established as an increasing number of new television delivery systems have been developed. Early televison had only a few over-the-air channels—so programs had to appeal to more general audiences. Now, with literally hundreds of channels from which to choose, the number of general interest shows has declined and highly specialized channels have sharply increased. Now there are special channels devoted to cooking, home renovations, gardening, or other highly specialized interests.

Will the new systems dominate our lives to a greater extent? Americans now have their sets on more than seven hours a day in one mode or another (cable, video, direct broadcast, Internet, etc.).

Increasingly, television, cable, and satellite platforms are merging with digital, on-demand, and Internet platforms. Further changes are ahead for our global, digital media.

However, it is becoming increasingly difficult to determine patterns of television viewing because television sets can be used in so many ways for multiple purposes, such as for watching broadcast television programs, cable channels, for playing DVDs or video games, or to connect to the Internet. Some analysts claim that television and the PC will merge eventually into one system.

The Internet and the World Wide Web. It was not until after World War II that computers began to be routinely used in science, education, business, and government. By comparison with what we have today, they were large, difficult to use, and intimidating to nontechnical people. However, they were extremely efficient, at least compared to anything available earlier, as a means to store vast amounts of information or to analyze complex mathematical problems.

The arrival of the desktop computer in the early 1980s changed all that. Today, with computer use becoming common, small desktop, laptop, and tablets are not only in virtually every workplace but also in an ever-increasing percent of American homes.

The Internet—initially developed during the 1960s by the federal government for scientific and military uses—is now used by millions of citizens for a remarkable array of purposes. This technology is not technically a mass medium in the same sense as radio, television, movies, and newspapers. True, it can provide point-to-multipoint transmission in terms of some content. However, it is also a medium by which people contact one another with millions of email messages every hour, or search for recorded information in databases. Thus, it combines features of both mass, interpersonal and reference media.

FIGURE 14.5

Percent of Households in the United States with Internet Access, 1997–2010

Source: http://ntia.doc.gov/files/ntia/publications/ntia_internet_use_report_february_2011.pdf

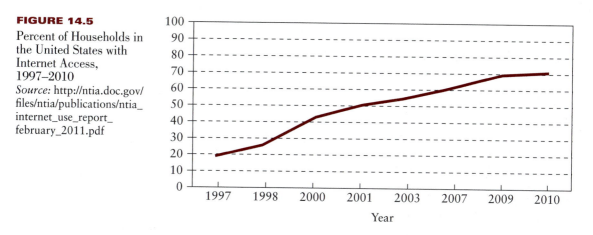

Despite these differences, the Internet—and especially its World Wide Web (the part that can carry multimedia content)—has developed many of the characteristics of traditional mass media: advertising, entertainment and educational content, federal regulation, and so forth.

At present, those using the Internet tend to be somewhat better educated and more affluent than the majority. As the system was developing, more men used it than women. That began to change as prices for computers continued to drop, as technological advances allowed simpler machines to be hooked to the Internet, and as software made the system easier to use. Figure 14.5 shows the pattern of the increasing number of U.S. households going online between 1997 and 2010.

How will computers and the Internet affect the mass media that have been described in preceding sections? It is difficult to predict, but it seems clear that we can expect continuing technological change and more convergence in the years ahead, although the nature of the content we receive may not change much.

Mass Communication as a Process

Like other forms of communication, **mass communication** is a *process* that depends on verbal and nonverbal uses of symbols and language—including the factors of context that have been discussed in earlier chapters. However, there are also significant features of mass communication that set it apart. The stages in the process can be summarized as follows:

1. Messages are formulated and encoded into standardized formats by *professional communicators* for specific goals and purposes.

2. These messages are *widely disseminated rapidly over distance* through the use of point-to-multipoint media.

3. The messages are available to *large and diverse populations,* who attend to them selectively.

4. Individual audience members *construct interpretations*—experience meanings—that to at least some degree parallel those intended by professional communicators.

5. As a result of experiencing these meanings, individuals' feelings, beliefs, attitudes, and behaviors are influenced. That is, the communication *has some effect.*

These stages provide not only a definition of mass communication but also a set of criteria by which mass media can be distinguished from other types. In summary,

Mass communication is a process by which professional communicators use media to disseminate messages widely, rapidly, and continually over distance to arouse intended meanings in large, diverse, and selectively attending audiences who are influenced in various ways.

By this definition, the media reviewed earlier (print, film, and broadcasting) are mass media engaged in mass communication. Excluded would be a long list of point-to-point media, such as the telephone, and all of those that do not involve professional communicators, large audiences, transmission over distance, and regular dissemination. The Internet, with all of its applications, is a special mixed case.

Notably missing from this description of mass communication are two critical factors that were central in the interactional and simultaneous transactions models: *role-taking* and *feedback*. Recall that these factors are also not involved when people communicate with several other kinds of point-to-point media.

The absence of role-taking and feedback is particularly critical in mass communication because senders using, say, a newspaper, a film, or a television broadcast have no way of knowing specifically who will be reading or viewing. Thus, there is no way that their message can be altered *during delivery to you* on the basis of perceived feedback from you—as is the case with interpersonal communication. For example, when Diane Sawyer or Anderson Cooper deliver the evening news, they have no way of knowing that you personally are among the audience, and certainly no way of altering the message if you fail to understand, disagree with, or express anger about something they have said. Mass communication, therefore, is a *rigidly linear process*. The messages move from sender to multiple receivers without the simultaneous role-taking and feedback features of the interactive model.

One might argue that letters to the editor, formal protests filed with the FCC, boycotts of the box office, or complaints to the broadcasting station are feedback. They are, in a delayed sense. Indeed, newer digital-tracking media allow the media and advertisers to learn much more about an individual's media habits, consumer preferences, and more. However, such after-the-fact reactions provide little or no opportunity for professional communicators to modify their delivery *during dissemination*. As such, these reactions do not play a part in

shaping the ongoing encoding of messages, as is the case of immediate verbal and nonverbal feedback cues in face-to-face communication.

The same can be said about role-taking. Mass communicators often benefit from research on their audience's composition, interests, and tastes. However, such statistical data are not the same as knowing the personal characteristics of an individual receiver in a face-to-face situation.

The Great Debate over the Influence of Mass Communication

All during the 1800s there was an enormous outpouring of complaints about the effects of mass newspapers. These complaints were based on the widely held assumption that newspapers had powerful influences on individuals in unwholesome ways. Similarly, all during the 1900s, people were deeply concerned about negative influences created by the newer media—movies, radio, and television. Recently, complaints about pornography on the Internet have resulted in similar complaints and restrictive legislation. Throughout these controversies, each of these media has been popularly assumed to have *great power*. These views result in a troubling conflict in our society and a great debate: People love the media, but there is also a **legacy of fear** that our mass media have widespread, unwanted and harmful effects.

If the media do indeed have great power to influence us individually and collectively, and if they have bad influences on us, we might be justified in controlling them far more than we do. It may not be in the best interests of our social and mental well-being to allow mass communicators to print, broadcast, or display whatever content they wish. However, censorship of media raises a very troublesome political issue. It goes to the very heart of our freedoms of speech and expression as guaranteed by the First Amendment to the U.S. Constitution.

How do we determine whether a particular form of mass communication content has antisocial or prosocial effects? Numerous critics of the media are convinced that their personal views provide answers. However, most contemporary communication scholars and social scientists think that *scientific research* is the best way to obtain answers. Understanding the nature of science and what it has revealed about the effects of the media is necessary for anyone who speaks out on the issue of the influence of the media. (For that reason, the nature of the scientific perspective and the methods by which communication research is conducted are discussed in Chapter 15.)

Early Research and the Magic Bullet Theory

Scientific research on the effects of mass communication began long after the media were well established. This was because the statistics and designs for surveys and experiments that are required for such research were not developed until the late 1920s. Well-conducted research begins with a theory, which in communication studies is often stated as a set of *propositions*. These propositions (statements) set forth what consequences are expected to occur if certain prior conditions are present. Thus, a theory is an *explanation* that indicates what *causes* a particular behavior, in the sense that it is a consequence of certain messages that have been received and understood by a person or audience.

Theories have to be tested against carefully assembled observations, and they must be abandoned or revised as necessary if they do not seem to get it right. Generally, then, the search for theories to explain the influences on audiences of mass media messages has been the guiding framework of scientific research on the process and effects of mass communication for many decades.

The earliest theory about the influences of mass communication—commonly called the **magic bullet theory**—stated that mass media messages (1) reach virtually every member of an audience; (2) penetrate every mind equally;

and (3) influence everyone's ideas and conduct, both uniformly and powerfully. Thus, message content—crime stories in newspapers or portrayals of sexual conduct in the movies—was thought to penetrate all persons' psyches and influence all persons' behavior in uniform ways.

This theory, which was accepted beginning in the early decades of the 1900s, now seems naive. At the time, the theory was based on what were thought to be correct assumptions about the nature of human nature. These were Darwinian-based assumptions that stressed biology and the inheritance of instincts that were said to control human conduct in uniform ways. Influenced by this genetic perspective, scientists of the time expected human beings to react to their environment instinctively, unconsciously, and uniformly.

This view of human nature led media scholars of the time to *fear* the power of mass communications. They assumed audiences could easily be controlled by demagogues through the clever use of the media.[27] Furthermore, startling influences, such as media advertising and wartime propaganda, seemed to confirm the worst fears of media critics, and they alarmed the public.

When research began, then, the magic bullet interpretation of media power still seemed logical. Eventually, however, communication scientists conducting empirical research found that it was seriously flawed. Indeed, it came to be totally abandoned by communication scholars. The public, on the other hand, in some ways still embraces this kind of thinking about the effects of mass communication.

Ironically, the first major research project on the effects of mass communication seemed to support the magic bullet theory! In the late 1920s, a group of social scientists investigated the influence of the movies on children. It was a massive project aimed at uncovering the influences of motion pictures on youth called the Payne Fund Studies.[28] The results seemed to indicate that children imitated forms of behavior, became sexually excited, and learned about crime and alcohol from these movies. Horror movies seemed to disturb their sleep, and attitudes about minority groups reflected in the movies seemed to have parallel influences on the children's attitudes. As research continued, however, those findings were not supported and a new general theory of media influences was needed.

Evidence of selective influences. It did not take long for the magic bullet theory to be questioned, as new evidence indicated that mass communications might have **selective influences**—that is, effects on some people but not on others. For example, in October 1938, a dramatic radio broadcast based on H. G. Wells's *War of the Worlds* (about a Martian invasion) panicked millions. Many people heard the broadcast and thought that creatures from Mars actually were invading. However, research right after the program showed that many others did not panic and were able to determine that it was only a radio play.[29] Thus the effects were selective. Those who panicked tended to be less educated and less able to make critical decisions. In addition, those with strong religious beliefs were especially likely to have panicked. This research refuted the claim that everyone is similarly influenced by the media.

Evidence of limited influences. Additional evidence of nonuniform effects, and new evidence of weak effects, came from impressive studies conducted during World War II. The goal was to determine the influence of films on *attitudes*. A now-famous series of films (*Why We Fight*) was prepared to teach army recruits about the enemy and the reasons for the war. The films were then evaluated to assess their influences on the soldiers, in meticulously planned and highly controlled experiments. The results were clear: Exposure to the films did little more than enable some subjects to *learn more facts* and modify a few *minor opinions* about the enemy and the war. Exposure to the films did almost nothing to change their attitudes in any deeper sense.[30] Clearly, there were no magic bullets at work here. At this point, the magic bullet theory was essentially dead.

A Theory of Selective and Minimal Influences

The studies of the *Why We Fight* films also were important because they showed that soldiers with higher educational levels learned more from the films than did those with less schooling. This led to an interpretation that *individual differences* in personal ability and social background made a difference in determining influence from mass communication.

Another famous study (*The People's Choice*) contributed historically to theories about the effects of mass communication.[31] The results of this remarkable research project, conducted in Erie County, Ohio, investigated how people make up their minds when voting in a presidential election. Although it was conducted many decades ago in the 1940s (Franklin Roosevelt versus Wendell Wilkie), its results are still remarkably meaningful today. The emphasis was on the role of media in the political campaign, and especially on which media voters turned to for information about the candidates and their ideas. (Television was not yet a reality.) The researchers found that the media (newspapers, magazines and radio) did have effects, but they were *minor* and *selective* rather than uniform and powerful. Those findings might be somewhat different today, with both TV and the Internet added to our national media—but most social scientists believe that the original results are still quite valid.

In the Erie County study, hundreds of citizens were interviewed in polls repeated over several months concerning their media use, how they learned about the candidates and issues, and how they made up their minds about whom to vote for.

Two kinds of effects of media were revealed: One was that the media campaign *activated the predisposed*. That is, for those whose social characteristics predisposed them to vote for a particular party's candidate, the mass-communicated messages from that source helped them reach and act upon their decision. For example, the media campaign did influence poor, Catholic, urban, blue-collar workers (the characteristics of many Democratic voters at the time) to go to the polling place and vote for Roosevelt—the Democrat's candidate. Similarly, rich, rural, Protestant farmers (typically Republican voters) were also activated by exposure to the media campaign to vote for Wilkie. Thus, *activation* was a major effect of the media.

A second, and different, influence was also detected. Many citizens in Erie County had already decided tentatively for whom they would vote, even before the campaign started. For these people, mass communications provided for **reinforcement** of a tentative decision they had already made. Thus, the campaign messages had the effect of keeping the party faithful from changing to the other side. Very few were converted by the media campaign from the Democratic to the Republican side, or vice versa (which would have been a powerful effect). Thus *reinforcement* was a clear effect of the media campaign.

Still another important finding from this historic study was that people's attention and interest in the media campaign was *highly selective*. Few indeed attended equally to both party's campaign messages. They selected the stories, speeches, and radio programs that were consistent with their own predispositions. Those predispositions, in turn, were influenced by their *social relationships*. Their ties to other people, in other words, influenced how much and how often they attended to the campaign's media messages. Specifically, family ties, friendships, and relationships at work or school often led people to listen to or read political media messages that they would otherwise have ignored. Thus, the web of social relationships in which a person is involved causes selective exposure.

These three effects—*activation, reinforcement and selectivity*—as well as the significance of predispositions and social relationships, have since that time been confirmed by studies as important effects of a mass-mediated political campaign. They will remain as important influences in many elections to come that rely on the mass media to convey candidates' messages to voters.

An unexpected outcome of *The People's Choice* research was that the media are not the only channel by which political messages reach voters. What the Erie County study showed clearly was that many voters got their information about the campaign *indirectly from other people* during discussions of candidates and issues. Many paid little attention to the news stories, speeches, and political ads presented by the media. They got their ideas and interpretations from other people by word-of-mouth.

Those exposed directly to ideas from the media were passing on information and interpretations to many others who did not attend to the campaign. This process came to be called *the two-step flow of communication*. The first stage in that flow was from the media to those who attend to the media more avidly. The second stage was the interpersonal transmission of ideas and influences from those people to others. Political messages, then, moved along word-of-mouth chains of tellers and retellers, influencing people as they went on. This discovery led to numerous studies of the diffusion of information by word-of-mouth, and the theory of the **two-step flow of communication** became well established.[32]

From these political studies, and many later ones that investigated other forms of mass communication content, came a new general theory of media effects, called **a theory of selective and minimal influences**. It completely replaced the older and outmoded *magic bullet theory*. The new theory explained that there were three major factors determining (1) *exposure* to particular presentations by mass media and (2) the *effects* such exposure would have on individual members of an audience. These three factors are:

1. *Individual differences*. People's psychological makeup—their personal configuration of interests, attitudes, intelligence, opinions, and prior beliefs—causes them to attend selectively and to interpret and respond to media messages in different ways. (This set of factors came to be called "consumer psychographics" in advertising and market research.)

2. *Social category memberships.* People's distinctive positions in the social structure—their age, race, education, political affiliations, income, gender, religion, and so on—lead them to share orientations with others like them. These produce selective patterns of attention and response to messages presented by the mass media. (Such category memberships are now called "audience demographics" by market researchers who assess radio and TV use and print media circulations.)

3. *Social relationships.* The web of ties to other people, such as family and friends, brings people to attend selectively to particular media content. Those ties also expose them to a two-step flow of ideas and interpretations of mass communication content in ways related to patterns prevailing among friends and family.

Above all, it became clear that when people were exposed to a particular movie, newspaper story, advertisement, television show, or other mass-communicated message, it was very unlikely indeed that they would suddenly be changed in any significant way.

Research support for selective and minimal influences. Thousands of studies of the effects of mass communication have supported the above interpretations, including intensive research on the influences of television on children.[33] Many studies explored the same issues— violence, sexual depictions, and antisocial behavior—that were the focus of the early research on films.[34]

In 1960 there was a massive study based on systematic observations of more than 6,000 children, plus 1,500 parents and teachers in both the United States and Canada.[35] People were startled to learn from this research that, even by 1960, children were, on average, devoting about one-sixth of their waking hours to television—more time than they spent in school! Still, *no direct and powerful influences on these children were identified!*

Perhaps no other research has had as much impact on the thinking about television and children as the 1971 government-sponsored *Report to the Surgeon General.*[36] This was a five-volume report on a related set of 23 independent projects (including some 60 specific studies), plus reviews of hundreds of prior investigations. It was funded with $1 million by the federal government (a massive outlay at the time). The goal was to determine whether portrayals of violence on television created a "public health problem" by causing children who were exposed to become more aggressive.

Violence shown on television did seem to influence some children, but not others, and only under some circumstances. Furthermore, the influences were often subtle and hard to identify. Overall, the Scientific Advisory Committee (composed of distinguished social scientists) concluded that television could lead *some* kinds of children to *some* kinds of aggressive conduct under *some* conditions. Thus, the theory of minimal and selective influences was generally supported. This less-than-clear conclusion was a disappointment to many critics of television, who "just knew" that it was harming the nation's youth.

At the end of the 1980s, there was a new *Report to the Surgeon General* on the issue of television and children.[37] The government-funded report did not sponsor new research but thoroughly reviewed the findings of more than 2,500 studies on the issue that had been published between 1979 and 1981. A major conclusion was that television did have some influence in raising rates of aggressive behavior among children whose viewing tended to be high. On the other hand, it appeared that viewing prosocial behavior tended to increase the probability of altruistic behavior. A considerable variety of other influences and effects were studied, but the bottom line was that although some influences could be detected, they were not powerful and uniform but limited and selective.

Conclusions. More than 70 years of research between the late 1920s and the 1990s supported the overall conclusion that *the magic bullet idea has no merit,* even though many people outside the scientific community still believe it. Far more strongly supported by research is the *selective and limited influences theory*—that people's individual psychological differences, social category identities, and web of social relationships lead them to attend to some media content some of the time. When they do so, they interpret the meanings of media messages within frameworks related to their psychological, social, and cultural backgrounds. Overall, however, the influence of any particular exposure to a specific mass-communicated message is likely to be minimal.

During more recent years, attention has focused on the Internet as a new medium. At present, the theory of selective and limited influences still seems to be one valid way to interpret the consequences of attending to messages from this source.

The Power of the Media: Alternative Interpretations

Although an impressive accumulation of research offers compelling evidence that our media are limited in their influences, everyday observation seems to suggest a different conclusion—that they are actually quite powerful! In fact, there does seem to be evidence that this is the case. But how could two such totally contradictory conclusions both be true? The experiments and surveys done in past decades seem both valid and impressive. However, a number of significant changes in both society and culture over the past years suggest that mass communications probably have had some significant influences.

The answer to this paradox lies in recognizing the difference between *short-term* and *long-term* effects. This section considers explanations of *long-term* and *indirect* influences of the media. It will look at both audiences in the United States and at people in other countries who have access to mass communication

entertainment products. The purpose is not to refute the findings from more than 70 years of research but to show that the situation is different when examined within a long-term perspective.

Long-Term Influences on Society and Culture

One way to understand long-term media influences is by considering how *minimal effects add up.* That is, over a long period of time, the media can have a great deal of influence in shaping people's shared ideas and interpretations, even though any particular message received by audiences on a specific day will probably have only minimal immediate effects. Two processes are involved in this adding-up effect. They are the **accumulation process** and the **adoption process.** Both have been explained by specific theories.

Mass communications have played a vital role in bringing about social and cultural changes over extended periods of time.[38] One need only look back at what has happened since World War II to see a number of long-term modifications in the way people interpret certain conditions in society. These could not have occurred without the mass media. Note carefully that this does not mean that the media directly *caused* these changes, but they served as a "necessary condition" in the processes that brought them about.

A clear example of the accumulation process is provided by the great changes during the 1960s in extending civil rights to African Americans and other minority citizens. A strong case can be made that the media played a critical role at that time (a necessary condition), as the majority of the country began to redefine their democracy to provide for more equality for all citizens, regardless of race, culture, gender, and age.

As noted earlier, during the 1950s, television developed as a household medium. It thus became ready to play a key role in fostering public support among the white majority for the civil rights movement of the 1960s (which focused mainly on black Americans). The movement, led by Dr. Martin Luther King, Jr., and others, truly changed our society.

It is not difficult to understand why television was especially important: Night after night, the TV network news showed scenes of people being denied basic rights. Their reports showed racist and segregationist treatment of African Americans—how they had to go to the back of buses, how they were refused service in restaurants, how they were not allowed in "whites-only" public schools, and how they were kept from voting by unfair laws.

As change was resisted by some segments of society, vivid and horrifying scenes were shown via TV in the nation's living rooms—scenes of men, women, and children being menaced by dogs, blasted with fire hoses, and mistreated in other ways. Television also showed both black and white people gathering in dramatic but nonviolent demonstrations to protest the existing situation of unequal status based on skin color. TV carried live the memorable "I Have a Dream" speech of Dr. King, which touched emotional chords in millions of viewers of all colors.

These portrayals did not immediately change everyone. But slowly, *public support began to accumulate* for changes in laws that would protect the rights of African Americans to vote, to work, to go to integrated schools, and to exercise freedom of choice in housing. It was an old cause, but the new medium played a critical role in increasing the pace of change. In time, then, change came. The principles at stake—freedom and equality for all, regardless of gender, age, and other personal characteristics—were defined in law.

Another classic example of accumulated effects leading to change is the historic Watergate scandal of 1972, in which an inept team of burglars tried to bug the Democratic National Committee Headquarters in the Watergate building in Washington, DC.[39] The *Washington Post*—and later the news media in general—presented *consistent* and *persistent* reports about political wrongdoing and cover-ups, said to be engineered by the White House.

Eventually, these media reports resulted in the resignation of Richard Nixon—the first time a president of the United States had been forced out of office.

The news media did not do this alone; they did not create the actual events that finally led to the resignation of Richard Nixon. What happened was that for almost two years the press engaged in relentless investigation of Watergate and repeatedly disclosed their findings in newspapers, on television, in magazines, and in books. This went on day after day and month after month, as the story unfolded. Thus, multiple exposure by various media created a *corroborative* effect, making the charges seem more valid.

At first, the public was not aroused, but President Nixon slowly lost support as the reports in the press raised more questions about his honesty. Finally, Nixon's political adversaries were about to start an impeachment process. President Nixon resigned on August 9, 1974, rather than face impeachment. By any measure, bringing down a president of the United States—the most powerful country in the world—is a remarkable effect.

Other examples could be added. A number of scholars have suggested that consistent, persistent, and corroborative presentations by the media played a part in changing the American population's beliefs, attitudes, and actions regarding the war in Vietnam. At first the war was portrayed and interpreted as a gallant effort to keep evil Communists from overwhelming a small ally. As the conflict escalated and dragged on year after year, television presented bloody war scenes and grim body counts, on a nightly basis, along with scenes of antiwar demonstrations, draft card burning, and campus protests. These reports—plus corroborating accounts in newspapers, magazines, radio, and film—helped bring about widespread negative interpretations of the morality of the war. As these interpretations accumulated, public support for the war gradually eroded. Finally, the nation's political leaders had little choice but to terminate it. By any measure that was a significant effect.

The accumulation process is common in our society. For example, during the past 25 years, large proportions of the population gave up smoking, developed a concern for the environment, began to worry about fat and cholesterol in their diet, began to wear seatbelts in the car, and changed their views about drunk drivers. Obviously, the media did not single-handedly invent and bring about these changes, but their messages clearly played *a necessary part* in altering our collective thinking and behavior patterns in each case. Without the media's attention to each of these issues, many more people in our society would probably be smoking, trashing the environment, eating fatty foods, ignoring seatbelts, and driving while texting or under the influence. These were standard behaviors three decades ago. Insofar as the media helped bring about these changes, they had a powerful influence.

The Adoption Process as Long-Term Influence on Change

A second form of media-related behavior that illustrates the role of mass communications in long-term change is the *adoption process*. Theories of how it works originated in sociological studies of how new technology comes into use in a society. The central concept is *innovation*—anything new, borrowed from other people, or invented within the society. It might be technology, an idea, a word, or even a new way of dancing. The patterns of adoption of the mass media themselves are illustrated by Figures 14.1 through 14.5.

Obviously, people do not immediately adopt every innovation as soon as it becomes available, even if it is rational to do so. Innovations come into use individual by individual as people make up their minds to change. The pattern is easily recognized in such innovations as DVDs, instant breakfasts, microwave ovens, cable TV, cellular phones, and home computers. Other innovations are social rather than material; that is, innovations need not be things. New meanings, slang terms, and shared ways of thinking also qualify.

How does the adoption process actually take place, and what is the part played by mass communications? By the 1950s, research on this process was an established tradition, and the process was well understood.[40] Adoption theory states that innovations spread in an accumulating pattern of use as a result of specific decisions made by growing numbers of individuals.

This process takes place under certain conditions. First, potential adopters become *aware* of the innovation's existence. Second, this arouses their *interest,* bringing them to *seek further information.* Third, the innovation is then *evaluated* in terms of possible *uses and costs versus benefits.* Fourth, if feasible, it may then be *tried briefly.* Fifth, *adoption takes place,* and the innovation is routinely used.[41]

These five stages do not apply exactly to every individual and every innovation. Some new things—opinions, for example—cannot be tried out on a small scale but require an all-or-none decision. Others may be adopted temporarily but then abandoned.

What is the role of the media in this process? The stages discussed above suggest that the presentation of information via the media and the adoption and diffusion of innovations are closely related. Although information about a new thing, idea, or form of behavior can be provided without people adopting it, the first stage in adoption is learning about its existence (and potential utility). This is precisely what mass media provide in modern society. If they present new ideas and interpretations of realities under the conditions outlined in the accumulation process, they can play a significant role in bringing about social change.

Socialization Theories

At least two additional influences of the media can be identified that would be difficult to document in experiments or surveys. Both are examples of media contributions to mass communication's long-term influences. Two aspects of *socialization*—the learning process by which the rules of behavior and all the demands of general and specialized cultures are acquired by an individual—are particularly influenced by portrayals in media content. In one, people are exposed to depictions of behavior that are seen as attractive and worth copying. In the other, people learn patterns of social expectations.

Modeling. This perspective derives from a general psychological theory of *observational* or *social learning* that explains how new patterns of behavior are acquired by seeing them acted out by others (whether in media presentations or elsewhere).[42] In connection with mass communications, **modeling** explains how actions that are observed in media portrayals can be adopted by people to become part of their personal habit patterns.

The basic idea is that various actions are "modeled" (that is displayed) by attractive people in media content. If these are imitated by an individual and prove to be rewarding by solving a problem for them, they can become a permanent part of that individual's habitual activities.

Thus, over time, an individual can adopt a number of habit patterns from observations of behavior portrayed in media presentations—ranging from how to dress for various occasions to more serious behaviors, such as the treatment of women and minorities.

Social expectations. Another way of looking at the long-term accumulation of influences on audiences is to point out that people learn the *rules* and *requirements* of various groups by seeing them portrayed in the media. That is, by seeing such groups as families, courts, the army, police departments, or law offices, receivers can see in action their norms, roles, ranking patterns, and systems of social control. They can even learn how to behave as a member of a criminal gang.

By seeing such portrayals in media content, then, even though they have never been members of a criminal gang or any of the other groups, they have a pretty good understanding of what behaviors are accepted or punished within such settings. This kind of long-term influence on people is the **social expectations theory** of media influences.[43] These effects would not be easily detected in a short-term experiment or survey, but they are very real nevertheless.

Generally, then, contemporary mass media may have limited and selective influences on people in a short-term and immediate sense. However, if audiences attend to media content over a long period of time, they can be profoundly influenced as they construct interpretations of reality, adopt new forms of behavior, imitate models, and learn how to behave in group settings.

Chapter Review

- Each of the major print media grew out of the technological, social, and cultural changes that produced modern capitalism and the Industrial Revolution. Books, newspapers, and magazines have a common origin of print development. The electronic technologies in radio, television, and computer networks are more recent.

- Early research on mass communications was based on the magic bullet theory of media effects. Some early research seemed to indicate that the media had immediate, universal, and powerful effects.

- A huge accumulation of research over several decades indicated that on a short-term basis the media may have minimal and highly selective effects.

- A number of long-term influences can be identified: the accumulation of minimal effects, adoption processes, the social construction of reality, the modeling of behavior, and the learning of social expectations.

Key Terms

dependency	penny press	theory of selective and limited influences
pictographs	mass communication	accumulation process
parchment	legacy of fear	adoption process
vellum	magic bullet theory	modeling
papyrus	selective influences	social expectations theory
colonial press	reinforcement	
freedom of the press	two-step flow of communication	

Notes

1. For a discussion of the broad implications of the influences of media on individuals and society, see: Bryant, J., & Oliver, M. B. (Eds.). (2009). *Media Effects*. New York: Routledge. For an analysis of the issue of media dependency, see: Smyth, D. W. (1981). *Dependency road: Communication, capitalism, consciousness and Canada*. Norwood, NJ: Ablex.

2. For a comparison of televised violence and its implications in Britain and the U.S., see: Gunter, B., Harrison, J., & Wykes, M. (2003). *Violence on television*. Mahwah, NJ: Erlbaum.

3. Guinea, M. A. G. (1979). *Altamira: And other Cantabrian caves*. Madrid: Silex.

4. See: Gauer, A. (1984). *A history of writing*. London: Scribner's.

5. Jackson, D. (1981). *The story of writing*. New York: Taplinger.

6. The Sumerians who lived in what is now Iraq took this important step around 1700 B.C., making use of a system of *cuneiform* writing. They made impressions in soft clay tablets that could be baked. They used a stick with a wedge-like end to form stylized symbols that stood for what we would call syllables. This required hundreds of separate symbols. The Greco-Roman alphabet we use today is much simpler, with each of our 26 letters standing for a brief sound element. See: Naveh, J. (1982). *The early history of the alphabet*. Jerusalem: Magnes.

7. See: Innes, H. A. (1950). *Empire and communications*. New York: Oxford University Press.

8. McMurtrie, D. (1943). *The book: A history of printing and bookmaking*. New York: Oxford University Press.

9. Clapper, R. H. (1934). *Paper: An historical account of its making by hand from the earliest times down to the present day*. Oxford: Oxford University Press.

10. Moran, J. (1974). *Printing presses: History and development from the fifteenth century to modern times*. Berkeley and Los Angeles: University of California Press.

11. Estimates of the number of books produced during the *incunabulum* (the period between 1455 and 1500) range between 8 million and 20 million copies, with an average press run of about 500 copies per book. This was a truly remarkable outpouring of publications. See: Eisenstein, E. (1979). *The printing press as an agent of change* (vols. I and II). Cambridge, England: Cambridge University Press.

12. Madison, C. A. (1966). *Book publishing in America*. New York: McGraw-Hill.

13. These criteria are based on definitions of a newspaper suggested in: Emery, E. (1972). *The press in America* (5th ed., p. 3). Englewood Cliffs, NJ: Prentice-Hall.

14. For a thorough understanding of the development and current status of the mass media, see: Dennis, E. E. & DeFleur, M. L. (2010). *Understanding Media in the Digital Age*. New York: Allyn & Bacon.

15. Growth trend continues for newspaper websites. (2012, June 11). Editor & Publisher. Retrieved from http://editorandpublisher.com

16. Edmonds, R., Rosenstiel, T., & Mitchell, A (2012, April 11). The state of the news media

2012: An annual report on American journalism. The Pew Research Center's Project for Excellence in Journalism. Retrieved from http://stateofthe-media.org/print-chapter/?print_id=10490.

17. Wood, J. P. (1949). *Magazines in the United States* (pp. 3–9). New York: Ronald.

18. Mott, F. L. (1930). *A history of American magazines* (vol.1, pp. 13–72). Cambridge, MA: Harvard University Press.

19. Quigley, M. (1948). *Magic shadows: The story of the origin of motion pictures.* Washington, DC: Georgetown University Press.

20. Eder, J. M. (1948). *History of photography.* New York: Columbia University Press.

21. For an account of early film-making, see: Talbot, F. A. (1923). *Moving pictures: How they are made and work.* London: Heinemann.

22. Specific data on these trends can be found in the Motion Picture Association of America's annual reports.

23. For an excellent discussion of these technological developments, see: Head, S. W., & Sterling, C. H. (1987). *Broadcasting in America* (5th ed.). Boston: Houghton Mifflin. See also: Dennis, E. E., & DeFleur, M. L. (2010). *Understanding media in the digital age.* New York: Allyn & Bacon.

24. Archer, G. L. (1938). *History of radio to 1926* (pp. 112–113). New York: American Historical Society.

25. For a readable account of the history of television up to the mid-1970s, see: Barnouw, E. (1975). *Tube of plenty: The evolution of American television.* New York: Oxford University Press.

26. Stelter, B. (2011, May 3). Ownership of TV sets falls in U.S. *The New York Times.* Retrieved from http://www.nytimes.com

27. See, for example: Lasswell, H. D. (1927). *Propaganda technique in the world war.* New York: Knopf.

28. These studies were published in 13 separate volumes. A short and readable overview is contained in: Charters, W. W. (1933). *Motion pictures and youth: A summary.* New York: Macmillan.

29. Cantril, H. (1940). *The invasion from Mars: A study of the psychology of panic.* Princeton, NJ: Princeton University Press.

30. Hovland, C. I., Lumsdaine, A. A., & Sheffield, F. D. (1949). *Experiments on mass communication.* Princeton, NJ: Princeton University Press.

31. Lazarsfeld, P. F., Berelson, B., & Gaudet, H. (1948). *The people's choice.* New York: Columbia University Press.

32. DeFleur, M. L. (1987). The growth and decline of research on the diffusion of the news: 1945–1985. *Communication Research, 14,* 1, 109–130.

33. Maccoby, E. E. (1951). Television: Its impact on school children. *Public Opinion Quarterly, 15,* 421–444.

34. Rubenstein, E. A. (1981). Television violence: A historical perspective. In *Children and the faces of television* (p. 114). New York: Academic.

35. Schramm, W., Lyle, J., & Parker, E. (1961). *Television in the lives of our children.* Stanford, CA: Stanford University Press.

36. Surgeon General's Scientific Advisory Committee on Television and Social Behavior. (1971). *Television and growing up: The im-pact of televised violence.* Report to the Surgeon General, United States Public Health Service. Washington, DC: U.S. Government Printing Office.

37. Pearl, D., Bouthilet, L., & Lazar, J. (1982). *Television and behavior: Ten years of scientific progress and implications for the eighties* (Vols. I and II). Washington, DC: U.S. Government Printing Office.

38. This section is based on the theory of accumulation of minimal effects. See chapter 15 of: DeFleur, M. L., & Dennis, E. E. (2002). *Understanding mass communication* (7th ed., p. 453). Boston: Houghton Mifflin.

39. The burglars apparently were looking for material that would be useful in the forthcoming presidential campaign. They were discovered, and two were arrested and convicted. It then became clear that the perpetrators and certain co-conspirators had ties to the CIA and to some of President Nixon's immediate aides in the White House. A persevering investigation by the *Washington Post* eventually revealed a complex plot that included attempts to discredit Mr. Nixon's political opponents. There were attempts to cover up the plot

and any involvement of the president in the scandal. At its peak, virtually all the media in the United States gave the story extensive coverage.

40. Rogers, E. M., & Shoemaker, F. F. (1971). *Communication of innovations: A cross-cultural approach* (pp. 52–70, 100). New York: Free Press.

41. Ibid., p. 100.

42. See: Bandura, A. (2001). Social cognitive theory of mass communication. *Media Psychology*, 3, 265–299; Bandura, A. (1977). *Social learning theory*. Englewood Cliffs, NJ: Prentice-Hall.

43. See the formal statement and explanation of this theory in DeFleur & Dennis *Understanding mass communication*, p. 455.

Chapter 15

Understanding
Communication Research

H ow can you make such a claim?" Martin protested. "There is no way that you are going to convince me that you can study human communication scientifically. Communication is far too complex. Besides, people have free will and that means they do not follow regular patterns, like trained seals, in any of their behavior, including communication."

"Well," Hanna replied, "first of all, it depends on what you mean by science. If you think of science only in terms of white coats, laboratories, microscopes, or electronic instruments that go bleep, bleep, bleep, then you're absolutely right. However, if that were the only type of setting in which science could be pursued, you would have to leave out about 75 percent of the fields that are now conducting scientific research."

"Take astronomy or meteorology," Hanna continued. "You can't get solar systems and galaxies, or warm fronts and hurricanes, into a laboratory—and microscopes would make little sense for studying them. Indeed, in the majority of scientific fields, it is not the place where investigations are pursued or not the instruments that are used for various purposes that defines it as a science."

"You will have to admit, though," Martin countered, "that people really are unpredictable. They can choose whether, when, and how they will communicate, and with whom. Because all that behavior is so random, there is just no way that you can develop any kind of formulas or laws that govern communication. After all, that is precisely what they do in sciences like biology, chemistry, and physics. Look at Newton's laws and the atomic table. What do you say to that?"

"I say that they are wonderful examples of how the scientific method paid off in physics and chemistry, and why it is so important to use it now in other fields," Hanna replied. "However, because those traditional sciences have already developed such laws does not mean that parallel discoveries cannot be made in newer areas, such as the study of communication. After all, the use of a scientific approach in studies of communication began only a generation or so ago. The physical and biological sciences got their start centuries earlier."

"Maybe," said Martin, still resisting, "but I still say that communication research just can't be scientific because it studies how people talk and act, and everybody knows that it is impossible to predict human behavior."

"Martin," Hanna sighed, "if you are willing to make the effort, I can show you how the scientific method has already revealed patterns in human communication, as well as explanations that help predict how people are likely to communicate in a great variety of contexts and circumstances."

Like Martin, many people are reluctant to accept the idea that human communication can be studied using the logic and methods of science. That is understandable, because communication behavior is indeed very complex, difficult to observe, and not always predictable. But difficult is not the same as impossible, and few would argue that the search for better ways to communicate is unimportant. The development of a body of trustworthy knowledge concerning ways to communicate more accurately and effectively is essential, which is why it is important to conduct research on the process and effects of human communication.

The present chapter has the goal of providing an understanding of how the rules, logic, strategies, and methods of science are applied to the systematic study of human communication and its consequences. It is not designed to train you, the reader, as a research specialist. However, the use of **research** to try and find answers to important problems is increasingly common in almost all fields.

Science had its beginnings in the study of the physical world—where it obviously has had remarkable success. It then came into use in medical fields—with additional great success. Later, during the later 1800s, the logic and procedures of science came into use in such fields as psychology, anthropology, sociology, and the study of political behavior. In these fields valuable insights into and understandings of human behavior were developed using scientific strategies. At present, communication scholars make use of scientific methods and procedures to study a great variety of problems in human communication.

At the same time, the scientific perspective provides one way to examine human communication; the humanistic or rhetorical perspective offers another. Humanists focus on how internal, psychological processes affect how we communicate. To observe, report, and explain objectively how we communicate is insufficient to humanists; instead, they want to know how we subjectively interpret the world we live in. Humanists argue that we cannot exactly observe how people feel, how they love or hate one another, and why a film should be interpreted in a particular way.

Both perspectives offer important methods for understanding how and why we communicate. Humanistic methods continue to be used to inform the study of communication

When was the last time you were asked to complete a survey? Survey research is one of the most common methods for assessing public opinion.

and scholars in the field also examine human communication using scientific strategies of measurement, theory building, and testing from the scientific perspective. This chapter will focus on the scientific perspective, and includes both quantitative and qualitative methods of research.[1]

As noted, the use of a scientific approach to understanding human communication began during the last century. Great strides have been made in developing methods of research that can be used effectively in this important task. Many of these methods were originally developed for use in the physical sciences (for example, the experiment). Later they were adapted for the basic social sciences, such as psychology and sociology. Other methods originated in the social sciences themselves (the survey) and were found to be very practical for communication

research. Still others have been invented by communication researchers themselves.

Whatever the origins of these methods, researchers who study human communication within the scientific perspective now use procedures that can be called *the scientific methodology of communication research*. Collectively, those procedures can be thought of as a kind of "tool kit." The kit has many useful methods for gaining knowledge. These consist of logical strategies of observation, techniques of measurement, criteria for assessing the quality and importance of what is observed, and rules for making conclusions known to others. Through the use of that methodological tool kit, trustworthy knowledge can be accumulated about how people communicate and what consequences such behavior has for them. This chapter describes some of the main features of communication research methods and provides examples of how studies are conducted when these tools are used. It adds an important dimension to knowledge about the human communication process that is so important in daily life.

The Postulates of the Scientific Research Perspective

We begin by asking a very basic question: What is meant by *research*? As the opening vignette suggests, for some people the term conjures up images of scientists with thick glasses wearing white coats and working in laboratories with electronic gadgets and glass tubes. This image misses the point completely. Research has little to do with where it is conducted or what gadgets are used.

In its broadest sense, research is simply a strategy for studying some aspect or feature of the real world in such a way that trustworthy knowledge can be gained and errors can be minimized. What is studied may be physical or biological, or it may be a form of human behavior—such as communication. Thus, it is not the object of study that defines research but the way one goes about it.

Simply stated, then, *research* (in any field) can be defined as *a set of systematic procedures for gathering credible information about some object or process.* In our discipline, the object or process consists of the verbal, nonverbal, and contextual features of human communication that have been discussed in previous chapters. Moreover, research requires that we study communication under carefully controlled conditions of observation in such a way that objective conclusions can be reached with a minimum of error.

Communication researchers conducting a scientific investigation are committed to three essential *assumptions* about the nature of what they are investigating and how they go about it. Broad assumptions of this kind are sometimes called *postulates*, and they apply to all fields in which scientific research is conducted.[2]

Research Postulates about Communication

Communication researchers using the scientific method agree on the following postulates or assumptions about the nature of human communication and the methods they use to investigate it:

1. *The assumption of an orderly universe.* Communication behavior is not a jumble of random events. How and what people say, with whom, and when they say it follows some orderly, discoverable rules or patterns.
2. *The assumption of cause-effect relationships.* Communication behavior does not just happen. There are identifiable, discoverable causes for why people communicate the way they do, when they do it, and with whom. Theories help explain the probable causes and consequences of a particular communication event.
3. *The assumption of scientific integrity.* Science is self-policing. To trust research findings and conclusions about human communication, studies must be made public with all the procedures, findings, and interpretations spelled out. Such studies are then screened by experts before they are accepted for publication. Unpublished studies that do not disclose their methods or findings are ignored.

The term **postulate** means a shared belief of a very fundamental nature—so basic that it is not subject to proof or disproof. The following assumptions are the postulates of the scientific research perspective. (Box 15.1 gives an overview of these assumptions.)

The Assumption of an Orderly Universe

Communication researchers using the scientific method must first assume that what they are studying *follows regular and discoverable patterns*. Indeed all researchers must assume there is order in what they study. Human communication behavior is no exception. It follows orderly patterns, just as physical and biological phenomena do.

The importance of making the assumption of an orderly universe is that it provides the basic reason for the very existence of science. Without this assumption, scientific research on any subject would be completely unnecessary. For example, in a chaotic world of communication behavior, no patterns could be discovered—it would be merely a jumble of random events. This is clearly not the case. Each of the chapters in this book has shown that a great deal of order in communication behavior has been identified.

Research aimed at revealing and describing order—stages, tendencies, configurations, or processes of human communication—is called **descriptive research**. Descriptive research studies reach conclusions that demonstrate some significant pattern or other orderly way in which people relate to one another using verbal, nonverbal, contextual, or mediated communication. The models of the communication process presented in Chapter 1 are examples of the end product of such research.

The Assumption of Cause-Effect Relationships

A second assumption (postulate) subscribed to by communication researchers is that it is possible to discover, through scientific investigation, *why* events occur. That is, their causes can be uncovered. This postulate is common to all fields of science—whether they are researching dreaded diseases, financial recessions, nuclear reactions, or failures in communication between people who are not alike. At any particular time in the ongoing development of science, their causes may be poorly understood or even unknown, but scientists reject the idea that things just happen randomly and that there are no causal sequences in events.

The need to develop explanations of causes and effects points directly to the role of **theory** in the research perspective. Theories are the form in which cause-effect relationships are stated, once they are discovered. In other words, if they have been verified, theories provide *explanations* of how one set of events brings about or influences another. Even before they have been verified, candidate theories provide invaluable *guides* to what needs to be studied in order to gain understanding. Much research is focused on testing and evaluating theories to see whether they really work. Thus, one major goal in communication research is to formulate (put together) theories that explain the consequences and influences of various kinds of communication. A related goal is to test and evaluate those theories to see if they are adequate. Throughout this text, theories have been used to explain particular effects in communication.

The Assumption of Scientific Integrity

The third assumption (postulate) of the research perspective is based on what researchers call the rule of *experto credite,* which means literally "have confidence in the expert." The assumption of scientific integrity refers to the confidence that scholars have in one another's published research findings. Scientists are perhaps the world's greatest skeptics, and they demand the highest standards of proof to ensure the information is credible. They abhor the idea that anyone would falsify data or findings.

The assumption of *experto credite* rests on three requirements concerning the nature of research reports, plus the skeptical and self-policing nature of science. These requirements are that science must be *public,* research reports must be rigorously *screened* before publication, and secrecy in research is *unacceptable.*

Science must be public. Scientific skepticism is nowhere more evident than in the requirement that research findings be published—spelling out exactly what was being studied, the methods used, the findings observed, and their implications. To meet this requirement, research reports are usually submitted as articles for publication in technical journals. Such journals are specialized magazines devoted to reporting research findings and related matters in various fields.[3] An acceptable article must describe in detail how the research was done and exactly why the conclusions were reached. One benefit of this requirement is that it enables other researchers to check the author's conclusions by **replication** of the study using the same methods and conditions. Findings that cannot be duplicated in this manner are regarded as controversial and are under suspicion.

Research reports must be screened. Editors of scientific journals receive many reports for publication from researchers all over the world. Each report is then *assessed* (screened) by a panel of peers, selected by the editors. These are experts in whatever has been studied. This means that the report is closely scrutinized by highly qualified researchers to detect errors in procedure or in how conclusions were reached. Only if the research report gets by this demanding review can it be accepted for publication. To protect the integrity of the assessment, this is almost always done "blind": That is, neither the author of the report nor any of the judges know the names of the others. Because many journals reject 90 percent or more of the reports they receive, this is a rigorous system.

If reports on scientific findings and conclusions survive this screening process, they become *public* knowledge. Those that are published are usually referred to as being in the "literature"—the body of research reports on any particular topic that appear in reputable journals, dissertations, or other publications. In this manner, *a body of trustworthy knowledge accumulates*. This accumulative feature keeps the cutting edge of science moving forward.[4]

Secrecy is unacceptable. The requirement that research reports be made public eliminates from the literature secret findings of projects conducted by industry, government, advertising agencies, or any other organization that does not publish its reports. Although this type of **proprietary research** (research owned by those who pay to have the research conducted) can provide a competitive edge to the particular industry that generates it, such studies may not be conducted with meticulous attention to scientific procedures and methods. Because they escape scrutiny, proprietary studies contribute nothing to science as a "shared" body of knowledge.

One of the advantages of these self-policing features of science is the belief that published research reports have *scientific integrity*. Although misconduct such as deception or fraud does occur, it is rare.

This system for achieving scientific integrity does not mean that there are no inconsistencies or controversies in published research reports on various topics. They are abundant. Honest researchers, diligently using sound methods, often reach different conclusions on the same issues. However, the system described above, which is based on accepting conclusions only after they are consistently supported by a body of research, is the best one yet devised to develop shared, accumulated, and trustworthy knowledge.

Steps in the Research Process

Communication research is conducted step by step. The six basic stages listed here are followed by researchers in all fields, from planning what they are going to study to publishing their results. Box 15.2 provides a brief overview of each of these steps.

Specifying the Goals of the Research

One of the most critical steps in the research process is specifying the objectives of the

BOX 15.2   A Closer Look

Steps in the Research Process

Research is a systematic process. Six basic steps are followed when conducting a formal research study.

1. *Specify the goals of the research.* The researcher begins by asking, "What problem do I want to solve? What exactly do I want to look at? What are the variables that I want to observe? What do I want to find out?"

2. *Review prior research reports.* The researcher searches the relevant literature to see what is already known about the research problem. This way, the researcher avoids duplicating research or reinventing the wheel. The literature can also give the researcher clues about procedures or special problems to consider in designing the study.

3. *Make the necessary observations.* The researcher is now ready to observe the relevant phenomena and record observations in some symbolic (often numerical) way. The researcher does this directly—by observing what people are doing or saying now—or indirectly—by noting what people say they did after the fact.

4. *Analyze the data.* To make sense of the obtained observations, the researcher must input the numerical data into the computer and perform statistical calculations. In this way, the researcher can reduce large amounts of information into a manageable index, average, or quantitative summary.

5. *Reach conclusions.* After statistically analyzing the data, the researcher must interpret the results by asking, "What does this mean? Do I accept or reject my hypothesis? Was the theory correct? Given these results, what alternative theoretical explanation can I make?"

6. *Report the results.* Finally, the researcher is obligated to make the study public by presenting and reporting each of the five previous steps. In this way, others can judge the merits of the study, learn more about the topic investigated, and teach or use the obtained information. Over time, this study and others like it contribute to the accumulated body of knowledge.

---

investigation—the reasons for which it is being undertaken. This includes stating exactly what is to be studied and why. First, the problem has to be identified in a general way. Then, each phase has to be stated clearly in a carefully defined *plan* so that the research can be conducted realistically with the greatest level of precision that resources will allow.

Identifying the relevant variables.   The first consideration in planning a research project is to understand what *variables* are to be observed. A variable is a concept, factor, or condition that can take different numerical values. Recall from the meaning triangle in Chapter 2 that each concept has a label (name) and some set of meanings that people experience in

response to that label. A simple example would be age. By convention, this term labels the number of birthdays an individual has had since birth. Other variables may be level of education, household income, or amount of time spent viewing television.

Looked at this way, age, income, education, and TV viewing time are concepts, and they can vary quantitatively from one individual to another. Thus, each is a variable concept. Researchers shorten this phrase and say that age, income, and so on are variables.

When relationships between variables are studied, some are *independent* and others are *dependent*. These terms can have two different implications. In some cases, variations or changes in the **dependent variable** are thought to be due to the presence and influence of a particular **independent variable.** That is, the two variables are in a relationship that implies cause and effect. For example, in a medical study the number of fatty hamburgers a person eats in a week can be related in a causal way to the probability that the individual will gain weight. However, the reverse would not be considered causal. In other cases, two factors might merely vary together in some coordinated manner with each other (a correlation), without implications of causation. In communication terms, a variable like communication apprehension might influence an individual's level of social efficacy. On the other hand, such apprehension might be correlated with an individual's lack of education, which it could not possibly have caused. It is very important for the researcher to understand which of these two cases is implied by the findings—potential cause or only a correlation.

In a research project, variables are *observed*—following the scientific requirement that knowledge is founded on observation, as opposed to traditional wisdom, speculation, or religious interpretation. Observation in research usually consists of *measurement* in some form—deciding whether a variable is present or absent or present to some degree. The measurement process is discussed in greater detail in a section that will follow.

Identifying the general objectives. Research begins with a decision as to the project's overall goals. If it is simply a descriptive study, the problem is to specify what must be observed and described. If the research is designed to develop, or to test, one or more theories, the problem becomes more complex: The researcher has to identify the exact observations that will be needed, how each variable will be measured, what patterns are expected in the results, and how to decide whether the findings support the theory being considered.

Often, a research problem can be formulated in terms of a **hypothesis**—a statement that poses tentative and expected relationships between variables. Ideally, a hypothesis is derived from a theory that predicts what variables are related to others. Assembling careful observations on those variables makes it possible to *accept* or *reject* the hypothesis, as long as standard procedures for making such judgments are followed. If the hypothesis can be accepted, then it provides *support* for the theory. If it must be rejected, then the theory is called into question.

In many research projects, it is difficult to derive hypotheses in this way because there are no well-articulated theories from which to obtain them. In such cases, researchers turn to the body of evidence that has been accumulated by other researchers about what they want to study. If the evidence is not sufficiently clear, researchers can formulate a "working" hypothesis that indicates what they expect to find, given the evidence to date.

Reviewing Prior Research Reports

Researchers review the all available sources to locate reports of others who have already studied the problem. Reviewing the previous research prevents duplication and can help researchers avoid the problems of the earlier studies. Such reports can be found in many sources. In addition to the technical journals in the field, research may be reported in books, monographs, convention papers, and government documents. All of these sources must be scrutinized before finalizing research plans. This is no easy task. One aid to review the literature is the *Communication Abstracts*, which abstracts (summarizes) all the articles in communication journals each month. Fortunately, electronic database systems available through college libraries and other online sources, including Academic Search Complete, EBSCO, JSTOR, and Google Scholar, are helpful for finding previous studies on a topic.

With computers and searchable electronic databases, a review of prior publications that formerly would have taken days or weeks to accomplish can be done much more efficiently and thoroughly. Commercial database providers offer electronic duplicates of printed abstracts and publications. Summaries and the full text of virtually all journal articles, books, reports, and monographs are posted promptly into these databases soon after publication.

Making the Necessary Observations

Yogi Berra, the famous baseball player, perhaps said it best when he reportedly remarked, "You can observe a lot by just watching!" His analysis actually has a great deal of merit. In scientific research, watching is called **empirical observation.** More specifically, researchers observe whether certain behaviors under investigation are present (in some amount) or absent. This means that researchers watch and make judgments as to how to classify what has been observed by deciding where the behavior fits in some set of qualitative categories, or along some numerical continuum. To illustrate, imagine a researcher who is watching a person talking to another individual in a small group experiment. One goal of the researcher's observations is to decide whether that person has played an *active* or a *passive* role as a communicator. On the basis of those categories, the judgment is recorded. A series of such recorded observations are *data.*

The nature of "data."   The term **data** means *information known as fact*. To make something known as fact requires that it be communicated. Therefore, observations that are to become scientific data must be *recorded* in symbols in some way, so that other scientists can see and understand what was observed. This can be done with detailed verbal descriptions for subtle qualitative observations, or it can be done with numbers for quantitative observations.

Transforming observations into recorded data can introduce distortion and change, so the procedure has to be designed with care. For example, when researchers depend on interviewing subjects, *questionnaires* are normally used for recording purposes. Traditionally, these pose each question in a standardized way so that all subjects are asked the same questions

in the same way. This, in turn, helps the interviewer to observe each case uniformly.

However, such standardization can obscure subtle and important information. For example, suppose the interviewer asks, "Are you single, married, divorced, or widowed?" Suppose that a male participant is still legally married but has long since separated from his wife. Suppose further that he is now living with another woman and they intend to marry. All of these subtleties are lost when he answers, "Well, technically I'm married." The interviewer then records the observation "married" on the form—missing all the rest. Later, when the data are analyzed for interpretation, that particular subject will be included in the "married" category, presumably living in a stable marital relationship with his legal spouse. If a number of such cases were encountered, the conclusions drawn from the category "married" might be incorrect, based on such responses.

Qualitative versus quantitative observation. There is no perfect way to make empirical observations. Many techniques and strategies can be used to observe communication behavior, and each has its advantages and limitations. Some scales and questionnaires produce remarkably precise numerical data that can be analyzed with statistics, but such procedures may miss subtle aspects of communication and may fail to explain very much about why people communicate as they do. On the other hand, purely qualitative techniques may provide sensitive insights into complex human feelings and values, but they do not produce numerical data that can be easily summarized and subjected to statistical tests. This means that it may not be possible to evaluate the truth of a conclusion reached from purely qualitative observation. Despite the limitations of these approaches, both play an important part in the accumulation of knowledge about human communication.

Direct versus indirect observation.   Behavior can be observed *directly* or *indirectly*. In direct observation, researchers watch communication

How do you make sense of data? One way is to demonstrate a trend.

behavior as it is openly acted out by the subjects. Here, the subjects know that they are being observed, and this condition can alter their behavior in some circumstances. In indirect observation, the participants do not know that they are being watched, so their behavior is not affected by the research. However, indirect observation without subject awareness is difficult, if not impossible. Few people would want to be observed communicating in natural settings—as they eat, watch TV, feed the cat, work, play sports, and generally carry on their daily routines.

A less direct form of observation is *unobtrusive* measurement. Here, communication activities are "inferred" from information obtained after the fact. For example, people's preferences in radio stations were studied by having auto repair shops record the stations to which their customers' car radios were tuned when the vehicles were dropped off.

Although there is no ideal observation method, **participant observation** has many advantages.[5] In its classic form, the investigator actually joins the group that is under study and participates fully in its activities—so as to observe its communication patterns directly. The group may or may not know that the person is a researcher. This form of unobtrusive data gathering is called *participant observation.*

Participant observation is both difficult and time consuming, because the researcher must learn the special language, norms, roles, and lifestyle of those being observed. It's also difficult for the researcher to make an accurate and secret record of the behavior under study. Consider the researcher studying communication behaviors among prison inmates (which has been done). Participant observation in such circumstances would be dangerous as well as difficult.

Analyzing the Data

Once recorded, data must be processed in various ways before they can be analyzed to determine their implications. In quantitative research, **data entry** generally refers to transforming recorded observations (such as from questionnaires) into numbers that can be entered into statistical software in a computer. The next step, **data analysis,** takes the numbers and subjects them to a variety of statistical tests, with a computer doing the drudgery of extensive calculation.

Not all communication researchers use a quantitative approach with statistics to determine what they have found in a research project. If participant observation or another qualitative procedure such as a focus group has been used, the findings do not consist of a mass of numbers to be manipulated. Instead, the "data" may consist of a transcript of the recorded responses and discussion that took place during a focus group session or in-depth interviews. Many sensitive and significant studies have been completed by communication researchers using qualitative observational strategies for complex problems.

Extensive planning is always completed *before* the research is undertaken. This is always at the beginning, rather than at the end, after the data have been obtained. This means that a complete plan for data entry and analysis must be developed before observations begin.

Whatever the topic of the research, when the analysis is complete, the researcher has reduced large numbers of observations to numerical indexes, coefficients, averages, or other convenient quantitative summaries. Findings of a qualitative nature usually are set forth in more lengthy descriptive reports with verbal summaries provided at the end.

For example, a study of social network "resisters" (those who do not have or want a Facebook or other social networking account) could be conducted by using a quantitative or qualitative approach (or both). A researcher could invite a sample of resisters to complete a questionnaire online, indicating the reasons for the refusal from a prepared list of possible choices. The responses could then be analyzed using quantitative statistical procedures. Alternatively, a researcher could invite a small group of resisters for an-depth discussion of the topic during a qualitative focus group session, later summarizing the comments made by the participants.

Reaching Conclusions

The bottom line in research is the set of *conclusions and interpretations* that the data imply. However, moving from data analysis to interpretation is done with great care. Various criteria may be used to ensure that unwarranted conclusions are not reached.

Descriptive generalization.   In descriptive research, where theory testing and hypothesis acceptance or rejection are not at stake, conclusions are likely to be stated in the form of a **generalizations**. *Generalizations* are accurate statements that communicate in precise language what was found with respect to any regularities or patterns observed. Generalizations do not address any specific case or subject under analysis. They focus on what was "generally" the case in the observations—what tendencies, trends, relationships, or differences between categories of subjects seemed to thread through the findings.

Many generalizations apply only to the particular people or situations that were involved in the study. However, based on the assumption of the research perspective that there is "order in the universe," investigators may think that what was found in their particular study is an accurate description of what exists among similar people and situations. In such a case, the generalization may extend beyond the data. There is always the danger of **overgeneralizing**—extending the implications of the results too far by claiming that the study's conclusions also apply to categories of people who were not examined and who are not sufficiently similar to those studied.

Accepting or rejecting hypotheses.   In testing hypotheses to determine whether they can be accepted, statistical procedures are invaluable. Statistics provide information based on *probability* for making a clear-cut decision about whether the results of a data analysis are likely to have occurred "by chance alone," rather than as a result of a cause-effect relationship between variables. If chance seems to be as good an explanation as any other, the rule is to conclude that chance has indeed been at work. That means rejecting the hypothesis that the findings are due to causal influences. It is a good system, primarily because the standards for accepting a hypothesis are very conservative. Thus, the use of statistical reasoning and difficult standards of proof is another example of the skeptical nature of science.

Assessing the theoretical implications.   There are several stages when the goal of the study is to test a theory: First, researchers must decide what conclusions are indicated by the findings. Were the research hypotheses accepted or rejected? Then, researchers need to determine the implications of those results for the theory. Are the findings *consistent* with the theory? What *alternative* explanations might account for the same results? Finally, researchers must consider any limitations or *flaws* in the study that may have contributed to the obtained results.

The role of replication. Repeating the study—that is, *replication*—helps researchers achieve reasonable conclusions. If the same kind of communication behavior is repeatedly studied and the same general conclusions emerge time and time again, the trustworthiness of the findings is enhanced greatly. This is particularly true when independent investigators arrive at the same results.

Sometimes in research a single study has dramatic findings, and the conclusions are taken as trustworthy, in violation of the principle of necessary replication. A classic example of this is a well-known study of fear appeals in persuasion. Social psychologists Irving Janis and Seymour Feshbach exposed high school youngsters to slide-illustrated lectures about dental hygiene.[6] In one condition the lectures contained a strong fear appeal, with gruesome slides showing terrible mouth conditions caused by poor dental hygiene. A second condition presented similar subjects with a moderate fear appeal. Here, the slides showed troublesome but less severe mouth problems. Finally, a third group of subjects received a minimal fear appeal, with slides showing only very minor mouth difficulties and cavities caused by poor dental practices. The goal was to see which level of fear produced the greatest personal concern and actual change in dental practices. The results were dramatic: Those subjects who were exposed to the strongest fear messages changed the least. Those who received minimal fear messages changed the most.

This unexpected topsy-turvy conclusion took on a life of its own and was frequently quoted in textbooks even after replication studies often found opposite results.[7] In the end, the relationship was found to be more complicated.[8]

Reporting the Results

When a research project has been completed, it must be made public and reported to other interested scientists. Their assessment of the importance of the findings is in a real sense the ultimate test of its merits. A lone genius working in isolation may solve the communication problems of humankind, but if he or she never makes the results public, they do not become part of the accumulated knowledge of science.

Research reports published in journals have a standard organization. Although there are variations, most good articles contain the following: (1) a statement of the problem under investigation, (2) a summary of what previous researchers have found, (3) a description of the research methods used, (4) a presentation of the findings, and (5) a section on conclusions, implications, and interpretations.

The accumulated "literature" is of critical value not only to researchers, but to professionals in many areas as well. People in business and government also rely on research journals.

Research Designs as Strategies for Controlled Observation

A research design is a *detailed plan* that indicates very specifically how each of the preceding steps in the research process will be carried out. Among the designs frequently used by communication researchers are *experiments, surveys, field observational studies, content analyses and focus groups.*

Experiments

Experiments originated in the physical sciences many centuries ago. They remain the major research strategy of modern physics, chemistry, and biology. However, experiments were not considered a suitable strategy for observing human behavior until well into the 1900s. They were pioneered by social psychologists who brought small groups of subjects into laboratory-like settings to simulate real-life experiences so that they could be studied under highly controlled conditions. After World War II, small group experiments were adopted for research in many other fields, and they have become a standard observational strategy suitable for communication research.

The logic of experiments is straightforward: Empirical observations are made on a number of human subjects, some of whom are designated as a *control group* and others as an *experimental group*. There may be more than one experimental group. An experimental group receives some sort of "treatment" deliberately introduced by the experimenter. The control group does not receive this treatment but usually undergoes some experience of a neutral nature. The treatment applied to an experimental group is some *manipulation of an independent variable that is suspected of having an influence on a dependent variable.* Measures of the dependent variable are made both before and after the treatment. The goal is to see whether the experimental group exhibits a change in the dependent factor. If a change occurs, it will be attributed to the independent variable involved in the treatment. Because the control group did not receive the treatment, it (logically) should not show any change.

There are dozens of variations, including several independent variables, a number of different treatments, and elaborate controls. Nevertheless, the underlying logic is the same: With extraneous variables eliminated or controlled, researchers can see if the treatment caused some observable effect or consequence. The experiment is an enormously powerful research design for assessing cause-and-effect relationships. Communication researchers rely on small group experiments conducted in laboratory-like settings. They also conduct large-scale experiments "in the field" (natural settings), and **quasi-experiments,** in which the treatment occurs naturally.[9]

Small group simulations. Studies of small groups in laboratory settings can be used for a variety of research purposes. The laboratories are rooms where small numbers of subjects can be carefully observed as they engage in particular forms of communication behavior. These labs are often equipped with elaborate technical apparatus that present various independent variables to subjects and measures dependent variables. Often, the labs are equipped with one-way viewing screens so that direct observation is possible without the subjects' awareness.

In such experiments, the investigator typically tries to create a miniature version of some important communication process and study it within a tight system of controls. For example, beginning in the 1960s, a substantial number of experiments has been conducted on the process of decision making in juries.[10] Because it is neither ethical nor legal to observe juries actually deliberating real cases, the laboratory experiment provides a way to study this important practical problem.

Jury deliberations are recreated *in simulation* in the laboratory by first selecting participants and instructing them that they are to act "as though" they were a jury. The mock jury is usually shown a summary of a legal case via videotape, film, or some other medium and asked to render a verdict after suitable discussion. By selecting subjects with specific characteristics, or by presenting different versions of a trial, a considerable amount of control can be exercised over the situation. A host of independent and dependent variables that can influence jury deliberations has been studied with this experimental strategy.[11]

One limitation of such experimental simulations is that, even though they do provide for a great amount of control over the variables under study, they are by no means *natural* settings for studying communication behavior. Many impose **demand characteristics**—activities the subjects are required to perform, or other conditions they experience, that are not the same as they would be in normal circumstances. Such characteristics can potentially produce influences other than those brought about by the independent variables. This is a troublesome issue because researchers may not suspect their influence. Moreover, subjects may suspect that they are serving as guinea pigs and misbehave deliberately. In many cases, they are convinced that some form of behavior is *expected* of them. This can lead them to either comply with what they think the researcher wants or to deliberately resist. Even if subjects are prevented from guessing the true nature of the research goals, biases may be introduced. There can be no assurance that the communication behavior being observed is identical to what would be found by an invisible observer in a completely natural setting. Thus, simulation experiments have many limitations.

Large-scale experiments in natural settings. Another type of experimental design—and one that has fewer problems concerning simulation versus real life—is the large-scale **field experiment.** In this research design, the subjects to be treated and observed are people living in a community, working in a factory, going to school, or carrying on their normal activities in some natural setting. The control group is a similar community, factory, school, or the like that does not get the treatment. Although this tends to avoid the issue of simulation, problems of measurement and control can be difficult.

An interesting example of a large-scale field experiment was conducted by mass communication researchers Sandra Ball-Rokeach, Milton Rokeach, and Joel Grube.[12] In overview, two communities in Washington State (Tri-Cities and Yakima) were designated as Experimental City and Control City, respectively. The investigators used a survey approach to measure sample residents' attitudes from each community before the experimental treatment. Then, the treatment was presented to the Experimental City, but not to the Control City. The treatment consisted of a special 30-minute television show that included persuasive messages aimed at changing viewers' attitudes and persuading them to donate money. Afterward, the same residents from both cities completed the survey again. The differences between the two groups regarding attitude change, and the amount of money donated, showed the influence of the treatment.

Quasi-experiments. This research design is difficult to use because it depends on applying the logic of the experiment without actual intervention by the researcher. To illustrate, suppose that you want to do research on how people communicate after a large-scale natural disaster, such as a hurricane, strikes. Your goal is to find out what communication networks survivors rely on to get medical attention, find loved ones, seek shelter, obtain food, and understand what happened.

Obviously, there is no way you can (or would want to) intervene and cause a hurricane, an earthquake, or a volcanic eruption. But such natural events do occur. If you are in an area where such a disaster does strike, you could organize a research effort to interview survivors and record their accounts of how they communicated; the role and impact of the media before, during, and after the event; the response of government agencies; and so on. Fairly elaborate data could be gathered in this way, using questionnaires, possibly supplemented with in-depth interviews for more qualitative assessments of what happened. In fact, after Hurricane Katrina devastated New Orleans and the Gulf Coast in 2005, a number of studies were conducted in order to learn important lessons from that disaster. For example, why did so many individuals fail to evacuate even though they were ordered to do so? How could more lives have been saved? What happened when normal channels of communication failed? What can be learned from the performance of the media in times of disaster such as this?[13]

At this point, however, you would merely have interesting *descriptions* of what people did after the disaster. You would not have any way of comparing your findings with what they did before, to really assess the differences. To turn your descriptive study into a quasi-experiment, you would have to take additional steps. First, you would have to identify a community or an area that is *very like the one in which the disaster occurred,* but one in which no such event took place. This can serve as a control group. You can interview people in that area who are like the survivors (in a sampling sense) whom you questioned. It is reasonable to assume that they will behave the way those in the disaster community behaved *before* the tragedy struck. By looking at your project in this way, you have "before" and "after" data to compare. Thus, the logic of the experiment can sometimes be applied after the event through the use of a quasi-experimental design.[14]

Surveys

This research strategy developed out of the idea of a *census*—a procedure for counting and assessing attributes of an entire **population**—and out of *statistical theory,* especially the concept of **sampling**.[15] Essentially, surveys provide ways of selecting a *limited and manageable number* of people from populations in such a way that they have the same distribution of personal and social characteristics as the entire population itself. Then, researchers can contact and question that limited number.

Sample surveys are used frequently in communication research, including public opinion polling, election trends, response to persuasive techniques, consumer attitude and behavior assessments, and a variety of other topics. For example, a recent study investigated whether adults in a Midwestern community believed that certain kinds of television programming, such as news magazines, situation comedies, science fiction, or law enforcement shows, had influenced their views about the federal government. The researchers cited the fact that, in earlier decades, most people felt that the "government" could do just about anything, from putting an American on the moon to solving major social problems such as poverty. In contrast, many people today feel that there is little that the government can do, or can do well. In recent years, media depictions of the federal government have become increasingly negative, and the researchers

wondered whether such depictions were at least partly responsible for negative perceptions of, and a lack of confidence in, the federal government. The results of their survey indicated modest support for their hypothesis.[16]

Thus, surveys are one of the central strategies used by researchers for investigating communication behavior when the purpose includes uncovering relationships between independent and dependent variables in relatively large populations that cannot be observed otherwise.

As in any kind of investigation, the initial steps in conducting surveys are to ensure that the purposes of the surveys are entirely clear, that the independent and dependent variables have been fully identified, and that decisions have been made concerning procedures for analyzing the results and reaching conclusions. Once these have been achieved, additional steps must be taken, including (1) using a procedure for picking the specific people to be studied, (2) contacting those selected and getting their cooperation, and (3) extracting the relevant information from them and recording it as data.

Selecting representative samples. *Sampling* is a procedure for picking from a population (usually a very large number of people with clearly defined characteristics) an adequate and manageable smaller number who, on average, are like those in the larger population. This smaller number can then be contacted and observed. A *population* (for research purposes) is *all the people about whom generalizations are to be made from the results of the survey.* Obviously, it is not possible to study every member of a large population, given the resources of most researchers. For example, the residents of a small city of 25,000 people would pose a formidable task if each one had to be contacted personally. Even contacting a few thousand people who work for a large corporation could take considerable time. Fortunately, researchers discovered that careful study of a small part of such a population can yield results nearly identical to those obtained from observing all members. For example, public opinion pollsters and market researchers (all of whom use the survey design) know that a meticulous study of 1,200 to 1,500 people selected with great care from the entire U.S. population can reveal the basic patterns of behavior and belief that characterize the entire nation. Doubling or tripling the number of people studied might make the results slightly more stable, but it is not always worth the expense or trouble because it certainly would not double or triple their accuracy.

The key to obtaining accurate results from the study of a relatively small number of subjects, rather than the entire population, is to select them so that they "represent" the population as a whole. A **representative sample** is one that has been chosen in such a way that the people included are like those in the entire population in all important aspects relevant to the research. Usually this means that on average they are generally of similar age, gender, income level, years of education, religious affiliation, political preference, and so on.

Choosing a representative sample is not easy because researchers usually do not know the exact nature of the personal and social characteristics of the population. Even if these characteristics are known, it would be difficult to screen people one-by-one to pick a small number who accurately represent the population as a whole. Fortunately, a representative sample can be obtained in a much more efficient way—by using a **random sampling procedure** to select people to study, even if the characteristics of the population are not fully known. To do this, researchers apply the same laws of probability that make games of chance—like poker, roulette, and dice—so much fun.

There are many different **random** procedures for selecting samples that are likely to be representative. All are supposed to ensure that *only chance factors* dictate the specific individuals who are selected. A completely random sample is one in which every person in the population has *an identical chance of being selected*. This can be accomplished in several ways. The simplest is the classic (but not practical) idea of using slips of paper and a big rotating drum.

Suppose, for example, that small slips of paper could be placed in the drum—one for each member of the population, with that person's name written on it. When all the slips and all the names have been placed inside, the drum is closed and turned over and over until all the slips are thoroughly mixed. Finally, the sample is drawn out (one slip at a time) until the number wanted for the sample has been obtained. Although the slip and drum procedure illustrates the idea, it is not practical because the mechanics are very cumbersome. Although it was used historically, today, statistical software programs and random number generators that are available online can accomplish the task with great efficiency.[17]

A purely random and totally representative sample is more of an *ideal* than a reality. It is a sort of "model" that one works toward—such as the concept of a perfect score on the SAT, a flawless performance by an athlete, or a straight-A record through four years of college. Such events are rare in real life. The same can be said about the samples used in actual research, which approximate, but probably never attain, perfection. A number of practical alternatives have been developed, because of this problem, to approximate the results obtained from purely random sampling.

Face-to-face interviewing. Once the people who make up the sample have been identified, obviously they must be *contacted*. Although this sounds simple, the question is *how*? One way is to go to the address of each person and conduct an in-depth, face-to-face interview. This ensures that those selected are actually those studied.

The face-to-face interview as an observational strategy has its problems. For one thing, it is expensive: Interviewers have to be recruited and trained; they have to travel to where the subjects live. They have to be paid; and they might just cut a few corners if not closely supervised. There is also the problem of those subjects who are not at home. It becomes prohibitively expensive to return many times trying to catch a missing survey subject. And, when subjects know that they are being studied, they may change what they claim. In addition, interviews often probe recollections of past behavior, which may or may not be recalled accurately. The interaction between interviewer and subject may also have an influence on the answers that are obtained. For example, a subject who is asked a question about his or her annual income by an attractive member of the opposite sex may exaggerate to impress the interviewer. These problems are well understood by researchers.

On the other hand, many people like to be interviewed and have their opinions known. As a result, they are usually willing to cooperate and provide interviewers with information. When interviewed face to face, they tend not to exaggerate or conceal information excessively. Thus, this procedure is the observational strategy of choice for surveys—if resources permit.

Telephone surveys. If it is impractical or too expensive to interview subjects face to face, telephones may be used. Many surveys are conducted in this manner, but the quality of the results is often in question. For one thing, a sample drawn from a telephone book cannot truly represent the entire population in an area, since many numbers are unlisted and many households have abandoned landlines altogether and rely on cell phones. Furthermore, it is not always clear who is being interviewed. If the subjects are supposed to be female heads of households, it may actually be a daughter or the next-door neighbor who answers the phone. Also, in this age of dual-income families, it is increasingly difficult to reach people at home. Finally, what about answering machines or voice mail? Many people screen their calls!

To get around the problem of unlisted landline numbers, survey researchers can use computer programs that select and dial telephone numbers randomly—reaching potential respondents even if their numbers are not listed. However, the increasing number of households that use only cell phones presents another problem. Until 2008, there was little evidence that the increasing use of cell phones had a significant impact on survey results. At that time, individuals who used only a cell phone were a small fraction of the general population. Thus, cell phone users were not routinely included in most surveys. By the end of 2008, when approximately one in five U.S. households was cell-only, national pollsters began to detect significant differences in election poll results when cell-only users were excluded, compared to polls in which they were included. As a result, pollsters now include cell-only users, as well as traditional landline users in national polls.[18]

Although telephone surveys are widely used for many legitimate research purposes, they have gotten a bad reputation in recent years. Many salespeople pitching their wares by telephone begin by claiming that they are "conducting a survey." This deception has resulted in suspicion, a loss of credibility, and frequent unwillingness by respondents to cooperate in legitimate research.

Mail surveys. A survey technique that can potentially limit costs and avoid other problems is to send subjects questionnaires by mail. This technique is cheaper per subject than face-to-face interviews, and subjects can complete the questionnaires at their own convenience. On the other hand, the people in the sample may or may not cooperate. The number of people who voluntarily return a mailed questionnaire can be hopelessly low. What if fewer than half the people in the sample send their questionnaires back, even after repeated appeals? They may be quite different from the others who did not respond, and there is no way to know this. Any loss to the sample, and especially an exceptionally low return, reduces the researcher's confidence in the final results.

On the other hand, for some purposes the mailed questionnaire can work reasonably well. A study conducted recently illustrates the point. The research problem was to discover whether bachelor's degrees earned online from a "virtual" university (one that has no campus or classrooms, and that provides instruction only via the Internet) were an acceptable criterion to gain admission to a graduate program in a traditional university. A questionnaire requesting views on this issue was mailed to a population of graduate deans, associate deans, and other administrators of graduate programs. Well over two-thirds returned the questionnaires carefully filled out. This was a return rate high enough to give confidence to the results.[19]

Internet surveys. In recent years, posting questionnaires online has become commonplace. A sample of respondents is contacted first by phone, mail, or e-mail and asked to participate in a survey research project. Those who agree are sent a questionnaire by e-mail, or given a link and a password to access the questionnaire online. Websites such as Survey Monkey (www.surveymonkey.com) and Qualtrics (www.qualtrics.com) allow researchers to create and post questionnaires on the website. Such websites have become very popular with professional researchers and even with students.

Internet surveys offer many advantages, including very low cost and convenience. Respondents can complete the questionnaire at their convenience and can submit it with a simple click of a button.

Using structured questionnaires. Most surveys—whether conducted face to face, over the phone, or by mail or the Internet—use formal and highly "structured" questionnaires. These familiar printed lists of questions with response options vary in flexibility; some are open-ended, allowing the person to give more elaborate answers. Most, however, require the subject to check boxes, answer "yes" or "no," or similarly fit themselves into the structured way in which the questions are posed.

Structured questionnaires have advantages and disadvantages. Critics maintain that highly structured questionnaires lead participants *lockstep* through a series of rigidly posed questions, reducing their answers to categories and boxes to be checked. As a result, the participants' subtle meanings, feelings, and perceptions are either lost or distorted. Defenders of such questionnaires maintain that they efficiently transform observations into data, and they make it easy to perform numerical computer analyses. Clearly, each side has a point.

Field Observational Studies

Sometimes referred to as **field research,** this design type for qualitative investigation is much less formal than the experiment or the survey. Field observational studies were pioneered by cultural anthropologists who went to live among peoples in remote parts of the world, often learning their languages and spending long periods of time learning to understand the subtleties of their cultures. Communication researchers are more likely to employ this approach to study various kinds of contemporary specialized cultures or sensitive social situations in urban societies.

The central observational strategy of the field study is *participant observation*. As indicated previously, this means that the investigator enters and becomes a member of—or at least is accepted by—some group. The first problem is to gain *rapport* with the other group members, which means gaining their trust so that they open up and talk. After this, the researcher seeks intimate familiarity with the communication patterns under study. The researcher comes to understand the communication strategies, tactics, assumptions, and meanings used by the members. If successful, the researcher can prepare detailed descriptions about how the members communicate and even think about the situations that occur.

An interesting example of the use of the field observational study design focused on instruction in the college classroom. Communication researcher Ann Darling studied ways that college students signal to professors that they fail to understand something in class. She sat in on and observed three different undergraduate classes for an entire academic quarter. She was introduced to the students as a researcher studying classroom interaction. At first, students were very aware of her presence, and this inhibited their behavior. However, within two weeks they were ignoring her. Darling then began to observe, code, and record all failures to understand—every time a student signaled "noncomprehension." By the end of the quarter, she had compiled an extensive body of data. Thus, by observing participants in a natural environment, and not imposing anything on the students, this researcher was able to describe accurately how students signal problems when they don't or can't understand the instructor.[20]

In another study, researcher Alexandra Murphy used the method of participant observation combined with interviews to study ways to improve communication between flight attendants and pilots. Her interest in this topic resulted from an airline tragedy in which 24 people were killed, including the pilot, the co-pilot, and a flight attendant. The official cause of the accident was attributed to "ice on the wings," but a National Transportation Safety Board (NTSB) investigation found that a lack of crew communication contributed to the accident. Apparently, a flight attendant did not convey information to the pilot about a build-up of snow on the wings that a passenger had brought to her attention. Thirty seconds after takeoff, the airplane crashed.

The researcher, who had been an employee of another airline, observed and interacted with flight attendants and pilots on 50 flights to a variety of destinations. She then conducted in-depth interviews with flight attendants in their homes. She wanted to understand the barriers to effective communication during in-flight emergencies, and made recommendations for facilitating communication.[21]

Content Analysis

Content analysis as a strategy for research began in World War II with Allied intelligence units routinely monitoring radio broadcasts from occupied Europe. They discovered that when the stations stopped playing music that was popular among the local population and began broadcasting songs that were popular among German soldiers, troops had moved into the area.

During the 1950s, communication researchers developed content analysis designs for systematically studying virtually any kind of message. These analyses begin with definitions of "units" relevant to the research goal. Such units might be a particular *word*, a *theme*, a *depiction of a social role*, an *act of violence*, or some other identifiable entity or episode. Once a set of categories defining such units has been developed, an analyst can count the frequency of each. These frequencies can then be subjected to various calculations and analyses. Content analysis is a useful way to obtain an objective summary of exactly what a complex message contains.

In recent years, the content of video games has received considerable attention. Researchers have used the method of content analysis to investigate the nature of the violent acts in such games, the lessons that may be learned concerning appropriate behavior, and other related topics.

Interest in the content of video games has increased, especially since the introduction of more realistic games. For example, in October 2001, RockStar Games released an entertainment product called Grand Theft Auto III. This game takes the player into a (virtual) American city. The player is depicted on the screen as a young male who is casually dressed in a leather jacket and jeans. He holds a baseball bat. The player, guiding the virtual surrogate, can walk around the city and engage in a variety of violent and illegal activities. The player can pick up prostitutes, beat them senseless and take their money. The user can commandeer a police car, and can be a bank robber, a hit man, or a car hijacker. One person, after playing the game for the first time, reported the following:

The world you roam is stunningly realistic, shadowy and gritty. When you drive beneath a streetlight, a pool of light reflects on your car. When you pass people on the sidewalk, you hear snippets of their conversation: "Damned foreigners." "Got any doughnuts?" If you jostle them, they glare at you. . . .

I walk around the streets with my bat until I spot an old lady and decide to see what happens if I hit her. She falls down. A pool of blood forms around her. A police officer arrives. In a panic, I hit him repeatedly until he appears to be dead.[22]

Reality television programs and social networking sites have also become areas of study recently, using the method of content analysis. For example, researchers Christopher Wilson, Tom Robinson, and Mark Callister examined the content of seven seasons of *Survivor*, one of the nation's longest-running reality television series. They wanted to determine the types, frequency, and context of antisocial behavior presented in the program, along with the possible effects upon long-time viewers. They documented 4,207 antisocial acts (45.7 acts per hour) during the seven seasons. This represented a higher rate of antisocial acts in a reality television program than a previous study had reported a decade earlier.[23]

Focus Groups

The **focus group** is a research strategy for gathering qualitative information. Approximately 6 to 12 people are interviewed simultaneously by a moderator, who leads the group in an in-depth and relatively unstructured discussion of a particular topic. The sessions are recorded, transcribed, and summarized.

There are many reasons for conducting focus groups. The primary use of focus groups, as mentioned, is to gather qualitative information for a more in-depth understanding of a topic or issue, such as a better understanding of the attitudes and behaviors of a group of people, and for answering questions such as "why?" rather than "how many?" In addition, focus groups allow researchers to collect preliminary information about a topic. For example, before designing a questionnaire for a survey, a researcher may want to know more about the topic under investigation and use focus groups to obtain a better understanding of the issues or problems involved. Researchers also use focus

groups because of the flexibility the format provides. Although the moderator prepares an initial list of questions to guide the discussion, he or she is free to probe other important points raised by the participants as well as clear up any confusing answers. Finally, another reason for the use of focus groups is that they can be conducted quickly and relatively inexpensively. After the participants have been selected and the moderator has been briefed, and all of the materials and recording equipment are prepared, a typical focus group session lasts about two hours.

Focus group research has several limitations and potential problems, as is the case with all research. First, the success of a focus group session depends heavily on the skills of the moderator, who must keep the discussion on track and deal with any problems that may arise. For example, one person may dominate the group and monopolize the conversation, which can have an adverse effect on the performance of the group. The moderator must control the situation and enable the participation of every member of the group. The moderator also must skillfully probe for more information when necessary. Most importantly, due to the small number of people involved and the ways in which they are selected, focus group participants may not represent the population from which they were drawn. To help with this problem, researchers usually conduct three or more focus groups on the same topic and then compare the results to determine whether any similarities or differences exist.

Focus groups are widely used in advertising and marketing research, for media and public relations research, and for business planning and decision-making purposes, as well as for academic research.

Observing by Measuring Variables

Measuring variables is the process of *observing numerically*. It results in data that can be analyzed quantitatively. Empirical research cannot be conducted without measurement. Even participant observation results in determining whether there are certain qualities, repetitions, or patterns present in particular messages or behaviors. At the simplest level, then, **measurement** may be little more than deciding whether some quality is *present* or *absent* in what is being observed. This is the most basic form of measurement (which may be symbolized as a 1 or a 0) in a particular instance under observation. At the most complex level, it may involve the use of sophisticated scales or tests designed to assess numerical differences among people in their personal or social characteristics. In these senses, measurement in some form is at the heart of almost any investigation of human communication, regardless of the research goals, designs, or the specific features under study.

Levels of Measurement

There are four distinct levels of measurement commonly used in research: *nominal, ordinal, interval,* and *ratio*. Figure 15.1 shows the basic differences among these four. Each has advantages and limitations.

Nominal measures. The first and simplest form of measurement widely used in communication research *classifies people into meaningful categories*. Examples are religious preference, gender, political affiliation, rural versus urban residence, employed versus unemployed, and so on. The number in each category can be counted, and simple percentages or other indexes can be calculated. In this way, **nominal measurement** provides a useful way for researchers to look at similarities and differences between categories of people.

Ordinal measures. In **ordinal measurement,** each person often has *more* or *less* of some quality or attribute than others in the same category. This permits them to be "ranked"—from first to last or most to least—with respect to the same attribute (for example, "class standing," a ranking system based on grade point average). This

was not the case with the nominal measurement example above. There, the people being studied were assigned to a particular category because they had an observable attribute (Republicans or Democrats, senders or receivers, males or females). Ordinal data can provide valuable information on the relative position—high, low, or somewhere in between—of subjects with respect to any variable being assessed.

Interval measures. At a more sophisticated level, **interval measurement** is based on a regular scale or *continuum* that is divided into equal intervals along that continuum. Subjects can be observed to see how much of a variable they have and then be assigned a particular point on the scale corresponding to that number. A familiar example would be assessing how attractive a person is on an interval scale between 1 and 10. Suppose you assign the individual an 8; another assessor gives the same person a 6. The average score, 7, is the numerical point where that individual is placed on the attractiveness scale. In communication research, many questionnaires are used to provide interval measurement. For example, attitudes are frequently measured at the interval level.

The only limitation on the numbers yielded by interval scales is that they *lack a true zero point*. Thus, even if you assigned a zero rating to a target, it would not mean that the person had absolutely no attractive qualities. This poses a problem only when sophisticated mathematical manipulations of the data are required.

Ratio measures. Although this is the most sophisticated level of measurement, it seems the simplest because it so familiar. Examples of variables assessed by **ratio measurement** are age, income, years married, and number of hours of TV viewing daily. Ratio measures are widely used in communication research.

Judging the Quality of Measurement

Whatever the level of measurement used in a research project, problems creep in. Measurement

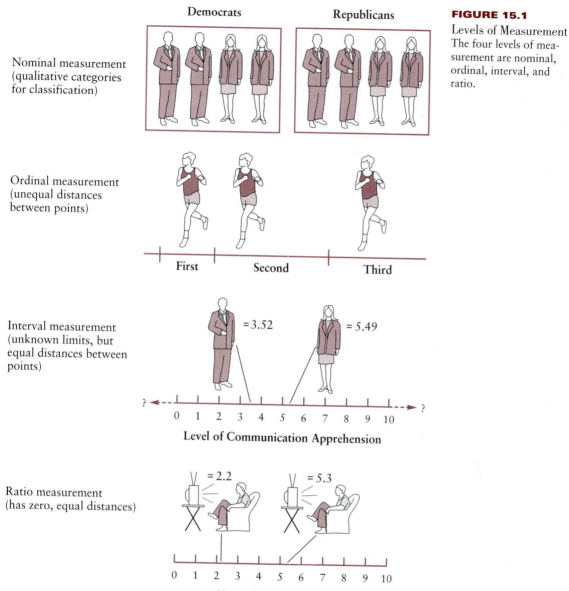

Nominal measurement (qualitative categories for classification)

Democrats   Republicans

FIGURE 15.1
Levels of Measurement
The four levels of measurement are nominal, ordinal, interval, and ratio.

Ordinal measurement (unequal distances between points)

First   Second   Third

Interval measurement (unknown limits, but equal distances between points)

= 3.52   = 5.49

? ← 0 1 2 3 4 5 6 7 8 9 10 → ?

Level of Communication Apprehension

Ratio measurement (has zero, equal distances)

= 2.2   = 5.3

0 1 2 3 4 5 6 7 8 9 10

Hours Spent Viewing TV

in communication research—or in any other field for that matter—is never perfect. There are always two basic questions to be asked concerning the *quality* of recorded observations: (1) Are they *valid*? and (2) Are they *reliable*? These may sound like two versions of the same question, but they are not. Each is an important

quality of measurement as a means of observation in research.

Validity.   A major concern about any procedure for measurement is whether it actually measures the variable for which it has been designed. For example, let's assume that you're studying

how to measure QUALITY

Measurement is at the heart of almost all research, including research on human communication. At the simplest level, measurement involves determining whether a particular quality or characteristic is present or absent in what is being observed. Yes, even an abstract concept such as quality can be measured!

meetings called by the administrators of a town, to allow citizens to comment on some proposal for the community. Your hypothesis is that high-prestige individuals are usually allowed to interrupt such a meeting or conference more than low-prestige individuals. But how can prestige or status be measured? One way would be to go ask everyone in the community under study to identify the level of prestige or status of all the individuals who might attend the meeting. If you had this information, you could calculate the average assessment or prestige ranking for each person present. Unfortunately, that approach would involve a massive undertaking, conducting hundreds of interviews.

Now suppose that you know the *assessed value of the home* of every family in the town (readily obtained from town records). You could decide to use home value (which is highly correlated with income) as a *measure of each individual's status*. So far, so good! You could justify this procedure by claiming that home value (and related income) is an important aspect of people's level of status prestige in the American society.

But wait a minute! Here is a question. Is home value based on income always a valid measure of prestige? The answer is probably not. Some people might have high incomes and expensive homes derived from socially disapproved sources—drug sales, gambling, or occupations to which people assign limited prestige. Others might have low-cost homes—for example, esteemed ministers, priests, and rabbis—but high social status. Thus, a person's home value and income would not be a true reflection of that person's prestige or status in the community. In other words, this particular measure could have *low validity*. Researchers may or may not know the **validity** of their measures. If they do not know it, this is a shortcoming that reduces the quality of the results.

Reliability. Measurement quality is also determined by **reliability**. Does the procedure used for measurement yield the same results *if used repeatedly* on the same subjects? Repeated measurements would be unusual, but if a procedure were repeated and if it gave one result today but a different result tomorrow—on the same people and using the same variables—it would not be a very useful way of recording observations. *Reliability,* then, is *the degree to which a measurement procedure yields consistent results with the same individuals.*

Importantly, a measure must be highly consistent (reliable) if it is to be valid. These two features of measurement quality—validity and reliability—are interrelated in this particular way. For instance, a bathroom scale that measures your weight consistently is reliable; but can it be reliably wrong—that is, invalid? Sure! The scale could consistently read 5 pounds low. Thus, reliability would be high but validity low.

Besides issues of measurement, the terms *reliability* and *validity* are also used to judge overall qualities of a research project and its findings. Researchers and critics alike are compelled to ask whether the project actually addresses the questions it is supposed to address. Can the results from the sample used in the study generalize to the greater population?

For example, are laboratory simulations of jury deliberations in small group experiments really valid representations of actual jury deliberations? If so, the experiment is valid. If it is consistently found that male jurors almost always find the attractive, young female defendant innocent and the old, unattractive male guilty, does this generalization characterize real juries? If so, the conclusion is valid.

Ethical Issues in Communication Research

Suppose that an enthusiastic researcher wants to understand how real juries work in reaching their decisions. One way to proceed would be to place hidden video cameras in jury rooms and secretly tape the deliberations. Doing this without telling the jurors or the judges would be deceptive, but our society needs to know whether there is anything wrong with the legal system. Would not this need justify the deception?

To take another example, assume that in a highly controlled, sophisticated experiment, the research findings did not support the investigators' theory. This would be a major disappointment—after all, a lot of time, effort, and money went into the project. Inconclusive results provide little glory. It would be easy to throw out some of the cases that do not fit the theory. Perhaps some data could even be invented so that the research findings look impressive. No one would ever know, and where's the harm? In a society where advertisers, politicians, and businesses all make exaggerated and deceptive claims, would such minor misrepresentation be so bad?

Both of these procedures would violate critical ethical norms governing scientific research and would not be permissible under any circumstances. Communication research is done within the same set of ethical norms that apply to all the social sciences.[24]

These norms are particularly important because human beings are the subjects of investigation. One category of scientific concern is for the *truth in research findings*. The second focuses on the *protection of human subjects from harm*—including deception, loss of privacy, and violation of confidentiality.

Truth in Findings

As this chapter has indicated, conducting research is a lot of work, and it takes a great deal of time. It can be very expensive, and often it yields results that are inconsistent with the researcher's personal theories. Because researchers' reputations are built in large part on publishing reports on significant research problems, some may feel a temptation to falsify findings to reap the rewards of scientific fame. However, there is an ironclad rule that research findings must be reported honestly, even though faked results might not be detected in the rigid screening described earlier. For example, in 2011, a respected medical journal reported that a study published earlier in the journal was fraudulent. The earlier study, which claimed that the measles, mumps, and rubella vaccine was linked to autism, raised public fears about vaccines and resulted in many parents declining to have their children vaccinated.[25]

Although hoaxes are extremely rare in any area of research, when they do occur they are cruel for several reasons. For one thing, they mislead other investigators who study the same issues. Naturally, they usually come up with different findings, which confuses everyone and wastes a lot of time and money. In addition, legitimate evidence consistent with the falsified findings will always be clouded by suspicion. Even more important, the central claim of science—that its data, conclusions, and explanations are *the most trustworthy* that can be obtained from any source—brings respect and financial support from the public. It is little wonder that scientists are outraged by the rare violations of ethical rules that do occur. They destroy the integrity of the research process and violate the rule of *experto credite*.

BOX 15.3   *Ethical Concerns*

INFORMED CONSENT AND DECEPTION IN RESEARCH

Is it ever ethical to deceive research subjects? One ethical position is that *informed consent* should always be obtained before any human being becomes a research subject: Obtain the subject's permission to agree to participate. In some cases, however, if the subjects know the purpose of the research before they participate, it may be pointless to conduct the study. Perhaps the most dramatic case addressing this issue was psychologist Stanley Milgram's famous study of obedience to authority.

In Milgram's experiment, subjects were ordered to administer electric shocks to individuals in another room. The design involved deception: No shocks were actually received by anyone. However, the subjects who complied thought that they were really administering powerful jolts to people. After administering a number of "shocks," subjects heard their "confederates" in the next room scream and cry out for relief. Even though many of the subjects were deeply disturbed at what they were told to do, they obeyed nevertheless, and continued to administer more shocks. Some bit their lips, dug their fingernails into their flesh, stuttered, trembled, or groaned. In some cases, anxiety continued after the experiment.

Is it ethical to cause such distress? As a result of the debate over this study, scientists now conclude that such deception was unethical. Recognizing that the reality factor would have been lost if the subjects had been fully informed about the nature of this particular experiment, it's better to abandon the experiment rather than cause people undue harm and anxiety.

Source: Milgram, S. (1974). *Obedience to authority: An experimental view.* New York: Harper & Row.

Protection of Subjects

Communication research is usually benign in a physical sense: It does not involve dangerous drugs, surgery, or confinement, as may be the case when human beings or animals are used in medical experiments. Nevertheless, there are several ways in which the research process may harm human subjects. Research projects may be based on deceptions that result in unusual stress and anxiety. Investigators may intrude on privacy to an unacceptable extent. Confidentiality may be violated concerning behavior that is socially disapproved, with a resulting loss of reputation. Communication researchers are concerned with all of these issues.

Risks versus benefits.   A very real problem is the issue of potential risk to people versus probable benefits to society from a particular research project. Where should the line be drawn? Clearly, research that results in death, injury, or illness is not tolerable under any circumstances, even if important information can be gained from it. The Nazis and the Japanese in World War II conducted medical experiments on human beings, and these experiments were widely condemned. This end of the scale is clear; but what about research that may merely annoy people or cause them embarrassment? If useful findings can be obtained, are such harms acceptable? Every specific project must be carefully evaluated before it is conducted by responsible and independent judges who determine whether the cost–benefit ratio is acceptable. In fact, colleges and universities and major private or government agencies that fund research conduct formal analyses for the protection of human subjects before allowing research to be conducted.

Privacy, confidentiality, and deception.   There are occasions when the disclosure of information gained in a research project may have serious consequences for the people involved. A classic case was sociologist Laud Humphreys's study of male homosexual activity.[26]

The initial observations were made in a public restroom located in a park. The researcher observed 100 men participating in homosexual activities, even serving as a lookout on occasion. As the subjects left, the researcher noted the license numbers of their cars. Later, after obtaining their addresses, he appeared at their homes (with a different appearance) posing as an interviewer for a survey. He obtained additional information about their family lives, work, and so forth.

Information about the research was later reported in a local newspaper. Many of the subjects were understandably concerned. At that time, unwanted exposure of their homosexual activities could have had a devastating effect on their families and jobs. Humphreys had burned the records of their names and addresses, so no disclosure occurred. Yet, a raging controversy arose over the violation of privacy of these subjects, plus the fear and anxiety that the research caused. This case helped clarify the ethical rules, making a similar situation unlikely today.

Generally, then, any research using human beings as subjects can raise complex ethical questions. In many cases, there are no clear answers to questions about what should or should not be done. The rules concerning faking evidence and causing substantial harm to people are clear enough. However, it is not always easy to calculate an acceptable cost–benefit ratio, and the development of adequate ethical rules remains an unfinished task. (See Box 15.3.)

Chapter Review

- The purpose of this chapter is to provide in summary a framework that will enable students to understand how research is conducted and to provide ways in which they can assess the methods and conclusions of particular research reports that they read.

- Research can be defined as a set of systematic procedures for gathering reliable information under controlled conditions of observation. The process is designed and conducted in such a way that objective conclusions can be reached with a minimum of error.

- The perspective used in communication research rests on a set of broad postulates or assumptions. It is assumed that human communication exists in an orderly universe and that there are cause-effect relationships between independent and dependent conditions. It is assumed that

the system for scrutinizing research reports supports the belief in *experto credite*.

- There are six general steps in the research process: (1) specify the goals of the research and the variables to be studied; (2) review prior relevant research on the topic; (3) make the necessary observations; (4) analyze the data; (5) reach appropriate conclusions; and (6) publish the results.

- A number of formal research designs are available to communication researchers, including laboratory experiments, large-scale field experiments and quasi-experiments, surveys, field observations, content analyses, and focus groups. Whatever the design used, observations must be measured and recorded in one of four ways: nominal, ordinal, interval, or ratio levels of measurement.

- The quality of any given measure is judged by its validity and reliability. A measure is valid when it accurately assesses the variable under study. It is reliable when the same results are obtained repeatedly with the same subject.

- Ethical considerations are critical in communication research. Scientific integrity demands that findings be reported truthfully. Other ethical considerations concern the protection of human subjects.

Key Terms

research	data entry	field research
postulate	data analysis	content analysis
descriptive research	generalization	focus groups
theory	overgeneralizing	measurement
replication	experiment	nominal measurement
proprietary research	quasi-experiment	ordinal measurement
dependent variable	demand characteristics	interval measurement
independent variable	field experiment	ratio measurement
hypothesis	population	validity
empirical observation	sampling	reliability
data	representative sample	
participant observation	random sampling procedure	

Notes

1. For a discussion of the social science research tradition as practiced in the communication discipline, see: Keyton, J. (2001). *Communication research: Asking questions, finding answers* (pp. 9–17). Mountain View, CA.: Mayfield.

2. These postulates are set forth in this section to explain clearly the logical foundation of science. Those who use humanistic, rhetorical, critical, or other approaches to the analysis of human communication also have the obligation to set forth their postulates, whether they are based on ideological convictions, shared frameworks of moral values, etc.

3. Most of the hundreds of journals in which communication research reports appear are published regularly by professional organizations, universities, government agencies, foundations, or other private groups. They are intended for professionals who are familiar with the technical terms and research methods of the field. Many of the technical journals in which the results of communication research are published have been cited in previous chapters of this book.

4. The accumulation and moving forward feature of any science is critical. The opposite is stagnation and obsolescence. Few people would be satisfied to stop research in their field and be content with a body of knowledge that would grow increasingly obsolete. This is as true in communication research as it is in physics or medicine.

5. Whyte, W. F. (1979). On making the most of participant observation. *The American Sociologist, 14,* 1, 56–66. A classic work is: McCall, G., & Simmons, J. (1969). *Issues in participant observation.* Reading, MA: Addison-Wesley.

6. Janis, I., & Feshbach, S. (1953). Effects of fear-arousing communication. *Journal of Abnormal and Social Psychology, 58,* 78–92.

7. For example, an analysis of over 40 texts on persuasion and public speaking revealed that

of the 25 texts mentioning fear appeals, only six made accurate claims. An additional four texts were unclear, whereas 15 continued to report the claims of the original Janis and Feshbach study. See: Allen, M., & Preiss, R. W. (1990). Using meta-analysis to evaluate curriculum: An examination of selected college textbooks. *Communication Education, 39*, 103–116.

8. See, for example: Perloff, R. M. (2003). *The dynamics of persuasion: Communication and attitudes in the 21st century.* Mahwah, NJ: Erlbaum; Higbee, K. L. (1969). Fifteen years of fear arousal: Research on threat appeals: 1953–1968. *Psychological Bulletin, 72,* 426–444. See also: Leventhal, H. (1970). Findings and theory in the study of fear communications. In Berkowitz, L. (Ed.), *Advances in experimental social psychology* (vol. 5, pp. 119–186). New York: Academic.

9. See: Saslow, C. (1982). Designing the experiment. In Saslow, C. A. (Ed.), *Basic research methods* (pp. 71–93). Reading, MA: Addison-Wesley.

10. Typical of such simulated jury studies is: Villemur, N. K., & Hyde, J. S. (1983). Effects of sex of defense attorney, sex of juror, and age and attractiveness of victim on mock juror decision-making in a rape case. *Sex Roles, 9,* 879–889.

11. For a review of an entire program of simulated jury studies, see: Miller, G. R., & Fontes, N. E. (1979). *Videotape on trial: A view from the jury box.* Beverly Hills, CA: Sage.

12. Ball-Rokeach, S., Rokeach, M., & Grube, J. (1984). *The great American values test.* New York: Free Press.

13. For example, see: Miller, A. & Goidel, R. (2009). News organizations and information gathering during a natural disaster: Lessons learned from Hurricane Katrina. *Journal of Contingencies and Crisis Management, 17,* 266–273.

14. Actually, the responses of a community to such an event were studied after Mount Saint Helens erupted in 1980. See: Pennebaker, J., & Newton, D. (1983). Observation of a unique event: The psychological impact of the Mt. St. Helens volcano. In H. Reis (Ed.), *Directions for methodology of social and behavioral science* (no. 15). San Francisco: Jossey-Bass.

15. See: Tankard, J. (1984). *The statistical pioneers.* Cambridge, MA: Schenkman.

16. Pfau, M., Moy, P., & Szabo, E. A. (2001). Influence of prime-time television programming on perceptions of the federal government. *Mass Communication & Society, 4,* 437–453.

17. For discussions of sampling, see: Wimmer, R. D., & Dominick, J. R. (2011). *Mass media research: An introduction.* Boston: Wadsworth; Kish, L. (1965). *Survey sampling.* New York: Wiley; Cochran, W. G. (1963). *Sampling techniques* (2nd ed.). New York: Wiley.

18. Mokrzycki, M., Keeter, S., & Kennedy, C. (2009). Cell-phone-only voters in the 2008 exit poll and implications for future noncoverage bias. *Public Opinion Quarterly, 73,* 845–865.

19. DeFleur, M. H., & Adams, J. (2004). Acceptability of Online degrees as criteria for admission to graduate programs. *Journal of Computing in Higher Education, 16,* 150–163.

20. Darling, A. (1989). Signaling non-comprehension in the classroom: Toward a descriptive typology. *Communication Education, 3,* 34–40.

21. Murphy, A. G. (2001). The flight attendant dilemma: An analysis of communication and sensemaking during in-flight emergencies. *Journal of Applied Communication Research, 29,* 30–53.

22. Weiss, J. (January 13, 2002). Connecting with your inner thug: Grand Theft Auto III gives you an on-screen crime spree—and too much fun. *The Boston Globe,* p. E1.

23. Wilson, C., Robinson, T., & Callister, M. (2012). Surviving *Survivor*: A content analysis of antisocial behavior and its context in a popular reality television show. *Mass Communication & Society, 15,* 261–283. doi: 10.1080/15205436. 2011 .567346

24. For a discussion and overview of such issues, see: Beauchamp, T. (1982). *Ethical issues in social science research.* Baltimore: Johns Hopkins University Press.

25. The autism vaccine hoax. (2011, January 8). *The Wall Street Journal.* Retrieved from http://www.wsj.com

26. Humphreys, L. (1975). *Tearoom trade: Impersonal sex in public places.* Chicago: Aldine.

Glossary

accommodating style A strategy for handling conflict in which people give in to their opponents. Accommodators are the opposite of competitors. They tend to be passive, and often allow their opponents to reach their objectives.

accumulation process A pattern in which mass communications have selective and minimal influences on a population, but over time they add up, and large numbers of people are changed when the messages are consistent and persistent.

accuracy In communication, the degree to which all elements of meaning incorporated into the message formulated by the sender are reconstructed in the interpretation of the meaning of the message constructed by the receiver.

adaptation Various ways in which message senders and receivers independently modify how they think and behave toward each other during the transmitting and receiving processes.

adoption process A pattern by which innovations spread through a population of potential adopters. They first become aware of the innovation's existence, which arouses their interest, causing them to seek further information. This leads to evaluation of possible uses and costs versus benefits. If feasible, it may then be tried briefly. Finally, adoption takes place, and the innovation is routinely used.

affinity-seeking The use of various communication strategies to get people to like you.

anomie (personal) A feeling of anxiety or distress arising from confusion concerning the social expectations of others.

arbitrary selection The random means by which sounds and letters used to form words within a given language are selected. Once selected and established in use, however, the relationship between words and their referents becomes fixed.

artifacts Physical objects—such as jewelry, handbags, pens, and briefcases, or even homes, cars, and offices—that provide meanings to others about our personal and social attributes.

assignment-based cohesion A type of cohesion based on the fact that members of a group have been asked or ordered to serve by their boss, are voted into membership by a valued constituency, or must serve for some other valid obligation.

assimilation A feature of the embedding process by which a message is reshaped into new interpretations (distortions) by the psychological characteristics and culturally learned habits of the receiver.

attitude A relatively enduring organization of affective beliefs about some broad object (such as a policy, social category of people, or situation) that increases the probability that an individual will respond consistently to that object.

attribution process The assignment to another individual of various personal qualities, conditions, dispositions, or external social pressures that we believe are the causes of or influences on that person's behavior. (see *implicit personality theory*)

audioconferencing Connecting people by long-distance telephone lines (sometimes with the parties in special rooms where they can make use of high-quality speakers) so that they can conduct a meeting.

authority The basis of legitimacy for the exercise of power.

avoidance style A strategy for handling conflicts in which an individual chooses not to be part of the confrontation or chooses to stay away from situations in which disagreements are likely to occur.

behavior-alteration techniques Persuasive strategies designed to arouse feelings of reward and punishment. These techniques are based on principles of behavior modification in learning.

belief A kind of statement of truth that an individual accepts about some object (thing, situation, or event). Some are factual (not involving positive or negative judgments or implying emotional orientation); others are affective (involving a positive or negative judgment).

body language The idea that body actions, gestures, and other nonverbal behavior reveal more of our true thoughts and feelings than does our verbal behavior.

bureaucracy A deliberately designed plan of the goals, norms, roles, ranks, and controls in an organization.

central route A pathway in the Elaboration Likelihood Model of Persuasion (ELM) in which an individual gives careful attention to persuasive arguments in a message, which may result in enduring attitude change.

charismatic authority An individual's unique personal attractiveness that makes people willing to accept the individual's leadership.

chauvinism A boastful, exaggerated form of ethnocentrism leading some groups to maintain that they are superior.

chronemics The study of the way in which people use time to transmit nonverbal messages.

Clever Hans effect The mistaken belief that an animal can use language as humans do because of the animal's responses or behavior. The animal may be responding to subtle cues, or its behaviors may be simply random occurrences.

coercion Compelling or restraining behavior that includes threatening people with unacceptable consequences.

cognitive reorganization A modification of an individual's feelings, beliefs, attitudes, or motivations (as a result of persuasion in the present context).

cognitive restructuring A form of treatment for fears (which can be used to reduce communication apprehension) involving changing a subject's personal interpretations of an anxiety-producing situation.

cohesion (group) The set of factors in every kind of group—large or small, intimate or formal—that motivates the participants to maintain their membership and to perform the activities required of them.

collaborative style A strategy for handling conflict in which people work willingly in cooperation with an opponent. The collaborative style is characteristic of those who have a sincere concern for their opponents as well as for their own goals.

collectivism A cultural orientation in which the group and its interests are valued over individual interests.

colonial press Generally, those newspapers that were published during the colonial period. They were small, usually subject to "prior restraint" laws, relatively expensive, and circulated to a small audience of elite subscribers.

communication (human) A process during which source(s) initiate messages using verbal and nonverbal symbols and contextual cues to express meaning by transmitting information so that similar understandings are constructed by the intended receiver(s).

communication apprehension Fear experienced in anticipation of or during communication encounters.

communication management strategy A communication strategy that uses interpersonal communication to maintain valued interpersonal ties in a close relationship.

communicator A person who either sends or receives a message during the communication process.

comparative perspective A strategy for studying behavior that assesses and contrasts modes of conduct (including communication) among various animals and human beings.

comparative psychologist A person who studies animals (including humans) as a strategy for recognizing laws of behavior common to many species.

competitive style A strategy for handling conflict in which people narrowly view all conflicts as win-lose events. Winning is their only goal and being concerned for their opponent is unnecessary.

compliance Yielding publicly or observably to an influence attempt without actually accepting the change privately.

compounding pattern A pattern of distortion whereby an original message passed word of mouth through a grapevine grows larger and more complex, gaining additional details and interpretations that were never part of the original message.

compromising style A strategy for handling conflict in which participants reach agreement by making mutual concessions.

computer network A number of computers linked by wires or a radio system so that their users can transmit data and other files or messages from one to another. Some are local and serve a given organization; others are large scale and reach many sites in a country.

conflict A dispute concerning rewards or resources that are in limited supply, when the participants' objective is to either neutralize or eliminate the opponents' prospects of winning what is at stake.

conflict style The manner that an individual is likely to exhibit when anticipating or engaging in a confrontation.

connotative meanings Personal or unshared meanings that an individual uniquely associates with a referent because of past experience.

constructive resistance A resistance to persuasion that contributes positively to a situation, especially when the behavior being solicited is against ethical norms.

content analysis A research plan in which recorded messages are the subject of the investigation. Various units of analysis are defined, whose occurrences can be identified and counted in the message.

context A physical setting or a sociocultural situation in which communication takes place. Examples are a church or an office (physical setting) and a wedding or a sales meeting (sociocultural situation). As a cultural factor, the relative amount of information implied by the setting or conditions of a communication exchange. In high-context communication, the message is inherent in the setting and is understood by the participants; in low-context communication, the information is communicated explicitly through the spoken word.

controls (communication) Messages that provide sanctions—rewards for compliance and punishments for deviation from the communication rules of the group.

convention A rule adopted within a particular cultural group (or language community) that specifies what patterns of meaning are to be labeled with what particular word or nonverbal sign.

corroborative effect An influence of mass communications in which presentation of the same facts and interpretations of news stories by different media adds credibility to what is being presented.

cost–benefit ratio The ratio of the efforts that have to be made in establishing or maintaining a relationship to the rewards that the relationship brings. (see *utilitarianism*)

credibility With regard to a source, the degree to which a receiver regards a source as trustworthy and a message as truthful; a perceived characteristic of a source based on a combination of beliefs about that source's competence, trustworthiness, extroversion, composure, and sociability. Also, the degree to which a message is judged to be valuable or worthless, critical or trivial, true or false, depending on the perceived sincerity and honesty of the source as evaluated by the audience.

criteria (in listening) The standards by which people decide whether a source is credible and whether a message is believable and important.

cultural exclusion An attitude or behavior based on people's belief that their way of thinking and acting is the only right way and those who think or act differently are wrong.

cultural inclusion The commitment to acknowledge, respect, and, when possible, adapt to others who may think, feel, and behave differently.

cultural pluralism A condition in a society in which members of diverse groups maintain their cocultural affiliations and identities within the larger framework of a common, shared culture.

cultural relativity A perspective for judging other people's cultures—recognizing and accepting the idea that people do things differently and that what works for them is all right; no absolute standard for how people should think or act.

culture An umbrella term that includes both the general or mainstream culture and specialized, unique co-cultures. A culture is not a group of people; it is their way of life, their language, the things they use, their traditional beliefs, and their distinctive norms and customs of behavior.

cushioning function The benefit derived from having friends or family members who provide emotional support when events make life difficult.

data Information known as fact. In science, this requires that the information be communicated. Therefore, observations that are to become scientific data must be recorded as symbols for other scientists to see.

data analysis The process of subjecting numerical data to a variety of statistical tests. Other, more qualitative analyses are sometimes performed.

data entry The process of assigning numbers to observations and feeding those numbers into a computer for subsequent data analysis.

decision-making group A group in which the goal is to arrive at orderly judgments, usually through a formal process of evaluation and discussion.

decoding The assignment of meaning to symbols perceived by a receiver in the communication process.

demand characteristics The activities of an experiment that subjects must perform, or conditions they experience, that may produce influences other than those brought about by the independent variables. These can be problematic if the researcher is unaware of their influence.

denotative meanings The meanings that by established convention are to be aroused and experienced by a particular symbol.

dependency With regard to mass communication, a condition in contemporary society in which people rely on mass media content—such as news, advertisements, and entertainment—for decisions they make in daily life.

dependency-based cohesion A type of cohesion characteristic of organizations with a complex division of labor. Members are bound to the organization and to one another because all members perform specialized tasks that are linked to and dependent on the tasks performed by others.

dependent variable A variable that is influenced by the presence of particular independent variables. In a cause-and-effect relationship, the dependent variable is the effect.

descriptive research Research aimed at revealing and describing some order—the stages, configurations, or processes of human communication.

destructive resistance Negative, subversive, or rebellious behavior in response to legitimate attempts at persuasion.

disassociation A strategy of transmitting messages to another that aims at reducing the use of the pronoun *we* and reverting to the individualistic *you* and *I*.

disengagement The communication strategies people use when they are attempting to withdraw from a close association with another.

distancing A strategy of transmitting verbal and non-verbal messages to another with the goal of increasing both physical and psychological distance between the two.

distortion An outcome of communication in which the source's intended meanings become compounded with, or displaced by, unintended interpretations as the receiver reconstructs the meanings of the message.

dyad Two persons in a relatively enduring social relationship.

elaboration The perceptual and cognitive processes by which a person receives and carefully considers the meaning of a persuasive message, and then appeals and arguments for change that it contains.

Elaboration Likelihood Model of Persuasion (ELM) A model representing the complex factors and psychological processes that are involved in achieving attitude change through the use of persuasive messages. The model depicts two main routes through which persuasion and attitude change may be achieved: the central route, which may result in enduring attitude change, and the peripheral route, in which any attitude change is likely to be temporary and less predictive of behavior.

e-mail A system for sending and receiving typed messages on a computer network. It consists of software that permits word processing and hardware that allows a message that is displayed on the sender's screen to be sent to the receiver's computer, where it can be displayed on screen and stored in both computers' memories.

embedding pattern A particular set of distortions—leveling, sharpening, and assimilation—that may occur in a message when it is transmitted orally from one person to the next serially.

emblems A category of nonverbal gestures that have established conventions of meaning, providing direct verbal translations.

empirical observation For the purpose of data gathering in scientific research, empirical observation is based on recording with the senses the presence or absence of certain attributes of a particular variable under study.

encoding The assignment of symbols to meanings that a source intends to transmit to a receiver.

enculturation The process of acquiring understandings of a person's general culture, including not only language skills but also shared beliefs, emotional orientations, attitudes, and values that make a person an accepted member of society.

engagement The communication process by which people move their relationship from an impersonal to a personal basis.

ethnocentrism A belief that one's own group and way of life are superior to all others.

exchange theory A formulation originally developed by George Homans to explain all forms of human social interaction. Applied to communication, it argues that people implicitly keep track of the history of benefits received from interacting with the other person, weigh that against the history of costs, and make an estimate of the worth of the relationship. If benefits outweigh costs for both individuals, the relationship is likely to continue; if not, the relationship is likely to terminate.

experiment A research design that involves systematic observations on a number of human subjects, some of whom are designated as a control group and others as an experimental group. The experimental group receives treatment deliberately introduced by the experimenter. The control group does not receive this but usually undergoes a neutral experience. Measures of the dependent variable are made before and after the treatment to see whether only the experimental group has changed. There are many variations to this design.

feedback The messages provided in an ongoing manner by a receiver in response to a message being transmitted by a source.

femininity A cultural orientation that emphasizes a traditional female gender orientation in which nurturance, cooperation, empathy, and collaboration are valued and sex roles are flexible.

field experiment A large-scale research design in which subjects to be treated and observed are people living in a community, factory, school, or other natural setting. The control group is a similar group that does not get the treatment.

field research (field observational study) A type of qualitative research in which the investigator lives, works, or regularly interacts with those being observed.

focus group A research strategy for gathering qualitative information, in which approximately 6 to 12 people are interviewed simultaneously by a moderator, who leads the group in an in-depth and relatively unstructured discussion of a particular topic.

formal communication A controlled communication among parties who are allowed or required by the group's coded rules to transmit particular messages to specific receivers using officially designated rules and restrictions.

forum A type of discussion group usually based on brief presentations by members of a small group, who are introduced by a chairperson. The presentations are followed by considerable participation by audience members, again coordinated by the chair.

freedom of the press A person's right to speak out in print or otherwise as specified in the First Amendment of the Constitution. This is an individual right, not a collective one giving newspapers special protections.

general culture The overall culture developed by a people within a society who speak a common language and share the same basic social institutions.

generalization   An accurate statement that communicates in precise language what was found with respect to the tendencies, relationships, or patterns among variables being studied.

grapevine   The complex social pathways within an organization through which informal messages are transmitted by word of mouth.

group   Two or more people who repeatedly interact, regulating their conduct within some set of rules for communication and social activity that they mutually recognize and follow.

haptics   The study of touch as a means of nonverbal communication.

human communication   [see *communication (human)*]

human relations perspective   A theory for managing organizations in which the personal and social characteristics of workers as individuals are critical factors in the work process. Managers try to motivate, encourage, and foster worker performance by taking advantage of human factors that make work more tolerable, under the assumption that this will increase output.

human resources perspective   A theory for managing organizations based on assumptions that bonds of loyalty can be created between worker and employer and that workers have insights into production processes that offer valuable clues as to how both quality and efficiency can be improved.

human use perspective   A theory of management in which workers are thought of not in humanitarian terms but simply as things that can be used, like machinery, and exploited, like raw materials.

hypothesis   A statement that poses possible relationships between variables. Ideally, hypotheses are derived from theories that predict the relationship between variables if the theory is correct.

identification   A yielding to influence that occurs because of a person's desire to emulate a particular individual or group.

implicit personality theory   An explanation of how assumptions are quickly formulated about a person one has just met. These assumptions are beliefs about qualities and motives that are projected onto an individual on the basis of limited information obtained in an initial encounter.

impression management   A transmittal of verbal and nonverbal messages that are deliberately designed to create a particular set of impressions.

independent variable   A variable that exerts influences on the dependent variable. In a cause-and-effect relationship, the independent variable is the cause.

individualism   A cultural orientation in which the individual is emphasized and autonomy, independence, and individual success are valued.

Industrial Revolution   A major change in a society or societies in which the production of goods in factories replaces agriculture as the major economic activity.

informal communication   Communication that takes place in the absence of deliberately designed barriers or constraints—communication that is spontaneous and unrestrained. In communicating informally, people feel relatively free to say what they feel and do not constantly worry that their meanings will be misunderstood or that they will arouse hostile responses.

information   Physical events that span distance—such as sound or light waves, electronic impulses, or electromagnetic radiations—into which symbols or other signs are encoded when a source speaks, writes, or uses electronic media to transmit messages to receivers.

informed consent   A requirement that research subjects know the nature of the treatments they will receive in a study and that they agree in writing to participate under those conditions.

intercultural communication   An exchange of messages between people of different co-cultures under conditions in which their co-cultural backgrounds influence the process.

internalization   A yielding to influence because it is personally rewarding or useful.

interpersonal communication   A communication that takes place between two people who come to know each other better as their relationship moves from impersonal to personal.

interval measurement   A rating that determines how much of a variable exists along a continuum and then assigns it a numerical point on a scale. Variables are placed in relationship to one another, and intervals on the scale are equal.

intimate group   People who make up either a human family or a peer group of close friends. The communication in intimate groups is extensive, self-disclosing, and uninhibited.

kinesics   The study of body movements—including gestures, posture, and facial expression—that are used to communicate nonverbally.

labeling theory   An explanation of the way people interpret an individual's characteristics and social worth after that person has been given a negative label by an official agency. For example, the term *mental patient* causes people to assign numerous negative characteristics to those so labeled, whether or not they have those attributes.

language   The shared words, nonverbal signs, and rules for their use and interpretation within a particular group or society.

language community   Members of a human group that speak a common language.

learned helplessness   A feeling of inadequacy and stress arising from an inability to communicate in a predictable way with people who are inconsistent in their responses to messages.

legacy of fear   A widespread conviction in U.S. culture that the mass media have the power to harm their audiences.

legal-rational authority   The basis of legitimate authority in organizations whereby leaders are selected for technical managerial skills that qualify them to exercise power within the limited sphere defined by official definitions.

leveling   A general shortening of a message—such as a rumor, story, or other verbal account—as it travels by word of mouth through a grapevine.

linear   Moving like a straight line, from a beginning to an end through specific stages.

linguistic relativity   The principle that people of different cultures, using different languages, may define and label features of reality in different ways.

listening   An active form of behavior in which individuals maximize their attention to, and comprehension of, what is being communicated through the use of words and actions.

magic bullet theory   An explanation of the effects of exposure to mass communications based on assumptions that media messages reach virtually every member of an audience and penetrate every mind equally, influencing everyone's ideas and conduct in powerful ways.

mainstream culture   A culture that consists of the most common language, the basic social institutions, the material artifacts and technologies in use, and the basic values to which most participants subscribe.

majority culture   A term originally intended to refer to the actual numbers of those groups that were most numerous in a population. Later it came to have additional connotative meanings including those groups that are most dominant, superior, or powerful in a population.

masculinity   A cultural orientation that emphasizes a traditional male gender orientation, in which achievement, success, ambition, assertiveness, and competitiveness are valued and sex roles are clearly differentiated.

mass communication   A process by which professional communicators use media to disseminate messages widely and rapidly, arousing meanings in large and diverse audiences to influence them in various ways.

mass media   The media that disseminate messages from professional communicators to large and diverse audiences. The major point-to-multipoint media are books, newspapers, magazines, radio, and television in its various forms. The Internet is a mixed case, incorporating some aspects of a mass medium.

meaning   The subjective responses that individuals learn to make to the things they directly experience in reality or to the particular symbols used to label that reality.

meaning (deep)   The basic ideas implied by a message that can be understood well enough for practical purposes.

meaning (surface)   The entire set of meanings encoded in a message, whether or not essential to understanding its basic ideas.

meaning triangle   A diagram showing that meaning, symbol, and referent constitute a system, with each element linked by a convention.

measurement   A process of observing that assigns numerical values to observations so that they can be quantified.

medium   Any device that extends the distance or time over which people can communicate. Media carry or store information into which symbols are encoded by senders and decoded by receivers.

melting pot policy   An early U.S. policy geared toward eradicating cultural differences among people and promoting rapid assimilation of immigrants into mainstream U.S. culture.

memorandum   From the Latin *memoro*, meaning "to call to mind." A stylized written document, widely used in organizational communication for the purposes of transmitting significant messages to one or more receivers.

message ordering   The question of whether or not it is more persuasive to put arguments favoring a position early in a message. Often called the primacy–recency question: Does more change result when arguments are inserted at the end of the message?

message sidedness   A feature of a persuasive message concerning the degree to which the arguments it presents explain one side only or refute opposing arguments as well.

minority culture   A term originally intended to refer to the actual numbers of those groups that were less numerous in a population. Later it came to have additional connotations, including those groups that were less dominant and less powerful in a population. In comparison with the majority, then, all so-called minority cultures were often regarded as somehow less significant, less dominant, or less important.

modeling   The acting out, description, or portrayal of behavior in mass communications in such a way that those activities serve as models for receivers.

natural sign   An event or situation occurring in nature to which an animal learns to respond or adjust.

negotiation   A process of conflict resolution that communicates back and forth between opponents.

nominal measurement   The method of measurement that names what is observed and places it into some qualitatively defined category, such as female or male.

nonsocial constraints   The nonsocial factors that reduce the consistency between attitude and action. For example, the act may be inconvenient, involve financial loss, pose risks, or be difficult to perform. Also, the person may lack opportunity or competence.

nonverbal communication   The deliberate or unintentional use of objects, actions, sounds, time, and space to arouse meanings in others.

nonverbal immediacy   A physical and psychological closeness with others; a condition that can be established through the deliberate use of nonverbal signals and actions.

normative confusion   A basis of group disorganization that occurs when communication norms have not been effectively clarified or when consensus breaks down about which messages, topics, or issues are approved or disapproved.

norms (communication)   The general rules that each participant in a group is expected to follow concerning the issues, topics, and modes of transmission that are acceptable to the other members.

oculesics   The study of eye contact and pupil dilation in nonverbal communication.

ordinal measurement   A rank ordering for what is being observed that assigns a number, such as first, second, and so on.

organization   A human group that has been deliberately designed to achieve a desired objective. Usually, an organization has a large number of participants whose activities are coordinated by complex rules for communication.

organization chart   A graphic representation of the chain of authority and command in an organization, which also provides a guide for the flow of formal messages. It is especially helpful in understanding the vertical flow of communication—up and down the organization.

organizational cohesion   The cohesion that binds members of an organization to one another and to the group as a whole. It is based on sentiment-based cohesion in small groups of work associates, reward-based cohesion in more temporary groups, assignment-based cohesion in decision-making groups within the organization, and dependency-based cohesion that is a product of task interdependencies in the overall structure.

organizational communication   The transmission of messages through formal and informal channels of a large, deliberately designed group, resulting in the construction of meanings that influence both individual members and the group as a whole.

overgeneralizing   The act of claiming that what prevailed among the subjects observed in an investigation also applies to people who were not actually studied.

panel   A more formal type of discussion group in which participants are often experts or representatives. The panel is usually coordinated by a moderator, and the discussion usually takes place before a live audience.

papyrus   A smooth writing surface first made in ancient Egypt from thin slices of a reed. When the slices were laid criss-cross and mashed together by pounding, and then rolling, pressing, and drying, a paperlike surface was produced. The word *paper* comes from this source.

parchment   A thin and smooth writing surface prepared from the skin of a sheep.

participant observation   A strategy of observation in which an investigator joins a group under study and participates fully in its activities in order to observe the group's communication patterns. The group may or may not know that the person is a researcher.

peer group   A small group of close and intimate friends, often of the same general socioeconomic characteristics, age, and gender.

penny press   The newspapers that followed the model of Benjamin Day's *New York Sun*—selling cheaply, making their profits on advertising, and aiming at large circulations by suiting the tastes of the common people.

perception   The psychological process of seeing, hearing, or feeling with the senses and then attaching meaning to what has been apprehended based on what is learned from the culture.

peripheral route   A pathway in the Elaboration Likelihood Model of Persuasion (ELM) in which careful attention to the persuasive arguments in a message is not given. Instead, an individual uses a variety of simple cues to make a quick decision to accept or reject the message, such as the number of arguments (rather than the quality) presented. Any attitude change that may result is likely to be weak and temporary, and less predictive of behavior.

persona (personal idea)   A set of beliefs, meanings, and understandings that an individual develops about another as a result of communicating with her or him. (see *implicit personality theory*)

personal space   The immediate zone people carry around during their daily interactions with others.

personality   The individual's enduring organization of meanings, motivations, emotional patterns, orientations, skills, and other attributes that make that person different in psychological makeup from all others.

personality trait   A person's individual characteristic, such as being smart, stingy, friendly, and so on. Specific attributes that make up his or her overall nature.

persuasion   The efforts to change people in some way by using strategies of communication. A transactional process in which a source encodes and transmits messages designed to influence a receiver's constructions of meanings in ways that will lead to changes desired by the source in the receiver's beliefs, attitudes, or behavior.

phylogenetic continuum   The idea from evolutionary theory that animals can be arranged along a scale in terms of the complexity of their bodily structures and organization.

pictographs   Crude drawings that are intended to represent objects or situations in reality. These were typical of the earliest attempts at writing.

population   A statistical term meaning the entire aggregate of what is being studied. In communication research, mainly all the people about whom generalizations are to be made in a study.

postulate   A shared belief of a very fundamental nature—a given that is so basic that it is not subject to proof or disproof.

power distance   As a cultural factor, the relative importance a group places on power, rank, and status. High power-distance cultures value social status, birth order, and occupational or political rank. Low power-distance cultures value equality and minimize the importance of power and status differences among members.

practitioner   A person who practices (works as a member of) a specific profession, such as advertising, law, education, etc.

predispositions   The tendencies to approve of some things and disapprove of others that are shaped by attitudes, values, opinions, preferences, and so on. These factors modify perceptions and interpretations because they lead people to like some stimuli and dislike others.

prejudice   A configuration of emotionally held beliefs that results in a person making judgments about another individual before he or she even begins to communicate or interact.

presentation of self   A way of formulating and transmitting verbal and nonverbal messages to other people about the kind of person you are.

primary groups   The intimate groups that are earliest in the experience of the human individual and that play a critical part in the person's psychological and social development. Essentially, these are the family and early peer groups. Peer groups in adult life can also be considered primary groups.

principle of delayed gratification   A belief that accepting costs or guarding resources in the present will pay off in significant long-term rewards.

propaganda   Messages, usually transmitted by media, that have the goal of shaping a receiver's interpretation or behavior toward a topic, issue or action.

proprietary research   Research conducted by industry, government, advertising agencies, or any other organization in which the findings are kept secret.

proxemics   The study of the meanings communicated by the use of space and distance.

psychodynamic strategy   A traditional approach to persuasion resting on the assumption that the route to achieving behavioral change lies in achieving cognitive reorganization. If feelings and beliefs can be changed by persuasive messages (cognitive reorganization), overt behavior will be changed correspondingly.

psychological reactance   The strong feelings of determined resistance that cause a person to react against an attempt at persuasion.

quasi-experiment   A research design that incorporates the logic of the experiment without actual intervention by the researcher. The treatment is a naturally occurring condition.

random sampling procedure   A set of steps for selecting a sample from a population in such a way that each subject has an equal probability of being included.

rank (communication)   The rules that define communication patterns based on authority, power, and privilege within a group. For example, rank determines who issues orders and whose messages are regarded as important.

rank ineffectiveness   A situation in which members of a group come to believe that the messages transmitted by those in positions of power and authority lack legitimacy.

ratio measurement   A measurement system that rates the value of what is being observed and then assigns it a number along a scale. The scale begins with a zero point, and the distances between any two numbers are the same.

receiver   A person who attends to, perceives, and interprets (decodes) the message information transmitted by a source.

receiver eccentricities   The personal attributes and individual differences that help or hinder a person's capacity to receive and interpret messages accurately.

referent   The object, situation, or event to which a symbol refers.

reinforcement   A term from psychological theories of learning, which implies that when a response to a stimulus is positive or rewarding, people will continue with the behavior, and it will become part of their repertoire, to be repeated in similar circumstances. Should the consequence be punishing, however, the behavior is likely to be dropped and replaced with some alternative response.

reinforcement learning theory   A theory of learning that explains how individuals try out various behaviors, which then result in consequences for the individual. If a behavior results in a positive consequence, the behavior is rewarded and reinforced, and may become a part of the individual's permanent repertoire and is likely to be repeated in similar circumstances.

reliability   A quality of measurement in research referring to whether a procedure will yield the same results if used repeatedly on the same subjects.

replication   The repetition of a study under the same general circumstances and with the same types of subjects to see whether the findings of the first investigation will prevail in the second.

representative sample   A sample that has been chosen so that the personal and social characteristics of those included are like those in the entire population in all important respects relevant to the research.

research   A set of procedures for gathering trustworthy information about some object or process that is studied under controlled conditions of observation in such a way that objective conclusions can be reached with a minimum of error.

resiliency factor   The propensity of human beings to be flexible in their learning histories and not to be rigidly shaped by a few negative consequences of their actions.

reward-based cohesion   A type of cohesion based on the personal satisfactions or rewards that flow to individuals because they participate in a group. This leads them to maintain membership and work toward the goals of the group.

roles (communication)   A cluster of rules in a group that define who has the right to transmit particular kinds of messages and who must pay attention to them.

role-taking   An activity whereby a source assesses the likelihood that a receiver will be able to interpret the intentions and meanings of a particular form of a message.

round table   A common format for informal discussion groups in which there is usually no audience and the participants are arranged in some sort of circular pattern.

salient characteristic   A feature or aspect of an individual that stands out in an initial encounter with another person and that serves as a dominant attribute around which that person constructs a pattern of initial impressions.

sampling   A procedure for picking from some population an adequate and manageable smaller number of people who can be contacted and studied, given the researcher's resources.

schema   A pattern or configuration of traces of meaning that have been organized and recorded in a person's memory.

scientific management   A theory for managing organizations in which managers themselves look systematically at the design of their group and its processes to try to communicate to workers ways in which incentives, work flow, and exercise of authority can operate most effectively and profitably. Early versions were concerned with time and motion studies.

scripted (or stereotypic) conversations   Conversations that are like highly standardized and predictable lines rehearsed in a play. These may follow clear, even rigid, rules in certain welldefined communication situations.

selective influences   An explanation of why only certain types of people attend to particular forms of media messages, based on assumptions about their individual differences, social category memberships, and social affiliations.

selective perception   An individual's assignment of a personally unique pattern of denotative and connotative meanings to some person, activity, situation, or thing. These personal stamps of meaning arise from people's different memories of meanings linked to signs, signals, and symbols, and to human characteristics, stored through experience.

self (self-image or self-concept)   The pattern of beliefs, meanings, and understandings each individual develops concerning her or his personal characteristics, capacities, limitations, and worth as a human being. A personal conception of who and where the individual is in the social order.

self-disclosure   The individual's communication to another that reveals the nature of the individual's past, private thoughts, personal views, or deep feelings. Also, the individual's telling another about beliefs, attitudes, values, accomplishments, status, and other personal and social characteristics.

self-talk   The internal dialogue you engage in as you go about your daily activities. Self-talk helps you to make sense of your experiences as you encounter them, and serves as an "inner voice" that determines how you listen, perceive, and process what others say or do.

seminar   A small discussion group now commonly used in advanced courses in universities. Usually, each student takes a turn at addressing a central question that is the focus of the discussion, and the mentor draws the important lessons out of various comments.

sender-receiver reciprocity   The successful adaptation to each other in a communication encounter by engaging in both role-taking and feedback simultaneously.

sender-receiver similarity   A condition in which the message's sender and receiver have similar learning experiences in their language community so as to have acquired parallel meanings for verbal and nonverbal signs and symbols.

sentiment-based cohesion   A type of cohesion based on bonds of affection that exist among members of a group.

sharpening   The counterpart of leveling in the embedding process. A verbal message shrinks as it is passed on by word of mouth. With each retelling, it becomes increasingly organized around its more salient details, becoming more and more concise until it is only a summary of the original message.

sign   An event that animals and human beings learn to associate with and use to anticipate subsequent events. Examples: clouds are followed by rain, the dog dish is followed by the dog getting fed, a red light indicates that one must stop.

signal   The noises or patterned movements that animals make to which others of their species respond. Examples: cries or postures that imply danger, the presence of food, or readiness to mate. Human beings also use many signals: whistles, bells, and waving flags.

signs   Stimuli to which people have learned to make a patterned response.

skills training   The form of treatment for communication apprehension based on the assumption that limitations in people's skills in communicating influence their apprehension levels. To reduce the apprehension, people receive training in public speaking skills or other communication behaviors.

small group   A group in which the number of members varies from two to perhaps a dozen or more; optimal size with all members participating fully in communication is five members.

small group conference   A small discussion group in which several participants are brought together, usually under private conditions, to share technical information or to discuss a problem in their area of expertise.

small talk   Discussions that focus on topics of general interest and have little emotional or personal significance, such as the weather, sports, or other matters not requiring self-disclosure.

social categories   A number of people who have a characteristic in common by which they can be classified. Examples are gender, age, education, occupation, and race. People in such categories are often said to be characterized by certain regularities in their behavior.

social construction of reality   A cognitive process by which a person acquires understandings of and meanings for some aspect of reality by communicating about it with other people (or from observing depictions of it in mass communications).

social efficacy   The condition of being competent as a social person—that is, being able to form, manage, and maintain all kinds of social relationships in an effective manner.

social expectations   The shared rules for conducting social activities within a group—norms, roles, ranking, and controls. These can be learned vicariously from media sources as well as by actual participation in a group.

social expectations theory   A theory that examines the long-term influences of the media. Specifically, this theory explains how individuals learn the rules of behavior from media content. People learn the rules and requirements of various groups by seeing them portrayed in the media. By seeing such groups as families, courts, the army, police departments, etc., we see in action their norms, roles, ranking patterns, and systems of social control. As a result, we learn what behaviors are accepted or punished in such groups.

social information processing theory (SIP)   A theory, articulated by Joseph Walther, that explains how users adapt to the limitations of computer-mediated communication and are able to develop close relationships with others by forming impressions based on the verbal content and other cues contained in online messages.

social institution   A broad configuration of closely related cultural elements and organized social activities that are essential to fulfillment of a perceived need of the social order.

social learning theory (observational learning theory)   An extension of earlier, more general reinforcement theories that was originally developed to explain how individuals learn—not by performing actions themselves but by observing the behavior and reactions of those who are important as models in their lives.

social network sites (SNS)   Web-based services that allow individuals to construct a public or semi-public profile within a bounded system, construct a list of other users with whom they share a connection, and view and navigate their list of connections and those made by others within the system. The term "social media" includes social network sites, social news sites, and blogs.

social pressures   The needs and desires to comply with social rules for behavior that are expected by others whose approval is sought in a situation of action. (see *social expectations*)

socialization   The long-term processes of communication within which deliberate or indirect lessons are internalized, enabling the person to become a unique human being, a functioning member of a society, and a participant in its general and unique culture.

source or sender   A person who formulates, encodes, and transmits a message to one or more receivers. In some cases, groups or agencies can serve as sources.

specialized culture   A specialized or unique culture that characterizes a particular group within a society; such groups are distinguished from one another by such factors as race, ethnicity, gender, age, or profession.

specialized organizational culture   The total pattern of beliefs, sentiments, attitudes, values, rules, and special languages shared by the members of an organization. These cultural elements set the organization off from other organizations and from the society as a whole.

stage fright   A special category of the more general condition of communication apprehension that specifically focuses on anxiety about a public performance or speech before a group or audience.

stakeholders   Persons who have some interest in the services provided by an agency or business.

stereotypes   Rigid and usually negative assumptions about personal and social qualities of people who are members of a particular social category.

stereotypic   (see *scripted or stereotypic conversations*)

susceptibility   The degree to which a person is influenced by others because of his or her personal characteristics.

symbiotic relationship   A relationship between two entities based on mutual dependency.

symbols   The labels used by participants in a language community to arouse standardized meanings for aspects of reality. The initial selection of a label for a referent is often made arbitrarily, but, once established, the connection between the label and its referent is permanent.

symposium A very formal discussion group whose participants are usually a small group of experts. They are individually introduced by a moderator, and each makes a speech about the theme. During or between presentations, the participants seldom talk; they simply take their turns in delivering their views.

syntax The rules for ordering words in a sentence so that their meaning is clear.

systematic desensitization (SD) A form of treatment that has been used to reduce many kinds of fears, including communication apprehension. It seeks to reduce apprehensions through muscle relaxation techniques.

task-oriented group A group in which people participate in order to get something done.

teleconferencing The use of media to link spatially dispersed people for the purpose of communicating in ways that approximate the conditions of a face-to-face meeting.

territoriality A common tendency or characteristic of both animals and humans in which they define or claim some space as their own.

theory The form in which cause-effect relationships are stated in scientific analysis. A theory provides an explanation of how one set of events brings about or influences another.

theory of selective and limited influences A theory of media effects that explains how people's individual psychological differences, social category identities, and web of social relationships lead them to choose certain kinds of media content. When they do so, they interpret the meanings of these media messages within frameworks related to their psychological, social, and cultural backgrounds.

therapy group A specialized discussion group in which participants who share a common difficulty meet with a coordinator who has some insight into the problem. The underlying assumption is that if these people get together and disclose their feelings to one another, it will help them feel better.

trace The imprinted records of experience registered in the brain by electrochemical or other activities of its nerve cells.

trait (personality) A relatively stable and predictable pattern of behavior that characterizes a person; a feature of an individual's personality that makes her or him different from others, such as stingy, honest, smart, and happy-go-lucky.

transaction Any kind of exchange. An activity that occurs between, and mutually influences, all individuals acting together in some way.

two-step flow of communication A process by which some individuals (opinion leaders) directly receive messages from the mass media and then pass them on to others by word of mouth, often influencing their interpretations.

unclear role definition The confusion that results from inadequate, ineffective, or unclear definitions about the roles played in a group. Whatever the type of group—from a family to a vast corporation—such role confusion can be a major factor leading to a loss of cohesion.

utilitarianism An explanation of human behavior in which people choose to engage in those behaviors that maximize pleasure and avoid pain. This idea is the foundation for contemporary psychological theories of learning that stress rewards (pleasure) and punishment (pain) as the basis for everyday, habitual behavior. Psychologists refer to this as a cost–benefit ratio for those punishments and rewards that ultimately guide our actions.

validity A quality of a measurement referring to whether it actually measures the variable for which it has been designed.

vellum A writing surface similar to parchment, except prepared from the skin of a calf.

vertical communication Communication that takes place within an organization. In vertical communication, supervisors send messages down to subordinates, and subordinates transmit requests or send reports up the line to supervisors.

vertical transmission The flow of formal messages either up or down in an organization, with clearly graded levels of power and authority.

videoconferencing The use of videocameras, long-distance cables, or satellite relays or the Internet to enable people to see and talk to one another in a close approximation to having them face to face in the same room.

vocalics The study of the way in which vocal cues signal meanings to others, such as showing people's happiness, nervousness, and so on.

wage incentive system A formula for paying workers in production settings in which wages are tied to personal output. Earnings for a worker in a production shop are determined by the number of units the individual produces in a given time period.

Credits

Text

Chapter 1 p. 5: "Raising the Bar: Employers' Views on College Learning in the Wake of the Economic Downturn." Survey of Employers conducted on behalf of The Association of American Colleges and Universities by Hart Research Associates. Used by Permission of The Association of American Colleges and Universities; pp. 28–29: survey based on "Explication and test of a model of communicative competence." Human Communication Research, 3, 195–213 by Wiemann, J. M. (1977). Used by permission of John Wiley and Sons.

Chapter 2 p. 50: Screenshot from www.forvo.com. Used by permission.

Chapter 4 pp. 104–105: Hamilton, Neil W., Effectiveness Requires Listening, "How to Assess and Improve Listening Skills" (2011). Florida Coastal Law Review, Vol. 13, Forthcoming; U of St. Thomas Legal Studies Research Paper No. 11–25. Available at SSRN: http://ssrn.com/abstract=1917059. Used by permission of Neil W. Hamilton.

Chapter 5 pp. 132–133: Berger, C. R., Clatterbuck, G.W., & Shulman, L. S. (1976). Perceptions of information sequencing in relationship development. *Human Communication Research, 3*, 34–39. Used by permission of John Wiley and Sons.

Chapter 6 pp. 162–163: Sargent, F., & Miller, G. R. (1971). Some differences in certain communication behaviors of autocratic and democratic group leaders. *Journal of Communication, 21*, 233–252. Used by permission of John Wiley and Sons.

Chapter 8 Figure 8.2, Kearney, P. & T.G. Plax. (1996). *Public speaking in a diverse society*. Mountain View, CA: Mayfield. Copyright © Patricia Kearney and Timothy G. Plax.

Chapter 9 pp. 256–257: Bell, R. A., & Daly, J. A. (1984). The affinity-seeking function of communication. *Communication and Monographs, 51*, 91–115. Used by permission of the Speech Communication Association.

Photo

Chapter 1 p. 4: © David Buffington/Blend Images LLC; p. 14: Stockbyte/Punchstock.

Chapter 2 p. 35: © Goodshoot/Punchstock; p. 52: Sabine Scheckel/Digital Vision/Getty Images RF; p. 58: John Dowland/Getty Images RF.

Chapter 3 p. 66: Design Pics/Darren Greenwood; p. 71: Ballyscanlon/Getty Images RF; p. 73: Purestock/SuperStock RF; pg. 75: Pixtal/AGE Fotostock; pg. 84: Fancy Collection/SuperStock RF.

Chapter 4   p. 95: Pixtal/AGE Fotostock; p. 101: © Brand X Pictures/PunchStock; p. 114: © Tetra Images/Corbis RF.

Chapter 5   p. 120: Pixtal/AGE Fotostock; p. 125: Design Pics/Kelly Redinger; p. 130: Brad Barket/AP Photo; p. 135: L. Mouton/PhotoAlto .

Chapter 6   p. 146: Digital Vision/Punchstock; p. 155: Onoky/Getty Images RF; p. 159: Ingram Publishing/SuperStock RF; p. 161: McGraw-Hill Companies.

Chapter 7   p. 175: Ingram Publishing; p. 192: Design Pics/Darren Greewood; p. 195: George Doyle/Getty Images RF.

Chapter 8   p. 208: © Corbis RF; p. 231: Bananastock/Alamy.

Chapter 9   p. 243: © Royalty Free/Corbis RF; p. 251: Ingram Publishing; p. 259: Shutterstock.

Chapter 10   p. 270: Image Source/Getty Images RF; p. 282: Tom Wang/Shutterstock; p. 284: © LWA/Dann Tardif/Blend Images LLC.

Chapter 11   p. 296: Historicus, Inc.; p. 300: The McGraw-Hill Companies, Inc./Christopher Kerrigan, photographer; p. 303: Jack Star/PhotoLink/Getty images RF; p. 309: Image Source/Getty Images RF.

Chapter 12   p. 322: Queerstock, Inc./Alamy; p. 326: Ingram Publishing; p. 329: © Ingram Publishing/AGE Fotostock; p. 333: Tatiana Popva/Shutterstock

Chapter 13   p. 344: Dimitri Vervits/ImageState; p. 355: Liquidlibrary/Dynamic Graphics/Jupiterimages; p. 362: ra2 studio/Shutterstock.

Chapter 14   p. 369: Angel Waye/Shutterstock; p. 382: cybrain/Shutterstock.

Chapter 15   p. 398: Photographer's Choice/SuperStock RF; p. 405: Design Pics/Don Hammond; p. 418: iQoncept/Shutterstock.

Names Index

Adams, J., 423
Addington, D. W., 92
Adler, R. B., 63
Adorno, T. W., 172
Aesop, 35
Agee, P., 320
Alder, R., 93
Algozzine, R., 91
Alkema, F., 91
Allen, M., 143, 266, 290, 292, 320, 423
Allen, T. H., 172
Allen, V. L., 117
Allport, G. W., 172, 204, 291
Almaney, A. J., 236
Alper, T., 93
Altman, I., 92, 143
Alwan, A. J., 236
Amato, Pr. R., 143
Anatol, K. W. E., 341
Andersen, J. F., 93
Andersen, P., 93
Anderson, A., 367
Anderson, C. M., 171
Anderson, J. F., 366
Anderson, J. W., 236–237
Anderson, N. H., 320
Anderson, P., 367
Appelbaum, R. L., 341
Archer, G. L., 394
Argyle, Michael, 91, 136–137, 143
Aristotle, 3, 43
Armstrong, Edwin, 379
Aronson, E., 117, 173
Asch, Solomon, 240–242, 243, 265

Athen, G., 236
Atkinson, R. C., 290
Atkinson, R. L., 290
Audet, A. M., 116
Auriemmo, A., 204
Axtell, R. E., 235
Ayers, J., 292
Azien, O., 319

Backlund, P., 237
Baddeley, A. D., 116
Bales, Robert F., 151, 171
Balfantz, G. L., 291
Ball-Rokeach, Sandra, 63, 291, 409, 423
Bandura, Albert, 117, 275, 277, 291, 395
Bargh, J. A., 32
Barker, D. A., 93
Barker, L. L., 91, 93, 116, 117
Barnes, H. E., 31
Barnouw, E., 394
Baron, Paul, 356
Bartlett, Frederick C., 31
Bateman, P., 63
Bateson, G., 142
Bauchner, J., 92
Bauman, I., 290, 292
Baxter, Leslie A., 143, 266
Bear, J., 91
Beattie, G., 31
Beatty, M. J., 291, 292
Beauchamp, T., 423
Beavin, J. H., 142
Becker, H., 31
Becker, H. S., 265

Beckwith, J., 172
Bee, H., 172
Beebe, S. A., 171
Bell, Alexander Graham, 352
Bell, D., 31
Bell, R. A., 257, 266
Benedict, Ruth, 155, 172
Benne, K. D., 172
Benne, Kenneth, 161
Bennett, C. I., 236
Bentham, Jeremy, 87, 93, 126, 142
Berelson, Bernard, 394
Berger, C. R., 132, 142, 143
Berkowitz, L., 320, 341, 423
Berkowitz-Stafford, S., 320
Berra, Yogi, 404
Berscheid, E., 91
Bertalanffy, L. von, 204
Bethea, L. S., 171
Bettinghaus, F. P., 319, 320
Bippus, A. M., 292
Birdwhistell, R. L., 90, 92
Birkner, L. R., 117
Blank, C. L., 141
Bloom, K., 318
Blumberg, S. J., 367
Bochner, A. P., 266
Bond, C. F. J., 92
Bond, J., 236
Bontempi, B., 31
Booth, A., 341
Booth-Butterfield, M., 116, 143
Borgatta, E. E., 320
Boster, F. J., 320
Bostrom, R., 116, 117, 320
Bostrom, R. N., 116
Bourhis, J., 290, 292
Bouthilet, L., 394
Bower, G., 31
Boyd, D. M., 367
Bradac, J. J., 237, 266
Bradley, P. H., 237
Brady, J., 63
Brehm, Jack W., 307–308, 319
Brewer, M. B., 235
Broadhurst, A. R., 32
Brock, T., 320
Brommel, B. J., 142
Bronowski, J., 31
Brooks, C., 63
Brooks, W. D., 117

Brown, J. D., 265
Brown, W. C., 117, 171, 237
Browning, Guy, 191
Bruner, J. S., 265
Brunner, C., 117
Bryant, J., 393
Bull, R., 92
Buller, D. B., 93, 265
Burgess, P., 91
Burgoon, J. K., 90, 91, 93, 265, 266, 290
Burkhart, J. C., 91
Burrell, N., 290
Burroughs, N. F., 319
Bush, George W., 15, 31
Buss, A. H., 291
Butler, B., 63
Butler, J. A., 203
Bylund, C. L., 142
Byrne, D., 142

Cacioppo, John T., 314, 320
Cai, D. A., 341
Calabrese, R. J., 143
Callister, Mark, 415, 423
Camarota, S. A., 235
Cameron, A., 91
Campbell, E. H., 320
Cantril, H., 394
Cantrill, J. G., 320
Carey, A., 204
Carletta, J., 171
Carol, J. B., 31
Carol, Lewis, 35
Carson, Rachel, 373
Cartell, R. B., 172
Casanto, D., 63
Casson, H. N., 367
Catgcart, R. S., 171
Cecchi, L. F., 172
Cegala, D., 117
Cermak, L. S., 31
Chaney, L. H., 235
Chaplin, W. F., 265
Charters, W. W., 394
Chenoweth, N. A., 367
Cherwit, R. A., 63
Cho, C. S., 235
Chory-Assard, R. M., 143
Clapper, R. H., 393
Clatterbuck, G. W., 132, 142

Hayes, Catherine, 38, 62
Hayes, J. R., 367
Hayes, Keith, 38
Hays, W. L., 265
Haythorn, W., 172
Head, S. W., 394
Heath, R. W., 117
Hecht, M. L., 236
Heider, Fritz, 252, 266
Heller, J., 92
Hellweg, S. A., 203
Henderson, A. M., 203
Henderson, Monika, 136–137, 143
Henman, L. D., 171
Henriksen, L., 318
Hertz, Heinrich, 378
Hesin, R., 93
Hess, J. A., 143
Hickson III, M. L., 91, 92, 93
Higbee, K. L., 320, 423
Higgins, E. T., 31, 32
Hikins, J. W., 63
Hilgard, E. R., 290
Hill, S. D., 93
Hirokawa, R. Y., 171
Hirschfelder, A., 227, 236
Hitler, Adolf, 181
Hjelle, L., 265
Hobbes, Thomas, 157, 172
Hocker, J., 341
Hocking, J. E., 91, 92
Hodge, C. N., 265
Hodges, R. I., 367
Hofstede, G., 235, 236
Hogg, R. V., 30
Hoijer, H., 63
Homans, George C., 133, 143, 170
Hornik, R. C., 30
Hortalsu, N., 143
Hosman, L. A., 266
Houston, J. B., 172
Hovland, Carl I., 313, 318, 320, 394
Howe, P., 367
Howell, W. S., 117
Hughes, D.L., 116
Humphreys, Laud, 421, 423
Hunter, J. E., 265, 290, 292
Hunter, J. H., 320
Hyde, J. S., 423
Hymes, D., 31, 63, 266

Ifert, D. E., 320
Infante, D. A., 337
Innes, H. A., 393
Iversen, M. A., 172
Ivy, D. K., 237

Jablin, F. M., 203
Jackson, D., 393
Jackson, D. D., 142
Jackson, L. A., 265
Jackson, R. L., 236
Jandt, F. E., 341
Janis, Irving L., 169, 313, 318, 320, 407, 422–423
Janowitz, M., 173
Janusik, L., 116
Jobs, Steve, 282
John, O., 91
Johnson, A. D., 88
Johnson, C. E., 265
Jones, J. P., 318
Jones-Corley, J., 292

Kaminski, E. P., 92
Karathanos, Patricia, 199, 204
Kaul, J., 204
Kearney, Pat, 117, 142, 172, 179, 221, 291, 292, 319, 320, 367
Keeter, S., 423
Kelley, Harold H., 143, 266, 313, 318, 320
Kellogg, Donald, 38
Kellogg, Louise, 38, 62
Kellogg, Winthrop, 38, 62
Kelly, L., 292
Kelman, Herbert C., 310–311, 319
Keltner, D., 91
Kendon, A., 91
Kennedy, C., 423
Keyton, J., 422
Khan, Genghis, 181
Khomeini, Rohollah (Ayatollah), 181
Kilmann, Ralph, 331, 332, 341
Kim, B. S. K., 236
Kim, Y. Y., 236
King, Martin Luther, Jr., 390
Kish, L., 423
Knapp, M., 63, 81
Knapp, Mark L., 91, 128, 142, 143, 265, 320
Knowles, V., 30
Ko, S. J., 265
Koehler, J. W., 341

Koester, J., 224, 236
Koontz, Harold, 182, 203
Kornblut, A. E., 31
Kramer, E., 92
Kraus, S., 320
Kreitner, R., 203
Kreps, G. I., 204
Krippendorf, K., 32
Krivnos, P. D., 266
Kuhn, T., 173
Kurland, N. B., 204
Kuwabara, A. Y., 291

La Gaipa, J. J., 143
Laing, R. D., 142
Lakoff, R., 237
Lambert, W. W., 320
LaPiere, R. T., 319
Lasswell, H. D., 394
Lavelli, M., 93
Lazar, J., 394
Lazarsfeld, Paul F., 394
Lee, A. R., 142
Lee, J. W., 92
Leen, R., 92
Lesser, C. S., 30
Leventhal, H., 423
Levine, J. M., 172
Levinson, D. J., 172
Levinson, W., 30
Lewin, Kurt, 172
Lieberman, P., 62
Liebowitz, K., 93
Linden, E., 62
Lindzey, G., 117, 173
Lippit, R., 172
Lippman, Walter, 142, 303, 318
Littlejohn, S. W., 31, 32
Locke, D. C., 236
Locke, John, 31
Loken, B., 30
Lollar, M., 367
Lowery, S., 318
Lowy, J., 367
Luchins, A. S., 320
Luke, J. V., 367
Lumsdaine, A. A., 394
Lundell, T. L., 237
Lustig, Ron, 224, 236
Lyle, J., 394

Maccoby, E. E., 172–173, 394
MacNeil, R., 63
Madden, M., 367
Madison, C. A., 393
Majors, R. E., 30
Malendro, L. A., 93
Mandel, W., 320
Mann, R. D., 172
Mannarelli, T., 265
Manstead, A., 92
Manusov, V., 91, 92
Marconi, Guglielmo, 378
Marin, B. V., 236
Marin, G., 236
Markoff, J., 367
Marler, P., 62
Martin, J. S., 235
Martin, K. A., 265
Marx, Karl, 373
Masterson, J. T., 171
Mayo, E., 203
Mazur, A., 92
McCall, G., 422
McCroskey, J. C., 60, 88, 91n, 92n, 93n, 203, 269,
    290, 291, 292, 315, 320
McCrum, R., 63
McDaniel, E. R., 235
McEwen, W., 32
McGuire, W. J., 320
McIntyre-Birkner, R., 117
McLaughlin, M. L., 320
McMillan, C. J., 204
McMurtrie, D., 393
McPhee, R. D., 319
Mead, George Herbert, 31, 57, 58, 59, 63,
    117, 142
Mehrabian, Albert, 87, 90–91, 93, 117
Merton, Robert K., 318
Messman, S. J., 292
Meyer, A., 117
Meyer, J., 116–117
Meyers, R. A., 320
Michela, J. L., 266
Milgram, Stanley, 309, 319, 420
Miller, A., 423
Miller, G., 143
Miller, G. R., 92, 141, 163, 265, 320, 423
Miller, K., 203, 204
Miller, L. C., 320
Mills, C. W., 203

Mills, J., 117
Mills, T. M., 265
Mineo, P., 91
Mitchell, A., 393
Modaff, D. P., 203
Mokrzycki, M., 423
Molloy, J. T., 91
Mongeau, P., 320
Montagu, A., 93
Moran, J., 393
Moreland, R. L., 172
Morris, C. W., 63
Morse, Samuel F. B., 45, 378
Mott, F. L., 394
Mottet, T. P., 291
Moy, P., 423
Mulac, A., 237
Munzio, E. G., 202
Murphy, A. G., 423
Murphy, Alexandra, 414
Murphy, Dan, 356
Murray, N., 30
Mussolini, Benito, 181
Myers, S. A., 171, 292

Nadel, L., 31
Nader, K., 31
Nadler, M. K., 320
Napoli, P. M., 30
Naveh, J., 393
Nelson, D., 142
Nelson, P. E., 117, 143, 341
Newcomb, T. M., 172–173
Newton, D., 423
Nguyen, M., 93
Nguyen, T., 93
Nichols, R. G., 116
Nicholson, H., 91
Nidich, P., 31
Nimmo, D., 93
Nixon, Richard M., 390, 394–395
Nofsinger, R. E., 266
Nydell, Margaret K., 229, 237

Ogden, C. K., 47, 63
O'Hair, D., 63
Okafor, T., 235
O'Keefe, B. J., 31
Oliver, M. B., 393
Ordman, L., 318

Oshinsky, J. S., 92
Oskamp, S., 319

Page, Carol, 354
Park, D. W., 366
Park, Y. S., 236
Parker, C., 117
Parker, E., 394
Parsons, T., 203
Patterson, Francene, 39–40, 62
Patton, B., 341
Paulus, P. B., 172
Payne, S. K., 291, 292
Pearce, W. B., 266
Pearl, D., 394
Pearson, J. C., 117, 142, 143, 237, 341
Pelled, L. H., 204
Pennebaker, J., 423
Perlmutter, D. D., 63
Perloff, R. M., 423
Petrullo, L., 265
Petty, Richard E., 314, 320
Pfau, M., 423
Pfungst, Oskar, 36, 37, 62
Phillips, G. M., 292
Phillips, Gerald, 288
Phillips, J. B., 265
Phillipson, H., 142
Piaget, Jean, 172
Pike, J., 63
Plato, 43, 52, 53, 55, 63, 160, 172,
    291, 303
Plax, Timothy G., 91, 116, 117, 142, 172,
    179, 291, 292, 318, 319, 320, 367
Poole, M., 117
Poole, M. S., 171, 173
Porter, L. W., 172, 203, 319
Porter, R. E., 235, 236, 237
Postman, I., 204
Powers, G., 30
Prager, K. J., 143
Preiss, R. W., 290, 423
Premack, A. J., 62
Premack, David, 40, 62
Previti, D., 143
Prisbell, M., 266
Putnam, L. L., 203

Quigley, M., 394
Quintillian, 3

Stafford, L., 292
Stafford, S., 320
Starbuck, R. R., 30
Steinberg, M., 141
Stelter, B., 394
Stephens, M., 367
Sterling, C. H., 394
Stevens, L., 116
Stewart, J., 30
Stewart, Jon, 130
Stewart, R. A., 290, 291, 292
Stiff, J. B., 320
Stogdill, R. M., 173
Storrs, C., 203
Stowe, Harriet Beecher, 373
Street R. L., Jr., 265
Strice, G. F., 172
Strodtbeck, F. L., 171
Stutman, R., 117
Sudnow, D. N., 63
Suh, E. M., 235
Sumner, W. G., 235
Sundberg, M. L., 62
Sussman, L., 203
Sybers, R., 91
Sypher, H. E., 31, 32
Szabo, E. A., 423

Tagiuri, Renato, 265
Talbot, F. A., 394
Tankard, J., 423
Tardy, C. H., 266
Taylor, A., 117
Taylor, D. A., 143
Taylor, Frederick W., 184, 185–186, 187, 203
Taylor, L. C., 91
Taylor, M., 30
Tenney, K., 116
Teven, J. J., 315, 320
Thayer, S., 93
Thibaut, J. W., 143
Thomas, E., 202, 291
Thomas, Kenneth, 331, 332, 341
Thomas, W. I., 304, 319
Thurman, B., 92
Ting-Toomey, S., 236
Titus, J., 318
Todd-Mancillas, W., 237
Tonnies, Ferdinand, 173
Towne, N., 63
Treece, M., 367

Triandis, H. C., 235
Truman, Harry S., 188
Tuckman, Bruce W., 151, 152, 171
Turner Bowkar, D. M., 266
Turner, L. H., 142, 171–172, 237
Tylor, Edward B., 207

Ugbah, S. D., 30
Urban II, Pope, 15
Ury, W., 341

Vale, L. J.,
Valencic, K. M., 291
Vander Houwen, B. A., 117
Vangelisti, A. L., 142, 143, 265
Vanston, L. K., 367
Verinis, J., 265
Vespucci, Amerigo, 234
Villemur, N. K., 423
Von Cranach, M., 92
Von Osten, Wilhelm, 36–37
Vrij, A., 92

Wakefield, M. A., 30
Waldeck, J. H., 117, 142, 172, 179, 367
Waldhart, E. S., 116
Walster, E., 91
Walther, Joseph B., 90, 346–347, 366
Wanzer, M. B., 116, 266
Wartella, E., 31
Watson, K., 116, 117
Watson, O. M., 92
Watson, W. H., 93
Watzlawick, P., 142
Weary, G., 266
Weaver, C. H., 117
Weaver, Warren, 24–25, 26, 32
Weber, Max, 180–182, 183, 185–186, 187, 203
Weider-Hatfield, D., 91
Weimann, J. M., 29
Weiss, J., 423
Wells, H. G., 386
West, R., 142, 171–172
Westie, F. R., 319
Wheeless, L. R., 266
White, R. K., 172
Whyte, William Foote, 422
Wiemann, J. M., 93
Wiener, M., 91
Wiener, N., 32
Wiggets, M., 92

Wilkie, Wendell, 386, 387
Williams, F., 117
Williams, Madelyn C., 74, 91
Wilmot, W. W., 142, 143, 341
Wilson, Christopher, 415, 423
Wimmer, R. D., 423
Wishner, John, 242, 243, 265
Witte, K., 320
Wolff, K. H., 143
Wood, J. P., 394
Wood, J. T., 142, 237
Wood, W., 319

Woodall, W. G., 93, 265
Wykes, M., 393

Yerkes, Robert, 40
Young, J. R., 367
Young, T. J., 320
Yousef, F. S., 237

Zajac, D. J., 318
Zenger, John Peter, 373–374
Zickuhr, K., 367
Znaniecki, Florian, 304, 319

Subject Index

Authority
  organizations, 181
  small group communication, 157
Automated behavior, 19
Avoidance coping style, 332b, 333–334

Barriers
  differences in interpersonal communication, 121
  to effective listening, 109–111, 112f, 116
Bees, food source directions, 38f
Behavior
  and attitudes, 305–307
  listening as, 97–98
Behavior-alteration techniques, persuasion strategy, 313
Behavior influence, mass communication process, 383
Behavior norms, cell phones, 353–354
Beliefs, 304
  shaping/altering, 302–303
Believability, source credibility, 314
Benefits and costs
  assessment, 134–135
  interpersonal relationships, 126, 141
Best alternative, principled negotiation, 338b, 339
Bias intimidation, 293
Blame, in disengagement, 138, 139
Body beautification, nonverbal message, 71
Body language, 70
Books
  during *incunabulum*, 393n.11
  information medium, 371
  U.S. developments, 372
Brainstorming sessions, 160
Breakdown and disorganization, group, 168–169
Brehm's theory of psychological reactance, 308b
Broca's area, 39
Bureau of Indian Affairs (BIA), Native American definition, 227
Bureaucracy, 177, 202
  Weber's classical theory, 180–182
  Weber's four principles, 180b

"Call-response" speaking response, 225
Careers, and communication apprehension, 281–283
Casual-personal zone, personal space, 79
Cause-effect relationship assumption, scientific research postulate, 399b, 400
Cell phones
  adoption speed, 352

behavior norms, 353–354
dos and don'ts, 354b
national polls, 412
versus landline, 353f
Central route, message processing, 315, 316f
Chair, *Robert's Rules*, 166, 167
Change, and conflict, 328
Charisma, 163
  authority source, 181
Chauvinism, 213
Chronemics, nonverbal behavior, 84, 85
Civil rights, changes and media, 389–390
Classroom, communication apprehension in, 279
Clever Hans, 36–37
Clever Hans effect, 37, 40
Closeness perception, affinity-seeking strategy, 256b
Clothing
  and impression formation, 250
  nonverbal messages, 73–75, 90
Co-cultures, 207, 235n.3
Coercion, 298
Cognitive functioning, 58, 300
Cognitive organization, 300
Cognitive processing, 55–56, 61, 300
  and language, 52
Cognitive reorganization, and persuasion, 299–307, 302b
Cognitive restructuring, 286, 288, 290
  steps, 287b
Cohesion
  groups, 167–168, 170
  organizational, 200–201
Collaborative coping style, 332b, 332–333
Collective living, and language, 52
Collective process, social construction of reality, 55
Collectivism
  Asian Americans, 226
  cultural value orientation, 217, 218f, 223b
  Latinos and Latinas, 225
  Native Americans, 227
Colonial press, 373
Comfort and reassurance, touch, 83
Comfortable self, affinity-seeking strategy, 256b
Common objective, group versus social category, 147
Communication
  accuracy in, 24–25, 107
  and conflict, 328–329, 340
  and technology, 372
  by computer, 355–361
  contemporary channels development, 44–45

Controls, social organization, 148–149, 149b
Convention, definition, 12
Conventions, 47–50
    meaning triangle, 47–48, 48f
    principle of, 46b
    schema, 48
Conversational rule-keeping, affinity-seeking
        strategy, 256b
Coping
    and intimate associations, 126
    styles, 331, 332b
Corantos, early English newspapers, 373
Corroborative effect, mass media, 390
Cost-benefit ratio, 126, 134
Credibility
    in communication construction, 263
    in initial encounters, 260–261
    persuasive source, 314, 318
Criteria, for effective listening, 99–100
Cro-Magnon people, 41, 51, 62n.11
Cues, in listening, 102
Cultural accumulation, 56, 57
Cultural conventions, 48
Cultural differences, and listening, 110
Cultural exclusion, 211
Cultural inclusion, 211
Cultural norms, conflict, 325, 330–331
Cultural pluralism, 211
Cultural relativity, 213–214
Culture
    communication influence, 214–216, 233
    definition, 206, 207b
    ethnic communication styles, 221–230
    gender communication styles, 230–232
    and language development, 54
    types, 208–210
    value orientations, 217, 218f, 222b, 223b
Cushioning function, 126
"Cybergossip," 197

Das Kapital (Marx), 373
Data, nature of, 404
Data analysis, research process, 402b, 405–406
Data entry, 405
De facto organization, 176
Deception, communication research, 420b, 420–421
Deciding on the message, linear communication
        model, 11
Decision-making groups, 151. See also Formal
        decision-making groups
    assignment-based cohesion, 168

Decoding, 8
    in linear communication model, 11, 20
    in simultaneous transactions, 21, 22f, 23
Deep meaning, 27
Demand characteristics, experimental simulations,
        408–409
Democratic group communication pattern, 157
Democratic leadership style, 161, 162
Denotative meaning, 15, 45
    and distortion, 26
Dependency-based cohesion, 167, 173.n 31
    organizations, 200–201
Dependent variable, 402–403
Descriptive generalization, 406
Descriptive research, 400
Destination, Shannon-Weaver conception, 25
Destructive resistance, 309–310, 317
Dexter, character likability, 259b
Digital broadcasting, television, 381
Digital Equipment Corporation, interactive
        computer, 356
Digital-tracking, 384
Direct broadcasts from satellites (DBS), television,
        380–381
Direct versus indirect observation, 404–405
Dirty tricks
    conflict, 340b
    deflection, 338b, 340
Disassociation, 140
Disclosure encouragement, affinity-seeking strategy,
        256b
Discussion group, reward-based cohesion, 168
Disengagement, interpersonal communication, 120,
        138–140
Disinformation, 68
Dislike and aggression, touch, 84
Distancing, psychological, 139–140
Distinctiveness, communication reconstruction,
        263
Distortion
    in communication, 25, 26b, 30
    in organizational communication, 197–199
Diverse population availability, mass
        communication process, 383
Diversity
    cultural, 209
    in United States, 210–211
Division of labor, bureaucracy, 180b
Divorce, conflict consequence, 325, 328
Dress codes, 73, 74
Dyad, definition, 120

Dyadic versus group communication, 150–151
Dynamism, affinity-seeking strategy, 256b

Economic model, causes of conflict, 324
Educational institution, 177, 180b
Effective communication, 3, 5t
  personal, 6
Effective listening. *See also* Listening
  actions required, 100–103
  barriers, 109–111, 112f, 116
  criteria, 99–100
  ethical concerns, 115b
  gains from, 98–100
  in health care, 95
  skills, 96
  strategic plan, 111–115
Effective online communication, 364–365
Effective self-presentation, 239, 264
  strategies, 247–251
Elaboration, definition, 314
Elaboration Likelihood Model (ELM), 314–317,
  316f
E-mail, 357–359, 366
  social norms, 357–358, 358b
Embedding pattern, organizational message
  distortion, 198
Emblems, gestures, 68b, 70b, 76, 91n.10
Emerging conflict, group development stage,
  152–153
Emotions
  and eye contact, 79
  vocalic cues, 77–78
Empirical observation, 404
Encoding, 8
  automated behavior, 19
  linear communication model, 11, 12–19
  in simultaneous transactions, 21, 22f, 23
Encoding and decoding, in simultaneous
  transactions, 21, 22f, 23
Encroachment
  prevention techniques, 81b
  space invasion, 80
Enculturation, 155
Endurance, attitudes, 305
Engagement, interpersonal communication, 120,
  127–131
English grammar, 49–50
Enjoyment facilitation, affinity-seeking strategy,
  256b
Entertainment, and social construction of reality,
  53–54

Equality assumption, affinity-seeking strategy, 256b
Ethical concerns
  communication apprehension, 288b
  communication dilemmas, 27b
  conflict dirty tricks, 340b
  effective listening, 115b
  groupthink, 169b
  informed consent and deception in research,
    420b
  responsible nonverbal behaviors, 89b
Ethical issues, communication research, 419–421,
  420b, 422
Ethnocentrism
  assessment, 212b
  definition, 211
  excessive, 213
European Americans, 210
  common characteristics, 222–224
  definition, 222
Evaluation situation, and communication
  apprehension, 272b, 274
Evidence weighing, formal decision-making groups,
  165
Excessive attention, and communication
  apprehension, 272b
Exchange, communication as, 9
Exchange theory (Homans), 133
Expectations, understanding, 58
Experiments, research design, 407–408
Expert assessments, formal organizational
  communication, 193
Expertise, source credibility, 314
Experto credite, scientific integrity, 400, 419
Explanation, in disengagement, 138–139
Exposure, mass media influence, 387
Expression, and conflict, 328
External conditions, attribution process, 253
Eye contact
  and listening, 96b, 102
  nonverbal communication, 78–79

Facebook, 361
Face-to-face communication, 22
  feedback, 345
  and media, 343–344
  nonverbal cues, 345
  psychological support, 346
  and videoconferencing, 360–361
Face-to-face interviewing, 411–412
Familiar versus unfamiliar place, initial encounter,
  246–247

Families, communication, 153–156
Family
  basic social institution, 180b
  and language, 57
"Fayol's bridge," crisis messages, 184–185
Fear appeals, persuasion strategy, 313,
    422n.7–423n.7
Feedback, 18, 21, 32n.19
  e-mail, 359
  in listening, 103, 104
  mass communication absence, 384
  and media, 345
  in simultaneous transactions, 21, 23
  receiver responsibility, 106
Feelings, and clothing, 74
Feminine Mystique, The (Friedan), 373
Femininity, cultural value orientation, 217, 218f,
    220–221, 223b
Field experiments, research design, 409
Field observational studies, 413–414
Fight response, and space invasion, 81, 83
Fighting, cultural support, 323, 341n.3
Fixed rules, bureaucracy, 180b
Flexibility, informal organizational communication,
    197
Flickr, 362
Flight response, and space invasion, 80–81
FM (frequency modulation) radio, 379
Focus group, 160, 415
Formal communication, 150
  official channels, 191–196
  organizations, 190–191, 202
Formal decision-making groups
  goals, 164–165
  patterns, 166–167
Formal situations, and communication
    apprehension, 272b, 273
Formal social organization, 175–176
Forming, group development, 151–152, 152b
Forum, task-oriented discussion, 160
Frame, verbal with nonverbal actions, 66, 91n.5
Freedom of the press, 373
Friendster, 362
Frustration, and aggression, 323

Gender
  cultural value orientations, 217, 218f, 220–221,
    222b, 223b, 230–232
  and persuasion, 312, 319n.28
General culture, 206, 208
General norms, 59

General transactions model, and conflict, 329
Generalizations, definition, 406
Gestures, nonverbal communication, 76–77
Goals
  as source of conflict, 330
  specification in research process, 401–402, 402b
Good guy-bad guy framework, disengagement, 138
Goodwill, source credibility, 314
Grammar, 9, 17
  conventions, 49–50
  significance, 51b
Grapevine
  message distortion, 197
  term, 196–197
Greetings, 259–260
Group, 171n.4, 171n.5. *See also* Small group
    communication
  breakdown and disorganization, 168–169
  cohesion, 167–168, 170
  common objective, 147
  development, 151–153, 152b
  formal decision-making, 164–167
  interaction rules, 58
  intimate, 153–158, 170
  size, 150–151, 169–170
  size and initial encounter, 245–246
  task-oriented, 158–164
Groupthink, 169b
Gua, chimpanzee, 38, 39

Haptics, nonverbal behavior, 83, 87
Harvard University, conflict negotiation, 335, 340
Hawthorne studies, human relations perspective,
    186–187
Height, nonverbal message, 70
Heritage, and word selection, 47
High apprehension, communication, 269, 270, 271,
    283
  consequences, 278
High context value orientation, 217, 218f, 219,
    223b
  Asian Americans, 226
  Middle Eastern Americans, 230
  Native Americans, 228
High power distance value orientation, 217, 218f,
    219–220, 222b
  Asian Americans, 227
Hispanic, definition, 224
Homo sapiens, sapiens, 41, 62n.11
Household Telephone Status, 2006–2009, 353f
Hulu, 381

Interval measures, research, 416, 417f
Interviewing, face-to-face 411–412
Intimacy, 133, 141
   maintenance, 133–138
   and sex, 137b
Intimate group
   informal communication patterns, 156–158
   sentiment-based cohesion, 167–168
Intimate relationship, conflict, 321–322, 327–328
Intimate zone, personal space, 79
*Introduction to the Principles of Moral and
   Legislation, An* (Bentham), 126
Invasion of privacy, 293
Irreversibility, interpersonal communication, 122,
   124b
Issei Japanese women, 211

Job termination, conflict consequence, 325
Judgment suspension, in listening, 113b, 115

Kilmann and Thomas' coping strategies for conflict,
   332, 332b
Kinesics, nonverbal behavior, 76, 87
Knowledge accumulation, and language, 52
Knowledge acquisition, from listening, 98–99,
   99b
Knowledgeability, source credibility, 314
Koko, gorilla, 39–40
Ku Klux Klan, 213

Labeling theory, 242
Labels
   encroachment prevention, 81b
   implicit personality construction, 242, 243, 264
   symbols as, 45
   words as, 13
Ladies Home Journal, 376
Laissez-faire leadership style, 161, 162, 163
Landlines, national polls, 412
Language
   as conventions, 47–50
   definition, 41
   impacts, 51–52
   learning in families, 154
   nature of, 45–47, 61
   relativity, 54–55
   and social construction of reality, 52–54
Language community, 37
Large groups, 175. *See also* Organizations
Large-scale experiments in natural settings, research
   design, 409

Latinos and Latinas
   common characteristics, 224–225
   definition, 224
Leader
   organizations, 181, 202
   task-oriented group, 161
Leadership styles, 161–164, 170
   assessment, 162b, 163b
"Learn, feel, do" advertising approach, 318n.4
Learned helplessness, 278, 292n.29
Learned internal behaviors, meaning as, 13
Learned signs, 37
Learning, and communication apprehension,
   274–278
Learning process, belief change, 303
Legacy of fear, mass media, 384
Legal-rational authority, 181
Letters, 349b, 349–350, 366
   legal protection and privacy, 349–350
Letters (alphabet), Greek, 42–43
Leveling, organizational message distortion, 198
Likelihood (ELM), definition, 314
Limited influences, mass media influence, 386
Linear communication model, 9–11, 10f, 29, 343
   stage one, 11
   stage two, 12–19
   stage three, 19
   stage four, 19–20
   stage five, 20
Linear model, definition, 10
Linear persuasion, 296
Linguistic relativity, 54
LinkedIn, 361
Listening. *See also* Effective listening
   affinity-seeking strategy, 256b
   barriers, 109–111, 112f, 116
   encounter, 103–108
   irritating habits, 96b
   misconceptions, 108–109
   as observable action, 102–103
   preparation, 112–113
   process, 97–103, 115
   strategic plan, 111–115, 113b
   visible characteristics of good and poor listeners,
      102b
Listening responsibilities, 106b, 116
Listening Strengths and Weaknesses Inventory,
   104b–105b
Local area networks (LANs), 357
Local languages, 54–55
Long-term effects, mass media influence, 389, 392

Long-term socialization, and communication apprehension, 274
"Looking-glass self" theory, 58–59, 136
Low apprehension, communication, 270, 271, 283
Low context cultural value orientation, 217, 218f, 223b
Low power distance value orientation, 217, 218f, 219, 223b
  African Americans, 225
Lying
  and eye contact, 78
  nonverbal cues, 68–69

Magazines, 375–377
Magic bullet theory
  mass media influence, 385–386, 387, 389
  persuasion, 296
Mail surveys, 412–413
Mainstream culture, 206, 207, 208
Majority, 210
Management, interpersonal communication, 120, 133–138
Manuscripti, 43
Markers, encroachment prevention, 81b
Masculinity, cultural value orientation, 217, 218f, 220–221, 222b
Mass communications. *See also* Mass media, Media, Mediated communication
  dependency, 369
  influence, 384–389
  modern and reality perceptions, 54
  power, 389–392
  as process, 383–384
  social and cultural factors shaping, 370–383
Mass media. *See also* Media, Mediated communication
  and simultaneous transaction, 22–23
  U.S. development, 372–383
  visual communication, 53
Massachusetts Institute of Technology (MIT), write/ edit computer programs, 356
Match.com, 362
Material culture, 207b
Meaning, 8, 9, 29–30
  active search for in listening, 113b, 114
  deep, 27
  definition, 13
  memory storage, 15–17
  social construction, 197
  surface, 27
  types, 14–15

Meaning construction/reconstruction, 301–302
Meaning triangle, 47–48, 48f
Measurement, research, 416
Media. *See also* Mass media, Mediated communication
  alternate cue systems, 346
  audioconferencing, 359–360
  censorship, 384
  in communication, 6, 343, 366
  computer, 355–357
  development, 44–45
  e-mail, 357–359
  and feedback, 345
  information transport, 344, 371
  relationship development, 346–347
  and role-taking, 345
  and sexual nonverbal messages, 76
  social network sites (SNS), 361–365
  technologies, 347–348
  teleconferencing, 359
  telephones and cell phones, 352–354
  traditional written, 348–351
  videoconferencing, 360–361
Mediated communication, 7, 366
  and simultaneous transaction, 22
  versus face-to-face, 343–348
Medium (plural media), definition, 344, 371
Melting pot policy, 210
Memoranda, 350–351, 366, 367n.9
  format, 351f
Memory
  cognitive process, 56
  and language, 51–52
  schemas, 20
  signs and symbols, 15–17
"Mental filter," message processing, 317
Message flow
  downward, 193
  large organizations, 190–191, 202
  official channels, 191–196
  upward, 192–193
Messages
  initial encounters, 259–260
  and persuasion, 312–314, 317
Middle Eastern Americans
  common characteristics, 229–230
  definition, 229
Minority citizens, status change and media, 389
Minority cultures, 210
Minutes, *Robert's Rules*, 167
Misconceptions, in listening, 108–109

Orders and instructions, formal organizational communication, 193
Ordinal measures, research, 416, 417f
Organization chart, 184, 185f
Organizations, 175–176, 201
  bureaucracy, 180–182
  communication consequences, 199–201
  communication designs, 182–190
  informal grapevines, 196–199
  institutions and social needs, 176–177
  internal cultures, 200, 202
  memoranda, 350–351
  message distortion, 193–196, 194b, 195b
  message flow, 190–191, 350
  official channels, 191–196
  theories, 177–180
Other Americans, The (Harrington), 373
Overgeneralizing, 406
"Owls," time schedule, 85
Oxford English Dictionary, 49

Panel, task-oriented discussion, 159–160
Paper, information medium, 372
"Paper trail," 361
Papyrus, information medium, 371
Paradigm, 7, 57
Parallel meanings, 9, 98
Parchment, information medium, 371
Participant observation, 405, 413
Passive listening, 101–102
Patterns
  and distortion, 25
  grammar and syntax, 9, 17, 45
Patterns of Culture (Benedict), 155
Payne Fund Studies, mass media influence, 385–386
Peer group, 145, 156
Peer screening, scientific research, 401
Penny press, 374
People's Choice, mass media influence, 386, 387
Perceiving the information as message, linear communication model, 11, 19–20
Perception, 19–20
  cognitive process, 55–56
  and language, 51
  and listening, 111
Performance evaluation, formal decision-making groups, 165
Performing, group development, 152b, 153
Peripheral route, message reception, 315, 316f
Personae, 121, 129
Personal autonomy, affinity-seeking strategy, 257b

Personal Report of Communication Apprehension-24 (CA), 280b–281b
Personal space, 79–80
Personality, 121, 154
  and communication, 5
  leadership, 163
  and persuasion, 312
Persuasion, 294
  alternative methods, 298–307
  compliance, 298b, 310–311
  definition, 297
  linear versus transactional, 296–297
  person-to-person, 294–295
  resistance, 307–310, 317
  strategies, 311–317
  tools of, 297
  yielding, 310–311
Phylogenetic continuum, 38
Physical attractiveness, affinity-seeking strategy, 257b
Physical responses, systematic desensitization (SD), 285
Pictographs, 42, 370
Pocket Manual of Rules of Order for Deliberative Assemblies (Roberts), 166
Policy formulation and change, formal decision-making groups, 165
Policy-shift directives, formal organizational communication, 193
Polygraph, 69
Population, surveys, 410
Positions bargaining, principled negotiation, 335, 338b
Postal service, 349
Postponement of gratification, 86
Postulate, definition, 399, 422n.2
Posture, nonverbal communication, 76
Power distance value orientations, 217, 218f, 219–220, 222b, 223b
Predispositions, 249–250
  and mass media influence, 387
Preexisting impressions, nature of, 261–262
Prejudices, and listening, 110–111
Presentation of self, 239
  construction, 263–264
  goals, 247–248
  impression pre-selection, 248–250, 251b
  initial encounters, 239–244
  plan, 250–251
Primacy-recency message impact, 313
Primary group, 145, 170n.1

Report to the Surgeon General (1971), violence on
 television, 388
Representative sample, 411
Research
 cause-effect relationships, 399b, 400
 definition, 399, 421
 designs, 407–415, 421
 focus groups, 415
 measurement, 416
 orderly universe, 399b, 400
 postulates, 399b, 399–400
 process steps, 401–407, 402b, 421
 quality, 416–419
 scientific integrity, 399b, 400–401
Resiliency factor, 277–278
Resistance, 307, 317
 constructive/destructive, 309–310
 psychological reactance, 307–308
Resistance coping, 338b, 339–340
Resistance to change, existing impressions, 262–263
Response, 8
Results report, research process, 402b, 407, 422n.3
Reward association, affinity-seeking strategy, 257b
Reward-based cohesion, 167, 168
Rhetoric, 3
Risks versus benefits, communication research, 420
Roberts' Rules of Order, 166
Role definitions, and persuasion, 299
Roles, 59
 and conflict, 330, 331
 confusion, 168
 intimate groups, 156
 social organization, 148, 149b
 task-oriented groups, 161–164
Role-taking, 18, 31n.16, 142n.6
 e-mail, 359
 learning, 145
 in listening, 103, 104
 mass communication absence, 384
 and media, 345
 and organizational messages, 193
 in simultaneous transactions, 21, 23
Round table discussion group, 159
Routine operational messages, 192–193
Rules of behavior, and language, 59
Ryze.com, 361–362

Salient characteristics, 18–19, 240–241, 247, 250,
 251b, 264
Sampling, statistical theory, 410
Sanctions, 157–158

Sarah, chimpanzee, 40
Sarcasm, 69
Saturday Evening Post, The, 376
Schemas, 16–17, 17f
 and conventions, 48
Scientific integrity assumption, scientific research
 postulate, 399b, 400–401
Scientific management (Taylor), 184
Scientific method
 communications research, 398, 399–401
 mass media effects, 385
 postulates, 399b
 research design, 407–415
 steps, 401–407, 402b
Scripted conversations, 127
Scriptoria, 43
"Secret tests," 136, 143n.26
Selective action, organizational messages, 195b, 196
Selective activation, reconstruction and anchoring
 (SARA) model, 16
Selective and minimal influences theory of
 communication, 387, 389
 research, 388
Selective attention, organizational messages, 195b,
 196
Selective exposure, organizational messages, 195b,
 195–196
Selective influences, mass media influence, 386, 387
Selective perception, 249–250, 264
Selective reception/perception, organizational
 messages, 195b, 196
Selective retention and recall, organizational
 messages, 195b, 196
Self
 description, 121, 142n.4
 in interpersonal communication, 124b
Self-concept, 58
Self-disclosure, 133, 135
 full, 136
 initial encounters, 255
 small group, 145
 and small talk, 129
 test, 258b
Self-image, 58, 121
 positive, 124–126
Self-inclusion, affinity-seeking strategy, 257b
Self-talk, and listening, 111–112, 113b
Seminar, task-oriented discussion, 160
Sender, 9, 10f
 listening responsibilities, 105–106, 106b
Sender-receiver reciprocity, 103–107, 116

Trait
    acquisition, 270
    definition, 269
"Trait theory," leadership, 163
Transactional persuasion, 296–297
Transactional process
    and conflict, 329, 339
    interpersonal communication, 122
    listening as, 103
Transmitter, Shannon-Weaver conception, 25
Transmitting the message as information, linear
        communication model, 11, 19
Trust, 135
Trustworthiness
    affinity-seeking strategy, 257b
    source credibility, 314
Truth in findings, communication research, 419
Tuckman's four stages in group development,
        151, 152b
Twitter, 361
Two-sided message, 313
Two-step flow of communication, 387

Uncle Tom's Cabin (Stowe), 373
Uncontrolled escalation, conflict, 326
Unfamiliar others, and communication
        apprehension, 272b, 272–273
Unintentional nonverbal contradiction, 68
Union-management impasses, conflict consequence,
        325
Unique personal meanings, 14
United States
    book development, 372
    diversity, 210–211
    foreign-born residents 2010, 209–210
    mass media development, 372–383
    value orientations of ethnic and gender cultures,
        218f
Universal principles of management (Fayol), 184
Unlearning, and communication apprehension, 275
Unproductive conflict, 326–327
    identifiers, 327b
Unresolvable conflict, 323
USDD Advanced Research Project Agency (ARPA),
        computer networks, 356
Utilitarianism, 126

Validity
    and intimate associations, 126
    research, 417–418, 422
Value orientations of U.S. ethnic and gender
        cultures, 218f

Values, culture, 207b
Variables
    identification, 402–403
    measurement, 415–419
Vellum, information medium, 371
Verbal communication, 7, 61
    time and distance, 41–44
    memoranda, 350
Vertical transmission, 192
Vicki, chimpanzee, 38–39
Videoconferencing, 360–361
Visible characteristics of good and poor listeners, 102b
Visual communications, 45, 53
Vocabulary, 49
Vocabulary differences, organizational messages,
        195b, 196
Vocal physiology, and speech, 39
Vocalics, nonverbal behavior, 77, 78
Voice, nonverbal uses, 77–78

Wage incentive systems, 183–184
War of the Worlds (Wells), 386
Wartime propaganda, and mass media power, 385
Washoe, chimpanzee, 39
Watergate scandal, and media, 390, 394n.39–395n.39
Weber's four principles of bureaucracy, 180b
Weight, nonverbal message, 71
Wernicke's area, 39
Why We Fight, mass media influence, 386
Wide dissemination, mass communication process,
        383
Wireless technology, 367n.12
Word-of-mouth communication, 387
Words
    definition, 12
    and distortion, 25, 26
    as labels, 13
    symbol representation, 42–43
Workplace
    communication apprehension at, 280–281
    nonverbal sexual communication, 75–76, 90
    relationship conflict, 321–322, 324, 330–331
Workplace perspective
    listening habits, 96b
    managing your manager, 191b
World Trade Center 9/11 attack, 213
World Wide Web, 356–357, 383
Writing, 42, 57, 348–349

"Yerkish," artificial language, 40
Yielding, 310, 317
    types, 310–311